ECONOMIC
AND SOCIAL
HISTORY
OF EUROPE
IN THE LATER
MIDDLE AGES

ECONOMIC AND SOCIAL HISTORY OF EUROPE IN THE LATER MIDDLE AGES

(1300-1530)

JAMES WESTFALL THOMPSON

FREDERICK UNGAR PUBLISHING CO.
NEW YORK

Republished 1960

Third Printing, 1969

Copyright 1931 by The Century Co.

Copyright renewed 1958 by Martha Landers Thompson

Printed in the United States of America

Library of Congress Catalog Card No. 60-9106

PREFACE

THIS volume is a continuation of my *Economic and Social History of the Middle Ages* (1928), which terminated in the second half of the thirteenth century. The terminal point of this work is not in a date, but in the economic and social condition of Europe in the early part of the sixteenth century, when the Reformation began to be caught in the coils of economic and social forces, and the flood of silver through Spain from America began to inflate the currency and raise prices in Europe to unheard-of levels.

Throughout these pages I have endeavored to show the close and intimate relations of economic, social, and political conditions and movements. For it is seldom in history that there was one of these phenomena without the others. It was written of the late George Unwin that he explained history "by reference, not to the large and dramatic combinations of statesmen, but to simple, constant and elementary motives." While I believe that, in the last analysis, all history is idea, nevertheless ideas are often the mental reflection of economic and social conditions, and the conduct of men is profoundly influenced by these conditions.

As in the previous volume, so in this one, I have purposely omitted consideration of England except when and in so far as England's relations touched the Continent. For there are many works in English on England's economic and social history, but none in the mother tongue upon the economic and social history of Continental Europe in this period. It is hoped that no reader will think that I believe that English medieval history is a provincial episode. Economy of space, not lack of interest, accounts for the omission.

JAMES WESTFALL THOMPSON.

CONTENTS

viii CONTENTS

ECONOMIC
AND SOCIAL
HISTORY
OF EUROPE
IN THE LATER
MIDDLE AGES

North of the Alps the tide of trade flowed from Lombardy in an ever increasing flood down the Rhine, whose affluents, the Main, the Moselle, the Ruhr, the Lippe, distributed it through all central Europe. At the same time Levantine goods found their way from Venice into south Germany, where the Danube and its affluents distributed them. The Rhône-Saône-Meuse route fed all eastern and central France with the same commodities. The river cities on these routes— Regensburg, Augsburg, Nuremberg in the Danube valley; Basel, Strassburg, Mainz, Coblenz, Cologne, on the Rhine; Lyons, Paris, Troyes, the Champagne Fairs in France, all grew rich and prosperous. Flanders, where the Rhine and Meuse routes converged and interlocked with the North Sea and Baltic trade routes, by the end of the thirteenth century was called the "Lombardy of the North." Here Bruges, Ghent, Ypres, Liège, Cassel rivalled the cities of the south in populousness and prosperity. Further east in Lower Germany Hamburg on the estuary of the Elbe, Bremen at the mouth of the Weser, Lübeck in the angle of the Baltic, and Brunswick and Halle in inland Germany, were close rivals of the Flemish group.

Not all this trade, however, was of oriental origin. Medieval Europe had also awakened to the development of its own natural resources, the stimulation of its provincial and local commerce, even international exchange of products between one country and another. Industrial development, too, grew apace. The cities were producers of manufactured wares as well as middlemen. The nature of these arts and crafts was usually conditioned by the environment. Thus Brescia in Italy, Nuremberg in Germany, and Liège in Belgium excelled in ironwork owing to the proximity of iron deposits. Laon, Ypres, Cambrai, Valenciennes specialized in linen goods to such a degree that their names are perpetuated to this day in such textile terms as *lawn* from Laon, *cambric* from Cambrai, *valence* from Valenciennes; the *diaper* pattern is derived from Ypres. Florence in the south and Ghent in the north were the two greatest centers of woolen goods, and the former led all Europe in the art of dyeing stuffs. The formation of merchants and craftsmen into gilds according to the kind of goods sold or the kind of wares manufactured contributed to the regulation of both production and distribution.

The result of this cumulative development was the growth of a new form of wealth derived in increasing volume from commerce and industry. In the thirteenth century Europe was in the throes of transition and economically becoming more and more commercialized and industrialized. Agriculture was still the most prevalent and productive enterprise, but it had lost its former almost universal character. Rural land values declined, owing to the competition of the new wealth and the drift of thousands of agricultural peasantry to the towns. The proprietary classes, the clergy and the nobles, wherever commerce and industry were active, were hard hit by these changes.

Every profound economic change also entails social change. Serfdom declined and in some parts of Europe had vanished before 1300. The civil condition of the European peasantry, especially in Italy, France, and Flanders, by the end of the thirteenth century was not so bad as commonly supposed in regard to personal and property rights. Many serfs who had formerly been taxable to the limit of the lord's wishes (*taillable à merci*) had risen to villein status so that their obligations were fixed by customary law and no longer variable and arbitrary; as for free villeins, they were practically rent-paying tenant farmers. Of course there were still many serfs, but the lot of few, if any of them, was as hard as formerly. Enfranchisement made substantial progress, not because of a new humanitarianism, but because it was becoming more and more manifest that free labor was more profitable than servile labor. Free villeinage was preferable to servile villeinage for the landlord, and of course for the peasant. The growth of towns, the development of industry and commerce, the slow improvement of agriculture, promoted this increasing material welfare of the peasantry. Along with these changes went an alleviation of the onerous *banalités* and *corvées* of the lords. Formerly servile villages in some cases became measurably self-governing communities with a rustic magistracy of their own. To this very day many French *communes* retain the territorial boundaries of the manorialized parish out of which they were formed, and the villages in name and location are identical with the name and location they possessed in the Middle Ages. Not only had personal serfdom greatly declined, but also the old vexatious "renders" had been regulated and the worst of them abolished. Local manorial customs might still be more or less onerous, but the fixity in the kind and mode of impositions was at least some guarantee against abuse. It is clear that much of the peasantry at the end of the thirteenth century was in very different condition from the serfs of former time. One must not be deceived by recurrence of the old-fashioned words. The words may have remained in usage, but the meaning of them had changed. Often they represented a theory of the law, and no longer reflected an actual historical condition. Even a noble might be the purchaser of a piece of property subject to villein tenure, as one may to-day buy a piece of real estate with certain old requirements attached to it.

The rise of commerce and industry stimulated town life, and the new town life gave birth to a new class in medieval society, the bourgeoisie or burgher class. Thus, again, the texture of society was changed. Servile peasants became freemen and burghers; crafts of many kinds developed which by better wages and more liberty lured the agricultural laborer away from the fields to a shop in the towns where he became an industrial worker; the feudal noblesse and the landed clergy, while they still retained their former social prestige, gradually lost that economic preëminence which had once been attached to privilege. Many of them were "land poor." There are some historians who think that the economic and social revolution of the twelfth and thirteenth centuries was more important than any later revolution, than even the Renaissance or the Reformation, for it altered the economic condition and the social structure of Europe more profoundly than they.

Political and administrative institutions, too, were changed by these new conditions. Aside from the important historical fact that the free, self-governing municipality introduced in Europe a new and original political unit which had nothing in common with the old and familiar feudal *cadres* like duchies, margraviates, counties, and other fiefs, the feudal governments everywhere were compelled to modify their old forms of administration and to adapt themselves to new conditions. It was not long before the rising burgher class intruded itself into the assemblies of the feudal "estates," as a third estate supplementary to those of the clergy and the nobles. In England the burgesses appear in the parliaments of 1265 and the so-called "model parliament" of 1295; in France the third estate appears in the first Estates General (*états généraux*) of 1302; in the Castilian Cortes we find the *communerós;* in the German Diet the burghers were recognized in 1356. At the same time we find the organs of executive and judicial administration like the Court of the King's Bench and the Exchequer Court in England, the Parlement of Paris, and the Chamber of Accounts in France, penetrated by this bourgeoisie. Even bourgeois councillors and ministers of state—whom we would call cabinet officials—are to be found, except in the case of the chancellorship, whose incumbent was always a churchman until the sixteenth century.

The decline of the medieval feudal economy and the development of a new economic régime based upon commerce and industry required the governments to adjust their taxation and fiscal practices to the new order of things. The new wealth made necessary new species of taxation and new machinery of collection. A money economy had very largely supplanted the preceding natural economy by 1300, for commerce and industry needed money to conduct them, whereas agriculture had long subsisted upon the exchange of one kind of produce for another. This decay of feudalism affected every branch of government: executive, legislative, judicial, military.

The practice of raising a large revenue from exportations and im-

portations—even the suggestion of tariffs for protective intention—
was common in Europe from 1300. Commercial enterprise pervaded
the whole of Europe and the Orient." [1]

The long established political and social theories which had sustained
by their sanction for centuries the political and social fabric of feudal
Europe were also naturally modified by these changes. Ideas of monarchy and nationalism began to discredit the old political theories derived from feudalism. The concept of mutuality and contract inherent
in feudal government began to be displaced by the concept of not
merely the superiority, but the supremacy of monarchical and royal
authority, while from below the voice of the newly risen bourgeoisie
demanded political representation and equality before the law. The
Church's wealth was the special target of protest, for the Church was
both the most privileged and the richest institution in Europe. The
enormous endowments of monasteries and convents, and in especial
the vast and irresponsible wealth of the military orders, excited the
resentment and cupidity of both kings and commons.

Politically the end of the Middle Ages was the downfall of the
feudal system; economically it was the triumphant effort of commerce
and industry to work themselves free from the manor and the farm
and to establish the cities as the centers of commerce and trade; socially it was the struggle of the lower classes to attain personal and
economic freedom with a measure of local self-government. Everything in fourteenth and fifteenth century history, even art and literature and philosophy, reflects these changes. What really passed in these
centuries was the whole medieval world.

It must be understood, however, that while the conditions above
described were general throughout medieval Europe about 1300, they
did not prevail with equal force everywhere. And the same observation
holds true of the new mental attitude. The "new thought" was not
equally keen and clear in all countries of Europe. Historical change
is partly the result of general conditions, partly the issue of particular
circumstance. Yet usually every particular is an example of the general. What deviations from the general trend occur are due to local
or national conditions, or the nature of the governing authority, or
the personal character of the ruler.

[1] "Mercantile conceptions are everywhere; the philosophy of utility is beginning to rule; in the material ambitions of commerce we find the mainspring of
the chief outward movements of the time."—Beazeley, *Dawn of Modern Geography*, III, p. 12.

"Too often do we forget to think of the Middle Ages as confronting problems
similar to our own, and considering solutions similar in spirit to those suggested
by our difficulties, however much the problems and their proposed solution may
differ in detail from those of the present."—Stephenson in *American Historical
Review*, April, 1930, p. 507.

Although in all central and western Europe at the end of the thirteenth century feudalism prevailed as a form of government, as a structure of society, as an economic régime, even as a psychology, there was great variation in the form of feudal government and the nature and degree of prevalence of feudal institutions. In England, France, and Castile, the trend was towards a growing sense of nationality, territorial expansion and consolidation, and strong monarchy. Germany and Italy were devoid of any national feeling, and the political drift was centrifugal. In Germany this tendency was expressed in the double form of particularism on the part of the feudality, and independence on the part of the burghers. The free cities were at strife both with the crown and the princes. In Italy on the other hand, feudalism was reduced to a mere gloss, except in the States of the Church and the Kingdom of Naples, owing to the preponderance almost everywhere of the city-state. The most medieval, the least modernized institution was the Church, both in its political theory, its administrative practices and its material circumstance.

In one respect, however, Europe of the fourteenth and fifteenth centuries lapsed. This was in manners. The progress of institutions was rapid in the fourteenth century, but it is a sad commentary that good manners decayed. This proposition is applicable to all Europe, not even excepting Renaissance Italy, in the fourteenth and fifteenth centuries. The comfortable, but fallacious doctrine of "progress" gets a rude shock when one crosses from the twelfth and thirteenth centuries into the last two centuries of the medieval epoch and the first of modern times. In sense of honor, in the amenities of gentility and courtesy, in kindliness, in feeling of responsibility, either to the individual or to society, in bearing and forbearing, in reverence towards the mysteries of life, the generations of these centuries were immeasurably inferior to their predecessors.

The passing of the old order of the high feudal age in government, law, institutions, economic conditions, social texture, and manners, was also accompanied by a change of morals. Morals were as unstable as prices and finance, and sometimes the lapse seems almost to have reached the verge of depravity. No class of society was exempt from this taint. Neither clergy nor laity, neither kings nor courtiers, neither baron nor priest nor bourgeois measured up to the character of men of these classes in the preceding period. Europe between 1300–1600 was, perhaps, the most callous age in the history of humanity.

Economically and socially the society of the twelfth and thirteenth centuries was composed of the great landed feudal aristocracy, nobles and clergy. The Church was the greatest landowner of all. It was an age of "natural economy," rather than of "money economy," in which the proprietary class produced little beyond its own wants and consumed hardly anything not locally produced. Market rights, toll rights, coinage rights, further eked out the feudal lord's resources.

This rich proprietary class also possessed another sort of wealth, in addition to land, in the form of family plate, church plate, bullion, hoarded coins, jewels, *etc.* The Church especially was rich in this kind of wealth. But it was idle wealth, immobile, unproductive.

The revenues which the landowners collect from their serfs or from their tenants are directed to no economic purpose. They are scattered in alms, in the building of monuments, in the purchase of works of art or of precious objects which serve to increase the splendor of religious ceremonies. Wealth, capital . . . is fixed, motionless, in the hands of an aristocracy, priestly and military.[2]

In the period of natural economy, royal and baronial households were organized for consumption only. Supplies were purchased for purposes of sustenance only, and not for trade to obtain profit. There may have been isolated instances where profit was indulged in; but as a general practice, it did not begin to develop until the twelfth century.

It was necessary for all this immobile and locked up capital to become fluid and to increase upon itself before real capitalism could emerge. Various theories have been propounded to explain this change. Sombart's theory is that the revolution was brought to pass by the monetization of manorial ground rents formerly payable in produce, followed by the conversion of much hoarded bullion and plate into currency. But this is only half an explanation, if so much. This theory of the rise of capitalism is largely belied by the facts, and remains but a theory. Overwhelming evidence shows that the first great private fortunes in Europe arose out of commercial and industrial enterprises conducted by men of the non-noble classes—the new bourgeoisie. The fact that nobles sometimes participated in these enterprises is proof of their penury, not their wealth. That large sums of money were in the hands of these men as the result of the conversion of ground rentals is not apparent.

The case of the Jews is evidence of the inaccuracy of this theory. The Jews were not permitted to possess land, and hence ground rents could not have furnished them the wealth which was unmistakably theirs. Only commerce and allied financial operations could have created their immense fortunes. Part of the wealth of the late medieval cities was derived from ground rents. But the fact that the mass of the small burghers were able to pay high rents implies that a certain

---

[2] Pirenne, *American Historical Review,* XIX, p. 494.

surplus already existed which must have grown out of commerce and industry.

The root of the change lay in the towns, not in the country; in business, not in land. This was forced forward by the revival of commerce in the twelfth and thirteenth centuries which was partly independent of, and partly stimulated by, the Crusades. We shall not stop to debate the question whether the Crusades stimulated commerce or commerce stimulated the Crusades; whether trade made the towns or the towns made possible the enormous growth of trade. It is sufficient to say that freer communication brought about by the Crusades, the progress of the town movement, and the rapid development of inter-urban and international commerce resulted in a condition which made necessary an adjustment of the methods of business to the new nature and scope of business transactions. Men began to realize the possibilities of "sowing their money to make it multiply," as Matthew Paris so aptly expresses it. Towns, trade, and capitalism emerged together in Europe. Merchandising, manufacturing, banking, business technique, credit—all are of urban origin. Then capital came to have a new sense; it was a value hatching a new value, or as Karl Marx put it, *"Mehrwert heckenden Wert."* Instead of being immobile, as formerly, wealth became fluid, mobile. Money became, so to speak, a means of production. Production was considered in terms of value in money as a means of gaining greater values. Services were no longer required of vassals and serfs, but were converted into money payments. Hired labor paid better than forced labor. Free workmen were found more productive than servile workmen. Business contracts replaced the old feudal and manorial ties. Monetized urban rents multiplied. "The continuous increase of the burghal population enriches them more and more. . . . In proportion as the wealth of the towns increases . . . they take up more and more an industrial character, the rural artisans flocking into them *en masse* and deserting the country." [3] The towns became commercial and industrial centers, the greatest of them having international commercial relations.

Italy was the earliest country in Europe in which a capitalistic régime and a capitalistic society appeared. The reason is twofold. In the first place owing to Italy's geographical position and peninsular shape the cities of Italy were able to tap the rich Levantine trade, a commerce essentially in luxuries like silk, spices, rare dyes, precious stones from the Orient, which returned enormous profits upon little bulk. A Venetian galley plying between Venice and Alexandria commonly paid one thousand per cent dividends upon a round trip, taking out iron and timber to ironless and timberless Egypt and returning laden with silk and spices. In the second place, the papacy drew down

[3] *American Historical Review,* XIX, p. 506.

into Italy the enormous ecclesiastical revenues of all western Christendom derived from Peter's pence, the census, tithes, indulgences, fees for appellate causes, *etc.* The annates alone represented the entire income of a diocese during the first year of a new bishop and were exacted as a fee for investiture. What these sums meant may be appreciated when it is said that the papal revenue out of England in 1252 was three times the revenue of the crown. The income of the Lateran in the thirteenth century must have far exceeded the income of all the princes of Europe taken together. Rome was not only the ecclesiastical capital of Europe; it was also the financial capital of Europe. In the thirteenth century the financial power of the papacy was like that of the great international banking houses of to-day.

When a money economy came to prevail in Europe, the most important financial men were the money-changers or *campsores.* Each state coined its own money. Therefore, whenever transactions were carried on by merchants of different countries, it was necessary to employ the services of the money-changers. There were tables for the money-changers in the principal towns, and always at the fairs. The merchants and money-changers assembled at some definite place to carry on their business. For this purpose we find the "old market" in Genoa; in Venice it centered around the Rialto and on the Piazza of St. Mark; in Florence a gallery was erected for financial business in the "Mercato Nuovo"; in Montpellier there was the *loge des marchands;* and in Bruges there was the famous *bourse.*

Banking, in its elementary medieval form as money-lending, first appears in Italy. In the Orient money-changing was an ancient profession, but it was new to the West, and crept into Sicily and then into Italy from the Arabs in the century before the Crusades. An Arabian geographer, Ibn Haukal, mentions money-changers at Palermo in 997. The Norman occupation of Lower Italy and Sicily and the Crusades, as we have seen, gave an immense impetus to commerce, especially to that of the Italian maritime republics. Money-changing and money-lending were an early by-product of this revival of trade. A gild of money-changers is found in Lucca in 1111. The tables of the money-changers are mentioned in a charter of King Fulk of Jerusalem in 1138. The word *cambio* was used in Genoa in 1156. The close relation existing between money-changing, money-lending and commerce is evident from the fact that before 1200 the words *cambiatori* (money-changers) and *mercatanti* (merchants) are used interchangeably. The *tavola* or "table" of the bankers and the counters of the merchants were often identical. We find Italian bankers financing the Crusades in 1191. There were branches of Genoese, Florentine, and Sienese banking houses in Egypt, in Cyprus and Syria. Pisa even had one in Armenia. The military orders and the kings of Europe made frequent use of them in the thirteenth century, notably St. Louis in his first crusade. The "letter of exchange" was still rare, but the "letter of credit" was common.

The widespread, popular—or rather unpopular—terms to denote this class were "Lombard" and "Cahorsian." The first testifies to the important historical fact that Lombard merchants, aside from the Jews, were the earliest to get into the money game in medieval Europe. The word "Cahorsian" was derived from Cahors in Languedoc, which seems to have been the earliest seat of the Lombards in France. With the rapid extension and development of money economy each term soon lost all local significance. Thus we read of "Lombards of Sens," "Cahorsians of Douai," etc. The Lombards and the Cahorsians were less detested than the. Jews, yet suffered like them on account of the prejudice against usury and because of the cupidity of the princes who frequently confiscated their moneys. They were expelled from France in 1269, 1274, 1277, 1291, but always returned because, perilous as their business was, the profits were large. Philip IV in 1295 permitted them to settle in any city in the kingdom. His bankers were the Guidi brothers, Biche and Mouche of Florence, who played an important part in his reign.

Besides loaning money the Lombards did a vast business in collecting money. They were the favorite bankers of the Church and were protected by the pope. In England, France and Germany they were collectors of ecclesiastical revenues. They maintained exchanges at all the great fairs in Europe, especially those in Champagne. If the Lombards, properly speaking, invented little, they enormously extended the financial practices of the time; they gave immense impulse to the system of mercantile and financial transactions. They stimulated, if they did not initiate, business.

The fiscality of the papacy was the first reservoir of the new capitalism, the wool trade of Florence the second. One of the most influential factors in creation of medieval banking was the necessity of the Roman curia to collect papal revenues in Europe beyond the Alps without exposing these sums to perils of travel, and further to relieve the *curia* from the delicate and difficult business of calculating revenues in terms of the complicated currencies of the age. In England and Flanders the wool and cloth trade helped the bankers by enabling the papal financiers to convert the papal revenues into either raw or woven cloth and to market it for benefit of the pope. From the pontificate of Gregory IX (1227–41) the important banking firms of the Italian cities had agencies in Rome and abroad, in France, Flanders, and England. Their chief function was to collect and to transmit the Peter's pence and other ecclesiastical revenues to Rome. These papal clients united papal authority with their own fiscal influence to promote and to protect their own business operations.[4] If an Italian merchant from Florence or Milan was robbed in France or England, or outrageously imposed upon by some noble, or could not collect a foreign debt, the pope intervened in his behalf, and usually papal pressure was successful. The Roman curia always protected the bankers against losses, so debts due the papacy or papal obligations were the safest form of banking activity to engage in.

The Italian banking houses not only invested their own profits in business and handled the collection of papal revenues, but acted also as agents of the Holy See to invest its enormous surpluses. No Italian city was so successful as Florence in its fiscal relations with the Holy See. The foundations of the great banking houses of Florence were laid in the thirteenth century—the Albertini, Albizzi, Ardiccioni, Bardi (the father of Boccaccio was a trusted agent of the Bardi), Bellicozzi, Ildobrandini, Borgo, Filippi, Gualfredi, Scala, Cerchi, Rimbertini, Frescobaldi, Acquerelli, Leoni, Monaldi, Rocci, Scotti, Marcoaldi, Tedaldi, Spigliati. The Florentine banking houses steadfastly supported the popes in their long political struggle with the emperor, Frederick II, and got their reward. Their loans to papal partisans in neighboring cities which were political and commercial rivals of Florence undermined those places. This is conspicuously true of Siena where the bankruptcy of the Gran Tavola ruined the city.

Siena made the blunder of backing the wrong political horse in supporting the emperor against the pope. Until she adopted this fatal policy Siena, and not Florence, had been the headquarters of papal banking. The chief Sienese banking house was that of Buonsignori, called the Magna Tavola or Gran Tavola, the name being derived from the table of the money-changers. In 1289 its capital amounted to the then large amount of 35,000 florins. It loaned money to popes, emperors, feudal princes, and cities. But when Siena espoused the imperial cause and forsook the papacy the popes removed their funds to Florence and left no stone unturned to discomfit Siena. In November 1260 all the Sienese banking firms went to the wall in the crash of the Gran Tavola. The tourist may still see in Siena a medieval house built in 1234 by one of the earliest of Sienese capitalists, Angliere

---

[4] The following apostolic letter is significant both in illustrating such use, and in showing the way the pope could wink at usury if received by those in his service. It was written in 1255 to Ralph de Rumiliaco, dean of the church of St. Mary of Troyes, concerning the bond of the abbot of Osney:

"If you find the money has not been paid, you will excommunicate the abbot and convent, announcing it on Sundays and feast-days, *pulsatis campanis et candelis accensis,* until satisfaction is made to the merchants, with just and moderate expenses and due recoupment of damages . . . *usuris omnino cessantibus.* If two months later the money has not been paid, you will suspend them from the administration of spirituals and temporals."

Solafica, on the front of which may be read the inscription: *Campsor Domini Papae Gregorii IX.*

Between the years 1260 and 1347 there were eighty banking houses in Florence, the greatest of which were the Bardi and the Peruzzi. The financial dealings of these two houses with the Angevin kings of southern Italy and with England were especially intimate. In 1268 they looked upon the expedition of Charles of Anjou for the conquest of the kingdom of Naples and Sicily as a profitable speculation and liberally financed it, in return receiving the right to collect *portoria* and to manage the mines and salt pans as security. But in 1282 the success of Aragon in promoting the Sicilian Vespers, which ruined the French domination in Sicily, seriously crippled them, in particular the Bardi, who were heavily involved. Fortunately for them it was to the interest of the popes to support the Angevin dynasty, and so the papacy rushed the Guelph bankers into southern Italy to the rescue of its royal protégés. The Florentines were in the vanguard of the rescue corps and by the end of the thirteenth century had done their work so well that Charles II was completely in their power. The king surrendered parts of the revenue and granted monopolies to cover the advances made by the bankers.

Whether the kingdom was at peace or at war, the result was the same: if at peace the rulers needed money for internal improvements or for keeping up their magnificent court; if at war cash was needed to pay the troops. In either case the Florentines reaped the benefit. Such a good thing soon became widely known and numerous houses sent their agents to partake of the rich profits which were to be made indirectly out of the royal patronage. Of these the Bardi were the most important from the standpoint of money advanced; they furnished 10,000 ounces of silver in 1291, for instance, for payment of the papal tithe. This gives an interesting illustration of the operations of the bankers. They were, as has been seen, agents of the papacy for the collection of the ecclesiastical taxes. They were at the same time the only ones possessing mobile wealth which was available for the making of loans. It thus happened that they would often loan needy individuals money with one hand and collect the same money with the other for transmission to the *curia.* All bankers became ardent Guelphs, "and their attachment to the Angevin family waxed with the profits which they derived from it." Arnold Peruzzi became counsellor and chamberlain of Charles II, and in 1308 his company paid a dividend of 40%. As time went on the main reliance of the throne came to be placed in a sort of syndicate which included the Bardi, Peruzzi and Acciajuoli, to which was added the Buonaccorsi about 1330.

The greatest financial operations of the Bardi and Peruzzi, however, were in England. Isolated instances of Italian loans to the English kings go as far back as the twelfth century. Richard the Lionhearted seems to have borrowed from them, for his brother and successor, King John, promised to pay the merchants of Piacenza a sum of money which they had advanced on the order of Richard to two English envoys sent to Rome, and in 1219 a certain Pietro Guibertini of Bologna came to Henry III and demanded payment of another loan which he alleged had been made by himself and others to Richard.

But the real period of Italian finance in England began in the thirteenth century. Then Italian merchants flocked to England to purchase wool or to negotiate loans secured upon wool. The first occasion on which they played a prominent part was in connection with the effort of Henry III to secure the German and imperial crown for his son Richard of Cornwall. Almost at the same time these Italian merchant-bankers made Henry III another loan of 135,000 marks, which was expended in the vain endeavor to put his oldest son, Edward, afterwards Edward I, upon the throne of Sicily. Edward borrowed Italian money to conduct his Scottish wars, and there is an intimate connection between the fall of William Wallace and the history of Florence. The king found loans more convenient than struggling with a reluctant parliament for subsidies. During the first four years of the reign of Edward I, the Lucchese merchants were largely employed in the financial operations of the crown. While many houses operated simultaneously, the Florentine influence grew steadily until it finally became dominant. The Mozzi of Florence became important during the period from 1277 to May 6, 1309, during which they lent £79,941 6s. 8d. During a shorter period (June 25, 1285–November 18, 1293) the Riccardi of Lucca lent Edward I £56,240 18s. 1d. The Spini of Florence were also prominent bankers in the later years of the thirteenth century, but data are lacking as to the extent of their operations. Other firms of lesser importance may be briefly noted: the Pulci of Florence, with whom were associated the Rimbertini of the same city, the Ammanati of Pistoia, the Ballardi of Lucca, the Cerchi Gianchi of Florence and the Cerchi Neri. The Bardi and Peruzzi of Florence also appear in this period laying the foundations of the royal favor which was later to be so disastrous to them.

The two firms which seem to have exercised most influence during the reign of Edward I were the Riccardi and the Frescobaldi, with the latter gradually forging to the fore. They virtually controlled the finances of the realm during this period. The king resorted to the device of turning over the revenues to the Italian merchants as security for their loans. In the year 1299 the whole of the revenue of Ireland was turned over to them in payment of a loan of £11,000.

And from April 1, 1304 to May 30, 1911, "nearly the whole of the receipts from the customs were handed to them."

The "Lombards" were as active in France as in England. It would be but repeating the names already cited to list them. They are frequently mentioned in French and Italian sources, both historical and literary, as for example by Villani, the Florentine historian and by Brunetto Latini, the Florentine savant who dwelt at the court of Louis IX for several years.

But Jews and Lombards were not the only people in Europe in the thirteenth century engaged in fiscal and banking operations. The Knights Templar were close competitors. Founded in Jerusalem in 1118 by Hugues de Payens, a nobleman of Champagne, and seven companions who first called themselves *Christi milites* or Soldiers of Christ, and later *Milicia Templi,* Soldiery of the Temple, the Templars—and the same is true of the rival Order of the Knights of the Hospital, or Hospitallers—were a curious cross between chivalry and monasticism. Technically they were regular canons, actually they were clerical-knights. Their tax collectors were to be under the protection of St. Peter. Since all their property theoretically was to supply the needs of pilgrims and of the poor, it was decreed that no one, either lay or cleric, should levy tithes on the income from their cultivated fields. The pope confirmed them in all the possessions which they might acquire in both Asia and Europe.

The patriarch of Jerusalem gave the Templars their first lands, but they obtained their first solid financial foundations in Champagne. In the thirteenth century they owned fifteen establishments in this region, and had gained control of about fifteen thousand acres of land. In 1228, a struggle began between them and the Count of Champagne, and the latter was finally able to prevent them from acquiring more landed estates in Champagne without his consent.

The enthusiasm for the Crusades had showered the two orders with wealth, not only in the Holy Land, but in Italy, France, Spain, Germany, England as well. In the middle of the thirteenth century Matthew Paris, the great English historian, estimated that the Templars were possessed of 9000 castles and manors. Indeed the riches of the Templars were so great that it excited the jealousy of all the monastic orders and even of Pope Alexander III. In 1179 the Lateran Council unsuccessfully demanded that the Templars renounce all the property which had been acquired within the ten preceding years. The Templars were especially favored in a financial way in the cost of labor on cultivated areas. This work was done by serving brethren who were admitted to the order in large numbers. These included husbandmen, shepherds, swineherds, mechanics, and household servants.

All historians have emphasized the enormous wealth and financial influence of the Templars. William of Tyre states that every province in the whole Christian world had given them money, and their possessions were equal to those of kings. Before the fall of Jerusalem in 1187 the Knights Templar owned estates scattered through the length and breadth of Europe, and a network of commanderies covered Italy, France, Germany, England, Spain. Possessed of manors in abundance, enjoying numerous market rights, and exemptions from tolls and taxes, sailing yearly fleets to the Orient with supplies of money and Crusaders for the unending struggle with the Saracens, its companies of armed knights riding over the roads of Europe, its fortified posts dotting the countries of Christendom, the realm of the Grand Master was already a monetary and military power of the first importance. He negotiated independent treaties with the Saracens and stood almost equal to the sovereigns of western Europe in power and dignity.

From the first the Templars pursued an avowed course of money economy in the administration and collection of the income from their landed possessions and privileges. Increasing sums flowed into the commanderies, supplemented by a continual flood of gifts and bequests which were invariably invested to yield a profit. Their endowments in East and West gave them a command of ready cash, much of which was employed at a profit, and not entirely consumed in fighting the Saracen. The duties of collecting, administering, and transmitting their increasing revenues required of the treasurers of the commanderies a skill that would match that of the bankers of to-day. Their commanderies were echeloned along the highways of Europe from the Scottish border to Christian Spain, from Bordeaux to the Rhineland, and down the Danube to Constantinople.

The wealth of the Templars, their pride, their exemptions and immunities, made them many enemies. Public opinion accused them of conniving with the infidel against their rivals, the Knights of the Hospital; of plundering Ascalon (1152); of betraying Frederick II (1229) and St. Louis (1250), when these two rulers were in the Orient. When Acre was lost in 1291 the Hospitallers retired to Cyprus, and still made a show of armed resistance to the Saracens. But the Templars abandoned the career of Crusaders, retired to their possessions in the West and with the enormous capital which they controlled, soon rivalled the Italian bankers and the richest Jews as financiers.

They became the bankers and treasurers of the papacy, of kings and princes, of many individuals. The Order furnished ministers and financiers to James I, king of Aragon, and Charles I, king of Naples. Money, jewels, wills, and even treaties were deposited with the Templars for safe-keeping. In England the Temple at London was early used as a place of deposit for papal subsidies, and for bequests and grants in aid of the Holy Land. Probably the practice of depositing treasure with the Templars in England began with this. By the beginning of the thirteenth century the custom of storing treasure at the New Temple was established. In its vaults lay the wealth of landed magnates, the surplus capital of the merchants, and papal subsidies. In 1204–1205, King John placed the seals and jewels of the English crown in the Temple at London for safe-keeping. In the next year he deposited there the church plate of the Archbishop of Canterbury. In 1263 when Edward, the son of Henry III, raided the Temple in London, he carried away 10,000 pounds belonging to many of the merchants and barons of the kingdom. In Paris the kings of France kept their treasure in the Temple for more than a century. In 1259, the original of the treaty concluded between Louis IX and the ambassadors of Henry III was placed in the Temple at Paris.

Since the commanderies were to be found over all Christendom, the Templars, like the American Express Company, received and transmitted goods, money, negotiable paper. They loaned money to nobles embarrassed to pay the feudal "aid" or wishing to confer generous dowries upon their daughters; to bishops hard pressed to pay the papal annates; to abbeys on the verge of bankruptcy, as many were in the thirteenth century; to merchants seeking funds; even to kings. The interest rates were lower than those obtainable from the Jews and Lombard bankers, for they had no taxes to pay and besides enjoyed immense protection and immunity. But they were merciless foreclosers of mortgages and enforcers of notes past due.

For all these enormous profits the Templars returned nothing to society or government. They maintained no hospitals like the Hospitallers; they had no schools; they supported no poor; they were untaxable in person and property; all of their business transactions were exempt from assessment. The costume of the Templars, a red cross on a white mantle, was regarded in many parts of Europe as a symbol of avarice, and the populace regarded their walled, moated, bastioned and turreted commanderies as their ancestors had regarded the sullen frowning castles of the robber barons. Richard Coeur de Lion said on his death bed, "I leave my avarice to the Cistercians, and my pride to the Templars."

By 1300 pope and king, baron, burgher and peasant feared and hated the Templars. In Paris, where the grand commandery was situated, the kings looked with ill-concealed resentment upon their inflated power. Exempted from the jurisdiction of the chancellery in 1191 by Philip Augustus after his return from the Holy Land, confirmed in all their possessions by Louis IX in 1258, though he was not a king who liked to see the royal authority abated, the power of the Templars continued to grow. Philip III, in an ordinance designed to prevent the acquisition of land in mortmain by religious associations, expressly exempted the Templars. In 1279 this king persuaded the Templars to resign the rights which they held within Paris through their many possessions, but in recompense they retained absolute power over their property in the faubourgs, high and low justice and extensive seigniorial rights. A whole "new town" (*ville neuve*) grew up within the shadow of their ramparts, the center of a state within a state, independent of all ecclesiastical or secular authority, having its own soldiery, its own police, its own magistrates, its own jurisdiction, its own taxes and finances.

The Paris Temple was the central bank of the Knights Templars in France, if not for western Europe. In it were kept the accounts of the various commanderies, of the pope, the king of France, the princes of the blood, the high noblesse, and the bourgeoisie. Considerable light has been thrown upon the system of accounts and methods of bookkeeping which were employed there by a document which M. Leopold Delisle discovered. This paper is the *Day Book* or *Journal of Receipts* of the Temple covering the period from March 19, 1295 to July 4, 1296.

Each page of this *Journal* begins with the date and the name of the Templar in charge of the cash-room that day. After this is entered the amounts of the deposits, the names of the depositors, the origin of the money deposited, the names of the persons to whose accounts the deposits were to be carried, and an indication of the register on which the receipt had been noted. The total receipts of each day, or the excess of receipts over outlays, was immediately borne to the central vault in the evening, an operation stated by the formula *Solvit in turre*. There was a separate book for a separate wicket that paid out cash, but the *Journal* mentions few payments. In addition, special registers were kept, which recorded, according to the nature of the operations, and grouped under the names of the different creditors and debtors, all the sums which the cashier received or paid on the accounts of the clients of the house. In general, the bookkeeping of the Temple was kept so as to indicate clearly the assets and liabilities of each of the parties to whom the accounts were open.

It is interesting to notice the number and condition of the persons who made deposits and kept accounts at the Temple as shown in the *Journal*. Delisle has divided these clients into five categories: (1) The officials of the Templars themselves, such as the master, the treasurer, the commanders of the houses in the provinces which had relations with the Temple; (2) different ecclesiastical dignitaries such as the cardinal legate, the abbot of St. Denis, *etc.*; (3) the king, the officials of the royal household—especially the officials responsible for the receipt of the royal revenues—the prévôt of Paris, the bailiffs of Auvergne, Orléans, Senlis, Sens, Vermandois, *etc.;* (4) members of the royal family and their agents, the bailiff of the queen, the count of Clermont and his bailiff; (5) the great nobles and different persons belonging to the noblesse and the bourgeoisie, the names of the latter sometimes more Italian than French.

There are 222 separate accounts of varying length, and belonging to persons of varying stations in life. More than sixty of these accounts refer to deposits made to the credit of another person. Following is an illustration of these accounts:

12 decembre 1295.—Dies lune.—Frater Johannes.
De Radulfo Messent, 25 £., ad debemus Omnium Sanc.
De Petro Messent, 25 £., super eundem Radulfum, ibidem.
De Richardo Messent, 13 £., super eundem, ibidem.
De Johanne Messent, 12 £., super eundem, ibidem.
  Summa: 75 £.
Solvit in turre.

A paraphrase of the above would read something like the following: Monday, December 12, 1295, Brother John, cashier of the Temple, received the following deposits: 25 pounds from Radulf (possibly Randolph) Messent, due on All Saints day; 25 pounds from Peter Messent, to be paid to the same mentioned Radulf Messent on the date above specified; 13 and 12 pounds respectively from Richard and John Messent, to be paid to the same Radulf Messent on the same date. Total 75 pounds.

An account of the king of France with the Temple, for 1286, indicates the general system whereby at the end of each year, each party could find out its assets and liabilities. This record was drawn up in the following form:

	OWED BY THE KING			DUE TO KING		
	£	s.	d.	£	s.	d.
1286 Ascension	101,845	7	6			
Toussaint	51,886	8	5			

"It is evident that in the unwarlike atmosphere of the counting-room, the soldiers of the Temple, for over a century, handled much of the capital of western Europe, becoming expert accountants, judicious administrators, and pioneers in that development of credit and its instruments which was destined to revolutionize the methods of commerce and finance." [5]

[5] Ferris, *American Historical Review,* VIII, p. 1.

CHAPTER I

FRANCE UNDER PHILIP THE FAIR (1285–1314) AND THE LAST CAPETIANS (1314–1328)*

At the end of the thirteenth century France was the most prosperous and the best governed country in Europe. The last decades of the long reign of Louis IX (1226–1270) had been years of unalloyed and continuous prosperity. The provinces of the South had long since recovered from the disastrous effects of the Albigensian Crusades; the protracted conflict with the English king over Guienne and Gascony had been settled in 1259. No foreign war and no internal strife had vexed the country for many years. The administration was honest and efficient. If Louis VII in the middle of the twelfth century could say, not without pride: "We in France have nothing but bread and wine and gladness," the statement would be twice-true of France in the thirteenth century. A single fact will illustrate the enormous wealth of France at this time.

According to statistics, in a single century between 1170 and 1270 the French built eighty cathedrals and nearly five hundred churches of the cathedral class, which would have cost, according to an estimate made in 1840, more than five thousand millions to replace. Five thousand million francs is a thousand million dollars, and this covered only the great churches of a single century.[1]

Brunetto Latini, the cultured Florentine scholar and tutor of Dante in his youth, who like his pupil suffered exile for his political convictions, found refuge at the French court in 1260 and there wrote his *Trésor*, a sort of encyclopaedia, in French instead of in Italian. He could not admire enough the peace of city streets, the quiet countryside which he saw, the commerce and industry of the towns, the farms and orchards and vineyards of the peasantry. Philip III (1270–1285) changed this condition in no respect. The short war with Aragon over the massacre of the French in Sicily in 1282, if without glory, was also without disaster. His reign was in some particulars a continuation of his father's policy, in others the point of departure of new tendencies. In his relations with feudal society the king followed

*For map see W. R. Shepherd, *Historical Atlas*, 7th ed. (Henry Holt & Co., New York, 1929), p. 76.

[1] Henry Adams. *Mont St. Michel and Chartres*, p. 95.

22

the maxims of St. Louis; he labored to maintain peace and justice within the kingdom, and like many other rulers of that time confused custom with law. But we detect the inauguration of a modern system of government and a departure from feudal tradition in the reign of favorites. Until the time of St. Louis and much so under his rule the royal government had been essentially personal; the king himself administered affairs, with the assistance of selected counsellors, but these did not take the initiative and never assumed any ascendancy in the administration. Philip III broke with this tradition. Pierre de Broce was the first of a long line of ministerial favorites in the history of the French monarchy. Henceforth the great administrative measures were devised and enforced by the king's ministers. The concept of the French kingship became less feudal and more royal; the royal prerogative expanded; feudal tradition was ignored or even crushed; the royal authority became increasingly arbitrary, and if this arbitrariness became so excessive as to provoke violent opposition or rebellion, the blame was put upon the unpopular ministers who were dismissed or even executed as a means of mollifying the populace.

Another indication that a new age was approaching in 1270 is found in the history of taxation during Philip III's reign. Except for the loans incurred for his ransom, Louis IX had met the expenses of his government with the ordinary revenues of the crown. His son was the first king of France to have recourse to the dangerous expedient of loans and the multiplication of new taxes. To be sure these taxes were almost wholly imposed upon the clergy in the form of tithes, but the next reign was to see the invention of a shoal of new taxes imposed upon both clergy and laity, especially upon the bourgeoisie. One may assuredly say that a reign which inaugurated unblushing taxation of the clergy, and in which the equilibrium of the old-fashioned feudal budget was so upset that it could only be restored by means of loans, was a modern régime.

A sharper change came to France, both in its internal condition and its external affairs when Philip IV came to the throne in 1285. Philip the Fair was a strong, ambitious, and sometimes unscrupulous king, far from content to rule after the placid manner of his grandfather. His concept of kingship was one of sovereignty, not suzerainty. He would be more king than overlord, more monarchical and less feudal in his prerogative. It would be an error, though, to ascribe this policy to mere ambition. Sometimes a great ruler—and Philip IV was a great ruler if not a great man—is a mirror of the shadows which futurity casts upon the present. Philip IV was the first modern king. He seems to have realized by intuition that feudalism was a bygone and obsolete institution as a form of government, if not as a social system, and set himself to adjust systematically a feudal régime already becoming antiquated, to the needs of a society demanding change. He seems to have realized that the old feudal economy based upon agriculture was giving way to a new economy based upon commerce and industry; that provincialism, which was of the essence of feudalism, must yield to territorial unification; that suzerainty must be displaced by real and national kingship; that the organs of both the central and the local administration must be tautened and tightened and local sovereignty give way to national sovereignty; that even the Church must draw in its horns and yield place in things temporal to the secular government. Philip IV's domestic and foreign policies, his diplomacy, his wars, and his administrative reforms are clear exemplifications of the modernity of the man. No great figure of history more incarnated the spirit of the age he lived in than he. In some things he was so modern that he anticipated by centuries a policy which later was to become commonplace.

The contrast between Old Europe and New Europe is most vividly manifest in the conflict between Philip IV and Pope Boniface VIII. Church and state had often been in collision before. But in the conflict of the emperor Henry IV with Gregory VII and that of Frederick Barbarossa with Alexander III, and the struggle of many temporal rulers to preserve their independence against the grandiose claims, promulgated by Innocent III, of the supremacy of the papal monarchy over all rulers and all states, the issue was clouded by doctrines and practices which were essentially medieval by tradition and in nature. Two forms of medieval sovereignty were at war.[2]

In the conflict of Philip IV with Boniface VIII the issue was not so compromised and complicated as with the Salian and Hohenstaufen emperors. Hitherto all ecclesiastical persons and property had been immune from secular taxation, although the papacy had sometimes sanctioned such impositions when the Church expected to derive benefit from them, as in the case of the Saladin tithe which was approved

---

[2] "The decisions in the course of the struggle were to a great extent affected by conditions of fact—by the feudal and municipal oppositions of the emperors, by the counterpoise of Norman and French politics against the aggrandizement of the imperial power; but at the back of these material conditions stood the immense influence of a dominating cultural idea—the belief in the spiritual leadership of the Roman hierarchy. As long as the claim of the Popes to organize the Christian world was contested by the emperors, the successors of St. Peter had much the best of the game. They were stronger in theory and better fitted to put theory into practice.

"The tables were turned against them when their great enterprise in the conduct of foreign policy—the Crusades against Islam—had signally failed, and when instead of the empire of the Hohenstaufen they were confronted by kings of consolidated national states—by Philip the Fair in France, by Edward I in England."—*Collected Papers of Paul Vinogradoff*, II, pp. 285–86.

by the pope as a means to finance the Third Crusade. But in 1293 France and England entered into war—the history of which is another matter—and both Philip IV and Edward I assessed the clergy for support of it. Boniface VIII at once vehemently protested on the ground that such taxation was a violation of the Church's liberty.

It is not without significance that the issue was so modern and so material a one as taxation. The pope did not base his protest upon the Augustinian doctrine that the Church was a superstate; he did not use the language of either Gregory VII or of Innocent III. Only later when driven to it by his ill success did Boniface VIII fall back upon Augustine's *City of God* and the doctrine of the Petrine Supremacy. The fact that both kings, in addition to providing themselves with revenue, were also interested in centralizing their authority and seeking to deprive the Church in their realms of immunities and exemptions regarded as deleterious and even dangerous to the welfare of the state, in no whit alters the fundamental nature of the issue. Moreover, Philip IV's taxation of ecclesiastical property was of a piece with his general resolution to tax the new wealth which had come into being through the growth of commerce and industry. The king exhibited a fertile ingenuity in devising new kinds of taxes to tap these new resources of government, and invented new administrative machinery to collect them. For the old machinery had been devised for an agricultural, not a commercial and industrial society.

We have an almost amusing complaint from Boniface VIII concerning such new-fangled taxes in the bull *Clericis Laicos* (1296) in which the pope forbade the imposition of lay assessments of any sort upon ecclesiastical persons and property of every sort. In part this famous pronunciamento reads:

By our apostolic authority we decree that if any bishops or other clergy, whether regular or secular, of any grade, condition or rank, shall pay or promise to pay or consent to pay any contributions or taxes, or the tenth or the twentieth or the hundredth or any other part of their income or of their possessions, or of their value, real or estimated, under the name of an aid, or loan or subvention or subsidy or gift or under any other name or pretext, without the permission of the pope, they shall by that very act, incur the sentence of excommunication. And we further decree that emperors, kings, princes, dukes, counts, barons, *podestà, capitanei,* and governors of cities, fortresses and all other places everywhere, by whatever names such authorities may be called, and all other persons of whatever power, or condition or rank, who shall impose, demand or receive such taxes, or shall seize or cause to be seized, the property of churches or of the clergy, or shall receive such property after it has been seized, or shall give aid, counsel or assistance in such policy either overtly or secretly, shall by that very act incur the sentence of excommunication.

The all-exclusiveness and the all-inclusiveness of this decree is evident. If literally enforced the Church everywhere in Europe both in person and in property was wholly independent of the states within whose confines it was established. The clergy was a great and independent society, the Church a great and independent polity, ecclesiastical property a vast and widespread immunity throughout Europe. Even the ancient feudal service of churchmen who were vassals was abrogated. If rigorously applied, the papal bull not only would have cut one of the oldest and longest roots of the tree of feudalism, it would also have cut back that nascent nationalism and modern government which at the end of the thirteenth century was in bud and on the verge of flowering. The bull nowhere mentioned either the French or the English king. The pope was too shrewd to give overt offense by so doing, although the intent is manifest. Moreover, if the pope's contention was true for France and England the principle was as valid for the rest of Europe.

The reply of Edward I and Philip IV to the papal prohibition was such as to be effective for their purposes and at the same time to evade by a technicality any embroilment with the Holy See unless Boniface VIII resolved to force the issue further. In England Edward I proclaimed all clerics and all church property to be outside the law—which was taking the pope's word more literally than he had intended—with the result that ecclesiastical property in many places was seized with impunity. The bishops' plate, the bishops' furniture, the bishops' horses were taken; abbey lands were invaded and the stock driven away. The outcry of the clergy soon became so great that the clergy were compelled in self-defense to compound with the king. In France Philip IV issued a royal ordinance forbidding the export of coin or the precious metals. While apparently of general application the particular slant of the prohibition was aimed against the pope, for it cut off the papal revenue in the form of annates and Peter's pence, of which France was an important source. Boniface VIII, however, more than neutralized this loss by declaring the year 1300 to be a Jubilee Year and granting plenary indulgence to all who visited Rome in that year. The result was crowds of pilgrims beyond anything ever seen there before, and overflowing papal coffers.

The controversy of the French king with Boniface VIII grew more and more acrimonious each successive year, for neither would abate a jot or tittle. It was wholly a political issue, however, in spite of the pope's effort to give it a moral aspect. Hence it needs only to be noted that French military intervention in Rome in 1303 resulted in the deposition of Boniface VIII and (1308) the removal of the papal seat from Rome, which had become an impossible place for the pope to dwell, to Avignon, which became technically a portion of papal patri-

mony beyond the Alps, but practically French territory. It was the fall
of the medieval papacy, the end of ends of the Middle Ages.

The spectacular collapse of the papacy in 1303 had an aftermath
of economic importance not only in France, but throughout all Europe.
This was the fall of the crusading Order of the Knights Templar.
In 1289 Philip IV had confirmed all the rights and privileges granted
to the Templars by his father. What changed the king's policy? Undoubtedly the fall of Boniface VIII strengthened his hands. Yet other
factors must be taken into account like the reverse to French arms in
Flanders, the monetary crisis and the king's overwhelming necessity
of money. The Templars ought to have read the writing on the wall,
for in the balance of public opinion they had been weighed and found
wanting. But they were overconfident and their eyes were holden.
In 1305 the grand master, Jacques de Molay, had haughtily rejected the
suggestion that the Templars and the Hospitallers be united. It might
have saved the Templars, for although far richer than the Templars
(in 1244 the Templars possessed only 9,000 manors while the Hospitallers owned 19,000), the Knights of the Hospital had escaped popular condemnation. A Norman lawyer of Coutances named Pierre
Dubois published a pamphlet entitled *De recuperatione Terrae
Sanctae* (On the recovery of the Holy Land) in which he advocated
that the Templars be compelled to dwell in the East, to put all their
lands to farm, to convert their commanderies and priories into hospitals and especially schools in which science and the arts, manual
training and oriental languages should be taught. It was a statesman-
like suggestion.

William de Nogaret, the king's astute minister who had been the
moving spirit against Boniface VIII, was also the chief instigator of
the abolition of the Templar Order. Pope Clement V was either persuaded or intimidated into acquiescence. The French king, though justified in the principle, resorted to shameful false charges and abusive
treatment of the Templars, as he had done in the case of Boniface
VIII. The case against the Templars has been summed up by a modern
historian:

The Templars administered their property well, they were themselves
persons of capacity, and they were probably far more formidable as an
organized society than either their numbers or their wealth might imply.
Wise men had long ago guessed at the possible danger this efficient and
determined society might become. . . . It is plain that the Templars were
a source of uneasiness to the rulers of Church and State in Europe. . . .
A body of professional soldiers with a powerful international organization,
with the purpose of their mission no longer capable of fulfilment, with
no special allegiance to the country in which they were living, with unusual financial resources at their command, if not in their possession, and

with the Templars' record of daring and insolence behind them, such a body could not but menace the stability of Europe, and above all the stability of the French state.[3]

The Templars were accused of gross immorality, of practising sorcery, of heresy. On October 13, 1307, Jacques de Molay and all the knights in Paris were arrested and brought before the Inquisition. Torture extorted outrageous and preposterous confessions of wrong doing. The grand master was spared until 1314. In the interval the pope, who in a papal bull in 1308 had branded the Templars heretics, had in 1310 called a council at Vienne as the result of whose deliberations processes were undertaken in all the ecclesiastical provinces of France against the Templars. Fifty-five knights were burned alive in Paris on May 10 of that year and nine at Senlis four days later. The enormous wealth of the Templars was confiscated by the king, who thereby cynically cancelled his own heavy debts to the Order.

Meantime the contagion of fear, hatred and covetousness had spread to other countries of Europe, but the abolition of the Order in most cases was more moderately accomplished. When news of Philip IV's action reached England Edward II hastily wrote to the kings of Portugal, Castile, Aragon and Sicily and to the pope, inquiring as to the truth of the allegations against the Templars. But before replies were received from these sovereigns a papal bull dissolved his doubts. The Templars in England were spared the infamous charges made in France, except that of heresy, and were not put to torture. But all their property was confiscated. In Spain the two "provinces" of the Order extended over five kingdoms: Aragon, Castile, Leon, Navarre and Portugal. James II of Aragon at first hesitated, then was convinced by letters from the French king and the pope. The knights put up a fight, but in the end succumbed. Castile followed the example of Aragon. In Germany the suppression of the Templars was accomplished with less violence than elsewhere, owing to the fact that since the German bishops were also feudal princes and calculated to profit by the extermination of the Templars, many of the baronage, who hated the bishops, sustained the knights. Our knowledge with reference to Italy is slight. It would seem that one must distinguish between the south of the peninsula and the north and center. The Angevin kings of Naples naturally followed the French precedent. The city republics of Tuscan and Lombard Italy were less drastic in their policy, for the good reason that the Templars had never acquired a firm grip upon the business and finance of these regions. The Lombard and Tuscan bankers were too well established to suffer seriously from the competition of the Templars.

[3] Edward J. Martin, *The Trial of the Templars* (Allen and Unwin, 1929).

However, everywhere in Europe and in the Latin Orient the Knights Templar were abolished as a military order and their property confiscated. Much of it fell to the Hospitallers. In Spain the two ancient Spanish military orders of Calatrava and Santiago profited by their fall. The bishops everywhere, the Dominicans, who were bitter foes of the Templars, the kings and the great nobles got large slices of the spoil. The French and English kings in especial lavished much of the ill-gotten wealth upon favorites and in this wise built up a pliable party of nobles around their thrones. Many of these fortunate persons were small nobles and in France even influential bourgeois, so that we see the phenomenon of the formation of a parvenu nobility dexterously utilized as a counterweight to the old feudal noblesse whom the kings steadily shouldered out of important offices of the crown. The history of the abolition of the Templars in spirit and in practice strikingly reminds one of Henry VIII's abolition of the English monasteries two hundred years later.

That Philip IV's motive in extinguishment of the Templars was primarily an economic one is shown by the fact that a similar fate soon overtook the Jewish and Italian banking firms doing business in France, the latter denominated "Lombards" although some were from Siena and other commercial towns of Italy. The Jews controlled a considerable portion of French commerce, owing to their possession of a mobile capital. But they had no assurance of legal protection. They were not regarded as subjects, but as chattels of the feudal noble in whose territories they dwelt and who might exploit or expel them as he chose. There were some Jews on the royal domain. Hitherto Philip IV had been tolerant of them on his own lands, but had exacted a special tax from them, which the Jews made up among themselves and brought to the king as the price of royal protection.

But in 1306 Philip IV, being hard pressed for money, enacted a general measure concerning the Jews. He claimed that all the Jews in France pertained to the crown, that they formed part of the regalia. (One thinks of General Ben Butler's famous declaration during our war with the Southern States that slaves were contraband of war.) The act is significant of the intensely monarchical conception of the royal prerogative cherished by Philip IV. On the same day royal officials, bishops, and barons, received a letter bearing the seal of the chancellor informing them that all the Jews in the kingdom were to be seized and all their property, fixed as well as movable, was to be confiscated to the royal treasury. The Jews were given until St. John's Day (June 24) to convert their movable property into cash for the king, but all fixed property was confiscated at once.

A similar fate overcame the Lombards in 1311. The Jews had been expelled; the Templars were either dead or in prison. The king was irresistible and his avarice insatiable. The Lombards lost their property and money and were expelled like the Jews. Those who owed the treasury were detained until they had paid their obligations. Those who had creditors were compelled to surrender their bills payable to the king. No apology or palliation of this atrocious policy can be offered. It must be put down to medieval intolerance, the king's avarice, and the false economic ideas which prevailed at that time. As a matter of fact the Jews and Italians promoted commerce.

The realization of Philip IV's cruelty and folly was shown soon. In 1315, the year after his death, Louis X permitted the Jews to return, forbade the clergy to harass them, and established the rate of interest they might exact, two pence per pound per week. This is the earliest example of formal regulation of interest in the Middle Ages. Even yet the conditions were hard. The Jews were required to wear a distinctive mark, a yellow target on their clothing. They were authorized to collect their old debts, but on condition that the king got two thirds of the amount. They also were permitted to repurchase their former synagogues and cemeteries. Under Philip V there was another persecution, and Philip VI later expelled them. Cruel and variable treatment of the Jews was like this all over Europe. The worst anti-Semite king of the period was Edward I of England.

One must pass almost wholesale condemnation upon Philip IV's policy towards the Templars, the Jews, the Lombards. But in the regulation of industry the case is quite otherwise, for the king's industrial policy was both politically and economically sound. In order to understand it we must go back to the reign of Louis IX. In 1261 Etienne Boileau, the provost of the merchants, which is to say the mayor of Paris since the municipality was governed by the great gilds, compiled a famous book, the *Customal* of one hundred and one métiers or trades of Paris, in which the statutes of the gilds were recorded. The crown in no wise interfered with the internal practices of any of the gilds. The gilds were free with regard to everything pertaining to the craft of each. They made their own by-laws, regulated hours of work, wages, terms of apprenticeship, prices, *etc.*

Under Philip IV, however, a new conception of the kingship was developed. The legists in the royal service convinced him that the crown had authority to regulate everything, to control everything. But it is to be added that the king in these regulations was not actuated as in his dealings with the Templars, the Jews and the Lombards, by purely selfish interest. It is true that sometimes he legislated for his own benefit, but truer that he legislated for the general interest of the community. We know of three ordinances of Philip IV in regard to gilds and other associations. In the first the king legislated concerning religious confraternities within the boundaries of Paris. These associations, which had a patron saint to whom an altar in their lodge was dedicated, and who was specially venerated on the day commemorative of his memory, were a sort of mutual benefit associations. In the next ordinance (1305) the formation of all new associations whatsoever was prohibited. The text of these ordinances has not been preserved, but we know their import by allusions to them in letters-patent of his successors who rescinded them. Drastic as these ordinances may seem, there can be no doubt that they were police ordinances designed to forestall possible rioting on the part of these semireligious groups at the time when the suppression of the Templars was in process.

Quite different in spirit is Philip IV's legislation concerning the bakers' gild in Paris, which for its time displays remarkable perception of government as a social agency. In 1305 there were "hard times" in Paris. Wheat rose to a famine price. The king took prompt measures to relieve the condition. He ordered a survey to be made of the standing and stored grain around Paris and compelled the owners to put all of it on the market except enough for home necessity and for seed against the next sowing. Nevertheless, because of the rapacity of the bakers, bread still remained very high. Accordingly commissioners were appointed to supervise the bakers, to see that good flour was used, that the lawful weight of loaves was not evaded, and that the bakers did not try to force up prices unwarrantably. Thereby Philip IV struck at monopoly, the very heart of gild motive. The measure was of temporary application, but it was ordained in the general interest of the public and in opposition to selfish interest.

Something similar happened at Pontoise. There the bakers were in feud with the town government. It had long been customary for bakers from adjacent towns and villages three times each week to bring their bread to Pontoise to sell. The bakers' gild in Pontoise endeavored to curtail this competition by preventing such outsiders coming into town, and claimed that the gild, not the local town government, had the right to control the price and sale of breadstuffs. The town magistrates appealed to the parlement of Paris, that is to say to the high court of the king, which decided that outside bakers had the right freely to sell bread in Pontoise.

Of more importance because of more general application is the Great Ordonnance of July 7, 1307 (Fagniez II, No. 9). This law applied only to Paris. It was declared at the instance of the provost of the city. Its purpose was to reduce the generally prevailing high prices, partly induced by crop failure, partly aggravated by a recent alteration of the coinage. The king had returned in 1306 to the coinage system of Louis IX. But many contracts existed which had been drawn up when his own baser coins were in circulation. Those who held notes and contracts of others demanded payment in the new coin; real estate owners made a similar demand of their tenants. The result was that tenants and the lodging house class in Paris revolted and a riot ensued. The king himself was beset in the streets and was blockaded in the Temple until the provost of Paris, Firmin de Coquerel, rescued him. Twenty-eight of the rioters were hanged on the eve of the Epiphany, seven at each gate of Paris. But turbulence continued all through the year 1307. There was complaint of the high price of foodstuffs, and it was mainly with a view to regulating these that Philip IV legislated as he did.

The whole ordinance dealt with the gilds (*métiers*) and contains fifty-eight articles. Every debt more than ten years old was cancelled, a provision which struck the Lombards and the Jews heavily. Ten articles (46–56) regulate a multitude of fees, especially of notaries and recorders. Many sections deal with regulation of markets and fixation of prices. Vintners, tavern keepers, fish dealers, bakers and millers were especially singled out. The article with reference to fish is interesting since it shows how largely fish was the poor man's meat in the Middle Ages, and the economic importance of fish food owing to the many fast days imposed by the Church. Bread had to be sold by weight. But no tax might be put on fresh meat, game and venison, as these were viands of the rich. Article 44 deals with clothing, on which there was a sale tax; for cutting and sewing three costumes a tailor might charge 3 *sous*, for a *robe de valet, 2 sous*. In Article 54 Philip IV interfered with the very constitution of the gilds. The gilds limited the amount of work a member might do and forbade night work. The king abolished these rules. Further, in many trades he forbade a master to have more than one apprentice and that one preferably was to be the son of a master. This measure was to protect apprentices from exploitation by masters and to ensure good technical instruction to apprentices. The term to be served and the wages of apprentices were fixed. It had been the practice of many masters in this time when journeymen workmen were common, to employ only apprentices of French birth. The king ordained that Flemings, Italians and Germans coming into France to learn a craft, might be apprenticed. This article displays real vision on the part of the king. The whole ordinance of 1307 was radical, even revolutionary of existing industrial conditions in Paris. But it was only of temporary and local application. When the "hard times" were relieved it fell into desuetude and the gilds reverted to their former selfish and arbitrary practices.

In the regulation of weights and measures, however, Philip IV's legislation was of wider scope, touching the whole royal domain, and since this included the greater portion of the kingdom, one may say that it was of almost national application. We have an ordinance of this kind in regard to spice merchants and dealers in comestibles (*denrées au poids*), which forbade them to use the *livre de précision*, this system of weights being reserved for physicians and surgeons. Just weights had to be employed, and sale must be free from fraud. For example, it was forbidden to mix tallow with wax candles, or to put too big wicks in candles so that they would be consumed with undue rapidity. Article 12 provided that "in every town of our kingdom where there are merchants four persons shall be appointed, namely a master and three others, to be guardians of the *métiers*. These four officials shall supervise the spicers, visit their stores at least four times each year, examine weights and measures, and summon delinquents before the local magistrates. All who wish to become sellers of merchandize shall take an oath to the master of the *métiers*."

Unfortunately the fiscal policy of Philip IV negatived the good effect of his measures and was detrimental, even disastrous, to French commerce. Philip IV more than any other sovereign of the time, was the creator of modern administration. It was in his reign that the parlement of Paris, the chamber of accounts and the council of state became three distinct bodies, all emanating from the old *curia regis*. But in order to establish these institutions and to keep his head above water in the midst of his great expenses owing to the double war with England and in Flanders, the king had prodigious need of money. Part of this he got from the Templars, the Lombards and the Jews, as we have seen. It is now necessary to observe the other means to which he resorted in order to increase the revenue of the crown. These means were of four sorts: (1) commutation of feudal military service for money payment, (2) a general tax upon sales, (3) the imposition of export and import duties, (4) manipulation of the coinage.

In the feudal period expenses of the crown had generally been inconsiderable and the domain lands sufficed for the maintenance of a simple court. Now, on the contrary, in the reign of Philip IV, when the royal domain comprehended the greater portion of the territory of the kingdom, heavy direct taxes began to be imposed in the king's name. The royal *taille* became perpetual. It had not been so before. When imposed at all it had always been expressly stated that it was for exceptional purpose and reason. *"Salva etiam tallia pro rege per capitulum facienda quocienscumque fieri contigerit"* ran the words of the ordinance of 1263. In the edict of 1268 the language was even clearer.

In 1292 war broke out between Philip IV and the emperor Adolf of Nassau over Franche Comté, or the Free County of Burgundy, which the reigning count, although a vassal of the Empire, ceded to France. The king gave the nobles the alternative of serving in person with their feudal contingents, or of commuting such service for a money payment. The practice was not novel, for scutage or "shield money" had been accepted by the English exchequer from barons and bishops in lieu of military service from them and the knights enfiefed upon their lands since the time of Henry II, who used the cash to hire mercenaries. But scutage was new to France. In addition Philip IV imposed a war tax of one penny in the pound (*livre*) (the *livre* was composed of 20 *sous* containing 12 pence each, or 240 pence in the *livre*) upon all sales, the tax theoretically to be divided between purchaser and seller, but of course the consumer really paid it. It was collected at markets and fairs, or of storekeepers; even when a peasant sold his harvest a government notary had to be present. The tax was very unpopular and was called the *maltôte* or "bad tax" by the people. Many of the French towns compounded by paying a lump sum in order to be freed from its inconvenience, though, of course, there was no relief from taxation since the towns had to raise the sum paid to the king in one way or another by local imposition. Paris purchased this privilege for a hundred thousand *livres* in spot cash. Numbers of nobles, too, compounded in similar wise. Contrary to what is generally written, Philip IV was not the inventor of this unpopular *taille du denier* or "last penny" tax. It was levied in Genoa as early as 1141, found at Montpellier in 1174, and on record in Aragon in 1247.

In the years which followed Philip IV also had recourse to taxes upon the importation and exportation of goods which, although war measures, possibly for the first time in medieval history are indicative of the protective principle. In 1302, a year of insufficient harvests, by an ordinance of November 3rd, the king forbade the exportation of wheat, wine and all other foodstuffs. Cloth was not included in this prohibition, but all commercial communication with the enemy, the English and the Flemings, was forbidden. That this measure was something more than one of temporary expediency is shown by the fact that even after the war was concluded, a new ordinance of February 5, 1305, forbade the exportation of wheat, vegetables, wool, and woolen cloth, horses, and arms. All merchandise of this kind which attempted to pass the frontier was to be confiscated together with the teams and wagons transporting them. In short, an economic barrier was erected between France and other countries in the form of an export instead of an import tax, as with tariffs to-day. Five days after the promulgation of this ordinance a bourgeois of Paris was appointed "master of ports and passages." Under him were two supervisors, and below them provincial commissioners, inspectors, wardens of bridges and fords, sergeants on foot and on horseback to patrol the roads and to watch at crossings.

It would be unjust historical interpretation to regard these *douanes* as merely fiscal expedients and not to take certain economic conditions and purposes into account. Little by little we discern a distinction being made between classes of merchandise, and sometimes licenses to export were sold in modification of the general prohibition. In the latter case a fixed rate of four pence *ad valorem* was established, as in the case of cloth, or else a certain sum according to weight or quantity was exacted. Payment was made at the frontier and a permit or letter of quittance given by the inspector to the exporter. This tax was called the *droit de haute passage* or "right of high passage." Exportation of raw wool was absolutely prohibited. This was a blow to the Flemings. Later, with the purpose of stimulating sheep-raising in Champagne, the law was modified so that wool-growers there might export raw wool to Valenciennes and Maubeuge for making into cloth on condition that the manufactured product be returned to France. But this protective measure excited the complaint of French drapers who demanded complete protection. The same friction arose in the Midi where Languedoc was an important wool-growing and cloth-manufacturing region with thousands of weavers and looms in Albi and other towns. As the drapers and textile gilds of the North protested against competition from Hainaut, so those of the South protested against Italian and Spanish competition and demanded a protective tariff.

It thus appears that the reign of Philip IV wrought a revolutionary change in medieval taxation. It was the inevitable result of the transformation of an agglomeration of fiefs, such as old France was in the feudal age, into a compact and royally ruled territory. The former distinctions of feudal status of the classes of society, whether nobles, bourgeois or peasants were becoming blurred, and more and more all classes of people were being regarded as subjects. The pressure of the crown tended to weld even hitherto semi-independent feudal territories with the royal lands and make the new taxes uniform for much of France, whether royal or feudal in nature. Thus in 1299 the fiftieth and the hundredth tax imposed for the war with Flanders were levied impartially upon crown lands and upon lands of the great feudatories. These royal taxes were laid in addition to those levied by the great nobles in their fiefs, which of course meant an increased burden of taxation upon the people at large, small nobles, tenantry and serfs. They represented the increased price paid for increasingly national or monarchical government. The benefits arising from improved administration had the disadvantage of costing France more than the old order —and disorder—of things.

The odium attached to Philip IV's name owing to his destruction of the Templars and expulsion of the Jews and the Lombards has a just measure of truth in it. But the notorious charge that the king was "a false moneyer" has been disproved by close modern research into the history of the coinage in his reign. The monetary policy of Philip

IV was not dictated by avarice, although it must be admitted that the king profited by it. The history of medieval coinage is a very difficult one, and never more so than in the late thirteenth and early fourteenth centuries when the long and complex accretion of economic and social changes engendered during the epoch of the Crusades reached a peak, and a new Europe was in process of formation. Factors like transition from an agricultural to a money economy, development of commerce and industry, growth of towns, rise in the standard of living, changes in the purchasing power of money, decay of feudalism and formation of monarchy, must all be taken into account in formulating a truthful historical interpretation and forming a just judgment. In the case of France—this is not so with England at this time—the difficulty is increased by the fact that the actual accounts of the French mints are wanting. The records of English currency reveal the exact amounts of coin issued of every kind of coin and the weight thereof. No such record exists for France.

In order to understand Philip IV's problem of the coinage it is first of all necessary to remember that in France the great feudatories had the right to issue currency, so that France abounded with a variety of coinage systems, each of which was composed of various coins.[4]

In France only insofar as the provinces fell into the crown and became royal domain could this feudal and provincial coinage be supplanted. On the contrary in England all coins emanated from royal mints and the king alone had the right of coinage. In 1263 Louis IX had dealt this feudal coinage a hard blow by ordaining that it might not be current outside the lord's fief and that royal currency should have parity with it within the fief. As the king's coins were sounder currency than that of the feudality the effect was to curtail the circulation of the latter, but the evil of a complex, vexatious, and debased coinage still persisted. Philip IV's first coinage act suspended the feudal right

---

[4] From the time of Charlemagne money was reckoned in terms of pounds (*livres*), solidi (*sous*) and deniers (*pence*). The pound or libra was valued at 20 solidi, and the solidus at 12 pence. But no coin of pound value and name was in circulation. The pound was a "money of account" like the English guinea today. Solidi were silver coins known as shillings in England, as marks or silver pennies in France and Germany. Gold coinage—angels in England, *écus d'or*, or *mouton d'or* in France, ducats in Italy—did not appear until the last half of the thirteenth century. But although the names of these coins remained constant, the value of them materially altered. This was due to two processes, first a reduction of the precious metal in them, and second, a great change in the purchasing power of money from the time of the Crusades. From the tenth century to the substitution of Napoleon's coinage everywhere upon the continent the *livre* was always estimated at 20 *sous* and the *sou* at 12 pence. But these coins had greatly shrunk in estimated value by 1300.—Cf. *English Historical Review*, XXV, p. 768.

to coin silver and gold into money and limited the right of feudal coinage to one copper piece only.

The justice of the king's next coinage act is more open to question. He demonetized all the royal money in circulation and replaced it by a new issue. Holders of the previous coins could recover only the intrinsic value of the metal in them. Not only was this done once, but twice and thrice.

The importation of bullion was favored, its exportation forbidden; the employment of gold and silver in the industrial arts was restricted by sumptuary law . . . Various attempts were made to prevent the market price of bullion from rising above the mint price, and in certain cases gold and silver were even seized and coined by force.[5]

At each emission the king strove to procure more gold and silver to put into circulation. At the same time Philip IV changed the estimated value of the new coins—he could not of course change their real value—and compelled the people to take them at the artificial value attached to them. For example, the *gros tournois,* which was valued at one *sou* in the reign of St. Louis, was now made to pass at three *sous.* In some cases these alterations were accompanied by a "crying down" of existing currency, in other instances no such depression took place. In addition, there was a considerable diminution of the metallic content of the coins. The effect was a violent derangement of prices and rents and turbulence of the populace. Between 1277 and 1309 rents in Paris rose enormously. This tendency was partly owing to increasing concentration of population in Paris and the larger towns because of the growing activity of commerce and industry which drew tradesmen, artisans and craftsmen from the outlying regions into the towns; but more on account of the alterations of the coinage and the decline in the purchasing power of money. At the same time there was a reduction of land values and of rents in the rural areas, which hit the landowner and the man who lived from the profits of rent, but was of benefit to the renting class. No satisfactory determination can be made with reference to the price of foodstuffs because of the bewildering variety of local weights and measures. Perhaps the price of comestibles went up; but it must be borne in mind that the first quarter of the fourteenth century was depressed by crop failures owing to abnormal and adverse weather conditions.

It is undeniable that Philip IV profited immensely by these manipulations of money, and this is the ground of the charges made against him. The profit from seigniorage, or the royal monopoly to coin money, was itself a large one. Moreover, the king had enormous debts. In

[5] *Ibid.*

order to pay a debt of one hundred *livres* before 1295 the sum of 2000 *sous tournois* would have been required. After the alteration of the coinage he could have paid the same debt for 666 *sous tournois*, a saving of two-thirds. He profited in another way also, for he compelled taxes to be paid in the older and better coin, or in bullion, and so realized immense other profit. We know, for example, that in 1298–99 the mint netted him 1,200,000 *livres tournois*, or three fifths of the revenue of that year. Again, during the period of fluctuation before equilibrium was established between the new and baser coinage and the price of commodities and commercial wares, he must have realized considerable profit.

In 1306 there was a monetary crisis. On June 8 Philip IV declared that he would return to "the money of St. Louis," and that this money should circulate at its old value. Thus the coinage was depreciated by two-thirds at least. Prices rose enormously, especially fixed prices like rents. Property owners demanded that their rents be paid in the better coin, that is to say they raised rents to three times the previous rate. An article which had cost three *sous* in 1305 was now worth only one *sou*. The king's manipulation reduced wages in the same proportion and the working classes naturally suffered. The result was that Paris was filled with rioting. There were also revolts in other cities as Rouen and Châlons-sur-Marne. A complaint to the king from the abbot of Cîteaux casts vivid light on these conditions. "Now we have to pay as much of the better money to hired laborers," he wrote, "as once we gave them of the worse, so that agriculture costs more than it brings in." Nevertheless Philip IV adhered to his ordinance, but tried to reduce the cost of manufactured objects by permitting masters to have as many apprentices as they might choose, a radical departure from his previous industrial legislation. It should be noted by the student that soon after this event the Templars were crushed and the Jews and the Lombards expelled from the realm.

How are we to evaluate these practices, and what judgment are we to pass upon Philip IV's monetary policy? While admitting that the king greatly profited by these operations and that need of money made him terribly avaricious, modern writers are inclined to exonerate him from the charge of deliberately debasing the French coinage. They find the explanation of Philip IV's course in the current economic fallacy of the time that the precious metals in themselves and intrinsically constituted wealth—a fallacy which lasted well down into modern history—and regard the royal alterations of the coinage not as wanton derangements for his own profit, but as endeavors to establish a stable coinage in an age of rapid and often violent economic changes. A reviewer of the last and most authoritative work upon this difficult subject has summed up the author's conclusions as follows:

The kings of France were continually anxious that their mints should be at work. . . . Two methods of stimulation were open to the king: by altering the currency and especially by crying down the coins in circulation, he might compel bullion to flow to the mint; or in various ways he might attempt to prevent it from being used elsewhere. Various measures of the latter kind were put in force. . . . With great justice he refuses to admit that the kings of France (he includes the last Capetian kings in this survey) debased their coins either to increase the value of accumulated treasure, or to evade paying their debts in full, or to diminish their expenditure, and he points out that in all probability any attempt of the kind must have resulted in failure, or have probably, if not certainly, diminished the king's revenue as well as his expenditure. The author's own view is that the debasements of the currency aimed at a double purpose, namely to bring bullion to the royal mints and so secure the king a large, if temporary revenue from the seigniorage, and to enable the mint authorities to make the ratio of the gold and silver coin correspond with the ratios of the market price of those metals. . . . He refuses to admit dishonesty as a general motive and prefers rather to refer these increases (in the metallic content of the currency) partly to a desire to regulate the ratio of the gold and silver coin, and more commonly to a desire to comply with the popular cry for a return to "good money." In those cases in which the increases were accompanied by a crying down of current coins he supposes the main motive to have been a desire to make a profit from the seigniorage upon the new issues. Here, too, as in the case of debasements, he finds real causes in the financial and economic needs of the time without attributing to the government a cynical and stupid dishonesty.[6]

Philip IV's constant need of money beyond the normal revenue compelled him again and again to resort to practices prejudicial to commerce, although his better judgment must have been against them. An instance is the persecution of Florentine traders in France at the instigation of the brothers Biche and Mouche. These two Florentines had received, as financial agents for Philippe le Bel, such rich concessions for the collection of taxes and had so largely exercised their rights by squeezing French and Italians alike, that to avoid any danger of competition they persuaded the king to arrest all Florentines in France, honest and dishonest alike, as usurers. The luckless traders had to buy their way out of prison.

But the king was a chronic opportunist and prone to exalt expediency above policy, and he never was troubled with conscientious scruples. A glaring illustration of this short-sighted course is in his treatment of the famous Champagne Fairs.[7] Champagne was the great-

[6] *English Historical Review*, XXV, p. 768, a review of Adolphe Landry, *Essai économique sur les mutations des monnaies dans l'ancienne France de Phillippe le Bel à Charles VII*, Paris, 1910.

[7] See Thompson, *Economic and Social History of the Middle Ages*, p. 589, for the origin and development of these fairs.

est commercial area in middle Europe in the twelfth and thirteenth centuries. It lay midway between the Mediterranean and the North Sea, between Lombardy and Flanders. The Champagne Fairs were the chief point in Europe upon which converged the trade from Italy and that from Flanders, the two most commercialized areas in Europe. The network of rivers there or adjacent to its territory—the Rhône, Saône, Seine, Marne, Meuse, Moselle, powerfully contributed to this prosperity, which was enhanced by the excellent government and liberal policy of the counts of Champagne. There were six of these fairs: In January at Lagny, in Lent at Bar-sur-Aube, in May at Provins, in July at Troyes, in September again at Provins, in November again at Troyes. As each fair lasted from six to eight weeks it may be said that the Champagne Fairs were almost permanent. Merchants came to them from all over Europe. The Italians brought oriental imports and manufactured articles; the Spaniards horses, steel, woolens, leather goods, and Saracenic importations; the Germans furs, linen, wooden ware; the Flemings woolen and linen cloth. All the fine wines and products of Europe were sold there. Under the counts of Champagne the fairs were enormously prosperous.

In the reign of Philip IV the prosperity of the Champagne Fairs began to decline. Henry III, count of Champagne, died in 1274 leaving a daughter named Jeanne. She was married to prince Philip, second son of the French king, who by his brother's death became king of France in 1285. Champagne was not annexed to the royal domain; Jeanne down to her death bore the title of countess of Champagne, and the great county passed to her son, the future Louis X, and to his daughter who married Philip, count of Evreux. Nevertheless, the king's influence in Champagne was preponderant and this influence was disastrous. Philip IV saw in the Champagne Fairs a goose which laid a golden egg and nearly killed the fairs by excessive taxation. He multiplied the taxes upon commodities, he imposed new taxes on sale, he increased the number of inspectors, notaries, and wardens of surveillance in order that no penny escape him. Consequently trade was strangled by the meshes of the administration and crushed by the weight of the taxes imposed. Moreover, the suppression of the Lombards and the Jews adversely affected the fairs. Notably the Italian merchants fell away, and after 1320, disappeared. Instead of continuing their route down the Seine to Paris or down the Meuse to Flanders they struck eastward to the Rhine, via the Doubs, and thus reached Flanders. More disastrous still was the king's fiscal policy. The war with Flanders broke off its commercial communication with the fairs, and seriously crippled them. A degree of relief from this condition came in 1305 when a part of Walloon Flanders—Lille, Bethune and Douai—was ceded to France by the treaty of Athis-sur-Orges. But the prosperity of these places was impaired when they were thus separated from Flanders, and these Walloon cities were not enough alone to feed the fairs. So the Flemings disappeared, like the Italians, from Champagne. The tariffs of the bureau at Bapaume at the intersection of the old Roman road from Cambrai to Amiens and that running from Rheims to Arras, through which the bulk of all goods from Flanders and Northern Germany passed, between the years 1301–22 show the fluctuations in and the decline of the commerce of the Champagne Fairs. The price of the farm of the *péages* at Bapaume fell so low that there was no bidder for it. The loss of Bapaume by the French crown in 1330 and its annexation by the counts of Flanders almost consummated the ruin of the fairs.[8]

Too late Philip IV endeavored to rectify what he had done. He planned to make the Seine navigable to Troyes and to canalize the little river Vouzie that goods might reach Provins by water. In an ordinance of March 23, 1303, he promised to observe "the ancient customs of the fairs." But it was an empty gesture. In 1315, 1322, 1326, 1327 his sons and successors legislated vainly in hope of resuscitating the fairs. Of equally adverse importance is the fact that the Italians at this same time began to reach Flanders by the sea. In 1317 a Venetian galley reached Bruges. In 1318 Venice signed a commercial treaty with Bruges. After 1325 a Venetian fleet of fifteen vessels annually sailed, part for England, part for Flanders. Champagne had been the focus of trade north of the Alps in the thirteenth century. Bruges became the same kind of center in the fourteenth. Thither the Italians brought their products, those of the Levant and the Far East, and carried back those of Flanders and the countries of northern Europe. More and more the Italians preferred the sea route. They brought directly to Flanders the products of Italy and the East and carried back cloths, wool and metals from the North. The merchants of La Rochelle also corresponded more and more directly with Flan-

---

[8] Bapaume had originally belonged to the counts of Flanders and from the eleventh century the latter imposed a *péage* there upon all merchandise which passed through this cross-roads. At the end of the twelfth century Bapaume was united to the royal domain with all Artois when Philip Augustus married Isabel of Hainaut. It fell to France in 1200 by the treaty of Peronne, and about 1202 after an inquiry into the toll the king determined to exempt merchandise passing by this town. But Artois with Bapaume, after having been governed by Louis VIII, was ceded in apanage by him to his son Robert of Artois, and from 1237 to 1330 belonged to the descendants of Robert. At this latter date the House of Artois was united with that of the Counts of Flanders, Louis of Nevars having married Marguerite of France, daughter of Philip V and heiress of Artois and Franche Comté. Through the counts of Flanders, Bapaume and Artois passed to the second House of Burgundy and did not return to the crown of France until after the conquest of 1640. Bapaume itself did not become a French town until after the treaty of Aix la Chapelle in 1668.

ders. The route from Aigues-Mortes to Flanders henceforth became of minor importance.

The Champagne Fairs were on the verge of expiring. By the fourteenth century the fair as a commercial institution was becoming obsolete and new methods of business were supplanting it; trade routes had changed or were changing. Finally the outbreak of the Hundred Years' War in 1337 and the terrible invasions of France by English armies in the ensuing years ruined the Champagne Fairs. Philip VI in 1349 issued a long ordinance dealing with them. The preamble, which describes their former history, might be regarded as their obituary notice. The fairs were nearly dead by that time; commerce was moving in new channels.

In the south of France the commercial conditions of Marseilles and Montpellier approximated those of Italy. There was direct communication between Alexandria and Marseilles, Aigues-Mortes, and Montpellier, although the merchants of these towns played a much inferior rôle at Alexandria to the Venetians. Lyons profited by the trade over the Great and Little St. Bernard passes.

There were four fairs each year at Lyons. Nuremberg merchants and those of other free German cities came thither in such numbers that they established permanent warehouses and a German company. They were even so favored there that they had the right freely to sell for fifteen days after the term fixed for the fair.

The chief natural port of entry into France from the Mediterranean was Marseilles, but Marseilles in the thirteenth century did not belong to France; the rule of it was divided between the count of Provence, the bishop and the abbot of St. Victor. Ever since the Crusades Marseilles had prospered and had an important trade with the opposite African coast. But the counts of Provence were also kings of Naples, so that the king of France derived no profit from this great prosperity. Arles, though situated on the embouchure of the Rhône, was a bishopric. Montpellier belonged to the king of Majorca. The only other natural port was Maguelonne which belonged to the bishop of Montpellier. Hence it was that Louis IX, in order to reach blue water unimpeded, had built an artificial port at Aigues-Mortes in the marshes of the Mediterranean littoral, from which a canal was cut to connect it with the delta of the Rhône. There were many Italian merchants in all these places, and the fair at Beaucaire was the greatest commercial center in the south of France. There was a prosperous Italian colony at Nîmes. In 1278 Philip III and Fulcio Cacia, a citizen of Florence, who called himself "captain of the university of the Lombard and Tuscan merchants"—the use of the word *universitas* to denote such an association is of interest—and who acted as resident agent at Montpellier for merchants of Genoa, Venice, Florence, Pia-

cenza, Lucca, Bologna, Pistoia, and Milan, signed a contract by which
the Italian colony in Montpellier agreed to transfer their headquarters
to Nimes on condition that they should have the same privileges as
merchants of Paris and could freely trade in the *senechaussée* of
Beaucaire. Beaucaire and Nimes were the first stage of the commercial route which began at Aigues-Mortes or Marseilles. Avignon was
the second. In 1309 this city had become the seat of the papacy. Under
Pope John XXII the fiscal system of the Holy See was reorganized
and imposed upon the whole church. The pope imposed regular tithes
upon all Christendom. Money flowed in and Avignon was the
scene of intense commercial and financial activities. The pope built
a magnificent palace there; the cardinals erected palaces in the city
and country homes in the country. Avignon has therefore in the history of art, as in that of commerce, a special place in the fourteenth
century. From Avignon the great commercial route went up the Rhône.

The towns of the northeast doubtless drew their merchandise from
Brabant and Flanders. Those of Lorraine drew partly from the Low
Countries and partly from the Rhine. Italian merchants had direct
connection with all these provinces, as is proved by a regulation of
Louis X in 1315 in which this king of France laid down the privileges
of Italian merchants or rather limited them for the purpose of restraining the great commerce of which they were already in possession.
By these privileges the Italians were free, subject to the payment of
ordinary duties, to frequent the Fairs of Champagne and Brie in the
north of France and those of Nimes and Narbonne in the south. Outside of these towns only Paris, St. Omer, and La Rochelle were open
to them. This legislation shows that Italian merchants at this time
supplied not only the south but the north of France including Paris.

We have described the chief route followed by the Italians. We
have also seen how and why the commercial current was diverted from
this course, but it is to be added that this route was not the only one.
Sometimes the Italians instead of going to Aigues-Mortes preferred
to cross the Alps. The pass most frequently used was that of the Mont
Cenis. Over this pass in the valley of the Doria Riparia the travellers
found refuge at the hospice of St. Michel de la Cluse; at the summit
of the pass was the hospice of Mont Cenis which the counts of Savoy
richly endowed; they had an interest in attracting merchants because
the duties there collected were a lucrative revenue. But sometimes the
Italians preferred to cross by the Pass of Largentière, north of the
Massif of Champeaux.

We have the proof of this in a curious document of May 12, 1312.
It is a contract signed between an Italian merchant and a freighter
of Paris named Guillaume Gasconne, who undertook to transport to
Savona sixty-four boxes of cloth having a value of 10,000 *livres*. The

charge was ten *livres* for each box and the route to be followed was Paris, Macon, Savoy, the Col de Largentière. The length of the journey was fixed at thirty-five days. Gasconne did not follow this route. Instead he took the Mont Cenis, reached Piedmont at the moment when a war was in progress, and lost his boxes. He was haled before the provost of Paris by the Italian merchants who demanded 20,000 *livres*, being the price of the goods with 10,000 *livres* additional as indemnity. The defense alleged the instructions given, arguing that in reality he had taken the shortest path, that a servant of the plaintiff who went with him had approved the change of course, and that what had happened was through no fault of his. He was in consequence acquitted.

Philip IV's excessive taxation of commerce ruined every project conceived for the promotion of French trade. As the Italian merchants forsook the Champagne Fairs, so he drove them out of the cities of the Midi, where they were the life of the fairs of Beaucaire. In 1292 when Philip IV first imposed the detested *maltôte* upon the sale of all merchandise the Italians in Nimes protested. The king's financial minister, Mouche, adjusted the grievance, but in 1315 Louis X imposed the *maltôte* again, even increasing the tax to four pence instead of a penny as before. The result was that the Italian merchants forsook Nimes and removed back to Montpellier or went to Avignon, to the great advantage of the papacy. Every trace of this Italian merchant colony in the south of France seems to have disappeared early in the fourteenth century.

At the same time, in the far south conditions adverse to commerce developed. The great southwestern commercial route began at Narbonne whence it passed through Toulouse and so via the Garonne river to Bordeaux. But in 1320 Narbonne suffered severely. The river Aude, a very capricious stream, broke its banks and overflowed the country. The basin of the port was silted up. The ship owners at Narbonne in the beginning of the fourteenth century struggled against this hopeless decay; they repaired the dike of Salelles; they dredged the bed of the river; but it was all useless. The branch of the Aude by Narbonne silted up more and more; the harbor was soon nothing but a marsh, and the despairing inhabitants dreamed of creating a port at Leaucate to replace that of Narbonne. A survey was made and work begun, but nothing was done. Leaucate might have become the trading point between the Mediterranean and the Atlantic.

The Italians, as has been said, had already begun to enter into direct commercial relations with Flanders and England around the Straits of Gibraltar. But if they could unload their merchandise in a Mediterranean harbor, and ship them down the Garonne to Bordeaux, they could avoid both the long sea route and the pirates of the Barbary coast. But the local authorities with amazing shortsightedness were unwilling to do anything. The people of Narbonne petitioned the king and offered an annual sum of 10 *sous tournois* per inhabitant to aid the project. They only asked that the crown would contribute to the expense all the incomes from the *péages* between Leaucate and La Réole. But the Hundred Years' War broke out; the king of France had other cares, and in the fourteenth century Narbonne sank to a provincial town.

However, in spite of the silting up of Narbonne's harbor the Garonne route was still followed in the early years of the century. It was the shortest road from the Mediterranean to the Atlantic. Moreover this route was through industrial and agricultural country. Languedoc did not market all her goods at the local fairs of Beaucaire and Carcassonne; much of it was sent to Bordeaux where it found English buyers. Even the cloths of Roussillon where cloth manufacturing was active, took this road. Finally this country produced much wine, and the wines of Toulouse and of Foix competed with those of the Gironde. Commerce, at least for the products of the interior of Languedoc, therefore continued, even after the silting up of the port of Narbonne.

The reign of Philip IV can point to a few positive commercial gains by France to redress this balance of adversity. The most important of these was the acquisition of Lyons at the junction of the Saône with the Rhône, commanding the head of the Rhône valley and the point of convergence of routes from over the Alps and from southern Germany. It was the first stage in the slow annexation by France of the old medieval realm of Burgundy which had pertained to the Empire since 1032. Another measure taken by Philip IV which was beneficial to French commerce was a treaty with Portugal and the establishment of Havre as a free port of entry for Portuguese goods.

In Normandy Rouen was a flourishing port. From the time that Louis VIII granted the city control of the quays of the Seine, the latter continually dredged the bed of the river so that the vessels of great draught could reach the town. The markets were situated on the quays. The harbor of Rouen was thronged. Havre did not then exist. Harfleur was of no importance. The English brought to Rouen tin from Cornwall and wool for cloth making. Dutch merchants were numerous also. The Hanseatic towns sent to Rouen furs, timber, eiderdown (*edredon*), martin skins, falcons, with which the ladies and gentlemen of the noblesse went hunting. As to the merchants of Portugal and Spain they brought sweet wines, and leather from Seville and Cordova. The little ports of Picardy had also a certain activity especially in smoked and salt herrings and in whale oil, for the whale then was hunted in the English channel.

The commerce of the provinces along the Atlantic seaboard was prosperous. But Gascony and Guienne were English, not French provinces. The only two maritime provinces possessed by France in the West were Poitou and Brittany. La Rochelle, the port of the former province, had been possessed by the French crown since 1224 and was the point of export for the rich Poitevin hinterland behind it. Through it passed the wines of St. Jean d'Angley and Niort, wool from Saintonge and salt from Aunis. Most of these products found their way to Bruges whence Hanseatic merchants carried them to the countries around the Baltic, the Flemings acting as middlemen for their distribution. The only important port of Brittany was Nantes, the natural outlet for the commerce of the Loire river, especially of Touraine and Anjou. Nantois merchants were in trade connection with Portugal, Castile, Flanders, Denmark, and German ports on the Baltic. But hostilities between France and England jeopardized this commerce and when the Hundred Years' War began in 1337 the mariners of Nantes, St. Malo, Vannes, Quimper, and Treguier became ferocious privateers, and Breton commerce sank to a mere coast trade.

In spite of the oppressive policy of Philip IV, commerce and industry had a great extension and historians agree in recognizing that the years which preceded the Hundred Years' War may be counted among the most fortunate which France has known in its long history. The population reached a high figure; according to calculations more or less ingenious it has been estimated at from 20 to 22 millions, and France was much smaller then than to-day. The density of population may have been almost equal to what it is now. Large cities were few. Paris had 200,000 inhabitants at the most; Rouen 70,000. But these were exceptions. The majority of the towns did not exceed 10,000 inhabitants; the villages were more populous than now; and in particular there were many isolated villages which disappeared during the Hundred Years' War. The fields were flourishing; in a great number of the provinces every trace of serfdom had disappeared and the peasants had become free. Agriculture was prosperous and remunerative. New towns or *bastides* were created everywhere, and fixed to the soil that wandering population always numerous in the Middle Ages and often dangerous.

In endeavoring to estimate the debit and credit side of the balance, so to speak, in Philip IV's administration it is undeniable that the improvement of public security, efficient policing in town and country, and other enlightened administration promoted the general welfare of France. Yet even before the calamities of the Hundred Years' War upset or destroyed almost everything, it is evident that the progress made was seriously impaired by heavy taxation and frequent alteration of the currency. Philip IV's administrative reforms were justified

by the conditions of the time, but the increase in the cost of government was itself a serious economic factor. Yet the king's intentions
were not so absolutistic as usually said. His model in many respects
was his grandfather, Louis IX. Thus the ordinance of March 1303
prohibiting private war is almost literally that of St. Louis in 1258.
He follows Louis IX's great ordinance of 1254 in restraint of possible
abuses creeping into the provincial administration by forbidding sene-
schals, bailiffs or prévôts giving office under them to relatives "for
fear lest such persons might not be just and honest in fulfillment of
their duties." Philip IV had a wholesome dread of favoritism and
graft. Royal surveillance of officials was vigilant and appeal facilitated
from lower to higher officials or courts.

Philip IV modified the forms of French administration less than
is usually said. But his endeavor to acquire Flanders lost him the fruit
of his first success in Guienne and if it did not compel, at least it
aggravated his taxation and fiscal policy. However, it must be kept
in mind that heavy taxes and violent fiscal practices were nothing new.
For centuries feudal nobles and petty chatelains had locally acted thus.
What was new to France was the royal nature of such exactions, the
magnitude of the scale, and the conspicuousness of the authority
whence the policy emanated. Perhaps if we knew the whole history
of provincial taxation of previous times as fully as we know the history of the reign of Philip IV we might have a more moderate and
a juster judgment. We judge him severely because he is clearly known
to us. We do not see him in true proportion or perspective.

This chapter may be concluded with a relation of the important
economic and social events which transpired in France under Philip
IV's three sons, Louis X (1314–16), Philip V (1316–22), Charles IV
(1322–28) with whom the Capetian dynasty terminated. Much economic and social discontent prevailed in France in 1314. Philip IV's
ravenous fiscality had provoked all classes. The clergy had been subjected to enormous exactions; the bourgeoisie was angry over the taxes
imposed upon commerce and industry; the masses furious owing to
constant manipulation of the money and high prices; the wealthy were
indignant at the sumptuary laws; the peasantry restive. In the
provinces local leagues were formed composed of nobles, clergy and
tiers état. Even the monastic orders took a hand, notably the Cistercians. The crown took alarm, hastily united the provincial estates in
assembly, and promised redress of grievances and strict inquiry into
complaints aimed at the royal officials against whom there was universal protest. Charters of enlarged liberty were granted to the estates
general of Normandy, Burgundy, Champagne, Picardy, Languedoc
and Auvergne, and guarantees given to the clergy and nobles. But
the reaction of the nobles went too far when they demanded restora-

tion of the judicial duel and the right of private war. Enguerrand de Marigny, the all-powerful minister of the late king, was hanged by Louis X as a sop to the populace.

No effective measures were taken, however, to remedy the general situation. The king permitted the exiled Jews and Lombards to return under licenses sold to them at a high price and with them contracted loans hypothecated upon the revenues of the *senéchausées;* he obtained a loan from the city of Paris and finally sold "commissions of freedom" by whose terms serfs on the royal domains were permitted to purchase their liberty. Nineteenth century liberal historians attached great significance to this action of the king. In 1830 Guizot declared that "the emperor Alexander of Russia would not dare to promulgate a similar ukase," and signalized the famous phrase of the pompous preamble of the ordinance that "all men are by nature born free" as a medieval anticipation of the rights of man. But the "rights of man" as a vague social abstraction were cant utterances of legists and churchmen all through the Middle Ages. The doctrine of "natural law" had no more to do with the reality of things than later glittering generalities of social visionaries of the eighteenth and nineteenth centuries.

It was a misfortune for France that the reign of Philip V (1316–22) was so short, for in character and ability this king recalls the best of the Capetian sovereigns. If his reign had been a long one it is not improbable that France might have been spared many of the appalling miseries of later years. An untoward symptom with which the king successfully coped was the appearance again of leagues of the nobles. These movements were wholly selfish reactions of the feudal nobility which for a century had regarded the growth of the royal power with sullen resentment; if successful they would have thrown France back again into the violence of the tenth and eleventh centuries. Neither the clergy nor the people viewed them with favor. They were class and sectional disturbances detrimental to the general welfare of France and deserved to be crushed. Private war, judicial duels, "high justice" of the great feudatories without right of appeal to the king's court for review or redress, provincial coinage rights, were obsolete feudal rights which had no place in the larger, more compact, more national France which was in process of formation in the fourteenth century.

In combating this feudal reaction Philip V leaned upon the clergy and the bourgeoisie. Distrusting the nobles he filled the civil offices of the government with clergy who were loyal to the monarchy and even used church militia in the subjugation of feudal insurrection in the provinces. In the estates general the representation and influence of the clergy was enlarged, in return for which the clergy in convocation granted the crown liberal subsidies out of ecclesiastical revenue. The accord between the crown and the clergy was so complete that the bishops and abbots not only of the royal domain, but of the entire kingdom became less and less feudal barons and more and more devoted subjects, not actuated by class consciousness but by loyal interest in the common good and general welfare of France. National feeling was stronger among the clergy than among the French nobles.

Towards the communes Philip V was at once masterful and liberal. Many of the municipalities owing to mismanagement of their finances, were on the verge of bankruptcy. Into these the king sent royal investigators to inquire into their finances and methods of taxation. In others —and this included all the larger towns—the cleavage between the patriciate and the people with the attendant exploitation of the lower working classes by the rich gild-masters provoked political turbulence. In these, too, the royal authority intervened. Thus the king suppressed the communes of Sens, Senlis, Laon and Compiègne and reduced them to prévotés under immediate crown control. On the other hand Philip V confirmed popular privileges in the towns of Languedoc, the *fueros* of French Navarre, the franchises of Paris, Calais, Troyes, Vitry, Meaux, Chaumont, Gisors, Evreux, Lisieux, Caen, Orléans, Bourges, Niort, *etc.* Between the peril of feudal reaction and the abuses which the populace of many towns suffered from the patriciate, the welfare of the people as a whole was promoted by the extension of royal authority over the towns. In the case of some of the larger towns the political pretension of the patriciate which ruled them was as great a menace to the union of France under the monarchy as the insurrectionary movements of the feudality in the provinces. In compensation for the loss of their political liberties the prevotal towns gained in administrative honesty and efficiency and economic prosperity. Between communes whose independence disappeared and the prevotal towns whose condition was ameliorated the distinction is a narrow one. The former ceased to be free municipalities, the latter ceased to be domainial communities, and both became *villes du roi*. The concept of the supremacy of the state triumphed over political particularism.

In his administrative activity Philip V was a demon of energy and was the author of an almost incredible amount of legislation. The completeness of each ordinance for the end in view, and the exactness of the language employed are remarkable features of this body of legislation. It is noteworthy that most of these laws were issued only after careful consultation with the estates. If Philip V ruled with an iron hand, the hand was enclosed in a velvet glove. The improvements which Philip the Long made were much less of a political nature than of material progress and social amelioration. Unlike his predecessor he did not make a mere gesture of interest in the condition of the servile class, but genuinely labored for relief of their condition. The devastation wrought by the feudal leagues in Champagne, Picardy, Artois, Nivernais, was enormous. Cottages and whole villages were destroyed, vineyards cut down, cattle, sheep and working oxen driven off, the peasants maltreated. Agriculture, commerce and industry were alike ruined in these provinces. The king labored hard for the remedy of these conditions, even going so far as to suppress the dearly beloved and ancient privilege of the nobles to hunt as they pleased across the peasants' fields, and to keep rabbit warrens, pigeons and hunting dogs, all of which were destructive of the peasants' crops and poultry. Not until the French Revolution swept these abuses away did France ever again see so drastic legislation in suppression of manorial abuses. Similarly Philip V established greater security of travel, improved roads and bridges, abolished tolls on road and stream. All *péages* and tolls which had been established without authorization were abolished. Where they were exacted, whether interprovincial douanes or tariffs at the frontier, the rates of all articles taxed were placarded in the bureaux for all to see them, the collectors were required to keep a complete register of all who passed through the bureau, with their names and the quantity and nature of what they had with them; and finally all commissioners were admonished to be polite towards all merchants and travellers. In order to defray the expenses of local improvements, local taxation was sometimes remitted, and in the case of the towns they were given permission to sell their common lands around the town from which the town's supply of timber and firewood came, in addition to a revenue derived from rents of tracts to truck gardeners. Philip V also reëstablished charitable confraternities which his father had suppressed for fear they might be made foci of popular agitation, but kept the gilds under close if benevolent supervision.

The effect of this energetic and intelligent legislation upon commerce was striking. The Champagne Fairs had a new lease of life, short indeed, but prosperous while it lasted. In the royal ordinance issued to the bailiffs of Champagne the king enjoined upon them *"que les gens du pays et d'autres pays, marchands, et autres, puissent surement aller et venir avec leurs marchandises."* In the matter of the fairs the government issued safe-conducts, patrolled roads by day and night, and provided escorts of soldiery to protect merchants and goods. The archives of Philip V's reign abound with evidences of the prosperity of the Champagne Fairs, of those of Brie, Lendit, Beaucaire. Many towns on the royal domain were given the right to have a fair. Philip V manifested greater and more intelligent interest in the promotion of commerce than any other French king before Henry IV. He combated the snobbish prejudice of the nobles against trade as socially demeaning by encouraging the rich bourgeois in his official family to keep on in the business which had made them rich in spite of the fact that they had become government officials, "as if they were not in my council and in my service." But the king did not promote the commerce of his subjects to the prejudice of foreign merchants in France. He looked with favor upon these, whether German Hansers, or Flemings or Spaniards or Italians. Towards the last he was especially liberal, and reversed all his father's prohibitive legislation. The result was an influx of "Lombards" into France, and colonies of Genoese, Florentine and Sienese merchants and bankers again flourished in Nimes, Lyons, Troyes, Paris and many other towns. All such foreign merchants who became "bourgeois of the king," or naturalized, were exempted from the tax on sales and the tax upon their goods which were imposed upon other foreign merchants in France.

In the matter of the Jews Philip V was almost as narrow as his predecessors. His brother Louis X had permitted the Jews to return for nine years, but limited their colonies to Paris, St. Omer, Nimes and La Rochelle, and in addition to the old tax of two pence in the pound exacted of them, imposed a *taille* upon both their real and personal property. Philip V made no change in these regulations. But if he was narrow, he was not intolerant. He would permit no popular molestation of the Jews, and protected the Jewries and the synagogues in them. But the Jews were still required to wear a yellow tabard. In a word, Philip V's protection of the Jews was hard and scant, but the heavy hand of the king was better than the claws of the fanatical populace.

Only with regard to heresy and heretics was Philip V fanatically intolerant, and the fourteenth century was prolific of heresies, for what reasons we shall find in another chapter.

The most radical reforms which Philip V contemplated were so revolutionary that they could not be effected. These were the establishment of a uniform system of coinage in France and a uniform system of weights and measures. To-day such conditions seem elementary to the promotion of commerce. But when we reflect that the metric system, in spite of the incontrovertible evidence in its favor, still does not obtain in the United States and England on account of tradition and prejudice, then we can understand how great an opposition Philip V encountered when he proposed this reformation of the coinage and weights and measures in France. Volumes have been written by scholars who have had the patience to explore the mystery and confusion attached to the history of medieval coins and medieval weights and measures. The variety was almost infinite. Philip V's purpose was a laudable intention which does honor to his intelligence. The weights and measures varied from one province to another, and from one town to another. Each used its own, the standards of which

were kept in the feudal castle or in the hôtel de ville. Sometimes in
the same city, the weights and measures varied. In Paris there was a
special measure for grain and another for liquids. The *setier* of rye
was not the same as the *setier* of salt. It is easy to understand the
difficulties arising from this condition. In every locality it was necessary for a man to make a new measurement of his merchandise; this
entailed new expense for the merchants which increased the price of
goods. At Paris the public scales in the Rue des Lombards was an
hereditary fief. What a service the king would have rendered if he
had been successful in establishing uniform weights and measures!
In 1321 Philip V submitted the question to the clergy, barons and
deputies of the towns whom he convoked at Poitiers. He asked them
if it would not be convenient to establish uniformity of money and of
weights and measures throughout France. But the deputies refused
to commit themselves. Then the towns which were individually consulted replied that their measures suited themselves. Thus in the face
of the general indifference, in the face even of the hostility of certain
towns, the reform failed. It took the French Revolution to bring about
the change.

One has no hesitation in saying that Philip V was an able and intelligent monarch, and deserved the popularity which he enjoyed among
the masses of his subjects. The poet Geffroi de Paris writing sometimes
in Old French, sometimes in Latin, certainly interpreted the general
opinion when he wrote that the king protected the "little fish" against
the voracity of the "big fish," and hailed him as "a shepherd, not a
wolf." He praises the king for avoiding unnecessary wars:

> *De la viennent toustes et batailles*
> *Quant le roy chevauche en tailles.*

He rejoices over the subjugation of the rebels in 1316. They are "un-
natural men" who fight against their motherland. A king is meant
to rule for the public weal and not in the interest of a privileged social
class. Philip V is a true king and the people will support him with
all their strength—*populus est tibi propitius.*

Nevertheless in spite of Philip V's intelligence and application the
distress of France was little relieved. The times were out of joint.
The instability of all values in a time of sharp economic and social
transition, derangement of prices, unstable currency, novel forms of
taxation, spasmodic outbreaks both of rebellious nobles and of a turbulent bourgeois and peasantry, characterized the reign. To add to these
adverse conditions Nature herself was faithless. The winter of 1314–15
was an unusually severe one, while the spring was too dry and the
summer too wet. The result was a crop failure in 1315. The year
1316 was no better. Both the spring and autumn seedings were frozen

in many places. Vineyards almost everywhere suffered from frost. Crowds of half-starved peasants in bare feet perambulated the stricken fields carrying sacred relics and imploring God to grant a return of the sun. France was the prey of famine for two years and prices did not become normal until 1318. A measure (*setier*) of wheat which ordinarily cost from ten to fifteen *sols parisis* in these years sold for from sixty to eighty *sols*. The poor ate bread made of leaves and straw. "Many men and women, poor creatures, died of hunger in the streets of Paris" records the *Chronicle of St. Denis*. Men, women, and children fought over heaps of offal in the streets. The sewers and ditches of many towns were choked with rotting corpses. Superstition added mental suffering to this privation and wild tales were current of demons, sorcerers, witches.

Out of this ferment in 1320 sprang a revolt of the peasantry, a new Pastoreaux, similar to that in 1251. Crowds of rudely armed peasants suffering from hunger and mystically exalted, forsook the farms and thronged together to the villages and towns bearing crudely made crosses and banners. Some wanted to go to the Holy Land, others to the shrine of St. James of Compostella, some to petition the king. As in the days of the Peasants' Crusade in 1096 and in 1251, these wretched hordes were made the dupes of depraved leaders, in this case of a defrocked monk. In addition the riff-raff of town and country-side joined them, "men without faith or law or hearth or home," high-waymen, cut-purses, thieves, poachers, runaway serfs, fugitive crimi-nals. "Like a violent wind," says the chronicle, these turbulent hordes marched upon Paris, where they looted the abbey of St. Martin-des-Champs, broke into the Châtelet, released the prisoners there, and mur-dered the provost of the city. The king shut himself up in the Louvre, the nobles took refuge in their castles, the bourgeois kept the shutters up on their houses and stores until this fury was passed. Finally the Pastoreaux quit Paris and broke up into separate bands which in-vaded the provinces: Berry, Saintonge, Languedoc, carrying rioting and pillaging with them. The Jews especially suffered from their fury. Five hundred men, women and children were massacred at Verdun-sur-Garonne. In Albi the town councillors shut the gates, but the popu-lace within opened them and welcomed the Pastoreaux "for the love of Christ against the enemies of faith." The same sort of fanaticism was almost everywhere. In vain the pope anathematized and excom-municated. Finally the largest band of Pastoreaux got as far as Aigues-Mortes with the fantastic idea of emulating St. Louis and going to the Orient to fight the Mussulmans. Here in the heavy marshes hunger and fever made an end of most of them, but for a long time isolated bands of these brigands infested the Midi. Elsewhere, too, the roving bands were cut to pieces or perished of hunger and privation. A brutal aftermath of this movement was a wave of popular fury against lepers. In many places communities of these wretched pariahs of medieval society were cruelly murdered. Even when spared, new laws imposed such terrible restrictions upon lepers that life with them was a living death.

The Capetian house ended in the person of Charles IV (1322–28), whose death terminated an epoch. Under the Valois kings the dominant historical event was the long war with England known as the Hundred Years' War (1337–1453). But the preliminaries of that conflict are to be found in the reign of Philip IV, and to the external history of France and the relations of Philip IV with Edward I of England we shall now turn.

CHAPTER II

AT the end of the thirteenth century the ancient feud between France and England which had existed ever since the Norman Conquest in 1066 assumed a new color. Hitherto all the wars between them had been wars of a feudal nature arising from the circumstance that the English king held in France, though in vassalage to the French king, the provinces of Normandy, Anjou, Maine, Touraine, Poitou, Guienne and Gascony, in addition to controlling the policy of certain other fiefs adjacent to these territories, of all of which the French king coveted possession. In 1204 Philip II had conquered the lands north of the Loire from John of England; in 1224 Poitou passed to France. But in the southwest the great rich territories of Guienne and Gascony still were held of England. These two provinces were an object of French territorial ambition in the reign of Philip IV. But the inducement was now not so much of a feudal nature as of an economic nature.

The entire character of the rivalry between England and France was changed by the end of the thirteenth century. Once feudal and political, the antagonism between them now became primarily a commercial one, in which the stakes were the wine trade of Gascony and the woolen manufactures of Flanders, which were dependent on English raw wool. A conditional factor was sea-power or maritime supremacy in the Bay of Biscay and the English Channel, then often called the "Narrow Sea." A glance at the map will show that the bond of connection between England and Flanders and between England and Gascony was the sea. It was absolutely necessary in the interest of English commerce that England be able to keep the sea lanes open between the eastern ports of England and the ports of Flanders, and between Southampton or Portsmouth and Bordeaux.

Another ground of dispute between the two nations was the fisheries in the North Sea, the Channel and the Bay of Biscay, the last the greatest whaling ground of the Middle Ages. Bayonne throve on whaling. The hardy Basque fishermen were famous whalers, and to this

* For map see W. R. Shepherd, *Historical Atlas*, 7th ed. (Henry Holt & Co., New York, 1929), p. 76.

day a whale is on the city seal of Bayonne. The North Sea possessed the most important fishing ground in northern Europe. From remote times the cod, haddock and herring fisheries of the North Sea were famous. The North Sea is a shallow sea at best, but off the east coast of England there is a low submarine plateau with an average depth of twenty fathoms, formed of deltaic mud, teeming with minute organisms which make the best food for young fish. This is the Dogger Bank. Here English, Frisian, Flemish, Norman and Breton fishing vessels were wont to gather in the spring and summer months. Clashes were frequent between the fleets of the various nations and piracy an almost chronic practice. It was a hard and daring life. For centuries no official cognizance was taken of these violent affairs since the fisher folk of each nation was equally an offender and the sea was regarded as a sort of "no man's land." But the growth of maritime commerce by the thirteenth century, combined with the development of stronger governments, led to legislation in restraint of evils like wrecking and piracy. The First Statute of Westminster (1275) of Edward I reënacted a law as old as Richard I, providing that when a ship was stranded it should not be accounted a wreck if a man, a dog, or a cat escaped alive from it. But since no police of the sea existed except what the warden of the Cinque Ports [1] was able to assure, such legislation was more honored in the breach than in the observance.

The history of Anglo-French rivalry in Flanders and that of French encroachment in Gascony, while originally separate and distinct chapters of history, by the end of the thirteenth century became united into a single issue, or rather may be considered as two different angles of the commercial rivalry between France and England in the reigns of Philip IV and Edward I. We shall first follow the history of Flanders and the territories adjacent to it, commonly and collectively known as the Low Countries, or in French, the Pays Bas.

The lowlands of Central Europe along the coast of the North Sea, made by the detritus of the Rhine, the Meuse and the Scheldt rivers, formed a cluster of feudal and ecclesiastical principalities. South of the Rhine the most important of these states were the counties of Flanders and Hainaut, the duchy of Brabant and the bishoprics of Cambrai and Liège. North of the Rhine lay the counties of Zeeland, Holland, Guelders and Zutphen and the bishopric of Utrecht. The

---

[1] Ever since the Norman Conquest, for fear lest that feat might be attempted by another, the five south-coast towns of Sandwich, Dover, Hythe, Romney and Hastings, to which later were added Rye and Winchelsea, formed a peculiar organization of chartered towns whose special mission was to protect England from foreign invasion. The ships of the Cinque Ports were the nucleus of every English fleet and the warden of the Cinque Ports was admiral thereof. The charter of 6 Edward I (1278) was the palladium of the Cinque Port liberties.

population of all these territories was historically of Low German stock, but considerable variation of blood and especially of language had developed in the course of the centuries. North of the Rhine the population was Friesian or pure Low German (Dutch) blood and speech. South of the Rhine it was Flemish, speaking a language midway between German and Dutch, except in Flanders west of the Lys river, where French was spoken. Broadly speaking this was Walloon Flanders, although in a closer sense Walloon Flanders was applied only to the territory around Lille. These Low Countries or Pays Bas shaded off on the east into Germany and on the west-southwest into France. The frontiers were a penumbra of wavering principalities, since geography denied any natural frontiers to the Low Countries except along the sea. These lowlands in the Middle Ages were separate political entities, though to-day united as the kingdom of Belgium. But whether in medieval or in modern times both in history and language they have always been transitional. Their political history has been largely that of other countries, of France and Germany in the medieval period, of Spain and Austria in the modern period. The romance Walloon speech stands between the romance language of western Switzerland and the romance tongue of northeastern France, while Flemish bears a similar intermediate relation between the German and the Dutch languages.

Of all these loosely agglomerated territories the county of Flanders, at the end of the thirteenth century, was the most important. The mixed composition of this principality admirably illustrates the heterogeneous nature of the Low Countries as a whole. Part of Flanders, known as the "lordship," of which the count of Flanders was *dominus* but not *comes,* was imperial and the count held it as a fief of the Empire; the "county" of Flanders was a fief of the French crown, while a third part of the territory ruled by the count was allodial or the "Free County of Flanders." Even these distinctions do not exhaust the variety of territories which formed the territory of Flanders. For the imperial portion was divided into no less than five regions: (1) the county of Alost between the Scheldt and the Dendre, (2) the little district of Over-Schelde, or the Land across the Scheldt (Terre d'outre-Escaut), (3) the estuary of the Scheldt along the Hond, composed of four small districts known as the Quatre-Métiers or De vier Ambachten, (4) the Zeelander islands of Walcheren and North and South Beverland, which the count of Holland held as vassal of the count of Flanders, (5) the Waes or Waesland.

The origin of imperial Flanders and the nature of the bond which united it with the Empire are very obscure. It was natural that the county of Alost pertained to the Empire. It was, in fact, a portion of Brabant which the counts of Flanders had seized in the middle of the eleventh century, and of which the emperors had recognized their possession subject to homage. Similarly Over-Schelde, situated between the two arms of the Scheldt, so near to Ghent that it almost seemed a part of it, was naturally German. As to Zeeland and the islands off its coast, though the counts of Flanders had acquired them in 1018, in reality from the middle of the thirteenth century (1253) they were considered as part of imperial Flanders attached to the county of Holland. The four districts known as De vier Ambachten, situated between the estuary of the Scheldt and Waesland and the parcel of territory called Over-Schelde, east of Ghent, were curious archaic survivals of Carolingian jurisdiction in this area—hence the name applied to this territory. The Waesland, though now every rood of it is cultivated, was in the Middle Ages a wide, sterile moor about thirty miles in length lying between Ghent and Antwerp. It was a fief of the French crown though the emperor claimed to be overlord of the count of Flanders for it.

Of all these confusing and confused territories the County of Flanders or French Flanders was far the most important. Here were clustered more towns than in any other region of the Low Countries. In the Flemish part (*Flandre flamingante*) were Ghent, Oudenarde, Courtrai, Ypres, Bailleul, Cassel, Bourbourg, Bergues, Furnes; in French Flanders were Bruges, Lille, Douai, and Orchies. The dividing line between the two idioms—and the latter was the Picard dialect— was roughly the Lys. This demarcation, however important, did not correspond to any political frontiers.

Flanders was one of the great fiefs of the French crown. Under the early Capetian kings the counts had been in amicable relations with the kings of France. Baldwin V had been regent of France during the minority of Philip I (1060–66). The commercial relations between Flanders and France were close. There is a record of the year 1066 relating how "merchants and wine dealers of the Flemish nation" resorted to the French provinces bringing Flemish woolens to exchange for French wines, and of French traders from Noyon, Vermandois, Amiens and Santerre journeying to Flanders to buy Flemish cloth. Flemish merchants thronged the Champagne Fairs. In the twelfth and thirteenth centuries French culture spread prodigiously in Flanders. Flemish students in great numbers attended the schools of Rheims, Laon and Paris; the noble families of the two countries were closely intermarried; high clerical offices in Flanders were often occupied by French incumbents; the French monastic orders of Cluny and Cîteaux had many houses in the land; the spread of the French language steadily limited the sphere in which Flemish speech was current. At the end of the thirteenth century the linguistic line of demarcation was practically identical with the condition to-day.

French was sung by *trouvères* in court and at cross-roads. French was the official language of the counts of Flanders before the kings of France abandoned Latin for the vernacular. It was the language of all but petty and local commerce.

But this growth of French influence was strenuously contravened by Norman influence. William the Conqueror's queen was Matilda of Flanders; many Flemings were in the invasion of England in 1066; considerable numbers of Flemish colonists settled in England in the time of the Norman kings.[2] Anglo-French rivalry in Flanders became acute in the reign of Henry I of England, who was the first king of record to establish money-fiefs, and this in the Low Countries where several vassals of the count of Flanders, notably the duke of Louvain, were in English pay. In 1127 when count Charles the Good of Flanders was murdered, news of this assassination first reached London through Flemish merchants. Henry I, Louis VI, and the emperor Lothar II each strove to establish his own candidate in the county, and the struggle terminated with English ascendancy. But the policy of Stephen, in hiring Flemish mercenaries, whom he billeted on the English people, and the paralysis of both agriculture and commerce during this epoch of anarchy, estranged England and Flanders. The count of Flanders supported Louis VII against Henry Plantagenet. At the death of Louis VII (1180), Philip of Flanders was regent during Philip II's minority. But when the young king married a daughter of the count of Hainaut, a niece of the count of Flanders, upon whose death the count of Flanders claimed her estates, war ensued which culminated in French annexation of Artois and the important town of Arras. Thereafter, for good reason the Flemish counts felt alarm lest France covet and acquire Térouanne, Béthune, Lille, Lens, Douai, and other towns of Flanders adjacent to the French border. This fear threw the counts of Flanders into the arms of the English kings and accounts for the alliance with John of England and the emperor Otto of Brunswick, an alliance which was smashed at the battle of Bouvines (July 27, 1214) where the count of Flanders was made a French prisoner. After her husband had suffered twelve years of imprisonment, the Countess Joan, to obtain his release, signed the treaty of Melun in 1226, which ceded Lille, Douai and Sluys as pledges for the payment of his ransom, and the Flemish barons swore on their fealty to compel the count to fulfill this obligation.

At the end of the thirteenth century the reigning count of Flanders was a pure Frenchman, Guy de Dampierre, a Champenois by birth, and related to the house of Bourbon, a junior branch of the French royal line. The Flemish court was modelled after that of the French

[2] See Thompson, *Economic and Social History of the Middle Ages,* p. 309.

kings. But although Flanders thus had gradually become politically
and culturally more French, commercially and industrially she gravitated more and more towards England. Simultaneously an acute social
cleavage developed. The Frenchified Flemish aristocracy enjoyed
feudal rights of justice and taxation, imposed *péages* and tolls upon
local trade, collected manorial "renders" in natural products, and quit-
rents and tenths in money from the non-noble classes. If the latter
had been mainly peasantry they would have been inarticulate and helpless in the face of the lordly class. But this was not the case. For in
Flanders earlier than anywhere else in Europe outside of Italy an
energetic commercial and industrial activity had developed. Like Lombardy, Flanders was a land of towns peopled by burghers who were
merchants, tradesmen and artisans. The civilization was predominantly
urban in nature, not rural. Ghent, Bruges, Ypres, Douai vied with
Milan and the towns of Lombardy. Commerce and manufacturing
were of more importance than agriculture. The population was denser
than anywhere else in Europe north of the Alps. Even as early as
1127 Flanders was described as *valde populosa*—"densely peopled."
A capitalistic régime predominated. The country, though wholly
French, had an industrial organization very different from that of
France, so that M. Pirenne can write:

> It was industry which gave these regions their characteristic physiognomy
> and which assigned them a unique place in Europe. Nowhere, not even in
> Italy, could be found so many manufacturing centers in so small a space.

The great towns of Flanders were practically free cities, for the measure of political authority which the counts still preserved over them
was slight. In the cities the rich merchants and industrialists formed
a political and social patriciate, or merchant aristocracy, which controlled the municipal government. Between them and the lower working classes a sharp distinction was made. These "poorters" or burghers
were rich and influential. Socially they were the town aristocracy,
economically they were the employer and capitalistic class. They were
organized into gilds or hansas, which had long since ceased to be
mutual associations of masters and workmen, and instead had become
great commercial and manufacturing corporations from which the
lower working classes were totally excluded. Such was the situation
in Flanders at the end of the thirteenth century.

The history of the fourteenth century, down to 1382, when the
domination of the French dukes of Burgundy was firmly established
in Flanders, is marked by great political, economic and social events.
Nowhere else in Europe, not even in Italy, did economic and social
questions have so much importance as in Flanders. Between 1300 and
1385 three great revolutions took place in which the divergent forces

played a large part. In the first phase the artisans and Count Guy de Dampierre were allied against the merchants. The gilds were almost destroyed and the working classes forced their entrance into the *échevinage*. In the second revolution, which was marked by the great name of Jacques Van Artevelde, the artisans and the bourgeois were combined against the count who, in the interest of France, sacrificed the commercial and industrial interests of his country, which relied upon English support. Finally, in the third revolution, from 1379 to 1385, the working classes became involved in violent feud with the bourgeois and were crushed by French military intervention. In the first revolution Bruges was the leader of the movement; in the other two Ghent played the leading rôle. We shall follow in detail in their proper places, the history of each of these revolutions in Flanders.

The internal and external history of Flanders was conditioned by this feud between the lower working classes in the towns and the merchant aristocracy, and in turn the policy of the French and English kings was influenced by it. This merchant aristocracy everywhere was a narrow-minded caste who imposed long hours of work, reduced wages and were indifferent to the material welfare of the masses. Hence it was that the working classes clamored for representation in the city governments. The *minores* were opposed to the *majores,* as in Italy the *populo minuto* was pitted against the *populo grasso.* There were some popular risings during the second half of the thirteenth century. For a long time such ebullitions were isolated and local in nature. But they became a general and chronic phenomenon. The whole artisan class rebelled against the patriciate.

If there is one word that expresses the life of Flanders during this period, that word is "cloth."

"All the nations of the world," we are told by Matthew of Westminster, "were kept warm by the wool of England made into cloth by the men of Flanders."

Flanders was dependent for its prosperity on the manufacture of cloth, and on the commerce resulting from that manufacture. The foundation stone of every town in Flanders was its cloth industry, and Flemish textiles were everywhere famous for their quality and the beauty of their colors. They were unexcelled in Europe and could be purchased in the bazaars of the Orient. This cloth was indispensable for the clothing of the nobility and the rich bourgeoisie, so much so that when Philip IV, during the war with the Flemings, closed the French frontier to the products of their industry, Flemish stuffs that the royal court could not do without, were nevertheless imported. They were of a surpassing variety: there were common cloths, black or gray; browns and cloths of a bright black; linsey-woolsey; cloths that showed streaks of changing colors. Every town had its products which were recognized by the length of the bolts and by the lead seals that were appended to them. At Ypres nearly 800,000 of these lead seals were used yearly. The market of Flanders was a world market. The manufacture of cloth became so important that other kinds of industry, regardless of their prosperity, tended to decline.

Since all Flanders lived upon cloth-making, wool was the all-important article of importation. Some of it came from Artois; some was purchased by Flemish merchants at the Champagne Fairs. But it was insufficient in quantity and inferior in quality. The greatest amount of wool, and that the best, came from England. The rich English land-owners, sure of their market for wool, developed sheep pastures to the detriment of agriculture. The abbeys, especially the Cistercian abbeys in Yorkshire, owned enormous flocks of sheep. The king himself was an extensive sheep-raiser on the royal domains; the *receptores lanarum regiarum* were important revenue officials. One of the richest incomes of the crown was derived from the export tax imposed upon wool. In consequence we early find resident in Dover and London groups of Flemish buyers who were agents of the Hanse of Bruges. Originally the various gilds in the towns of Flanders had been separate and distinct. But in process of time they had become fused together as the Hanse de Londres. The core of this association was the gild of Bruges, whence it was sometimes called the Hanse of Bruges. The director of this corporation or *hansgraf* was always a Brugeois. When Ypres was affiliated with it, it had the privilege of furnishing the *schildrake* or standard-bearer. Curiously enough Ghent was never a member of it. In its largest capacity the Hanse of Bruges was composed of the gilds of some fifteen Flemish towns engaged in the English wool trade. This London or Bruges Hanse must not be confused with another hanse in Flanders which was an association of seventeen merchant gilds from seventeen towns and which was spread all over the Low Countries. For besides the Flemish towns of Bruges, Ghent and Ypres, we find towns like Lille, Valenciennes and Cambrai in it. This Hanse of Seventeen Towns, formed of localities which were subject to different feudal princes, never had the solid organization of the other hanse. Its principal business was trade with the Champagne Fairs and with their decay it perished. It certainly ceased to exist after the middle of the fourteenth century. When the Champagne Fairs ceased to be of importance the merchants of this hanse confined their activities to local fairs in the Low Countries, the largest of which was that of Thourout. But this fair shrank as Bruges grew in commercial importance. Other fairs were at Ypres, Ghent and Lille. The last disappeared when Lille was annexed by the French crown. Bruges in time absorbed so much of the commerce and exchange of the north that all fairs in the Low Countries decayed. The conditions of business were changed.

Exploitation of the mineral wealth of the Low Countries also dates from this epoch. The basin of the Meuse is rich in iron, copper and coal. Liège was early famed for its iron work, Dinant for its copper. Coal was mined as early as 1198.

The rich woolen and cloth merchants, through their double control of the gilds and the town government, manipulated things to their own profit and to the exploitation of the workers. A weaver could not be a weaver and a dyer too; nor could he have more than one apprentice, though a wool-clipper might have seven; a patron could not have more than three apprenticed "companions" or assistants working under him; small tradesmen were restricted in the kind and quantity of goods they might sell; the purveyance of foodstuffs was similarly differentiated and limited; raw materials were exclusively controlled by the great gildsmen and doled out to the workers as piece-work, which was more profitable—to the employers—than the wage system. The workers were subject to crises and unemployment. The wool did not pass immediately from the big merchants to the working-man, but through the intermediary "cloth merchant," also a capitalist who procured the wool from the big merchants and divided it among the master weavers, who in turn sold the finished product. Finally, the "blue nails," as the lower working population was contemptuously called by the rich bourgeoisie, were shut out from all representation in the local government, being denied the right to vote or to hold office. Thus acutely antagonistic elements of class conflict, political, economic and social, existed in the Flemish towns as in every other European town, for that matter. Far from narrowing the gulf which separated the upper and lower classes, the patriciate in its pride widened the breach. From year to year town laws and gild rules aug-mented the privileges and the power of the gild monopolies, and re-duced freedom of labor, lowered wages. For fear of rioting by the workers no more than seven were permitted to assemble together; they were forbidden to form associations or to bear arms. The *keures* or customals of the towns witness to this class tyranny. In some towns a patrician could strike a workman with impunity, while an insult to a patrician was punished with heavy fine. In consequence of this strained condition we find terrible outbreaks recorded. In 1280–81 there were riots in Bruges, Ypres, Douai and Tournai. Nevertheless something favorable remains to be said of this merchant aristocracy. They paved the streets and canalized the sluggish streams; they built magnificent hôtels-de-ville, or city halls, like that still to be seen at Bruges; they erected stately gild halls like the great Cloth Hall at

Ypres, which was destroyed in the World War; they founded churches and hospitals and they erected for themselves palatial houses whose architecture and decoration still delight the observer.

Count Guy de Dampierre looked with apprehension upon the large political authority exercised by the patriciate in the great towns. In 1280 when the working classes rebelled, he took advantage of the situation and refused to renew the charter of Bruges which had been burned with the town archives in the riot, and the "XXXIX," i.e., the Thirty Nine patricians who had governed the town since 1228 hated him accordingly.

Already may be seen—and this is the key to the history of the next century—the alliance, becoming traditional, of the ruling class with the French sovereign, they to maintain their power alike against the count and the craftsmen, he to strengthen his hold upon the country. When, therefore, in the next few years, the governing class showed their readiness to accept the rule of the French king, the artisans, struggling against them, became of necessity the defenders of the independence of the country and the staunch supporters of that count.[3]

Philip IV, who resented the quasi-independence of Flanders, coveted Flemish territory not merely for territorial aggrandizement of the French kingdom, but also for the purpose of gaining control of the rich revenues of Flanders. He made skilful employment of the discordant elements in the country. With the fine fiscal machine he possessed, the commerce and industry of Flanders would pour treasure into his hands. But Edward I of England regarded the prospect of French political control over Flanders with grave apprehension, for it would be certain to be injurious to the English wool trade. Hence it came about that the cleavage within Flanders affected the relations of France and England. The count and the lower classes inclined towards England; the nobles and the patriciate in the towns favored France. Philip IV high-handedly established "guardians" in Bruges, Ghent, Douai and other Flemish towns to protect the échevins, all of whom it must be appreciated were under patriciate domination, from "injustice" on the part of the count. This not only lessened Guy's political power, but had its economic aspect in that it decreased his financial resources. Guy was financially dependent on the towns, and felt the superimposition of the "guardians" keenly.

An additional grievance of the count of Flanders against France was the Valenciennes question. Valenciennes had recently expelled the garrison of the count of Hainaut there and offered its allegiance to the count of Flanders. The French king gave out that he

[3] Ashley, *James and Philip Van Artevelde*, p. 43.

would restore Valenciennes to the count of Hainaut and cherished the hope of uniting Hainaut and Flanders under the house of Avesnes by driving Guy de Dampierre to revolt against his suzerain. The emperor Adolf of Nassau declared that he would regain the imperial lands taken by France in late years, and especially Valenciennes. It was an empty boast, as both Philip IV and the Flemish count knew. Desperation made the count bold. Guy de Dampierre turned to Edward I of England as an ally. Political hatred of France threw him into the arms of the English king in 1294, but both the count and the king must have felt the force of the mutual economic relation between English wool-growing and Flemish cloth-manufacturing. It was a timely moment for the proffer of such an alliance by the count of Flanders. For already France and England were at war.

Guienne and Gascony were another bone of Anglo-French contention. These provinces were the last portion of the once great Angevin Empire and had been possessed by the English crown ever since 1152. But for them the English king had to do homage to the king of France. There was the rub. Philip IV looked with covetous eyes upon Gascony and Guienne and plotted to despoil the English sovereign of them. Behind this natural tendency of a strong monarchy to expand its territorial domination and to consolidate the loosely agglomerated provinces of feudal France into a more compact form, a subconscious sentiment of dawning nationality also was working. For even making every allowance of difference in blood, language and local institutions, the population of Guienne and Gascony was yet French of a sort, and however content that population might be under English rule, the French monarchy regarded that rule as a foreign domination within their realm. We discover an evidence of this nascent sense of nationality in French propaganda of the reign of Philip IV that the "natural frontiers" of France were the Rhine, the Alps, and the Pyrenees. The authorship of this political doctrine, with true monarchical genius, was ascribed to Julius Caesar. For had he not said that these were the natural boundaries of Gaul, and what was France but Roman Gaul under a new name?

But there were also economic motives in the French king's ambition to annex Guienne and Gascony to the crown. The latter province excelled any other region in Europe as a wine-growing country. The rolling downs and lush meadows of Gascony made it a veritable paradise for stock-raising. Gascon horses were famous, while the fisheries and whaling of the Bay of Biscay were exceedingly profitable. Salt-making, too, was an important industry along the Biscayan coast. Geography and geology contributed to the prosperity of these English provinces in southwestern France.

The variety of the climate and territory—mountain and meadows and fertile valley, the unique river-system, fed from the Pyrenean snows and spread like a network over the whole country, gathering up into the stately Garonne and centering in Bordeaux, the queen of French maritime cities, the long seaboard and navigable estuaries which bred a race of hardy seamen, the aptitude of the soil for the growth of the vine.[4]

These were the factors. Bordeaux was a capital worthy of its political and commercial importance, and singularly adapted to be the point of union between a maritime people and a dependency which could only be reached by sea. Situated far up the estuary of the spacious Gironde, and yet not so far but that the largest fleets could ride safely on its "noble tide"; capable, too, of the strong fortification which the English took care to provide, this place was pointed out by nature as the center of a great civil and military administration.

No commercial city in France or England could compare with Bordeaux. London was wealthy and squalid; Bordeaux was wealthy and beautiful. On its ample quays were landed the corn, cheese, butter, skins, fish, leather, rope, and, above all, the tin, the wool, and the cloth of England. From thence issued forth to the British and Flemish ports great fleets of wine ships, generally sailing together for mutual protection, and governed, like men-of-war, by codes of laws. Free trade between the English and the Gascons anticipated by centuries the modern lessons of political economy and gave unfettered vigor to the commerce of both countries. Not only did all the roads of the province converge on Bordeaux, but it was the center of that remarkable river system already mentioned. The Garonne, the Dordogne, and the Adour, with their numerous affluents, circled throughout the whole extent of the land, and afforded admirable means of communication with the neighboring provinces. Hence the extraordinary magnitude of the Gascon wine trade. This formed the staple commodity of the whole province, and bestowed life and wealth on the whole population. The merchants sailed with their own wines in their own ships. Of such value were these wines to England that the nobles, bishops, clergy, the king himself, and the queen, all traded on their own account. Sure of a hospitable welcome in the English ports, this fine Gascon commerce, not unnaturally, attracted the jealousy of the French, and numerous were the conflicts in which the Gascon and English traders fought on the same side against their rivals of the northern and northwestern coasts of France.[5]

The technique of grape cultivation all through the Middle Ages was so special that vineyard dressers were the freest among the peasantry. This was true in the Rhine and Moselle lands, in the Côte d'Or in Burgundy, and above all in Gascony where the freehold system of landholding obtained very widely. In the country districts all alike,

---

[4] Burrows, *Brocas de Beaurepaire,* p. 19.
[5] *Op. cit.,* p. 21.

nobles, small landowners and peasantry were born and bred to an
inheritance of freedom which greatly differed from the economic
condition and social structure of other provinces of feudal France.
So dearly was this freehold right cherished that popular opinion attributed the blessing of it to Charlemagne. "When the great king
Charles," runs a chronicle, "came to conquer the country from the
Saracens he was compelled to pay the nobles who otherwise would
not serve him; but the common people served without pay and asked
for nothing. That is why, when he bestowed the conquered lands upon
the nobles, Charlemagne bound them to do military service and other
feudal aids. But to the lower classes, out of gratitude, and in order
to encourage population, he granted their properties free from all
manorial obligation and declared them to be freeholds henceforth."
The provisions of feudal law, moreover, were more liberal in Guienne and Gascony than elsewhere in the matter of wills, wardship,
marriage, succession and the right of accused persons to bail.

The English rulers of the country supplemented this unusual condition of free institutions by promoting the communal system, notably
in the *bastides* or "new towns" which were laid out in geometrical
forms, the ground-plans being square, hexagonal or octagonal as the
case might be, with straight streets running across the town from gate
to gate, and a broad piazza in the middle of the town. These new
towns were free from the crooked streets and narrow alleys of older
medieval towns and had better sanitation. Trade received a real impetus from these improved conditions. The *bastides* of Aquitaine ought
to be better known than they are, for many of them still exist, and
challenge attention by their peculiar construction. Libourne (on the
railway between Paris and Bordeaux) is the chief, and one of the
earliest, of these places. It still contains 15,000 people. Selecting
a splendid situation at the confluence of the Dordogne and the Isle,
and attracting inhabitants by a liberal charter of privileges, Edward,
in 1270, with a view to defense, built the town in a regular form,
consisting of a central square and eight streets radiating from it. It
had more regularity than picturesqueness, the public buildings in the
center being the rallying point. Such *bastides* formed cities of refuge
for the people of the country in time of war. The policy of the design
was well tested in Libourne, the leader of the group, which, like Bordeaux, offered, both in 1370 and 1451, the most strenuous resistance
to the French.

Unfortunately the English provinces in France were not bounded
by any natural frontier and the nobles of the border were always
tempted to play fast and loose across it, a condition which easily
gave the French king room to interfere. Of these inland proprietors
Froissart wrote:

Such is their unstable nature that they are never loyally attached to either rule. The very necessity under which the English are to grant concessions, pardons and privileges forms an incessant inducement to turbulence.

The vast wine trade out of Bordeaux was a gold mine to the English kings, as the export of wool was from the English ports. Upon every cask of wine was imposed a high export tax called the *grande coutûme*, which was graduated according to the quality of the wine. The once familiar signs chalked or charred upon the head of a liquor cask, X, XX, XXX, came down to modern times from these insignia. Every hogshead paid a *gauge fee* and every vessel a ship toll or *keelage*. The ship captain was given a branch of cypress which he was required to fix to the mast as a clearing signal. An additional tax was one for maintenance of the lighthouse at the mouth of the Garonne. But these were not all the assessments upon the wine trade.   The English king had the right of prize. He took two hogsheads in every cargo of thirty hogsheads and furthermore collected two *sous* per hogshead on the balance of the cargo. The vineyard owner was subjected to minute regulation in cultivation of the grape. The processes of tillage, pruning, picking, straining, barreling, shipping down to Bordeaux from the up-country were all supervised by inspectors. The wines were carried to all the ports of England and sometimes Flemish vessels came to Bordeaux. The production was very great around Bordeaux; but the wines of Haut-Pays, of Quercy, of Albigeois were much sought on English tables and among the most celebrated were those of Gaillac and Rabasteins.

It was forbidden to ship these wines from any ports except Bordeaux and Bayonne, but the latter was not permitted to compete with Bordeaux. That is why there were so many tolls there. Moreover, the wines could not be floated down the Garonne before November 11, St. Martin's Day. The bourgeois of the city had the right of first sale, the *banvin*. In certain years the date was extended even to Christmas. Nevertheless all this wine ended by being well sold.

Aside from wine the exports of Bordeaux were fine cloths from Languedoc, plants for dyeing, like pastel and madder, and arms. In the fourteenth century Bordeaux was celebrated for its manufacture of arms, and Froissart in his accounts of battles speaks in various places of the swords of Bordeaux. The ships which bore all these products returned from England with wool. Later when the English themselves began to manufacture cloth, the cargoes were often of salted fish, herring, codfish, and mackerel, so much so that in these medieval times when fast-days were numerous England nourished Bordeaux which was its continental colony. Wheat also came in part from England. For everything was vineyards around Bordeaux and the people would have died of hunger in the midst of their riches. Finally upon these ships travelled thousands of pilgrims bound for the shrine of St. James of Compostella.

Froissart showed shrewd judgment of conditions in Gascony when he wrote:

It is worth more for the Gascons to be under the English who hold us openly and free, than under the subjection of the French. They have more trade in wine, wool and cloth with the English than with the French; they are inclined towards them naturally.

This relation between the towns of Gascony and the English wine trade is what preserved English rule in Gascony at a time when Normandy, on which England seemingly had had a stronger hold, was lost. Unable to take a large army to Gascony or to depend upon the feudal lords in that area, the king relied upon the towns.

But popular and prosperous as the English rule in Gascony may have seemed, party or class feeling ran high in the Gascon towns and opened a breach for the entrance of French influence. We have seen how intestine divisions rent the Flemish towns and the reaction of these upon the political history of the time. The situation was much the same in the towns of southern France where the merchants constituted the patriciate and the craftsmen formed the popular party. But in the south the condition does not appear in such sharp relief as in the north, for the reason that these internal clashes did not recoil upon general history to the same degree. In Bordeaux, for example, we find no such events as the Massacre at Bruges and the battle of Courtrai; at least no chronicler has related such incidents.

Nevertheless, the class antagonism prevailing in Bordeaux in the time of the Edwards was sufficient not merely to give the French king plausible occasion for intervention, but even to warrant the legal exercise of his overlordship of the English duchies in France. English historians have universally condemned Philip IV's policy in Gascony as unwarrantable abuse of prerogative. The facts will not bear out this contention except in part.

Like most European towns in the thirteenth and fourteeth centuries, Bordeaux was divided into two factions, the patriciate and the popular party. The Colomb were the leaders of the latter. The Del Soler were chiefs of the patriciate. One is reminded of the great feud in Florence between the Blacks, or Guelfs, and the Whites, or Ghibellines, the partisans around the Donati and the Cerchi families. During the reign of Henry III municipal politics in Bordeaux oscillated for mastery between these two factions. When Simon de Montfort was made governor of Aquitaine, he brought with him the popular tendencies which he later exhibited in England during the War of the Barons and so favored the Colomb to the prejudice of the Del Soler. On June 28, 1254, an armed rising took place in Bordeaux. It was sternly repressed by Montfort, and in the charter of the English king, imposing peace upon the rival families, they were advised to intermarry in order to abate their differences.

The "Solerians" remained exiled from Bordeaux until 1257. When they returned they found the Colomb entrenched in local power. The mayor was Jean Colomb. The strife was renewed and attained such dimension that Henry III suppressed the commune and the mayoralty in Bordeaux, and put the city under the direct authority of the seneschal of Gascony. The dragon's teeth thus sown were destined to spring up early in the fourteenth century.

The chronic condition of turbulence in Bordeaux was perhaps enough of itself to justify Philip IV in stepping in in his capacity as suzerain of Edward I, who seems to have been unable, owing to distractions elsewhere, to suppress it, although English accounts have invariably represented Philip IV's course as high-handed outrage. Be this as it may, the French king installed his judges (enquêteurs) at Bordeaux. This was the introduction of a form of appeal to the parlement of Paris. The embarrassment of the English government in Gascony was very great, not only because of this assertion of royal suzerainty, but because at the moment the English king was not sustained by the popular party. For the Colomb family and all their following went over to the French side, while the Del Soler adhered to England. Another Jean Colomb was Philip IV's sergeant in Bordeaux and in that capacity became a local dictator, having the lower masses back of him.

The previous situation was completely reversed. The English government from then on was identified with the patriciate in the Bordelais, and the French crown with the people. The condition was a complete reverse of the condition in Flanders where the French king was sustained by the patriciate and the Flemish noblesse, and the working classes adhered to England. Nothing could better illustrate the "practical" nature of English and French policy; how each king made local politics subserve his own immediate ends; how each was indifferent to any high moral principle; how each played to win; how cynical each was in his public professions.

An additional source of aggravation between France and England was piracy. All nations and seamen were equally bad. We hear of the evil wrought by pirates of Germany, England, Scotland, Brittany, France, and Spain. Indeed, the granting of letters of marque and the practice of reprisal gave apparent sanction to these robberies. Thus, when Bordeaux merchants had their wines taken from them by Flemish pirates, they procured letters of reprisal against Flemish merchants in England. As a result of this high-handed policy trade suffered enormously. Pirates and privateers swarmed in the North Sea and in the English and Irish Channels. The crews of these vessels were sometimes French and Flemish, Scotch and English, a motley band of outlaws, "sanctuary men" and desperadoes of the various countries, who seldom cared about the nationality of the vessels they captured. All that could be swept from the sea was considered the fair prize of war. There seems to have been little or no law as to capture at sea. Crews and passengers of captured merchant vessels were frequently tossed overboard, sometimes with their hands tied behind their backs, or were hung up along the yards of their vessels, or even murdered upon the deck in cold blood. No truce on land was of force at sea.

Piracy entailed no stigma upon the adventurer. The name pirate was not one of reproach and we often find the bearers obtaining a high rank, as mayor or other official. In the fifteenth century even an abbot of St. Augustine in Canterbury was convicted of plundering a wine vessel and forced to pay the aggrieved parties for the loss of goods and the expenses of prosecution. Such cases were not uncommon among the clergy.

Not only the sea but even the shores of both countries were kept in a constant state of alarm by these rovers. Private treaties gave a fitful and precarious peace, but in spite of treaties, in spite of booms and chains thrown across the mouths of harbors, in spite of the vigilance of the watch by night and day and the beacons along the cliffs, town after town was sacked and destroyed, the townsmen killed, and the crops burned by the crews of these privateers. In England almost every town along the southern coast as far as Bristol was burnt during the war with France. Sandwich never recovered from the ruin wrought by these buccaneering attacks. People on the coasts fled inland, fields were left untilled, farmsteads fired and small ports fell into decay. It was perilous to dwell near the sea for every sea was infested and marauders even lurked in the rivers for a considerable distance inland. In ordinary times local resources could often repel the incursions, and whenever the French fleet was seen from the cliffs beacon fires lighted on the neighboring hilltops soon called together a sufficient company of peasantry and gentlemen to prevent a landing. But the continual state of alarm which reigned hindered the regular and peaceful pursuit of trade and agriculture and reduced the lands exposed to the rovers to a barren waste without inhabitants. The mouth of the Rhine and Calais and St. Malo are mentioned as being chief haunts of pirates at different times.

The piracy of the times resulted in various attempts to check and prevent it. One of these was the convoy system. Ships were forbidden to go out singly—though some did go—but were to meet at a certain port and travel in a group to Bordeaux, keeping in deep water to prevent attacks. There were also other attempts to solve the problem. Letters of reprisal against goods of the merchants of the country engaging in piracy were issued in 1320; their main result was to act as a deterrent of trade. In 1293 all former depredations at sea were cast into the shade when a combined Norman, Poitevin and Breton fishing fleet fell upon an English merchant fleet off the Breton coast, captured most of the ships, slew the crews, and then paraded before the English ports with the bodies of the slain sailors hanging alternately with the carcasses of dead dogs from the yard-arms. Edward I at the time was engaged in war with the Scotch. He had no mind to take on a new enemy and so did nothing. But the seamen of the English Channel ports were furious and sent a challange to the Normans and Bretons proposing to fight it out among themselves.

On April 14, 1293, the Cinque Ports fleet, reinforced with Irish, Dutch, and Gascon ships met a Norman, Breton, and Flemish fleet— for all maritime peoples were drawn into the fray—off Point St. Mathew near modern Cherbourg. It was an English victory. Nevertheless Edward I was alarmed. He knew the character and ambition of Philip IV. In spite of the fact that in 1279 England had at last renounced all claim to Normandy, which had been lost in 1204, and obtained formal possession of the fiefs of Gascony and Guienne, Edward I was well aware that the French king coveted possession of these territories, and would seize upon any plausible pretext to get them.

Accordingly the English king summoned the barons of the Cinque Ports to account. Part of their elaborate reply must find room here. After recapitulating a long series of outrages which English shipping had suffered, the memoir goes on to relate how a French fleet of eighty vessels had posed at Bordeaux as peaceful wine ships, but after leaving the Gironde had rigged themselves out as warships by putting up "castles" fore and aft and hoisting their "banners." Thus arrayed they fell upon a flotilla of Bayonne and Irish vessels and captured seventy of them. The warden of the Cinque Ports, the protest recites, forbade reprisals, so that in self-defense all English shipping was compelled to assemble at Portsmouth "for a peaceful voyage," and while lying at anchor in the harbor of St. Mathew was attacked by the French. Then follows a brief but spirited account of the engagement.

On the Friday before Pentecost they came in sight with two hundred ships, crammed with armed men in bow and stern, and with banners of red cendal flying, each of two ells in width and thirty in length, which are called "baucans," and by the English "streamers," and these signify amongst all men of the sea death without quarter and mortal war. In this way the Normans came down upon your people and feloniously attacked them contrary to the peace. Your people defended themselves and God by His grace gave them victory.

This carefully drawn account suppresses the fact that the battle was a prearranged duel and the rendezvous at Portsmouth out of the way of the lord warden is significant.

The cards were in Philip IV's hands. He demanded redress with a veiled threat concerning Gascony. In reply Edward I offered to adjust the matter in a personal interview with the French king as soon as his war with the Welsh was terminated, or to leave the matter to arbitration by the college of cardinals, since the papal throne was then vacant. Philip IV's answer (December, 1293) was to cite Edward I to appear in Paris. Instead of himself coming Edward I sent his brother Edmund of Lancaster, who weakly yielded the *"seisin"* of the border fortresses of Gascony and Guienne as security for his royal brother's appearance when his hands were freed of the Welsh. Knowing well Edward I's embarrassment at home the French king sent a second, then a third summons, and when Edward I failed to appear, declared the English duchies in France forfeited to the French crown (May 7, 1294). War followed along the Anglo-French border of Guienne and Gascony, in the Bay of Biscay and in the Channel.

We have already observed the bearing of this war upon the history of taxation culminating in a conflict of both sovereigns with Pope Boniface VIII. What is of interest now is the causes of the war, especially those of an economic nature.

The war raged along the border of Gascony and Guienne and in the Channel. "There was no law imposed upon the sailors," runs a contemporary narrative, "but whatever any one could carry off, that he called his own." Gascony was well-nigh overrun by the French, a French attack on Dover was disastrous and Prince Edmund ravaged the French coast of Poitou and burned Cherbourg.

In 1294, when news of the betrothal of the daughter of Guy to the English crown prince reached Paris, Guy was summoned there and retained in prison for six months. Although he was then allowed to return to Flanders, his daughter was left in the hands of the French king. Also all of his English retainers had been seized and their property confiscated. Then followed a period in which Philip IV tried to win over Guy. This had its result in the treaty of January, 1296, between France and Flanders, which provided for commercial privileges for Flemish merchants, for many concessions to Guy de Dampierre, for a lessening of the political power of the French king in Flanders, and the raising of a *cinquantième* for the war, to be divided equally between Philip and the count.

No permanent effects, however, resulted, because the root of the problem had not been touched. The personal antagonism, which Guy felt keenly, was emphasized by the constant recurrence of the old problems: the frequent interference of the king in the Flemish cities, the difficulty over the wool from Scotland which Philip IV, as the ally of Scotland, wished to favor; a dispute between Hainaut and Flanders over Valenciennes; the differences over the ordinances on money. The collection of the *cinquantième* also led to difficulties, for Philip exempted some of the towns on the payment of a specified sum without communicating with Guy, and there was friction over its division. Matters were made worse when Guy was called before the parlement of Paris to give up Valenciennes.

As relations between Guy and Philip IV became more and more strained, Edward of England made use of every opportunity offered to secure the alliance of the Flemish count. Since the war progressed very unfavorably for him in Guienne, he hoped to create a diversion in the north, and appealed to all the ambitions of Guy; he offered the count large subsidies; he held out to him the prospect of territorial aggrandizement at the expense of the French crown. In addition, although it had a disastrous effect on his own kingdom, Edward I forbade the exportation of English wool to Flanders, hoping thus to gain the support of the Flemish people who would blame their loss of prosperity on the French king who had got them into war with England.

Guy thus had a difficult policy to decide upon. To fulfill his vows of homage meant that he must be subjected to the acts of encroachment of a hard master whose war was ruining his country. To join England seemed to promise plenty of money and economic prosperity for his people. He postponed decision as long as possible. In 1294 he signed articles betrothing his daughter to the son of the English king, which is not conclusive evidence of treason. During the following years his imprisonment, the increasing encroachments of the French king in spite of some of his softer words, and the smooth talking of the king of England made Guy's decision almost inevitable. At the end of 1296 it was perfectly evident which way his decision was going. He tried to conciliate the Flemish *métiers*, causing a sort of loyalty for the dynasty to grow up among them, of great importance later. He refused to appear before the parlement of Paris and demanded that he be allowed to come before a court of peers, asserting that unless the claims were granted his bond of vassalage was broken by the French king.

With that defiance he signed a treaty with Edward in January, 1297. Politically it provided for a perpetual union between England and Flanders, a large subsidy and the marriage of young Edward, Prince of Wales, with one of his daughters. A commercial agreement was signed also, stipulating in substance that all English ships and those of the count would each be received in the ports of the other. It also provided for disputes and prizes. This treaty with later privileges was to make Bruges the center of the woolen trade for the whole continent. Edward continued to follow this policy and in the next year gave large concessions also to merchants of Ghent in England.

But the war did not fulfill the promise seemingly indicated for Guy at the beginning. Most interesting is the alignment of the various social groups within Flanders, which were influenced by economic and social factors. Most of the nobles followed the French king, although there were a few who elected to follow the count. The higher clergy also adopted the cause of France as their own, while the lower clergy allied themselves with the lower classes, and sustained them. The towns split in their adherence. Ghent, Ypres, and others favored the count of Flanders, after very lavish concessions from Guy. Bruges and Lille, still angry at Guy because of his attitude during the revolt of 1280, adhered to France. The full strength of the class struggle had not yet become apparent. There is absolutely no evidence that patriotism, as we understand it, determined the action of any one of these groups.

In the summer of 1297 a French army invaded Flanders. The garrison in Lille, encouraged by Robert de Béthune, made a stout fight, but the French victory at Bulscamp (August 20) prostrated all Flemish resistance to France. Two days later (August 22) without knowledge of this event, Edward I had sailed for Sluys. Quarrels among the men in the fleet were added to the French victory at Bulscamp to trouble the English king. For during the landing of the English forces, records Walter of Hemingburgh,

As soon as ever the king had anchored in Swyn port, the seamen of the Cinque Ports, inflamed by their inveterate hatred of the men of Yarmouth, which dates from olden times, rushed to arms and in the fury of the attack burned over twenty of their ships, putting to the sword as many of their crews as they could lay hands on. Nor, though the king commanded them to desist, was he able to restrain their mad violence.

This outbreak was the famous "Yarmouth Feud." Other broils followed. The English men-at-arms in Sluys picked a quarrel with the citizens, plundered their houses and the magazines of the merchants, and killed two hundred of the inhabitants. In Ghent the Welsh archers got into a fight with the people. His hands tied by the French victory and the insubordination among his troops, Edward I was only too glad in October to conclude a two years' truce with the French, for which Philip IV was little less solicitous, owing to the then formidable nature of his conflict with the pope.

The count of Flanders, abandoned by the English king, was left to his own resources. He foresaw what was coming, and vainly tried to save himself from the encircling band of alliances that Philip IV was creating, but to no avail, and in 1300 Flanders was again successfully invaded by Philip IV. The count of Flanders and his two eldest sons surrendered themselves to the French king, and Flanders came under the direct administration of the crown.

All Flanders was united with the royal domain. In 1301 Philip IV visited his newly acquired territory with the queen, who was immensely impressed with the wealth displayed by the wives of the rich burghers of Ghent. But the French governor, Jacques de Châtillon, was lacking in tact and angered the crafts. A terrible rising took place at Bruges under the leadership of a weaver named Peter Coninck. On May 18, 1302, the French garrison was massacred by the infuriated mob. This was the "Matins of Bruges." Most of Flanders was soon in insurrection, but Ghent adhered to France. Many of the smaller towns were intimidated by Bruges and reluctantly furnished militia, money and supplies for the rebellion. Mercenaries were hired from Zeeland, Limburg, Brabant and the German provinces. On July 11, 1302, the French army was defeated at Courtrai in the so-called Battle of the Spurs, from the circumstance that the victorious workingmen stripped the fallen French knights of their spurs which they hung up as trophies in the local church. The battle-field was a maze of irrigation and drainage ditches which made it impossible for the French cavalry to maneuver. Consequently they fell victims to the nature of the terrain rather than to the prowess of the foe.

It was not so much France which succumbed at Courtrai as the Flemish patriciate. It was a social war in which the crafts triumphed over the gilds. The victorious artisans promptly seized control of political and commercial administration in the towns. The property of the patricians was confiscated; the "deans" of the crafts (*métiers*) were put at the head of the town government in Bruges, Ypres, Furnes, and even Ghent. The crafts everywhere shook off the authority and regulations of the gilds.

The victorious crafts were now so confident that their armed forces invaded Artois. But the battle of Mons-en-Puelle (August 1304) reversed the success at Courtrai; the Flemish army melted away.

The king was master of almost all of Flanders that spoke the French tongue. . . . From Gravelines to Mons-en-Pevèle the Flemings had met a series of defeats that had altered the confidence created by Courtrai. At Zierikzee their war fleet, equipped at great expense, had just been destroyed. All of the foreign allies had abandoned the Flemish one after another. . . . As for Flanders itself, the artisans worked no more. There was black misery in the households once so prosperous. Merchants abandoned the country. The passage of the armies had ruined the peasants. One saw only the uncultivated fields, closed shops, deserted markets, in a country where the dense population could exist only by the constant labor of the merchant, the workingman and the laborer.[6]

The register of tolls at Bapaume shows a decline of two-thirds in 1303–05.

A reaction followed against the dictatorship of Bruges in several towns, notably in Ghent. One reason for this was jealousy of Bruges because she insisted on her right of free trade throughout all Flanders and exemption of all her commerce from local tolls. In the treaty of Athis-sur-Orges (June 23, 1305) Flanders was compelled to cede Lille, Douai and Orchies to France.

But the victory of the artisans was more apparent than real. In fact, economic conditions were not greatly altered. The working classes were given a share in local administration, but they were poor. Although the great gilds were supposed to be abolished, the rich ex-gildsmen still retained control of wool importations. The merchant class, having lost its former political privileges, became retail sellers or petty employers. The artisans were still dependent upon the capitalists, although theoretically these no longer enjoyed political privilege or legal monopoly. But "money talked." These rich importers purchased great supplies of wool abroad and sold it to the weavers who returned the finished cloth to them. It was then marketed through drapers and other small cloth merchants. They made no effort to restore the former gilds, but formed less formal combinations in regulation and restraint of trade by which they kept control of Flemish commerce and industry in their own hands. The analogy between Flemish capitalism at this time and modern capitalism is not a strained one. These shrewd operators manipulated importations, markets, prices and made money make money. To sum up: the artisans who had wanted to effect an economic revolution accomplished only a political one.

The war also resulted in other changes in Flanders. Commerce and industry became so centered in Ghent, Bruges and Ypres that the lesser towns declined in population and importance. In essential respects these three lordly cities became Flanders. They endeavored to monopolize trade and manufacturing and reduce the small towns and rural areas to small farming and truck gardening. Hence the social cleavage between town and country became sharper. In the three great towns we find a densely settled proletariat living on daily wages dispensed by rich employers, often the victims of wage reduction and unemployment in slack seasons, prone to strike, economically discontented and socially restless.

[6] Funck-Brentano, *op. cit.,* p. 482.

It is not necessary to trace in detail the relations between France and Flanders from 1305 to 1314. The problems had not been solved by the treaty of Athis, particularly the economic and social problems. On the whole these years were spent by the Flemings in attempting to avoid, or to make less stringent, the hard terms of the treaty, and by Philip IV in giving concessions more or less graciously. One of the biggest questions was that of raising the French indemnity. Count Robert put the collection of this in the hands of an Italian banker, who established a bureaucratic organization not liked by the Flemings.

Philip IV had gained the support of the sons of Guy de Dampierre, and Robert de Béthune tried to restrict the privileges given by his brother to the communes. He inclined towards the patricians and supporters of France. Gradually strained relations developed, and for the same reasons as under his father. The king had not yet given up the thought of getting control of Flanders. The cities began appealing to the king of France over the attempt of Bruges to make them pay part of the special fine imposed upon her for the Matins. So things went on. Affairs seesawed back and forth during the remaining years of Philip IV. In 1312 he won a considerable victory, for he was able, because of the financial difficulties of the Flemish count, to secure the cession of Walloon Flanders to France.

Yet in spite of its turbulence, this period after 1305 is characterized by the "astonishing vitality of industry," as the registers of Bapaume show. Commerce with France gradually picked up. After the Treaty of Athis, Philip IV asked the English king to reëstablish the commercial relations which had formerly existed between his subjects and Flanders. Edward I assented, provided Scotch goods were excluded from Flemish ports. The count of Flanders was opposed to this because his ports had always been open to merchants of all nations. Edward I did not insist, and on the whole relations between Flanders and England were good.

One reason why the French king was anxious to have peace with Flanders was because of the effect of the turbulence in Flanders upon the provinces in the northeast of the kingdom. Artois and Champagne had been the chief fields of activity of the reactionary nobles who had formed rebellious leagues against the crown, and that rebellion encouraged the Flemings in their resistance towards France. Robert of Béthune, count of Flanders, had signed the treaty of Athis in 1305 with the secret determination not to execute the terms imposed upon him by it. He had yielded Lille, Douai and Béthune to France, but cherished the hope of recovering them; he refused to destroy the border fortresses, to surrender Cassel and Courtrai, to pay the tribute stipulated in the treaty, or to send six hundred Brugeois to participate in a crusade in expiation of the massacre of 1302. In 1314-15 a new war of France with Flanders seemed imminent. Louis X undertook, in alliance with the count of Hainaut and the duke of Brabant, to bring the count of Flanders to terms, but was driven out by floods. The king's death and the troubles of the brief regency before Philip V's accession emboldened the count, who was not deterred by the collapse of the feudal league in Artois and Champagne. He had men, money, a fleet; he relied on the support of the communes: Ghent, Bruges, Ypres, Furnes, Bergues, Courtrai, Audenarde, Nieuport, Dixmude, Sluys and Ardembourg. In the summer of 1316 war raged along the Franco-Flemish border until the count of Flanders sued for peace. At the same time in the Bay of Biscay the Bayonnais, allied with the Flemings, attacked a fleet of Norman merchantmen and burned four vessels. Fortunately for France, owing to the crushing victory of the Scotch over the English at Bannockburn (1314) and the perilous state of the Anglo-Scottish border, England's hands were tied so that she could not intervene and so widen the war. Flanders paid a war indemnity of two hundred thousand livres and agreed to the demolition of the fortifications of Bruges, Ghent and Ypres. While France annexed no new territory from Flanders in this war, the dismantling of the fortifications around the three great cities of Flanders exposed the country to any future French aggression. This peril of French ascendancy in the Low Countries and of consequent jeopardy to the English wool trade there, sensibly brought the coming war between France and England a step nearer. The limits of Flanders had been pushed back to the Lys; Arras and Artois and the French-speaking districts of Lille, Douai and Orchies (Walloon Flanders) had been acquired by France; Flanders had lost, too, the homage of the county of Boulogne. But Philip V's support of the urban oligarchies had made the masses in the towns strongly anti-French in sympathy. This irritable relation between France and England at the same time was aggravated by dispute between Philip V and Edward II over the latter's homage for Guienne and Gascony, and the piracy of the Bayonnais, the Rochellois and the Bretons. In 1320 Edward II came across the sea to do homage for his fiefs in France, and an Anglo-French commission was created to adjust the claims for damages of merchants of each nation. It was a futile proceeding. For privateering and piracy in the Channel and the Bay of Biscay were of appalling dimension, and the grievances of the two nations against each other played a part in provoking the Hundred Years' War.

New tension arose in 1323 over alleged French trespass in Gascony. Charles IV proclaimed *in France only* a summons commanding Edward II to do homage once more for the English fiefs in France, but Edward did not receive information of the summons until it was too late. The French king, owing to the other's failure to respond, declared

Gascony and Ponthieu (the dowry of Edward II's mother) forfeited. War seemed imminent in 1324. French troops overran Ponthieu, Agenois and Oleron. The English coast was looked to in anticipation of a French descent, and all French monks in alien priories near the seaboard were removed inland. Queen Isabel deserted her husband, crossed over to France and refused to return to England. When Charles IV, in view of a new truce, ordered her to leave France she found refuge with the count of Hainaut to whose daughter, Phillipa, young Edward, prince of Wales—afterwards Edward III—was betrothed, although her father had married a daughter of Charles IV of France.

In Flanders, the cleavage between the count, whose dependence on the French king increased, and the craftsmen fighting for political rights and Flemish independence, continued to widen. In 1320 Robert of Béthune signed a treaty in which he bound himself never to claim Lille, Douai and Béthune. Soon afterwards Louis de Crécy, the eldest son of Louis de Nevers, married Marguerite of France, the eldest daughter of Philip V. Two years later both count Robert and his son Louis de Nevers died (1322) and the latter's son became the new count of Flanders. Instead of choosing Flemings for his administrators, he chose French ministers, who introduced the fiscal machinery of Philip IV into Flanders. The result was that there was an agrarian rising in the Franc of Bruges in 1324 which soon extended to west or maritime Flanders. The artisans of Bruges fraternized with the insurgent peasantry so that nearly all Flanders was soon in an uproar. Ghent alone adhered to the count. A battle ensued between the militia of Bruges and that of Ghent at Deinse (1325). Meanwhile the count fled to Paris. But Charles IV had too much on his hands with the English king to venture to intervene and a sort of settlement was patched up in 1326.

The situation between France and England was this: France feared to intervene in Flanders or to seize Gascony lest war ensue with the Flemings in support of England, while England feared to intervene in Flanders lest she lose Gascony.

Then quite suddenly the situation changed. In 1327 Edward II was murdered and his son Edward III succeeded. The French influence of queen Isabel and her paramour Mortimer was terminated by the imprisonment of the queen and the execution of Mortimer. In France in the next year (1328) Charles IV died and his cousin Philip VI of Valois came to the throne. A new page in history was turned.

CHAPTER III

In 1328 the tension between England and France over their rival political and economic interests, a rivalry in which the Low Countries and Gascony were the chief stake, was strained nearly to the breaking point.

John XXII refused to grant a papal dispensation for the marriage of Edward III and Philippa of Hainaut, since they were second cousins. Back of this objection lay two oppositions. The new French king, Philip VI, wished to obstruct the political combination of England, Flanders and Hainaut. The pope's objection was of a different sort. He was strenuously opposed to the policy of the emperor Ludwig of Bavaria in Italy, where the ancient Guelf-Ghibelline feud was still carried on. As the emperor had married another daughter of the count of Hainaut there was a prospect of the emperor joining the anti-French alliance. The pope feared that the union of Edward III with Philippa of Hainaut "might place all the industrial and commercial power in the Low Countries, where the most powerful, the Flemings, had been for several years in full revolt against their suzerain, the king of France, at the side of the excommunicated king of the Romans." [1] Second judgment, however, convinced him that it was wise to grant the dispensation in hope that it would alienate Edward III from the emperor and mend English relations with France. Rumors were rife in the summer of 1328 that Edward III intended to aid the Flemings. Certainly he did his best to cultivate friendly relations with Bruges and Ypres by compensating Flemish merchants for losses which they had sustained from English pirates. Some of the rebel Flemish leaders even went so far as to offer Edward III the lordship of Flanders. French money was refused circulation.

In this second revolution in Flanders the count was not, as before, allied with the artisans; on the contrary the artisans, with some bourgeois, were united against him. Nevertheless, the count did not want French assistance in crushing the rebellion, for he knew it would be costly to him. But he could not prevent French intervention in Flanders. The battle of Cassel (August 23, 1328) compelled the rebellious

---

* For map see James Westfall Thompson, *The Middle Ages,* 2 vols. (Alfred A. Knopf, New York, 1931), Vol. II, p. 910.

[1] Lucas, *The Low Countries and the Hundred Years' War,* p. 62.

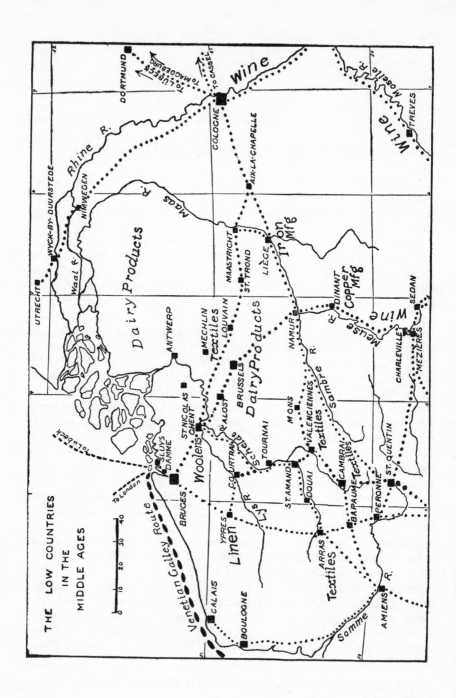

THE LOW COUNTRIES
IN THE
MIDDLE AGES

Flemings again to submit. Bruges and Ypres, which had acclaimed the revolt, opened their gates without resistance.

Emboldened by French military and diplomatic success in the Low Countries Philip VI hardened his policy towards England. In July, 1331, Edward III was commanded to appear before the parlement of Paris on the ground that his allegiance to the French king was liege homage. It was a technicality calculated to inflame the relations between the two countries. Edward III turned towards the Low Countries for support and especially made overtures to the count of Hainaut, who was growing alarmed over the increase of Valois power in the region north of the bend of the Meuse. The French king countered this English policy by an endeavor to secure the support of the duke of Brabant, well knowing that no love was lost between Brabant and Hainaut. The strategic situation of Brabant between Flanders on the west and Liège on the east might link up these territories with the county of Namur, and thus form a solid array of territories under French influence in the Low Countries. "The duchy, with its towns and industry, was sufficiently like Flanders to have similar social and economic problems. The duke, who ever jealously restrained the aspirations of the crafts, might possibly be counted upon to aid in checking any future democratic movement of the Flemings. . . The economic ties with England made him little inclined to turn a deaf ear to Edward's insinuations." [2] But in the end French diplomacy triumphed. The alliance of Brabant and Luxemburg with France made a solid block of pro-French principalities in the Low Countries, and French power in this region was all the greater because the count of Hainaut, now all but surrounded by French influence, prudently stayed neutral. France had won the first hand in the game.

Further French aggression followed. The count of Flanders resented having his country under the episcopal jurisdiction of the bishop of Tournai, which was situated in Hainaut, and preferred the bishop of Mechelen instead. This ambition was sustained by the French king and the pope. But there was an underlying commercial intention in the purpose. Mechelen, though close to the eastern boundary of Flanders, was entirely within the territory of Brabant. There was commercial motive in the Flemish policy. But the duke of Brabant

regarded the transfer of Mechelen as a serious challenge to his entire political policy. . . . Situated on both banks of the Dyle and near the Ruppel, it commanded access for many towns in Brabant to the greater centers of commerce. The counts of Flanders might seek to throttle the progress of Antwerp, sever its connection with its economic hinterland and even divert some of its ever-growing volume of trade to their own

[2] Lucas, *op. cit.*, p. 112.

towns. . . . This policy becomes impressive when viewed in the light of the duke's wider economic connections, especially with England. The staple of English wool and woolfels at Bruges had been abolished on May 1, 1326.[3]

Since the fixed English staple at Bruges no longer existed, the duke of Brabant determined to secure that commercial advantage for his own territory. The English government naturally favored this course. In 1329 the town of Diest was given special commercial privileges and the merchants of Louvain were taken under English protection; in 1331 similar privileges were given to merchants in other Brabantine towns; in 1333 the duke of Brabant, in return, invited English merchants to trade in Antwerp. France's reply to this extension of English commercial influence in the Low Countries was to cover the narrow seas with French privateers. It was manifest that war between England and France was not far off, and Edward III crossed over to Germany to meet the emperor at Coblenz where an Anglo-German alliance against France was entered into. The expense to England was terrific. Ludwig IV was to receive four hundred thousand florins in four installments; the archbishop of Trier got one hundred thousand. In his new capacity as a vicar of the Empire the English king was in a position to put the screws upon all the feudal princes in the Low Countries who held territory within the Empire, even Louis of Flanders.

The weak point in Edward III's position was financial, for these costly alliances imposed an enormous burden upon the English wool trade. In order to secure the ready money to effectuate his alliances abroad Edward III negotiated loans with Italian bankers in England, notably with the two famous Florentine banking houses of the Bardi and Peruzzi, offering wool as security. Accordingly all shipments abroad of wool were forbidden, and the ports of Kingston-upon-Hull, Newcastle, Chicester, Bristol, Yarmouth, Lynn, Boston, Ipswich, Hartlepool, London and the Cinque Ports designated as "ports of deposit" for the storage of wool. The five great or "staple" commodities exported from England were wool, woolfels or sheep skins, leather, lead and tin. These could be exported only by a licensed corporation known as the Merchants of the Staple, which had its own laws and officials and was exempt from the jurisdiction of ordinary magistrates. "The history of the 'English Company' . . . is the history of an early, if not the earliest attempt by a group of English merchants to take over the collection of the taxation on wool and to manipulate the wool trade to their own and the king's advantage." It was forbidden by law

[3] Lucas, op. cit., p. 136.
[4] George Sayles, "The English Company of 1343," Speculum, April 1931, p. 179.

to carry merchandise of the staple out of the country at any other places than those specified, and a felony for any but authorized merchants to deal in staple goods. This high-handed measure to make the English wool trade a royal monopoly angered the wool-growers, the greatest of whom were abbots and bishops. Great quantities of wool were smuggled out of the country, while the licensed shippers had difficulty in transporting the wool across sea on account of French privateers in the Channel. Many of the English seaports were in a panic of fear lest they be attacked by these rovers, and with good reason, for raids on them were frequent. Even London trembled. The sheriffs of all counties along the coast were commanded to arrange for alarm bells and signal fires in order to notify the inhabitants of French attack.

Louis of Nevers had been educated at the French court and had married a French princess, Marguerite, a daughter of Philip V. Unlike his ancestors the new count was a pronounced *leliart*, that is to say he regarded himself as a *seigneur des fleurs de lis,* or vassal of the lilies of France. In other words Louis was pro-French in sympathy and policy. It was a turning-point in the history of Flanders, and no less in the relations between France and England. The new count in 1336 formally declared his adhesion to the French king and ordered the stoppage of all commerce between Flanders and England, besides arresting English merchants in Flanders. In retaliation Edward III arrested Flemish merchants in England and seized their goods. War was brought a notch nearer and, anticipating that it would soon break out, Edward III sought to foment another rebellion in Flanders by which he might profit. The policy was a bold one. In spite of the count's edict, English wool might have been smuggled into Flanders and the working classes thereby kept from starving. But Edward III determined to starve the Flemish people into submission to English policy and resistance to France. The consequence was that an embargo was laid on all English wool except that intended for Brabant and the Hanseatic cities of Germany, and Flemish cloth-workers were allowed to settle in England (11 Edward III c.i. 1337). Incidentally it was hoped that the prosperity of Brabant next door to Flanders would open the eyes of the Flemings to the desirability of embracing the English cause.

Hard times ensued in Flanders. Deprived of English wool the crafts ceased to work; the employés of the drapers who were dependent upon their daily wages for sustenance, were reduced to a starving condition, and wandered into the countryside where their depredations inflamed the rural peasantry; small patrons in turn were hard hit and retailers, who lived off their petty sales to the working classes, were compelled to put up the shutters on their stores. Discontent became general. Deputations waited upon the count and petitioned, even demanded, renewal of commercial relations with England. But Louis of Nevers declared that his honor to the king of France would thereby be attainted. He thought, and many in France also, that England would be compelled to yield; that she could not afford to lose the lucrative wool trade with Flanders.

On October 7, 1337, Edward claimed the crown of France on the ground that he stood nearer the royal succession than Philip VI. It was a mere pretext for war. The religious houses in England loaned their jewels and plate for support of the war with France. The North Sea, the Channel and the inlets of Zeeland and Flanders swarmed with French, and doubtless also Flemish piratical craft, with which English sea-power could ineffectively cope. In the next year the French burned Portsmouth in June (1338) and made an attack on Southampton in October. Between these two dates Edward III had sailed for Flanders (July), where he hoped to profit by the discontent. For the English policy of isolating the Flemings had brought about a social and industrial crisis. As Bruges and Ypres had been ruined in the previous rising in maritime Flanders, Ghent was the most important city in Flanders.

The traditional account of what happened in the first week of January, 1338, in which the events are treated in the light of the later conflict between the patriciate and the commons, must be discounted. The personnel of the revolutionary government in Ghent was composed of patricians and men of the lower classes. There is no evidence that the movement which ensued was a popular movement against the aristocracy. On this occasion, at least, the solidarity of all classes in Ghent seems to have been a fact. The leader of this pro-English movement in Flanders was a remarkable man, Jacob Van Artevelde, who was appointed captain of Ghent by the partisans. He was not a brewer of mead, as Jean le Bel and Froissart, the chroniclers, have alleged, and the democratic romanticism of the nineteenth century was in error in hailing him as a "tribune of popular liberties." Modern terms like "democracy" and "popular rights" must be used with caution when applied to medieval social conditions. Actually Van Artevelde was a wealthy cloth merchant, and something of a landowner besides. In other words he came from the bourgeois aristocracy of Flanders and not from the lower classes.

Beyond doubt Van Artevelde was one of the great statesmen of the later Middle Ages. His policy was not a revolutionary one at first. We can discern the various stages in its development. At first (winter-summer 1338) he advocated neutrality for Flanders, and even Philip VI consented to an agreement between Flanders and England in order to relieve the economic pressure in Flanders. Few except the nobles were opposed to his policy, but among these was the count. With a

little army improvised of town militia, weavers, fullers, dyers, Artevelde labored "to pacify the land and to restore to it its peace, order,
liberties, and its industry, for honor of the count." But though sedulously striving not to offend the count, Artevelde's *de facto* power
made him enemies. With better intelligence than the count of Flanders
the French king perceived that, "confronted with Edward's hostility
and fearful of the enmity of Flanders in case of conflict," it was wiser
to let Artevelde have his way. Between a hostile or a neutral Flanders
in the approaching war prudence dictated choice of the latter.

What defeated this course was the obstinate opposition of the
Flemish nobility and the patriciate in the great towns which were allied
together against Artevelde. This compelled Artevelde, one thinks
against his judgment, to draw closer to the crafts and the proletariat.
As the months wore on it grew more uncertain whether Flanders could
be kept out of the political vortex. The wind from France also veered.
The caution—or procrastination—of England in coming to blows with
France, or perhaps hope of effective reliance upon the loyalty of the
Flemish noblesse and patriciate, made Philip VI change his mind.

In this predicament Artevelde astutely labored to win the count of
Flanders to his support by proposing that the count demand the restora-
tion to Flanders by France of the lost territories of Artois, Lille,
Douai, Tournai, Béthune and Orchies which Philip IV had annexed.
This would have given Flanders its ancient frontiers. His hope was
that Philip VI would yield. But the project failed, and Artevelde saw
that henceforth it would be impossible to maintain the neutrality of
Flanders, and that alliance with England was necessary. Brabant already had declared for England. The dire necessity in Flanders forced
Artevelde's hand. The last quibble was removed when Edward III,
who had claimed the crown of France in 1337, now in 1339 assumed
the title of king of France, "a card he was forced to play in hope of
winning the game." The great war, the Hundred Years' War, was
on between England and France, and both Flanders and Gascony were
swept into the whirlpool. On January 26, 1340, in the market-place
of Ghent, the English king received the oath of fealty from the
échevins of Ghent, Bruges, and Ypres, and in return the king swore
to maintain the rights of the people of Flanders and give them commercial advantages. He even promised to restore Artois, Lille, Douai
and Orchies, or Walloon Flanders.

The Hundred Years' Was was a dynastic and political conflict, and
a commercial and industrial struggle between France and England for
supremacy in western Europe. In this sense it was not different in
principle from later great wars in the sixteenth, seventeenth, and
eighteenth centuries which did not terminate until Waterloo.

It is not the province of this book to narrate political and military history except in so far as these data are requisite to give a frame to the picture of economic and social history. Yet wars, as the world has recently learned only too well, result from commercial rivalries and entail important economic legislation, and economic and social changes. The Hundred Years' War was no exception. It was waged in part for commercial reasons. England's territorial empire comprehended Britain (less Scotland) and Gascony and Guienne in France; but her commercial empire included the Low Countries with them.

Two actions of England in the inception of the war bear out the theory of her paramount commercial interest. These were the issue of a special gold coin for currency in Flanders, and the famous declaration of English "sovereignty of the seas." Undoubtedly the aggravation of piracy was so great that police of the high seas was necessary to the prosecution of trade. Sovereignty of the sea was an almost compulsory English policy, given her triangular commerce—England, Flanders, Gascony—which only maritime supremacy could unite into one whole and protect. It would be idle, though perhaps interesting, to speculate upon how different European history would have been if France had had no provinces which were in closer economic relation with England than with the mother-country, or if England had been wholly an insular power.

The doctrine of the sovereignty of the sea was not an *à priori* or theoretical one, but, like all great political doctrines, developed out of facts. It was a formulation of principle based upon historical conditions. Its origin, although clear record fails us, must go back at least in practice to the Norman and Angevin kings. The Lord Warden of the Cinque Ports was officially called *custos maris*. The integrity of the Angevin Empire, lying as it did on both sides of the Channel, required English dominion of the sea. In the twelfth and thirteenth centuries the intention of the doctrine was political, for England had not as yet a great overseas commerce. But in the fourteenth century England had less territory abroad and much more commerce than before. Hence, the primary intention of the doctrine of sovereignty of the sea was commercial protection and advantage. The treaty between Edward I and Bruges, in 1297, is the earliest document which formally asserts it. That the intention then was primarily a commercial one is borne out by the legislation of all three Edwards, tending to require all cargoes bound for English ports to be carried in English bottoms. As early as 1300, we catch a glimpse of the great Navigation Act of 1651. But it was a tyrannical policy. A modern French historian has caustically observed, in regard to this English policy in the fourteenth century:

It is one of the habitual proceedings of English politics, of which many examples might be cited, to know how to combine conditions and incidents which enable England to pose as the champion of the cause of right, of civilization and of humanity under color of promoting her commercial interests, of extending her colonial dominion and crushing those suspicious of her sincerity. . . . In the fourteenth century it was under the pretext of suppressing piracy that she concealed her desire and secret purpose to ruin the maritime trade of the French, the Spanish and the Flemings.[5]

There is a measure of truth in this charge. The most recent historian of the royal navy has frankly admitted it:

The space of sea over which the sovereignty of England was held to extend was counted to stretch from Finisterre to the coast of Norway. When the words "sovereignty of the sea" are used as meaning the king's effective superiority to any force which could be brought against him, there can be no question as to its reality. . . . He passed and repassed at will to and from his kingdom of France. . . . The rule was that when the monarchy exerted its strength it could sweep the seas. . . . No serious resistance, however, was made to this claim till the reign of Louis XIV. . . . The Venetian and Basque traders submitted to the claim. . . . The Flemings were generally our allies and the northern powers were not concerned.[6]

To be sure the English kings made no effort to impose duties on all shipping which passed through the Narrow Seas as the Danish king taxed vessels in the Skaggerak and Cattegat. But they could and did distrain competing commerce when it pleased them.

The commercial possibilities inherent in the establishment of England's domination over the sea will be more apparent if we examine in some detail the nature of the sea-borne commerce of the time, especially with reference to Flanders, and look upon Bruges and Ghent as international marts. Flanders was the Lombardy and Venetia of the North. As all Mediterranean commerce focused upon Italy, so all the commerce of northern Europe focused upon Flanders. From England came wool, woolfels, lead, and tin; from Scandinavia, fish and peltry; the merchants of the German Hansa brought furs, pitch-pine, ship stores, hemp, beeswax and bowstaves from Russia and the Baltic strand. Iceland contributed dried and smoked fish; Greenland, whale oil and walrus ivory. At the same time products of the hinterland of central Europe—not the least important of which were German iron and copper—found their exit via the Rhine, the Meuse and the Scheldt. The mouths of all three rivers were found in Flanders. Moreover, as European commerce became more international in scope, a vast volume and variety of products from the Mediterranean lands and the Levant, Oriental stuffs and dyes, spices and condiments, perfumes, unguents and medicines, found their way to Flanders. Venice and the

[5] Finot, *Les relations commerciales entre France et Flandre,* p. 112.
[6] David Hannay, *Short History of the Royal Navy* (1929), p. 17.

Lombard cities were in intimate economic relation with Bruges; Genoa at first shipped her importations from Syria, Egypt, Byzantium and Africa via the Rhône, the Saône, the Champagne Fairs and the Meuse to Flanders. When the Champagne Fairs began to fail, in 1317, Genoa opened the daring "Flanders Galley Route," the all-sea route through the Straits of Gibraltar, across Biscay water and up the Channel to Bruges, an inauguration which Venice soon imitated. At the same time the commerce of Spain and Portugal—chiefly wines, olive oil, leather goods and Castilian wool, dried fruits and nuts—found its way to Bruges and Ghent by the same route out of Cadiz, Seville, Lisbon and Oporto. The ubiquitous Italian merchants and money-lenders, roughly called "Lombards," were to be found in Paris, London, Bruges, and almost everywhere else where trade flourished. Sea-power might not only protect the Gascon-English wine trade and the Anglo-Flemish wool trade; it might be employed to stifle competition, as for example, the competition of Spanish wool and wine; it might be used as a weapon of war in sweeping French commerce off the sea. As early as December, 1336, in anticipation of the coming war between France and England, and irritated by the high-handed practices of the English on the high seas, where so early as this they attempted to stop delivery of Spanish wool to Flanders in order to protect the English wool trade, Castile entered into an alliance with France by the terms of which the Castilian fleet was put at the service of France.

The social condition established by the care of the Capetian kings of France from St. Louis forward may not have been of halcyon quality, yet security had prevailed almost everywhere in France for the hundred years previous to the inception of the great war with England. To be sure there was still some pillaging barons in remote quarters of the kingdom, in mountainous provinces like Auvergne and regions like the Cévennes. But the flat plain country where agriculture was highly developed, like the Basin of the Seine, the Beauce, Touraine and Poitou, Champagne and Burgundy, and the great plain of Languedoc enjoyed general tranquillity.

Everything in these rich areas changed when the English invasions began. Before 1346, the year of the first invasion, France was the most peaceful and prosperous country in Europe. A population which had not known the horrors of war was suddenly visited with evils which recalled the direst epoch of the feudal period. Henceforth the evil knew no cessation until 1380—a whole generation of constant war. To the foreign invasion was added civil war and social revolution. Even after the treaty of Bretigny in 1360 the evil was not relieved. For then mercenaries in both armies, left without pay, pitilessly plundered the country. Not a province, scarce even a town of all France except in the far south escaped depredation and destruction in the long period between 1346 and 1380. An analysis of the events of this epoch will distinguish three periods or stages of the war: (1) the epoch of the grand invasions, 1345-56, in which the battles of Crécy and Poitiers are the spectacular events, (2) civil and social war simultaneously with a new English invasion. It is the period of the revolt of Paris under Etienne Marcel, the peasant revolt of the Jacquerie, the invasion of 1359 and the settlement of Bretigny, (3) the long conflict of Charles V first against the Free Companies and then against the English (1360–80).

The war began in the North with a naval [7] battle of the English and French fleets at Sluys (1340). The French had twenty thousand men and two hundred and two ships, one hundred and sixty of which were furnished by seventeen Norman ports. The whole fleet was destroyed, only thirty vessels escaping. This disaster ruined French commerce. There was no longer any French marine in the Channel. After the battle of Sluys it is significant that Edward III extended the jurisdiction of the English admiral, which up to that date had been "mainly disciplinary and administrative," so as to enable him to hold an independent court and administer plenary justice in piracy and other maritime cases.

Six years later in 1346 the great English invasion took place. Edward III landed in the Cotentin and then systematically pillaged Normandy. The English burned St. Lo, and the cloth industry there, which Jean Le Bel praises, was ruined. Caen resisted although it was an open city only protected by a castle. The English found there forty thousand pieces of cloth and serge which were shipped to England. The battle of Crécy took place on August 26, 1346.[8] Calais surrendered on August

[7] Neither England nor France possessed a navy. The custom was to impress merchant and fishing vessels into government service and to man them with soldiery. Neither "navy" nor "marines" yet existed as a separate service in the administration. France was more deficient than England in shipping and the deficiency was made up by hire of Genoese, Basque, Castilan, Catalan, and Provençal ships and mariners. The coast of France then exposed to attack and therefore requiring defense was much less than that of modern France. Gascony and Guienne pertained to England and the Mediterranean coast was never endangered by an English fleet. In Picardy the ports were Boulogne, Montreuil, Abbeville, Saint Valery and Calais (until its loss in 1347); in Normandy the ports were Dieppe, Havre, Rouen, Pont Audemer, Harfleur, Touques, Caen, Barfleur and Cherbourg; Brittany proved incapable of defense, especially after the war of succession broke out there when one party was supported by France, the other by England. In Poitou, Aunis and Saintonge there were but four ports: La Rochelle, St. Jean d'Angély, Tonnay and St. Savinien.

[8] The Hundred Years' War is distinguished in history as the earliest war in which gunpowder was used, but it was effective, and that only to a slight degree, in siege of towns. It did not revolutionize field warfare until the last half of the sixteenth century. The first evidence of the employment of gunpowder is

4, 1347, after a year's siege. Nearly the whole population had vanished. The fine houses were given to English merchants and English colonists were sent out. Calais became the continental emporium of England, which thenceforth had a port near Flanders. Edward III returned to England after the capture of Calais.

"He found the country in a state of unparalleled prosperity. The harvest had been good." But the modern historian who so writes neglects to record the observation of the contemporary English historian Walsingham that when the campaign of 1346–47 was over almost every house in England, even peasant cottages, were resplendent with spoil out of France; that women of fashion went gaily decked with some portion of the looted towns of Normandy; that cupboards shone with plate from French monasteries and castles; and wardrobes were crammed with furs, silks and draperies of French manufacture.

While the primary motive of England in capturing Calais was to have an entrance into France at the nearest point opposite to England, especially since the murder of Van Artevelde in 1345 made English use of Flanders as a base of military operations difficult, there was also commercial interest in its capture. In the twelfth century Calais had been a small and unimportant channel port. Its prosperity began in 1196 when Henry of Louvain, duke of Brabant, constructed a new harbor. Though Calais did not pertain to him, Richard I, during his reign, granted it letters of safeguard and exempted its merchants from tonlieux in Normandy. In 1196 a gildhall was erected. Calais was then an important center of the herring fishery, and English wool-ships and Spanish and Portuguese wine-ships resorted to it. Between 1328 and 1340 from five thousand to six thousand sacks of wool passed annually through Calais.

The English people were under the impression that the possession or acquisition of considerable transmarine dominions by the English king would lessen the burden which the exigencies of the king's exchequer called upon them to bear. The advocates of foreign empire pointed to the benefits which would accrue to trade by the possession of a country the supply of whose produce was a matter of necessity to England, and whose people might be purchasers of English produce. In any case, it was of great military importance that the country should have for itself some means of entrance into France. Thus Calais was conceived to be of the highest value to England. It was garrisoned with extraordinary care. The charge of maintaining it was a heavy burden on the English exchequer.

in 1338. The French fleet which assailed Southampton in that year carried some bombards on board. In 1339 Cambrai was defended by ten mounted cannon. From this time forward mention of cannon and gunpowder is frequent in the records, but always for siege purposes or for defense of walled towns. The tale of gunpowder having been employed with field artillery at Crécy in 1346 seems to have been a canard.

It was made the principal mart for English produce, or in the phraseology of the time, the Staple was fixed there.[9]

Moreover, possession of Calais gave Edward III almost undisputed supremacy over the Narrow Seas. "This enabled him to throttle the maritime commerce of the south with the north at will" complacently observes a modern British historian.[10] The Spanish and Basque fleets of merchantmen which were used to coming up in the spring, unloading and reloading at Bruges or Antwerp where goods from northern Europe were exchanged for goods from southern Europe, and returning towards autumn, might now be stopped.

From 1347 to 1355 there was a long cessation of hostilities between the combatants, although no peace was made. Piracy and occasional forays of Englishmen into Brittany where there was a war of succession in which France supported one claimant and England the other, continued. The reason for this interval was the prostration of both countries by the Black Death.

The most significant event in this period for the student of commercial history was the battle of Les Espagnols-sur-Mer in 1350. Deprived of sea-power herself France made a double alliance, one with Castile, the other with Waldemar III of Denmark, who cherished a romantic dream of conquering England as the Danes had done in 1000 under Sweyn of Denmark. Philip IV had projected such a Franco-Danish alliance in 1295. The plan was to utilize the naval power of Castile, Denmark and the Hanseatic cities to overwhelm England. Already in the previous year (1349) a Spanish fleet had voyaged as far as the Baltic, made a raid on the Esthonian coast, and on the return home had attacked English shipping in the Channel. So it happened that on August 28, 1350, an English fleet off Winchelsea intercepted and destroyed a Spanish merchant fleet under convoy, laden with wares out of the North and homeward bound from Flanders, whither it had come in the spring with cargoes of Spanish wool. The Basque sailors had been warned but had confidence in the superior size of their vessels. Moreover, as a precaution they had hired at Antwerp crews of fighting men so easily picked up in every port in Europe in those days. Thus had the famous sea-fight of Les Espagnols-sur-Mer befallen. Edward III might have pleaded technical provocation. But behind that lay the firm conviction of England that she would suffer no competition with her wool trade with Flanders. She thoroughly believed in the maxim that trade followed the flag.

When the war was resumed in 1355 it went from bad to worse for France. In this year the war shifted to the south of France. The Black

[9] J. E. Thorold Rogers, *Work and Wages*, p. 196.
[10] Hannay, *op. cit.*, p. 16.

Prince raided Languedoc as far as Narbonne. There was no organized defense and the English pillaged the towns of the south at their leisure. In the next year, 1356, the English invasion penetrated to the heart of the kingdom, into Périgord, Limousin and Auvergne. On September 18, 1356, John the Good lost the battle of Poitiers and the English spread over all the country. Poitou was a province rich in natural products and had prosperous manufactures such as cloth trade and metal working. All this activity decayed and the country was ruined. The war was everywhere at once. The terrible rout at Poitiers in 1356 in which King John, three princes and hundreds of nobles were made prisoner, reduced France to the verge of dissolution.

The capture of King John left the rule of France to the crown prince Charles, a precocious youth of eighteen years of age. The dismay felt in Paris when the disaster at Poitiers became known soon gave place to furious anger against the crown and the nobles, and instead of rallying around the prince in defense of the country the bourgeoisie began a class conflict against the government. Popular grievance against the extravagance and corruption of the Valois government was inflamed by the catastrophe coming so hard after the defeat of Crécy and the loss of Calais. Commingled with this feeling was resentment towards the noblesse, whose prestige was ruined and whose numbers were decimated at Poitiers. The wildest rumors were afloat, which were added to by panic-stricken refugees, escaped prisoners, deserters, who thronged into the capital.

The duty of Prince Charles was clear—to get a new army into the field against the invader and to effect the release of the king. But it was clear that the captivity of John would not terminate without an onerous peace on France's part, and no new war measures were possible without money. This meant that the states general of the northern provinces (*Langue d'oil*) must be called at once.

The heydey of the states general was between 1355 and 1360— the darkest period of the war with England, when France was financially and economically on the verge of exhaustion. Since in the states general, which met on October 17, 1356, there were more than eight hundred deputies, the assembly at once took the bit in its teeth by electing a commission of eighty members from the three estates to investigate the past policy of the government. Under normal conditions it might have been expected that the clerical and nobiliary representatives of the commission might be counted upon not to manifest hostility towards the court. But the condition was exceptional. Many of the clergy and the nobles were partisans of the ambitious and unscrupulous prince Charles of Navarre [11] and intrigued to make him regent.

[11] Charles the Bad was a French prince, a grandson of Louis le Hutin who claimed that his mother, and hence himself, too, had been excluded from the

Though the crown prince was spared, the speeches of the orators bitterly denounced the king's ministers and the frivolity, extravagance and corruption of the government. The violence of the language added fuel to flame. The estates general demanded that the administration be put into the hands of a commission composed of four prelates, twelve nobles and twelve bourgeois. This was political revolution, for it amounted to suspension of the crown prince and the abolition of a monarchical form of government. Young Charles was firm. He replied that he would deliberate with the proposed council, but that he would not dismiss his father's ministers and dissolve the lawfully constituted council of the realm. But how could the dauphin resist? Only the estates general could provide funds for the conduct of the war, and they refused to do so unless consent was given to the creation of the proposed commission.

The dauphin dissolved the estates general and appealed to Étienne Marcel, provost of the merchants of Paris, that is to say to the mayor and corporation of the city of Paris, in hope of securing funds. This brings upon the scene one of the most striking persons and important political events in French history. Marcel was a rich cloth merchant of Paris, as Van Artevelde had been of Ghent. The hanse of Paris of which he was chief (*prévot*) was legally not a commercial association but a police organization, which controlled the traffic on the Seine and exercised police regulation of commerce in the city. However, since its members were merchants, the hanse, through the enjoyment of its rights of civil and criminal jurisdiction, could and did practically control the commerce and trade of Paris. It was at once the municipal government, the police system and the chamber of commerce of the city, and its power was enormous.

There was a considerable colony of Flemish cloth merchants resident in Paris, whom Marcel naturally knew and besides his business had called him frequently to Flanders. These facts are significant. There can be little or no doubt that Marcel was fired with the ambition to be another Van Artvelde, another Rienzi; through his domination

French succession in 1328. Consequently he turned traitor and connived with Edward III for the conquest of his country. He held that his own right to the French throne was superior to that of Edward III—each it must be remembered, was a claimant through the female line—but he was willing to divide the realm with Edward III in the circumstances. We have a full record of this treasonable correspondence, which on the part of England was conducted by the duke of Lancaster and the bishop of London in the years 1355–56, first at Bruges which was conveniently situated both with reference to Calais and the count of Hainaut, and later with great secrecy at Avignon in the private apartments of either the cardinal of Arras or the cardinal of Boulogne, both of whom were partisans of England in the war. The pope was totally unaware of these negotiations. Secret diplomacy is nothing new in history.

of Paris to dominate the other great cities of France as well; to create a strong bourgeois party in France able, not only to dictate to the government, but to make the government subservient to it; in short Marcel projected a gigantic bourgeois revolution at once political, economic and social. It was a bold anticipation of 1789. He counted upon the strait of the government, the widespread unrest and dissatisfaction, the economic discontent, the social antagonism of the time to abet his designs. The exigency of money and the hardships arising from the flood of "weak" coin which King John had emitted afforded him plausible pretext to pose as the friend of the people, the advocate of popular rights. But Marcel's sincerity in these professions is belied by his acts. In the end his alliance with Charles the Bad was fatal both to his success and to his character. He was a shrewd and unscrupulous demagogue, although his memory was idolized during the French Revolution and he has been the hero of every revolution in France since then, 1830, 1848, 1871.[12]

The crown prince was compelled to temporize and to go with the stream. In the spring of 1357 the states general were again convoked. If they had confined their attention to the finances only, there would have been justification of their policy of wishing to centralize the financial administration in their hands. But, dominated by the partisans of Charles of Navarre and Marcel, they subordinated the welfare of the country to political ambition. Under the guise of "protecting the rights of the people" Marcel played a daring and unscrupulous hand. He could afford to be daring. For Paris was in the hollow of his hand, and Paris had been formidably walled and fortified within the past year. The states general refused to grant any general tax unless the government would surrender to its demands for investigation and control of it, but merely permitted short-time collections which required constant renewal. Paris was in a condition of such suppressed turbulence, the political tension was so great, that the dauphin could no longer remain there with safety and the court removed to Compiègne. No funds were available except precarious ones from the royal domain. The crown dared not impose taxes, for the word had gone out and was magically current among the masses that only the states general had the right to lay permanent taxes; that government rested on the consent of the governed. It was new and revolutionary doctrine for a feudal age—if it may be said to have been a feudal age in the fourteenth century—to hear.

12 The French historian Henri Martin in the middle of the last century proposed the erection of a statue to Étienne Marcel "for having first endeavored to establish representative government in France." An equestrian statue of him in the Place de l'hôtel de ville is cherished as a symbol of French democracy and every May-day is decorated with flowers by radicals, marxists, third internationalists and soviet sympathizers.

The condition in February, 1358, when the states general again convened was almost sinister—"the country ravaged by foreign invasion, the town of Paris at the point of insurrection, the government divided between the parties of peace and war, the States General themselves disunited, for the nobility had withdrawn, the dauphin and the representatives of the assembly at odds. . . . The demands of the popular leaders remind one in several respects of those put forward by the baronial party in England exactly a hundred years before, and repeated in substance on later occasions." [13] But there was this wide difference between the condition of England under the misrule of Henry III in the thirteenth century, and France in the middle of the fourteenth century. Baronage, country gentlemen and burgesses were then united and actuated with ideas of constructive reform. In France there was antagonistic cleavage of the classes, and the least politically experienced class had the government by the throat. Moreover, Marcel and his ilk were mainly struggling for power, not for reform of the administration. "Reform" was a smoke screen behind which they hid.

An additional factor of alarming nature was the formidable ascendancy of Paris. The great city of revolution was this early beginning to manifest its claim to rule all France. The dauphin was compelled to consent that the deputies of from twenty to thirty towns should be assembled in Paris. One of the most remarkable clauses in a law passed by this states general, and ratified by the dauphin because he could not do otherwise, provided for the suppression of all provincial assemblies throughout France and the establishment of one "general assembly to be held annually in the town of Paris." This early connection between democracy and centralization anticipated the attitude of Paris in the revolution of later years.

In the midst of the political events of the time it is worth while looking at the part which the gilds of Paris played. The city of Paris put itself at the head of a movement directed, not against the crown, but against the incapable and wasteful government of King John. It attempted to organize resistance to the English at the very moment when the states general were claiming the right of the supervision and control of the royal administration and creating a new financial system. This was the movement inspired by Marcel, who drew the gilds to his support. We have already seen that these gilds maintained armed watchmen in Paris. Accordingly the artisans had arms. After the battle of Poitiers this militia rose in defense of the capital and formed a veritable army under Marcel's orders.

One measure taken, however, had genuine intention back of it. This was a law requiring the razing of the *petites forteresses* which had sprung up all over the country, except in Languedoc. Many of these

[13] *English Historical Review*, XI, p. 567.

were local efforts to ensure security, but the remedy had proved worse than the evils of anarchy they were intended to mitigate. Numbers fell into the hands of the English, others were captured by bands of mercenary soldiers who lived by banditry; others represented a recrudescent feudalism natural to troublous times and under weak government. These structures were as dangerous as the enemy and more destructive of commerce and agriculture. For they were abodes of rapine. The relaxation of the war, though as yet there was no peace, released thousands of the mercenaries in both armies, men who were ruffians and cutthroats by nature. They were a motley of English, French, Bretons, Flemings, Brabantines, Spaniards, who lived by pillage.

However, instead of taking immediate and effective steps to destroy the scourge from which the country was suffering, the states general, which was under Marcel's thumb, played politics. The municipal colors of Paris, *parti de rouge et de pers,* that is to say red and blue, were displayed everywhere in shop windows and on the streets; the deputies, even those who were reluctant so to do, were intimidated by the mob into wearing them. The dauphin, who showed courage in coming to Paris, attempted in a speech to the populace to stem the rising current of revolution. He was replied to by an échevin of Paris, a henchman of Marcel, who impudently said that "there were so many bad weeds in the realm of France that they choked the good herbs." The first revolutionary reign of terror was not far off. The provost had curried favor with the working classes in Paris and, under the guise of organizing them patriotically, had under his command several thousand armed men, not all honest artisans and craftsmen, but men drawn from the dregs of Paris. With this improvised militia, which was far from being the true militia of Paris, Marcel resorted to intimidation and force. The states general was pliant and cowardly; honest law-abiding citizens, tradesmen and artisans, were cowed. In the last week of February, 1358, Marcel at the head of his armed array and followed by the rabble of the city, marched upon the royal palace. On its way through the streets the mob murdered a poor pastry-maker, and, having tasted blood, invaded the palace. Charles, who was without fear, faced the ominous crew. Marcel demanded the dismissal of the king's ministers and acceptance of the revolutionary statutes passed by the states general. The two marshals of the prince, fearing that violence might be done him, interrupted Marcel's harangue, upon which the furious band of his retainers threw themselves upon the marshals, cut them down, and dragged their bodies into the courtyard where the mob indulged in a gruesome orgy.

A few days later Charles of Navarre arrived in Paris. He was master of the situation. His army of mercenaries, many of them former English troops, controlled Normandy and the Ile-de-France as far west as Chartres. His safe-conducts were more honored than those of the dauphin. His plan was to bully his cousin into the cession of Champagne or Normandy to him, in addition to an enormous bonus of money, and so he made common cause with Marcel. As for the latter, he was in a state of elated ambition bordering on intoxication. He wrote triumphant letters to Ghent and Ypres apprising them of the revolution which had been achieved in Paris, and expressed the hope that the great burgher cities of Flanders would make common cause with him and Paris. Democracy—heaven save the word!— had run riot. At the same time he wrote to the *bonnes villes du royaume* demanding that they join the revolution and make their people wear the red and blue chevrons of Paris. The plea of every red revolutionist was in Marcel's epistles: "They who have been killed are so few . . . for the which thing and other evils of his counsellors," he wrote to the échevins of Ypres, "a small number of them have been justly put to death." One is reminded of Barnave's sneer during the massacres in Paris in September, 1792, when so many innocents of noble blood were slaughtered by the furious mob: "Is their blood so pure?"

Meantime, while these violent events were happening in Paris, a peasant revolt had broken out in the valley of the Oise. Luckily for France it was a local affair and the movement was crushed before it could spread to other provinces. The episode was a terrible symptom of that class hatred and economic distress which prevailed more or less throughout the country. This was the Jacquerie, so called from Jacques, the customary name for a peasant. The revolutionists of Paris and neighboring towns like Senlis, Amiens and Meaux were not indifferent to this rural insurrection.

The Jacquerie was not inspired by the same motives as the rebellion in Paris, but there was enough of common grievance and common purpose in both movements to unite them if sufficiently successful. Peasant hatred of the nobles was an old sentiment in France. After Poitiers, in which battle thousands of nobles had been slain or taken prisoner, thus leaving country houses, manors and châteaux defenseless, this hatred broke out around Beauvais, and the exasperation was accentuated by the ravages of marauding brigands and prowling robbers. In addition the captured nobles had to ransom themselves and could not look to the government for their release, so that everywhere in France the manorial peasantry suffered from exorbitant exactions.

The immediate occasion of the rising sprang from the efforts of the regent to cut off Paris from supplies and so to break it. To this end Charles attempted to garrison the points around Paris with the small troops at his disposal and to intercept the transportation of supplies into the city. One of these companies which was scouring the countryside making requisitions—for they were compelled to live upon the country—was set upon by a band of infuriated peasants. It was the spark which kindled the conflagration. The peasants were ignorant, without discipline, unused to arms and having none except what could be picked up. Many wore improvised armor made of boiled leather and carried swords formed out of scythes and billhooks. Their "captain" was one William Cale or Karle. The cruelties and brutalities of the Jacques were what might be expected—burned houses, murdered families, torture of defenseless men, women and children. At least one nobleman was roasted on a spit before the eyes of his wife and children. The valley of the Oise was at once an oven and a shambles. With more wit than his fellows, Karle recognized the futility of the insurrection unless it received outside support and endeavored to get assistance from the towns roundabout. If his appeal had been hearkened to, if the bourgeois had made common cause with the peasants, above all if Paris had given them support, a social revolution of portentous dimension would have resulted. But the towns rejected the appeal, except Paris. Marcel had grown alarmed over the effort of the regent to starve Paris into submission and saw in alliance with the Jacquerie a means to foil that design.

But such a project was repugnant to Charles of Navarre, who was a noble, indeed a prince of the blood, and Marcel's plan split the partnership between him and Charles. The tide of revolution in Paris was beginning to ebb. The suppression of the revolt of the peasants, itself a terrible chapter, did not cause the fall of Marcel, but his policy had so compromised him that his failure was inevitable. His very excesses estranged his own followers and honest men in Paris took courage from the signs. The regent saw more clearly than any which way the water was running and realized that if Navarre could be satisfied in his demands and his brigand army, *un ramas d'aventuriers*, be removed from around Paris, then Marcel and the revolution he had engendered would collapse. Paris could then be starved into submission. So far it had been these forces, not Marcel's, which had prevented the execution of the regent's plan.

With the object of estranging Navarre from Marcel, Prince Charles in a conference with the disreputable prince of Navarre proffered him a bribe—for this is what it amounted to—of ten thousand livres' revenue out of the royal domain and four hundred thousand additional in annual installments of fifty thousand to be taken from the aids levied for support of the war. The renegade prince accepted the offer, though be refused to partake of the sacrament which was solemnly to bind the bargain, satirically saying that he was "not hungry." The blasphemy was of a piece with his character.

The blockade around Paris was now made closer. The pinch of

hunger began to be felt by the populace. The anger of the mob which Marcel had fomented against the dauphin now turned against himself. In desperation Marcel sent messages to the échevins of the Flemish towns imploring them to intervene in behalf of "the liberties of the people," but nothing resulted. In July the cordon of loyalist and royalist troops, supplemented by the *routiers* of Charles of Navarre, many of whom were English, ringed Paris. The Parisian infantry militia made several disastrous sorties against them in order to relieve the siege. When Marcel returned from one of these disastrous sallies with the broken remnant of his troops he was hooted and pelted in the streets. One hope remained to Marcel—to alienate the prince of Navarre from his alliance with the dauphin, and this he planned to accomplish by surrendering Paris to him. In possession of the great capital on the Seine, Navarre might dream of overthrowing the house of Valois and making himself king. It was Marcel's last card. This design was suspected by some of Marcel's officers. On the night of July 31, that favorite month of revolutionary Paris, as Marcel was on the point of delivering the keys of the Porte Saint-Antoine to Josseran de Macon, the prince of Navarre's treasurer who had been secretly introduced into the city, he was cut down by one of his own men. Within an hour the counter-revolution, favored by forces and feelings which hitherto had been latent through fear, leaped to furious expression. The mob of Paris veered, as mobs always do. A bloody reaction was soon under way which was not stopped until the prince regent entered the city on the second day of the events (August 2). His hand was on the helm.

But for France this consummation was no more than a budding morrow in midnight. All of northern France was in a condition bordering upon anarchy. Charles of Navarre was in possession of Normandy and conniving with the English enemy to support his claim to the throne of France. In November (1359) Edward III landed at Calais with a new army. The fact that he presumed to start a campaign in the winter and expected his army to live upon a country almost utterly reduced to desolation shows his military incompetence. The invader avoided Paris whose new walls stood it in good stead, but cut a huge swath of destruction around Paris from Rheims to Chartres. France had no army to oppose him. But what arms could not accomplish, that the wintry weather did. A terrible blizzard in the early spring, on April 13, 1360, destroyed men and horses by thousands. That "Black Monday" lived long in English memory. "Thanne beynge a foul, derk day of mist and hayl," disconsolately records a chronicle, "and so bitter cold that manye men deyde for cold, wherefore unto this day manye men callen it the Blacke Moneday."

The prince regent seized the opportunity to negotiate for peace, which was concluded on May 8, 1360, at Bretigny in Anjou. By the terms France yielded its claim to suzerainty over the English king for the fiefs of Gascony and Guienne, which were henceforth to be held in free possession, and in addition ceded Poitou, Périgord, Quercy,[14] Saintonge, Rouergue, Agenois, Limousin and Bigorre to the English crown, in return for which Edward III renounced his claim to the throne of France. The next important provision of the treaty was the arrangement made for the ransom of the captive John, who had been living in royal splendor in England, having the Savoy palace on the Strand for a residence and an annuity of two thousand pounds for his hôtel. The ransom of Louis IX came vividly to the minds of many in these days and John's own address to the nation recalled it. But so ignorant was the king of past history that St. Louis was said to have been captured at Tunis, whereas as a matter of fact it was at Mansourah in Egypt in 1248, and he had died on the sands before Tunis in 1270. Also the highly colored statement was made that so much of the precious metals had then been withdrawn from France to pay for Louis' liberation that leather money was substituted. France was again to discover that kings were costly personages. The ransom was fixed at three million *ecus d'or*. But this huge sum represented only a portion of the money exacted from France. For the captive French princes and marshals besides hundreds of nobles had also to be ransomed. The royal ransom was to be paid in installments, save six hundred thousand *ecus d'or* which were payable almost immediately.

So important is the history of the collection of King John's ransom, which made an indelible impression on French taxation, that it is now in order to examine the history of this imposition in detail. But first a glance backward at the history of French taxes before 1360 is necessary.

The receipts of the royal treasury in the time of Philip IV, as has been seen, were derived from two sources. They were those of the royal domain or crown lands,[15] proceeds from court fines, emoluments

[14] The towns in Quercy when called upon in fulfillment of the treaty of Bretigny to renounce their allegiance to the French king patriotically, though hopelessly, protested their patriotism.

[15] In 1328 the royal domain or the territory administered directly by the king, comprised the Ile-de-France, Normandy, Champagne, Artois, Orléanais, Touraine, Anjou, Poitou, and a part of Berry. In the South the king possessed Languedoc, Auvergne and the Lyonais. Administratively these territories were divided into thirty-six bailiwicks and *sénéchausées*, as they were denominated in the South. The rest of France was represented by fiefs of the crown which were directly governed by their respective feudatories. The largest of these were the duchy of Burgundy and the counties of Flanders and Brittany, and in this category must also be included the English fiefs in France, notably the duchies of Gascony and Guienne.

of the great seal, tolls, coinage or seigniorage. These receipts supported the court and paid the salaries of administrative officials. By the time of Philip of Valois, owing to wastefulness and negligence, the ordinary revenues of the crown arising from the royal domain, supplemented by administrative fees and taxes imposed upon the conduct of trade, were insufficient for the royal needs. The king had no power of taxation outside of those provinces included within the royal domain, and even within some of these, like Normandy and Languedoc, he could not impose taxes without deliberation with the local estates. These ordinary revenues failed to suffice for Philip VI's extravagant tastes and especially for support of the war with the English. Consequently the crown was compelled time and again to solicit "aides" from its subjects. In these cases the king had to walk warily, for the great nobles, the high clergy which enjoyed many privileges, the towns which possessed recognized "franchises" were jealous of their rights, and the crown was often required to reduce, even to give up a proposed subsidy, to certain nobles or to certain towns.

These aides, however, had a more general character than other taxes. The manner of levying them varied according to the sort of accommodation agreed upon between the king and the nobles and the towns. The clergy's assistance invariably was in the form of special tithes. Philip VI's first taxation was imposed in 1328 for the campaign in Flanders which culminated in the battle of Cassel. For this he collected the sum of 231,078 *livres* from twenty-two bailiwicks and *sénéchausées* of the royal domain. The document which informs us of this amount lists the collection from each bailiwick and also tells us how it was raised. In some places the assessment (*fouage*) was laid upon "hearths," *i.e.*, upon households. In Sens every hundred "hearths" were assessed four *sous per diem* for four months; in Troyes a *per capita* tax was levied, with a minimum exemption and a graduated rating rising to a tax of four *livres*, 10 *sous* for those having five hundred *livres'* worth of property or over. In Rouen a lump sum was spread over each parish, and each inhabitant paid according to his means; some parishes paid in installments; others paid at once. In a word, no uniform system of taxation existed. The king left local ways and means to the discretion of the local officials. Most towns laid a special assessment and collected the amount with their own machinery. In many instances the towns took advantage of the king's need to demand royal confirmation of their franchises. The half-independent nobles in provinces outside of the royal domain also demanded assurance of their privileges.

War taxes were unpopular but explicable. However, when Philip VI undertook to impose new *aides* merely to pay the extravagant cost of knighting the princes, or to provide dowries for his daughters, he

met with great opposition. Nevertheless, he was measurably successful in raising these revenues, a fact which is evidence of the growing
power of the monarchy.

Finally, the war with England made an immense call upon the
revenues of France. Real and personal property, improvements, incomes either in kind or in money, households, parishes, towns, domains, commerce and industry were all taxed. Philip IV's old "penny
in the pound" tax on sales, popularly called the *maltôte*, was increased
to four pence in the pound, the seller being supposed to pay two pence
and the purchaser the other two pence. The vineyard provinces especially suffered from this tax. It was specified that in the seaboard
provinces the amounts raised were to be expended for protection of
the coast and not for ordinary purposes of war. Nobles who were summoned for military service in person might compound by paying a
fifth of their revenue; the same rate held for freeholders; towns had
to contribute a fifth of their revenue raised in the customary way.
This was an enormously heavy tax imposed upon the whole realm,
and actually could not be collected. Everywhere adjustment and composition took place, particularly in the provinces not comprehended
within the royal domain. This meant that the tax was not uniformly
laid and varied from province to province, from town to town, from
fief to fief. Paris paid a lump sum of eighteen thousand *livres tournois*
in order that bread, wine, cheese, herring and ordinary woolens might
be exempted. For there was always fear of rioting in Paris in event
of high prices or hard times. But the other forms of assessment stood
fast, except that nobles, clergy, collegiate houses, colleges, professors
in the University of Paris, and public officials were exempted. These
variegated general taxes which began to be imposed in 1337 were
renewed nearly every year in one form or another. But as the war
continued and the provinces were ravaged the returns diminished.
Local resistance was not unusual and successive edicts witness to the
penury of the government. In the provinces outside of the royal domain there was friction with the great feudatories. What was needed
was a general tax providing substantial income combined with ease
of collection. These considerations brought forward two especial taxes
destined to become permanent: the *fouage* and the *gabelle*.

The *fouage*,[16] as intimated before, was a householder's tax; technically it was a tax of ten *sous* spread over five years imposed upon
every hearth and estimated upon a family of five persons per hearth.
Thus the family hearth (*feu familial*) might not coincide with the
feu fiscal, for the latter was a sort of fiction, a unit for purposes of

---

[16] From the word *focagium*, smoke and not from *feu*, fire, although *feu* and
fouage were used interchangeably to signify "hearth-money" or "smoke-penny";
hence a family, a household, a house.

assessment. A large house might be assessed for two or more "hearths." It was a profitable but unpopular tax. The *gabelle* was even more so, for it was a tax upon salt, of Spanish origin, adopted by the Valois government. But back of old Spanish usage, the *gabelle* had a long tradition. A tax upon salt seems to have originated with Alexander the Great and subsisted under the Roman Empire. Then it vanished for nearly a thousand years until St. Louis imposed it as an extraordinary tax. Its unpopularity was so great that not even Philip le Bel, for all his avaricious ways, ventured to resort to it. But in obscure ways the *gabelle* seems to have persisted in Spain where Roman tradition was strong. Indubitably the French kings learned of this tax when French and Spanish politics were in close relation. Probably it was of Aragonese, not Castilan origin.[17]

The *gabelle* made the manufacture and sale of salt a government monopoly; salt springs and salt-pans along the Mediterranean seashore where salt was produced by evaporation were made regalian rights. This highly provocative tax was established by royal edict on March 16, 1341. Immediately the king sent into every province commissioners to buy up available salt, to acquire storehouses and establish offices. These officials acted with extreme rigor. Complaints poured into Paris; but they were not listened to and the *gabelle* was imposed almost everywhere. The complaints of the people became louder, so that in 1346, when the states general was convoked, Philip VI suavely informed them that he had no intention of making the *gabelle* permanent, but that it was a "war tax." The assembly believed him and adjourned. But the tax remained. Unlike the English parliaments, which vigorously demanded concessions of the royal prerogative and imposed limitations upon the crown in return for grants of taxes and subsidies, thereby laying the foundations of parliamentary government in England, the French states general pliably yielded to the demands of the king, and so forfeited the opportunity which the war gave to establish the elements of constitutional government in France.

The collection of these taxes became more and more difficult as the war went from bad to worse, while the expenditures for the war steadily mounted. An added evil was the corruption of the currency. There were twenty-two monetary laws modifying the currency between 1328 and 1355. In 1343 Philip VI gave out that the government would return to the "good money of St. Louis." It was a barefaced pretext and had not even the plausibility of the same practice in the reign of Philip IV. It merely gave the government the opportunity to pay its obligations in debased coin and to collect taxes in the better coin. Moreover, in order to sustain the war Philip VI had recourse

[17] Finot, *Essai historique sur les origines de la gabelle*, 1866.

to other expedients like sale of privileges, legitimization of bastards— for a fee—processes of mortmain, by which persons desirous of leaving property to the Church could do so only upon payment of a high fee.

Early in 1346, the year of the Crécy campaign, the king, having learned that the *gabelle* and the four-penny tax *"estoient moult deplaisans a nostre peuple, que tant par icely comme pour les prevoz, fermiers et les excessis nombre des sergenz et les commisaires envoyez par nostre royaume, sur plusieurs cas, nostre dit peuple se tenoit moult agravez,"* as the preamble of the royal proclamation recites, convoked "the prelates, barons, chapters and good towns of our kingdom in order to remedy all these things." This time the states general were double: those of Northern France (*Langue d'oil*) were convened at Paris in the king's presence; those of the South (*Langue d'oc*) at Toulouse. In both assemblies it was again asseverated that the *gabelle* and the four-penny tax were only temporary taxation measures. In these assemblies it is worth observing that each province voted separately. In other words each province was a voting unit having one vote, and in the provincial representation each class, *i.e.*, clergy, barons, bourgeois, voted as a group. By this system the small provinces had equal weight with the larger ones, but as there was greater affiliation between the two privileged orders than between either of them and the third estates, the preponderant vote was usually that of the clergy and nobles in each provincial assembly. Moreover, as the king was the first of nobles his relation with the privileged orders was less strained than his relation with the commons.

The dire strait of the country after the disaster at Crécy and during the siege of Calais (1346–47) enabled Philip VI to adopt drastic means of raising revenue and of silencing complaints. In summoning a provincial assembly at Pontoise in 1347 the king merely said "we are under certain necessities which we cannot well describe." The battle of Crécy had shown the military incompetence of the nobles, so that the French government inclined towards the employment of mercenary soldiers instead. Accordingly in 1347 we find a measure for enlarging commutation of military service on the part of the nobles. After the loss of Calais, with the intention (or under the pretext?) of equipping a fleet for a naval attack upon England, new moneys were extorted, but no employment of this revenue for this purpose was made.

The incompetence, the waste, the graft, inseparable from all these fiscal measures, was so great that if Philip VI had not been able to rely upon the church tithes and papal loans he would have been even worse off financially. Fortunately ever since the time of Philip IV the tithes could be counted upon as a permanent resource by the government. They were collected every year. Theoretically the popes at Avignon always consented to them. As the church collected them the tithes were broadly imposed and apparently collected with more honesty than was the case with the government's taxes. One example will give an idea of what the tithe brought to the royal treasury. In 1330 it furnished 278,832 *livres*, 10 *sous* and 5 *deniers tournois;* the cost of collection amounted to 12,841 *livres*, 15 *sous* and 9 *deniers*, leaving a balance for the king of 265,990 *livres*, 14 *sous* and 8 *deniers.* The monastic orders, which pretended to possess an immunity the secular clergy did not enjoy, vigorously protested against this exaction of tithes for government purposes. "The abbeys of the order of Citeaux," wrote the chief abbot to the master of the chamber of accounts, "with difficulty make a living from their fields, their vineyards and their flocks and herds. Farming in some years costs more than it brings in, especially since the new coins have been put in circulation; for we have to pay our laborers and hirelings in it instead of in the old money." The flagrant waste of the tithes upon fêtes and favorites, however, by Philip VI in the early years of his reign stirred the anger of the pope and in 1336 their payment was stopped, and the privilege not regranted until the war with England began. Philip of Valois, furthermore, derived a pecuniary profit from the sale of royal "letters of safeguard" to a great number of towns, notably in Picardy, which assured them special protection of their franchises and liberties in return for financial assistance. The protection was illusory, but it had the substantial effect of confirming the liberties of the towns and so ministered to the growth of the bourgeoisie.

Philip VI also had recourse to loans from Italian bankers and to forced loans from his own subjects. The rates of interest on the former were very high; the latter often proved to be arbitrary confiscations. The largest banker of the king, though, was the pope. The papal incomes being derived from all Christendom were of a prodigious amount, and the popes, being Frenchmen, were liberal in making loans to the French kings. In the early years of the great war, between 1345-55, the papacy advanced the enormous sum of 3,392,000 gold florins. These sums were the fullest and readiest resources of the French monarchy. The English government, while it had no proof of these loans, had a shrewd suspicion that papal gold was financing the French kings, and since the papacy drew large revenues from England as well as from other countries, the feeling of the English people that they were supporting the French enemy against themselves was not a consoling sentiment.

After the treaty of Bretigny, in 1360, the loss of some of the richest provinces of the crown and the alienations of revenue due to the disastrous policy of establishing appanages in favor of the princes, the government's income was more crippled than ever. The people, now that the war seemed ended, clamored for the restoration of *les anciennes franchises et libertés* as in the time of Philip le Bel, and demanded the suppression of the extraordinary taxes which had been imposed by the Valois kings. This demand was mingled with an economic and social discontent among the lower working classes because of the great gilds and a vague spirit of rebellion among the peasantry, in whom memory of the Jacquerie was not dead. We shall soon see that if France escaped a peasant rebellion like that in England in 1381, she was to experience, along with Flanders and Florence, a widespread revolt of the crafts in the chief cities, a revolt characterized by the manifestation of certain antisocial tendencies of a really revolutionary nature.

In order to explain the resentment with which the people regarded the taxes imposed upon them at this time, it is necessary to remember that the taxes which were most unpopular, like the *gabelle*, the *fouage* and the four-pence tax on sales, were new, and the nation looked with anger and dismay upon the prospect of their becoming established forms of taxation, which is exactly what happened. The enormous sum required for the ransom of King John made permanent and fixed the various expedients of taxation resorted to by Philip VI. An ordinance of December 5, 1360, established under the name of *aides pour deliverance du roi* the three taxes already familiar from occasional previous imposition, but which now became permanent features of French taxation.

The *fouage* has an especial interest for the economic historian as the figures of it give statistical information which otherwise he would be without. After the separation of the provinces renounced in 1360, eliminating Burgundy and Dauphiné which were not subject to the system, it has been estimated that the *fouage* was imposed upon about one half of the present *départements* of France. The number of hearths so taxed was between 2,000,000 and 2,300,000, and the amount collected between four and five million dollars. It is impossible to arrive at a more accurate figure for the reason that the *fouage* was not always a personal assessment, as has been pointed out before. In Languedoc, for example, it was sometimes a tax upon real property, sometimes a tax upon goods estimated as a unit to be *of the value of* a hearth or cottage, but still called a *fouage*. Again, the property of related families might be lumped together and estimated to be taxable at so or so many *fouages*. In other terms, the *fouage* was a fictitious unit of tax estimation, by the aid of which the collector determined the taxability of the varied and mixed resources of the locality taxed. This fixation without doubt was subject to frequent exemptions and irregularities. The *fouage* was necessarily less collectible in the devastated provinces, and Languedoc, which never suffered from invasion by the English, enjoyed certain privileges. The product of the *fouage* in proportion to other taxes has been calculated to have been as eight to twenty-five (8:25).

These taxes created by the necessity of the king's ransom had an important influence upon the future history of France. They were the first attempt to establish a regular and permanent series of taxes. But collection of them was not the same everywhere. In the Ile-de-France and Normandy the collection most nearly conformed to the letter of the law. A well-working fiscal organization was there developed, the chief agents of which were a receiver-general and treasurers, having under them local collectors called *élus* and "diocesan receivers." The last collected tribute from the clergy, of which all branches except the Mendicant Orders were taxed. But in certain provinces, notably Languedoc, which enjoyed a certain degree of autonomy, collection was made by local and not by royal officials. This also was done by some of the greater cities.

The sum total of war taxes borne by France in the reign of Charles V has been estimated by a careful French historian at thirty-three millions of francs (*i.e.*, when the franc was worth 19.25 cents as before the World War) or about $6,500,000. But this sum signifies little unless one knows that the purchasing power of money in the fourteenth century was at least four, perhaps as much as six times the purchasing power of money to-day. Accordingly the total burden of taxation imposed by the crown for the war of liberation in the years 1369–80 was at least $25,000,000 and may have been nearly $40,000,000. But this is not the end of the tale. For it must be remembered that in addition to these royal taxes the French people of all classes were subject to church tithes; that nobles were liable for "aides" or had to compound for them; that the unfree peasantry was subject to service or pecuniary "renders" and *banalités* to manorial landlords. What the volume of such taxation amounted to is mere conjecture.

The question now arises: What was the population of France in the Valois period? By taking the figures in the *Registers of the Fouage* imposed in 1328, which applied to forty-eight *départements* and more than half the population of modern France, and comparing these figures with the census of 1851—which it is better than using the last French census since the great modern urban development, with consequent important displacements of population had not then taken place in France—it is found that 2,465,948 hearths in 1328 represented a population of 18,767,000 people in 1851. Allowing five persons for each hearth in 1328 and multiplying the number of hearths by five we get 12,329,740 inhabitants, exclusive of the clergy, university professors and students who enjoyed ecclesiastical privilege, paupers and the very poor. The population of France, therefore, in 1328, was a third

below what it was in the middle of the nineteenth century. This difference, however, disagrees with the evidence furnished by some provincial sources. For example, Burgundy, in 1328, possessed 32,000
hearths or 160,000 inhabitants (estimated) while the population an-
swering to that region to-day numbers over 400,000. Yet, since in
modern times the principal increase of population has been in cities
and towns, it may be justly inferred that the rural population of
France has not sensibly increased since the fourteenth century, and
even that it has diminished in certain areas.

But Charles V had no such area of territory and no such population
to assess as Philip VI had in 1328. The treaty of Bretigny in 1360
had ceded Poitou, Périgord, Quercy, Saintonge, Rouergue, Agenois,
Limousin, and Bigorre to England. The provinces yielded to Edward
III represented a loss to France of thousands of hearths which otherwise would have been subject to the *fouage*. Deduction also must be
made of French Navarre and Normandy which pertained to Charles
the Bad, of Ponthieu which was part of the dowry of Edward III's
mother and hence practically an enclave of English territory within
France, and of the Pale of Calais. Moreover certain regions which
had suffered heavily from devastation by the English were exempted
from the *fouage*. Most of these areas were in the Ile-de-France and
had been ruined by the campaign of 1359. All these deductions taken
together constituted an enormous deprivation for Charles V. In
fact, he had only slightly over half as many hearths and no more
than half the population from which to derive revenue as Philip VI
had.

Contrasted with the wealth of England, however, in this time, if
the condition of the French provinces had been normal and not one
of ruin, France would have been approximately three times as rich as
England. For England, after 1360, had not over 8,600 parishes against
France's 22,000. The tax upon movables imposed in the second year
of the reign of Richard II (1378)—two-tenths in towns and two-fif-
teenths in the country—must have been heavier than French taxes
of the same kind. The conclusion is unavoidable that the military collapse and the misery of France in the reigns of Philip VI and John II
were due the criminal negligence and waste of these kings. No worse
sovereigns ever cursed France.

The burden of the excessive taxation on account of the king's ransom was so great upon France that time and again the provinces were
on the verge of revolt, which was averted by the honest and efficient
administration of Charles V. As peace and prosperity grew this burden was gradually relaxed. In 1370 the *fouage* in the *sénéchausée* of
Carcassonne was reduced from 90,000 hearths to 35,623; that of Beaucaire from 70,000 to 23,478; that of Toulouse from 50,000 to 24,830,

or a total of 83,000 hearths instead of 210,000. By 1378 the *fouage* had sunk to a total of 30,000 hearths.

This consideration of the history of taxation has carried us forward of the narrative. It is necessary to return to the year 1360.

After the treaty of Bretigny the English invasion gave place to a new scourge, no less terrible for France. Bands of armed men, "Free Companies" they were called, a sort of residue of the regular armies, both English and French, brutally practised the fruitful business of pillage and ransom of the distracted population. Even towns were sacked and the pope in Avignon was not immune from paying blackmail to these marauders. The "Free Companies" were formed of adventurers of all nationalities, those who had been in the pay of France, of England, and of the renegade Charles of Navarre. They never had a single chief, but a great solidarity existed between the several bands. The rapidity of their movements and the prostrated condition of the country made it easy for them to concentrate for any determined operation. The principal object of their ambition in 1360 was to intercept the sums of ransom to be dispatched from Languedoc to the abbey of St. Bertin in St. Omer, which the treaty had fixed as the place of deposit of the ransom. Fortunately this treasure was saved. But the desperadoes forthwith turned upon the pope in Avignon, whose treasure was reputed to be fabulous, and held Urban V up for a staggering sum of money. It was this experience which led the popes to fortify Avignon so formidably with those walls and towers which are still preserved.

Charles V found a man capable of dealing with these ruffians in a Breton captain, Bertrand Du Guesclin, whom he made constable or commander-in-chief of the French army. It took seven years of unabated effort to rid France of these guerrillas. Some were driven to seek new fields of activity in Italy; some went over into Germany where the hardy civic militia of the German towns exterminated them; the last drifted over the Pyrenees into Castile, where a war of succession between Pedro the Cruel and his half-brother Henry Trastamara gave them occupation on one side or the other. The Black Prince, whom Edward III had made viceroy of Gascony and Guienne after the battle of Poitiers, with foolish ambition for more military renown intervened in this conflict in behalf of Pedro, and mortally offended his subjects by laying the new-fangled French hearth-tax upon the provinces under his rule.

Thus English intervention in Spain caused new and heavy taxation in Guienne and Gascony. The sting of this *fouage* imprudently exacted by the Black Prince was not only in its novelty, but in the weight of it. For it was heavier than that customary in France, and amounted to 1,200,000 *livres* for a territory no greater than nine *départements* of France to-day. The revolt was initiated by certain nobles who for personal reasons cherished sentiments of discontent and were fomented and bribed by French gold. The towns followed their lead in order to escape the extraordinary subsidies from which they asserted their privileges exempted them. They were also tempted by Charles V's offers of still larger franchises.

Meanwhile, under the wise administration of Charles V France had been slowly recovering from the wounds of war, and when, in 1369, a deputation of Gascon nobles appeared in Paris and complained to the king of the Black Prince's injustice, Charles V lent a willing ear. The tables were turned when the war was resumed. Every important French town had been walled, provisioned and garrisoned against attack; Du Guesclin had remade the army; France had become agriculturally and commercially prosperous; there was money in the treasury. When the forces of the Black Prince invaded the French provinces the peasantry fled with their cattle and their belongings into the walled towns. Villages and hamlets, farms and crops might be burned, but the population was safe and the fortified towns, all except Limoges, resisted attack. The invaders were soon reduced to starvation as a result of their own ruinous policy, while Du Guesclin, avoiding pitched battle played the game of hanging on their rear, cutting off stragglers and foraging parties and generally harassing the English without loss to himself. Finally the English gave it up and began to retire. Then the French armies took the offensive, invaded the English provinces where much of the population, for the first time, displayed a real French national sentiment, fraternized with the French soldiery and abetted the conquest. Within a few years Charles V annexed all the English provinces beyond sea and France was a territorially united country. France had realized her dream and had reached the Pyrenees. All the French territory which remained to England was the Bordelais—the city and territory of Bordeaux—and the Pale of Calais. France had not sufficient sea-power to take these. In 1380, when Charles V and his heroic captain Du Guesclin both died, the first period of the Hundred Years' War really terminated. Bretigny had been but a mere armistice, although officially called a peace. It had given France nine years in which to recover strength.

The internal administration of France during Charles V's enlightened reign now requires consideration, for except in the matter of taxation, which was inseparable from the history of the war, this subject has not yet been examined.

A word is first in point concerning Charles V's restoration of the coinage. Manipulation of the currency was one of the most despicable practices of the Valois kings. The crown thereby escaped payment of at least a part of its debts. John le Bon was a worse debaser of the coin than his father. Charles V clearly realized that the foundation stone of economic well-being was a sound and stable medium of exchange. St. Louis in establishing a sound and good money had furnished a royal precedent which his successors had unwisely neglected to follow. At the beginning of his reign, Philip VI had, it is true, attempted to restore *une bonne et forte monnaie—comme le temps de St. Louis*, but between the years 1337 and 1350 the exigencies of war necessitated no less than twenty-four distinct changes in the coinage of the realm. Even Charles V, as dauphin, after the defeat at Poitiers, had been compelled to resort to the same expedient. An ordinance of December 5, 1360, created a new coinage, a stronger and stabler money than that then in circulation, coins of unalloyed gold or silver whose values represented the ratio between the precious metals. This new coinage was a victory for the ideas of Nicolas Oresme, the great economic writer of the age, who inspired and directed the monetary policy of Charles V. This remarkable man had been rector of the College of Navarre in the University of Paris and become bishop of Lisieux. He is the intellectual glory of France in the fourteenth century. His works include theology, natural science, physics, politics, political economy and a translation of Aristotle's *Politics* made for Charles V. But his most important work is the famous *Traité de la première invention des monnaies*, the foremost treatise on economics of the Middle Ages. It was first written in Latin, at once translated into French, and shows strong Aristotelian influence. Indeed, Oresme's translation of the *Politics* and his *Traité* appeared almost simultaneously, in 1372. The latter opens with some reflections upon the origin and use of money, and having shown its necessity from antiquity, passes to the Middle Ages. In this portion Oresme protests against a theory often expressed that money is the property of the prince. Money, he says, is the property of the possessor of it, and represents his labor in salary or wages, his possessory heritage. He admits the justice of seigniorage, or the charge made by the prince for coining bullion into currency, but protests against the medieval abuse of this prerogative, such as the scandal of frequent emissions, alloyment of the precious metals, alteration of weights, *etc.* It is unjust and tyrannical for a prince to change the natural ratio between gold and silver, or to issue "weak" money, since bad money will drive good money out of circulation, and if the proper ratio is not preserved, hoarding ensues. "Strong" money must preserve the just balance between the metals and be sound currency. Charles V, who divides with Louis XI the honor of having been the most intelligent of the Valois kings, was a convert to Oresme's ideas. He suppressed the bad money of his predecessor and put France upon a sound money basis, at least during the term of his administration.

In 1364, the Hôtel des Monnaies was founded at Tours, and the succeeding years were filled with monetary ordinances. In 1379 the king forbade the circulation of foreign coins within the realm, suppressed all previously issued coin, laid down other provisions for a sound coinage, and forbade the manufacture of gold and silver except for the church.

The policy of Charles V was to increase the royal power and to establish the authority of the king uniformly throughout the kingdom. Since the town was in effect a feudal person whose rights and duties were expressly defined by a charter, the king attacked and limited the independence of the towns as well as that of the feudal lords. As dauphin and regent he claimed the right to establish "consulates and communes." As king he approved a great number of old charters, but created only one new commune. His authority over the towns was more frequently exercised by the suppression of communes, either as an act of grace when the town was too impoverished to pay the taxes, or as an act of justice when the town had not been faithful to the king. The communes thus suppressed became part of the royal domain and could only be reëstablished by royal authority.

The towns were in some measure compensated for the rigid exaction of taxation by concessions of one-sixth, one-fourth and, in certain instances, one third of the *douze deniers* to be used by the town for fortifications and for defense. The strict administration of the king gave to the towns security and peace. Under these conditions industry flourished. In the main the towns were loyal throughout his reign.

In addition Charles V carried out a most thorough reorganization of the administration of the royal domain. Evidence that the regulations concerning the domain were strictly enforced is found in a mandement of 1372, removing one Edouart Thadelin from office as *maistre de nos monnaies* for violation of an ordinance which required that the entire profits of the domain be brought to the royal treasury at Paris before the proportion due to the *maistre* for his own services should be deducted. Many permits granting the right to gather dead wood in the royal forest give conclusive proof of the adequate supervision to which the domain was subjected.

In the course of the fourteenth century the crown endeavored to maintain the monopoly of sale in the *halles* of Paris one day in each week and to make its control more perfect. It rented stalls at an annual rent to the Parisian corporations. These corporations had to make all necessary repairs and enlargements at their own expense and even to rebuild the edifice if destroyed by fire. Arrangements of this kind were common and soon almost all the *corps de métiers* had their separate *halles*. The king tried to increase the number of market days in order to augment his revenues. An ordinance of October 3, 1368, made

Wednesday, Friday and Sunday royal market days. There was violent protest and some of the gilds were exempted from use of the *halles* except on Sunday; others had to use it two days, Friday and Sunday. Thus the king for fiscal reasons controlled the market. In the beginning merchants had gone voluntarily to these markets where they were sure of finding buyers, but these buyers deserted the *halles* during the Hundred Years' War. The merchants who paid rents and sold nothing dropped away and the crown entered into new conflict with them.

What we have said of Paris is true of the other great cities. Commercial life withdrew from the markets and the time came when the character of commercial intercourse was changed. In the early days the chief articles of commerce were cloth goods, furs, jewels. But in the fourteenth century foodstuffs were sold in a separate place and before long the market itself was reserved for foreign merchants. Charles V still retained the regalian rights and specified that the king alone could police and tax all markets and fairs.

However, if the principle was asserted it did not always prevail. The king was not always successful in forcing this recognition by the great feudatories like the count of Flanders and the dukes of Burgundy and Brittany. In the fourteenth century when the markets were falling into decay the king could not make good his claim except in the case of fairs and important markets. Markets which were held on regular days fell under the authority of the municipalities and we find the municipal authorities establishing markets, changing them, regulating them. This shows that the markets had ceased to be of general importance and were falling into decline.

From markets and fairs one naturally passes to a consideration of commerce. And first it is to be noted that France in the fourteenth century made two important territorial acquisitions, one of which, at least, was of great benefit to commerce. These were both made in 1349. They were Montpellier and Dauphiné. Montpellier belonged to the kingdom of Majorca. Previous to its acquisition the French kings even attempted by force to prevent vessels from putting in at Maguelone and Montpellier. When the watchman descried a sail out at sea he sounded his horn. A ship which was always ready went out to meet the vessel so signalled and forced it to come into Aigues-Mortes and to pay a navigation tax of one penny *per livre*. The captains often tried to avoid the vigilance of the watchmen and sometimes sailed at night, which was absolutely contrary to the medieval practice, but having been compelled to pay harbor dues it was then cheaper to unload their merchandise at Aigues-Mortes. A canal was early cut to connect Aigues-Mortes with the chief branch of the Rhône; later another canal opened communication with Montpellier. Thus all the importations were centralized at Aigues-Mortes; many exports could only issue from this port, such as wool and all kinds of merchandise subject to the "right of high passage." But the port of Aigues-Mortes was an artificial creation; and easily silted up. In 1336 it was necessary provisionally to grant vessels permission to enter by other canals of Languedoc.

In 1293, Philip le Bel had paved the way for the annexation of Montpellier to the crown by acquiring from the bishop of Maguelonne the old part of that city, suzerainty over the rest of the city, and the castle of Lattes, which belonged to the king of Majorca. This fact gave rise to a good deal of political friction. In 1341, the last, egged on by Peter IV of Aragon, refused to recognize French overlordship of Montpellier on the ground that the act of the bishop of Maguelonne had not been approved by the pope. But in 1349 Majorca was conquered by Aragon, and James III, its expelled king, wishing to procure means to recover his island realm, sold Montpellier to the king of France for 120,000 *ecus d'or.* It was an advantageous purchase by France. For Montpellier opened by a canal upon the Mediterranean. When Montpellier became a royal town in 1349 the privilege of Aigues-Mortes ceased.

The purchase of Dauphiné in 1349 from the childless count Humbert II, because it rounded out French territory between the Rhône and the Alps, was of more political than economic benefit, although it gave France control of the western end of the minor pass of St. Jean de Maurienne from Grenoble and Chambéry to Piedmont Italy (Modena and Turin). But it was a costly acquisition compared with the other annexation.

As dire need of money compelled the king to heavy consumption taxes like the *gabelle* and the *octrois,* so it drove him to onerous taxation of commerce. In this particular Charles V's reign initiated a new and vicious policy which became permanent like the *gabelle* and lasted as long as the monarchy. Hitherto, as the royal domain had progressively grown and become consolidated, the crown had abolished the old and vexatious interprovincial tolls which the feudality had imposed upon commerce. The sole taxes upon internal commerce were bridge and ford taxes, a few ancient *péages,* market dues and of late the *octroi.* Charles V revived these old interprovincial impositions on the commerce of France. It was an old tax with a new name, the *douane.* The *douanes* were bad enough when imposed on general commodities, but absolutely evil in effect when applied to wheat, the chief cereal of France, and wines. It is a pity this vicious precedent ever was established. For the weight and abuse of the *douanes* were one of the great popular grievances under the *ancien régime.* They were not abolished until the revolution in 1789.

The economic recovery of France in the reign of Charles V was not as complete as one might have expected. There was an internal crisis caused by the taxes which became permanent between 1360 and 1380; then the systematic ravages of the English from 1369 to 1373 ruined part of the country. And yet industry and commerce made great progress. With peace there was a migration of artisans from one town to another, and these workmen carried knowledge of the processes of manufacture with them. Charles V promulgated a series of ordinances relating to industry, yet always with a qualification of increasing the king's authority over the corporation, and favored certain industries pertaining to luxury.

There are a great number of ordinances of Charles V dealing with the trades. In September, 1364, he confirmed the statutes of the confraternity of the drapers and the regulation of their *métier;* in February 1367 he approved the regulations of the hatters of Paris; in 1371 those of the barbers. The rules were sometimes very liberal, at other times very strict. The rule governing the poulterers provides that whoever is a poultry dealer in Paris may have as many apprentices as he wishes. On the contrary that for the hatters provides that no master may have more than one apprentice, and the latter is forbidden to work for any other patron. The time of apprenticeship is fixed at five years. Charles V sometimes limits the number not only of the apprentices, but even of the masters, thus creating in favor of the latter a regular monopoly. But the king was always watchful to enlarge his rights over the *corps de métiers,* for it was an easy method of giving his provost supervision over all the trades of Paris.

The barbers of the city held of the king's barber, who had the rank of a *valet de chambre* in the royal household. The king's barber was judge of violations or infractions of the rules of the corporations; but only in cases of first instance. An appeal was possible from his decisions to the provost of Paris. The same practice obtained in cases arising in the other trades. The king's baker (*pannetier*) had jurisdiction over the Paris bakers, and the marshal of the stables over blacksmiths, but appeal lay to the king's provost. The power of the provost was therefore largely increased. He was consulted about the drawing up of statutes governing the trade and about fines; he issued ordinances applying to this or that trade which were executive throughout the whole city. He instituted *gardes jurés* and received reports from them.

As might have been expected Charles V threw upon the provost the general police of commerce and industry in Paris. Ordinances were published on this subject in 1371, in 1372, and after his death in 1382. The first and the last are lost, but we have that of September 25, 1372. In this document Charles V provided that the provost of Paris alone has power to inspect trades, provisions and merchandise throughout the whole extent of the city and its *banlieu,* and to watch over the observation of the statutes and customs by recommending necessary reforms and condemning bad regulations.

Charles V gave great attention to the services required of the gilds. The weavers in Paris were subject to the watch, and as the corporations were rich, the weavers had redeemed themselves from the obligation by paying a certain sum to the king. But, impoverished by the wars and decimated by disease, they could no longer pay this tax. They evaded it by establishing themselves upon the land of the Church, which enjoyed immunity. There were left only sixteen families of weavers on the royal domain instead of three thousand that had been there before. In April, 1372, Charles V declared that all the weavers under his immediate jurisdiction should be enfranchised from this obligation of paying for the watch; he remitted the taxes which were due from them on condition that they would provide watchmen themselves in person like the other gilds. Each *métier* was required to stand watch for three weeks in each year; if one failed the clerks of the watch made another appointment at the expense of the culprit. Moreover, outside of these watches which the *métier* had to sustain, a guard of twenty mounted sergeants and twenty-six foot sergeants under command of a knight had to be kept up every night. In February, 1368, the king modified the royal watch by prescribing twenty mounted sergeants and forty footmen instead of twenty-six. They were to have no other profession and their pay was fixed. The king also compelled certain *métiers* who had hitherto been exempt to stand guard, but from this requirement the barbers were expressly exempted "because they were often called in the night to attend the sick in place of doctors and surgeons."

Charles V also confirmed the statutes of a great number of the corporations of Paris and augmented the royal power over the trades. But he also interfered in a great number of towns on the royal domain. In June, 1375, he approved the regulation for the corporation of the turners of Sens; on May 16, 1376, he issued a regulation for the manufacture of cloth at Honfleur; in July, 1356, he gave out letters regulating the length and breadth of bolts of cloth and every manner of linen goods at Marvejols. Thus we see that the king, as Eberstadt has proved, interfered more and more in matters which the gilds had hitherto regulated for themselves.

In the beginning, each group of workmen had a trade-mark. The weavers for example wove a special sign upon the selvage of their pieces of cloth. The signs were certificates of both the origin and the fine manufacture of the goods. The gild master, after examining the cloth, approved it, and affixed a wax seal or mark, which attested its excellent quality and indicated its origin. The king began by guaranteeing these trade-marks for certain articles. Thus in January, 1365, he granted to Evrard de Boessay, a cutler, and to all his heirs who exercised the same craft, the exclusive right to put a deer's horn upon their blades. Formerly this mark had belonged to one Jean de St. Denis, a knife-maker, who had worked for the said Evrard, but who died without leaving legitimate heirs. Charles V forbade all other makers to use this mark. He even guaranteed the mark of the corporation.

But the king did not limit himself to guaranteeing these trade-marks. He exacted them in the interests of the public. In all his confirmations of the statutes of the weavers he decrees the mark of the corporation. Later he claimed this mark was a royal concession; he claimed that it was an invention of the royal authority, done for its interest and not devised by and intended for the interests of the corporation. Thus the granting of trade-marks became a royal monopoly, and for every piece so marked a like tax was imposed which was called the *droit de marque*.

Charles V was the author of so many regulations governing industry that with good right he has been said to have had a real industrial policy. But above all he favored certain industries having to do with luxury. He was also a great builder. In the east of Paris, beyond the wall of Philip II, he had purchased many contiguous properties and combined the whole into a splendid piece of property with a chapel, galleries, carefully laid out gardens, a cherry orchard, a menagerie with lions and other animals, wild birds, *etc.* He likewise employed a great number of workmen in building the castle and the chapel at Vincennes, which still stands and the Bastille in Paris, which was destroyed in 1789. He built the convent of the Celestins, at the entrance to which one may still see his statue and that of his wife. On the banks of the Marne he erected a beautiful country house. In fact, so energetic a builder was he that, as Christine de Pisan says, "*Il maçonna fort.*"

In partial compensation for his meticulous regulations of trade, Charles V endeavored to restore freedom of trade on the great rivers of France, notably on the Seine, but did not succeed. In 1315 the monopoly of the hanse at Rouen had been suppressed by Louis X. Liberty of commerce was established in the region of the lower Seine. But the monopoly of the hanse at Paris between Mantes and Ville Neuve-St. Georges continued. No one could use this part of the river without putting himself under the patronage of a member of the Parisian hanse and using the Parisian company. Here evidently was a great injustice; it was necessary to suppress these privileges. But the government was unable to do so and the ordinance of Louis X remained a dead letter. The hanse of Rouen claimed a monopoly and ended by winning its point. In 1378 Charles V recognized the right of the Rouennais to intercept navigation on the lower Seine and confiscate merchandise which was not transported by them. The Parisians protested, and petitioned the king, who, reversing his preceding decision of 1367, confirmed Louis X's ordinance. Then the Rouennais claimed that they could freely pass Mantes to Paris. The Parisians stopped the boats from Rouen which penetrated into their zone, and a legal case resulted which was brought before the parlement of Paris. This case dragged on until 1450, when Charles VII abolished the privileges of both the Norman and the Parisian companies and declared the free navigation of the river throughout its length. On January 11, 1462, Louis XI confirmed this decision. Henceforth the course of the Seine was free.

Charles V also was the author of another series of measures which it is important to notice. He recalled the Jews, perceiving the function they had in keeping money in circulation. The Jews had been expelled again from the kingdom in 1349 after the Black Death on account of popular hatred. Charles then had been a boy. In 1359, when regent, he let them come back. He granted them privileges and appointed the count of Étampes guardian of these privileges. There was a similar guardian for Jews in Languedoc. The Jews were divided into three classes: (1) those who were established in France and who were subject to certain periodical taxes; (2) those who simply came to France for commercial purposes and who were required to pay an entrance fee of four gold florins each; (3) finally, those who came to France simply for pleasure, who were exempt. But soon after the treaty of 1360, when John II returned from England and had to raise an enormous sum for his ransom, these taxes were increased. Every Jew had to pay 14 gold florins for himself and his wife to come into the kingdom, and two *gros tournois* for each of his children. He had to pay a tax of seven florins annually to stay within the kingdom. But he was exempt from all other taxes.

The Jews had to contract not to demand more than 4 pence *per livre* weekly interest. This was 86 per cent annually! It is true that in exchange they obtained some great privileges. They could own houses in which to live and had their own cemeteries; they were not judged in either criminal or civil causes by ordinary judges, but by the king or their guardian, unless they voluntarily accepted another jurisdiction. They had the right to do business, to follow any trade. They could also, aside from the conditions governing interest mentioned above, loan money on pledges, but on condition that they did not take objects used for religion or tools or instruments of labor. A Jew's deposition made under oath was valid evidence for the collection of a debt unless satisfactory proof in opposition could be presented. The guardian of the Jews was required to give them assistance in the recovery of their debts. Jews of the same nationality could assemble and make collections for common expenses, that is to say for their synagogues and cemeteries, and for the royal taxes. However, later Charles withdrew certain material advantages, and compelled them to wear a mark upon their clothing consisting of a band of yellow. (December 29, 1368.)

In 1367, at the moment when the war was about to begin against the English, there was a new movement to expel the Jews. An ordinance to this effect was even drawn up, but the king recognized that his good faith would be compromised, and refused to sign it. In 1369 the people of Languedoc clamored for some measures against the Jews, but Charles V protected the Jews, for they were an element of prosperity to the kingdom. The Jews were again expelled in 1410 in the reign of Charles VI.

On June 2, 1380, Charles V granted five German merchants permission to establish themselves for fifteen years in the city of Troyes for purposes of commerce and loaning money. They were to pay to the king twelve hundred francs for their entrance and two hundred francs per year thereafter. Other Germans soon obtained similar privileges. The emperor Charles IV of the House of Luxemburg was a friend of Charles V and himself came to Paris in great pomp in January 1378.

Some Spaniards and Portuguese in the early part of the reign had obtained analogous favors. In April, 1364, Charles V had granted the merchants of the kingdom of Castile a general safe-conduct whenever they wished to enter the kingdom of France and especially to bring merchandise to Harfleur and Leure. Whatever dispute or war might arise between France and Castile was not to compromise these Castilians. They might not be thrown into prison until brought before a judge, and they were to be permitted to be released on bail. All contests between the Castilians were to be judged by two or three merchants or sailors of the kingdom of Castile or by some party whom the contestants might choose. If a case arose between a Frenchman and a Castilian, the case was to be judged by the provost of Harfleur and two inhabitants of Harfleur and two Castilians were to act as bench judges with him. Appeal lay to Rouen before the deacon of the church of Rouen, the bailiff and the viscount of the city. Thus there was an exceptional jurisdiction established for these merchants as for Jews. Moreover the Castilians were granted warehouse privileges and dockage at Harfleur and Leure. They could enter any port of France without paying dues. In case of death among them the *droit d'aubaine* was abolished in favor of their heirs. The rent of warehouses which they leased was to be fixed by the *prud'hommes*. In June, 1364, Charles V confirmed the privileges of some Portuguese merchants.

Thus the Jews and foreign dealers formed colonies of merchants and bankers with special privileges, often very large. These merchants brought money to the burdened treasury of the king; they created or developed foreign relations and sustained national industry. It is evident that a large commerce was in their hands. Charles V wanted to restore the commerce of France, and as the French, ruined by war and taxes, were in want of capital he had recourse to these foreign colonies.

We have no general ordinance from Charles V upon commerce. But yet we can see in the many particular ordinances preserved, that he attempted to favor it. The king was also interested in roads and ports. He undertook harbor improvements at Aigues-Mortes, which was silted up and practically abandoned for Marseilles or Montpellier. The cost of these improvements was estimated at 56,000 *livres*. A third was to be furnished by the royal treasury, a third by the merchants of Beaucaire, a third by the *claverie;* that is to say by the Bureau of Receipts at the fort of Aigues-Mortes. On November 2, 1364, he revived the ordinance that all vessels at sea near enough to see the lantern of the great lighthouse of Aigues-Mortes must land there and pay the old harbor dues. But life had left the port in spite of royal ordinance, and it was the same for all the other French ports of the Mediterranean. Montpellier and Narbonne saw the number of their hearths diminish in a disquieting degree. The project of creating a new harbor at Leucate to take the place of Narbonne was even revived.

The Atlantic ports on the other hand were prosperous. Rochelle received spices directly from the Italian colony established at Nimes. It took seventeen days to make the journey overland, but the merchants had no other tax to pay except the penny charged for *pesage* (weighing). Merchant vessels at this time generally travelled together for protection against pirates. We find ship owners petitioning the duke of Brittany for Breton pilots to guide them along the dangerous coasts of the peninsula; they also asked for letters of safeguard and permits to revictual. The first emancipated them from the right of wreckage; the second gave them the right to take food and water in the country.

On account of the heavy taxes collected by Charles V, France did not recover as rapidly as it ought to have done. But in extenuation of his policy it must be remembered that the prudent military tactics which the king adopted in the war against the English were terrible for the country, though politically successful. The French avoided pitched battles and let the English wander through the land, living upon it, despoiling it, exhausting it. Thousands of houses, towns and villages in France were burned between 1369 and 1373; the population of the country areas was terribly diminished, while commerce and industry lapsed outside of the walled towns.

Moreover, even the urban population declined in the smaller towns. One needs only to read the ordinances of Charles V to be convinced of this. Since the *fouage* was collected by hearths, the towns had to return a census of these, and the number of hearths steadily diminished. Nor did the population increase anywhere except in the largest cities. It is evident therefore that industry did not have a great revival and that commerce languished.

And yet everything did not decline in the reign of Charles V. Some progress was made even in industry and commerce. In the first place, in regard to industry, there was a diffusion of artisans which carried new methods of work into new regions; then the crown confirmed certain regulations of trade and forced the introduction of more liberal policy. It intervened in the organization of trade, sometimes in the minutest way, and finally, the crown patronized those industries engaged in the manufacture of articles of luxury. The artisans of the small towns in the open country, driven out by the English, or by the general misery, sought work in the walled towns where, however, they were not always welcomed by the local workmen, who were jealous of competition.

This whole body of new taxes which became permanent weighed heavily upon the people and prevented the kingdom from recovering. Charles V perceived it and on his deathbed felt remorse for having maddened the people, as the chronicle of the *Quatre Premiers Valois* says. "He caused the hearth tax to be reduced which weighed upon the poor people of his kingdom and because of which the people was grievously moved."

Historians are still much in the dark in regard to the question by whom and how the cost of the Hundred Years' War was paid. The chroniclers give only the vaguest impression. Froissart drew upon his imagination. The *Chronicle of St. Denis* imitates classical rhetoric. Documents in the archives alone enable us to establish how and in what measure the cost of the war weighed upon the various classes of society. Of all sources of information the papal archives are the richest.

Although the clergy suffered much in loss of property, their privations were wholly relative when compared with those endured by the people as a whole. This is not saying, however, that their losses were not great. In the fourteenth century churches and abbeys were but slightly fortified. The long peace of the reigns of St. Louis and Philip le Bel had made walls unnecessary and those which existed when the conflict began were much decayed. Everywhere the soldiery of each combatant established themsleves in the churches and monasteries and utterly plundered them. The nobles had their chateaux, but many of these were not proof against marauders, though priests and monks flocked into them for refuge. As for the peasantry, when possible they fled into the depths of the forests or into the marshes. Most of the towns, even the greatest, were sacked, many of them more than once.

The peasants possessed little property; the upper bourgeoisie were well-to-do; the lower classes in the towns poor. Materially the Church suffered immense losses, for it had most to lose; the nobles next. In so far as it was practicable, both the king and the pope still attempted to wring money out of the Church. The pontifical government had created and perfected an elaborate system of ecclesiastical exactions which drained a large portion of the revenue of the clergy. General impositions were levied by the popes and by the kings, notably the tithes. Moreover, it must be remembered that the upper clergy for the most part were feudal proprietors and, as such, subjects of the king, so that the upper clergy had to submit to a double taxation, for purposes of local or national defense.

The fluctuations and debasement of the coinage also contributed to the impoverishment of the clergy, although in this respect every class in French society suffered. Finally, the Church almost everywhere was a great landowner, and the war destroyed agriculture in every province the invader entered, and scattered the working peasantry upon the Church's lands. From the point of view of duration the Hundred Years' War was worse than all others in history. In some parts, except for a few slight interruptions, it lasted for one hundred and twelve years, and even in the regions least affected it lasted hardly less than eighty or one hundred years. The name it has taken in history is only too well justified. It was an endless and terribly monotonous succession of massacres, burnings, pillagings, extortions, accompanied by the destruction of harvests and cattle, assaults, and calamities of every description. Fire was the expedient of every general, every captain, every man-at-arms during the Hundred Years' War. And what made the consequences more terrible was the almost inconceivable activity of the soldiers of the time, in spite of the bad state of the roads and the insufficient means of transport. With what rapidity the most cruel of the leaders flew from one place to another! The people enjoyed scarcely any rest, and even when they were left alone for a time they lived in precarious safety, amidst constantly renewed agitations and fears.

The effects of the Hundred Years' War favored the frequent appearance of the plague and other epidemics, scourges which in their turn decimated the population. Poor harvests and heavy taxes heightened the prevailing poverty; high prices and famine were inevitable. It was in the fourteenth century, from 1355 to 1370, that the fighting was the most cruel. The period from 1355 to 1364 especially is distinguished above the rest for its frightful ravages.

The Hundred Years' War was more disastrous for the great

churche̞s and abbeys than the religious wars. In the fourteenth century they still held dependencies and very considerable estates, comprising a great part of France. But in the Hundred Years' War a great number of the abbeys were forced to give up much of their property and income; others were seized by the nobles; and those that the war had spared were often despoiled by the commendatory abbots. In the sixteenth century when the religious wars were about to break out, the abbeys had lost much of their old domains; they had been divided and dismembered. In this respect the Hundred Years' War made an epoch in the history of the feudalism of the Middle Ages. But often the death of one means the life of another. So the decline of the feudal system brought prosperity to the communes, the cities and private individuals who before were only farmers.

As far as the destruction of their convents went, the mendicant orders suffered hardly less than the abbeys. As these convents were situated for the most part outside of cities or in the outskirts, the citizens would demolish them either for the fortifications, which generaly date from the Hundred Years' War, or so that they might not serve as a point of vantage for the enemy. It is impossible to give all the mendicant friars' changes of place during the Hundred Years' War. Their convents were scattered by the enemies' troops. But the friars owned nothing outside of their convents, and their losses were naturally much less than those of the abbeys.

CHAPTER IV

TOWN LEAGUES IN GERMANY

THE greatest historian of the economic history of medieval Germany, Inama Sternegg, in the preface to his concluding volume uses these words: "More than a thousand years have been traversed, a period long enough and surely significant enough to enable us to understand how Germany developed into one of the leading civilized nations of Europe, richly endowed with wealth."

Germany in the thirteenth, fourteenth, and fifteenth centuries was *par excellence* the burgher country of Europe. It was a land of free cities, as neither France nor Italy was. In the upper middle valley of the Rhine for a long time towns were established only on the left bank. Not till the fifteenth century did numerous market grants increase the importance of localities on the right bank. Until this time the bishops had jealously maintained their rights, and in seigniorial localities town life was slow in developing.

Certain urban communities were transformed rural communities, though it is impossible to ascribe the origin of all municipalities to such a source. One must distinguish between towns properly commercial and certain fortified towns, which uniquely owed their physiognomy to the walls surrounding them. The immunity which they possessed distinguished them from the country roundabout. Military necessity originally conditioned the grouping, but in ordinary times the inhabitants devoted themselves to agriculture.

The commercial cities on the other hand were essentially of market spirit, if not of market origin; their interior organization seems to have rested almost entirely upon the *jus fori, i.e.,* the special law governing the market. This law was not formed spontaneously, but was the issue of royal concessions. The merchant in fact could not ply his trade without a formal authorization, the strict formalism of the old popular law having engendered in civil matters a spirit of narrow exclusiveness. At first applicable to rigorously determined circumstances, it ended by becoming the common law. The importance in this evolution of the transformation of primitive annual markets into weekly markets is to be observed. The privileged situation at first given wandering merchants in time became that of sedentary merchants also, and the judicial prerogatives which were accorded them became the basis of urban law. Tribunals whose original purpose was to settle commercial questions in market-time gradually arrogated to themselves the right to judge processes relative to property situated anywhere within the *banlieue* at all times. Thus the merchant class compelled the development of a common civic spirit among the inhabitants of the town, and the formation of new municipal guarantees.

While the beginnings of this fecund development of the cities in Germany go back as far as the late eleventh century, the thirteenth century was the period of most rapid growth. Frederick II, in order to purchase the support of the bishops and great nobles, sanctioned the anti-urban legislation of the diet of the princes in 1231, but it was an empty gesture, for neither the emperor nor the princes and prince-bishops could arrest the growth of the German cities.

In 1250 when the brilliant Hohenstaufen dynasty's career terminated in the vanishment of the dreams which it had cherished, Germany politically dissolved into a swarm of semi-independent principalities—duchies, margraviates, landgraviates, counties palatine, feudalized episcopal and abbatial states, and free cities peopled by sturdy burghers. But this political decomposition did not entail social disintegration or economic decadence. On the contrary the extreme particularism of all German life intensified the economic and social activity of the time. In 1279 Rudolph of Habsburg made a vain attempt to preserve the ancient right of the king over merchants by trying to impose the "thirtieth penny." But the German towns threatened to rebel and Rudolph dropped the idea. The *gemeine Pfennig* of Maximilian I was to fail two hundred years later for the same reason.

No country in Europe possessed so many free cities nor so energetic a burgher population as Germany. These cities of Germany, unlike French cities, but like the Italian towns before they fell under the yoke of local despots, were corporate and sovereign political entities.

Geographically they may be distinguished into three groups: (1) the Rhenish cities, like Mainz, Cologne, Frankfort, Worms, Strassburg, Basel; (2) the North German cities like Bremen, Hamburg, Lübeck, Stettin, Danzig, situated along the North Sea and the Baltic coast or near the mouths of the German rivers, with which must be associated certain inland cities upon these rivers which were natural foci for the trade roundabout them and at the same time stations on through routes from west to east or from north to south, like Brunswick, Soest, Goslar, Halle, Magdeburg, Brandenburg, Leipzig and Frankfort-on-the-Oder; (3) the cities of south Germany in the Danube·valley like Ulm, Augsburg, Munich, Nuremberg, Regensburg, Passau, Vienna.

While all of these cities were essentially similar in political forms and social ingredients, historically they were of different origin. Some had sprung up on episcopal lands, others on abbey lands, still others on feudal lands, and finally there were those which had arisen on crown lands. In each the town council (*Rat*) was a sovereign body; each was a self-governing burgher community making its own laws, laying its own taxes, administering its own justice, possessing its own coinage, even forming political alliances and making war or peace as it pleased.

The episcopal cities were the first to rise. They early freed themselves from the yoke of the bishop and forced him either as the result of a revolt or free concession to grant them regalian rights, as coinage, justice, taxation, *etc.* In this conflict the cities were aided by the emperors whom they sustained in the quarrel of investitures, and during the struggle between the Guelfs and the Ghibellines. This is the history of the Rhine cities—Strassburg, Basel, Speyer, Worms, Mainz, Cologne, and Magdeburg on the Elbe. They had a stormy history, and if one could go into details many dramatic scenes might be related. But the bishops almost never freely renounced their prerogatives and always awaited an occasion to recover control of the city. Trier and Würzburg returned to the bishops. In 1462 Mainz was subdued by the archbishop, and Magdeburg had the same experience in 1486.

By the side of these episcopal cities were other cities—not subject to a special lord, but a direct portion of the empire. Originally they formed part of the imperial domain, just as in England after the Norman conquest William the Conqueror reserved the cities for himself. But after the fall of Frederick II Germany was in a state of anarchy and these cities of the imperial domain easily won complete independence. This is the origin of the free imperial cities of Germany—the *"Nostrae et imperii civitates"* of the imperial charters. Examples are Aachen, the city where the emperors were crowned, Frankfort-on-the-Main, where the imperial election was held, and Nuremberg.

In the third place there were cities which sprang up on lands of the nobles. These were numerous in Bavaria, Bohemia and Austria.

The imperial and episcopal cities soon became confounded in the degree that they became independent. They all are often called "free cities" without regard to historical distinction. The episcopal cities cast off even the last semblance of allegiance to the bishops, but the imperial cities always retained the imperial eagle in their arms.

The medieval town, even in the earlier stages of its development, was not an isolated community, and the German towns least of all were of a "closed" city economy. Far from content to draw their sustenance from the radius of territory around them, they had early and eagerly reached out to get contact with other towns. Interurban commercial relations are a distinguishing mark of the German cities. This policy was partly due to the necessity for protection caused by the breakdown of royal authority and the upgrowth of a predatory baronage all too prone to batten upon trade; and partly due to the ambition of almost every town to expand its trade and establish reciprocal relations with other towns. Even when the lay and clerical feudal nobles did not actually prey by violence upon trade, the restraints which they imposed upon it in the form of tolls amounted to exploitation.

In the palmy days of the medieval Empire river tolls had been exacted for the purpose of improving and protecting navigation. Imperial toll stations were established at fixed points, usually where navigation was difficult. Henry IV (1056–1106) in particular, had a high conception of the royal prerogative to regulate commerce and navigation on the Rhine in virtue of the crown's regalian rights (*Oberzollregal*). The tariff lists of 1104 and 1209 show that payments of the toll were made in kind, as a *fuder* of wine, a certain number of bushels of wheat, *etc*. These payments were taken from the cargo. Merchants were not permitted to transport their goods in their own boats, but were required to employ professional bargemen or carriers who were licensed (gilded) corporations. Such associations, which are found upon every navigable river in the Middle Ages, were monopolistic corporations. We find mention of them as far back as the Barbarian Codes, but whether there was connection between these medieval transportation companies and the ancient Roman *collegia nautarum* or river corporations is not certain. After the dissolution of the Frank Empire these associations multiplied and feuds often developed between rival groups, with the result that a river was divided into "reaches" beyond which the boats of another association might not go. Thus the Seine was divided into an upper and a lower reach, Mantes below Paris being the division point between the *nautae* of Paris and those of Rouen. Similarly the Rhine was appropriated and divided above and below Mainz. These transportation companies sometimes were at feud with robber barons who had castles along the river, and sometimes shared their profits with them. Occasionally a company worsted a baron so that the whole length of the river, or a long reach of it, might be subject to their control only. These vexations greatly increased in the thirteenth century when the Hohenstaufen power in Germany was waning. The anarchy of the Interregnum (1250–73) aggravated this condition. The number of tolls on the Rhine rose from 19 to 62. The practice became one of exorbitant exploitation, as much as 60 per cent of the cargo being taken as toll. For as commerce and trade increased, predatory nobles turned from blackmailing of landowners and peasants to exploitation of merchants and burghers. In addition the river swarmed with pirates.

Accordingly, as a means of self-protection and mutual advantage, the German cities in the thirteenth century began to form leagues or confederations. This practice profoundly distinguishes German history from French history of the same time. The French cities never acquired the same degree of independence as the German cities; they never coined money, nor enforced high justice; nor did they ever develop that spirit of organization and association which we see in Germany. Etienne Marcel, in 1358, vaguely dreamed of such a coalition, but the idea came to nothing.

In 1226 Mainz, Worms, Speyer, Strassburg and Basel formed a league for the common defense of their commerce upon the Rhine. Thereupon the archbishop of Mainz appealed to the diet, and Prince Henry, acting as regent for his father, the emperor Frederick II, who was afraid to antagonize the bishops and powerful nobles, ordered the dissolution of the league. The cities, however, refused to obey the decree, much as the Lombard cities in the previous century had defied Frederick I, for there is record of its continued existence in 1236. What finally disrupted the league was the excommunication of the emperor in 1239 by the pope. Then Worms, Speyer and Oppenheim—all old Franconian towns with memories of loyalty to the emperor Henry IV in his conflict with Gregory VII—sided with Frederick II while Mainz went the other way and allied itself with the emperor's enemies. But short-lived as this first Rhenish league was it had introduced a new principle into German history. Similar leagues arose elsewhere, or at least combinations between two or more towns. Thus in 1246 Basel and Mühlhausen combined, in 1248 Braunschweig (Brunswick) and Stade; in 1252 Cologne and Boppard; in 1253 Boppard and Coblenz.

The anarchy of the Interregnum increased the number and dimension of these town leagues. In 1253 the Westphalian League was formed by Münster, Dortmund, Soest and Lippestadt.

In the next year (1254) Mainz, Worms and Oppenheim revived their former association out of which was born the League of the Rhine, the first great commercial league of medieval Germany. It expanded so rapidly that within a few years it embraced seventy towns in the Mittel Rheinland, spreading up the Moselle to Trier and up the Main to Bamberg. This league established a river patrol, both on the stream and along either bank, for maintenance of which a Bundzoll was imposed to defray common expenses. The League of the Rhine was formally recognized in the next year (1255) by William of Holland, one of many aspirants for the imperial crown who was anxious to promote the commerce of his country, in the *Formula pacis* in which the Rhenish cities are described as *civitates conjuratae*. Tradition, supported by good historical authority, ascribes the formation of the League of the Rhine to the genius of a Mainz burgher named Arnold Walpado. The declaration of the League of the Rhine is an interesting document:

"Since now for a long time many of our citizens," so runs the preamble, "have been completely ruined by the violence and wrongs which have been inflicted on them in the country and along the roads, and through their ruin others have also been ruined, so that innocent people, through no fault of their own, have suffered great loss, it is high time that some way be found for preventing such violence, and for restoring peace in all our lands in an equitable manner. Therefore, we have mutually bound ourselves by oath to observe a general peace for ten years from St. Margaret's Day. (July 12, 1254.)"

Among the members of this league are mentioned the judges, consuls, and all the citizens of Mainz, Cologne, Worms, Speyer, Strassburg, Basel and other cities—the venerable archbishops, Gerhard of Mainz, Conrad of Cologne, Arnold of Trier, and the bishops Richard of Worms, Henry of Strassburg, Jacob of Metz, Berthold of Basel, and many counts and nobles. The first provision of the peace was that the members themselves agreed to give up the "unjust tolls which we have been collecting both by land and water, and we will collect them no longer." Furthermore beneficiaries of the peace were to be all classes—"the small with the great, the secular clergy, monks of every order, laymen and Jews." Quarrels between members of the league were to be settled by a board of arbitration. On September 29 at a *Städtetag* at Worms further provisions were made for the working out of the new confederate system. Two centers were selected for the transaction of the business of the league—Mainz for the lower and Worms for the upper Rhine. Four representatives were to be sent by each city or lord to each meeting for the transaction of the league business. Besides several general peace provisions each member of the league was to prepare itself for war; the cities between Coblenz and Basel were to equip one hundred war boats and those below Coblenz five hundred war boats.

The next year further developments were made in the constitution. By the action of the league meeting of October 14, 1255, it was decided that quarterly meetings be held each year—January 6 at Cologne, eight days after Easter at Mainz, June 29 in Worms, and September 8 at Strassburg. At these meetings all representatives were to be given full powers of representation. At the same time the league began to draw to itself new members, so that by 1255 it embraced the whole Rhineland and, besides the members already mentioned, included Cologne, Thurgau, Freiburg, Breisach, Colmar, Schletstatt, Hagenau, Weissenburg, Neustadt, Wimpfen, Heidelberg, Lauterberg, Frankfort, Friedberg, Wetzler, Gelnhausen, Marburg, Alsfeld, Grünberg, Herschfeld, Wolda, Mühlhausen, Aschaffenburg, Seligenstadt, Diebach, Bacharach, Wesel, Boppard, Andernach, Bonn, Neuss, Aachen; in Westphalia, Münster with more than sixty other cities and Bremen. The next year in October Regensburg was taken into the league. A large number of lords and churchmen also joined.

The Rhine League had come into being largely because of the oppressive tolls on the river and because protection against the attacks of robber knights and barons was necessary. Consequently its first work was to rid the river of the illegal tolls. The next step was naturally that of disciplining unwilling or recalcitrant members. One of the earliest members, Archbishop Gerhard of Mainz, had himself caused the initial organization of the three cities by his unjust raising of tolls. Significant in this connection is article 15 of the first peace established by the league—"We firmly promise that if any member of the league breaks the peace, we will proceed against him at once as if he were not a member, and compel him to make proper satisfaction."

One of the first joint efforts against an outsider was undertaken by the burghers of Worms allied with Philip of Hohenfels, Wernher, lord high steward of Alzei, and the burghers of Mainz and Oppenheim against the baron of Strahlenberg in which they burnt his village of Shriesheim and destroyed his vineyard.

Another expedition by Mainz and other cities was made against a castle of Wernher of Boland near Ingelheim—a center of much oppression. The castle was completely destroyed. As fast as friendly counts and lords united with them the towns pushed their policy. Many of the lords were compelled to give up their illegal practices and tolls.

In 1255 two events occurred of considerable importance to the league. There had been a *Städtetag* announced at Strassburg for St. Michael's Day. Mainz had sent her treasurer and the mayor, Worms, two councillors. As these came to Harde in the vicinity of Mainz they were attacked and captured by Emicho of Leiningen and taken to Burg Landeck. But the count thought better of it and in ten days set them free. In the other instance, William of Holland and his wife arrived at the beginning of December in Worms. One day as the empress in company with Count Waldeck was on a horseback ride to the imperial castle Trifels, she and her escort were captured by Hermann of Riedburg, robbed of her jewels and taken captive to Riedburg castle. But when the burghers of Mainz and Oppenheim and other cities arrived before the castle, the courage of the robber sank; he set the captives free and surrendered unconditionally.

The next year again we take notice of the league compelling law and order. In the year 1257 the league made an expedition against Rudolph of Baden and besieged him in Seltz. But the margrave was the victor and took eighty-five captives. These were later redeemed through the mediation of Strassburg so that each town was able to ransom them. The last of the efforts of the league of which we have record occurred in the year 1260. Already by 1258 there seems to have been a union of robbers and peace disturbers formed—from which Worms especially suffered. Finally in July the militia of Worms with many lords of the land surrounded the robbers' den, the castle Alzei. Walls and battlements were pulled down and destroyed. The Alzeinsers were forced to renounce all their former practices and it was stipulated that if ever one of these at any time injured any one of those who had been in the siege, all of them would suffer.

Naturally, since the league had become so important in the Empire from its enforcement of peace and power in war, it dared to exercise its power in other things also. With the defeat of William of Holland by the Friesians a new imperial election was held. The towns held two meetings, one on March 12 and another on May 26, in which it was resolved that the league would not support any one as king who was not unanimously elected and would wage war against any king not so elected.

They not only decided upon this, but sent delegates to the imperial election at Frankfort and assured the princes of peace and of their desire to further the welfare of the Empire. Several of the princes answered and assured them of their interest to further the welfare of the Empire at the coming election. However, at the election no person received all the votes of the electors. As a result there was a divided election. Politically the power of the league was at an end. In August, 1257, Speyer, Worms, and Oppenheim refused to recognize Richard as emperor. Oppenheim was later won over by the Bishops of Mainz and Strassburg, and finally Speyer and Worms agreed on January 16, 1258, to adhere to Alphonso of Castile, who was not even in the country!

The League of the Rhine was the first instance in the history of Germany when the third estate—the burghers—played a part in German history. Further than this it became the antecedent not only of the Swabian League of the following century, but also of the great organization of the Hanse and the formation of the Swiss Confederation.

The sources of the Swabian League naturally go back to the Rhine League of 1254. The same forces and conditions which produced the one produced the other. The underlying causes for movements of union and mutual protection can readily be seen from a glance at a map of the time. The stages in its evolution are clearly discernible. As early as 1285 we find a league on the upper Rhine between Strassburg, Basel and Freiburg. This was many times renewed. In 1307 a *Landfriede* was established between the nobles and the cities of the upper

Rhine. In 1312 Constance, Zürich, St. Gall and Schaffhausen united. On May 20, 1327, Constance, Zürich, Lindau, Ueberlingen, and St. Gall, joined with the middle Rhine cities, Worms, Mainz, and Speyer, the upper Rhine cities, Strassburg, Basel, Freiburg, and Bern, to form a league which was to last until April 23, 1329. On June 5 they were joined by the Swiss cantons of Uri, Schwyz, and Unterwalden.

The next step in the evolution of the Swabian League came through a *Landfriede* established by Emperor Ludwig IV. He was in a painful position because of his relation to the papacy and realized that the cities could help him in his need. Consequently he favored them many times, seeking to win their support. He often required financial support, and never limited their freedom, but in every way possible extended their privileges and supported them with the necessary power to protect them from the nobles. On June 29, 1331, the cities of Esslingen, Reutlingen, Rotweil, Heilbronn, Hall, Gmünd, Weil and Weinsberg formed with the emperor's consent (*mit Gunst, Gebot und Willen*) a league to promote peace. Twenty-two cities, including those named above, and Augsburg, Ulm, Biberach, Memmingen, Kempten, Kaufbeuren, Ravensburg, Pfullendorf, Überlingen, Lindau, Constance, St. Gall, Zürich and Wimpfen allied themselves on November 20 with the emperor's sons, the Margrave Ludwig of Brandenburg, Dukes Stephen and Ludwig, and Bishop Ulrich of Augsburg.

The constitution (if such it may be called) of the league is reminiscent of the Rhine League and foreshadows the greater Swabian League of 1376. The league was to last two years after the emperor's death and was organized to make the election certain. To the general council of the league each city sent a representative excepting Augsburg. However the bishop of Augsburg and the duke of Bavaria sent delegates.

The cities were divided into three groups, each one of which had the privilege of taking in new members, although such members could send no representatives to the general council. The group around Augsburg was required to counsel with the duke and the bishop, but the group around the Alps and the group around Constance was not required to do this.

This was the first league which included all the cities of Swabia, and the importance it lent to them on that account is very great. Several evidences in regard to its enforcement of peace are of interest. The emperor had promised in the articles of union that it would be his will and bidding that if any were robbed all should unite to punish the guilty one. Thus in the spring of 1340 the league destroyed the robber castles of Brenz and Statzingen. But the power of the league created fear and hatred on the part of the nobles. This developed a division within the league, and since it was impossible to remedy it, the emperor reorganized it in June of the same year, binding the twenty-two imperial Swabian cities to his sons and the Bishop of Augsburg and soon also the counts of Württemberg, Oettingen, Hohenberg, Werdenberg, and other lords. He appointed nine men to arbitrate in case of disputes between the members. Thus was averted the danger of having Swabia split into two opposing camps, for the league was an imperfect union.

After the emperor's death the wider league dissolved, but nineteen cities (Constance, Zürich, and St. Gall having withdrawn) formed another league, agreeing to mutual protection and common interest in the recognition of a new emperor. When the cities were mutually agreed in regard to the recognition of a new emperor—then the union was to be dissolved. The next year (1340) the league was confirmed by the new emperor Charles IV, who found little pleasure in the proud behavior of the towns, but was forced to recognize the cities in order to obtain a firm hold on the throne. As soon as he was firmly established he expected to permit no such powerful city organization. He hoped to put in place of such a league, a *Landfriede* under his direction.

Between defensive leagues, which held a definite position in the Empire on equality with the other estates while protecting their own freedom, and a league which was supported by the emperor's power, there was a great difference. An emperor like Ludwig IV, who had to battle with extraordinary forces, could afford to use extraordinary means to obtain his end, which in ordinary times would not be permitted. Charles IV, then, as soon as he felt himself able began to act. In May, 1350, he dissolved the city league and substituted a league of cities *and nobles*. His attitude is clearly shown in the Golden Bull of 1356 in which he not only failed to recognize the burgher element, but forbade all unions or leagues of cities or between cities; or between persons or between a person and a city with the exception of a *Landfriedensbund* organized directly under his authority.

It was hard to carry out this policy, however, because the emperor's power was not very great. In September, 1351, he had been forced to permit an alliance to be made between Nuremberg, Ulm, Augsburg and the Swabian cities, thus allowing the Swabian League to renew its organization for three years. In May, 1351, the example of Nuremberg was followed by Schaffhausen. By December, 1351, the cities were able to compel Count Ottingen to preserve the peace and abolish his unjust tolls.

In September, 1352, Charles IV appeared in person at Ulm and instituted the general peace already mentioned. An imperial ordinance was promulgated governing cases of trouble between the cities. In such cases the three towns nearest the disorder were to act as arbitrators, and in case this failed a general diet was to be summoned at Augsburg to settle the matter.

A third general peace was established by Charles IV in 1359. By this the league was brought immediately under the jurisdiction of the imperial court. All tolls were to be abolished and the cities were guaranteed freedom from interference of the local lords, both spiritual and temporal. In the course of the year Charles finally was able to bring a large number of nobles, including the bishop of Augsburg, the Wittelsbachs and the counts of Ottingen, into the league of twenty-nine cities. A general council of eleven was to be the executive body of the league—five members from the cities, five from the nobles, and one imperial representative. This was to last until November 11, 1361. Until 1370 the emperor had no other relations with the cities of Swabia. However, in February, 1362, the Swiss cities Constance, Zurich, St. Gall, Lindau, Ravensburg, Ueberlingen, Wangen, and Buchhorn united for the period of Charles' life and two years after his death. Because of the fixed duration of time of the league Charles IV confirmed its organization.

In 1370 the emperor again took the lead in ordaining peace. Through his agent, Voresch of Riesenburg, on December 6 a *Lanfriedensbund* was organized for all of Swabia which was to last until April 23, 1375. Thirty-one towns became members of the league. Count Ulrich of Helfenstein was placed at the head. He had direct control of all the league's affairs. All requests for help and all meetings were called through him. The upper group met at Ulm and the lower at Essingen, while regular semiannual meetings were held at Ulm and St. Gall. Strict rules were made in regard to the breaking of the peace and compensation for injury. It was not to be an exclusively city league, but right of joining it was allowed spiritual and secular lords. As members they were to have their ordinary privileges with their customary laws and freedom, as well as a share of the common business of the association.

The nobles, however, thought that the league was aimed directly at them. The truth was, the breakers of the peace were in most cases nobles (*Raubritter*) who raided the freight trains of the towns. To the great nobles the wealth of the towns was a thorn in the flesh. The poor noble, on the other hand, threatened by the princes, appreciated the league. As a result of the feeling on the part of the nobility, on January 6, 1372, at Weissenhorn, a counter league of the nobles was organized. A week later, the leader of the league, Count Ulrich, as he was returning from the court of the Pfalzgraf Ruprecht, was attacked by some nobles and captured, taken first to the castle Neipperg in Zaberger and later to Falkenstein in Schwarzwald. The cities took up arms, but before they were fully prepared Count Eberhard of Württemberg, called the Quarreler—the soul of the opposition to the cities—attacked some of the confederation's troops at Altheim near Ulm, April 7, 1372, and more than a hundred burghers with their captain, were killed. A large number were also captured. This defeat caused great discouragement in the cities. In Ulm the cries of the people were such that a riot was feared, and many left the city to avoid paying their share of the cost of the battle. The Augsburgers paid the count four thousand florins so that he would not march into their territory.

The death of the count of Helfenstein, as well as the attack on the league's troops, caused intense bitterness between the towns and the nobility. The league, however, did not outlive its leader. The emperor now forbade organizations of both nobles and cities. A new *Landfriede* was declared May 27, 1373. This league was to last until June 24, 1376, and Count Eberhard of Württemberg, the enemy of the towns, was placed at the head. Sixteen towns joined the new league.

There seems to be no doubt that Charles IV was utilizing both the nobles and the towns in order to carry out his policy of having his son elected as emperor before his death. He used first the cities and then the nobles, bringing them into opposition, so that the position of the princes would be favorable and that the election of his son would be ensured. To raise the necessary money by which he could bribe the electors, he turned to extortion. As his agent the count of Württemberg was very effective. The money for the acquirement of Brandenburg was wrung from the cities in 1373 and was twice as heavy on the cities as the war had been. Then began the exactions for the imperial elections. In this the emperor went so far as to mortgage a number of the towns.

On June 10, 1376, Wenzel was elected emperor because his father had bought the princes with heavy bribes, as every one knew. On June 27, Charles IV pledged the city of Donauwörth to Duke Otto of Bavaria. In the preceding April he had pledged Feuchtwangen to Frederick of Nuremberg. To the cities it seemed that others would soon follow. If they wished to preserve their liberties they had to act quickly. July 4, 1376, upon the advice of a wise burgomaster of Ulm, a new union was formed called the Swabian League. It was composed of the cities of Ulm, Constance, Ueberlingen, Ravensburg, Lindau, St. Gall, Wangen, Buchhorn, Reutlingen, Rowteil, Memmingen, Biberach, Isny and Leutkirch, and was to last until April 23, 1380.

From the very nature of the articles of agreement it was a league organized for war and not for peace. It was a league of the towns to preserve their integrity and identity in the Empire. Their relations with Charles IV as well as with Ludwig IV had taught them how to organize effectively. Now in direct contradiction to the Golden Bull they were organizing a league without the imperial sanction. Ostensibly it was to preserve peace and make commerce safe and certain; but there seems to be no doubt among historians that it was also to protect the towns against the oppression of the emperor himself.

Then began a twelve years' war against the nobles and princes. For the most part it was not fought against great lords, but against the lesser nobility. There were no great battles and no long sieges. The aim of each side was to do the most damage possible, destroying fields of grain, and vineyards, stealing cattle, plundering and burning villages, and occasionally capturing a few soldiers. The surrounding towns soon became interested in the league. Weil and Esslingen were driven into the league by being pledged to the count of Württemberg. Plainly the movement was going against the emperor. To overcome this Count Eberhard decided to threaten the towns, particularly Reutlingen and Achalm. One day his son, Count Ulrich, with a couple of hundred pikemen and spearmen came between the burghers of Reutlingen and the town. In the battle that followed the Württembergers lost seventy-three men while the burghers lost only three and took many prisoners.

A truce was then arranged as there was nothing else that the emperor could do. The towns were freed from the ban and promise was given that they should not be alienated from the Empire by sale or pledge. This, however, did not establish peace. Of the emperor's policy it may be said that he had no understanding of the struggle of the cities for freedom according to the modern idea of the state, but "considered them as milch cows from which he yearly received taxes; or which he might pledge for money." Of the cities under the control of bishops, he could not demand taxes. He did sell to them gladly, however, the privilege of coinage; for the chancellery of Charles IV was a pastmaster in the art of raising money by tricky legal methods.

The immediate effect on the towns was to increase the power of the league. New members increased the league to twenty-seven, including Augsburg, Heilbronn, and Appenzell. Through a new organization formed December 20, 1377, to last until April 23, 1385, the union which had been formed to meet a momentary danger took on the character of a permanent institution to preserve the interests of the cities. Many nobles, seeing the growing power of the cities, desired to enter also. Thus we find Duke Leopold of Austria and Duke Albrecht III desiring to become members. By 1378 the total number of members was eighty-four cities.

The increasing power of the Swabian League led to the organization of counter-associations by the feudality. The most important of these associations was that of the Lion (*Löwenbund*) established October 13, 1379. Its name was derived from the gold or silver lion which the members wore. Other similar associations of nobles were also organized about this time, such as the Society of St. William.

These societies as a usual rule did not endure very long. The greatest danger to the cities lay in the fact that the princes hired them for service against the burghers. Trouble soon came. In 1380 the Lions besieged Frankfort, which had captured some robber members of the Bund and compelled the city to surrender the captives. The fear of the cities because of these bands led to the creation of a new city league at Speyer on the Middle Rhine. It is not strange that the next step should be a union with the Swabian League. Each had the same aims and the same enemies. July 17, 1381, the union was completed. They pledged themselves mutually to honor the Empire, to benefit the land by furnishing what was necessary, and to help in any way against the attacks of robbers and nobles. Upon demand the Swabian cities were to send two hundred pikemen and the Rhenish cities in their turn were to send one hundred. No party could conclude a separate peace in which the league was concerned without the others' knowledge and will, and no one could be taken into the league without the consent of all. The league was to last until Christmas 1391. The Swabian League lengthened the period of its duration until April 23, 1395. Its membership also increased so that by 1385 it included forty cities.

The emperor naturally was opposed to such a powerful organization, as were the electors, but it succeeded in spite of their opposition. As a counterweight Wenzel and the electors organized a league of their own. Its purpose was to prevent the further organization of city leagues in their territory and to unite in mutual defense. At a diet at Frankfort in September, 1381, a *Landfriedensentwurf* was suggested whereby the power of the cities should be broken and the soldiers of the cities be scattered throughout the various territories of the Empire. This proposal was impossible, and new steps were taken. Through the mediation of Duke Leopold of Austria a truce was arranged to last from January of the next year until Easter. Leopold proposed that the city league in full strength should be incorporated in the imperial league. This was consummated by an agreement at Ehingen, April 9, 1382, in which the joint league, the three orders of knights, Duke Leopold and Count Eberhard, were united into a peace league until January 6, 1384. The different interests of the different groups, however, soon drew them apart. The league was hardly formed before Duke Leopold fell to fighting the duke of Bavaria. The count of

Württemberg soon drew away, as did the three orders. By the next October Leopold was completely alienated from the cities by his appointment as imperial tax collector for Swabia.

Again the emperor's policy had failed. He was more successful, however, in his policy of organizing general peace agreements (*Landfrieden*). By these he hoped to accomplish two purposes—first, to reduce the need for other leagues of either nobles or cities; and, second, to draw away from the city leagues those cities which were not in open opposition to him and thus weaken the city organization. Already in 1377 he had established such a peace in Franconia and Bavaria. The *Landfriedensbund* of 1381 has been mentioned. At a diet held in Frankfort the next year he ordered the cities of Wetzlar, Friedberg and Gelnhausen to join the league. Just the opposite occurred, however. More cities joined the city league in open opposition. A greater effort was made the next year. The emperor then sought to unite the cities and princes in one great *Landfriede* under his leadership. Perhaps one reason for the fear of the emperor was that if entire Germany became organized voluntarily in one great league he might find himself superfluous. The scheme embraced the whole Empire and was to last twelve years. No member could join another league without the emperor's consent. The cities, however, were left on the outside. The whole arrangement was for their opponents. Their entrance would have meant that their league would have been dissolved. New plans were made by a number of the princes. The princes openly spoke at this time of the deposition of the emperor and the ruin of the city league.

However, a four years' peace (the so-called *Heidelberger Stallung*) was patched up. It was a peace agreement between the princes and the Swabian-Rhine league. The difference between the new league and the foregoing organizations lay chiefly in the fact that while the others were leagues of cities, nobles and princes as individuals, this was a league of the noble and city leagues as such. Archbishop Adolf of Mainz, the elector prince Ruprecht (der Ältere), Bishop Gerhard of Würzburg, Duke Leopold of Austria, Burgrave Frederick of Nuremberg and Count Eberhard of Württemberg, were the representatives of the princes. The towns were represented by Mainz, Strassburg, and Frankfort, for the Rhine League; and Augsburg, Nuremberg, and Ulm for the Swabian League. The cities at last had the satisfaction of seeing their league recognized by the princes. It was a victory for the cities. Never had the burgher element had greater influence in Germany than in 1384.

The emperor, being informed of the deposition plan of the princes, turned to the cities. One of the chief grievances of the cities had always been that of tolls exacted on river traffic. Those which had been levied by the emperor were removed. Worms was especially favored by being granted the privilege of collecting tolls upon the Main between Frankfort and Mainz on water and land, on every measure of wine and other goods, in payment of a debt of six thousand florins which it had loaned the emperor. The league was unable to suppress the gilds of bargemen, but its opposition reduced the worst features of their monopoly and compelled a more just regulation.

In June, 1384, Nuremberg entered the league of the Swabian cities, as did Basel, and a union was attempted with the Swiss Confederation. In the Confederation, however, the jealousy of the rural element kept the Swiss cities from uniting as a whole with the league, but at a meeting at Constance, a nine years' association was formed (February 21, 1385) with Zurich, Bern, Solothurn, and Zug.

Duke Leopold saw in this a declaration of war and prepared for it. In order to obtain the necessary finances, the Swabian cities, at the suggestion of the emperor, began to rob the Jews. Nuremberg obtained by this disgraceful operation more than sixty thousand florins, forty thousand of which were given to the emperor. The Rhenish cities took no part in this plundering of the Jews, not because of Christian or humane considerations, but because the Jews had not yet recovered sufficiently from the last catastrophe.

Soon after the pact of Constance the outlook became threatening. The Swabian cities were in favor of an offensive policy, while the Rhenish cities and Nuremberg advised for peace. Lucerne, on account of a burdensome toll, had made an attack, December 29, 1385, upon Austrian territory and through that provoked war with Duke Leopold. It seemed as if a general outbreak were unavoidable, but before a declaration of war was made by the Swabian League, a truce was negotiated. The Swiss had to depend upon their own strength, which proved to be sufficient to win the battle of Sempach on July 9, 1386.

Shortly after the battle the Rhenish cities were summoned to Mergentheim by the archbishop of Mainz, the Pfalzgraf and Duke of Bavaria, the bishops of Bamberg and Würzburg, the burgrave of Nuremberg and Count Eberhard of Württemberg, to send to the help of Austria fifty pikemen against the Swiss. The emperor hearing of the matter hurried to Würzburg in order to gather the friendly nobles, and from thence to Nuremberg, where in March, 1387, he concluded a defensive and offensive alliance with the Swabian League. This was succeeded on 5 November by the so-called *Mergentheimer Stallung* which was essentially a renewal of the Heidelberg agreement. The difference between the new league and the old lay in the strict provision that all cases must be arbitrated. The Swabian League joined and the Rhine League refused to do so.

Three weeks after the conclusion of the Mergentheimer agreement, the peace was again broken by the three ducal brothers of Bavaria. The Archbishop Pilgrim of Salzburg had been friendly, and on July 25 had allied himself with them in a defensive league against the Bavarian dukes, who had proven to be embarrassing neighbors. After the alliance was made the brothers invited him to a conference in which he was taken captive by them. Besides this the brothers had attacked a number of Augsburgers, robbed the Regensburgers of a load of wine and the Nurembergers of nine wagons loaded with merchandise. Thereupon the league declared war. The army of the league was increased and a leader chosen—Count Henry of Montfort. On January 17 the declaration was sent to the dukes. On January 19 the burgher army began to assemble at Augsburg.

Then began a devastating war on both sides. The emperor seemed to have neither the courage nor the ability to do the right thing, and played the part of a neutral spectator, allowing the war of the cities to go on. All the enemies of the cities now joined together. During the course of the summer the league's troops made a plundering expedition diagonally across Württemberger territory to the city of Weil on the edge of the Black Forest. Here on August 23 at the fortified churchyard of Doffingen, the league's forces were attacked by Count Eberhard. Although his army was smaller he gained a complete victory.

The character of the war now changed. No more battles were fought. It was a war of raids and reprisals. The most striking deed of arms on either side was the repulse of the besiegers by the burghers of Regensburg. The war lasted until the spring of 1389 and was concluded without any treaty of peace. The damage arising from the war was very great. It was estimated that over two hundred villages in Swabia were burned and in many places for ten or twelve miles the devastation was complete. The war was not confined to the Swabian cities alone. The Rhine cities had sent help from the beginning and war was carried on later in their own territory.

In the spring of 1389 the emperor took steps towards peace. On May 5 at Eger he declared a general peace-league for the entire Empire. Representatives were to be selected from the different territorial groups—eight in number—and with the king they were to settle all complaints of robbery, murder, arson, capture, and injustice, and to administer punishment. These men were to meet four times a year for that purpose. All other leagues were placed under the ban.

The Swabian League collapsed. Its lack of success in battle, misunderstanding between the cities, the lack of a binding force, and different city aims all tended to break it to pieces. The emperor's ban completed the work. He declared that the league had been erected "against God, against him, against the Empire, and against the law." The cities, as they reconciled themselves individually with their opponents, one by one joined the general league. The first to do this was Esslingen, the last Ulm. The seven Lake Constance cities—Constance, Ueberlingen, Lindau, Ravensburg, St. Gall, Wangen and Buchhorn, however, still clung together.

Once more the cities had failed in their effort to obtain a share in the political control of the Empire. If the Swabian League had succeeded, its importance could hardly be overestimated; since it failed, it is important chiefly as another indication of the new democratic spirit abroad in Europe during the thirteenth and fourteenth centuries.

Beginning as associations for protection of their interurban trade, the League of the Rhine and the Swabian League soon put political aspirations ahead of commercial, and endeavored to compel constitutional recognition of their status and representation in the German diet. In this purpose only the imperial cities succeeded; all the other cities were shut out. This astute concession of the emperor split the leagues and at the same time left the cities within the diet so few in number that their influence was negligible.

Historically the origin and formation of Switzerland is of a piece with the history of the formation of the League of the Rhine and the Swabian League, with this difference, that Switzerland was a fusion of rural cantons *and* towns, whereas the Rhenish and Swabian Leagues were urban associations only. The Swiss Confederation is the one league of thirteenth-century formation which became permanent and has endured to this day. While political freedom on the part of these hardy mountaineers was their primary purpose, there were economic interests which promoted that intention. The Swiss wanted independence in order that they themselves might control the traffic over the Alpine passes and reap the profits thereof instead of letting it be enjoyed by the local bishops and abbots, who had been granted this right from early medieval times. The chief of these were the bishops of Chur, Zürich, Lucerne and Basel, and the abbot of St. Gall. One famous valley in Switzerland in its very name recalls the memory of the lucrative Oriental trade which once passed up it. This is the Valtelline in the valley of the Ticino river, which was known as the Val Levantina in the Middle Ages, because of the Levantine goods imported by Venice and trans-shipped over the Alps (. . . *que ducuntur per valen leventine*).

The Alpine passes may be resolved into two systems, one that of the Simplon, the other that of the St. Gothard. The opposition between these two systems long retarded the growth of the Confederation, and is a fundamental fact of Swiss history. It was a rivalry of influences coming from Central and Northern Europe, the Rhine and the Danube, with western influences coming from the Rhône, the

Saône and the upper Po rivers. In the issue the St. Gothard won. For the forest cantons, the cradle of Swiss liberty, were determined to maintain close relations with the markets which fed the traffic of this pass—the greatest in Switzerland.

It is not without significance that the inception of the movement towards liberty by the Swiss—perhaps even the conception thereof—

originated in the Forest Cantons, the natural guardians of the St. Gothard, and that the date of the opening of this pass (1237) falls between the two initial dates in the history of the formation of the Confederation, viz., the recognition of the independence of the canton of Uri in 1231 and that of Schwyz in 1291. "The Forest Cantons . . . were anxious to maintain close relations with the markets that kept up the traffic of the St. Gothard Pass whose guardianship was the essential and fundamental reason for their liberties." [1] On the Italian side of the Alps Milan especially wished a direct route through the Central Alps.

Neither the Romans nor the early Middle Ages knew the St. Gothard Pass. Until the thirteenth century the gorges of the Schoellenen proved impenetrable. Between 1125 and 1237, when the St. Gothard is first heard of, we have details of eighty-seven crossings of the Alps. Between 1125 and 1170 there were thirty-four crossings, four via the Mont Cenis, one via the Lukmanier, seven via the Great St. Bernard, three via the Septimer, twelve via the Brenner. Others cannot be determined with certitude. Between 1171 and 1200-01 there were twenty-three crossings via Mont Genèvre, two via the Mont Cenis, one via the Lukmanier, six via the Septimer, three via the Brenner. Of the rest of the routes in this period we are uninformed. Between 1201 and 1237 we have thirty itineraries; of those of which details are given, two were by the Mont Cenis, ten by the Brenner. There were possibly two crossings of the St. Gothard before 1237, one in 1212 by Abbot Emo of Floridus Hortus on his return from Rome—he had come into Italy via the Mont Cenis—the other in 1226 by Conrad of Urach, cardinal bishop of Porto, who went from Germany to Italy in that year via the St. Gothard. Each of these journeys must have been fraught with great peril and hardship. For the sombre defile of the Schoellenen is two and a half miles long and is flanked by vertical granite cliffs at the base of which the turbulent Reuss flows. Tradition recites that in 1237 an ingenious blacksmith of Urseren near Andermatt constructed a wooden gallery suspended by chains along these cliffs. This was the Stiebende Brücke or Teufels Brücke—the Bridge of Foam or Devil's Bridge. If this tale be true, then this unnamed smith, and not William Tell, is the hero of Swiss liberty, for the successful trade connection established between the Forest Cantons and Italy, especially Milan, is a central fact in the history of the formation of Switzerland.

[1] Muirhead, *Switzerland* (Blue Guides), introd. p. xix.

CHAPTER V

THE HANSEATIC LEAGUE *

THE remarkable inclination and ability of the German cities to form urban leagues for the protection of their commerce, manifested in the history of the League of the Rhine and the Swabian League, found its greatest manifestation in the Hanseatic League of Northern Germany. The two former associations lasted far less than a hundred years and their sphere of activity was a restricted one. But the Hanseatic League, in addition to spreading over all North Germany also expanded its sway into Flanders, England, Denmark, Scandinavia, the Baltic lands of the Teutonic Knights—Prussia, Kurland, Livonia and Esthonia—and even into Russia and Finland. It was international in its operations, and sea-power even more than land-power was the mainspring of its domination. Nothing like the Hanseatic League had ever existed before, and no other similar achievement in the history of commerce, whether for extent of influence or duration, has been seen since.

Like every other great historical institution the Hanseatic League, although seemingly a quite sudden and spontaneous phenomenon, had its roots deep in the past. A great tradition of commercial enterprise lay behind its creation.[1] In this place we need only observe a few of the most important facts preliminary to the formation of the Hanseatic League. They have to do with four cities of North Germany—Cologne, Hamburg, Bremen and Lübeck. Even before the Norman Conquest of England in 1066 commercial relations between merchants of Cologne—and this means the whole area of the lower Rhine—were intimate with England. The Norman Conquest, by binding England closer to the continent, stimulated that trade so much that in 1157 Henry II granted chartered privileges to a colony of Cologne merchants resident in London which were renewed by many subsequent English kings. Richard Coeur de Lion, remembering their generous contributions toward his ransom, granted letters of freedom to his "beloved burghers of Cologne," exempting them from the annual rent on their gildhall in London, and freeing them from all taxes due the king. Succeeding kings subsequently confirmed and extended these liberties

---

* For map see Shepherd, *Historical Atlas*, 98–99.
[1] See Thompson, *Economic and Social History of the Middle Ages*, pp. 527–31.

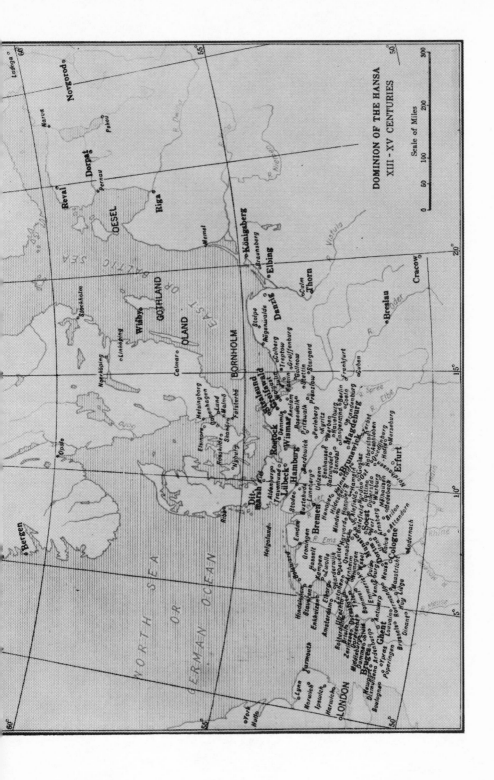

DOMINION OF THE HANSA
XIII - XV CENTURIES

Scale of Miles

0   50   100   200   300

to the merchants of Lübeck. In 1267 the merchants of Hamburg, Lübeck, and Cologne resident in London joined together.

Henry the Lion, duke of Saxony, in 1158 had captured Lübeck, which had been founded in 1143 by Count Adolph of Holstein. This gave the thriving towns of Saxony an opening upon the Baltic, which was fast becoming a German lake through the enterprise of Low German merchants who had established a colony at Wisby on the island of Gotland and already had ventured as far as Finland and Novgorod. This was an old colony of German merchants trading with the Baltic lands as the Cologners traded with England. These adventurers originally came from Alt-Lübeck and their organization antedated the founding of Lübeck.

Wisby seems to have inherited a considerable portion of the maritime commerce of early German merchants trading with the Baltic Slavs and to have been the successor of Veneta in the island of Usedom which was destroyed in 1043. The island of Gotland, of which Wisby was the capital, was peopled originally by Swedes and Germans, the friction between whom brought about intervention on the part of the emperor Lothair II. Later in the same century the great duke Henry the Lion of Saxony, after his occupation of Lübeck, in 1163 endeavored to establish friendly relations between Wisby and Lübeck by a charter granting protection to the merchants of both places. There is historical evidence that early in the thirteenth century the joint community of Swedish and German merchants at Wisby had a commercial factory at Novgorod. When Lübeck acquired the ascendancy over Baltic commerce Wisby and Novgorod became, as it were, extensions of Lübeck in these regions. As Wisby also had had commercial ascendancy over Riga—for the earliest charter of 1200 provides that merchants trading in Riga must observe the laws in use by the merchants of Gotland—it follows that Lübeck by 1299 had acquired control of the commerce of Riga also.

Wisby was the chief link in the chain connecting Russo-Baltic trade with that of the North Sea ports. The commercial contact of Novgorod with the West was older than the Hanseatic League. Certainly as early as the twelfth century Gotlander merchants from Wisby were established there, with the church of St. Olaf as their center. At the same time there was probably a Novgorodian (Greek) church in Wisby. The oldest treaty preserved recording this relation is inscribed on the same parchment with another treaty of later date. The next is badly mutilated and some parts are missing, including the dates. Internal evidence afforded by the proper names which occur, fixes the dates of these two instruments between 1189-95 and 1257-63. A third similar commercial treaty of 1270 written in the Low German tongue is still preserved intact. In the twelfth and thirteenth centuries the German merchants in Wisby formed an association with a common fund to which four of their number carried keys; it was called the "Association of the Navigators of the Holy Roman Empire to Gotland." Wisby's walls still stand. Of the forty-eight towers which once surrounded the city, thirty-eight remain, and in this fortification a modern town is situated. The old town was much larger. In the days of its prosperity Wisby had eighteen churches, in one of which, Sancta Maria Teutonica, service is still held. Two others, St. Catherine and St. Nicholas, are beautiful ruins.

The German merchants of Gotland acted as intermediaries between the east and west of Europe. They carried the cloths of Flanders, salt, beer, *etc.*, to the Slavonic peoples bordering the Baltic. In return they carried back furs, hides, wax and amber. By the Neva the Germans entered Lake Ladoga; through this they reached the Wolchow and upon the banks of Lake Ilmen was situated the city of Novgorod. The Wisby merchants founded here the most celebrated of their factories, the Peterhof, next to the church of St. Peter—Peterskirche.

What Lübeck was for Baltic commerce, that Hamburg and Bremen were for North Sea and North Atlantic commerce. Both inherited trade relations with England, Norway, Iceland and Ireland from old viking times and the Anglo-Danish Empire of Knut the Great (1000–35). All this land-borne, river and maritime commerce of Northern Europe found its focal point in Flanders, where the vertical and horizontal axes of trade crossed. Here Bruges was the terminus of Transalpine-Rhenish trade; of other Mediterranean trade up the Rhône and Saône, through the Champagne Fairs and down the Meuse to Flanders; of Russo-Byzantine trade; of Venetian, Genoese and Spanish galleys; of Baltic, North Sea, English and Icelandic commerce.

It was natural, then, for the enterprising merchants of Cologne to have a colony at Bruges as they had one in London. We do not know exactly when the Brugeois group was established, but it must have been about the same time that the London group was chartered. For we have a charter of the emperor Frederick Barbarossa in 1173 granting Flemish merchants market privileges at Aachen and Duisberg with right of free navigation of the Rhine; in 1178 Philip, archbishop of Cologne, "with the unanimous consent of that city" granted merchants of Ghent right of staple in Cologne and free navigation of the Rhine below—but not above—Cologne; between 1209 and 1215 the Emperor Otto IV extended this privilege "to all merchants of Flanders"; in the beginning of the thirteenth century we find the Saxon towns of Brunswick, Goslar, Halberstadt, Hildesheim, Hanover, Lüneburg, Quedlinburg and Werningerode united with Bremen and Hamburg in a petition to Ghent for mutuality of trade. This "Hansa of German merchants" was first established at Ghent; but as Bruges,

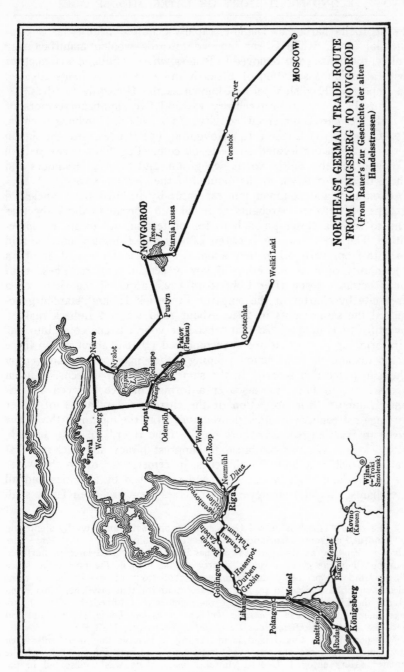

NORTHEAST GERMAN TRADE ROUTE
FROM KÖNIGSBERG TO NOVGOROD
(From Rauer's Zur Geschichte der alten
Handelsstrassen)

MANHATTAN DRAFTING CO. N.Y.

149

owing to its harbor at Damme, rapidly acquired priority as a commercial center while Ghent inclined towards woolen manufacturing solely, the hanse soon removed to Bruges where it became a competitor with a similar association of Flemish and French merchants engaged in importing English wool and known as the Hanse de Londres.[2]

Thus in the thirteenth century we find five significant centers of North German commercial activity: (1) Lübeck-Hamburg-Bremen, (2) Cologne, (3) London, (4) Novgorod, (5) Bruges, with the Saxon cities strategically located so as to be connecting links between both Cologne and the Baltic-North Sea group, and between Flanders and these three port towns at the mouths of the German rivers.

Proximity and common interest naturally inclined these nucleated groups of German merchants at home and abroad to draw together and to form a closer union both for protection and to abate competition. The close relations between Lübeck and Hamburg may be said to date from 1210, when they adopted by a common act of accord a community of civil and criminal law in certain matters. These relations became closer after Lübeck, in 1226, acquired the rights of a free city by charter of the eniperor Frederick II, and Hamburg acquired the same rights in 1232. About 1230 we find Lübeck making overture to Hamburg "so that whenever your citizens come into our city bringing goods that are unencumbered (that is about which there is no dispute or legal action pending), they may possess and enjoy them in peace and security in the same way as our citizens." Eleven years later, in 1241, we discover a formal alliance between Lübeck and Hamburg "for protection of the citizens (merchants) of either city against robbers or other depredators from the mouth of the Trave river to Hamburg or anywhere on the Elbe river." In 1259 Lübeck, Rostock and Wismar combined to suppress piracy and declared that "all who rob merchants in churches, in cemeteries [3] or on the water or on the land shall be outlawed and proscribed by all cities and all merchants . . . and whatever city receives them and their booty shall

---

[2] The word "hansa" is an old German word originally and literally signifying a "handful," a group, association or collection of things, and in this sense survives in English, as when we say a "handful." It was used later in northern Europe when the gilds arose to signify a gild. But in the mercantile sense "hansa" did not primarily signify an associated group of merchants, but technically signified a right to trade and a tax paid for that privilege. Thus when Henry the Lion wished to encourage the commerce of Lübeck he allowed foreign merchants to leave it *absque theloneo et absque hansa, i.e.,* without toll and tax. (Schaube, *Historische Vierteljahrschrift,* 1912, Heft ii.)

[3] Even so late as this time it is interesting to observe that merchants when travelling sought the protection of ecclesiastical edifices for the sake of the greater safety enjoyed. Use of churches as markets was widespread in the feudal age.

be held equally guilty with them and be proscribed by all cities and merchants." In 1252 Lübeck and Hamburg entered into a treaty with Bruges, an agreement which is sometimes regarded as the date of emergence of the Hanseatic League.

By 1265 one may say that the Hanseatic League, at least so far as the German cities in it were concerned, was formed. For between 1260–65 we have substantial legislation on the part of the concerted cities of North Germany "which have the law of Lübeck"—a striking evidence of Lübeck's initiative in the whole movement—for the protection of their merchants both in person and in their goods "against robbers, bandits, pirates and feudal war," together with provision "to hold a meeting once a year to legislate about the affairs of the cities." Although the specific word "hansa" was not to appear yet for a century to denominate this union of North German cities for promotion of their trade, nevertheless by 1260–65 the Hanseatic League was more than half formed. The intra-German element in the league at least was constituted.

But, as pointed out, the Hanseatic League, unlike the other city leagues of Germany, was of international scope. In order to understand the actual character of the Hanseatic League we must also regard its foreign origins. For the Hanseatic League was of double nature. *The Hanse was the fusion of associations formed by German merchants abroad, as in London and Bruges, with similar associations formed in Germany.* These two factors in combination gave birth to the new association known as the Hanseatic League. The completed, full-rounded Hanseatic League comprehended the German merchant groups abroad in Bruges, in London, in Wisby, in Novgorod.

In the reign of Edward I, Lübeck, Hamburg and Bremen imitated Cologne and established each its own hansa in other English towns along the east coast, as Lynn, Newcastle and Boston, which were staple ports for shipment of English wool across sea to the continent. But Lübeck determined to break the monopoly of the Cologne merchants in London. For the Cologne men allowed other German traders to share their privileges only on the payment of heavy fees. As a result this Cologne Hansa had expanded to admit most of the traders from the Rhine valley and Westphalia, but merchants from other regions of Germany found it most difficult. In 1282 all the German hansas in England were brought together into one organization. This combination brought the Rhenish merchants and the Baltic-North Sea merchants close together. German merchants abroad had now reached the point of combination for common purposes in a foreign land. We do not know when or from which group the suggestion emanated for this wider union, for the documents fail us. But there is ground to believe that about the time that Lübeck and Hamburg were effecting their combination with Bruges, the Hanse in London and the Hanse in Bruges united into a single coöperative group, and that soon after 1282 these separate associations of Germàn merchants—those at home and those abroad—combined. Then, and then only, one may say that the Hanseatic League was fully formed.

The fact that the word "hansa" was originally attached to the German merchant groups in London and Bruges might seem to justify the conjecture that the suggestion for a union of the two associations —that within Germany and that without—emanated from the London-Brugeois group. But on the other hand Lübeck had broken the monopoly of the men of Cologne in London. There can be no doubt that the Hanseatic League primarily owed its creation and formation to Lübeck. It was Lübeck which effected the first combination of merchants both at home and abroad; Lübeck was the seat of government of the Hanseatic League; and Lübecker Law the common law of the league when formed. In 1293, in response to the persistent pleas of Lübeck, a congress of merchants from Mecklenburg and Pomerania, assembled at Rostock, resolved that in future all causes in which they were interested should be tried by the laws of Lübeck. It is significant that twenty-six towns voted for this resolution.

By this time a marked change had taken place in the spirit of the Hanseatic League. It began as an interurban society of the towns situated on or near the Danish isthmus, across which there was a short transit between the Baltic and the North Seas, for the protection of their commerce, by suppressing brigandage and piracy and abolishing unjust tolls. It speedily became ambitious to suppress competition in the interest of monopolistic control of the commerce, not only of North Germany, but of England, Flanders, and Russia as well. There is no doubt that some towns would have wished to remain free, but were constrained to come in by deprivation and even destruction of their commerce. For the Hanse was not averse sometimes to practising violence and even piracy as a compulsory measure less patent than actual war. The League apparently kept no records in its early days or else found it prudent to destroy them, for they are continuous only from 1361. Mastery of the Baltic and the North Sea—*imperium maris*—was necessary to this monopolistic control. Sea-power and commercial domination in the countries bordering these two seas were united as a single policy.

There were islands conveniently placed at the mouths of the Vistula and the Niemen; and Wisby, with its excellent harbor, now filled in and covered with gardens, seemed fitted by nature to serve as a stepping-stone across the Baltic and to focus within its walls most of the trade between Novgorod and Bruges. . . . The League forced their way into Norway and Sweden, dotted fishing centers on the peninsula of Scania, then under

Danish suzerainty, and extracted privileges from the various rulers, of such a far-reaching character that the inhabitants soon found they could no longer fish in their own waters.[4]

The Hansa played an important part in Scandinavian history. The economic domination of the German towns soon weighed heavily on the North. To the former period of audacious expansion of the Norse peoples had succeeded a period of inertia. Little by little the Hansa acquired control of all the commerce of Denmark, Norway and Sweden. It dominated in all the important towns in which it organized municipal life to suit its interests.

This achievement was not the enterprise of a year, but required many years to consummate, and was not attained until 1370. For Denmark, Norway and Sweden strenuously resisted. These three kingdoms were separate states, but the ruling houses in them were intermarried and the resultant dynastic and territorial feuds weakened their resistance to the League. The position of Norway was weakest, and in 1285 when Erik Priesthater was at war with Denmark over the dowry of his mother Ingeborg, who was a Danish princess, the Hanseatic League forced the king to grant it commercial privileges in Norway, and especially at Bergen. In 1293 the league showed its teeth to Sweden. The island of Gotland nominally belonged to her, though Wisby was practically independent. Already as far back as 1280 Lübeck and Wisby had entered into an alliance for protection against pirates, joined two years later by Riga. But now Lübeck demanded the incorporation of the Gotland merchants with the Hanseatic League. She was determined to break the monopoly of Wisby in Russia as she had broken the monopoly of Cologne in England and to incorporate the one as she had incorporated the other. When Wisby resisted this dictation a Lübecker fleet captured the island and forcibly annexed the eastern trade (1293).

From England to Russia the Hanseatic League had become the heir of the ancient Norsemen. It was in possession of the ancient Holmgaard (Novgorod) of the Norsemen in Russia, of London and the chief ports of the old Danish Danelaw in the eastern shires of England. It was heir, through Hamburg and Bremen, to their ancient intercourse with Ireland, Iceland and Greenland. By 1300 the Hanseatic League included practically every port town of Germany along the North Sea and Baltic seaboard from Bremen at the mouth of the Weser to Danzig at the mouth of the Vistula. The Prussian and Livonian towns of the Teutonic Order soon entered. Inland, in Mecklenburg, Westphalia, and Saxony the progress was slower because

[4] *London Times Literary Supplement* (a review of E. Gee Nash's "Hanseatic League").

the Hanseatic League had to go more cautiously lest they encounter the opposition of the feudal princes. But by 1360, at which time we have a list of the towns which were members of the League, there were 52 cities included within it.

The extension of the Hansa was retarded at the beginning of the fourteenth century by a double opposition. On the north Denmark, on the south Brandenburg, renewed their efforts to expand. Of these, Denmark, under the energetic Erich Menved, was by far the more dangerous. In 1300 Rostock, fearing an attack from Erich, acknowledged his overlordship. Lübeck did not dare to resist and in 1307 it also submitted. Then Erich incorporated Rostock with Denmark. Resistance was useless. Other cities and many princes yielded. The ambitious Count Gerhard of Holstein acquired ascendancy in Denmark and in 1339 the combined fleets of Denmark and Holstein undertook the conquest of the western Baltic. The combination was far more dangerous to the Hansa than Denmark had been alone. Lübeck and the Wendish cities therefore threw their support to the legitimate heir of the Danish throne, Waldemar III, a fearless and diplomatically gifted man. In 1340 with the aid of the Hansa he expelled the usurpers from the German mainland. But Waldemar soon revived the dangerous expansionist policy of the Danes. Simultaneously Charles IV was seeking to acquire control of Brandenburg. If he had succeeded, the result would undoubtedly have been the adoption of a far-reaching Baltic policy. To oppose this Waldemar, in 1349, proceeded to Brandenburg with an army. This forced Charles IV to give up his Baltic policy and also convinced the Danish king that a policy of conquest towards the South would be far too difficult and dangerous. Therefore he turned to the North. Here in 1359–61 he deprived Sweden of Schonen, Oland, and Gotland. Thereby he again came in contact with the Hansa.

It was necessary to break Denmark if the monopolistic dreams of the Hanseatic League were to be realized. Denmark's position was a double menace to the League in that she possessed Schleswig on the Danish isthmus, thereby bringing Denmark uncomfortably near to the transit of trade across Holstein from Lübeck to Hamburg; and also possessed Scania, Schonen, Halland and Bleking, which had once belonged to Sweden. Denmark thereby had absolute control of both sides of the Sund, the narrow strait between Denmark and Scandinavia. Politics and geography united gave Denmark the power to tax all shipping passing through the straits. Yet the imposition of these tolls was not the primary grievance of the Hanseatic League. The real ground of complaint was that Schonen was the chief seat of the herring fisheries.

We have already seen in a previous chapter how important the fishing grounds of the Dogger Bank in the North Sea were, and how strife over fishery rights was one of the sources of friction between France, Flanders, and England. But cod and hake and flounder were less important fish foods than herring. A modern historian has wittily said that "in the Middle Ages the herring was an historical personage." The Reformation, by displacing the Catholic religion and abolishing the fast days of the Roman Church throughout all Northern Europe, was prejudicial to the herring industry of the Baltic and North Sea. Until the Reformation reduced the demand, enormous quantities of herring were consumed throughout Europe. For in dried or salted form herring were exported even to the Mediterrean countries. Herring was the poor man's meat in medieval times; armies in the field and sailors at sea were fed upon it.

The Sund was the most famous herring ground in the world. There the great annual harvest of the sea was reaped. Every summer from August to October prodigious shoals of herring passed through the straits. We have a most interesting account of this zoological phenomenon from the pen of Philip de Mezières, one of the most travelled men of the fourteenth century, who once passed through the Sund at the height of the herring season, on his way to Prussia. He saw forty thousand *schuts* (flat-bottomed boats), each having a crew of from six to ten men, and five thousand larger vessels at work hauling, salting and packing the herring. He calculated that there were three hundred thousand men employed. For nearly fifty miles along the shore of the peninsula of Schonen there were wooden huts for housing the men, who besides the fishermen included gangs of ropers, shoemakers, watchers to prevent overloading, coopers to make the herring tuns, carpenters, salters, packers, smiths, *etc.* To feed this host ships were constantly plying back and forth between the markets of Skänor, Malmö and Falsterbö carrying wine, beer, flour, vegetables. Each town had its own allotted station (*vitte*) along the shore. The herring ran so thick that "you could cut them with a sword. Such a big battle of folk to catch such little fish."

In Waldemar III (1340–75) of Denmark, the Hanseatic League found a redoubtable antagonist. He, like them, was ambitious to acquire the mastery of the Baltic and fixed his eyes upon Wisby. It was easy to find a pretext for aggression. Haakon, crown prince of Sweden, was married to Waldemar's daughter Margaret. The island of Gotland was politically a part of the Swedish kingdom. Accordingly Waldemar plausibly claimed that Sweden, now practically an appanage of Denmark, was the rightful ruler of Gotland and that the Wisby merchants were Swedish subjects. In 1361 Northern Europe learned with astonishment that Wisby had been captured by the Danes. The Gotlanders, who were primitively armed with pole-axes and swords, but who were without body armor, strove valiantly but unavailingly to defend the city. How grimly the battle was fought has been disclosed by modern archaeological discovery. For within the past year, outside of Wisby's walls the graves of eighteen hundred men who fell in this siege have been uncovered. The dead were interred in two different fields and the identity of the combatants is revealed by the fact that the Danish dead were killed by blows upon the head, whereas the dead among the Gotlanders had perished chiefly of body wounds. A vast amount of rusted armor and arms and mouldered spearshafts and arrows was unearthed.

At once the Hansa called a council, made ready a fleet and provisions, and effected an alliance with Norway and Sweden against their common foe. In May of the following year, it attacked and plundered Copenhagen. The commander, John Wittenborg, expected at this juncture that the two northern powers would send reinforcements to him, but this they neglected to do. He was then obliged to leave the fleet with a weak support, while he prosecuted the campaign on land. But on the sixteenth day, Waldemar and his fleet suddenly appeared off Scania and carried away twelve of the best ships and most of the provisions. After this defeat, the Hansa made negotiations for an armistice, but Waldemar again broke faith, and attacked some herring fishers at Scania. A little later he succeeded in marrying his daughter to the heir of Norway and Sweden, thus making any further alliance between those powers and the Hansa impossible.

The Hansa towns saw that their safety depended on their own resources, and on September 19, 1367, called the famous diet at Cologne. There were delegates from Lübeck, Rostock, Wismar, Kulm, Thorn, Elbing, Kempen, Elborg, Harderwijk, Stralsund, Amsterdam, Briel. A veritable alliance was formed against the kings of Denmark and Norway, which culminated in a military expedition in the spring of 1368. This meeting was the foundation of the constitution of the Hansa, and the first known congress of that body as a recognized whole. They bound themselves to unite and furnish ships and supplies. The cities which were too distant had to furnish money. Any town which declined to join the League was forbidden trade with any other of the Hansa.

At the same time Mecklenburg allied itself with Holstein and Schleswig against Waldemar, who sought in vain to break the alliance. While he went in person to Germany for that purpose, his opponents overran Jutland. The Hanseatic fleet seized Copenhagen and, with Swedish aid, also seized Schonen, excepting Helsingborg, which resisted until the next year. Then the fleet proceeded against the Danish islands and soon all Denmark was in the possession of the League. Meanwhile another Hanseatic fleet had attacked Norway and plundered and burnt Bergen. Denmark as well as Norway lay at the feet of the victor.

Waldemar fled and the kingdom was overrun by the Germans, until every fortress except Helsingborg had fallen into their hands. Denmark was wearied with the long strife and drained of her resources. The council and deputies of the kingdom forced Waldemar into signing the peace of Stralsund in 1370, declaring that if he refused they themselves would carry out the conditions. The treaty was degrading to the king's honor. The Hansa claimed for the next fifteen years two-thirds of the revenue of Scania, possession of its strongholds, free passage of the Sound, the right for fifteen years to veto the choice of a Danish ruler, and numerous other concessions and privileges. This successful war at once opened the eyes of Europe to the power of the Hansa. From a mere commercial organization it had expanded to the point where it had become a powerful political federation. To safeguard the provisions of the treaty of 1370 it was obliged to maintain armed forces in readiness and to continue to collect revenues. The power attained by this treaty meant complete freedom of Hanseatic trade on land as well as sea. The cities realized that they had secured this triumph only through common action and there was no more thought of letting the union fall apart. On the contrary it was extended through the admission of other cities. The year 1370 marked the climax of Hanseatic power. The emperor Charles IV gave public recognition to this in his address at Lübeck upon his visit there in 1375.

The long dimension of the Hanseatic League by this time extended from Novgorod on the east to London and Bruges on the west, while its vertical axis was measured by a line drawn from Cologne to Bergen. Within this vast area were comprehended Northern Germany, the provinces of the Teutonic Order, Northern Russia, Finland, the Scandinavian kingdoms, Denmark, Flanders and the Netherlands, and England. The sea-power of the Hansa reigned almost supreme over the Baltic and the North Sea, in Hanser parlance usually denominated the "East Sea" and the "West Sea." But a sharp distinction is to be perceived historically and was preserved administratively between these components which formed the Hanseatic League. The League had roughly the shape of an inner and outer parallelogram, or an ellipse within an ellipse. The inner was North Germany; the outer was formed by the countries in which the Hansers possessed "factories," and which embraced North Germany like a picture frame. One must not, however, stress this form too geometrically. For the inner portion included Denmark, Gotland and the adjacent territory of the Teutonic Order in addition to North Germany.

The territory of the Hanseatic League in Germany was administratively distinguished into three—later, four—circles (*kreisen*): (1)

The Wendish Circle, of which Lübeck was the capital, comprehended Mecklenburg and Pomerania, and included such towns as Hamburg, Wismar, Rostock, Greifswald, Kiel, Haddeby, Stralsund, and Stettin. (2) The Prussian or Livonian Circle, of which Danzig was the chief town, included the territories of the Teutonic Knights together with the island of Gotland. The principal towns were Wisby, Elbing, Königsberg, Thorn, Libau, Riga, Reval, Pskov, and Dorpat. (3) The Saxon Circle, of which Brunswick was the head, comprised within it that prosperous group of towns which owed so much to the enterprise of Henry the Lion, like Goslar, Hanover, Nordhausen, Nordheim, Hameln, Halle, besides the old episcopal towns of Bremen, Magdeburg, Halberstadt, Minden, and Hildesheim. This Saxon Circle extended eastward into the New East which had been created by German eastward expansion and colonization in the twelfth century, where were Berlin, Brandenburg, Leipzig, Frankfort-on-the-Oder, Breslau, and thus possessed a distinct historical identity. It represented alike Old Saxony and New Saxony. (4) The Westphalian Circle, of which Cologne was the chief seat, was not created until the crisis of 1367. It comprehended Westphalia, the Lower Rhinelands and the Netherlands. As the only part of Germany within the dominion of the Hansa whose history went back to Roman and Carolingian times, naturally there were many places of commercial importance in this circle, old towns such as Münster, Osnabrück, Dortmund, Soest, Paderborn, Coblenz, Wiesbaden, Aachen, Nimwegen, and Utrecht; and in the Low Countries along the Yssel and the Vecht or around the indentations of the coast, Zutphen, Arnheim, Deventer, Zwolle, Venloo, Groningen, Stavern, Middelburg, Dordrecht, Duisburg, Briel, Wessel and Amsterdam. Emden on the estuary of the Dollart was the farthest port of the Westphalian Circle.

For the internal commerce of Germany the Hansa preferred water courses to roads. German river commerce was relatively greater in the Middle Ages than to-day. Even very small streams were used; their beds were straightened; their channels marked by stakes; and canals constructed. The most famous of these canals was the Graden, between the Trave and the Elbe rivers. It was made between 1390 and 1398, primarily to transport salt from Lüneburg to Lübeck, but was used for the transportation of all kinds of merchandise. A canal between Hamburg and Lübeck was planned, but negotiations ended in nothing in 1448. Brunswick in 1459 made considerable improvements on the Ocker in order to have river communication with Bremen, and this in spite of the opposition of Lüneburg and Magdeburg.

It is difficult to say how many cities were in the Hanseatic League, for the number fluctuated. But at the height of its power there were between seventy and eighty of them. The governing authority never disclosed the exact number at any time.[5] The mnemonic figure "seventy-seven" was widely current. Sometimes a city did not find its connection of sufficient benefit to warrant paying its dues or incurring the expense necessary to send deputies to the diets, and voluntarily withdrew. Other towns, neglecting to meet their customary obligations, or violating some established law or custom of the League, which were always rigorously enforced, were "unhansed," and it was a matter of great difficulty to be restored to good standing. The organization of the Hanseatic cities was a loose one, and in no way did it correspond to the present idea of a federal union. It was organized primarily for trade, and varied in its control as commerce fluctuated. By a union of these separate units greater privileges could be demanded and trade made safer. Temporary unions were made, as the one between Hamburg and Lübeck for protection against pirates and robbers. Then the larger cities often aided the smaller cities in commercial ways and in private wars. "There was no Hanseatic assembly that can be proved to have been attended by all cities, no resolution by which all the towns usually considered Hanseatic were bound, no membership roll in accordance with which regular contributions flowed in from all sides, no universally recognized statute, no common policy of defense and no war in which all the members were engaged. In short the so-called Hanseatic League was a union of cities, similar in every respect to the German States called the Holy Roman Empire." [6]

Certain prescriptions governed admission to the League. No town was admitted which was not situated on the sea coast, at the mouth of a river, upon a navigable river, or which did not keep the keys of its own city gates. No city might go to war without the consent of its four nearest neighbors, and the diet only could decide whether the Hanseatic League as a whole should participate in such a war. New cities were from time to time admitted into the League. Their applications for membership, which were usually addressed to Lübeck, were always considered by the diet, and their rejection or acceptance determined therein. The claims, resources, etc., of any city seeking entrance were examined with extreme care. The Hansa was never averse to increasing its strength or dividing its expenses, so the applicants were generally accorded admission, which, however, was granted upon very unequal terms, depending upon the resources, location and general importance of the city. These inequalities constituted a source of considerable trouble and misunderstanding, leading to frequent

[5] The total number of cities which *at one time or another* were comprehended within the Hanseatic League throughout its whole history has been determined to have been 96 (*Hansische Geschichtsblätter*, VII, p. xxxi).

[6] Helmolt, *History of the World*, VII, p. 26.

clashes and ruptures in the League. This was particularly the case on questions of levying war, for which there had to be a general appropriation. Self-interest was the motive which prompted each city to join the League, and it was always ready to withdraw in case it appeared that no benefit was received from a sacrifice for the common good. Individual advantage was all that held the cities together; and when new conditions in the world of trade and industry, attendant upon the advent of modern commerce, wrought a change in the interests and life of many of the Hansa towns, the power of the League was ended by swift dissension within.

The flexible nature of the Hanseatic League also admitted to privileges individual or associated merchants who were resident in towns outside of the perimeter of the League proper. So merchants in Spain, France, Ireland, Iceland, parts of England enjoyed membership when local conditions were mutually advantageous.

The government and administration of the League furnish a most interesting feature of its study. The League was governed by a diet, meeting theoretically every three years in Lübeck, the time of meeting being known as the "Hanse Days." Between 1363 and 1550 there were fifty-three general assemblies. The first took place in 1363 and from that date to the end of the century there were thirty-four of these diets in thirty-seven years. Between 1400 and 1460 there were only twelve, and between 1461 and 1550 only seven. The decline is significant.

The number of these diets progressively diminished because the executive power of Lübeck was more and more substituted for the legislative power of the general diet. A large number of questions were regulated by local assemblies which dealt directly with Lübeck. Of the forty-three assemblies before the end of the fourteenth century thirty-five were held at Lübeck, which proves the preponderance of the city in the League. Lübeck was the most central city and the most natural place of meeting of the delegates. The diets could be held at any season, but there was a preference for Eastertide. The towns were not all represented. The larger and more important cities were represented directly; the smaller and less wealthy, which did not consider themselves able to incur the expense of sending a deputy of their own, were represented through the more powerful cities with which they were connected. Thus Rostock spoke for practically all the cities of Brandenburg, though all were equally entitled to the League's protection and shared the common rights and privileges. In case a city had no deputy properly authorized to represent it at a session of the diet, some excuse had to be forthcoming for its failure to send one, which, if deemed insufficient in any respect, rendered the town subject to a heavy fine. For three failures to send deputies it might be "unhansed." Also, if a deputy did not reach the meeting place of the diet in time for its opening, he had to pay a gold mark for each day's delay, a fine which was not remitted unless careful inquiry revealed an ample and justifiable cause for the late arrival. In 1447 thirty-nine towns sent deputies, and this is the highest number recorded. Rarely more than thirty were represented, and the average varies from ten to twenty.

Naturally in these diets there was a fight for leadership. Cologne attempted without success to deprive Lübeck of first place. Hamburg claimed third place. Lübeck had to send out notices at least three months in advance and indicate the questions that would be discussed. When the delegates arrived, they were met by members of the local council and escorted to the Gildhall, where they were given the wine of honor. The meetings began at seven or eight in the morning and lasted until three in the afternoon. The burgomaster of Lübeck was president. First the excuses sent by the cities were inquired into and the proper fines placed. Next the questions of foreign factories were discussed; questions involving money were settled; and private cases were heard on appeal. Close records were kept. As the oligarchic organization of the League was perfected, the diet met less often, thus giving more and more power to Lübeck.

Observance of the statutes of the League was not always successfully enforced. Delegates sometimes left the diet prematurely in order that their towns might have a pretext for not observing the decisions taken. The representatives in general were members of the municipal corporations of the towns from which they came. The decisions were taken by a majority of the towns represented, and all the Hanseatic cities had to submit. Many tried to evade this submission by pretending that their delegates were not authorized to accept such and such an article. Thus the selfish interest of the towns often injured the general interests of the League. As a means of coercion the League could exclude from the Hansa the towns which did not fulfill their obligations. The merchants of such towns lost their privileges. They were arrested and their merchandise confiscated in every town of the League. Cologne once stayed outside of the League for five years and ended by yielding. However, the Hansa preferred to rule the recalcitrants by softer measures, for it feared internal dissensions and was afraid lest the feudal princes might have a pretext to intervene. The Hansa controlled the fines collected from those cities which did not obey the statutes, the indemnities paid by foreigners, and finally the tolls. The first of these revenues went to Lübeck to pay for the expenses of administration. The second went to special bureaus; the third were only levied under exceptional circumstances. The Hansa was able, by lending money to bankrupt princes, to obtain large political liberty. It was never pressing about debt if a privilege were tended instead and was always ready to purchase a new opening. All the findings of the diet were engrossed upon parchment and carefully preserved in the municipal archives. In many of these towns collections of these sources have been made and thus a large number have been preserved. The archives of Lübeck are practically continuous from 1361; those of Stralsund from 1363.

The deliberations of the diet dealt with the most varied subjects—measures to be taken for the protection of merchandise; wars to be made; treaties to be signed; methods of protecting roads and seas; the question of securing broader privileges from foreigners; opening new avenues of traffic by land and water; establishing common regulation for coinage, weights, and measures; disposition of stranded goods; and methods for the settlement of disputes. The diet also decided on peace and war; it sent dispatches to foreign kings and princes; and threatened, warned, and exhorted those who had failed to fulfill treaty obligations.

The diet aimed to maintain civil order and to uphold the aristocratic city governments. Toward the rising artisan class the League showed a positive hostility; it was decidedly the champion of the old oligarchy.[7] The League was far from being a democratic institution. The most important administrative posts were reserved to certain families known as patricians, who were noted for their wealth or had performed some particular service. Under such a system it was but natural that friction often arose, especially between the coast and inland towns. The marvelous thing is that things functioned as well as they did, for we must remember that after all the Hansa attained its great power by means of the resources of the different cities and their coöperation.

There was but one real tie that held the different members of the League together and that was the principle of mutual advantage. It was this principle which had called the organization into being late in the thirteenth and early in the fourteenth centuries—the desire to see the highways of trade safeguarded, and the further desire to secure broad trading privileges in foreign countries and safeguard these. But this also was an element of weakness, especially since the

---

[7] In 1374 in Brunswick an uprising took place against the Council with the result that several members were executed and others driven into exile. The League retaliated by expelling Brunswick, excluding its merchants from all markets under Hanse control. Full reparation had to be made before Brunswick was readmitted. Lodge, *Close of Middle Ages,* p. 440.

membership of the League was scattered over so wide an area. Not all of the towns had the same interests. As a result there arose feuds between the coast towns and the inland towns, between those in the east and those in the west.

Technically speaking, the Hansa had no army, but made war with the troops and naval forces of the towns. Moreover all did not take part in a war, but simply those cities most directly interested. The militia of the towns formed an effective army, and for maritime purposes the seaports abounded with sailors. Exactly as each city had its particular justice, exactly as the German merchants abroad were judged by special justices, so the Hansa claimed the right to judge all causes arising in Hanseatic towns. The diet of 1381 decided that in case of quarrel between towns the cause should be submitted to the neighboring Hanseatic towns. Under no pretext were appeals to be made to the feudal princes. If the neighboring towns were not successful in establishing peace the matter was brought before the diet or the council of the Hansa. Various injunctions repeat this prescription, which proves that it was not always observed. Yet it is evident that processes judged by the Hansa were more and more numerous. Even the princes brought their differences before the Hanseatic diet. Judgments were according to local custom and there was no uniform law, but the "customs of Lübeck" tended to spread over the Baltic coast, and the "law of Dortmund" was applied at Magdeburg and the towns of the Lower Elbe. There was therefore a sort of uniformity in these customs, and even when differences existed a species of uniform jurisdiction was ultimately established. The "Laws of Wisby" were most complete. Lübeck later codified her own ordinances.

The statutes of the Hansa were strict. Any person who captured a member of the League could trade in none of the cities. The citizens of one town could obtain justice in another. A member of the League could demand help from a city if molested. One who broke his word with one city was boycotted by all. Any one who purchased stolen goods was likewise held guilty. Whoever married a foreigner forfeited his rights in the League. Not only was marriage prohibited with foreigners, but not even a foreign commercial partnership could be formed. In the markets of the League sales could not take place between two merchants not members of the League. In this way the Hansa acted as a middleman. Foreign merchants in vain sought permission to settle in Hansa towns. In Cologne foreign merchants were permitted to reside for only six weeks at a time and that only three times a year, and other cities had similar restrictions. The Hansers were always exceedingly jealous of competition, and employed every means to keep absolute and exclusive commercial control so far as possible. To this effect decrees were issued forbidding any German to go into partnership with a Russian, Englishman or Fleming, their great rivals for the Baltic trade.

The relative economic importance of the cities of the Hanseatic League may be determined from an analysis of the assessment in thalers levied upon each town in 1364. The bracketed figure before each name indicates the "circle" in which the town was situated.

(1) Lübeck	100	(3) Göttingen	30	(4) Thorn	20
(2) Cologne	100	(2) Zutphen	30	(4) Elbing	20
(1) Colberg	95	(2) Arnheim	30	(4) Braunsberg	20
(1) Hamburg	80	(2) Harderwick	30	(4) Dorpat	20
(4) Danzig	80	(2) Bolswerd	30	(4) Pernau	20
(3) Bremen	60	(2) Emmerick	30	(2) Duisberg	20
(1) Lüneburg	60	(2) Osnaburg	30	(2) Venloo	20
(4) Königsberg	60	(2) Dortmund	30	(2) Paderborn	20
(1) Rostock	50	(3) Hildesheim	30	(2) Unna	20
(1) Stralsund	50	(3) Goslar	30	(1) Anclam	18
(3) Brunswick	50	(2) Wesel	30	(2) Hervorden	15
(4) Reval	50	(3) Minden	30	(2) Lemgo	15
(2) Deventer	50	(1) Wismar	25	(2) Warberg	15
(4) Riga	50	(1) Greifswald	25	(4) Culm	11
(3) Magdeburg	40	(3) Hanover	25	(4) Bommel	10
(1) Stettin	40	(1) Stargard	25	(2) Tiel	10
(2) Kempen	40	(2) Ruremond	25	(2) Lipstad	10
(2) Münster	40	(2) Hamm	25	(2) Bielefeld	10
(2) Nimeguen	35	(2) Zwolle	25	(3) Eimbeck	10
(2) Staven	35	(3) Hamelin	20	(1) Golnow	8
(2) Groningen	35	(3) Stadt	20		
(2) Soest	35	(3) Buxtehude	20		

From a further analysis the following comparison results:

29 cities of the Westphalian Circle	838 thalers	average, 28.9
12 cities of the Wendish Circle	576 thalers	average, 48
12 cities of the Saxon Circle	365 thalers	average, 30.4
11 cities of the Livonian Circle	361 thalers	average, 32.8

Thus it would apparently seem that the Westphalian and Saxon Circles were not so rich as the other two. But this would be an erroneous inference. In this early period of the history of the Hanseatic League the Saxon and Westphalian Circles had but recently entered into the Hansa. The volume of commerce was more in raw products from Russia, Livonia, Scandinavia, and England—wool, furs, pitchpine, hemp, bow staves, barrel staves, and fish—than in more refined or manufactured commodities. In the fifteenth century the balance between these sorts of commerce was more even.

The four great "factories" [8] of the Hanseatic League, which as we have seen were all of the thirteenth-century foundation, were, with approximate date of origin: London, in 1267; Bruges, about 1252; Novgorod, in 1272; and Bergen, in 1278. Except Bruges every one of these factories was a base for the collection and export of raw stuffs. Each factory was a foreign concession exempting the merchant colony there from jurisdiction of the country in which it was established and so was an extra-territorial extension of the motherland, administering German law among the members thereof. For these privileges the Hansa paid nothing. Reciprocity was not in the order of its thinking.

The most famous factory was the Steelyard [9] in London, which at least rivalled that of Bruges in importance, and lasted until 1579, when the English government abolished the liberties of the Hansa. The Steelyard was situated on the banks of the Thames, just above London Bridge, so the merchants had their own docks. The houses of the company were protected by a high wall strongly fortified. For although the kings granted them privileges this did not mean protection also. Individuals or corporations had to furnish their own protection. The Gildhall was most worthy of notice. It was a huge building of many stories with a gabled roof. On the north side which looked towards Thames street were three round portals, clamped with iron. Only the center one was opened and that seldom. This building served as a dining room and was also used as a meeting place for the merchants. In a strong tower at one end the documents were kept. In a second stone building near the river the master lived. Here also were kitchens. Connecting the two buildings was the garden, planted with vines and fruit trees and a very few flowers. This garden was famous. There the merchants recreated themselves, drinking wine and playing bowls, but they were not the only ones to be found. Londoners came to buy Rhenish wine at three-pence a bottle. It was the assembly place of the greatest men of the time—bishops, mayors, statesmen, generals and naval officers flocked there.

[8] The word "factory" is here used in its original sense of a trading post. As late as the nineteenth century the trading posts of the British East India Company were so called, and the fur posts of the Hudson's Bay Company in Canada are still known as "factories."

[9] The origin of this term is disputed. It was probably so called because the chief German import was steel in ingots or billets, but possibly was derived from the steel-yard or weigh-scales employed; or the word may be a corruption of Stapelhof, or the House of the Staple. This derivation seems to some historians more probable than that the name came from the sale of German steel there. The Steelyard stood on the present site of Cannon Street Station. Long after the Steelyard was abolished the adjacent tavern lasted, where Rhenish wines, caviar, smoked ox-tongues and smoked fish were sold. It was known as the Stilliard and is frequently mentioned in Elizabethan plays.

Besides these buildings and the garden there were many more, closely grouped together and guarded. Neighboring buildings outside of the Steelyard proper were rented and controlled by the League. The clerks and servants lived here as in a monastery. The working staff of employees was divided into units designated as "families," each having a head called a "husband" who was responsible for the conduct of the members thereof. Each "family" had its own table and its own sleeping quarters. Discipline was severe. There were heavy fines for disobedience of rules, for drunkenness, for keeping late hours, for going out of bounds. No woman was allowed within the compound under any circumstances. Married members had to leave their wives at home. No outside person could be admitted unless with the "factor's" consent. Like a medieval baron, the factor held court within the precinct from time to time for adjudication of disputes and for imposition of penalties for violation of the regulations. Arms and armor sufficient to equip every man in the place were kept in an arsenal room. For the Hansers were not popular in London and rioters not infrequently attacked the quarters. No Hanser's life was safe in the streets of London, for the English workingmen looked with hatred upon the Germans and Flemings in their midst. On Sundays and saints' days no work was done; relief from the grueling grind of hard labor was found in rough games which were played in the wide market square within the compound.

In the Steelyard were representatives of at least sixty Hanseatic cities, who were variously known to Londoners as Easterlings [10] (Osterlingi), Hansers, Pruciers (Prussians), or Teutonics of Almain. While London was the headquarters of the Hanseatic League in England the Steelyard had forty-five *kontors* or counting-houses affiliated with it in England, Wales and Ireland. The most important of these were at Boston, Lynn, Yarmouth and Hull. The Scottish *kontors* dealt through Bruges. Wool was far and away the most important export.

The extent of the trade between England and the Baltic towns may be gathered from the fact that in 1392 three hundred ships cleared from Danzig alone with cargoes of grain, honey, salt, potash, skins of Russian beaver, rabbit, marten, weasel and ermine, and Danzig beer. Besides this there was a vast and growing trade in timber (especially yew from which the famous England bow-staff was made), pitch, tar, amber, tin, osmund (or Swedish iron), Hungarian copper. England in turn supplied the Hansers with woolen stuffs, worsteds, coverlets, and frieze from London, Bever-

---

[10] The monetary word "sterling" was derived from this word, a fact which testifies to the financial importance of the Hanseatic trade to England.

ley, Hull, Colchester, Dublin and Münster, which thus found their way to Novgorod for distribution throughout Russia.[11]

The following table represents the Baltic trade, as listed by Macpherson and Gibbins:

IMPORTS Woolen cloths, linen, yarn, works in metal, needles, salt, Rhine wines, beer passing to the West				EXPORTS Wax, tallow, hides, corn, leather				
NORWAY		SWEDEN		DENMARK		BERGEN		
Exports	Imports	Exports	Imports	Exports	Imports	Exports	Imports	
Timber	Corn	Pitch	Corn	Herring	Linen	Butter	Flax	
Resin	Wine	Ashes	Meal	Salt-fish	Wax	Salmon	Cloth	
Pitch	Metal-	Iron	Wine	Horses	Honey	Dried-	Ale	
Furs	work	Hemp	Linen	Cattle	Beer	cod	Corn	
Fish	Beer	Copper	Cloth	Corn	Wine	Fishoil	Malt	
Blubber	Salt	Timber	Metal-		Cloth	Fine	Biscuit	
	Spices	Salt-fish	work			furs	Flour	
	Fruits	Meat				Timber	Wine	
							Spirit-liquor	
							Copper	
							Silver	

During the reign of Edward III the power and prestige of the Hansa merchants expanded enormously in England. The English king was in dire need of funds to carry on his war with France. The huge crown debt to the Bardi and Peruzzi, the Italian bankers, was repudiated; and in 1345 these banking houses failed. Whatever profit had previously been enjoyed by the Italians was reaped by the Germans, who eagerly stepped forward to help the king. They were only too glad to advance him large sums of money provided he gave them the valued export privilege. For a time the Germans even got into their hands the management of the export duties in different ports, and one firm for several years held the valuable tin mines of Cornwall. So hard pressed was Edward III for money that on one occasion the crown jewels were pledged in the city of Cologne. England found the Hanser merchants a valuable asset in her wars with France.

[11] Wylie, J. H., *History of the Reign of Henry IV.*

A view of the customs of England will illustrate the commodities handled. Macpherson gives the following table of exports and imports for the year 1354:

EXPORTS AND IMPORTS TO ENGLAND—1354

EXPORTS:

						CUSTOMS		
Wool—31,651½ sacks of wool, @ £6...£189,909	0	0						
3,036 cwt. (120 lb. wool, @ 40s..	6,072	0	0					
65 wool-fells.............	1	1	8					
	£195,982	1	8			£81,624	1	1
Hides............................	89	5	0					
Cloth—4,774½ pcs. @ 40s......	9,549	0	0			6	17	6
8,061½ pcs. worsted @ 16s. 8....	6,717	18	4			215	13	7
	£212,338	5	0			£81,846	12	2

IMPORTS:

1,831 pcs. of fine cloth, @ £6........ £10,986	0	0			£97	12	0
397¾ cwt. of wax, @ 40s........ 795	10	0			19	17	5
1,829½ tuns of wine, @ 40........ 3,659	0	0			182	19	0
Linens, mercery, groceries, etc......... 22,943	6	10			285	18	3
	£38,383	16	10			£586	6	8

Balance in favor—£173,954 8 2

This list represents the great staples of English commerce, but there were many lesser items. A few of these appear from time to time, as follows (*i.e.,* dates at which mentioned):

1284—lead from Wales.
1291—coal mines worked in Scotland.
        Almonds, raisins and figs from African coast to England.
        Wheat, oats, malt, ale from Ireland to England.
1325—coal from Newcastle to France.
1338—tin from Cornwall and Devon.
1348—Calais staple for tin, lead, feathers, English made woolen-cloth, worsted stuffs.
1350—13,429 tuns of wine from Bordeaux.
1355—Scottish pearls to France.
1357—Avesbury (a contemporary) estimates annual export of wool above 100,000 sacks.
1463—wheat, rye, barley, cordage, hemp, flax, pitch, tar, masts, pipestaves, steel, iron, wax, wainscot, linen, cloth are listed among the imports of the Easterlings to England.

Unfortunately for the English merchants the Hanseatic League was in a position where it could practically dictate to the crown. The same fact appears even more strikingly in the last half of the fifteenth century. Edward IV, when driven out in 1470 by the Lancastrians, was brought back through funds furnished by the Hanseatic League. The price paid by the English king was high, for exceedingly liberal terms were given to the Hansers.

The Hanseatic "factory" in Bruges was very different from the Steelyard in London. Bruges was preëminently a seat of international commerce, the converging point of almost all the important trade routes of Europe. It was not immediately on the coast, but a few miles inland—which gave it protection from pirates—and was connected with the seaport of Damme by the canalized river Zwyn. Here a huge dyke and tide-gates formed a harbor renowned in Europe. Dante (*Inferno*, canto xv, lines 4-7) compared the barrier which separated the river of tears from the desert in Hell with this great dyke. In Bruges the Hansers exchanged the raw products of the North for southern and Levantine products.[12] Bruges was the greatest mart of Europe outside of the Mediterranean. The Hansers here were primarily commission agents and brokers (*maeklers*). They had no monopoly, but were in strong competition with other merchant groups. The *comptoir* at Bruges when the prosperity of the Hanseatic League was at its height, had three hundred merchants on its roster. Here, where an air of internationalism was diffused over everything, a walled compound was unnecessary, and the warehouses of the Hansers along the waterfront were open to the town. An adjunct to trade and brokerage in Bruges, as nowhere else among the Hansers, was a banking business of large dimension, details concerning which we shall come upon later.

The "factory" at Bergen in Norway was as great a contrast to that in Bruges as is conceivable. Norway in the fourteenth and fifteenth centuries was still of a crude civilization. It was, so to speak, a frontier country of Christian Europe. Accordingly the "factory" was a warehouse and distributing center for the raw products of the whole North. Concentrated in Bergen was the trade of Greenland, Iceland, the Orkney, Faroe and Shetland islands. Almost everything had "an ancient, fishlike odor." Herring, cod, hake, fish oil, whale oil, whale bone, walrus leather and ivory, eider down, skins, pitch-pine and rosin were the chief articles of trade. Hither enormous quantities of salt were brought from the Biscayan and Spanish coasts for curing fish. In the season fish racks for drying fish extended for miles along the shore by Bergen. The factory consisted of twenty-two separate courts called "gardens," in blocks of nine or thirteen buildings to each court, each court accommodating fifteen "families." Forty-eight chambers of Hanseatic merchants from forty-eight towns were represented there. Like Denmark, the Hanseatic League held Norway as in a vise. The Norwegian people were reduced to a species of servitude by the exploitive policy of the Hansers, who compelled a nation of

[12] The cargo of a Catalan ship bound from Genoa to Bruges which was wrecked on the island of Cadsand near Damme consisted of sulphur (from Sicily), ginger, lemons, dried prunes and raisins, rice, wood, Egyptian linen, cinnamon, sugar and paper made in Mohammedan Spain.

fishers, trappers and hunters to sell their catch to them at the lowest price, and forced onerous service from them in cleaning fish and skins. Competition in the northern trade by the English, Scotch, Dutch and Icelanders was suppressed by retaliatory methods, strongly savoring of actual piracy. The Hansers were feared and hated by the Norwegians, who were powerless against them. The complaint of one of their puny kings is eloquent of grievance:

We are thankful for those merchants who bring us wheat and meal and cloth and linen and flax, for these are things we cannot produce and which do the land good. But the Germans come hither in great ships and take away butter and dried fish unto the desolation of the land. For which they offer in return strong wines which intoxicate and demoralize my people. Out of this trade much evil has come and no good. Many through strong drink have got into brawls; many are injured by blows; others have lost their lives; and all have done foolishly. Therefore I have no thanks for these Germans.

When Lübeck overcame Wisby in 1293 the Hanseatic League fell heir to the trade of Wisby with Russia. It was a fortunate moment of acquisition. For the Tartar sack of Kiev in 1239 and conquest of southern Russia had driven the oriental trade out of Asia far to the north of its customary route. Novgorod then became the chief emporium of all the Russian lands, where German, Polish, Hungarian, Greek, Armenian and Tartar merchants all gathered—a rendezvous facilitated by the admirable river system of Russia. Novgorod at this time was a free city and the citizens gave the Hansers liberal privileges. They had even the right to acquire pasture lands. Their quarter in Novgorod was known as the "Court of the Germans at Great Novgorod," or the "Court of St. Peter" from St. Peter's Church in it. The factory was enclosed within a huge stockade made of thick planks with timbered bastion towers. The Code of the German colony, known as the *skra,* is preserved and presents a lively picture of the life of the Hansers in Russia.

The Court of St. Peter contained besides the living houses, stores and other buildings, a hospital, a brewery, a bakery, *etc.* The main building was the church. The priests were not only engaged in the church services but helped the merchants in their writings and accounts. Moreover, the church being more strongly built than the rest of the buildings, served as a guarding place for the weights and measures, for the written documents and for the treasury. The entrance to the court was jealously watched. At night the whole place was locked and guarded by watchmen and fierce dogs. Every member of the court was under obligation to guard the place when his turn came. These fortifications seem to have been necessary because the

Russians hated the merchants, who were foreigners and people of a different belief, or rather disbelievers, which was about the same in the eyes of the mass of the people.

There were two kinds of travellers who usually visited Russia: these were the "summer and winter guests." The former usually arrived in early spring and left in autumn; the latter stayed in Russia over the winter. The "summer and winter travellers" elected from out of their number the alderman of the Court of St. Peter. He was the head of the settlement, the highest dignitary and, with four others, judged all quarrels, personal and commercial.

The "great room" was common to all. The rules were rigid, but some special privileges were permitted to the "winter travellers," who were secluded from all the world during the long Arctic nights. On the whole it was a monotonous life, interrupted only in the spring and autumn by the arrival of new comers with their rich wares. The merchants beguiled their time in the common room by drinking beer and listening to anecdotes and tales. The subordinates who accompanied their masters had a certain degree of protection and security, because the master could not dismiss them until he had brought them home. He was also bound to care for his servants in sickness, and might not punish them arbitrarily nor on his own authority alone.

In case of disagreement between Russians and Germans the parties were to be judged in the city courts; but the Germans carefully sought to avoid such quarrels. They treated the Russians with contempt and never had business transactions with them without two witnesses. In general the rules against the Russians were severe and offensive in the extreme. A Hanser enjoyed the first privileges in all respects. For instance, if a Russian became bankrupt, the German merchants to whom he was in debt had the right to be paid before Russian creditors. The whole attitude of the Germans was haughty and overbearing, and therefore risings against them were of frequent occurrence.

Operating through Novgorod there seems also to have been a subordinate "factory" at Pskov on the Vilikaya and perhaps a depot at Moscow; but Novgorod was always the stronghold of the League's Russian trade.

The currency used was mainly metallic, but as the lower classes of the Russians used leather money, this form of currency was also accepted in payment by the Germans.

The export products of Russia were wax, honey, flax, hemp, hops, leather, timber, and furs. In especially good years the Hansers exported grain, but agriculture in Russia was very little developed and therefore grain was sometimes imported. The imports consisted of stuffs from Flanders, England, Germany; the smaller trade was made up of articles such as linen, gloves, dyed thread, needles, parchment, salted fish, metals and wine. Red wine was preferred, but white wine and beer were sold in barrels upon the market. Of the metals the most important were iron, copper, tin, silver, and gold. Another article of great importance was salt.

The monopoly which the Hansa exercised in Novgorod began to be broken down when the Teutonic Knights established Kovno on a tongue of land between the Vilikaya and the Niemen. This gave Russian merchants who chafed under the tyranny of the Hansers a new outlet and the powerful protection of the Teutonic Order as well. This bitter competition sometimes made the Baltic as dangerous as the North Sea because of the retaliatory practices—to give it no harder term—of both rivals. As Venetians and Genoese cut each other's throats in the Mediterranean in the thirteenth century, so the Hansers and the Teutonic Knights were often at feud over the commerce of the Baltic lands in the fourteenth century. In 1438 the murder of a Russian interpreter in Novgorod led to the rebellion of the town against the Hansers. Finally, in 1478 Ivan III, prince of Moscow, the real founder of modern Russia, captured Novgorod, and its glory departed from it.

While the field of the Hansa's greatest commercial activity was confined to the Baltic, the North Sea and the countries bordering thereon, its ships penetrated as far as La Rochelle, Bordeaux and Bayonne in France, Lisbon and Oporto in Portugal, and to Cadiz and Seville in Spain, whence they returned laden with dried fruits, Spanish wool, olive oil, wines and salt. The first mention of a Hanseatic merchant in Spain is in 1372 with a cargo of iron.

When England and France were at war the Hansers, as neutrals, carried the wines of the Gironde to England. Salt was most important. The salt marshes along the low Biscayan coast produced enormous quantities of evaporated salt, especially at Blaye and the Baie de Bourgneuf just south of the mouth of the Loire river in Poitou. This bay belonged to the Bretons, who sold the salt without ever dreaming of transporting it themselves. The salt ships sailed as a regular fleet, for the English sometimes stopped them and on one occasion captured fifty vessels. The sailing and arrival of the "Bay Fleet," as it was called, was an important event in Hanseatic annals. The salt industry at Bourgneuf can be traced as far back as the ninth century and may have been begun by the monks. A salt trade is first recorded in the twelfth century. Most of this salt was carried to Bergen for salting fish. For the salt mines of Lüneburg supplied Lübeck. The salt trade of Lisbon rivalled that of the west coast of France, and in 1450 there was a Hanseatic colony there. No Hanseatic ships, however, endeavored to enter the Mediterranean or to establish shipping relations with Genoa or Venice. They would have competed with the Venetian and Genoese galleys and given umbrage to those governments. Yet indi-

vidual German merchants, or merchant groups who enjoyed membership in the Hansa, had direct commercial connections with both these
places. We have the correspondence of a firm of Hanseatic merchants
in the first quarter of the fifteenth century. One of them was resident
at Venice, a second at Bruges, a third at Cologne, and a fourth at
Lübeck, while three others travelled for the firm. In 1420 Stralsund
tried to get privileges for her merchants in Venice but little came of
these efforts. For the South German merchants of Nuremberg, Augsburg and Regensburg were jealous of the Hansers and pretended to a
monopoly of commercial relations with Venice, especially Nuremberg.
In 1411 the emperor Sigismund prohibited North German commerce
with Venice except by sea.

Most of the trade of the Hanseatic League was water-borne commerce. Even between inland towns barges on the rivers were used
where possible in place of transportation by road. For the roads were
liable to be infested with brigands, and almost invariably barred with
toll-gates. Every merchant or merchant chamber owned its own ships,
though all flew the Hanseatic flag. Ships were often built and operated
on shares. This was a common form of investment in Hanseatic towns.
Sometimes these shares were divided into as many as sixty-two por-
tions. The captain and the crew were almost certain to own stock in the
ship. If so they would struggle hard to save her in event of storm
or attack by pirates. As there was no insurance in those days, this sense
of responsibility on the part of the crew was an asset. The total number of vessels employed must have been very large. We have already
seen that 392 ships cleared from Danzig for England in a single year.
The vessels varied in size from small ones of 40 tons burthen engaged
in coasting trade to sea-going ships of from 1500 to 2000 tons. In
1474 the *Peter von Danzig* had a tonnage of 2,250 tons burthen. Vessels of deep draught did not pay since many harbors were shallow.
Danzig was the chief ship-building port. While meant for peace, these
ships, by the erection of bow and stern-castles, could be converted into
warships capable of defending themselves against attack. Every ship
carried small arms. If times were especially dangerous vessels sailed
in squadron. Discipline on shipboard was strict.

The inception of such combinations as that of the Hanseatic League
was due to the necessity of self-defense. On land, the condition of
roads (if not the lack of them), the exorbitant tolls, the danger from
robbers; on sea, systematized wrecking, uncharted coasts, the principle
of treasure-trove, the swarms of pirates, the fluctuating currency, the
difficulty of enforcing contracts—all these things necessitated merchant leagues. The Hansa worked many changes, especially in maritime commerce. In important ports the Hanseatic League built lighthouses, marked channels, fixed buoys off reefs and rocks and estab-

lished licensed pilots. In the fifteenth century a "Sea Book" was compiled which described channels, harbors and lighthouses, even the tides, from Reval to Cadiz. The Hansa played a two-edged game in regard to piracy. If it paid to tolerate or even to promote piracy in order to destroy competitors, the Hansa did not hesitate to do so. For example:

The English traders, chiefly from Lynn, who had formed a factory in Bergen were exposed to constant attack. The doors of their houses were battered in; their stock-fish, which they had bought for export to England, were seized; and they themselves were robbed and beaten. Ninety-six Cromer and Blakeney men were captured by the Hansers in their fisherboats off the island of Hitteroë, at the entrance of the Flekkefiord. Their hands and legs were tied together and they were drowned knee-bent in the Vindefiord in six fathoms of water.[13]

The Norwegians saw their trade ruined, and obtained no assistance from their oppressors when pirates sacked Bergen in 1428. On the contrary, they had to stand helplessly by while the pirates' loot was sold openly in the streets of Hamburg. After this Bergen was practically a German city. No Norwegian could buy fish there except in the quarters of the League. The bridge leading to the Hanseatic harbor was called contemptuously "the Bridge of Lice." Even in a great independent center such as Bruges a threat of boycott was generally sufficient to bring the burghers to their knees. The Hansers were unscrupulous, self-seeking and brutal, but they knew all the secrets of inland and export trade; and it was in their hard school that the rest of Europe learned its lessons.

Otherwise the Hansers labored to destroy the nests of pirates which infested the coasts. It must be understood, however, that in those days piracy was looked upon as a sort of knight-errantry of the sea. It was glorious, if dangerous adventure, but not crime. The most notorious corsair was Klaus Stoertebeker, who still lives in northern saga. In 1394 when the Norwegians laid siege to Stockholm (Sweden and Denmark were then united) Klaus and his band of pirates victualled the city, and hence became known as the Vitalienbrüder. For seven years he terrorized the Baltic and North Sea until he was captured near Helgoland, taken to Hamburg and there hanged.

The Hanseatic League exerted great influence upon the formation and development of international law in Northern Europe in the later Middle Ages. This evolution supplemented the progress already made earlier in the Mediterranean lands during and after the Crusades. The "Gotland Sea Laws" or the "Wisby Code" was the northern analogue of the "Rhodian Code," the "Amalfitan Tables," the "Laws

---

[13] Wylie, *op. cit.*, IV, p. 11.

of Oléron," and the "Consulate of the Sea," all of which were Mediterranean codes of maritime and international law. In theory and in practice medieval sea laws were local and had jurisdiction over limited areas. The sea was regarded as a part of the adjacent land. Venice claimed lordship over the Adriatic as the Venetian Sea. Until the rise of the Hanseatic League maritime law in Northern Europe was almost non-existent; even England's claim to the sovereignty of the sea was enforced by a rudimentary body of laws. The warden of the Cinque Ports and the admiralty court always construed the law adversely to the foreigner. Sea law, as practised by the Hansa, consisted of two classes of laws. The first comprised the legislation of the individual cities of the League. Local codes were issued by the town of Wisby as the "Wisby Code"; by the Teutonic Order as the "Sea Laws of the Teutonic Knights"; by the cities of the North Sea as the "Maritime Law of the Osterlings"; by Danzig as the "Danzig Sea Laws"; by Lübeck as the "Ship Laws of Lübeck." Among foreign codes affecting the Hansers or which the Hansers influenced were the Danish, the Russian, the Swedish, the Norwegian, the "Black Code of the Admiralty" of England, the "Purple Book of Bruges," the "Sea Laws of Flanders," and other compilations.

Hanseatic maritime practices and laws are interesting both because of what their provisions indicate of conditions under which navigation was conducted, and because of their general tendencies toward the development of international law. For convenience in reviewing their content, the regulations may be divided into three groups, namely, the general provisions affecting all engaged in commerce, the provisions affecting only the shipmaster and merchant, and the provisions affecting only the shipmaster and mariner.

The protection of the property of the merchants is obviously the tendency in the provisions of general interest. In order to increase the safety of cargoes, winter voyages were not recommended; experts were required to supervise the construction of vessels; ships that were not navigable were destroyed; vessels were not permitted to sail without a proper amount of man-power on board; and shipmasters were compelled to stay together until the end of the voyage if they had previously agreed upon such an arrangement. In order to promote coöperation between shipmasters, one crew was required to help another save its goods in case of danger or trouble. In order to protect Hansers against foreigners, all ships were required to be registered in the home port. Foreigners were not allowed to share in the owning of merchant ships under the protection of the League, and no foreigner was allowed to be a sailor on a League ship. No ship was allowed to make its departure on any religious holiday. In order that visiting mariners and masters might be protected against impositions by townsmen, cities were forbidden to make unreasonable charges upon their visitors.

Merchants were protected in various ways against infringement resulting from actions of masters of ships. The master was responsible for damage resulting from overloading of ships, for damage done if the ship went out of its course, for damage done if the ship landed at any other port than that to which it was consigned; and if the voyage were delayed through default of the master, a penalty was imposed. The master was expected to report immediately in case of jettison, and was required to use his crew to save the goods in event of an "act of God." The merchant was compelled to pay half of the freight charges for half or less than half of the journey, and for the rest of the journey he was compelled to pay in proportion to the amount completed. In bearing the risk of losses from any and all causes, apparently no set rule was established as in the case of the "Code of Oléron," in which the loss was borne by those losing goods in proportion to the total amount lost.

The mariner was dependent upon his master in many ways after the contract between the two parties was once framed. The general rule for the payment of wages gave one-third of the total amount of wages due from the master to the mariner before the beginning of the journey; in case the mariner for any reason could not complete the journey, he was obliged to return the money to the master. If disagreement arose over wages the matter was to be settled by judges in the next port. The mariner was granted extra pay for extra work, such as extra loading or unloading of cargo. The mariner at sea was obliged under penalty to assist the master in saving goods, and in fighting when called upon. He was under the constant supervision of the master; he could not leave without the master's consent; disobedience was followed by dismissal, trial or torture. He was severely dealt with if he deserted; if the cause was a wage difficulty, he was brought to trial and if guilty sentenced to jail; if in case of peril, he was put in the pillory and whipped. He could not use or carry arms except with his master's consent. In case of protest over food he was discharged if the claim was unjustified. If the sailor was arrested and thereby became a deserter, he was to be put to death; if he killed another, he was given the same penalty.

In reviewing the content of these laws, two tendencies are manifest: First, the aim of the laws was the protection of commerce; regulations of sea vessels and discipline of the men had in the main the purpose of guaranteeing the safe passage of the cargoes; the severe discipline of the crew was a means to that end. Second, the head officials of the League saw the need for extending the scope of the sea laws, and tried to improve them. This development was slow and the laws inadequate; as is plainly shown by the fact that Lübeck, the capital of the League, passed and put into effect as part of the League's code, several laws of her own without sanction of the diet.

Relations between the Hansa and England afford a good example of the practices between two countries on the sea. Cases were frequently brought to the attention of one government because of violation by the subjects of the other. The existence of these instances shows mutual interest and mutual effort. The principle of freedom of the seas was not established, but the presence of Hanser merchants in so many foreign ports indicates a very wide acceptance of freedom of trade to privileged merchants. The independence of the Hansa within the Steelyard was a germ of the modern theory of extraterritoriality. The English had to deal with the problem of foreign residents within their country, and began to formulate general principles to govern such conditions. It is fortunate that the Hansa had such extensive relations with England, the country which was to secure the supremacy of the sea and to take a leading part in establishing law between nations. The most laggard development was in the matter of citizens dying abroad, whose property was confiscable by *droit d'aubaine*, and in the question of neutral rights.

In general the Hanseatic League made important contributions to international law. In particular three points should interest the student of the history of the law of nations: In the first place, the Hanseatic League secured the acceptance of the importance of increased protection of commerce in the north of Europe. In the second place, the Hansa influenced the development of practices for protection of merchants resident in a foreign country. In the third place, a start was made in the development of respect for neutral shipping trade; the Hansa emphasized the protection of commerce and used its influence to this end. English maritime law is fundamentally the old Hanseatic law of the sea.

The decline of the Hanseatic League was far slower than its rise and due to many different forces, some within it, some external. In the first place it was an international corporation, whose executive office was at Lübeck, whereas the drift of political development in the fourteenth and fifteenth centuries was towards nationalism, and the nations of Europe at the end of the Middle Ages were jealous, even enemies, of one another. Hence the prevailing sentiment of the time grew increasingly hostile to the commercial activity of a group of foreign merchants in its midst, especially a group swinging so much power, enjoying such large liberties and immunities, and so little subject to the law of the land. The original business of Lübeck had been to ship across the isthmus between the Elbe and the Trave rivers cargoes of cloth and salt, the former from Flanders, the latter from

Lüneburg, for transfer to Baltic ports. They received in return wheat, dried and smoked fish, and furs. For a long time Lübeck controlled this traffic. But at last Lübeck began to decline. English and Dutch merchants penetrated the Sund in spite of the Hanseatic League's efforts to prevent it, and this process was aided by the growing independence of Denmark. The opening of this route ruined the isthmus route because freights were cheaper although the route was longer. Notably French salt passed this way and competed disastrously with the Lüneberg salt springs which had long enjoyed a monopoly of production in North Germany. To the opening of the Sund to free navigation must also be added the closure of the market at Novgorod.

The Hanseatic League suffered a blow in 1363 when King Albert of Sweden acquired possession of the island of Gotland, dominion over which was coveted by both Swedes and Danes. However, Sweden was so exhausted by a long series of wars that Albert almost at once mortgaged the island to the Master and Brethren of the Teutonic Order. They remained in possession of it until it was redeemed by Queen Margaret the Great in 1408, after she had united the three northern kingdoms. This control of Gotland by the Teutonic Knights was in the time of the famous grandmaster Conrad von Jungingen, who made the maritime court at Danzig so famous for its justice that it was the favorite court of resort for merchants of the eastern Baltic.

The union of Denmark, Norway and Sweden under Queen Margaret of Denmark effected at Calmar in 1397 seriously impaired the power of the Hanseatic League. She forced it to renounce its direct political control in Denmark, to deliver up its castles, to abolish its tolls. The Hansers had to submit to great losses in Danish waters. When they made trouble for her she doubled trouble for them by secretly encouraging piracy against them. The "old Amazon" was regarded as a saint by the Danes, but "the Swedes consigned her to the deepest hell." For the Danes exploited Sweden fearfully. Even when the old queen died in 1412 it brought no relief to the Hanseatic League. In 1423, Denmark, perceiving that geography and history together had given her possession of both sides of the Sound and thereby conferred upon her an incomparable opportunity to tax all ships passing through, became bold enough to enforce such dues. The Hansers threatened to go to war, but they dared not push their threat to the hilt. Denmark's "international quasi-river" became the envy of all other kings.

Even long-suffering Bergen grew bold enough to reduce the privileges of the factory there. In desperation the Hansa offered the Swedes their assistance in breaking the grip of the Danes upon them and aided the revolt of the nobles in 1520–23 under Gustavus Vasa against Christian II of Denmark. But once upon the throne Gustavus

Vasa repudiated the Lübeckers who had helped him, saying that "the crown of Sweden has been too long an object of merchandising by the Hansers."

In Prussia and Livonia the decline of the Teutonic Knights operated detrimentally to the Hansa, while in Russia first famine, then a war between Moscow and Pskov, damaged Hanser interests. Finally in 1478 after the capture of Novgorod, Ivan III flung the Hansers out of Russia.

Even nature seemed to have conspired against the Hanseatic League. About 1417 it was observed that the herring schools in the Baltic were becoming thin. By 1425, for some mysterious reason never explained, the herring had quit the Baltic entirely and instead were spawning in the North Sea. The loss to Lübeck owing to this phenomenon was enormous. On the other hand the change made for the prosperity of Holland, especially of Amsterdam, whose streets were said to be paved with herring bones. The Dutch towns forsook the League.

These accumulated reverses made the Hansers cling all the more tenaciously to Flanders and England. But in 1451 the German merchants quitted Bruges and removed to Antwerp to escape the exorbitant taxation of the luxurious duke of Burgundy. The failure of Ghent's rebellion against Philip the Good in the next year was a blow to the liberties of all the Flemish towns and made permanent the removal of the previous year, which had been intended as a threat. But in 1477 Charles the Bold was killed and the Burgundian state dissolved. As long as the wars of the English in France lasted, so long both countries had need of the Hansers. But when the Hundred Years' War terminated in 1453 their position became unstable. The War of the Roses in England for a season delayed their fate. In 1485 Henry VII ascended the English throne, and the Company of the Merchant Adventurers was founded to compete with the Hansers. Their day was nearly over. Alien merchants were no longer popular in England, though the Hansa was "tolerated" for nearly a hundred years more. Not until 1579 were their privileges suppressed, although before the great discoveries at the end of the fifteenth century revolutionized the trade routes the Hanseatic League had been reduced to a shadow. An English envoy in Germany reported that "most of its teeth were out and the rest loose." In last analysis it may be said that the Hanseatic League finally succumbed to the demands and conditions of a modern business world which it was unable to understand or to which it was unable to adjust itself.

CHAPTER VI

THE Boro-Russians, or Prussians, whom the Teutonic Knights conquered and nearly destroyed in the thirteenth and fourteenth centuries
were a people of Lettish race, kindred to the Finns, who dwelt along
the Baltic between the Vistula and the Pregel. Not merely remoteness,
but natural features had isolated their country for centuries from outside contact. Salt marshes, lagoons and sand dunes obstructed the coast
through which the rivers had to worm their way to the sea. The
hinterland was a vast area of undulating plains, forests and swamps.
Between Poland and Prussia was nothing but a low line of hills, mark-
ing the terminal moraine of the great glacier which once covered the
country.

History more than geography, however, explains why this region of
Europe had remained isolated for so long. For both Prussians and
Letts, or Livonians, were fiercely pagan and resisted all incomers. In
the ninth century a daring merchant from Haddeby in Schleswig,
after sailing for seven days and nights, reached this inhospitable shore
and brought back to the West the earliest knowledge of the manner
of life of these peoples. They were fisher folk and fur-hunters and,
like all Slavs, bee-keepers. They lived in ring-villages or *runddorfen*,
within the enclosures of which they sheltered their cattle at night.
The only industries besides petty farming and cattle-raising were the
making of linen, in which they were adepts. With the exception of
Esthonia, which was conquered by King Canute the Great of Denmark (1000–35) the Slavonic peoples of the Baltic from the mouth
of the Vistula to that of the Neva remained pagan and independent
down to the end of the twelfth century.

The Prussians were divided into eleven separate tribes, each having
its own chieftain. A common religion gave them unity, at least against
all outsiders, although among themselves fierce intertribal conflict divided them. The priests were very influential, and they had a high
priest called a *criwe* whom the Germans regarded as a heathen pope.
Their temples were set in sacred groves.

It was Livonia, however, and not Prussia which was first settled by a
new wave of colonization out of Germany at the end of the twelfth
century. The movement is closely related to Henry the Lion's second

* For map see Shepherd, *Historical Atlas*, p. 77.

founding of Lübeck in 1158, and was primarily influenced by German commercial aspirations. For from as far back as the ninth and tenth centuries and even earlier, an ancient trade route had run from the upper Dnieper over Polotsk and Smolensk to the basin of the Dwina. The prospect of tapping this Russo-Byzantine trade was what tempted German merchants in the Baltic.

As previously, priest and merchant were banded together. An extract from the *Chronica Slavorum* of Arnold of Lübeck, an historian of this colonization, pictures the process.

In the year of the incarnation of the Word, 1186, the episcopal see in Livonia was founded in the place called Riga. And because that region abounded in many things owing to the beneficence of the soil, Christian settlers never failed there, and planters of the new church. For the land was one of fertile fields, of abundant pastures, well watered by rivers full of fish, and densely wooded. . . . Moved by the impassioned preaching of the lord abbot Berthold of Loccum not a few well-to-do and gentry, for to break the strength of the heathen and to establish the religion of Christ, took the road of migration. . . . A vast number of them came from Saxony, from Westphalia, from Frisia, prelates and priests, soldiers, merchants, rich and poor, unto Lübeck where were vessels laden with arms and foodstuffs, whence they went to Livonia.

Bishop Meinhard, who received the name of apostle of Livonia, constructed a church and a castle at Uexküll in 1187. But Bishop Albert of Buxhovden (1198–1229) was the real founder of German domination in this remote country of the Baltic. In 1201 he established Riga at the confluence of the river Riga with the Dwina and built a wall around the community of priests, soldiers, and traders gathered there. To-day this site is marked by the Inner or Old Town of Riga, around which was clustered the servile native Lithuanian population. It was not long, however, before there sprang up outside the walls a suburb composed of Moscow merchants who had soon found their way thither.

The Hamburg Code was the local law, which points to the provenience of most of the settlers, and in 1282 Riga joined the Hanseatic League. The gild of merchants was known as the Great or Virgin's Gild, and dated from the second half of the thirteenth century. It was in commercial connection with both Moscow and Novgorod.

But the whole country, Livonia, Esthonia and Kurland, were yet to be subdued. To this end, in 1202, Bishop Albert established the Military Order of the Brethren of the Sword, or the Sword Bearers, which Pope Innocent III confirmed in 1204. For this was the period of the Crusades. The public opinion of Christendom no longer would tolerate heathenism in Europe. Served by the intertribal rivalries of the native Letts, infinitely superior in arms and equipment, the Sword Bearers, who were liegemen of the Holy Virgin, rapidly accomplished the conquest of Livonia, Kurland and Esthonia. Their motto was

> Das Schwert empfang durch meine Hand
> Schütze Gottes und Marienland.

Within twenty years after the colony at Riga was established the territory was dotted with German fortified towns, such as Dünamunde, Holm, Uexküll, Lennewarden, Kokenhausen in the valley of the Dwina, Venden on the Aa, Fellin and Dorpat, the last founded in 1224. Reval was purchased from the Danes.

The territory of the heathen Preussen between the Dwina and the Vistula rivers was physically nearer to Germany than Livonia, though harder than Livonia to subjugate on account of the fierce nature of the people. But ringed by Germanized Pomerania, a dependency of militant Brandenburg on the west, by Poland on the south, by the territory of the Sword Bearers on the north and east, the German conquest of Prussia was inevitable.

The first German and Christian colony planted in Prussian territory was the monastery of Oliva, near Danzig, which Duke Sobieslaw of Pomerania established in 1170. For fifty-four years it was unmolested, but in 1224 the Prussians, alarmed at the growing menace of Christianity, sacked the community and then with fire and sword invaded Poland, which at this moment was more feared than the Germans. At this time Poland was divided between the two sons of the late King Casimir. One of them, Conrad of Mazovia which was adjacent to Prussia, bore the brunt of this invasion. Remembering that the bishop of Riga had appealed to the Order of the Sword Bearers, Conrad appealed to the grand master of the Teutonic Knights for assistance. It was a turning-point in the history of Northeastern Europe and an almost fatal event for Poland, as the future was to show.

Though founded in 1190 as a military order to combat the Mohammedan in the Holy Land, early in the thirteenth century the Teutonic Knights had left the Holy Land and found a new sphere of activity in Southeastern Europe where the frontier of Hungary was beset by savage Cumans from Southern Russia. In 1211 when the Burzen district of Transylvania, which was peopled not by Hungarians but by German colonists, was imperilled, King Andreas II of Hungary called in the Teutonic Knights. But the Teutonic Knights speedily developed so arrogant and independent a policy and manifested such an appetite for lands and privileges, that in 1225 the king expelled them. The grand master at this time was Hermann von Salza, one of the most stalwart figures of the thirteenth century, who in this predicament saw the "open door" afforded by Conrad of Masovia's invitation. Profiting by his experience in Hungary he exacted very definite rewards in advance of the conquest. To make these promised cessions doubly sure Hermann von Salza secured imperial confirmation thereof, and then to negate the possibility of imperial interference, offered to hold the prospective conquests of the Teutonic Knights in Prussia of the pope as suzerain. This adroit policy was of great advantage, as it reduced episcopal and feudal opposition.

In 1231 the castle and walled town of Thorn was founded on the right bank of the Vistula; in 1232 Culm was established, in 1233 Marienwerder. Then began fifty-three years of almost unremitting war. It is the last chapter in the history of German eastward expansion and colonization, an heroic history invested with the aura of romance in German annals and legend. Nothing in medieval history is so comparable to it as the dogged and gallant advance of Castile in the Spanish peninsula against Islam. The *Chronicle* of Petrus of Duisburg, written long after the events, though written in prose, is analogous to the poetical *Chronicle of the Cid*. In both the drama of the frontier is unfolded in successive acts, each of which is of years' duration. The sombre glory of the *Eddas* invests these pages like the glow of the North's own winter sun. Religious mysticism, racial pride, contempt of the Slavonic barbarian, prowess and treachery are commingled. One almost sees the pointed firs silhouetted against the wintry sky and columns of mounted warriors moving across frozen marshes where the ice breaks beneath the hoofs of the horses. A hundred and fifty years later Peter of Duisburg, writing long afterwards but looking back, viewed this chapter in East German colonization in true focus:

For they had left the sweet soil of their native country and entered into an alien land, in which their future was to be, where for many years they were destined to endure hardships without hope of return homeward even unto the fourth or sixth generation of them. They came from a fertile homeland, peaceful and quiet, and penetrated a country of horror and vast solitude, and filled with baneful war. In a word, putting behind their backs an abundance of everything in this world, liberty, home, honor, they accepted hunger and thirst, endured infinite poverty, endless discomfort, failures and perils.

The method of the conquest was a repetition of the practice by which Mecklenburg, Brandenburg and the eastern marches had been conquered from the Slavs of the Elbe two centuries earlier—to throw out successive lines of castles and walled towns, and then to colonize the protected area behind them with settlers. In this way, zone by zone, the territory was won, the Prussian population either subdued or driven out. The wonder is that it was so effective. For in these early days the number of the Teutonic Knights was not large. The *Chronicle of the Order*, which is anterior to Petrus of Duisburg and less romantic, relates how ten years after the conquest was begun, when Culm was endangered, the garrison there sent three times for assistance to Reden, asking for *a* knight, and how when ten knights appeared with thirty horses, joy was matched by astonishment. Even in 1400 when the Order was at the height of its power, there were not more than a thousand knights in all Prussia. Effectiveness was not in numbers, but in the prowess, arms, armor, and tactics of the knights. Against these mounted warriors, each of whom was a moving castle, against these walled towns, the ill-armed and armorless Prussians had scarcely a chance.

The Teutonic Knights effected their first and strongest establishment in the angle formed by the Vistula between the mouths of the Drevenz and the Ossa, where Thorn, Culm, Marienwerder and Elbing were situated. The ruins of the castle of Thorn, which was destroyed by fire in the fifteenth century, are of cyclopean dimension. These edifices were built of brick, for Prussia is a stoneless land.

Through Elbing the Teutonic Knights maintained communication by sea with the motherland to the west. For Slavonic, though Christianized, Pomerania—a doubtful neighbor—lay between the territory of the Teutonic Knights and real Germany. The Slav duke of Pomerania looked askance upon the upgrowth of this new territory along his eastern border, and his attack upon the Order in 1241 was the signal for the first rebellion of the Prussians. It was a precarious year. For the Mongols had invaded Silesia and a united German and Polish army was disastrously beaten by them at Wahlstatt. Fortunately in this crisis Ottokar of Bohemia lent assistance to the knights. For the first time the sacred wood of Romowe was penetrated. The only remaining pagan people left were the Lithuanians, powerful and warlike neighbors to Poland on the east.

Bohemia and Poland both resented the spread of German domination in Prussia, for each was ambitious itself to reach the Baltic. But in the circumstances they were compelled not merely to acquiesce in the conquests of the Teutonic Knights, but even to help promote them. For with the Mongol domination so near to them in Russia, no other choice was left them. Accordingly, in 1254, when the pope issued a bull commanding the crusade of the Teutonic Knights and ordering support of them by the Poles and Bohemians, compliance was necessary. As a result of the triumphant campaign of that year Königsberg was founded by the Bohemian king. For the first—and last—time in history the "Coast of Bohemia" was not a literary conceit but an historical reality. Soon afterwards Memel, too, was founded.

But Prussia was not yet subdued. In 1261 a second and more formidable revolt broke out which soon inspired the Livonians also to revolt against the Sword Bearers, who were defeated by the Lithuanians. Kurland was liberated, while behind the Teutonic Knights the duke of Pomerania gave aid to the Prussians. For ten years the history is one of reverses. Finally the enormous losses of the Prussians in this long and unremitting war were so great that the tide turned from defeat to victory and in the next decade the Teutonic Knights recovered all that had been lost. The conflict terminated when the Sudavians, a little people living in thick forest and swamp land, rather than submit to conquest, migrated to Lithuania under their terrible chieftain, Stardo.

So terminated the neroic era of the Teutonic Knights. The shattered batallions, whose members, when besieged, had been reduced many a time to eating their horses, and even boiled leather and parchment, had exhibited an almost sublime faith that the Virgin would save them, and had been justified of that faith. Petrus of Duisburg's pages in this particular reflect the feeling of the twelfth rather than of the fourteenth century. But although Europe rang with the repute of the victories of the knights, there were not wanting voices of protest raised against their cruelty. One of the fiercest of such denunciations is that of Roger Bacon.

The mass of the vanquished Prussians who had survived were depressed to a servitude lower and harder than that in older parts of Europe. What the Germans had done in Mecklenburg and Silesia in the twelfth century was repeated in Prussia. Duisburg is as tragic in particularizing the hardships of Prussian serfdom as he is romantic in recounting the history of the conquest. Years later, when the Teutonic Order had lost its power and passed under the vassalage of Poland, the grand master, Paul von Russdorf, opened an inquest into the profound social degradation obtaining in Prussia, and the resultant finding is a picture of terrible distress. The Teutonic Knights made but slight pretense of promoting Christianity among the conquered Prussians, with the result that paganism in broken and mutilated forms survived everywhere. Tithes were rigorously exacted, but the gospel went begging. The grinding process finally Germanized the population. In the sixteenth century the Prussian speech was extinct, and Prussia had become a thoroughly German province.

Marienburg was the capital of Prussia and the seat of the Teutonic Order, whose domination, with the incorporation of the territory of the Sword Bearers in 1237, extended over Livonia, Kurland and Esthonia. In addition, it bought Pomerelia with Danzig, when the duke of Pomerania died in 1295, and Neumark from the margrave of Brandenburg in 1308 in order to reach the Oder, and so established direct territorial connection between Prussia and Germany. With the subjugation of Semigallia in 1290 the period of conquest terminated, and Low German was spoken from the mouth of the Scheldt in Flanders to the mouth of the Neva in Russia.

The territory of the Teutonic Knights was a novel state in Europe. It was not governed by a king, nor by a bishop; it was not a republic. Its ruler was the grand master of a corporation, an associated aristocracy of knights. The German historian, Leopold Von Ranke, has compared the government of the Teutonic Knights with that of Venice, with this difference, that the Venetian government was that of a merchant, not a military, aristocracy. The territory was divided into commanderies, subdivided into districts. The subordinate officials in these districts were entitled either "forest-masters" or "fishery-masters," which points to the economic resources of the Order. The discipline of the knights was severe and their manner of living austere. They were half monks, half soldiers. Life within the commanderies, if not in the field, was like that in a monastery. The head of the Order, the grand master, according to the law, held almost unlimited power as regarded the general government of the Order. His other self was the land-master, who travelled through the country with superior authority accorded him in the district in which he was visiting. The council of five was chosen by the grand master and the chapter. Each member served also as a departmental head: the chancellor was at the head of the administration of the land, the marshal was commander of the army, the treasurer was head of the finances, the hospital warden supervised relief work, the chamberlain was over the commissary and, later, trade relations. The chapter held the ultimate power, as it was superior to the grand master and the council. The membership consisted of the masters of Finland and Germany, the commanders of the commanderies, and later the governors of the provinces. The council met but once a year or upon extraordinary occasions.

The population under the sway of the Teutonic Order was composed of Prussians, Poles and Germans. The last were of most importance, not in number but in wealth and influence. The Germans were drawn from every part of Germany, and every Germanic dialect was current in Prussia. Low German was spoken at Danzig, high German at Thorn. These incomers brought with them the tribal antipathies of Old Germany. The North German Saxons railed at Bavarians and Swabians; the Rhinelanders were contemptuous of Swabians and Bavarians; it was the traditional attitude of the Franconian stock. These antagonisms and cleavages became dangerous in the fifteenth century and to some degree impaired the resistance of the Order against its enemies.

Theoretically the pope possessed suzerainty over Prussia, but was content merely with drawing certain revenues. But Peter's Pence was not collected in Prussia. As for the emperor, Prussia was not included in the German kingdom and hence was not comprehended within the empire. Ecclesiastical authority and the "dead hand," which bore so heavily upon the rest of Europe, fell lightly on Prussia. There were only three bishops in Prussia and three in Livonia. They were richly endowed, but minded their own business and did not mix with politics. As for monasteries, the only monasteries east of the Vistula were those of Oliva and Peplin, both of which were in Pomerellia. The Mendicants only had free run in Prussia.

The towns in Prussia enjoyed large local liberties and were almost burgher republics. Historical circumstances accounted for this. The conquest had been largely made possible by planting walled towns peopled with burghers. In order to populate these places large local liberties had been promised to those who would come and settle in them. Naturally the most important towns like Danzig, Culm, Königsberg, Elbing, Braunsberg, were the most privileged. These incomers were from towns which were members of the Hanseatic League. Hence all these Prussian towns were soon within the Hanseatic League and sending deputies to the diet; Lübecker or Magdeburger law was the prevailing law within them. At first only taxes in kind were levied, but by the fourteenth century the Order had developed a taxing system based on a monetary régime. The money income was estimated at £275,000.

Officials of the Order collected the land tax in each district, subject to the limitations imposed by terms of the charters given the towns when founded. The corporation possessed rights over mines, waters, forests, hunting, fishing, etc., and drew a large revenue from these sources. During the fourteenth century, the most prosperous period of the Order, its government was not heavy upon the governed. Neither taxation nor military service was onerous. The currency was sound and stable, and nothing like the alterations of the coinage in France obtained, a fact of great importance to commerce. The severe police of roads and rivers by the Teutonic Knights was another factor which promoted prosperity.

In Prussia proper, exclusive of Livonia, Esthonia and Kurland, there were eighty-five chartered towns, of which seventy-two were founded in the fourteenth century. Internal improvements like road-making, swamp-draining, and diking, contributed to the development of agriculture. The *Registers* reveal that in addition to the staple cereals and vegetables, the Teutonic Knights introduced saffron culture and hop-raising. Even the grape and mulberry were introduced; but the hard winter of 1392 revealed the impracticability of such cultivation. Sheep were imported from England, horses from Flanders and Germany, and the vast forests of oak supported thousands of swine. The *Registers* show that at the beginning of the fourteenth century the Order possessed 16,000 horses, 10,500 horned cattle, 61,000 sheep, 19,000 hogs. The Order forbade the export of raw wool, preferring to keep it at home in order to develop independent cloth manufacturing. But grain and timber were exported in enormous quantities. Furs, potash, wood ashes for soap-making, wax, tallow, honey, and wooden ware, were other exports. Great importance was attached to mills, saw-mills and flour mills, which the abundant water-courses furthered. The *Registers* again reveal that the Order owned 390 mills capable of grinding 2,400,000 bushels of grain, sufficient flour to nourish over half a million people. Some of these mills were most substantial structures costing from twenty to thirty thousand thalers. The bakers formed an important gild, followed by brewers, shoemakers, leather workers, and butchers. There were 376 gilds in Danzig alone, among them a gild of physicians, who even treated cataract and stone in the bladder. Art was furthered by the churches and castles. We have record of payments to painters, sculptors, glass-makers, organ-builders. One painter of Marienburg received 2,880 thalers. We also find mention of amusements and professional entertainers like singers, acrobats, bearwards, clowns, and sleight-of-hand performers.

In the heroic days when the conquest was in progress, adventurous princes from all over Europe came out to Prussia to break a lance in service of the Virgin and to have a roaring time, as in the eleventh century the same sort of adventurers had flocked to Spain, and in the twelfth century to the Holy Land. Among such visitors were John of Bohemia, Louis of Hungary, the emperor, Charles IV, in his salad days, Günther of Schwarzburg, Ruprecht of the Palatinate, two kings of Bohemia, two dukes of Austria, two counts of Holland, Boucicault, the famous marshal of France, adventurer and swashbuckler *par excellence*, the Scottish earl of Douglas and the English earl of Bolingbroke, afterwards the first Lancastrian king, Henry IV.

The effective organization of this territory and the period of military rest enabled the Order to participate in the world movements of the time. As the knights had colored the character of the German colonization eastward, so now they began to be influential in the growing commerce of the time. The rich natural resources of their provinces, as well as the strategic location in relation to the Russian trade, made them a factor worthy of consideration. The grand master was quick to realize this, and statutory and charter provisions were made for the purpose of promoting commerce.

The Teutonic Order was almost pushed into trade by the abundance of its revenue in raw materials. But it had to petition the papacy for permission to enter into commerce. In 1263 Urban IV gave it power to sell its products and to purchase others in place of them, but forbade business for profit (. . . *dummodo id causa negociandi non fiat*). This restriction seemed unsupportable in the fourteenth century when the Order reached the height of its prosperity. The French popes of this period, however, were not favorable to the Teutonic Knights, nor indeed to anything pertaining to Germany. Accordingly the Teutonic Order resorted to forged documents and fabricated a false bull which was attributed to Alexander IV, dated 1257, permitting the knights to go into commerce, "on account of their poverty." This apocryphal bull is still preserved in the archives at Königsberg and is attributed to the grand master Werner von Orselm (1324–30), who seems to have first organized the commercial policy of the Teutonic Order.

The commercial agents of the Order were known as *Schaeffer*. There were two Grand *Schaeffer* (*Grosschaeffer*), or ministers of trade, one at Marienburg, under the supervision of the grand master and the treasurer; the other at Königsberg under the grand marshal. The most profitable trade was in grain and amber. The valley of the lower Vistula then, as now, was a granary, and wheat was shipped by sea to Scotland, England, Flanders, and even to Spain. The coast of Samland was the center of amber production, and amber was a jealously guarded monopoly. Most of it was shipped to Lübeck and Flanders for distribution.

Below the *Grosschaeffer* were lesser *Schaeffer* (*Kleinschaeffer*), one of whom was resident in each important town. Finally below these were various kinds of employees called *Knechte,* subdivided into many classes of particular nature. For example, the local agents or factors of the Order abroad were known as *Lieger*, and commercial travellers were called *Diener*. In 1379 the Teutonic Order joined the Hanseatic League.

In exchange for exports the *Schaeffer* received products from every country of the north, besides Spain. Commercial relation with France was slight. Danzig, Thorn, Elbing were most important commercial centers in Prussia. Through the ports of Riga and Reval flowed a large volume of the Russian trade. The founding of Kovno was especially injurious to Novgorod. Polish trade found an exit on the Baltic through Danzig and Elbing. Silesia and Bohemia shipped wares down the Vistula to Danzig, which was the most important emporium of Prussia. The bargemen on this river formed a powerful gild. The shipping of the Teutonic Knights rivalled that of the Hanseatic League, and when the herring ran through the Sund their fishing fleet numbered a hundred ships.

Although the Prussian and Livonian towns were members of the Hanseatic League, the grand masters of the Teutonic Order often pursued an independent commercial policy—one which so competed with the Hanseatic League that sometimes resentment was engendered. For example, Pskov was a republic like Novgorod, having acquired its independence during the Mongol invasions. It was an important emporium of trade between Russia and Germany and a member of the Hanseatic League. The German factory lay on the left bank of the Velikaya, and German merchants were forbidden to cross the bridge of boats which connected it with the town. The Teutonic Order coveted possession of Pskov so that with the exception of Novgorod they might have complete control of the inland trade out of Russia. But the Lithuanian princes time and again foiled this purpose.

The knights could be as high-handed and dictatorial as the Lübeckers. In 1404 the grand master expelled the English merchants from Danzig and forbade any Englishman from marrying any Prussian woman in Danzig, Elbing, Thorn, Culm, Königsberg or in any other Prussian town. Henry IV retaliated by an order excluding Prussian goods from entry through English ports. "But the Danzigers outwitted it by shipping wood in ballast, potash in beer barrels, pitch and tar in false packing cases, and other goods stowed away under their cargoes of grain." [1]

The *Grosschaeffer* in Königsberg handled 30,000 marks' worth [2] of business in the prosperous times of the late fourteenth century, an enormous sum for the time. In common with every other institution of the epoch, whether ecclesiastical or not, in spite of the prohibition of the canon law, the Teutonic Order conducted a banking business also. Michael Kuchmeister, Grosschaeffer at Königsberg in 1402–04, loaned money openly at from 8 to 10 per cent interest. The exactions and rapacity of the fiscal and commercial agents of the Order without doubt were part of the cause of its ruin in the fifteenth century.

Poland and Bohemia regarded Prussia with hostile eyes as an intruder into the Slavonic sphere of Eastern Europe. Both kingdoms resented being shut off from the Baltic—the Poles from Danzig, the Bohemians from Königsberg—and being compelled to pay commercial tribute to the Teutonic Knights. Poland in addition had good reason to fear that the Order secretly cherished the ambition to conquer her. In 1343 Casimir III was compelled to renounce to the Teutonic Order the rights which his predecessor had reserved over Culm, Michelan and Pomerellia.[3] Indeed, the partition of Poland was actually con-

---

[1] Wylie, *History of the Reign of Henry IV*, II, p. 75.

[2] One Prussian mark was equal to 6 shillings, 8 pence. (Wylie, *op. cit.*, IV, p. 19 note and p. 307.)

[3] When the Teutonic Order declined, the Poles seized Pomerellia with Danzig; and this territory again was "revindicated" by Frederick the Great in the first partition of Poland in 1772. The history of the "Danzig corridor" since 1918 is the last chapter in this eventful region.

templated in the middle of the fourteenth century when two German princes of the house of Luxemburg, Sigismund and Wenzel, reigned in Hungary and Bohemia, and Brandenburg was an appanage of the latter. In 1378 the duke of Silesia came to the grand master at Thorn and said: "My master, the king of Hungary, the margrave of Moravia, the duke of Korlitz, the duke of Austria, and I have agreed to attack the king of Poland. The king of Bohemia will give help. Will you participate in the proposed enterprise?" The grand master hesitated and asked for more explicit information. The answer was: "Everything on this side of Kalish, with Massovia, shall go to Prussia; everything on the other side of Kalish shall go to Hungary, and all the territory of the Wartha shall be divided between the margrave of Brandenburg and the king of Bohemia."

The dread which Poland and Lithuania felt lest both be conquered by the Teutonic Knights drew them together, although one was Christian and the other yet heathen.

The political balance against the Teutonic Knights changed in 1386. By a singular combination of circumstances, the reigning houses in Poland and Hungary died in the middle of the century, that of Poland in 1370, that of Hungary in 1382. Between 1370–82 there was a short union of the two kingdoms under Louis the Great of Hungary. In 1382, when Louis died, Hungary fell into the hands of Sigismund of Luxemburg, but the dead king's daughter Hedwig in 1386 married Vladislav II, Jagello, duke of Lithuania. Poland and Lithuania thereby were united, and the Lithuanians formally accepted Christianity. Thereby the *raison d'être* of the Teutonic Knights in Lithuania was removed; Prussia only was left to them, and the now united Poles and Lithuanians looked with hostile eyes upon the Teutonic Knights.

This event had an even deeper significance in that it changed the status of the Order and thus placed it upon the defensive. Poland was in a position to make active progress against the aggressive action of the Order. Hitherto the Order had almost smothered Poland's existence. Apart from this external peril, inherent internal weaknesses in the Teutonic Order appeared, foreshadowing its decline. For the Order was primarily not a state, nor even a government, but a corporation. It was a company organized for promotion of trade and colonization, an artificial creation, not an institution. It had not even a dynasty to incarnate its purposes and its will, and in the Middle Ages kings made states, and princes principalities.

The "state" of Prussia, if it may be so called, was formed of a landed and military aristocracy, superimposed upon a population of burghers and peasantry who had no word in the management of the country, and each class bore its grievance against the Order. The merchants resented the competition of the great trading corporation which the Teutonic Order was in one of its capacities, chafed under its regulation of trade, and resented its manipulation of imports, exports and markets. As for the peasantry, they were discontented because they could own no land of their own, but were all tenants on long leases of the Order, which to them seemed a great land company. Moreover, to both burgher and peasant the Teutonic Knights formed a caste which they resented. In the very nature of things the Teutonic Order could not inspire devotion, nor could the sentiment of patriotism be developed under the conditions prevailing in Prussia. Finally, the notions of chivalry and monasticism, which were at the root of the Teutonic Order, in the fifteenth century were obsolete ideals. Even Petrus of Duisburg ridiculed the pretensions of the Teutonic Knights to chastity. "No man can be chaste unless God give him the power (*castus nemo potest esse, nisi Deus det*)," he writes. Chastity was a counsel of perfection even for priests and monks, for whom a special providence was supposed to provide; among knights and nobles the idea of chastity was merely ridiculous. And the glaring licentiousness of the knights, their worldly life, their gross prosperity affirmed the justice of the opinion. Still another grievance against the Order was its indifference to education in an age when Europe everywhere was awakening to a new life of the mind. Prussia had few monasteries or cathedral sees, and in none of these was there any school. In an age of universities there was no university in Prussia. Ambitious youth had to go to Prague or Heidelberg or Cracow—in Poland! Once the white mantles of the Teutonic Knights with the red crosses upon them had been signs of a militant and heroic Christianity, emblems of social protection; but now they seemed a reproach. The Teutonic Order was as an alien in Christian Europe in the fifteenth century, and its crusading pretensions a parody. There were no more heathen Prussians, for they had been exterminated; the Lithuanians had become Christian.

But the Teutonic Knights were too blind to see that times had changed, and that they had not changed with the times. They were living in a fool's paradise, out of which they were rudely awakened. Early in 1410 the Polish king, Vladislav Jagello, sent out an emissary, who made the round of the European courts presenting a series of complaints against the Teutonic Order. Before each sovereign he laid a paper written in German containing twelve indictments. Nothing resulted so far as prospective assistance was concerned. But Vladislav was not daunted by the apathy of the West. In July, at the head of a motley army composed of Poles, Ruthenians, Letts, Lithuanians, Tartars—the last of which were described not without justice by the emperor Sigismund as "rabid pagans,"—invaded Prussia. A great battle was fought at Tannenberg on July 15, 1410, from nine until five o'clock. Of seven hundred knights only fifteen came out alive; sixty thousand of their other troops are said to have perished. It was an appalling slaughter of knighthood such as that which had happened at Nicopolis in 1396. But the Turks were infidels; the Poles were Christians. The death-blow of medieval knighthood was in this event. Europe was staggered by the news of Tannenberg, and the wildest tales were rife.

For eight weeks after the battle the huge fortress of Marienburg under the heroic Henry of Plauen, succeeding the grand master who had fallen at Tannenberg, held out against siege. When at last Marienburg succumbed, the Teutonic Order was a shattered thing. A war of the burghers against the castles or commanderies ensued. The greater part of its dominions and numbers of the towns and the noblesse went over to Poland, but preserved their chartered liberties. "Danzig, after having destroyed the castle of the Teutonic Knights which adjoined the Altstadt, placed itself under the protection of the king of Poland. In this anomalous position as an independent state under Polish supremacy, the city enjoyed extensive privileges and absorbed almost the entire trade of Poland." [4] By the peace of Thorn, February 1, 1411, the Teutonic Order covenanted to pay to Poland the enormous sum of one hundred thousand *"schock"* of *groschen*. Vain endeavor was made to collect due bills in Flanders and England to meet a part at least of this amount. But Philip of Burgundy and Henry IV of England turned deaf ears to the entreaty, and both repudiated their debts to the Order, which was at this point powerless to enforce collection. Calamities multiplied. "Prussia was, indeed, in the direst straits. The fields were untilled; the herrings turned westward and left the Baltic; the Vistula was flooded; the country was plagued with mice; the coinage was debased; the Vitalians were on the seas. . . . Monstrances, chalices and other silver vessels were melted down or sold; but nothing could satisfy the demands of the victors." [5]

The Teutonic Order passed almost into dissolution. In 1466 the partition of what was left of its territories took place. West Prussia and Elmeland were ceded to Poland. The Order retained only East Prussia as a Polish fief. In vain the Teutonic Knights endeavored to organize the remnant of their holdings into as close a union as possible. Tradition and their own statutes negatived such a policy. Effort was made to establish a diet in order to pacify the burgher element of the population. But it was frustrated by the law which forbade the Order to recognize any lay authority. The military policy had lost its preëminent quality of knighthood, and was based upon mercenaries rather than knights. Herein finances played an important part. Often the soldiers would open the gates of a city to the enemy, since they

[4] Baedeker, *Northern Germany*, p. 239.
[5] Wylie, *op. cit.*, IV, p. 8.

had not received their pay. The tax levied to pay for this military service aroused the greatest protest. The inhabitants of the district controlled by the Order had, by this time, lost their sympathy for the Order; and, by degrees, bands of the nobles and the cities fell away from allegiance to the Order and offered their allegiance to Poland.

The outstanding figure in this last period is that of Albert of Brandenburg, who became grand master in 1512. He bent every effort toward gaining alliances that would strengthen the Order against Poland. Poland insisted upon the full recognition of the Second Treaty of Thorn in 1466. In the civil war that followed little aid was furnished by outside countries. Europe was concerned with more important movements: it was the period of the contest between Charles V and Francis I; of Martin Luther and the Reformation in Germany. The grand master saw in the Reformation a solution of his difficulties. He embraced Protestantism, thereby dissolving his allegiance to the pope, secularized the Teutonic Order, and converted himself into a lay prince, duke of Prussia under Polish overlordship.

CHAPTER VII

THE COMMERCE AND INDUSTRY OF SOUTHERN GERMANY IN THE FOURTEENTH AND FIFTEENTH CENTURIES

THE commerce and industry of Southern Germany profoundly differed from the commerce and industry of Northern Germany in the last centuries of the Middle Ages. Fundamentally, this difference was due to different geographical conditions. The upper Danube corridor is a natural highway across Southern Germany. The middle Danube carries the route on eastward through the plain of Hungary, traverses the Wallachian flats and so leads to the Black Sea and the Balkan peninsula. Moreover, access is easy from the Danube trough to North Germany. The vertical routes northward across the watershed dividing North and South Germany to the Saale and the Weser were not difficult carriages. The broad plain of the March offers access to lowlands bordering on the sources of the Oder and Vistula. The upper waters of the Elbe were less accessible owing to hill and forest. The second geographical factor is the deep indentation of the Adriatic, which gave Germany, through Venice, the shortest route to the rich marts of the Levant. Finally, South Germany had in the Brenner, the Splügen and the Septimer passes over the Alps—after 1237 also the St. Gothard Pass—short and direct connections with the great commercial and manufacturing towns of Lombardy and Tuscany. Germany's nexus with Italy was far closer than that of France.

Italian industries were the first to flourish, but Germany soon responded to the stimulus from Italy. Presently one German city after another produced more than was required for home consumption, and sought an outlet for surplus products as well as an inlet for foreign wares. The Italian cities were the nearest market-places for Germany. It is quite probable, as Falke suggests, that the Italian campaigns by the German emperors were not merely expeditions for conquests and for the gratification of personal ambition, but attempts to make secure the advantages of the oriental trade, though the motive was vague and not clearly understood. For the trade of the South German cities with Italian cities was a source of great wealth. Regensburg, Augsburg and Nuremberg became the principal cities carrying on trade with Italy, and thus continued well into the sixteenth century. As early as the fifteenth century Nuremberg developed its toy industry, which furnished no small part of its exports.

When we turn from geography to history, again we find very different historical conditions governing South Germany. The Hanseatic League for two centuries gave North Germany a large degree of commercial unity. No commercial league was ever formed in South Germany except in the extreme southwest, where the Swabian League came into being, as we have seen in a previous chapter. The reason lies in the fact that the Hanseatic League essentially was built up on sea-power, and South Germany had adjacent to it no such great bodies of water as the Baltic and the North Seas. South German commerce was a land-borne commerce; North German commerce was chiefly sea-borne commerce. The fact that no commercial league was ever formed in South Germany makes a profound difference in commercial policy when the North and the South are contrasted. In Western and Northern Germany the League of the Rhine and the Hanseatic League to some degree neutralized the cutthroat policy of the cities towards one another and established mutuality and reciprocity in interurban relations. But in the case of the great cities of Southern Germany the condition was wholly different. There the absence of any common commercial association, supplemented by the feudal particularism which prevailed, gave room for fierce, and sometimes retaliatory competition between the cities. Regensburg, Nuremberg, Augsburg, Ulm, Munich and other towns, with the aim of promoting their own local commerce and industry, imposed exorbitant tariffs upon all merchandise not imported by their own merchants or produced by their own craftsmen. Commercially their policy was an extremely protective one; industrially it was the principle of the "closed shop."

According to the theory of the times, broadly stated—though more often acted upon than phrased—the town held the right to practice trades as a feudal tenure from the emperor, who held it from God. This tenure—the right to practice trades—the Rath, or town council, parceled out between the gilds or groups of citizens, each gild having the right to practice only that art or even subdivision of art granted it by the Rath. Finally, in its turn, the gild granted to its different individual members the right to practice the trade, conditioned, however, upon restrictions and within very definite limits. Subject to the rule of the town council and the overrule of the emperor, the trade gild held the right to control any detail it would of its especial craft. The gild had the right to say who should practice the craft, and when and where and how. The gild determined what raw material might be bought and how much. The gild determined the number of apprentices any master might employ and the conditions under which they should work. It determined the number of journeymen in any shop, and the wages they were paid. It held the right to determine, and often did determine, the very methods and mechanism of production. Above all, it fixed the price of the finished product and scrupulously controlled the market. Anything more contrary to the principle of the free shop it would be scarcely possible to conceive; equally plainly, the system was paternal, if not socialistic. . . . The gilds measured and weighed and tested all materials, and determined how much each producer could have. The gilds said where materials should be bought. They favored the home market. No open market or free trade for them. They equally measured or counted, weighed and tested, the finished product. No dishonest goods, no adulterated wares, were to be foisted on the market to deceive the purchaser or lower the price. . . . To buy in the cheapest and sell in the dearest market was not Nuremberg's commercial law.[1]

From the time of the Fourth Crusade in 1204 the Danube route vied with the sea route from Venice as an important artery of trade between Constantinople, the Orient, and the cities of South Germany. Until the last half of the fourteenth century when the invasions of the Turks into Europe began, tolls at many points along its length show that products of the Orient reached Europe by this path. An example of such tolls is the one authorized by Duke Leopold for the benefit of the Abbey of Stein on the Danube. These toll records specifically mention pepper, ginger, saffron, cannell, cloves, and raw and manufactured silk. The towns situated on the Danube in South Germany became important places of commerce, and flourished by reason of their fortunate position. Above all, Vienna and Regensburg were advantageously situated. We see by the privileges which the duke of Austria granted Vienna how much it prospered from this advantage. A notable grant is that of Frederick the Fair in 1320. Regensburg was for a time the chief commercial place of all South Germany and even before the end of the twelfth century was already called the richest of German cities. Vienna and Regensburg also, unlike all other cities of South Germany, tapped the Russian trade at Kiev until its destruction by the Mongols in 1240.

As the commerce of Venice with the Levant increased, and as Venice became the general depot for all the products of the East, the South German cities found it more advantageous to get their goods from Venice than to procure them via the Bosphorus and the Danube. The German cities of the Middle Danube accordingly gravitated towards Venice for Levantine goods, luxuries like spices, rich silks and cotton goods. On the other hand, for manufactured wares they turned to the Lombard cities, notably Milan, and to Tuscan Florence. The masterly situation of Milan, commanding every one of the Alpine passes to Germany except the Brenner, which Verona commanded, gave Milan first place in the eyes of Augsburg and Nuremberg, whose own situations were so advantageous to the northern entrance to these passes.

[1] Bliss, "Nuremberg, the city of the closed shop," *Outlook*, March 17, 1906.

Augsburg and Nuremberg, accordingly, became points for the distribution of Italian commodities to the cities of the Rhine and the Main, to Westphalia, Saxony and all North Germany. In this wise they touched hands with the Hanseatic League. The archives of many Lombard towns, notably of Milan, contain many records of privileges granted by the Italian princes to German merchants.

Regensburg became a free city in 1256, having profited by the suspended state of the kingship during the Interregnum (1250–73), as so many other German cities did. It was the earliest city of Germany to establish direct commercial connection with Italy, for there is evidence of a colony of Lombard merchants in it as early as 1038. Regensburg seems also to have been the first German city to deal with Venice, though we do not know when this intercourse began. Our information on this head is derived from a contest which arose in the fourteenth century between Regensburger and Nuremberger merchants over priority of commercial privileges in Venice. The case came before the Venetian Senate, which decided for the Regensburgers as "the authors of the Venetian route" (. . . . *quasi auctores itineris Veneti*). This route was up the Inn river, over the Brenner Pass and down the Adige through Verona to Venice. A document in the Venetian archives mentions Leogard von Ransborg and Heinrich von Münen as Regensburger merchants in Venice in 1330–31, and the account book of a Regensburger merchant covering the years 1383–1407 which has been preserved shows close intercourse with Venice. Woolen cloth and especially furs (*pelles varie et alia*) were the chief articles dealt in by Regensburger merchants and exchanged at Venice for oriental imports. These furs came from Bohemia, Prussia and Poland, for Regensburg's location opposite the mouth of the Nab river gave her convenient connection with the upper Elbe and Oder rivers. In this particular Vienna was Regensburg's only rival. For the valley of the March was to Vienna what the valley of the Nab was to Regensburg.

In the fourteenth century Augsburg and Nuremberg followed in Regensburg's steps and established trade with Venice. As early as 1308 we find Venice complaining of the detention at Füssen of goods which were bound for Augsburg. These sufferers obviously were Venetian merchants en route to Augsburg. However, Venice soon abandoned sending out her merchants to Germany and instead compelled German merchants to come to her.

The richness of the country around Augsburg, united with her favorable geographical situation on the Lech, which gave her access both to the Danube and the Tyrol and so to Italy, materially contributed to her prosperity. Linen and woolen goods, metal ware and saffron were important products. From the tariff accounts of the bridge over the Lech at Augsburg we may infer that the trade of Augsburg was almost as old as that of Regensburg. Moreover, the Venetian letter of complaint refers to "an ancient friendship long observed" (*antiquam amictiam . . . diutius observatam*). The route of these Augsburger merchants followed up the Lech river to Füssen[2] in the Tyrol, to Innsbrück, which had enjoyed *stapelrecht* (*jus depositionis mercium*) since 1329, over the Brenner Pass through Brixen and Bozen, down the Adige to Trent and Verona and so to Venice. A short cut was via the Brenta, but it was a steep climb from Trent over the ridge to the headwaters of that river. After the establishment of burgher government in 1368 and its union with the Swabian League, Augsburg grew rapidly, and by the fifteenth century was the greatest banking city of South Germany, where the Fuggers and the Welsers had their headquarters. In the fifteenth century sugar and paper were imported in great quantity from Aragon. We have the journal of a merchant of Augsburg named Lucas Rem who lived early in the sixteenth century. He relates his business trips to Italy, Spain, Portugal, Flanders, the Azores, Cape Verde, and the Madeira islands as an agent of the great house of Welser.

The etymology of the word Ulm (from Olima, a marshy place) gives a clue to the nature of its most important industry, namely flax-raising and linen-making. Like Nuremberg, it was originally an imperial domain whose denizens shook off their manorial dependence on the crown and acquired municipal freedom. Again, as in the case of Nuremberg, this process towards municipal freedom was facilitated by the fact that it had not to contend with either bishop or baron, and during the Interregnum there was no king to coerce the cities. In the fifteenth century Ulm added cotton-spinning to its industry, which brought it into contact with Venice, the principal importer of Egyptian cotton. Ulm belonged to the Swabian League, but never became a place of widely varied industry like Nuremberg, nor a banking center like Augsburg. Ulm's history is simpler than Augsburg's. In linen goods she surpassed any city in Germany, and hardware of all kinds was manufactured. In 1431 Ulmer dealers in metal ware received imperial permission to trade in any fair in Germany, and soon controlled the market. Ulm greatly profited when, late in the fifteenth century, the Fuggers got possession of the Habsburg mines in Tyrol, Austria and Bohemia.

Historically, Nuremberg is a far younger city than Regensburg or Augsburg. In this respect it is like Vienna. The earliest mention of Nuremberg is in 1062, when the emperor Henry IV granted it market right. It was not then a free town, but a crown land community. Nuremberg must have been a city of considerable importance by 1163. In this year it was guaranteed the same security and freedom of trade

2 The name was derived from *fauces* = the jaws.

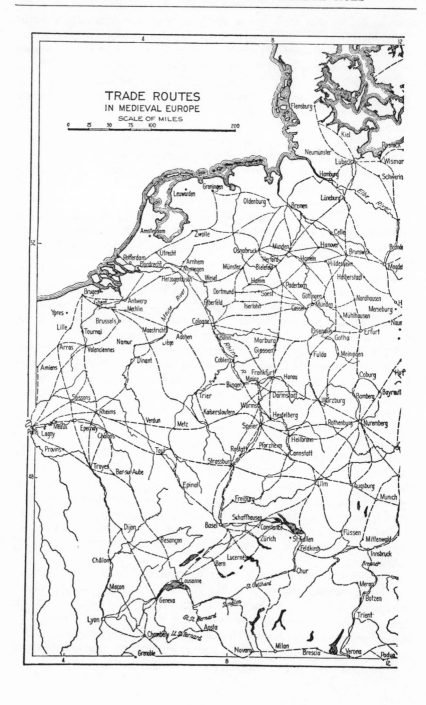

TRADE ROUTES
IN MEDIEVAL EUROPE
SCALE OF MILES

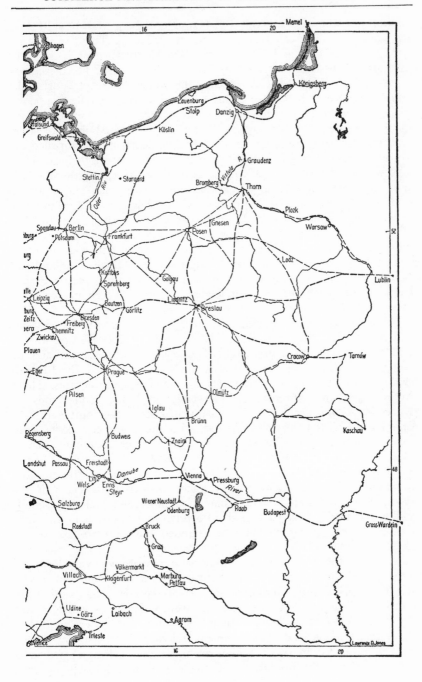

as was guaranteed Bamberg. By 1219 Nuremberg was permitted to use gold and silver coins as mediums of exchange. These coins were used in Nördlingen and Donauwörth. The significance of Nuremberg as a great industrial center is also seen by the fact that her merchants were exempt of toll between Passau and Regensburg. At Worms the merchants of Nuremberg were only required to pay annually one pound of pepper and a pair of gloves. In Nuremberg the development of industry preceded that of commerce. "Our city is situated on hard, sandy and unfertile soil," recites a document. This deprivation compelled the Nurembergers to supplement the niggardliness of nature by hard work. The wood and metal industry made Nuremberg rich, and the city was famous for its manufacture of various kinds of weapons. The armorer's craft was the leading one in the city. After a home revolution in 1348, in which the armorers were leaders, they were expelled from the city and scattered all over Germany. The weapons and arms made in Nuremberg were considered the best in the world and were in great demand, not only in Germany and Italy but also in Spain, England and Poland. All sorts of metal work was manufactured, brass basins, grates, locks, censers, candlesticks, candelabra, statues of iron or brass, or carved wood.

In 1219 Nuremberg entered into tariff agreements with Regensburg and Speyer; in 1264 with Mainz. No town in Middle Europe was so centrally situated as Nuremberg. The trade of the Levant and of Northern Europe met there. It was a distributing point for Flemish cloths, Baltic herring, French wines, and Italian manufactures. There were colonies of Nuremberger merchants in Venice and Lyons. A Nuremberger merchant named Ulmann Stromer in the fourteenth century traded with Cracow in Poland, with the Black Sea ports, with Genoa, Bruges and Barcelona. A Nuremberger merchant named Matthew Ebner in the fifteenth century operated in France, Spain, and Hungary. The Behaims traded with Portugal, and Martin Behaim, the famous fifteenth century geographer, was in the service of the Portuguese crown. He and two other Nuremberger merchants, Imhoff and Hirschvogel, took part in the Portuguese expedition to India. It was Nuremberger merchants who founded the German *fondaco* in Milan in 1472.

In Venice the Nuremberger colony of merchants was very large, so large indeed that the trade route between Nuremberg and Venice was sometimes called the *"Caminum de Norimberga."* Merchants from the *"stati liberi"* or free cities of Germany were welcome in Venice where the *Fondaco dei Tedeschi* gave them hospitality. We know a great deal about this famous institution from no less than 821 documents of its history preserved in the Venetian archives, the earliest of which is dated 1225. But the *fondaco* itself probably existed as early as 1200.

The government kept the house for the reception of German merchants; and officers were appointed to look after the trade transacted in the house; a house-master, a cellarman, and cooks were employed to attend to the wants of the guests; rent was taken for the rooms, and in 1497 the *fondaco* was said to bring in a revenue of 100 gold ducats a week. . . . The *fondaco* was an inn, but it was much more than an inn; it was an exchange-house and store as well. The Venetians compelled all German merchants to live in the *fondaco* or in houses especially appointed for the purpose when the *fondaco* was too full; moreover, no commercial transaction was legal which was conducted outside the *fondaco*. The reason for this is obvious. The customs both on the import and on the export of goods bought or sold by Germans were assessed and levied in the *fondaco* by officers of the Venetian government. If the merchants were allowed to lodge where they chose, it was probable that they would smuggle. A merchant accordingly was compelled to bring his goods to the *fondaco,* where they were stored in vaults or in the passages and corridors.

The Venetian government kept control over the *fondaco,* both externally and internally. At the head of the establishment was a committee of three nobles called *visdomini;* they were entrusted with the entire control of the house, and had power to punish its inhabitants for breaches of their rules: the Germans might appeal to their *consoli* against a ruling of the *visdomini,* and if the *visdomini* were dissatisfied with the finding of the *consoli,* they again might carry their case to *proveditori di comun.* Under the *visdomini* came a number of officials attached to the *fondaco,* and employed in the various operations of commerce and of taxation. Among these officials we find the *sensali,* or agents, without whose intervention no merchant was allowed to transact business; the boatmen, porters, weighers, stampers, and packers. The packers, or *ligadori,* formed an important guild of themselves, and had their altar, burying-place, and special masses in the church of SS. Giovanni e Paolo.

The internal order and management of the house were entrusted to the house-master or *fondacarius,* who was responsible to the *visdomini.* It was his duty to see that the merchants gave up their weapons when they entered the *fondaco;* to shut the house door at sunset; to provide beds and sheets for the merchants, for which he was paid; to keep the keys of the various rooms; to supervise the kitchen and its cooks, the wine-cellar and the cellarman. The German merchants were, on the whole, well behaved; they gave the government far less trouble than the Turks in their *fondaco.* It is rarely that we come across any serious quarrel inside the house. On one occasion the merchants of the imperial cities objected to sitting at the same table with the merchant subjects of princes, while the Cologne merchants claimed a separate room and table for themselves. On another occasion the merchants insist that the wine-cellar in the *fondaco* shall remain open all night, or they will break open the door. But on the whole their conduct was remarkably quiet.[3]

---

[3] Quoted from a review of H. Simonsfeld, *Der Fondaco dei Tedeschi in Venedig und die deutsch-venetianischen Handelsbeziehungen* (1887), in *English Historical Review,* III, pp. 563–66.

The conditions under which the various German cities carried on trade with the Italian cities depended on the diplomatic skill they could bring to bear to get concessions. There seems to have been no consistent policy except with Venice. Whatever regulations there were, were made merely to meet momentary exigencies. Along toward 1500 Venice reduced tolls on certain articles, apparently to all German merchants. These reductions were due, no doubt, to the rise of competitors along the northwest coast of Europe, and in the sixteenth century many other reductions were made. In 1462 Augsburg could boast of having had concessions "from time immemorial." On the other hand, there were often restrictions on trade. The Germans were forbidden to carry any wares to Venice that were not produced in Germany. The Venetians reserved the right to themselves to handle non-German wares and often transported them through German territory. In 1449 the Germans were permitted to carry only raw copper to Venice, for she wanted no competition with her own copper industries. The Germans curbed the competition of Venice by not allowing Italians to purchase in person in Germany, thus promoting their own power as middlemen. There are no reliable records of the value of the commodities that were exchanged. A Venetian letter of 1472 says wares worth 1,000,000 ducats were exchanged by the Germans annually. Another letter says that tolls yielded 20,000 ducats annually. Still another letter says the tolls amounted to 100 ducats daily. These estimates may give some idea of the volume of trade. More reliable are the reports about individual merchants. In 1499 the Fuggers were reported to have had copper in Venice worth 60,000 ducats. A Venetian merchant bought 45,000 pieces of linen in 1358. In 1426 a Nuremberg merchant sent 425 fox pelts to Venice. Another evidence of the enormous volume of trade during the fifteenth century is the number of bankruptcies with liabilities as high as 25,000 ducats, at a time when business on credit was not yet extensive.

In Southwest Germany Basel was the most important town. Originally an episcopal town, it acquired the immunities which made it a free city more by peaceful purchase than by conflict with the lord-bishop. By 1360, later than most German cities, it had the right to elect its municipal council, to lay its own taxes, manage its own finances, police itself, administer its own justice, to make alliances and to make war according to its own interest. Even yet, however, the territorial superiority pertained to the bishop, who also had "mean justice," while "high justice" pertained to the emperor, who appointed his burgrave. The bishop still collected tolls on imports into the town and coined the current money, nor could the town establish new taxes without his consent. Considering the number of rights which the bishop preserved it is remarkable that no conflict developed between the burghers and the bishop. Fortunately the bishops of Basel were a liberal sort who had the best interest of the town at heart and who worked harmoniously with the burghers. Basel owed its prosperity to its advantageous situation at the head of the valley of the Rhine and on the great roads leading to the passes of the Jura and the Alps, which gave it a lucrative transit trade. There is record of a Basel merchant in Genoa as early as 1216. This natural stimulus to trade was improved when Bishop Henry of Thun built the old bridge across the river. In 1274 Basel joined the Swabian League, and not until 1501 was it united with the Swiss Confederation.

The last city to be mentioned as attaining commercial importance in Southwestern Germany is Strassburg. Its history in every particular is much like that of Basel. Even its situation reminds one of Basel. For it, too, was in the upper Rhine valley (though on an affluent of the Rhine), conveniently located for roads over the Alps, the Jura, and the Vosges; in addition the upper Danube was more accessible to Strassburg than to Basel.

It was natural that these cities of Southwestern Germany should join the Swabian League and that their chief trade should be down the Rhine and with France, where the fairs of Lyons were a great attraction. The same observation may also be made in regard to the fairs of Geneva. For Geneva, situated at equal distance from France, from Italy, from Upper Germany, and located within the territories of the duke of Savoy, who ruled on both sides of the western Alps and controlled the Great St. Bernard, the Little St. Bernard and the Mont Cenis passes from end to end, was an international rendezvous of merchants.

While one thinks of Austria and its attendant lands of Styria and Carniola as German provinces, nevertheless the phrase must be qualified. For the Austrians in blood, institutions, and culture are a happy mélange of German, Slav and Latin influences. These influences, in turn, were reënforced by long commercial relations with Byzantium, Italy and Germany. The foundations of Austria both politically and economically were laid by the intelligent and efficient Babenberger dukes of the feudal age. Leopold V (1177–94), who acquired Styria in 1184, brought both distinction and prosperity to the duchy. Leopold VI (1198–1230) gave Vienna her first municipal code and made her for a brief time the most brilliant capital in Germany. During the savage and foolish wars of his son and the anarchy of the Interregnum, men looked back to his reign as Englishmen looked back to the reign of Edward the Confessor. When the Babenberger dynasty died out in 1246 a time of trouble ensued in Austria. In 1278 this was ended by Rudolph of Habsburg's lucky victory on the Marchfeld over Ottocar of Bohemia, who had seized the territory. The prize was worth winning. For Pope Nicholas III borrowed 200,000 gold florins from bankers of Florence and Pistoia in 1277 to support Rudolph's expedition.

The fourteenth century was, in the history of Austrian commerce, the happiest time in the whole Middle Ages. Import and export trade and trade in manufactures increased. Though the import of salt declined because of the opening of the salt mines at Hallstadt and Aussee, the import of textiles greatly increased. Not less than 8,500 pieces of wool alone came in from the North in one year, most of it destined for the Hungarian trade. Wool was greater in amount than any other cloth, but trade in all other textiles was lively. The most noticeable feature of the export trade was the mighty growth of the wine export. Austrian vine-growers had found wine so profitable that it had come to overshadow every other product of the land. While the trade with Hungary benefited chiefly the Viennese, the wine trade made for a powerful industrial strengthening of the whole land. The importance of wine may be seen from the fact that during this century the commercial condition changed so that the balance of trade between Austria and Upper Germany came to be greatly in Austria's favor. Furthermore, Viennese manufactures drove foreign-made goods, with the exception of cloth, out of the land. Toward the end of the thirteenth century Flemish fustian weavers had been imported into Vienna, and by the middle of the fourteenth century foreign tailors, weavers, knife-makers, saddlers, goldsmiths, furriers, purse-makers and sword-forgers had developed their trades in Vienna. Through this means Vienna got a monopoly of the Austrian and Hungarian trade in manufactures, for no native craftsman equalled the foreigners in skill. In all directions then, Austrian commerce expanded and flourished. Hundreds of boats annually plied upstream to Passau or down the Danube to Hungary. The worth of the wares they carried was so great that it was scarcely exceeded by that of the goods freighted upon the middle Rhine at the same time. In the fifteenth century, when sources are richer, we find record that Viennese merchants penetrated even into small villages. They developed trade not only in Austria, but also in Styria, Carinthia, and Salzburg. This brought them into competition with merchants from other cities like Nuremberg and, vice versa, outside merchants began to compete with those of Vienna. Vienna's peculiarly advantageous situation with reference to Hungary and Venice made her an object of commercial jealousy. In order to abate this feeling Albert I of Habsburg granted liberal trading privileges to Regensburg merchants. But in the time of Albert II, Vienna not only regained her former monopoly, but also extended her commerce with Venice through the acquisition of Carinthia. The great saffron market established at Aquileia in 1390 was later removed to Crems in Austria.

Bohemian resentment towards Austria was so great that it developed a new trade route between Bohemia and Hungary through Germany. In 1236 King John of Bohemia, whose relations with the Habsburgs had for some time not been particularly cordial, granted the Nurembergers trade privileges and a safe conduct through his country. Of greater effect upon the Austrians, certainly, were the counter-restrictions which their neighbors began to make in the second half of the fourteenth century. In 1387 King Wenzel passed a law forbidding merchants of Vienna and other Austrian cities to trade with Bohemia until the roads to Venice should be opened to citizens of Breslau and Prague. This energetic defense must have hit Vienna hard. Doubtless the Bohemian rulers hoped to make Brunn a great staple like Vienna. This result, however, was not accomplished because, when the Hussite wars broke out, the trade through Bohemia was entirely cut off, and nothing more is heard of it for almost a century. It could not, indeed, have had much effect upon Vienna, for no Viennese complaint against it is recorded.

Although Austrian trade in 1400 was in a flourishing condition, signs of trouble ahead were many. A whole mass of complaints against invasions of their monopolies, made by the gilds of Vienna, show that foreigners were already disturbing their peace. One of these complaints, that of the knife-makers' gild, may be taken as typical. The knife-makers complain that knives have been brought by strangers to the city, have been smuggled in without paying the tax, have been sold to visitors from Hungary and other lands as Viennese goods and that, being of inferior quality, they have thereby brought the wares of Vienna into disrepute. The gild asks redress in the form of restrictive laws. These complaints show that the effort of foreigners was especially directed toward breaking down the old trading monopolies, and that their effort was succeeding. The real trouble of the Viennese was that they were depending upon their vested position and were not exerting themselves to meet the new conditions. That they could hold their own when they did make the effort was proved by the fact that trade with Venice as late as 1433 showed little decline.

One thing which made it hard for the townsmen to keep the foreign traders out was the fact that the rural population wanted them to come in. On several occasions, when there was a shortage of the grain supply in Upper Germany, Austrian farmers found a lucrative market for their grain there. This export, however, worked to the disadvantage of the towns because the whole surplus of grain was thus consumed, and a famine occurred among the townspeople at home.

The Austrian vine-growers, too, liked to sell to the German traders.

This direct trade between the Austrian producer and the Germans was interrupted in 1390 by the grant to the city of Passau of the staple right in wine, designed to make the burghers of that town the middlemen in the Austrian wine trade, as the staple of Vienna had made its citizens the middlemen for all German goods going to Hungary. Naturally the monopoly was not established without opposition, but the tax records of Passau show that by 1430 at least the monopoly was fairly complete. The economic condition of Austria was greatly hurt thereby, for the prosperity of the Austrian wine trade was a fundamental condition of the development of Austrian economic life.

The Passau tax records show also that the Viennese were no longer active in the trade with Upper Germany. Evidently, at about the same time, the Viennese were losing their immediate trade with Hungary. Foreign merchants established in Vienna resident representatives called *Lagerherren* or factors, who, in spite of weak efforts to stop them, developed into influential business men. Even the Habsburgs borrowed from them.

The organization of the trade of foreigners in Austria is illustrated by the history of three men. Every year at fair time a ship was fitted out at Regensburg by a merchant named Runtinger (1383–1407) and loaded with all sorts of wares, especially cloth, to trade in Austria. The trade itself was carried on by the old method in a retail market; it was confined to imports alone, for Runtinger, strangely enough, did not carry a return cargo. Sometimes he or his agent stayed a long time in Vienna. His transactions were usually on credit, a circumstance which somewhat lessened the profit.

In contrast to Runtinger, Ulrich Stark of Nuremberg (1426–36) was not primarily a merchant, but a landholder with a large income from rents. Occasionally he gave his trading friends money or wares to use in trading far and wide in the Southland. They usually brought back other products for sale in Nuremberg. They sometimes ventured into Austria for wine and even went through Austria into Hungary with cloth and jewelry. It is evident that they did not bother themselves about the Viennese staple right. Otto Ruland of Ulm (1444–64) represents the first of capitalist entrepreneurs. He made contracts to buy the whole product which craftsmen could produce in a certain time and handled the sale of the whole output himself. The methods of these men have some common features. They all confined themselves no longer to trade in single cities and lands, and they all used somewhat large amounts of capital.

From the recently discovered Pressburg book of the receipt from the *Dreizigste,* we know something about the Austrian trade with Hungary. The *Dreizigste* was a tax collected at Pressburg on all articles of import or export. Being originally one-thirtieth of the value, it furnishes a measure by which values may be reckoned. It records also the name and place of residence of the traders.

The value of the trade from Austria to Hungary by way of Pressburg was about 130,000 *fl. ung.*, and the trade to Austria from Hungary about one-tenth as much. The balance of trade was thus strongly in Austria's favor. To the worth of about 3,000 *fl. ung.* such articles as pepper, southern fruits, ginger, saffron, figs, nuts and lemons were carried in, but by far the greatest amount of import trade was in textiles and hardware.

Wool constituted 75 per cent of the whole import, and linen 11 per cent. This was usually cloth of fine grade, and it came immediately from Vienna, though originally it came from Italy, England, the Netherlands, and the German cities of Aachen, Cologne, Eichstätt, Mainz, Nuremberg, *etc.* The price varied, the Italian and English products costing most. A considerable tax also was collected on metal ware—chains, nails, knives, and kitchen and farm utensils of all sorts. The trade in leather and pelts was small. There might have been a larger trade in wooden ware had it not been for a prohibition placed by the Austrian duke on its export.

In contrast to this somewhat extended import trade was the small export trade, mostly cattle, oxen, sheep, horses, fresh fish, copper, hides and honey. The most important export, however, through the whole of the Middle Ages, was precious metals. Hungary had as yet no manufactures.

We cannot doubt that the number of merchants engaged in this trade was large. Hungarians from Pressburg, Ofen, and Raab carried goods into Lower Austria; Austrians, chiefly Viennese, came into Pressburg at fair time in May and August; but no Germans came in. The merchants usually travelled in companies of not less than four or five. The trading at the Pressburg fair was entirely retail. It appears that here, as at Passau and Vienna, wholesale trade developed independently of the yearly markets. The widening of the area of production, which made necessary a carrying trade between producer and consumer, promised greater profits to the wholesaler than to the retailer; and thus developed in the fifteenth century the capitalist entrepreneur. The fact that wholesale trade developed first in such articles as cloth and knives, which were freighted via the Danube, suggests that wholesale trade develops first where means of communication were such that the small merchant had not capital enough to procure the necessary transportation. Some wine growers also engaged in wholesale trade, not as capitalist carriers, but as stationary merchants. There were four such firms in Pressburg. The change from market-place trade to wholesale trade, a development of the fifteenth century, shows that the old market monopolies were breaking down as trade expanded.

The decline in Austrian trade reached a crisis in the middle of the fifteenth century as is evidenced in a great number of contemporary sources. The reasons for this crisis were the obsolete methods used by the Viennese and the more energetic and effective policy of their foreign competitors, the wars between Kaiser Frederick III and his brother Albert for the inheritance of Ladislaus Posthumus, and the consistent debasement of the currency.

From the contemporary complaints of the Austrians against the foreign merchants and the demands that their unwelcome competition should be checked by legal regulations, it is evident that foreigners had succeeded in getting the lion's share of the trade of the land. That this should have happened is not surprising, for we have already noted their greater energy and initiative. Only gradually, however, were they able to break down staple rights. An edict to the Viennese issued by Ladislaus Posthumus, decreeing that retail trade in Venetian goods should be free to all, made an opening through which the traders from abroad had pushed forward. By evasion of the unpleasant monopolies they no longer respected the privileges of the townsmen, who made constant complaints that the foreigners were overstepping the bound allowed them. Complaints that they were selling goods out of market show that they had established relationships between themselves and the agrarian population. In increasing numbers they act as middlemen between the Austrian wine producers and the German consumers. Austrians gradually cease altogether to carry goods to Germany, and fall back more and more upon the production of wine. Thus the old Viennese monopoly had the unforeseen result of making the Austrians dependent upon foreigners by crushing out native initiative.

Additional ground for the great decline in Austrian trade is to be found in unfavorable political conditions. An examination of several statistical sources like the tax books of Vienna, for instance, show that there was a strong slump from the middle of the century on, which reached its greatest degree between 1481 and 1488. There is a direct connection between the years of decrease and wars, the greatest decline being the time of the occupation by the Hungarian King Mathias. Since the traders from Upper Germany could no longer get Hungarian wares in Austria, they sought a new route. And there is evidence that they went increasingly often through Bohemia and Moravia. This, of course, struck at the very root of the prosperity of the Austrian cities. But Austrian farmers also were hit by the war. Not only were their harvests destroyed, but at the same time their land rents were increased to pay the expense of war.

Another important cause of the downfall of Austrian prosperity was the condition of the currency. There was a universal tendency in the fifteenth century toward the debasement of currency. A direct connection always existed between debasement and war times. Nobles who had the minting right were likely to try, by clipping coins, to get the wherewithal to conduct their campaigns. This was true in Austria. One debasement followed another until confidence in the silver coinage of the land entirely disappeared. The evils of this were not so noticeable in domestic trade, but it made the Austrian silver *pfennig* no longer usable in foreign trade. The Hungarian gold *gulden* began to play the rôle of a standard of values.

Moreover, Austria suffered not only from the debasement of her own coinage, but also from the debasement of foreign coinage as well. We have seen that Austria sold more goods abroad than she bought and that, therefore, a balance of foreign coin was always coming into the country. But since Austria was entirely dependent upon foreign merchants for a market for her wine, she had to transact business in whatever coin the foreigners desired. And because everybody at that time was trying to get good money for bad, it is not surprising to find that the foreigners dumped poor money upon the Austrians and demanded gold in payment for goods sold. Everywhere, in all the sources, we find the evidence of industrial decline in Austria.

Our survey of conditions would be incomplete without a glance at prices. From the Viennese *Kammeramts* we find that wine stayed about stationary in price from 1430–1460. But the real worth of the *pfennig*, in which its value was computed, fell one-half between those dates. The same thing is true of grain. We have a fine source of comparison in the price of cloth. Every year at the races held in connection with the fair at Vienna, a piece of scarlet cloth from Verona was given as a prize. From the record of the price of the prize from year to year we learn that the price of cloth slowly fell until 1460, but remained almost constant from then on. There are no complaints about the rise in the price of cloth. Fustian and linen remained constant after 1438. Italian wine in general rose in price during this century, while pepper, ginger, saffron, nuts, figs, grapes, rice, cinnamon and other wares from the South fluctuated greatly. These articles did not, however, greatly affect the average person.

On the whole we see that the articles of Austrian production, especially wine, sank to one half of their former worth, though they remained constant in price because Austrian silver declined in value, while imported goods in general either remained a constant value or increased slightly in price. These values were measured in the Hungarian *gulden*. All these evidences tell the same story—that conditions of living for the Austrians were becoming harder and harder.

Some general observations upon medieval German town life may conclude this chapter. Certain German cities had a special law called the *stapelrecht*. No merchants could pass through a city without unloading his merchandise there, and he could not go on until the inhabitants of the city had purchased what they wanted. Even the territorium around the city was under the *stapelrecht*. For example, the boats which descended the Wartha to get to Kustrin on the Oder were compelled to go up this river to Frankfort and there to debark their merchandise before descending to the Baltic. Certain kinds of commerce were often forbidden within a determined radius around the city. It was forbidden to manufacture beer within the area, so that the brewers of the city could better dispose of theirs. This was a veritable monopoly. The town council supervised the market and regulated weights and measures, the standards of which were generally deposited in the city hall. The market was, moreover, the source of revenue, for the city rented the stalls and imposed a series of taxes upon the sale of merchandise.

The market was generally weekly. Thither the peasants came to sell their products: eggs, butter, fruit, *etc*. Ulm was famous for linen, Constance for hemp, Erfurt for the pastel, which was highly prized for dyeing purposes. The market had rigorous regulations. On that day all sale was prohibited anywhere else. Sale could not begin before the ringing of the bell in the town hall. The cities took great precautions to assure the success of the market. Purchasers were forbidden to leave the city before the merchants had, and the local bourgeois could only purchase what was necessary for their own consumption. Moreover, retailers could not purchase until the consumers had made their purchases. At the time of the Council of Constance in 1415 an immense floating population of clerks and courtisans were drawn to the city and it became necessary to open a special market for the sale of eggs in order that the poor could get them as well as the rich. The market on the opening day was the scene of extraordinary animation. Its extent was greater than to-day, although the population was less. There were special markets for grain, for cattle, for horses, for hay, for hops, *etc*. The last were very important in a country where beer formed the chief drink. There was often a market for woad, that plant so· much used for dyeing and so precious before the introduction of indigo into Europe. These markets were frequented not every week, but every year at determined dates intermediate between the annual fairs of spring and fall. They were often held in special buildings. In the fifteenth century in German cities there were often grain halls, and the floor of the city hall and of the *Kaufhaus* frequently served as a special market-place.

It is necessary to say a word about the *Kaufhaus,* for every city possessed one of these in addition to its *Rathhaus*, or city hall. The oldest known *Kaufhaus* is that of Mainz, dating from 1314 and demolished in 1813. But they are found everywhere: in 1355 at Cologne, and in 1358 at Strassburg. Sometimes these *Kaufhaüser* were popularly called *"Die Gred,"* a word without doubt coming from *Grad* because the market was established along the banks of a river. The outside merchant could only unpack his goods in the *Kaufhaus,* and there he sold wholesale to local merchants. There he paid the city toll so that the market street was sometimes called the *Tollstrasse.* In Strassburg it was called the *rue de la Douane* until the German capture. The cities appointed officials to govern the *Kaufhaus.* The bulky merchandise was sold on the ground floor; the more valuable goods on the floors above. The cellars were generally of huge extent, and the buildings very large. For example, the conclave which elected Pope Martin V in 1418 met in the *Kaufhaus* at Constance.

The impression which these cities made upon foreigners was great. The Russian metropolitan Isidore crossed Germany when going to the council of Florence in 1430, and was mightily astonished at the sight of such cities as Nuremberg and Augsburg. But he came from Russia. At the same time an Italian gives us other testimony. Aeneas Sylvius Piccolomini asserted that Germany had never been so flourishing. He praised Cologne for its admirable churches, its *Rathhof,* its monuments. He admired Strassburg with its many canals of limpid water, which reminded him of Venice, but a gracious Venice because it was without the nauseating odors of the lagoons. In Strassburg were many churches and convents, ecclesiastical houses, and palaces of rich merchants, good enough for a king to live in. Munich and Nuremberg appealed to him in like manner. Finally he ended with these words: "No country of Europe has more beautiful and more pleasant cities than Germany. They are so fresh and smiling that it seems as if they were built yesterday." Macchiavelli in his *Discourse on Livy* gave high praise to the German towns for the honesty of the citizens and the efficiency of municipal administration. He ascribed their virtue to the fact that the Germans were "uncorrupted" by the Italians, French and Spaniards, and, further, the German towns did not tolerate in their midst nobles or burghers trying to ape the nobles.

The free city of the Middle Ages in Germany had to bear the cost of maintaining a foreign policy and waging war in defense of itself. Hence it had to bear conditions and study problems which no modern city has to do. In 1387–88 Nuremberg spent for purposes of war 80,000 "pounds of Halle" in fourteen months, a sum triple its other annual expenses. On the other hand, a town often seized the opportunity afforded by the political or financial embarrassment of a neighboring noble to round out its territory, or in the case of a noble who still retained remnants of taxing rights over it, to purchase them of him. An operation of this kind in 1427 with Albert of Brandenburg cost Nuremberg 137,000 pounds in weight of metal alone, without taking into consideration the difference in the purchasing power of money then and now. And this was at a time when the population of Nuremberg probably did not exceed 15,000. For in 1449 when a census was taken, the population amounted to 25,000.

The political instability of the times and the rudimentary experience of the burghers in town administration made the preparation of a budget impossible. The towns lived from hand to mouth, relying on taxes and loans from their citizens, and when in great distress resorting to confiscation and pillage of the property of the Jews. In 1385 on a concerted day all thirty-six towns which were members of the Swabian League imprisoned the Jews until "satisfactory arrangements" for their release were made. Nuremberg being at this time indebted to the local Jews for a loan of 7,000 pounds thus cancelled its debt. The emperor Wenzel, the official protector of the Jews throughout Germany, since they constituted a portion of his regalia, had sanctioned this spoliation in advance for a bribe of 40,000 florins, of which Nuremberg contributed 15,000.

The German towns early had recourse to two kinds of taxes, direct and indirect. A direct tax was levied on comestibles entering the town. This tax, corresponding to the French *tonlieu*, was called *Ungelt*,[4] a term expressing the popular aversion to it as emphatically as the French word *maltôte* did. Many of these municipal tariffs have been preserved, the oldest being one of Augsburg for the year 1276. We have long lists of articles taxed according to weight or measure— lists which throw interesting light on the nature and circulation of commodities.

We find the *Ungelt* imposed on wine and beer, on cheese, grain, salt, metal wares and textiles. It was commonest, however, on wine and beer. A large proportion of the amount collected was consumed in maintenance of the town wall, always and everywhere an absolute necessity. But in spite of this fact the *Ungelt* was always highly unpopular. Time and again one finds it described as *"iniqua exactio quae ungelt dicitur,"* etc. The medieval burgher prided himself on the exactness and vituperative nature of his language when talking about the *Ungelt.* Every change in the rate of its imposition or extension of its application was greeted with fury. An honest chronicler of Augsburg, Bernard Zink, who lived in the latter half of the fifteenth century, records how he found "an old book" in which the history of a great riot in 1397 was related. The weavers, the bakers, the coopers, and

---

[4] The medieval Latin word for it, *indebitum,* indicates the same thing.

the smiths united to compel the abolition of an *Ungelt* which the town fathers imposed. Zink himself was an eye-witness of a similar rising in 1466, and gives at length the speeches of the leaders of the mob. Popular opposition was not merely due to the weight of the *Ungelt*. It was also a protest of the lower classes in the towns against the graft which often was attached to its collection. The *Ungelt* was also frequently a cause of disaffection with the clergy, who claimed immunity for the wine which they sold from their vineyards.

Sometimes the *Ungelt* was not collected in money but was "taken out" of the commodity itself. But this was not common, for a money economy very largely obtained in the towns. In South Germany until late in the fifteenth century the revenue arising from wine was greater than that from beer. Thus Ulm in 1478 collected 722 pounds on wine and only 5 on beer. In North Germany, on the other hand, where the vine would not grow, the revenue from beer was greater than that from wine. Hated and detested as it was, the *Ungelt* was the chief source of municipal revenue. At Nuremberg in the fourteenth century it was one-third of the town revenue; at Frankfort-on-the-Main it was one-fifth in 1404. Fifty years later at Basel it amounted to one-half of the town's income, and at Augsburg it was much more than this.

The relative importance of indirect *vs.* direct taxes in the German cities varied greatly according to situation and population. Cologne and Mainz and Strassburg gravitated towards indirect taxes by preference. But the general inclination was to preserve taxes on consumption almost everywhere. In Lübeck the property tax steadily fell between 1376 and 1405. By 1462 it was negligible. The following figures show the decline of the *Schoss* there:

Year	Total receipts	Receipts from the *Schoss*	Percentage relative to total revenue
1407–8	14,704	7,900	54%
1421–2	19,384	8,132	42
1430–1	22,810	8,149	36
1445–6	33,586	3,210	10
1470–1	42,819	2,975	7
1500–1	21,422	1,888	9
1520–1	52,753	1,380	2.5

The direct property tax, widely called the *Bede* (from *bitten*, to demand, was known as *Lösung* (release) in Nuremberg; *Gewerf* in Strassburg, Freiburn and Constance; as *Schaetzung* or estimation in the Rhenish towns, and as *Schoss* in towns along the Baltic like Lübeck. This obviously bore upon the upper and wealthy classes only.

In the case of taxes upon property which was rented to others, the tax of course was passed on to the tenant in the form of increased rent.

Some towns had municipal windmills on the walls and municipal sawmills which were rented out, as were also garden plots in the dry moats and house sites on or under the walls.

The problem of crime in the cities of Germany in the Middle Ages was probably greater than anywhere else in Europe, for the reason that Germany was so divided into separate principalities—feudal, ecclesiastical, urban—into one of which a fugitive from justice might flee and be immune from arrest by the authorities he had outraged. Goods stolen in Nuremberg could be sold in Furth on Bayreuth territory, almost within sight of the city walls. The very prosperity of the German towns attracted the criminal element. The *Nuremberg Malefactors' Books*[5] throw ample light on this subject.

Here came skilled cutpurses who had perhaps learnt their trade in a regular school (we read of such), card-sharpers and jewel thieves, impostors of every kind. Nürnberg was a centre whose wealth drew adventurers from all parts. They were ingenious and versatile. . . . Pretended knowl-edge of the unseen world was a never-failing card. Many rogues traded on their acquaintance with talismans, on their power of divining hidden treasure. The city's underworld was recruited from among home-bred sharks as well. The transition from legitimate to unlawful art was easy and nowhere were the legitimate arts better taught than at Nürnberg. . . . We read of locksmiths turned housebreakers, of goldsmiths turned coiners. . . . Nürnberg was rich and skilful; her rogues, native and imported, had a superb education and superb opportunities for crime. She was, of course, without police in the modern sense. . . . Hence no doubt one reason for the savagery of the code, which punished all felonies and many misde-meanors with death and practically condemned all prisoners by the un-sparing use of torture. Those who have visited the Burg at Nürnberg and seen the instruments of torment can form some faint idea of what this procedure and these death penalties could mean. It is easy to forget against what a world of violence and skill they had to war.[6]

In the matter of the Jews there was a wide difference between their legal status according to the laws of the Church and the edicts of the emperors and their actual condition in concrete dealings with their neighbors. Violent molestation was the exception, not the rule. They suffered most during the Mongol invasions in 1241 and the Flagellant outbreak which accompanied the Black Death. It was to the interest of the towns to maintain a taxable population and even to encourage their immigration. Although never entirely freed from imperial taxation,

[5] Theodor Hampe, *Crime and Punishment in Germany,* translated by Malcolm Letts. As illustrated by the Nuremberg Malefactors' Books. (London, 1930.)
[6] From a review in *London Times Literary Supplement,* January 2, 1930.

as a part of the imperial regalian right, actually the Jews in every city were subject to local legislation for or against them. On the whole their lot was not a hard one until the fifteenth century. At the beginning of the fourteenth century we find Frankfort Jews borrowing from the city chest and at the end of the same century the municipal government borrowing from the Jews. As late as 1458 the Jews of Frankfort dwelt in a good quarter of the town. The first ghetto, which the Jews bitterly called "New Egypt," was built in 1462. The change from measurable toleration to intolerance late in the fifteenth century may fundamentally be ascribed to economic jealousy, just as anti-clericalism was due to economic prejudice.

CHAPTER VIII

EASTERN EUROPE—BOHEMIA, POLAND, HUNGARY, WALLACHIA, MOLDAVIA

BOHEMIA, Poland and Hungary formed a bloc of lesser states in Eastern Central Europe whose historical and cultural attachments were primarily with Germany, but which, however, retained their own national life and culture, and from their situation naturally had commercial relations with Russia and Byzantium. Of these three Bohemia was most intimately attached to Germany, for the upper Elbe gave it direct communication with Germany. In natural products, especially in grain, timber and, above all, metals, Bohemia was a self-sufficient country. But salt had to be imported, and this was largely furnished by Venetians, who every year came to Bohemia with long strings of mules bearing salt evaporated in salt pans along the Venetian lagoons. Linen goods, leather work, especially gloves, and in the fifteenth century paper-making were Bohemian industries.

Commerce and industry were mostly in the hands of Germans settled in Bohemia. German immigrants cleared the forests, exploited the mines and plied the skilled trades. The German language so far penetrated into the public and commercial life of Bohemia that the native Czech idiom was current only among the lower classes and in the rural regions. There was an important colony of German merchants in Prague as far back as the thirteenth century. In the middle of the next century Venetian merchants pushed in in such numbers that a house or hotel was established for them on the bridge over the Moldau. It was called the *Walhenhof*,[1] like the German *fondaco* at Venice. This commerce of Bohemia with Venice was especially brisk during the reign of Charles IV (1348–76). One route to Prague followed by these Venetian merchants was through Vienna, where there was a *Stapelplatz*. The other passed via Nuremberg and Regensburg. Charles IV, whose favorite residence was Prague, did much for the material embellishment of this chief city of Bohemia. He aspired to make it the greatest mart of Eastern Central Europe, and to that end dreamed of connecting the upper Moldau with the Danube by means of a canal. The merchants of Venice exchanged wares out of the Orient and Italian-manufactured goods in Prague for furs and amber, which

---

[1] According to Erdmannsdorfer, p. 33, in Slavic "Voloh" or "Vloh" (Woloh or Wloh) means "Italian."

found their way to Prague from Russia and the Baltic coast. Charles IV's revenues were so great that he could afford to pay 500,000 ducats for the Mark of Brandenburg, which he bought in 1373 from Otto the Lazy, the last Bavarian margrave.

The chief source of Bohemia's wealth was in its mines, which produced iron, copper, tin and especially silver. At the end of the Middle Ages Bohemia was the Nevada of Europe. The greatest of the silver mines was that of Kuttenberg, opened in 1237. Its annual production in the beginning of the fourteenth century was 50,000 pounds. This wealth of precious metal explains the splendor of the reigns of Ottocar II (1253–78) and of Charles IV (1347–78), who owed his election as emperor, as did also his worthless son Wenzel, to the bribes he was able to offer. The king, the court, the high clergy and great nobles were all shareholders in this mine. Kuttenberg, Deutschbrod, Iglau and other mining towns were German communities. German miners flocked into Bohemia. But in due time it became evident that this prosperity of Bohemia was more apparent than real. While it provided capital and promoted immigration, the flood of silver wrought a revolution in prices by the inflation of the currency similar to that which took place on a far larger scale in the sixteenth century when the mines of Spanish America flooded Europe with bullion.

The result was economic and social discontent among the working classes, especially the weavers, commingled with religio-socialistic or communistic ideas, which came to a head in the Hussite wars of the fifteenth century (1419–36). These wars reduced the population, ruined Bohemia's commerce, prostrated industry, devastated agriculture and all but destroyed the country. Before this disaster nearly two-thirds of the soil of Bohemia had belonged to small proprietors and free peasants, who were ruined by the wars and whose posessions fell into the hands of great proprietors, so that a new serfdom developed. Thousands of the population fled the country and became wanderers, seeking for new homes in Germany and even in France. This was the time when the Gypsies first appeared in Central and Western Europe, and in the popular mind these Bohemian exiles were often confused with the Gypsies. Indeed in the French language to this day the word "Bohème" signifies a gypsy.

The political history of Poland in the fourteenth and fifteenth centuries was a very fluctuating one, a condition which is reflected in the history of its commerce. Under the last Piast kings, the kingdom, if not dismembered, was a loose agglomeration of provinces. Only the ecclesiastical organization held the kingdom together. When Casimir the Great died in 1370 a short union of Poland with Hungary followed under Louis the Great. Finally in 1386 his daughter Hedwig married Ladislas II, Jagello, grand duke of Lithuania. This union of what were formerly two hostile peoples and territories under a strong ruler resuscitated Poland.

The fact that Poland was a land without natural frontiers, and ringed roundabout by jealous or even hostile neighbors was her misfortune. The chief of these were the Teutonic Knights in Prussia and the duke of Pomerania, who cut Poland off from access to the Baltic. Accordingly Poland was almost at the mercy of its neighbors for ingress or egress of Polish trade. Thorn, Danzig and especially Breslau competed with Cracow and Lemberg, the most important Polish towns. Exportation and importation were in the hands of outsiders like the Hansers and the Venetians, who came up from Prague to Cracow or else over from Breslau. Other notable outsiders who traded in Poland were Armenian merchants, who came up the Dniester or Pruth rivers through Red Ruthenia (or Galicia) from Constantinople and the Black Sea area. Before the Mongols destroyed Kiev in 1240 it had been the farthest north that these progressive oriental merchants had traded. Deprived of that once great mart, they pushed on to Cracow and especially to Lemberg, where a large colony of Armenians became permanently settled, and where their descendants are still found. Even the Turkish occupation of Southeastern Europe did not arrest the prosperity of these Armenians.

As in the towns of Bohemia, so in those of Poland, the burgher population was largely composed of Germans. Between them, the rural peasantry, and the Polish magnates, a great gulf was fixed. The introduction of this German middle class into Poland was largely due to the Tartar invasions in which so many Polish towns and hamlets were destroyed. For then Boleslav the Pious encouraged German settlers in the towns to revive Polish commerce and industry again. The exports of Poland were almost wholly those of a natural sort like furs, hides, tallow, wool and a coarse cloth made of flax.

Louis the Great (1370–82) was compelled to conciliate the Polish magnates in order to carry out his political designs and so conceded many privileges to them in spite of the protest of the towns and the murmurs of the peasantry. Casimir the Great felt the futility of wasting Polish efforts against the Teutonic Knights and the duke of Pomerania, and turned his energy towards the East in hope of getting closer Polish connection with the Black Sea trade. He was the first Polish king who pushed the frontier eastward beyond the San river and acquired possession of the upper course of the Dniester and Pruth rivers, a route which soon became known as the "Armenian Way."

Besides these Orientals we find, quite unexpectedly, a considerable number of Italians in Poland. The salt deposits of Bochnia and Wieliczka were ceded in the fourteenth century as a monopoly to a Genoese company, whose headquarters were in Cracow. Fattinati, one of these

concessionaires, was the great capitalist in Poland in the reign of
Ladislas Jagello. About 1393 he also possessed at Kolomea a warehouse crammed with merchandise, especially silks. From Bruges, where
the Genoese had a branch bank, Genoese financiers came to Poland
on Hanseatic ships in the fourteenth century; and in the fifteenth we
find Venetians and Florentines, the latter agents of the banking house
of the Medici who were interested in salt concessions. Progressive
Genoese merchants also came up into Poland from Kaffa on the Black
Sea through Red Russia along with Armenian merchants. These
traders—two of them named Filippo and Jacopo—brought silk and
wine from the Morea, notably malmsey, but soon got mining and salt
concessions and gradually displaced the Jews in Poland as tax collectors. The Venetian merchants who found their way into Poland
over Nuremberg and Prague could not compete with the Genoese,
to whom possession of Kaffa gave a great advantage.

In the fifteenth century the defeat of the Teutonic Knights at Tannenberg (1410) and the subsequent (1466) cession of West Prussia
and Ermeland to Poland at last gave Poland an open door upon the
Baltic through Danzig, which though technically a free city, in a commercial sense became a port of Poland. In the time of Casimir Jagello
(1447–92) enormous quantities of grain, timber, ship stores and hides
went out through Danzig to Flanders and England. In 1471 Casimir's
son Vladislav became king of Bohemia, and the union of Bohemia,
Hungary and Poland seemed likely to be consummated in the near
future. If this triple alliance could have been accomplished, Germany,
the Turks, and Russia would all have been held in check and a great
state created, which would have touched and tapped the trade of the
Baltic, the Black Sea and the Adriatic. But it was not destined to be,
for the elements of discord within it were too great.

Unlike Bohemia, which was almost wholly mountainous, unlike
Poland, which was almost wholly plain, forest and swamp, the kingdom of Hungary was sharply divided between plain and mountain.
This double nature of Hungary's physiography sharply distinguished
the country's economic history. In the great plain of the Danube and
the Theiss cattle-raising and the industrial arts which spring therefrom, like leather work, tallow-making, etc., prevailed. Here the land
was owned in immense ranches by the nobles, who were great magnates; and the villages were peopled by servile herdsmen and shepherds. The markets were mostly cattle markets, weekly or monthly,
and were situated at points convenient for the ranches roundabout.
The appointed local day might be a Tuesday or Wednesday, or Friday or Saturday. In process of time a permanent village grew up in
such a locality, with the singular result that the hamlet was called by
the name of the day of the week on which the market fell. Szombat

(Saturday) is a place-name of fourteen villages in Hungary; Szerda (Wednesday) of nineteen; Pentek (Friday) of seven.

Even in Transylvania one finds similar instances. But Transylvania is mountainous, and the chief industry was mining. For after the discovery of silver in Bohemia, the discovery of similar deposits in the Tatra and the Zips rapidly followed, with the result that the dominant population in Transylvania was composed of German (or Saxon) miners. Transylvanian place-names are predominantly German. Hermannstadt was, in the Middle Ages and yet is, the most important town. It was once supposed that these Transylvanian Germans were important middlemen in the transit of trade from Constantinople and Central Europe. But we now know this view was erroneous. For there was no important commerce up the lower Danube in the early Middle Ages. The Avar, Slav, and Bulgar inroads into this region between the sixth and eleventh centuries effectually destroyed it, and the route was not opened until the destruction of the Bulgarian Empire in 1018 by Basil II. But the lower Danube route never seriously competed with Venice. Even in the Golden Bull granted by King Andrew II in 1222, the evidence of Hungarian and Transylvanian commerce is not great. What outside wares were imported were chiefly brought in by Venetian merchants through Zara, the seizure of which by Venice in 1204 deprived Hungary of its only seaport. Sigismund, king of Hungary from 1385, emperor after 1411, hated the Venetians who barred the Hungarians from the Dalmatian coast, and in order to humble Venice, turned to Genoa. His ambition was to open a route via the lower Danube and to effect a junction with the Black Sea ports of Genoa in the Crimea, especially Tana and Kaffa, and in Constantinople at Pera. In 1418 two imperial agents were sent to Kaffa and Pera. But the design was frustrated from the beginning by the hostility of the Tartars of the Kiptchak and the progress of the Turks, who steadily engrossed the territories of southwestern Europe and cut them off from connection with the West.

The Byzantine Empire from the thirteenth century forward was in a state of progressive dissolution, with the result that its border provinces in Europe fell away one by one. In this wise two principalities under native princes called *voevodes* or *voivads* came into being in Southeastern Europe, Wallachia and Moldavia, which in the nineteenth century were destined to be fused into the kingdom of Roumania. Of these two principalities Wallachia was founded first by a vassal of the king of Hungary about 1290. In subsequent years its territory was extended more and more towards the Black Sea, occupying all the area comprised in the delta of the Danube (Dobrudga) and part of Bessarabia. The chief town was Silistria. Moldavia was established about the same time in the mountainous region of Transylvania, but its consolidation was more difficult than that of Wallachia. It paid tribute alternately to Poland, to Hungary, and finally to the Turks in the fifteenth century, as did also Wallachia. Stock-raising was almost the sole industry. Wealth was estimated in terms of horses and cattle. Genoese merchants, before the Turkish conquest, did a brisk business in velvets and silks, for the Roumanian nobles were excessively fond of this sort of finery. The Roumanian town of Giurgevo derived its name from St. George, the patron saint of Genoa. The capitals of these two principalities slowly moved from West to East, in Wallachia finally becoming fixed at Bucharest, in Moldavia at Jassy. Bucharest being situated upon the main highway between the Genoese trading-post at Kaffa on the Black Sea and the Germanized towns of Galicia, in the fifteenth century grew into a not unimportant place of commerce; but Jassy remained nothing but a halting point for merchants. These merchants were mostly Germans or Armenians, for the Vlachs were exclusively a shepherd people. Wallachia and Moldavia were rich in raw products, but of primitive commerce and undeveloped industries. The prosperity of both principalities was almost destroyed by the invasions of the Turks. For after the great Turkish victory at Nikopolis in 1396 Wallachia, Moldavia, and all the territory on the right bank of the lower Danube was tributary to the sultan. Hungary's own day of disaster began with the catastrophe at Varna (1444), and the battle of Mohacs (1526) nearly obliterated the kingdom.

CHAPTER IX

AT the end of the thirteenth century Italy was a portion of the Holy Roman Empire. But the relation was only nominal. The Interregnum ceased with the election of Rudolph of Habsburg in 1273. The new emperor made peace with Charles of Anjou in 1278, and in the following year renounced all claim to the Romagna. Thus the loss of Central and Southern Italy was recognized by the Empire as a *fait accompli*. In the North, however, the emperor still preserved the right, at least theoretically, to appoint imperial vicars, to confer offices and titles, to claim the ancient regalia except in so far as they had been curtailed by the peace of Constance in 1183. The tradition of the Expeditio Romana was perpetuated without being effective. When the emperor came down into Italy the towns usually opened their gates and many nobles joined him. But these were merely ceremonial tours. Now and then an incautious ruler like Henry VII and Ludwig IV attempted to his peril to interfere in the fierce partisan strife within and between the Italian towns.

The dominant political and economic feature of Italy at the end of the Middle Ages was the vitality of town life. Italy being without rulers, the city-state emerged. In this Italy was like Germany. But there is an important difference to be observed. In Germany the nobles were excluded from the city. In Italy the nobles had huge fortified town houses like castles and the distinction between nobles and bourgeois was a blurred one.

Everywhere the dominant society was bourgeois. The old feudal nobility had lost its political authority in the twelfth and thirteenth centuries to the bourgeois of the cities, and been ruined by the economic revolution due to the decline of agriculture, a natural economy —on which feudal authority had for centuries reposed—and the rise of commerce and industry. One cannot separate economic revolution from social revolution. The old noble families when their castles in the country proved uninhabitable removed to the towns, where their sons and daughters married into the families of wealthy bourgeois. In Florence after the triumph of the Guelfs in 1267 knighthood was liberally bestowed on bourgeois. For the parvenu bourgeois aspired to social distinction. "Scratch a knight and you will find a merchant," the Italian historian Salvemini has written. The degradation of knighthood was further increased by the practice of the winning political party conferring titles as a reward of party loyalty.

"After 1330 in Florence the floodgates were thrown open. . . . Citizens became knights who could not break a straw, much less a lance; men upon whom, in Boccaccio's words, knighthood sat as a saddle on a pig, who were as devoted to knightly virtues as the devil to the cross."

The administration comprised a town council (*credenzia*), a small number of executive officials especially for war, justice, and taxation (usually denominated consuls [*consules*]), and the local board of trade, an association of the chief merchants called *consules mercatorum*.

In some towns we find various governments side by side or in apposition. Milan is a type. In 1198 the Credenzia Sancti Ambrosii appeared. Before this there had been two parties, the nobles and the people. The latter split in two and the artisans formed a separate group known as the Credenzia Sancti Ambrosii. After 1215 the podestà of Milan interfered in the struggle between the upper bourgeois or *popolo grasso* and the Credenzia, so that there were three governments competing for mastery.

The towns did not dominate all the territory, so that in the areas between them we find local authorities like feudal nobles, free proprietors, and free villages. This condition was less prevalent in Lombardy and Tuscany than in Piedmont and the Alpine regions. The free city in Italy, once so vivid and energetic in its life, survived only in small and remote mountain towns off of the beaten tracks of commerce. Southern Italy was devoid of independent town life. The Angevin monarchy was practically absolute except in so far as it had to compromise with a bellicose feudality. Naples was a kingdom in which political absolutism was more important than commerce and industry. It was the most backward, the most medieval part of Italy.

This altered political condition was due to the chronic civil wars. It is hard to say of these whether they were the cause or the effect of the division into parties everywhere. Were these factions hostile because they had been opposed to each other before? Or were they formed as the result and effect of the civil strife? It is difficult to pronounce. But it is clear that every town had two bitterly rival families or groups of families, who had first battened on the conflict between the popes and the emperors as Guelfs or Ghibellines, and when that conflict was terminated continued to fight each other. But by then the old party names had lost all their original significance. Sometimes further cleavage took place. For example, in Florence when the Ghibellines— of whom Dante was the greatest victim—were expelled by the Guelfs, the Guelfs split into two factions, which fought it out again on the backs of the populace.

It was this anarchic condition which gave rise to the podestà. The office was of imperial origin. Frederick Barbarossa had created a great number of them in the twelfth century. In the next century the institution acquired a new character. The podestà was introduced into many towns as a non-partisan ruler thereof and above faction. Bologna, a city of legists and jurists, seems to have provided the new model. The term of the podestà was usually not more than a year, often only six months. He brought with him his own staff of administrative officials and took an oath neither to favor nor fear any one in the community. At Piacenza such a staff comprised twenty-two persons, of whom seven were judges and three knights, in addition to a company of twenty-five men-at-arms. Almost every Italian town in the late thirteenth century except Rome, Venice and Genoa had its podestà at one time or another.

In the fourteenth century a new power arose. This was the *condottiere*, or soldier of fortune. Hitherto the towns had waged their wars with their own militia and their own knights. But from the time of Henry VII's Italian expedition in 1309 the use of hired train bands formed in companies and battalions came into practice. Most of this soldiery was composed of German *Lanzknechte*, Swiss pikemen, English or French adventurers out of France. Not until late were Italian recruits introduced. The employment of mercenary forces at this time was general throughout Europe, but in Italy the practice acquired a particular importance. Owing to constant warfare between the Italian towns the service of mercenary troops became more and more in demand, so that finally the greatest of these captains became Italian princes. The Gonzaga and the Sforza dynasties are examples. Some of these *condottieri* paid with their lives for their great adventure, like Carmagnola in the market square of Venice. Others like Francesco Sforza rode to fortune on the tide.

The despotisms all tended towards one type. But they did not cover all Italy. The republics must be sharply distinguished as a second type, of which the most notable were the two maritime republics of Venice and Genoa, and the republic of Florence. Lesser republics were Siena and Lucca. The physiognomy, so to speak, of these varied according to local geographical conditions. Venice and Genoa traded with the Levant; Florence, being inland, developed industry first, then commerce, and finally banking.

Unlike the despotisms, which all tended towards one type, the form and structure of these commonwealths varied. Venice was severely oligarchic in form of government. Genoa and Florence were democratic rather than aristocratic. But this democratic attitude was a wholly relative one, the larger part of the population having no voice in administration. Citizenship was hereditary in a limited number of families. In Florence, for example, a bourgeois had to belong to one of the major arts or gilds. For if the tendency in Renaissance society was towards the fusion of upper wealthy bourgeois families with impecunious nobles, on the other hand a sharp cleavage prevailed between the upper stratum and the lower stratum of the populace. The new aristocracy was composed of rich merchants, bankers, employers of labor, or entrepreneurs on a large scale, while the commonalty comprised the petty tradesman, the artisan class, the wage earner, the casual laborer, and the proletariat. The cleavage was due to economic forces, not to political conditions. Everywhere the artisans were grouped into gilds or arts. But the condition was one of sharp differentiation between the "major arts" and the "minor arts." The former were composed of merchants like drapers, mercers, spicers, apothecaries, *etc.*, who were not manual toilers. The latter were weavers, fullers, dyers, tanners, joiners, *etc.* The distinction was both of technique and of class. The Florentine historian Varchi accurately describes this qualification:

All Florentine burghers were obliged to rank in one of the twenty-one arts; that is, no one could be a burgher of Florence unless he or his ancestors had been approved, and matriculated in one of these arts, whether they prʿcticed it or not. . . . The arts were these: 1. Judges and notaries. 2. Calimala, or cloth industry. 3. Banking. 4. Wool. 5. Silk. 6. Physicians and apothecaries. 7. Furriers. 8. Shoemakers. 9. Blacksmiths. 10. Butchers. 11. Linen drapers and clothesmen. 12. Masons and stonecutters. 13. Vintners. 14. Innkeepers. 15. Oil sellers, rope makers. 16. Hosiers. 17. Armorers. 18. Locksmiths. 19. Saddlers. 20. Carpenters. 21. Bakers.

The last fourteen were called the Lesser Arts. The inclination of the *arti maggiori* everywhere was to identify themselves with the influential families and ruling party in the town, and thus get a share in the government and shut out the common people. What began as an economic differentiation thus became a social cleavage and terminated as a political conflict between local aristocracy or oligarchy and local democracy. This condition was most acute in Florence where it culminated in the rising of the lower classes or Ciompi in 1379. But it was not peculiar to Florence or to Italy. Everywhere in Europe we find the same mixed economic-social-political phenomenon. It was so important that a separate chapter later in this book is devoted to its history.

In every town class antagonism was bitter and each class fought to acquire exclusive control of the administration. The nobles were at feud with the *popolo grasso* or rich bourgeoisie; the *popolo minuto* with the *popolo grasso*. In the conflict the proud, but frequently impoverished nobles, married into wealthy middle class families and thus was formed a "patriciate," which was politically and economically supreme. The greater gilds controlled the town government. They were careful to give themselves and their class privileges and to impose the taxes upon the common people. The *popolo minuto* were politically disfranchised; their gilds were nothing but workingmen's associations subject to the greater gilds or *arti maggiori* which regulated wages and hours of work. In a word the familiar conflict of capital *vs.* labor, of employer or entrepreneur and workingman, was already staged by the fourteenth century. By the end of that century the patriciate-capitalist class was dominant, not only in the Lombard and Tuscan towns, but in Europe as a whole. In those few cities where the popular party triumphed, exclusion from franchise and public office, and even exile, was imposed. In Pistoia in 1285 the victorious lesser gilds proscribed all members of the *arti maggiori* along with the nobles. In Parma in 1284 the upper middle class (*otiosi*) were disfranchised.

But this conflict was politically ruinous to the rule of the patriciate, for it paved the way in many cities of Tuscany, Lombardy and the Romagna, such as Florence, Milan, Ferrara, Urbino, for the establishment of despotism, whether the despot was a local dynast like the marquises of Ferrara, the princes of Urbino, and the Malatesta of Rimini; or a former imperial vicar, who built an illegal power upon the basis of his office, like the Della Scala in Mantua and the Visconti in Milan; or a podestà who converted his authority into a one-man power; or a soldier of fortune like Castruccio Castracene, the hero of Macchiavelli's romance, and Francesco Sforza, who supplanted the Visconti; or a papal nephew intruded into rulership, like the Riario in Forli and the Farnese in Parma; or a citizen of eminence in this town or that who generally by his wealth acquired despotic ascendancy, like the Medici in Florence, the Bentovogli in Bologna, the Baglioni in Perugia.

In most of these cases great wealth was the original source of despotic ascendancy. It was not uncommon to buy cities together with their signory. Thus the Rossi bought Parma for 35,000 florins in 1333; the Appiani sold Pisa; Astorre Manfredi sold Faenza and Imola in 1377; in 1444 Galeazzo Malatesta sold Pesaro to Alessandro Sforza, and Fossembrone to Urbino; in 1461 Cervia was sold to Venice by the same family. . . . Towns at last came to have their market value. It was known that Bologna was worth 200,000 florins, Parma 60,000, Arezzo 40,000, Lucca 30,000. . . . The history of the bourgeois despots proves that Italy in the fifteenth century was undergoing a natural process of determination toward tyranny. . . . She instinctively obeyed a law of social evolution by which princes had to be substituted for municipalities at the end of those fierce internal conflicts and exhausting wars of jealousy which closed the Middle Ages. . . . Rank had nothing to do with their claims. Bastards . . . who had no pedigree, merchants like the Medici, the son of a peasant like Francesco Sforza, a rich usurer . . . had almost equal chances with nobles of the ancient houses of Este, Visconti or Malatesta. . . . Despotism in Italy, as in ancient Greece, was democratic. It recruited its ranks from all classes and erected its thrones upon the sovereignty of the peoples it oppressed.[1]

It is impossible not to believe that these usurpations were approved by the great majority of the inhabitants of these tumultuary communities. They were interested in commerce, industry and banking, vexed and worn out by these intestine feuds, and wanted peace and a firm and durable government instead of constant quarrels between Guelfs and Ghibellines, between nobles and the common people. Tyranny meant security for them, even if heavy taxes were imposed. Politically the rise of the Renaissance tyrannies was an evidence of the exhaustion of the factions within the towns and a reaction against oligarchy.

Almost invariably in history political struggle against oligarchy takes the form of a fiscal war. The Greek and the Renaissance despots alike employed taxation as a club to coerce the rich and the powerful in the community. Hence the income taxes imposed by the Visconti and the Medici. This practice had the added advantage that it provided them with great wealth, which was an indispensable instrument to a prince whose rule rested on no legal title, but was derived from force and usurpation. Moreover, at the same time this wealth was used to lull discontent among the masses. The magnificent palaces and public buildings erected by the Italian princes, the public improvements promoted by them—like roads and canals—were in part intended to provide labor for the unemployed. This trick of government-provided labor as a means of economic relief and as a social safety valve is old in history and may be traced back to the ancient monarchies of Asia. The policy is still with us, and at least it has more reason to sustain it than the dole system now so current in European countries which, like the ancient Roman practice of *"panem et circenses*—bread and the circus," breeds an idle proletariat.

The only two states in Italy which preserved themselves from despotism were the two maritime republics of Venice and Genoa, but in neither of these was liberty preserved. The intense commercial and industrial rivalry between the city-states of the Renaissance led to incessant war between them. This was a heritage from the epoch of the Crusades.

The last class of mediaeval wars—namely, the commercial—were intimately connected with, and in part a continuation of, the Crusades. The Italians had regarded the conquest of the Orient as a commercial venture;

[1] J. A. Symonds, *Age of the Despots*, pp. 89, 90.

the Venetians utilized the Fourth Crusade to establish their commercial monopoly at Constantinople. From this arose prolonged and desperate wars, especially between Genoa and Venice, whose common object was the advancement of their own commerce through the destruction of a dangerous competitor. . . . No one can read Macchiavelli's *History of Florence* or the early chronicles of any mediaeval city without perceiving that commercial rivalry shaped their whole policy. . . . The history of the intricate and incessant wars between Pisa and Florence . . . is merely an illustration of what went on all over Europe, especially in Italy, Germany and the Low Countries, where commercial interests were strongest. In fact, the history of the commercial cities from the eleventh to the fifteenth century reveals, on a small scale, all the features which have characterized the history of commercial nations from the fifteenth to the nineteenth centuries. The one all-important difference is that, by a wider division of labor and greater activity of the central government, the economic unit has grown from the city-state to the national-state.[2]

The history of Florence clearly illustrates this policy. The thirteenth century was a period of transition and preparation, prophetic of the future growth of her commerce and industry. In the beginning Florence's attitude toward other states was conciliatory and aimed to repress interurban reprisal. After 1250, with the accession of popular government there was unveiled a vision of mercantile supremacy by overcoming the competition of rival neighbors which led to wars. There was no knowledge in the Middle Ages of the laws of equity, of what to-day we call international law. Nothing seemed more legitimate than to close all passage to a neighbor, or to impose upon him prohibitive, intolerable taxes. From this sprang hatreds and quarrels without end, which the right of the strongest alone could settle. While Siena, Volterra and Pisa are invariably hostile, why did Arezzo oscillate between Florence and Siena? Because she is at an equal distance from them. Why did she end by pronouncing against Florence? Because she could hinder Siena from communicating with the South, while she overwhelmed with taxes the Florentine merchants going in the same direction, who could not avoid Siena except by passing through Arezzo. The same motives which unleashed war cemented alliances. Lucca was too jealous of Pisa not to be the ally of the Florentines. Genoa, having large interests on the sea, hated Pisa, which disputed its domination with her. Genoa broke her friendship with Florence only when Florence had overcome Pisa and reached the sea. Bologna was a no less faithful ally. Separated from the Arno by the Apennines, she had to open her doors to Florentine merchandise. And so Florence sought roads to the North by way of Bologna and Lucca; toward the sea by way of Pisa; to the South by way of Siena or

[2] *Political Science Quarterly*, XV, p. 603.

Arezzo. Even when they opposed her with refusals, when they marched in arms against her, there always remained to her the hope of a revolution in the Ghibelline cities where· she kept in touch with the Guelf party, and where the local Guelfs, after as before victory, had to buy her support. The most notorious example of this policy is the war with Pisa in 1405–06, which gave Florence an open door on the Mediterranean and stimulated her ambition to acquire sea-power so that she might avoid the necessity of sending her wares in foreign vessels.

In the beginning of the fourteenth century political enmities, embittered by commercial rivalry, had closed Pisa to Florence and she formed the project of shipping through the port of Talamone in the territory of Siena. "It was a windfall for the latter city, and she undertook with ardour the betterment of the port and the roads that lead to it." In 1311 Balducci Pegolotti of Florence asked for his compatriots the authorization of the government of Siena to ship their merchandise through this port by sea or by land. The treaty was renewed in 1356. It made the Florentines independent of Pisa in spite of her efforts to block the port. But Talamone was inconvenient and unhealthful. Florence was determined to have Pisa's port, and in 1406 Pisa was starved into submission after frightful sufferings heroically borne. Almost every house had been smashed or riddled with gunstones hurled from bombards and catapults; the place had been brought to well-nigh total ruin and two thousand of its principal citizens had been deported to Florence, where they had to show themselves in person twice a day at an appointed place under threat of execution. Swarms of Florentine troops were quartered in the town to check disaffection, and the process of rebuilding had gone on apace. But as long as Leghorn was held by the Genoese, Florence was disquieted over her galleys, and so in 1421 after prolonged haggling she bought that port for 100,000 gold florins.

These pages have been written as an introduction to the particular economic and social history of four states of Italy in the. fourteenth and fifteenth centuries whose history is of special interest and significance, viz.: Milan, Venice, Genoa and Lucca. The economic and social history of Florence is so important that a separate chapter is devoted to it.

The extreme diversity of the civilization of the trecento and the quatrocento, the infinite variation of local conditions, of form, of color, make it well-nigh impossible for one to get an understanding of the Renaissance as a whole. It must be studied locally and by selection of types. Florence was the typical manufacturing, industrial community, and specialized in woolen textiles; Venice and Genoa were typical commercial communities, particularly engaged in maritime trade and dealing in the luxuries imported from the Levant; Milan was at once an industrial and a commercial community, but her chief office was as a middleman for the transmission of wares over the Alpine passes into Germany; Papal Rome was an important fiscal center, owing to pooling of the enormous revenues of the Church there and the patronage of the Holy See. But banking was general in every big trade center of Italy—in Rome, Florence, Genoa and Venice especially; Lucca was preëminent for the silks which it manufactured; Brescia manufactured iron.

The economic interpretation of history has profoundly modified the views of older historians with regard to the origin and nature of the Italian Renaissance. The economy and the social texture of Italy was profoundly changed in the second half of the thirteenth century; a capitalistic civilization came into being, and out of this soil sprang that higher life of the Renaissance expressed in literature and in art. There is not merely a striking simultaneity between the new economy, the new society, and the new intellectual and esthetic life—there is a direct relation between them. Both the material and the moral civilization of the Italian Renaissance reposed upon the newly risen and rich bourgeoisie. The Renaissance, whether manifested in politics or trade or art or letters, had the seal of the new capitalism stamped upon it. It was a common phenomenon everywhere in Italy.

The city located in nearest proximity to an Alpine pass was Verona. The Italian entrance to the Brenner, the lowest pass between Germany and Italy, was at Chiusa, not more than ten miles from Verona where the Adige emerges into the plain through a narrow defile; thence the road ascended the Adige to Bozen, whence it followed the Eisack to Brenner Lake on the watershed between the Po and the Danube. The descent on the other side was via the Sill to Innsbrück. In addition to this advantage Verona possessed Legnago, the only point where the Adige could be crossed. This gave her control of more than half the navigable part of the river which served as the great highway of trade between Venice and Verona. Verona also controlled the upper Mincio through Peschiera situated at the point where the river flows out of Lake Garda. Verona's prosperity was gained as a commercial middleman though her industries were well developed, especially the making of woolen cloth. As early as 1228 a code regulated the *arti*. But there are much earlier evidences of Verona's commerce. The earliest of these codes concluded with Venice (1107) regulated the dues to be paid by the merchants of one city when entering the territory of the other. It was enlarged in 1274, 1306, 1310. In the twelfth century the House of Merchants (or Gild) tabulated all duties on exports and imports. German merchants were lightly taxed "because they had to come so far." Venetian merchants were even more liberally

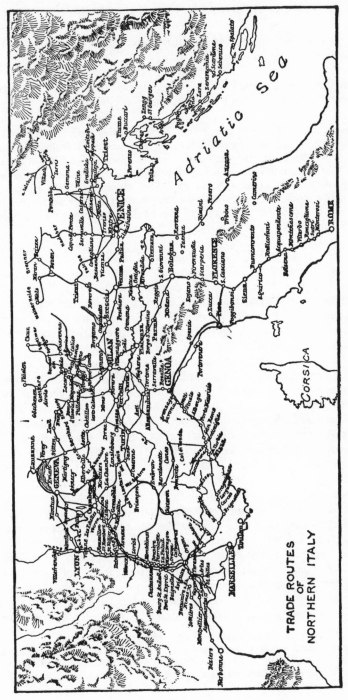

TRADE ROUTES
OF
NORTHERN ITALY

233

treated and were preferred creditors. Next to Venice, Verona's most intimate commercial relations were with Mantua, whose merchants were given undisputed passage through the lower Brenner on their way north. There was a working agreement between Verona and Vicenza to protect trade on the road between the two cities.

It may confidently be assumed that these treaties with Venice and Mantua were not isolated occurrences. . . . The normal relation between the Italian city-states at this period was one of passive hostility, that is, two cities were not regarded as being at peace with each other unless the fact was definitely expressed in some way. This accounts for the great number of treaties, societies, concords, leagues, pacts and other forms of alliance which date from the latter part of the twelfth century and the beginning of the thirteenth.[3]

As in Tuscan Italy Florence dominated the scene and dwarfed other Tuscan cities like Siena and Pisa into insignificance, so in Lombardy, Milan lorded it over the whole province after 1183. The commerce and industry of Pavia, Piacenza, Cremona, Brescia and other towns of the Lombard plain were of merely local importance. In a very true sense in the fourteenth and fifteenth centuries Milan was Lombardy and Lombardy, Milan.

We must go back to the thirteenth century, not for the origin, but for the development of this condition. The Lombard communes after the peace of Constance (1183) formed free self-governing burgher communities. Trade controlled politics. The powerful associations of merchants and money-changers—*mercatores, negotiatores, cambiatores* —through their elected officials, called consuls, practically controlled the local administration in each town. For the commercial and industrial prosperity of the Lombard cities gave great influence to the consuls (*consules mercatorum*),[4] all the more because the long and ruinous war waged with Frederick Barbarossa had exhausted the financial resources of the towns. Direct taxes, whose usage was introduced at this epoch, failed to meet the deficits, and indirect taxes were still in their infancy. In consequence the cities turned to the rich merchants for relief in the form of loans, or sold to them anticipations of taxes, or commitments of revenue arising from tolls, octrois, *etc.* Even church plate was pledged. These municipal notes circulated as negotiable paper, and we thus see how early, at least in Italy, the practice of issuing municipal bonds obtained. Whenever a new loan was

---

[3] A. M. Allen, *A History of Verona*, p. 42.
[4] These *consules mercatorum* in the thirteenth century are found at Milan, Modena, Lucca, Pistoia, Ferrara, Bologna, Mantua, Piacenza, Asti, in Lombardy; in Florence, Siena, Perugia and Pisa in Tuscany; in Genoa and Luçca in Liguria; even in Rome.

projected it was always advisable for the local government to confer with the consuls of the merchants.

The number of these commercial and industrial gilds was astonishingly large in every Lombard town, a fact which testifies to the prosperity of the country, although the medieval tendency towards meticulous differentiation of crafts is partly responsible for the number. In the thirteenth century the distinction between "major" and "minor" gilds, which later led to so much economic and social antagonism, had not yet developed. Pavia had twenty-five gilds; Bergamo eighteen, Bologna twenty-one in 1228, which were increased to twenty-six in 1386. Among the last we find specialization like wool workers in foreign wool, wool-workers in domestic wool, silk weavers, cotton weavers, linen weavers.

The Peace of Constance settled the struggle between the Lombard communes and the emperor, but it did not assure internal tranquillity to the cities. Thus in the process of time Lombardy fell under the despotism of the Visconti, who extended their sway over most of the territory and converted it into the Milanais or Duchy of Milan.

Milan and the other cities of the Lombard plain were more fortunately situated for purposes of commerce than Florence. The Po gave access to the Adriatic and the Levant. The proximity of the Alpine passes opened up Central Europe, and by extension nearly all Europe beyond both the French and German Alps, to Milanese merchants, who thrived as middlemen. We have striking evidence of this in two documents. In 1278 Folco Caci of Perugia, "Captain of the association of Lombard and Tuscan Merchants (*Capitaneus universitatis mercatorum Lombardorum et Tuscorum*)," in the name of the "consuls of the merchants" of Rome, Genoa, Venice, Piacenza, Lucca, Bologna, Pistoia, Asti, Florence, Siena and Milan, concluded a treaty with Louis IX, the king of France, which guaranteed merchants from all the enumerated towns business privileges in Provence. Ten years later Roger of Casace, a doctor of laws, who was also "captain and rector of the Company of Milanese ultramontane merchants trading at the Fairs of Champagne and in the kingdom of France" demanded redress of count Amadeus V of Savoy for injuries and losses sustained by the company in his states. Some idea of the extent of Italian commerce beyond the Alps with Flanders and Central Europe, as well as with the Levant, may be gained from the remarkable *Imposicio Officii Gazarie* written at Genoa in 1313.

The roads of the Milanais were crowded with vehicles and the rivers and canals with barges. The chief transalpine route of Milan was the Simplon Pass, but in 1341 we find application for a safe-conduct over the St. Gotthard. Milan was in constant intercourse with Augsburg, Zürich, Ulm, Nuremberg, Constance, Luzerne, Basel and Geneva. The

Morosini had a branch business house in Basel, the Busti one in Cologne, which is still commemorated by the Mailan there. Filippo Maria made special concessions to German merchants, who were exempted from "perforation" of their bales and parcels in order that smuggling of dutiable articles might be detected, which speaks volumes for the honesty of the German merchants. The great German houses, like the Fuggers and Welsers of Augsburg and the firm of Irma in Basel, had trading permits of two years which were renewed time and time again. Like most of the European states of this period Milan had her own protective system. The volume of trade with Germany was so great that in 1498 a special German-Italian vocabulary was issued. The duty on woolen goods, especially Anglo-Flemish and Florentine cloths, was the chief. The Segazoni firm of Como was the great dealer in woolens. By 1442 silk manufacture was so developed that 15,000 operatives were employed.

The divided political condition and the cutthroat commercial competition of the cities which had vexed Lombardy in the thirteenth century was largely removed as the result of the union of most of the Lombard cities into a single state under the rule of the Visconti in the fourteenth century.[5] Although the taxation of the Visconti was everywhere oppressive, the population was indemnified by the peace and good order which was made to prevail and the improved communications. At the same time the Visconti dukes were not actuated by a mania for uniformity. The towns retained their local government distinct from that of Milan. Each kept its own local institutions and local administrative bodies, which varied according to tradition. "The various Lombard, Tuscan and Romagnol communes which were united under the Visconti had no connection with each other." [6]

The Visconti were intelligent financiers and tax masters. They broadened the basis of taxation, abolished privileges, and spread the burden of assessments over many, thus lightening the load on each. The exaction of large sums was spread over a term of years. The duke's own officials were not exempt, but had to pay 12½ per cent of their salaries. In order to simplify collection this amount was taken out at the source, like some of our own income taxes. Neither clergy nor nobles were exempted. Giangaleazzo laid down the principle that every person must pay his share, and in 1387 initiated an investigation by *quo warranto* proceedings to detect evasions and pleas of exemption. When he found that the cities were imposing too heavy taxes upon the rural areas around them, he equalized the impositions. Reggio is

---

[5] These cities included Milan, Lodi, Como, Alessandria, Vercelli, Novara, Bergamo, Pavia, Cremona, Crema, Piacenza, Brescia, Asti, Guastalla, Tortona, Reggio, Vicenza, Verona, Feltre, Belluno and Padua.

[6] Dorothy Muir, *Milan under the Visconti*, p. 175.

an example. The duke could be considerate, but he was never easy going. In 1388 he wrote to Reggio: "I have waited as long as I can, and would be glad to give you a fresh respite if I could. But it is impossible, for I myself have reached the point when I must pay up." The modernness of both idea and execution represented in Giangalleazzo is striking. "I have seen," wrote Giovio, "in the chests of his archives, books on sheepskins which contained year by year the names of the captains, the *condottieri* and old soldiers, and the payment of each one, and the roll of cavalry and infantry." In commenting upon this passage Symonds has written:

His love of order was so precise that he may be said to have applied the method of a banker's office to the conduct of a state. It was he who invented bureaucracy by creating a special class of paid clerks and secretaries of departments. Their duty consisted in committing to books and ledgers the minutest items of his private expenditure and the outgoings of his public purse; in noting the details of the several taxes, so as to be able to present a survey of the whole state revenue; and in recording the names and qualities and claims of his generals, captains, and officials. A separate office was devoted to his correspondence, of all of which he kept accurate copies. By applying this mercantile machinery to the management of his vast dominions, at the time when public economy was but little understood in Europe, Giangaleazzo raised his wealth enormously above that of his neighbors. His income in a single year is said to have amounted to 1,200,000 golden florins, with the addition of 800,000 golden florins levied by extraordinary calls.[7]

In addition to extraordinary subsidies the chief taxes were the *gabelle* on salt, the *citimo* or income and property tax, and duties on wine, flour, flax and cattle. In the fifteenth century a tax commission was appointed to make revaluation of real and moveable property every five years. The method was just and thorough. Five *squadre*, each composed of six assessors, studied the whole matter, each independently of the others. Then the estimates were checked against one another and the mean taken between the highest and the lowest estimate.

In 1396 Giangaleazzo issued a code of laws which included in its provisions regulation of weights and measures,[8] food regulations, customs and duties, a mercantile code and the wool merchants' code. The duke was ahead of his age in the matter of public health and compelled isolation of infectious diseases. In 1447 Giovanni del Torgio, official "conservator of the health of Milan and the duchy," issued severe regulations in dealing with the plague. All persons who within forty

[7] *Age of the Despots*, p. 111.
[8] There is record of a revision of weights and measures as far back as 1228.

days had been in contact with infection had to report the fact. All instances of the disease were to be reported in writing to the head of the parish and by him to the public health officer. Suspected cases were to be reported and isolated. Every physician and barber called to attend a patient had to notify the health commissioner at once, and no unauthorized medicines could be administered. Milan's paved streets and good water must have made her more healthful than most Italian cities.

It is an eror to think that our problems of excessive urbanization are wholly modern. The towns of Renaissance Italy suffered from the evils of rapid increase of population owing to the relatively greater advancement of commerce and industry over agriculture, and the drift of the rural population into the cities.

Leonardo da Vinci produced an elaborate scheme for the rational reconstruction of the cities of Lombardy which would scatter the great mass of the people crowded "like goats one on top of another." . . . Many of Leonardo's ideas with regard to building and sanitation are those which are commonly regarded as the exclusive property of the present century. His insistence upon light, air, open spaces and wide streets might come from the modern social reformer, while his proposals for the regulation of traffic are in advance of what has been achieved to-day. There would be two kinds of streets in Leonardo's ideal city. Carts and heavy vehicles would be confined to the lower roads, upon a level with the basements of the houses, while elegant hanging streets would be reserved for pedestrians and light traffic.[9]

Lunatics were cared for in ward by the government. Family feuds, duelling and party strife were rigorously suppressed. It was against the law to use the ancient party terms Guelf and Ghibelline. Even a postal system was instituted. In emergency, letters could be sent express "by day or night." The slower post forwarded letters only in daytime. Every letter dispatched or received had to be stamped at the post office, and the postmaster was forbidden to read them except in suspected cases. Over one hundred horses were employed in the postal service, and relay stations were all over Lombardy by 1425. The service was even extended over the Alps. Aside from official business, most of the letters were missives of merchants and traders. Private correspondence was light. In 1398 Giangaleazzo systematized the public debt, and sold his subjects government bonds which bore interest at ten per cent. Letters of credit were current.

The remarkable system of canals in Lombardy constructed during the twelfth and thirteenth centuries [10] was maintained and improved

[9] Ady, *Milan under the Sforza*, p. 167.
[10] See Thompson, *Economic and Social History of Middle Ages*, pp. 445–46.

in the following centuries. Fortunately as Milan was situated with respect to the Alpine passes, it was not favorably located to benefit by the river system of Lombardy. But by the union under its walls of artificial rivers connecting the Ticino, the Adda, and the Po, this immensely progressive city made amends for natural disadvantage. Duke Giangaleazzo Visconti of Milan, after the capture of Pavia in 1359 began the construction of a canal between Milan and Pavia, which could not have been completed much before the beginning of the next century, for a document of 1411 mentions the "new canal which goes to Pavia." This, however, could have been nothing but an irrigating canal, since it was constructed before locks were invented. It was made navigable between 1473–75. In 1372 the Naviglio Civico of Cremona, having its head near Calcio, was constructed. In 1376 the same ruler unsuccessfully tried to reorganize the whole system of irrigation from the Naviglio Grande, but "these efforts were invariably met by such resolute opposition on the part of the powerful body of citizens of all grades and classes to whom grants had been assigned that even the despotism of the Visconti was foiled." [11] In 1472 we find Francesco Sforza, successor of the Visconti dukes, equally thwarted.

Francesco Sforza and his son, Ludovico il Moro, rank among the enlightened despots of Italy in the fifteenth century and as engineering rulers they were unsurpassed. The Martesana Canal was begun by Francesco I in 1457 and completed within a few years. Though not the earliest example of the invention of locks it was the first notable work of that kind. Tradition says that this device was invented and installed by Leonardo da Vinci but it is not trustworthy, since Leonardo was chief engineer of Ludovico il Moro in 1496. The earliest certain example of a lock is that of San Maria in Viarenna in 1439 which connected the Naviglio Grande with the Fossa Interna. It was built by Duke Filippo Visconti to facilitate the transportation of marble for the cathedral of Milan, which was brought by the Ticino and Naviglio Grande from the quarries on Lake Maggiore. In 1445 it is still called the "new canal." In 1452 the lock was minutely and technically described by Leon Battista in a work entitled *De Aedificatoribus*, which was dedicated to Pope Nicholas V, the founder of the Vatican Library. The locks of the Naviglio Grande which are described in a document of 1439 are probably the first practical instances of this invention. But it is of interest to learn that the device of locks was theoretically worked out as much as two hundred years before. For in the *Life* of Filippo Visconti (1265–73) mention is made of a project which he cherished of connecting the Naviglio Grande at Abbiategrasso with Vigevano on the opposite bank of the Ticino "by the employment of

11 Baird Smith, *Italian Irrigation*, I, p. 207.

the machine called locks (*colle uso delle machine che si chiamano conche*)."

Francesco Sforza constructed the Bereguardo Canal between 1460–70, and the Naviglio Interno, by which transportation within the walls of the city was improved, belongs to the same period. The former was a remarkable engineering feat. For five and one-half miles the bed of the canal was carried along the banks of the Adda over fifty feet above the level of the river, part of the line having been bored through solid rock and part through such loose earth that the walls had to be made of concrete. Nor was this all. The canal crossed the torrent called Molgora near Gorgonzola by an aqueduct of three arches each 64 feet in span.

The name of the last and unfortunate Sforza duke of Milan, Ludovico il Moro, whom Louis XII of France defeated and imprisoned for life in the dungeon of Loches in 1501, is immortalized by his relation with Leonardo da Vinci, his engineer, whose work on *Hydraulics* in nine books (*Del moto e mesura dell'acqua*) is a monument to his versatile genius. A long-cherished dream of the Visconti dukes was to unite the Ticino and the Adda. The construction of two locks at Gorla and Cascina di'Pomi on the Martesana in 1471 opened a line of navigation to Milan through the Martesana Canal. It remained to unite this stream with the Naviglio Grande by means of the Naviglio Interno. But the engineering difficulties were insuperable until Leonardo undertook and accomplished the feat in 1496. The solution for connecting the Naviglio Grande with the Martesana entailed the building of five locks on the former in a length of three and one-quarter miles with a fall of twenty-five feet. The completion of this great engineering enterprise fulfilled the long-cherished dream of the Sforza dukes to connect Milan with Lage Maggiore on the west and Lake Como on the east. Leonardo also improved navigation by inventing locks with double gates meeting at an obtuse angle as to-day. Three years after the work was accomplished the Milanais was conquered by the French.

These internal improvements facilitated commercial communication all through the Lombard plain, but especially stimulated the trade with Venice and Genoa. With the latter trade was free of tolls. Another benefit which followed the construction of this immense system of irrigation and transportation was rice culture. It was introduced into Lombardy, not as one would expect from Venice, but by the Irma firm of Basel which brought the first seed grain from Moorish Spain. The spread of rice culture in Lombardy is peculiarly due to the promotion of Lodovico Sforza. His great estate at Vigevano was a model farm and agricultural experiment station called La Pecorara or the Grange where cattle- and sheep-breeding, rice-, mulberry-, and grape-growing were studied.

The French chronicler Robert Gaguin gives the fullest description of the ducal farm. He waxes eloquent over "the marvellous number of beasts" that he saw there, and over the admirable system on which each farm was worked. Through the meadow land on which it stood ran "thirty-three streams of fair living water." Homes for the foremen of each department were provided in the central square of the farm, while beyond lay a block of dwellings for the labourers and their families. Hay, milk, cheese, butter were all carefully weighed and the farm was organized upon strictly scientific principles. Lodovico's experiments attracted the attention of Leonardo da Vinci, whose notebooks contain several references to details which struck him during a visit to Vigevano.[12]

In the first quarter of the fifteenth century a trade war broke out between Milan and Venice. Hitherto their relations had been peaceful and the trade between them enormous. In 1420 when the struggle impended the Venetian doge Tomaso Mocenigo in a vain effort to avert hostilities pleaded this fact as an argument for peace. "Every year," he said, "we receive 900,000 gold ducats from Milan, and cloth worth 200,000 ducats. We give the Lombards in return cotton goods, woolens, cloth of gold and silks, pepper, drugs, sugar, soaps, spices. This traffic employs so many ships in all parts of the world that Venice gets 2½ per cent in freight rates from it." Against this argument Foscari, the leader of the Venetian war party, urged the new policy of what may be called continental imperialism. For Venice, not content with her vast empire in the Levant, was now ambitious to become an Italian mainland power also. This was a revolutionary departure from her past policy, which had been one of "splendid isolation" and freedom from entangling alliances in the peninsula, and was commenced by Venetian seizure of Padua, Vicenza and Verona. This war vexed the last decades of the Visconti house. Florence, Savoy, Ferrara, Montferrat and Mantua joined the league against Milan. Begun in 1423, it lasted with intervals of truce until 1450. Its history is one of fierce battles of mercenary armies under hired *condottieri* and of that tortuous secret diplomacy so characteristic of the age. Venice pressed her attack with land troops and a river fleet which penetrated up the Po to Cremona, where a successful engagement enabled it to go nearly to Pavia. Meantime the duke of Savoy attacked the western frontier of the Milanais. Filippo Maria bought off Savoy by cession of Vercelli and pacified Venice by yielding Brescia and Bergamo. Florence got nothing and was both angry at expending three and a half millions of florins and jealous of Venice's imperialistic course. In 1430 the second war broke out. Savoy was bought off by a marriage alliance; Montferrat demanded Asti and Alessandria. Risings instigated by Venice

[12] C. M. Ady, *Milan under the Sforza*, p. 166.

took place on the Riviera di Ponente, and Genoa threatened to join Montferrat. Venice persuaded Florence to come in against Milan and both guaranteed Montferrat if he would join the league. But the Milanese won a big naval victory at Bina over the Venetian fleet. This made Florence and Montferrat pause, and the rest of Italy watched Venice's mainland policy askance. In the midst of things the Swiss, with an eye to expansion and commercial advantage to be gained by getting possession of the Italian end of the St. Gothard, took advantage of Milan's difficulties to invade Lombardy. They were badly defeated in the Valtelline. Savoy then became an active ally of the Visconti duke, while Genoa united with Venice and Florence against him. But it was a fragile alliance. Florence had gained nothing in the past while Venice had acquired Bergamo and Brescia. Gian-franceso marquis of Gonzaga, who had hitherto been an ally of Venice, turned his coat and allied himself with the Visconti. In 1439 it was written : "Venice stands in water up to her throat and is almost ruined." Nevertheless she fought desperately to get Cremona, which was the key to the river system on the frontier between Venetian and Milanese territory. In his apprehension Filippo Maria took a momentous step. He appealed to Alphonso of Naples and to Charles VII of France. It is a pity he so lost his nerve, for Cosimo de' Medici by that time dreaded Venetian ambition and reversed his policy. His theory, more than that of any other Italian statesman, was the "balance of power." He feared lest Venice might acquire Lombardy and so form an overwhelmingly powerful state in North Italy. The chief immediate effect of this long war, which was largely waged for trade purposes, was the succession of Francesco Sforza, the great Milanese commander, to the last of the Visconti in 1450. More momentous—as we shall see later—was the appeal which had been made to France, for it stimulated the French king's appetite to acquire the Milanais as a reversion to him from Valentine Visconti. Venice as a great Italian mainland power, by annexing Lombardy, might have kept out the French invasion in the next century.

We now turn from the history of the great interior commonwealth of Lombard Italy to the history of Venice and Genoa, the two great rival seaboard and maritime states. The contrast between the two great maritime republics of Italy, Genoa and Venice, and the two inland states of Florentine Tuscany and the Milanais is marked. Florence was largely an industrial community, Milan a middleman. But Genoa and Venice lived by the sea. Florence and Milan thrived on the land. Though Genoa and Venice were both maritime states with a far-flung commercial empire in the Levant, the contrast between them was striking. This was due to the difference of terrain. Owing to her situation on the mainland

Genoa could not avoid being drawn into the whirlpool of Guelf and Ghibelline politics which tore her neighbors to shreds. . . . Her great nobles were not merely merchant princes; they were landed proprietors as well. . . . Italian politics affected the life of Genoa and the feuds of great nobles broke the city into factions. Far different was the position of Venice. Isolated by her lagoons . . . the wind of Guelf and Ghibelline contention hardly rippled the surface of her placid estuary; no feudal system, with its arbitrary divisions of society, broke the solid body of the Venetian people; no powerful landed aristocracy presented a mark for popular jealousy. Venice was singularly united. The merchant noble, the clerks in her counting houses, the captains of her ships, the men who worked them, were all coöperators and shareholders in the joint-stock concern. The struggle with Genoa was terrible in its long-drawn drain upon the resources of either combatant, but the issue could never have been doubtful.[13]

The gigantic commercial duel between Venice and Genoa was for the mastery of the Black Sea and Aegean trade, and was fought out in Eastern waters and on the back of the Byzantine Empire after its restoration in 1261. It is simpler to consider this history in connection with that of the later Byzantine Empire. Here only the Italian relations of Genoa need be observed. Internal strife was Genoa's undoing. In the beginning the government was in the hands of certain noble families whose power rested, not so much on the possession of land, as upon a lucrative maritime commerce. The two most prominent representatives of this aristocracy were the Grimaldi and Fieschi families. The popular element in Genoa looked for leadership to the rival Doria and Spinola families. In the struggle between these two factions each, when worsted, resorted to the Italian practice of appealing to outside intervention. Thus turn by turn Genoa offered itself to the marquis of Montferrat, to the Visconti of Milan, and finally in 1396 to the king of France, who established permanent French domination there. Only when war with Venice was on were the rancors temporarily forgotten. As soon as peace was made the intestine quarrels were renewed with no party strong enough to dominate the rest. From 1350 to 1355 war with Venice was constant. Thereafter it dragged along at intervals until the duke of Savoy mediated the Peace of Turin in 1381. After that date Genoa ceased to be a first-rate power either in Italy or on the sea. In 1396 the French occupied Genoa and it practically became an annex to France. No commonwealth of Italy during the Renaissance was so grossly materialistic as Genoa, and her passing need not be mourned. Unlike Florence, unlike Venice, unlike Milan, her greatest rivals, Genoa never manifested the slightest interest in higher culture. Letters and art were alien to her. She had no interest except trade; no aptitude except for business.

[13] *English Historical Review,* XII, p. 348, a review of Caro.

Venice has been described as "the mightiest example of working energy and purposeful action which history knows." The greatest secret of Venetian commercial importance, the cause which indicated Venice as the mart through which East and West were to exchange their produce, was her geographical position. A glance at the map shows us that Venice is the seaport nearest to the center of Europe; the German merchants touched the sea soonest there, and the Levantine merchants brought their cargoes nearer to their markets there than at any other point.

Venice was the earliest commercial and colonial empire of history. Situated on a cluster of islands at the head of the Adriatic, like Great Britain since Tudor times, Venice maintained an aloofness from the continent during the Crusades. She spread her tentacles over the eastern Mediterranean, Aegean and Black Seas, and established *fondachi* or trading-posts in the Balkan peninsula, in Asia Minor, in Syria and the Holy Land, in Egypt. The overthrow of the Latin Empire in Constantinople in 1261, the loss of the Holy Land and much of Syria in 1291, injured her. But in the face of these adversities the republic hardened her government and heroically rose superior to calamity.

From the inception of her history Venice had been a nation of merchants. Not a thread of feudal class existed in her social texture. In form the old constitution of Venice was like a pyramid resting on the Doge, the College, the Senate or Pregradi, and the Grand Council. The doge was chief executive of the government, and in the eleventh and twelfth centuries was a real monarch, but a constitutional one. For his power was checked by the Collegio, which was a sort of cabinet or executive committee without judicial or legislative functions, but with the right to propose laws to the Senate. It was composed of several ducal councillors and twenty other persons, members of various boards of great officials. The Senate or Pregradi (the invited) may be called the upper house; it was preëminently the legislative body. It included 246 members and decided questions of peace and war, made treaties, laid taxes, regulated finance, and passed all legislation. The Consiglio Maggiore or lower house consisted of hereditary nobles. It chose the doge, the college, the senate. From 1172 onward the richest of this commercial nobility had systematically consolidated political power in the Consiglio Maggiore or Grand Council, whose aims were to reduce the doge to a figurehead and to extinguish the people. In the thirteenth century the members pertained to both the older and the newer noble houses and an increasing number of wealthy *popolani* (one-third in 1275). From 1275 to 1321 a series of measures were passed, of which the so-called *Serrata* or Closure of the Grand Council in 1297 was the most important. The effect of these was to stereotype conditions. This law legally established an hereditary mercantile aristocracy and converted the government of Venice into an oligarchy. A rising of the people in 1300 and the more formidable conspiracy of Tiepolo in 1310 culminated in the creation of the famous Council of Ten, which consisted of seventeen persons: the doge, six ducal councillors and ten elected members. Originally it was an emergency committee of safety, with dictatorial powers temporarily conferred during the Tiepolo conspiracy. But it was never abolished and gradually absorbed most of the powers of the government, finally eliminating the doge and the six councillors.

Revolts, like that of Tiepolo, were due to family feuds and personal ambitions, not to democratic movements among the *popolo minuto,* and the policy of the ruling class was to prevent the formation of factions and the acquisition of predominant power by a family or an individual.

Tiepolo died, and with him died the old nobility as a dominant party in state. He and it were killed by the new aristocracy. Tiepolo's object had been to preserve the old constitution of Venice; for in it he and his order, by long prescriptive right of birth and rule, were powerful. But this party failed to make common cause with the people, they neglected to win their confidence, and they went down before the younger and stronger order. Had Tiepolo succeeded it is not impossible that Venice might have developed a constitutional government based on the three estates of prince, nobles and people; but it was not given to her to escape the tendency which was bringing all Italy under the power of individual families of despots.[14]

This brief dissertation upon the Venetian form of government has not been intended to elucidate political science. It is necessary to understand these changes in order to understand how clearly Venice in the Renaissance elaborated a despotism which in its own peculiar way reflected the drift of all Italy towards despotism. There can be no doubt that this hereditary merchant aristocracy powerfully contributed to the economic greatness of Venice. It was, as one has said, "indulgent to the subject, sumptuous in the public service, economical in the administration of the finances, equitable and impartial in the administration of justice, knowing well how to give prosperity to the arts, agriculture and commerce; beloved by the people who obeyed it."

The stability of the Venetian government was of benefit to its commercial policy. Venice had constantly in view its commercial supremacy and pursued this purpose with undeviating resolution and undiminished energy. Genoa might not have succumbed and might have maintained a parity with Venice in spite of the fact that its situation was not so favorable, if it had had a more stable government.

The Venetians have been charged with having been the most gainful, greedy, materialistic people of the Renaissance. But the allegation is

[14] Horatio Brown, *Venetian Studies.*

exaggerated, if not untrue. If she was indifferent to literature and can boast no great name like that of Petrarch or Boccaccio, yet she rivalled Florence in art.

Until the fourteenth century Venice sedulously avoided becoming embroiled in peninsular politics in Italy, except for an ancient trade feud with Genoa for commercial domination in the eastern waters. The years between 1284 and 1381 formed nearly a century of struggle for the mastery. With Venice defeated by Genoa in 1284 at Meloria and again in 1298 at Curzola, the conflict ebbed and flowed between the two antagonists until the end of the fourteenth century. In 1379 the Genoese defeated the Venetian fleet off of Pola and captured Chioggia, one of the main islands of the republic. But in the next year (1380) Venice decisively defeated Genoa, saved herself and so far weakened Genoa that by 1396 she had succumbed to French conquest. Possessed of unparalleled sea-power, mistress of a wide and rich commerce, Venice, from its island situation in the northeast of Italy, was, until the French acquisition of Genoa in 1396, without mainland interest except for the narrow strip of territory represented by Treviso. Genoa was the ancient and bitter commercial rival of Venice, and Venice thenceforth looked with apprehension upon the possibility of French-Genoese consolidation of policy and interest in upper Italy. Consequently Venice looked with relief upon the prostration of France after Agincourt. Her antagonism reawakened with the second French occupation of Genoa (1458–61). Then Venice appeared as a sudden and unexpected element in the conflict between Louis XI and Charles the Bold. In the course of events Venice was the foremost power on the Italian mainland in the north, eclipsing both Milan and Florence in this capacity.

Venice's commercial relations with Western Europe were almost wholly maintained by the sea by means of the famous Flanders Galley Fleet. The Flanders Galleys were the most remarkable of the state trading fleets sent out by Venice. They were built by the state and let out each year to the highest bidder. Each galley was in command of a captain and numbered among its crew two fifers, two trumpeters, a notary public, a physician, a pilot, scribes, and craftsmen of various kinds. There were thirty archers for defense and one hundred and eighty oarsmen. The archers and oarsmen were under command of four young patricians, sent out to see the world, get used to toil and danger, and learn to expose their lives for Venice. The oarsmen were chiefly Slavonians from the Venetian possessions. There is some dispute as to when the first Venetian galleys came to Flanders for purposes of trade. A. Bachet places the date as early as 1273; others think the annual galley voyages commenced in 1317; Adolf Schaube finds valid reasons for assuming the year 1314 as the one in which these voyages began. The route was across the Adriatic to Capo d'Istria, thence via Corfu, Otranto, Syracuse, Messina, Naples, Majorca and the principal ports of Spain and Morocco, finally touching Lisbon. From Lisbon part of the fleet went to England, landing at Sandwich, Southampton and London; the rest went to Bruges, Sluys, Middleburg and Antwerp. On the return voyage the entire fleet met at either Southampton or Sandwich. The voyage, strictly a trading one, lasted about twelve months.

The articles of trade are exceedingly interesting as throwing light on the state of European commerce and civilization. Silks were collected from Aleppo, Damascus, Greece, and dyed yellow, light blue, and green in Venice. These found a ready sale in England, raw silk being especially in demand. Spices came from Alexandria, Damascus, Aleppo and Constantinople, and included besides the regular spices and pepper, wormwood, borax, camphor, gum arabic, musk, seed pearls, and elephants' teeth. Spun cotton and raw cotton were collected at Damascus and Cyprus. The depot of currants was Patras. They were an excedingly important article of commerce and much in demand in England where they became known for the first time in 1317. At Venice the galleys were loaded with silks manufactured and dyed there; glass and earthenware. At Messina they took on sugar, molasses, preserved fruits, candy, silk yarn, spun cotton, saltpeter and large coral beads or buttons called paternosters from their resemblance to the large beads in the catholic rosary. Bow-staves also formed an important part of their cargo.

For the return voyage the galleys loaded in England with wool, tin, pewter platters and porringers, dressed calf-skins, and ox-hides. The calf-skin and ox-hides found a ready sale in Pisa and Sicily. The English cloth was taken to Venice, dyed and distributed by the Venetian merchants throughout the great fairs of Italy and Germany and the ports of the Mediterranean.

At Bruges the galleys unloaded silks, indigo, Barbary wax, rock alum from Constantinople and ostrich feathers, receiving in return cloth, brass- and tin-ware, cutlery, bowstrings, white thread and curtains. Antwerp bought sulphur, which the galleys had loaded at Sicily, ivory for combs, pearls, diamonds, rubies, and turquoise, and sent out cloth gloves, hardware and cutlery.

The Flanders Galleys made their last trip to England and Flanders in 1532.

The only western state with which Venice had war, except Genoa, was Hungary. For Venice was determined to make the Adriatic a Venetian lake, and with that intent labored long and hard for complete possession of the east Adriatic shore. As early as 1203 the capture of Zara had deprived Hungary of her only port. When Fiume too was taken by Venice in 1345, Hungary and Venice desperately struggled for possession of Ragusa.

Modern Ragusa is connected by a causeway with the mainland, but medieval Ragusa was on a rocky island. Though nominally subject to the Byzantine Empire, Ragusa was practically independent. In 866–67 she withstood a Saracen siege of fifteen months until relieved by the emperor Basil I. Ragusa's fleet even then was able to furnish transportation for imperial troops to Apulia in an expedition which broke the Arabic domination in the "heel" of Italy and resulted in creation of the theme of Lombardy. Ragusa got embroiled with Venice during the latter's war with the emperor Manuel, when he occupied Ragusa, and in 1221 Ragusa became a Venetian protectorate in pursuance of Venice's policy to make the Adriatic a Venetian lake. Ragusa shared in Venetian prosperity in the thirteenth and fourteenth centuries. Gilds of various trades were formed, and colonies of Ragusan merchants settled in the interior of the Balkan peninsula. The chief exports were live stock, skins, cheeses, and wax in return for salt, wine, oil and woven goods imported from Italy. Stephen Dushan, the czar of Serbia, gave Ragusan traders free access to his kingdom. In 1358 Venice yielded Ragusa to Hungary, which thereby at last got a door upon blue water. The Ragusans shrewdly foresaw the importance of the Turkish conquests and early got on good terms with them. In the fifteenth century Ragusa became the place of refuge of many who fled from the advance of the Turks in the Balkans. As many of these brought considerable wealth with them and engaged in trade, Ragusa prospered. She had factories in the main ports of the Mediterranean and made commercial treaties with Spain in 1494, with France in 1508, with Egypt in 1510, which last opened the way to the Indies to her. The fame of Ragusa to-day survives in alienated majesty in the English word "argosy" which is a corruption of Ragusa.

In order to have a double route open or to supplement the sea route when the Adriatic was too infested with pirates or impracticable in winter or storm, the Venetians attempted with some success to secure a land route for their commerce to Constantinople through Bulgaria and Serbia. In the jumbled mass of mountains and valleys formed by the convergence of the ends of the Dinaric Alps, the Carpathians, and the Rhodope mountains, the Serbian people had established a *de facto* independence. In the thirteenth century the Latin Empire of Constantinople had no sway over them, nor was the restored Byzantine Empire of the Palaeologi any more able to impose its domination upon them. They were a hardy, mountaineer people engaged in stock-raising and practising the domestic arts. They excelled in leather and metal work. For Serbia is rich in ores. But the miners were Germans from Transylvania. Self-sufficient and living in simple conditions which sometimes bordered upon primitiveness, the Serbians exported and imported little. Nevertheless the country was of commercial importance. For the Serbian mass is cut by the valley of the Morava river from the Danube to the plain of Nish, the junction point of the two great natural roads of the Balkan hinterland; one ran from Nish over Pirot and Sofia in the valley of the Maritza river straight to Constantinople. It was the old road of the Crusaders. The other cut this old road almost at right angles at Nish and ran down the Vardar river to the Aegean at Salonika. Thus Nish by this X-shaped road system was a great gateway of Southeastern Europe to the Orient. This transit trade was chiefly in the hands of the Venetians and Ragusans.

The oldest Balkan treaty of Venice is of 1352. It was concluded at Nicopolis with the Bulgarian Prince Alexander. This agreement stipulated that Venetian merchants should have free and secure passage through the country upon payment of a three per cent tax on the estimated value of the merchandise; that they should have the right to establish factories, to build churches, and hold landed property in Nikopolis. Twenty years later another treaty was made with Stephen, king of Serbia, which permitted them to pass through that country to Constantinople. But the progress of the Turks in Europe, and especially the disaster at Nikopolis (1396) stopped most commercial intercourse of Europe with the East through the Balkans. To this loss to Venice must be added the extinguishment of its Black Sea trade—or what the Genoese had left of it—when Tana was sacked by Timurlane in 1395.

In partial compensation, however, for these losses, Venice had greatly extended its domination in Italy, ruling the whole eastern shore of the Adriatic from the Alps to Trani together with the islands, and of course was still in occupation of the Morea and Crete.

Venice's most remarkable industry was glass-making. Venetian glass-workers have been traced to Germany, France and Flanders. In Italy glass-making reached a point of great excellence. Molmenti cites a document of 1090 which mentions a certain Petrus Flabianus, a glass-worker of Venice. Tradition dates the origin of the Italian glass industry at L'Altare from the eleventh century, though no reference appears of the manufacture of glass before the thirteenth century. In this century there is pretty certain evidence of the existence of a gild of glass-blowers, and Molmenti thinks the gild was even older than this date. At this period, also, there were regulations concerning the glass trade, and the establishment of furnaces at Murano, Trevisa, Ferrara, Padua and Bologna. Undoubtedly the art of glass-making, in common with the more artistic industries of Venice, received a remarkable impulse from the capture of Constantinople. Although by 1278 a large part of the glass-workers were settled in Murano under the protection of San Donato, yet a decree of the Consiglio Maggiore dated November 8, 1921, shows that there must have been a considerable number of glass-blowers in Venice itself. This decree, with a view to freeing the city from all industries which were either a nuisance or which were unhealthful "ordered the removal of the glass furnace at Castello to Murano, though in the following year leave was granted to make a certain kind of glass in Venice, but only in small furnaces which must be five paces away from any inhabited building." [15]

During the fourteenth century glass-workers' gilds became quite common. Many were subdivided—bead-makers, mirror makers, *etc.* It is likely that the government encouraged the subdivision as that would make it more difficult for single workmen to establish glass-works in foreign countries. The factories at Treviso, Belluno, and along the upper course of the river Piave, all of which were along the German trade routes, helped to introduce Italian glass-workers into the transalpine industry. But the Italian influence was of little weight in Germany before the first half of the sixteenth century.

Venetian glass of the fourteenth and fifteenth centuries was of three kinds: (1) beads, (2) hollow ware, for general use, (3) mirrors, lenses, *etc.* There were some attempts to imitate the brilliant enamels of the East but "the successful handling of these colors was not a matter to be easily learned. There were as yet no handbooks to teach the composition of the colored fluxes, to say nothing of the various devices and 'wrinkles' to be mastered before the enamels could be successfully applied to the surface of the glass." [16]   By the sixteenth century, however, Venice was producing three kinds of enameled glass: (1) the clear white glass, rather thick, ornamented with appliqué bases of colored glass; (2) a glass which was similar to the enamelled copper ware of Venice, having opaque solid enamels frequently applied upon a transparent colored glass. The most famous example of this is the Coppa Muziale in the Museo Civico at Venice. This work has been assigned to Angelo Berorieri, the greatest glass-worker of the fifteenth century, to whom is generally attributed the introduction or at least the perfection of enamelling on glass. (3) The third kind of enamelled glass was that in which opaque enamels were painted with a brush upon a thin, colorless glass. A pair of goblets in the British Museum is an example of this class and types of that long series of wine glasses so familiar in later days.

Beads, both in manufacture and in export, have always formed the very backbone of the Venetian glass industry. By the fourteenth century beads were a very important part of the cargo of those galleys which were yearly dispatched to the Black Sea, to the Thames, and

[15] Molmenti, p. 67.
[16] Dillon, *History of glass-making*, pp. 178–79.

to Flanders. Even in the thirteenth century bead manufacturing had become so highly developed as to arouse the jealousy of the *Cristollae di cristallo di rocea,* who produced the beads for rosaries. The authorities were induced to prohibit the imitation on the part of the glassworkers, but in 1510 the prohibition was revoked because of German competition. Bead manufacture, according to Molmenti, arose from the manufacture of spectacles in the thirteenth century. They were first made from the rock crystal or the yellow quartz, then they began to be imitated in glass.

As Venice has afforded room for a dissertation upon the history of glass manufacturing, so Lucca [17] illuminates the history of medieval silk manufacturing. Silk manufacturing was never important at Florence. In that craft Lucca led Europe. But brocades, cloth of gold, filagreed cloth, *etc.,* were made in Florence. The making of velours was a monopoly of the Velluti family. The Arabs had introduced silk weaving and sericulture into Spain in the eighth century and into Sicily in the ninth century. Roger II of Sicily developed and stimulated the industry by the introduction of Greek silk weavers into the Palermo workshops in 1147. The Normans either introduced or perfected the industry in Apulia and Calabria. During the latter part of the twelfth century and in the thirteenth century the art of silk weaving spread into central and northern Italy. Silk was woven on a small scale in Florence before the end of the twelfth century; and in Genoa, Venice, and Milan in the thirteenth century. For the latter century there is evidence of the silk industry in Paris, in several places in southern France, and in Cologne in Germany.

Silk novelties were manufactured in Lucca at the beginning of the eleventh century. Our evidence is the Latin poem, *Ruodlieb,* written in the German monastery of Tegernsee about 1030, in which silk garters made in Lucca are mentioned in the description of a festal costume. The approximate date of the beginning of the silk industry in Lucca and the source of its introduction are insoluble problems.

Before the end of the eleventh century Lucca was an important commercial center. Merchants from northern Italy and from beyond the Alps came to the city to trade. Many pilgrims came to visit the famous miracle-working crucifix, called *Volto Santo* or Holy Face. Lucchese merchants frequented the markets and fairs of Italy. In the twelfth century they were attending the fairs of Champagne. By a commercial agreement of 1153 Genoa got control of the transportation of merchandise between Lucca and the French fairs.

Close relations with a seaport were essential to Lucchese commerce and industry. Lucca was continually at war with Pisa. The latter cap-

[17] These paragraphs are an abstract of a dissertation of one of my students, Dr. Florence Edler, upon *The Silk Trade of Lucca.*

tured the small Lucchese port, Motrone, in 1159 and held it until 1356. Therefore Lucca used the Genoese harbor throughout our period. In 1166 Genoa admitted the Lucchesi to full participation in maritime commerce on the same terms as her own citizens.

The raw materials of the Lucchese silk industry were imported from the Caspian Sea region, the shores of the Black Sea, Turkestan, the interior of Persia, Asia Minor, Syria, Greece, and Spain. Much of the raw silk was purchased in Genoa, as the Genoese notarial records testify. Some of it was purchased in Asia Minor and Syria by Lucchese merchants who frequented Lajazzo and Acre during the period of the Crusades. Sericulture was gradually introduced into Italy and southern France, but there the supply of raw silk was very limited.

Lucca manufactured every kind of silk known to the Middle Ages, but she specialized in rich, heavy silk fabrics in which gold or silver threads were used. Lucchese baldachin, brocade, *camucha*, diaper, samite, velvet, and *zettano* were in great demand. The most popular of her light-weight silks was sendal, which was used for banners, dresses, linings, hangings, and cushions.

The silk industry in Lucca was capitalistic in its organization. The silk merchants or entrepreneurs gave the raw silk to be worked to the throwsters, dyers, weavers, *etc*. The artisans returned the material to the entrepreneur after each operation. The workers lived in the city and in the country. Most of them owned their implements and worked for wages, so much per piece or per pound. The dyers and weavers were organized into gilds. The master workmen of the artisan gilds, as well as all the merchants of Lucca, were members of one large corporative body, the College of Merchants, at the head of which was the Court of Merchants, composed of a magistracy and a council. The court exercised control and jurisdiction over all commerce and over those industries, as silk manufacturing, which were related to commerce. From the oldest extant statute of the Court of Merchants, that of 1376, one obtains a clear impression of the rôle played by the court in the regulation and control of industry and commerce.

Most of the merchants of Lucca were organized into companies, which at first had a distinctly family character. The companies employed factors or salesmen to represent them abroad. Annual lists of the merchants, with their partners, factors, and apprentices were kept by the Court of Merchants. A few of these lists are extant.

The great markets for Lucchese silks, as for most medieval export products, were the fairs—especially those of Champagne and Flanders. The merchants attended in person or sent their factors. Partners and factors also represented the silk firms in the important trading centers of Western Europe. Many Lucchese merchants were furnishers to royalty and to the nobility, as well as to the papacy.

In several cities—Genoa, Naples, Rome, Avignon, Montpellier, Paris, Bruges, and London—the Lucchesi residents were sufficiently numerous to form "nations" or colonies with a corporate organization and limited jurisdiction over their members. Each colony had a statute, but only that of the Bruges "nation" is extant. The colonies were governed by consuls and assistant officers chosen annually by the members. In Bruges there was a consular house owned by the colony in which the officials resided, meetings were held, and trading was conducted. Every Lucchese who resided even temporarily in a foreign city in which his fellow-townsmen were organized as a "nation" had to join the organization or be ostracized. Each nation had a chapel or a church dedicated to the *Volto Santo* and a confraternity devoted to the cult of the Holy Cross. The statute of the Bruges colony is at once that of a civil corporation and a religious confraternity. All the dues and fines collected by the "nation" in Bruges were used for the support and upkeep of the chapel.

The consuls had jurisdiction over the members of the colony in cases of violation of the statutes of the nation, of dispute between Lucchesi, and of offense against the welfare of the merchant community. Copies of decisions rendered in one colony were sent to the other colonies and to the mother-city, so that a Lucchese who fled from justice in one city could not take refuge with his fellow-townsmen in another city, but would be ostracized in all Lucchese colonies. Upon request of the officers of a colony, Lucca would seize a culprit's possessions in the home-city.

Besides the colonies founded for trade another type of Lucchese colony appeared in the fourteenth century—the colony founded for industry. Bologna, Florence, and Venice received large numbers of silk artisans and merchants who were exiled or who voluntarily emigrated from the Republic of Lucca during the years of civil war and political strife which began in 1300, and during the two periods of foreign rule, 1314–17 and 1329–69. Ghibelline Pisa ruled Guelf Lucca from 1314 to 1317 and again from 1342 to 1369.

The artisans and the merchants were welcomed wherever they went. Bologna granted them special privileges because they introduced a new source of wealth into the city. Florence welcomed the Lucchesi as brother Guelfs and as skilled workmen who brought improved methods of weaving and dyeing to the small Florentine silk industry. The Lucchesi in Florence were permitted to form a corporative body which was admitted as one of the "members" or divisions of the silk gild, the *Arte di Porta Santa Maria*. They had a chapel dedicated to the *Volto Santo* in the church of San Marco.

The largest group of emigrant silk merchants and artisans settled in Venice. The Grand Council permitted the Lucchesi to form a silk gild called the Corte della Seta, to which Venetian silk-workers and merchants were presently admitted and later compelled to belong. The Venetian silk industry was already an export industry in the thirteenth century. The Lucchesi who settled in Venice in the fourteenth century introduced improvements in weaving and dyeing and changed the economic organization of the Venetian industry which hitherto had not been capitalistic. The weavers had purchased thread and produced on their own account fabrics which they sold to merchants. The Lucchesi changed this system by introducing their method of merchant entrepreneurs. They owned the materials and gave them out to the artisans who worked for wages.

The merchants of the Lucchese colony in Venice prospered greatly. They formed and supported a confraternity dedicated to the *Volto Santo* with a chapel, an assembly hall, and a hospice for indigent Lucchesi.

Venice rewarded those Lucchesi who remained in the city at least fifteen years with rights of citizenship which enabled them to enjoy all the commercial privileges accorded to Venetians at home and abroad. The Lucchesi might retain their native citizenship by writing a monthly letter to the Council of Elders in Lucca.

The Lucchesi abroad did not lose their love for their native city. Those in Venice were especially active in endeavoring to free Lucca from the Pisan yoke. Some returned to Lucca after she recovered her liberty. Others were too firmly established elsewhere to return without great losses.

Like other Italian city-states, Lucca kept a watchful eye on her citizens abroad, both as individuals and as groups. She interfered on behalf of her citizens whenever their persons or their goods were unjustly attacked. She attempted to have lawsuits before foreign courts transferred to Lucca, if there were any grounds for making the request. She obtained safe-conducts from rulers for her citizens. She interceded on behalf of entire colonies with popes and lay rulers.

In return for this protection Lucca demanded certain forms of submission from her subjects while they were residing abroad. The colonies had to acknowledge the jurisdiction of the mother-city. All their statutes, ordinances, and resolutions had to be sent to Lucca for approval.

During the fourteenth century, owing to the loss of the independence of the republic and the resulting emigrations of merchants and artisans, the Lucchese silk industry suffered a serious decline. After the recovery of her independence the government of Lucca together with the College of Merchants made valiant attempts to revive the industry and to recover the former markets. For a century and a half there was a slow recovery, but Lucca was unable to regain her former position of supremacy in the silk industry because of successful competition of Florence, Venice, and other cities. After the period of recovery, which reached its highest point at the beginning of the sixteenth century, a rapid and fatal decline set in. In the sixteenth and seventeenth centuries one silk company after another failed. The last silk house closed in 1785.

CHAPTER X

THE FLORENTINE WOOLEN INDUSTRY IN THE FOURTEENTH AND FIFTEENTH CENTURIES

FLORENCE in the popular mind is usually thought of as a place in which arts of all kinds predominated; in which poets and writers, painters and sculptors vied with one another. In reality it was primarily a factory town during the Renaissance. There were whole streets devoted to certain industries, the silk street, the streets where stockings were manufactured, the dyers' street, the weavers' street.

The history of Florentine trade in the Middle Ages is in first rank the history of its cloth trade, which expands naturally into a history of Florentine trade in general. Commerce alone did not enable Florence to win primacy among the Guelf communes, to construct its magnificent buildings, to beautify itself with works of art, and to nourish such a prosperous merchant aristocracy and town life. Florence's prosperity rested upon the interaction and coördination of merchant activity and industry, of the banking business, purchase of raw material and delivery of industrial products to nearby and distant lands. As far back as the thirteenth century Florentine bankers had secured something like a monopoly of fiscal relations with the papacy. In all countries clerical and secular princes were their debtors. The Florentine woolen gild was the heaviest buyer of English wool and dominated the cloth trade of Europe.

The fact that Florence developed home industries, in particular the manufacture of wool cloth, is of primary importance in accounting for her greatness. As an interior city, without a port until late in her history, she lacked the natural conditions for extensive commerce. In compensation her home industries protected her from the bloody rivalries which existed between those other Italian states such as Genoa and Pisa and Venice, where the carrying trade played the first rôle. In time of the most severe crises—depression of markets, wars and disorders abroad—Florence prospered—at least more than her neighbors. When, for example, Philip the Fair in his war with Flanders and England closed the Fairs of Champagne to the Flemish cities and later on, in the interest of native industry by the acts of 1307 and 1311, drove the Italian merchants out of France under the pretext that they violated the canonical law against usury, the *Calimala*, or cloth gild was deprived of its most important cloth market. On the other hand, the *Arte della Lana* or woolen gild managed to obtain raw wool from England and other places; the home industries continued to flourish, and the trade in native cloth developed at an ever-augmenting rate.

If we accept the authority of Davidsohn, the distinguished historian of Florence, the Arno city was the first European city not on the sea, a navigable river, or at the entrance or exit of an important mountain pass to become a focal point of great commerce. At the same time Florence was not without advantages. She was in a central position through which passed routes of importance. From an early time, the Florentines realized their strategic position from the standpoint of internal commerce, and sought to make themselves undisputed masters of their surroundings. The conquest of the mouth of the Arno was always one of their prime ambitions in order to remedy the misfortune of being an inland city. The very obstacles they encountered created in them the characteristics of energy, determination, shrewdness, resourcefulness and civic pride.

To the foregoing factors may be added as ancillary causes: the highly developed technical experience of her industry, the quality of her purchased and transformed raw stuffs and dyes, the able organization of production with respect to the division, management and use of human labor, the profits in the finished product, the intimate knowledge and energetic use of all the conditions ruling in the world commerce of the time, the communal economic policy, "which left nothing untried, even to war itself," to enhance its industry and commerce.

In the dye industry Florence led the world. The barbarian invasions of the fifth century had caused an arrest of all the arts in Western Europe, and until the twelfth and thirteenth centuries dyed stuffs were obtained exclusively from the East. It was Northern Italy, Venice, Florence and Genoa which saw the rebirth of the art of dyeing in the West. In 1300 a Florentine of German birth, Federigo Oricellarii, brought from the Levant the secret which he had found out of extracting the orchella from lichens. The discovery of this process made the fortune of Florence. In 1340 Florence had no less than 200 manufactories which manufactured from 70,000 to 80,000 bolts of colored cloth each year, and in 1429 the first treatise on the art of dyeing was written at Venice. Later the discovery of America gave a new impulse to the dyeing trade by introducing the use of cochineal, which the ancient world had known, but which had been lost for centuries in Europe. At the same time the discovery of the Indian route introduced other coloring materials like indigo, campeche wood, redwood, *etc.*, and finally the cultivation of tincture plants, notably pastel, stimulated the dyeing industry.

The wool industry in Italy goes back to early Roman times when, to follow Mommsen, Italy supplied almost the entire Roman world with wool. But in the late Empire home-produced cloth no longer satisfied the fastidious taste of the wealthier Romans. The peasants and the plebeians of the cities continued to use native or homespun cloth, while the upper class made use of the fine, richly colored cloth of the Orient.

The art and practice of weaving wool never died out in the peninsula during either the barbarian inroads or in Langobardian or Carolingian times, and while the written evidence is exceedingly scarce, the investigations of Muratori for Italy as a whole, and those of Robert Davidsohn for Florence in particular, have established the unbroken continuity of the woolen industry in Italy since Roman days.

In the case of Florence the first trace of the industry revealed in written records appears in the convent of St. Andrea in the ninth century. Here the nuns had to deliver yearly to the bishop of Florence "a vestment out of goat's wool." The art seems to have been developed even further by the nuns of St. Michael. They were required to deliver "five pieces of strong stuff" annually to the abbot of Nonantola, who was overlord of the convent. Since there were only six inmates under the abbess, it is clear that the spinning and weaving must have been carried on by maid-servants, and that the nuns acted only as overseers. Besides the five pieces, the sisters were required to receive twelve maids from a Modena convent who, under their supervision, made vestments of wool and linen. This also went to Nonantola, but in this instance the latter had to furnish the raw material. From this, says Davidsohn, we must conclude that the art of wool-working was better understood or more skillfully practised in the Florentine convents than in those of neighboring places.

The records continue very scanty, not only for the woolen industry and trade, but for the general history of Florence. It is not until after the beginning of the second millennium of our era that we get any information at all concerning the inner life and growth of the city, and not until the thirteenth century, when the *Arte della Lana* and the *Arte de' Mercanti di Calimala* were already established, have we any fullness of information with regard to the wool trade and industry.

The woolen industry took its great swing upward in the thirteenth century, but in the eleventh and twelfth centuries it was undoubtedly already important. From the weaving loom and spinning distaff of the convent cells the industry passed through the stage of primitive home manufacture, carried on largely by women, to that of an essentially capitalistic enterprise with each detail in the complicated process, from the spinning of the raw wool to the weaving, fulling, dyeing, finishing and cutting of the cloth, carried on by separate crafts. In these early centuries, the industry was carried on more in the countryside surrounding Florence than in the city proper. In Florence itself we first hear of fulling-mills in 1062; by the beginning of the twelfth century, every stream had its fulling-mills. A leading article of manufacture in the weaving industry of those days was that of stockings, of which the sources speak as early as 1132, but which by that time must undoubtedly have been well developed.

The chief traders of Florence in the eleventh and twelfth centuries were those dealing in woolen goods. They were the first to attain political influence in Florence, from which fact we have additional confirmation that their industry was the first to attain a high development. Davidsohn has given us a wonderful story of how the moneyed men in Florence loaned money to the landed gentry, the abbots, and bishops, and then eventually when they were not able to pay their debts foreclosed on them and came into possession of most of the landed wealth of the gentry and the church, increased their own riches until they controlled the finances of the popes, and thus captured the money markets of the whole church. With this credit the Florentines went into the markets of Flanders and bought cloth, undyed, and brought it home to dye. Then they improved upon the cloth which they bought and made a business of taking the cruder cloth of the northern countries, and through processes which they developed, making a cloth that commanded the cloth trade of the whole western world, and eventually also the cloth trade of the Orient.

The importance of Florence's woolen industry and trade in these centuries may be gauged by the various measures undertaken by her neighbors to hinder her competition and spread. To please the merchants of Lucca, who loyally sustained him in his conflict with Gregory VII, Henry IV in 1080 forbade Florentine merchants to appear in the markets of Parma and Lucca, where the industry also had an early beginning. Since Florence at this time did not deal in luxuries —being still an inland trading city—the only conclusion to be drawn is that her home industries were already in a flourishing condition. Henry V in 1116, at the instigation of Bologna, enjoined Tuscan merchants from passing through Bolognese territory more than twice a year; and throughout the twelfth century the German emperors continued to pass discriminatory ordinances against Florentine and other Tuscan traders in order to please Venice.

The wool gild was the first corporate society or trade corporation in Florence, and was in existence before her wool and cloth merchants began to travel through Europe. The origin of both the *Lana* (woolen manufacturing gild) and the *Calimala* (woolen merchant gild) is shrouded in darkness, but the former appears to have been in corporate existence by 1138, and the latter by 1212. But while "in a very true sense the *Arte della Lana* was the mother of the *Arte di Cali-*

mala," as time went on, "the greater profits obtainable by the latter drew into membership the more considerable of the citizens, and hence the *Calimala* merchants took the first place in wealth and influence, whilst the native manufacturers had to be content with second place." [1]

Among the well-known names which occur in these documents are those of Giovanni Villani and Dino Compagni, the two chroniclers of Florence, each of whom had large interests in mercantile affairs; the elder Boccaccio, who was a trusted agent of the Bardi; and Giotto, the artist, who appears in an odd capacity as hiring out in September, 1312, at the zenith of his fame, a loom of English make, for six months to one Bartalo Rinucci in Florence.[2]

The Italians were among the first to appear at the Champagne Fairs where they purchased the wool products of northern France and Flanders, England and Spain, that were there sold. How far back this traffic in foreign wool and *"Panni Franceschi"* dates is not known exactly; certainly before the middle of the twelfth century and doubtless much earlier. The first recorded date is 1138. The cloth was then taken home, subjected to a refining process which greatly increased its fineness and value, and then resold.

After 1138 Florentine trade was no longer limited to Tuscany but spread to its neighbors in the peninsula, Europe at large, and the Mediterranean; her treaty with Pisa in 1171 giving her equal privileges with the native citizens in sea-export, furthered her traffic abroad. Florence by 1193 already possessed a trade colony in Messina and had a street there named after her.

By 1300 there was "hardly a large city, either in Central, East or South Italy, or in Liguria, where shipments from the Arno were not constantly under way, where the Florentines did not play a prominent part; especially was this the case in Genoa and Naples." [3] By that time the Florentines might have been found doing business in Sicily, Sardinia, Corsica, Pisa, Lucca, Sarzana, Genoa, Bologna, Ferrara, Padua, Venice, Vicenza, Bassano, Belluno and Treviso, Friuli and Verona, Brescia, Verona and Mantua; Parma and Piacenza, Milan, the Romagna, Ancona and Perugia, Umbria and Rome.

All the great houses had *fondachi* in the Italian cities, which, serving principally for the wool trade, were at the same time used for other operations, banking in particular. The Falconieri had a *fondaco* in Bologna in 1245; the Spini, the Pulci, the Canigiani, had *fondachi* in

---

[1] Staley, *Gilds of Florence,* p. 142. The investigations of P. Emiliani-Giudici in his *Storia dei Comuni Italiani,* and G. Fillippi, in his *L'Arte dei Mercanti di Calimala in Firenze ed il Suo Piu Antico Statuto* are in confirmation of this fact.

[2] Cf. Doren. *Studien aus der Florentiner Wirtschaftsgesch.* I. p. 68.

[3] Davidsohn, *op. cit.,* IV, p. 247.

Anagni by 1303, at the time when Boniface VIII had his court there; the Della Scalla had one in Venice, at least until its collapse in 1326; the Bardi had one in Perugia in 1329. The Velluti by the middle of the thirteenth century had *fondachi* in Bologna, Milan, Pisa, Genoa and Rome, as well as in Paris, other parts of France, and England; twenty-six Florentine firms had *fondachi* in Pisa in 1322.

In the kingdom of Naples the Bardi and the Peruzzi were supreme; next to them came the Acciajuoli. All the large societies there carried on commerce as well as banking. Besides the export of grain, the sale of wool cloth was the most important item of trade. The first record of a shipment of a large quantity of cloth to the southern kingdom occurs in 1267, when the Florentine firm, Asini-Carapesa, shipped by way of Genoa.

Florentine merchants in France and at the Fairs of Champagne are first heard of by 1152, though not in large numbers until 1211. In the latter year the Florentines were exporting considerable quantities of cloth to the French markets, and were already importing the famous Garbo cloth directly from the Spanish province of Algarve, partly from the Fairs of Champagne. By the middle of the thirteenth century the Florentine firms were carrying on a brisk banking and commercial intercourse with France.

At the outset the Florentine merchants had to combat many difficulties and hindrances in France. The French feudality and merchants were jealous of foreigners and sought to exclude them. Many, indebted for heavy sums, endeavored to renounce their obligations. Gregory IX (1227–1241) took the Florentines under his protection. At this time the Crusading preachers managed to obtain a decree granting a four-year moratorium for debts owed by the Crusaders, whereupon Gregory issued a declaration saying, "This refers only to the disbelieving Jews; to the faithful Florentines, however, the contracts must be fulfilled."[4] Under Louis IX (1226–1270) the treatment accorded the Florentines along with the other Italians underwent constant fluctuation. Owing to their help in financing the Sixth Crusade and to the intercession of Innocent IV (1243–54), that great protector of the Italian bankers, their stock went up, but towards the end of his reign the French king revived his early conscientious scruples and in 1269 passed an act against usurers and pawnbrokers which hit the general commerce as well as the financial operations of the Italians heavily.

The real blossom time of Florentine trade with France began with the accession of Philip the Fair (1285–1314). The Arno merchants and bankers were able to make use of the king's financial embarrass-

---

[4] Davidsohn, *op. cit.*, IV, p. 321.

ment in his wars with the Flemish cities to win for themselves positions of importance in the kingdom. This was the beginning of the fortune of the brothers Franzesi, and "with them began the ranks of those mighty Italian men of finance who lasted through the times of Mazarin until those of the intendant D'Emery." [5] But even the Franzesi were not concerned only with banking. One of their branches, the firm Baldofini e Fratelli, took a prominent part in the wool export by the beginning of the fourteenth century. This same period finds the Florentines settled in forty-three towns of France.

Coins from Provins found in Florence indicate Florentine participation in the Fairs of Champagne as early as 1211. These fairs, which in the course of the thirteenth century had attained a European significance, were especially important in the exchange of products of the Orient for those of northern and southern Europe. Here from one side appeared Provençals, Italians and Spaniards; from another, North French, English, Flemish and Germans. Already in 1209 Philip Augustus took the Italians coming to the markets under his protection, and this policy was continued by his successors. In the letters of privilege granted by the French kings, Florentines are among those mentioned most often.

The Tuscans and the Lombards were among the most important at the fairs for two principal reasons: the large exchange in wool cloth and the banking business, the Florentines being foremost in all the transactions. The house Berto Frescobaldi borrowed in 1295 for Edward I of England 200,000 gold florins, part of which was obtained in Florence, part in Champagne. The obligations of the Flemish princes to the bankers of the Arno were often made payable at the fairs.

The fairs date their decline from the time of Philip the Fair (1285–1314), who by his heavy taxes and duties, his forbidding of the Flemish to attend the markets, and his proscription of the Lombards, broke the chain between the merchants of Italy and the merchants of the North. It is to be kept in mind, however, that while the wool trade of Florence suffered by this act and the other acts of Philip, it was only a temporary setback. On the whole the period of Philip IV is one of expansion of Italian trade and banking, as we have already seen. Following the deterioration of the markets of Champagne, the Germans diverted their merchandise to Bruges and the other markets of Flanders; the Italians began to use the sea route and go directly to Flanders and England. The Hundred Years' War ruined the fairs. Despite the measures taken to restore them, notably those of Charles VII in 1445 and 1455, they never recovered.

The Florentines were in Marseilles from 1248; a decade later Feo

Leoni was active there; the Bardi were in the city by 1292. Many of the wealthier merchants, such as Simone del Befco and Mastino de Bardi, possessed their own lands and vassals in and around the city. About the middle of the thirteenth century, the Brunelleschi had an establishment in Nimes; in 1277 the Medici were active there— "their first contact with the kingdom whose crown certain of their members were eventually to possess." The Florentines soon triumphed over their competitors in both the general trade and the money-lending business, their raw wool and wool cloth forming the great bulk of the exports shipped from the city.

By the second half of the fourteenth century the Italians began to pass by many of the harbors of Languedoc on their way to England, and even La Rochelle on the Atlantic became less frequented. Another reason for this lay in the decline of the Champagne Fairs. Oriental goods destined for the latter had come largely through the southern ports. Nevertheless commercial exchange continued. Emporiums and trade routes merely changed. Montpellier gave way to Marseilles in importance; Avignon, a residence of the papacy, began to play an important rôle as a gold and merchant mart; the fairs of Beaucaire began to take the place of those of Champagne. In all these places the Florentines obtained a fair-sized share of the business.

In Paris most of the large, as well as the middle, Florentine houses had establishments at one time or another. Here also was the head-quarters of the *Calimala* consuls for France. Traders of the smaller Tuscan cities carrying on trade here passed themselves off for Florentines, just as in the Orient the latter gave themselves out for Pisans. Some of the merchants and bankers possessed plots of ground and property in the city.

In Flanders and Brabant, as in other regions, the Florentines were doing business very early. The trade centered in Bruges and Antwerp. In 1315 Francesco Pegolotti was factor of the Bardi at Antwerp. The sources are surprisingly silent, in regard to any woolen trade between Florence and Germany. Davidsohn and Doren fail to mention any direct connection whatever; Schulte, while clearly showing that the Florentines, including the Bardi, Peruzzi, Spini and Cerchi, carried on banking transactions with Germany, which originated with the collection of papal taxes, indicates that a considerable number of German artisans migrated to the wool establishments of Florence, and names a number of Florentines residing in Germany in the late Middle Ages. But he, too, fails to demonstrate any active, regular intercourse in wool products between the two countries. The two peoples certainly encountered each other at the Fairs of Champagne and in the Flemish cities, and it is hard to believe that some wool and cloth business was not transacted there. But the real explanation probably is that the

Germans found it much simpler and cheaper to buy their cloth from the home industries, where the art of wool-weaving and cloth-making was of old origin, or else from nearby Flanders, whose looms in the quality and quantity of their turnout were rivalled only by the Arno city.

As Schanz points out, the commerce between England and the Italian cities differed in its origin, basis, organization, political, and other relations from that which existed between England and the Low Countries. The origin of the trade relations between the former was not in the luxuries which the Italians principally sold in those days— the need for such luxuries was not sufficiently awakened among the rough inhabitants of the British Isles—but in the collection of church taxes which the papacy first turned over to the citizens of Siena, later also to the Florentines and the Lucchesi. This gave acceleration to the money system which the Italians so early developed. In a short while they had the entire foreign money business of England in their hands, and after the Jews were expelled, during the reign of the first Edward, in 1290, they controlled the domestic banking as well. Already in the eleventh century we have Italian settlements in England. Traffic in money was very quickly followed by traffic in goods; by the middle of the thirteenth century, the Italians held most of the offices connected with customs and money, and a cry went up against them.

Contrary to a tradition afloat in contemporary Florence itself that the Bardi were already carrying on money transactions with the English crown in 1183, the first Florentine trade relations with England do not begin, as the investigations of Davidsohn demonstrate, until 1223. In that year there is mention of Guido Spada and Simonetto, the latter probably of the firm Ugolini, engaged in the service of Henry III (1216–72). In 1226 we hear of two Florentine merchants at Dover; by 1243, the trade of the Florentines in the kingdom was already so developed that the crown granted, instead of individual permits, a general right of travel and trade to all Florentines for a period of two years. In the pontificate of Gregory IX (1227–41), the Florentine money-lenders did a thriving business with the Curia, during war with Frederick II (1212–50). By the early years of the reign of Edward I (1272–1307) the Florentines had overtaken both of their most serious competitors in the banking business in England, the Siennese and the Lucchesi. In this reign many large Florentine houses established branches in the country: the Della Scala, the Ghino Frescobaldi, the Cerchi, the Falconieri, and the Bardi.

The English wool trade quickly became a business second only to banking. The profits were enormous. We hear of two brothers, Giovanni and Donato, of the Ricomani family, who around 1273 brought to England 3,000 *librae*. At the end of twelve years in the country they had thirty-three separate contracts relative to the delivery of wool of future shearings, twenty-five of which were with monasteries. A document of 1273 mentions the total export of that year to have been 32,743 sacks, of which 35 per cent was exported through Englishmen, 21¾ per cent through French, 11 per cent through Brabantines, 4½ per cent through Germans, 1 per cent through Spaniards, 2½ per cent through merchants of Liège, and 24½ per cent through Italians, of which 3,960 sacks or 12 per cent was taken by the Florentines, and the balance divided between Piacenza and Lucca. Neither Venice, Genoa, nor Pisa is named at all. The total worth of the Florentine share of this export is estimated around 1,830,000 gold liras. The chief Florentine firms participating in the trade during that year were, in first rank, the Frescobaldi, in the second, the Bardi, Cerchi, Macci, Falconieri, Del Papa-Donati, and Guglielmi.

To assure themselves of an uninterrupted, continuous supply of raw wool for their industry, the Florentines would contract with the English producers for several years in advance, instead of the usual one-year contract engaged in by their Flemish, German and Italian competitors—a demonstration of the canniness of the Arno merchants which explains why they built up such a magnificent commerce.

Just when the full flowering of Florentine wool trade with England was reached and when its decline began is a matter of some uncertainty. If we are guided by the investigations of Schanz, Florence had definitely lost its supremacy in commerce with England to Genoa and Venice by the end of the reign of Edward III (1327–1377), retaining first place only as a banker. The repudiation of his debts by Edward had resulted in such a heavy catastrophe for the houses of the Bardi and Peruzzi and a great number of smaller firms, that, as a consequence, "the blossom of the Florentine trade with England and the rest of Europe was entirely destroyed, as well as the social and political conditions in Florence greatly changed." Doren thinks that the bankruptcy of the Bardi and the Peruzzi had only a temporary effect upon the wool trade itself, for the industry did not experience serious decline until the fifteenth century. But despite the gradual decline in commercial relations, the Florentines continued as the favorites of the English court until the time of the Tudors. From the first years of the fifteenth century English economic history is a story of the rise of English native industry on the one hand, and the struggle to oust foreign competitors from both the home and the international markets on the other. The jealousy of the English manufacturer became marked in the legislation of the Lancastrians, and by the middle of the fifteenth century Genoa, which had succeeded Florence as the chief trader with the Island Kingdom, had succumbed to the adverse legislation and given way to Venice. Venice then became the object of attack. The policy of protection of English home industry and discrimination against foreigners, begun under the Lancastrians (1399–1461), was carried on still more intensively by the Yorkists (1461–85) and the Tudors (1485–1603), and in the end achieved its goal.

The Mozzi, Spini, Cerchi, Abati-Baccarelli and Frescobaldi firms came to Scotland first in 1282 in connection with the papal revenue, but very quickly expanded their interests to include a general money-lending and wool business. Travellers to Scotland for the buying of wool were in subsequent years very numerous, coming both from England and from the Fairs of Champagne.

Relations with Ireland developed even earlier and more extensively than was the case with Scotland. The archbishop of Armagh was obligated from 1263 to the Ghilberti-Bellindoti, the archbishop of Tuma from 1263 to the Dal Borgo, for revenue due the papacy; the archbishop of Dublin to the Pulci-Rimbertini from 1266. Edward I, in 1275, named Banasio Buonotti and his partners to collect the wool duties at the harbors. Many smaller houses, such as the Simonetti-Jacopi, the Tinachi, the Marulli, the Guittoni, carried on a lively and very profitable trade, as well as a lending business, in Ireland. By the end of the thirteenth century and the beginning of the fourteenth Florentine firms had representatives not only in Dublin but in Cork, Limerick and Tipperary as well.

Florentine trade relations with the Iberian Peninsula began with the time of Innocent IV's (1243–54) residence at Lyons. The Dal Borgo in 1263 lent money to the bishopric of Palencia secured by the future income of the see; in 1264 Florentine merchants were among the most important in Barcelona. The Bardi were doing a lively money and merchandise business in Seville in 1327.

The chief article of import to Florence from Spain was wool. This was the famous merino wool which had established a high reputation for purity of color and silkiness of texture. No wool was so useful as this pure white variety for fine manufactures; it also went under the name of *"Lana di Garbo."* Another commodity was the fine Garbo cloth, the best cloth of that time. This came from the Sultanate of Algarve, as we have already seen. So large was Florentine trade in this article at the beginning of the thirteenth century that a street in Florence, where most of the dealers in Garbo cloth lived, was named "Via del Garbo"; it existed until modern times. Besides wool and cloth Florence obtained from Spain Castilian alum, Catalonian saffron, dye-stuffs, rice and mustard. Most of this came in by way of Pisa and Genoa.

The records for Florentine trade with Portugal are very scanty. The house of Doni carried on business with Portugal around 1325, but more than this we do not know. By the end of the fifteenth century, however, a considerable number of Florentines were already settled in Lisbon. This came about in part because the port was a convenient stopping point for galleys on their way to Flanders, in part because the possibility of trade with the country was recognized. One of the ships making up the expedition of Cabral to India in 1501, following the voyage of Vasco da Gama, belonged to a Florentine, Bartolommeo.

The trade with Majorca was more lively than with Portugal. The Bardi had one of their numerous factories here in 1332. The import of goods came partly by way of Genoa, partly over Pisa; for the most part it consisted of wool and wool fleeces. In the fourteenth century the island became an important emporium for the famous Garbo wool. Owing to her position Majorca became a center for products not only from the Iberian Peninsula but from North Africa as well. In addition to wool and cloth Florence traded in Castilian alum, many kinds of dyes, saffron, drugs, sugar, paper, wine, oil, honey, hides of Spanish and Berber horses, leather, various kinds of silk stuffs, elephant teeth, leopard and wolf skins, and various ornaments.

Florentine wool and general trade with Tunis goes back before the middle of the thirteenth century. In 1253 Florentine merchants, on account of the Guelf-Ghibelline feuds taking place in Pisa, did business in cloth, linen and cowls with the North African state by way of Genoa. Pisa from 1230 possessed *fondachi,* not only in the capital (Tunis), but also in Gabes, Bona, and Tripolis. Fleets from Pisa regularly sailed to La Goletta, and the Florentines would participate in these voyages, sharing the expenses and profits. In 1280, however, they began doing business on their own account, winning for themselves like privileges to those enjoyed by the Pisans. Already by this time they had overhauled their Tuscan rivals in the amount of trade which they did with the African state. By 1271 the large banking houses had branches in Tunis; the Mozzi carried on trade with Tunis by way of Naples in wine, fruits and various kinds of merchandise; by the second decade of the fourteenth century the Peruzzi had an establishment there; in the thirties of the same century a branch of the Acciajuoli is mentioned in the documents as existing in Tunis. The import of Tunisian wool fleeces through the Bardi via Genoa was heard of at that time also. The chief Tunisian exports to Florence consisted of wool, raw silk, cotton, flax, leather, wax; imports were chiefly grain and oil, both probably from South Italy.

As the trade relations of Florence with western and northwestern Europe were undertaken chiefly with the view of finding the raw material for the fabrication of woolen cloth, so we must consider her connection with the lands of the East as the most important market for the finished product of the industry. As Doren is himself careful to point out, this is not an absolute division. Raw wool was imported from Tunis, Asia Minor, Greece and Flanders; dyes and especially alum came from the East; Florentine cloth was sold in Bruges and Antwerp, in London and Paris. What Doren means is that just as the fine wool of England and Spain decided the entire character of the production, without which the greatness of the Florentine industry is unthinkable, so also did the love of the Orient for brilliant-colored, elegant cloth determine the selection of colors and the manufacture of expensive cloth in the Florentine home industry. The costly, warm colored cloth of the Florentine looms found its most important market in the East; with her cloth Florence paid for her spices, her drugs and dyes, and the other innumerable products from the Orient which she carried to the North and from which she reaped the usual golden harvest.

The *Calimala* gild reached the peak of its prosperity by 1300, about the time when the first codex of its statutes appears. By then its members were trading with all of France, Flanders, England—in the whole realm of the *"Oltra Monti"* (beyond the mountains), and with Spain. It delegated consuls to represent it abroad; on extraordinary occasions it sent ambassadors and representatives to France, or else the city of Florence did so for it; it had a regular messenger service with the fairs of Champagne; and supervised through its consuls a whole chain of inns and innkeepers in France for the benefit of its merchants.

Through this unique and singular process the *Arte di Calimala* became a tremendous business enterprise. By 1338, when at its height, it owned twenty large warehouses in Florence and received annually more than 10,000 pieces of cloth valued at 300,000 florins. In England and Flanders, at the monasteries and the fairs as well as in the craftsmen's shops, its agents continued to purchase the coarse cloth, while other agents were in the East selling through Venetian, Genoese, and Pisan stations their finished products. Through their agents, who were spread over all northern Europe and Spain, the *Calimala* merchants bought the roughly woven and poorly finished woolen cloth, transported it to Florence in this less bulky form where it was carded, shaved, dressed, and cut so as to remove all knots, thereby diminishing the coarseness. By a jealously guarded secret process known only to Florentines, this "doctored" cloth was dyed with beautiful eastern shades, carefully ironed, faced, and folded ready for eastern markets, where it brought a handsome price. Sometimes it was sent back to Flanders and England and exchanged for other coarse cloth. With the tremendous profits which accrued from this monopolistic business the *Calimala* merchants turned their surplus into banking channels.

The gild's membership was not made up of equals, with masters at the head and journeymen only a few years removed from mastership.

One did not pass from apprentice to journeyman and then to master as in the simple gild. Instead the corporation was composed of superiors and inferiors destined to remain in their stations, each class separated from the other by insurmountable walls. A small group of patrons had under their supervision and command the inferior workers. Of this latter class were the dyers and dressers, who were subjected to hard rules, low wages, and prohibited from combination. Nor could they seek work from other employers of the *Calimala*. These capitalists were the real rulers of the gild.

The Art was a state in itself: its consuls commanded an armed force; they passed statutes with the assent of their councils, held courts to redress the grievances or punish the offenses of its members. While obedience to the state was lightly held, disobedience to the Art implied exclusion from trade and total ruin. Within Italy and without, the Councils of the Art pushed its trade, protected its members, provided for their lodging, exercised unceasing pressure on foreign governments. Within the State the consuls, as has been said, sat in the councils and promoted the interest of the art. It had, moreover, federal relations with its fellow-arts, for the combined societies formed Le Capitudini, whose head was the Proconsolo.

The result of this system was . . . a widely spread political and industrial education. Every merchant was versed in the administration of important interests, in the discussion of statutes, and the decision of commercial suits; he had relations with all parts of the known world, he was himself liable to serve on foreign missions, for the furtherance of common interests. . . . To this political and industrial training must be attributed the full development at Florence, of all the powers of which the individual is capable, the wealth of art and literature which takes its rise in a body of traders, unchecked by chronic disorder in the constitution of the state.[6]

The *Arte di Calamala* had been formed in 1212 by merchants who left the *Lana* to produce cloth from the raw wool instead of refining the coarse material imported from the North and West. Their progress had been slow until near the middle of the thirteenth century when they adopted an improved method of weaving. By the middle of the thirteenth century they produced the finest quality of weave in Europe. They established a factory in the neighborhood of Florence in 1239. The coarse Tuscan raw wool was supplanted by a finer grade of English and Champagne wool, brought in 500-pound rolls over devious and expensive routes. Consequently their raw material was increased in price over 100 per cent. Agents and judges were sent to England to make these purchases. Sometimes English wool was bought up for years in advance. The wool was oiled when it reached Florence, washed, beaten, combed, carded, and refined in large plants which required numerous workers and costly equipment. The spinning

[6] *English Historical Review*, IX, p. 358.

itself was done in the workers' homes, but the other parts of the process were performed in the plants belonging to the gild members.

The Wool Gild (*Arte della Lana*) which lagged behind the *Calimala* in the early centuries, began to forge abreast of its rival by the beginning of the fourteenth century, and thereafter continued to prosper, whereas the *Calimala* began to decline. We have already seen how external circumstances, such as the discriminatory legislation of Philip IV, dealt a heavy blow to the *Calimala*. Her merchants continued to ply the wholesale trade—their real working field—but her industrial activity in refining foreign cloth continued to decline more and more with the growing competition of the home industries, which not only began to rival the dressed and refinished cloth of the *Calimala*, but even to surpass it in quality and fineness. With this conquest of home manufacture begins the rise of Florence as the first industrial city of the world at that time—the ground in which the roots of modern capitalism are found.

In this elaborate system the cost of production was reduced and the quality of cloth of the *Arte della Lana* became superior to that produced by the *Calimala*. In its prosperous days, 1338, this gild had 200 houses which manufactured 70,000 to 80,000 pieces of cloth, among which were magnificent brocades of gold and silver of fabulous values. The miners of Foglia in Asia Minor for these manufactures furnished silver to the value of 100,000 florins per annum. The value of the average bolt of cloth increased about 300 per cent after the introduction of fine grades of raw wool. Gradually as its wealth increased the *Arte della Lana* took the place of the *Calimala* in the government of the city. The Mercanzoria passed from the *Calimala's* control into the hands of the *Lana*. Finally the *Calimala* was completely disabled by the passage of a law prohibiting the importation of foreign finished goods.

Like the *Calimala*, the *Arte della Lana* was a capitalistic syndicate made up of associations, at the head of which were a few ruling figures, dominating and directing the less fortunate workmen of the various trades connected with the production of woolen cloth. The trust feature was worked out more completely here than in the *Calimala*. The *Lana* as a unit became a middleman of the English clothier type two centuries later. As an organization, directed by the merchants and manufacturers who headed it, this gild imported the oil, the carding irons, the raw wool, kermes, alum, and other raw products necessary in the manufacture of the cloth, and distributed these through commissions to its members and the associations as needed. The costs were divided proportionally. It possessed its own warehouses, shops, and drying plants. New workers, new fields of business, and new equipment were often engaged and entered into by the *Arte* as a unit.

Under these magnates—there were about 2,000 magnates in the days of prosperity—the manufacturing was supervised by commissions of their own selection. They distributed the raw products to workers, and each of these associations performed its particular function. There were about twenty-five such associations, all of which were under the direction of and responsible to the magnates. Wages, hours, and length of employment depended upon the heads. Some workers, however, enjoyed more privileges than others: the dyers had fixed wages, which could not be reduced, and eventually became a separate gild, at least for a few years; while the washers, beaters, fullers, and combers of wool were crowded together in great workshops, subjected to rigorous discipline by the foremen, and forbidden to organize into "unions," as they would be called to-day. Their plight, as we shall observe later, was indeed pitiful.

The fourteenth and the first half of the fifteenth centuries was the great period of the Florentine wool industry and trade. Already early in the fourteenth century a large portion of Florence was given up to the woolen industry. Streets were named after the various crafts and vocations connected with wool manufacture, as the *Via dei Cimatori*—Street of the Shearers; *Via delle Caldai*—Street of the Cauldrons; *Corso dei Tintori*—Street of the Dyers.

A large amount of capital was necessary. This explains why so many small businesses consolidated into larger firms and why from the three hundred relatively small firms which existed at the beginning of the fourteenth century, two hundred large establishments had developed in 1338. At the same time the value of the cloth doubled, despite the fact that production had fallen off from 100,000 pieces of cloth at the beginning of the century to 70,000 or 80,000 by that year. Villani estimates this value at 1,200,000 florins and figures that about one-third of this sum was dispensed as wages for the workers and to support a population of 30,000 persons. Besides these figures must be included twenty great warehouses of the *Calimala* gild with an import of over 10,000 pieces of cloth to the value of 30,000 florins. This was for Florentine use alone, and did not count the cloth which, after refining, dyeing and finishing, was exported, particularly to the Orient.

The history of the Florentine cloth industry has been subjected to widely differing interpretations because it has been written by those who have sought to find in it proofs of their theories regarding the advantages of free trade or the rise of capitalism. To prove their points they have associated facts and figures derived from several centuries, neglected the element of change in the trade, and questioned the authenticity of contemporary sources that do not agree with their arguments. Much of this confusion is possible because the fact has not been recognized that the golden age of the industry was limited to a comparatively brief period and was followed by a rapid decline. One need not, therefore, question the contemporary statistics which indicate the prosperity existing in the first half of the fourteenth century. The size of the city as shown by the extent of the walls and the figures of population, the political privileges enjoyed by the cloth-makers guild, and the support contributed by the trade to the public improvements of the period corroborate these statistics. But thereafter followed a series of disasters—pests, plagues, wars, dissensions within the trade, and popular uprisings. In the meantime, neighboring cities had fostered the industry and Florence was unable to regain the supremacy that had once been hers.[7]

In the fourth decade of the fourteenth century the trade experienced a decline due to a number of causes. Among these may be mentioned the continued persecution and expulsion of the Italian merchants from the trade centers of France; the pestilence and famine of the year 1340, a forerunner of the Black Death of eight years later; the unlucky war with Pisa over the occupation of Lucca; the short but heavy tyranny of the Acciajuoli duke of Athens; the bankruptcy of the Bardi and the Peruzzi, which affected a number of large and small concerns and brought poverty and distress in the land; the Black Death of 1347–48, which affected all the industries of Florence and the wool industry in particular, for the mortality among the workers forced the rise of wages and the absorption of smaller into larger firms.

The industry recovered, but experienced several setbacks in the course of the next twenty years, including the war with Pisa (1360–64), which shut off Florence from Porto Pisana and forced her to use the Siennese harbor of Talmone. The whole decade of the seventies was taken up in trouble with the workers, culminating in the fierce *Ciompi* uprising of 1379, which disorganized production, deliveries and credits, and led to the winning of many privileges by the workers.

In the decade 1380–90, due to the internal quiet of the city, the woolen industry took an upswing again, and by 1393 the wool gild was able to cancel the privileges won by the workers during the revolutionary years. The gild was benefited also by the law of October 25, 1393, passed by the government as a result of pressure applied by the gild itself. This law, "in order to prevent the impoverishment of the gild," sought to keep out foreign cloth by an almost prohibitive duty, exception being made of coarse or light cloth which was not manufactured in Florence, and of cloth from Flanders and Brabant, with which the *Calimala* merchants were chiefly concerned. This measure was aimed against the competing Italian cities,

[7] M. L. Hansen, comment on Robert Davidsohn, "Blüte and Niedergang der Florentiner Tuchindustrie." *Ztschrft. f. d. Gesamte Staatswissenschaften*, 85 (2) 1928; 225–256.

since aside from France, Flanders, Brabant and Germany, these were the only places supplying foreign cloth to Florence.

Following the acquirement of Pisa (1406) and Leghorn (1421), the last great hindrance was removed, and the Florentine wool trade again conquered the world.

Florence was no whit behind her Italian rivals in the oriental markets. Already in the twelfth century Florentine merchants were to be found in Palestine; around the middle of the thirteenth they were established in Acre; towards the end of the century they were in practically every city of importance in the Mediterranean, Black, Aegean and Adriatic seas. The Crusades, which initiated the period of expansion of medieval commerce, quickened the commercial life of Florence along with that of the other Italian cities; in the end no inland city of the peninsula could compare with her in the amount of trade transacted with the Orient. Before the conquest of the Byzantine Empire by the Ottomans her commerce with the Levant was conducted through Venice. When the Doge Tommaso Mocenigo, dying (1423), contemplated the rich resources of Venice, and developed the theme to the dignitaries standing around his bed, he said among other things:

> You know, that the Florentines each year give us 16,000 pieces of cloth which we distribute for them in the Barbary, in Egypt, Syria, Byzantine Empire, Cyprus, Candia, Morea and Istria; further, the Florentines bring goods of all sorts to the value of 70,000 ducats a month, therefore, 840,000 ducats a year, and fetch for that wool from France and Catalonia, *"karmoisinrothe"* (scarlet?) cloths, carded wool, silk, gold and silver, thread and precious stones.

At the time of the Bardi failure (1345) Pegolotti published his book *Descriptions of countries and of methods in business and of other things needful to be known by merchants, etc.* He spent the most of his life as a factor in the service of the Bardi, and his travels for the profit of that commercial house led him to North Persia. He was in Cyprus in 1324, and in 1335 he gained from the king of Little Armenia a grant of privileges for trade at Lajazzo. He secured privileges at Antwerp in 1315 and in London in 1317. So this Florentine gives us a view of travel along some of the greatest international routes. He is the first European to note the mercantile importance and give a detailed account of the Black Sea route to Cathay—that "shorter and safer way which Monte Corvino had recommended for mission travellers." [8] Pegolotti's work is one of our most important sources of information regarding Italian trading enterprises in the Levant, and from its details of his own doings we may judge of Florentines

[8] Beazley, *Dawn of modern geography,* III, p. 326.

in general. Besides business houses established in foreign cities there were three hundred or more men sent out yearly direct from Florence to carry their trade into foreign parts, and Florentine traders had been even to northern China. Before they had a single ship the indomitable Florentines had established houses and banks and introduced their merchandise in all the principal eastern ports. Pegolotti says they went through Astrakhan to Saracano on the Volga and thence crossed Asia to China.

In Adalia the chief trade was in cloth of bright colors, which naturally drew the Florentines there at an early date. In the thirties of the thirteenth century the Bardi obtained a reduction of the tolls to 2 per cent *ad valorem* for imports and had to pay nothing for exports, whereas the merchants of nearby Cyprus were compelled to pay 2½ per cent tax on both imports and exports.

In Little Armenia the Florentines by the thirteenth century were trading in fine wool cloth along with many other things. The Arno banking houses at the appointment of the papal curia stood in constant connection with the kingdom, the Holy See hoping that by subventions to the king of Cyprus he might stand as a last bulwark against the oncoming Mohammedans in the Holy Land. With this task the Franzesi in 1307, and later the Bardi, were entrusted. The latter succeeded in 1356 through Francesco Pegolotti, their representative in Cyprus, in obtaining free import and export rights, which placed them on equal footing with the Genoese, Venetians and Sicilians. The Peruzzi also won certain favors at this time.

In the case of Brusa, the Empire of Trebizond, Tana (Azov) and Sivas (Sebasteia), the sources, in describing the very considerable activities of the Florentines in these places, do not specifically mention trade in wool or wool cloth. That there was such trade is hardly to be doubted when it is remembered that in all the neighboring cities and regions, such as Constantinople, Acre and Lesser Armenia, wool cloth was the chief article of sale of the Arno merchants. In all these very important emporiums the Florentines had colonies; in both Tana and Trebizond they established *fondachi* and consulates.

Single and isolated references to the Florentine wool trade with Egypt appear in the sources first in 1220; again in 1245. In a notebook of 1278 belonging to a Pisan and in the writings of Balducci Pegolotti are mentioned some of the principal items of commerce with the Mameluke state in the thirteenth and fourteenth centuries. Exports to Italy consisted of ginger, rhubarb, incense, alum, saltpeter, lack, Arabian gum, rose-water, medicinal plants as aloe, roots of all sorts, dyestuffs, particularly indigo, dates, sugar from Alexandria; wax, gold in bars as well as minted or spun in thread; wool, raw silk, brocades, tapestries, camelot, linen and cotton; in return Egypt imported grain and oil from Apulia, nuts from Naples and Salerno, tin from Sardinia. Cloth from Florence was a constant object of import also.

Most of the European ships stopped at Alexandria. In this cosmopolitan and world trading center were found numerous merchant colonies and the most important market. Damietta was also important, largely because of the products of the Nile Delta, such as sugar, which could be more easily obtained here than in Alexandria. The Knights of St. John had a consul there; Venetian and Genoese colonies were found also, the consulate of Venice lasting until deep into the sixteenth century. The shipping service with Egypt started late and for a long time was irregular. The Council of Florence around 1444 began to bestir itself over the value of establishing regular sailings between the two lands, partly to give business to the state galleys, partly to insure circulation of its wool and silk goods, partly for the aromatics, spices and countless other products it obtained from the Levant. In that year it ordered its Consuls of the Sea (August 18, 1444) to send two trade galleys yearly in the spring to Alexandria and the neighboring regions. The route used was the following: from the Italian coast to Syracuse, then by way of Modon and Rhodes to Alexandria, Beirut and Jaffa. On the return voyage landings were made in Cyprus, Crete or Rhodes. In 1460 galleys going to Tunis were ordered to stop at Alexandria and Rhodes in the course of their itinerary.

Not until around 1465, however, may we speak of an uninterrupted connection between Florence and Egypt. In that year Mariotto Squarcialupi was appointed consul for Florence in Alexandria, and serious attempts were made to gain privileges for the Arno merchants. The negotiations continued for several decades, until in 1496 Florence received a "letter of privilege" from the sultan Kaitbai granting her equal rights with Venice. Egypt, facing at this time the menace of the Ottomans, sought alliance with the western nations and for this reason was more conciliatory. This document represents the last detailed trade treaty between the two countries. Thereafter the documents talk only in generalities or repeat certain chief points contained in the former treaties.

In contrast with the experiences of other nations, Florentine-Egyptian relations ran along smoothly on the whole, but, at that, one detects evidence of occasional friction between the Arno merchants and the Egyptian officials. The former asked repeatedly for a *fondaco;* it was as often promised, but apparently never realized, although there was a Florentine consul in Alexandria.

The famous book of Balducci Pegolotti is particularly important for the trade with Cyprus; as the agent for the Bardi he had the deepest insight into the commercial life of the island, and his account seems entirely trustworthy. The Florentine commerce with Cyprus attained great volume. As usual its chief competitors were the Venetians, the Genoese and the Pisans. The position of Cyprus made it an emporium for the Near East and a meeting point for trade between the Orient and the Occident. Famagusta, the capital, was the converging point for this commerce. For Florence the origin of trade with the island is to be found in the transaction of papal business. The Society Pulci-Rimbertini around 1275 granted a loan to the archbishop of Nicosia apparently at the behest of the Holy See; Bishop Guido of Famagusta contracted a loan with the Bardi at the court of Boniface VIII.

In 1299 the Bardi sent a quantity of grain from Naples to Cyprus and from that time forward began to do a large business in cereals and other commodities along with their banking business; the Peruzzi took part in commerce with the island from 1298 on. From the books of the Bardi and other sources we learn that exports from the island were chiefly raw silk, Egyptian wool, heavy silk stuffs worked through with gold thread, jewels, pearls, coral, squirrel skins, glassware, dye-stuffs, paper, sugar, dates and ginger. Most of these went to Italy, principally by way of Ancona, and in some quantity through Pisa and Naples.

With the exception of the Bardi and the Peruzzi, the Florentines living in Cyprus gave themselves out for Pisans as late as 1324, but after this date, at the intercession of Pegolotti, privileges equal to those enjoyed by the two large houses and to those possessed by the other foreign merchants, such as the Venetians, the Genoese, the Pisans, Provençals, Narbonnese and Catalonians, were granted all the Florentines.

Under the two kings of Cyprus, Jacob I (1382–98) and Jacob II, the Bastard (1460–73), the Florentines were given a cordial reception and various privileges. From then on—at least for a short while —trade flourished somewhat more extensively. The sources mention at least one Florentine consul appointed to Cyprus, Mariotto Squarcialupi.

The Peruzzi had a factory in Crete by 1317, probably at Candia, though this is not certain. The Venetians, lords of the island, exercised naturally the chief trade, but Florence came in with money operations, and the delivery of cloth played a considerable rôle.

Rhodes was not an important focal point of commerce like Cyprus; its importance rests much more on the fact that it was the seat of the Knights of St. John. In Cyprus the Bardi house played the leading part, but here it took a rôle subordinate to that of its rival, the Peruzzi. Both companies lent the knights the necessary money for buildings and forts when they first arrived in the island, and the Order continued to be indebted to them. A commercial exchange followed naturally, and in the thirteenth century consisted principally of caviar, which came in preserved form from the Black Sea, linen cloth, and soap made from olive oil; later on the commerce expanded to greater variety and volume.

By the end of the thirteenth century Florentine merchants were already established in Constantinople in considerable numbers, had their own settlement, and were considered as a separate trading nation —this at a time when as yet Florence did not possess her own harbor or her own galleys. In 1416 the Florentine, Bettino Bartoli, arranged a treaty with the emperor Manuel by which Florence obtained the church and the loggia as well as all the privileges formerly belonging to Pisa, whose star by this time had definitely set. After the acquisition of her own port, the commerce of Florence with the Byzantine Empire increased largely; her first trade voyage to Constantinople in her own ships took place in 1436. But the privileges accorded Florence did not come into full effect until the issuance of the Golden Bull of August, 1439, by the emperor John Cantacuzene in appreciation of the reception accorded him by the Arno city during the "Unification Council."

Like the other foreigners residing at Constantinople, the Florentines lost heavily in the sack of the city by the Turks (1453). Their good fortune lay in the fact that they possessed less property there to be plundered than did their fellow-traders. The Venetians are estimated to have been damaged to the extent of 40,000 ducats, the Anconitans 20,000, and the Florentines 20,000 ducats. The Genoese, living for the most part in Pera, sustained relatively small losses at the time, but in the end suffered more than any other nation from the Turkish conquests. This same fate eventually befell the commerce of the other nations, with the exception of the Florentines, who were clever enough not only to regain their trade but to increase its volume—if only for a short time. Following the conquest of Constantinople they transported their headquarters to Pera, which became the chief center of their activities in the Turkish Empire.

By a clever policy of bribing and diplomacy Florence soon won for herself first place in the empire. In 1488 the wool gild decided to make a present of 950 florins to the sultan out of its own means, and in later days the home government assisted the gild in this bribing process. The "presents" to the sultan became so burdensome that the Florentine administration found itself compelled to lay new taxes, not only on the export merchants and members of the Lana gild, but also on those who did only an import business with the Levant. But all this helped. By 1469 there were no fewer than fifty Florentine commercial and banking houses listed in the Turkish Empire. Bayezid II, who succeeded to the throne of his father, Mohammed II, in 1481, sent a delegate to Florence and among other things agreed to buy annually 5,000 pieces of cloth. Until the end of the fifteenth century Florentine commerce with the Turks continued in sizable volume; thereafter it underwent a quick decline. By the end of the century the state shipping had already stopped coming to Turkish ports; by 1520 private shipping also ceased.

Adrianople, which before the conquest of Constantinople was the chief city of the Ottomans in Europe, possessed a colony of Florentine merchants by the close of the fourteenth century; Chios, after 1447, was a port of call for Florentine galleys on the way to the Byzantine, Egyptian and Syrian ports, but undoubtedly Florentines did business there before then. Trade with the duchy of Athens sprang up in the fifteenth century at the time of Antonio Acciaijuoli, duke of Athens. Under him the Florentines were given equal rights and privileges with those possessed by the Venetians, Genoese and Catalonians. Negotiations for the establishment of trade relations with the Morea were entered into during the rule of the despot Constantinus in 1446; his successor, Demetrius, in 1450, continued the negotiations, promising certain inducements. Whether these privileges were actually made use of is not certain, for by 1460 the Turks had already put an end to the Greek domination in the Morea and carried Demetrius to Constantinople. With Corfu the Bardi were doing business by 1301; by 1319 at least three of the large societies, the Bardi, the Peruzzi, and the Acciajuoli, carried on trade with Valona in Albania. Florentine cloth was sold as early as 1252 in Ragusa. The Della Scala were established there in 1303, and a little later the Bardi also had a factory. Trade with Dalmatia goes back even earlier, but the first evidence of a lively intercourse with Zara in Florentine cloth appears in 1345.

The cloth trade was the focal point around which all the commerce of Florence originated, but how this trade was created, in what form it grew, whether it was designed before everything to meet the demand of the home consumer for finer cloth; whether at the beginning it served principally as a sort of medium for the exchange of eastern goods for western; how and why this cloth refining industry developed to such an extent that the world has not seen its equal—on all these questions the sources are silent. What is certain is that the Florentine cloth trade reached its full bloom only after it had succeeded, by a series of refining processes—especially in connection with dyeing and finishing—in improving the coarser northern cloth to such an extent as to satisfy the most capricious tastes of the Occident and Orient, and reducing the excessive transport costs, at that time one of the chief factors in raising the price of commodities.

Florence's commercial and industrial policy was one of strict protection of home industry, and the most developed and striking example of this policy, which became very general throughout Europe in the fourteenth and fifteenth centuries. This policy is clearly set forth in a political tract written in the middle of the fifteenth century by Lippo Brandolini entitled: *De comparatione respublicae*. He says:

Since we are in so large measure given to mercantile life and profess to supply others with an abundance of garments of every sort, we would surely seem to do ourselves an injury if we permitted others to carry on our own craft in our city. . . . If we admitted foreign goods of this sort we would not only lower our prices, but also our prestige. . . . We think that foreign woolens should under no circumstances be admitted. . . . Since our merchants are citizens, they have themselves sanctioned this law.[9]

Trade secrets were carefully guarded in Florence. With the development of the textile industry dyeing began to revive in Europe. The cultivation of color-producing plants, notably madder and saffron, the organization of important gilds, the gradual extension of the industry from southern Europe to the northern and central parts, are all indications of the activity of the dyers during the fourteenth and fifteenth centuries.

It has been said before that part of Florence's success in the textile industry was due to the attractiveness and efficiency of her dyeing processes. The industry was carefully regulated with a view to developing the quality of the output to the greatest possible extent. Any cloth which was badly dyed was either "remanipulated, cut and sold to hucksters, or burnt." As a result Florentine cloths attained a genuine excellence, surpassing that of all other Europeans in the beauty of their dyes.

As a rule vegetable dyes only were employed, and they were sought in every land.

The time and abilities of the most prominent citizens were given ungrudgingly to the discovery of new colouring plants and to their export to Florence. The acquisition of a new dye was just as much a question of state policy as was that of obtaining mordants and other adjuncts of the dyeing industry.[10]

The chief colors used by the weavers were black, blue, red, gold, brown, and white, though the sources mention many more. Exactly how the various shades were produced is not known, but the sources tell something of the kinds of dyestuffs used. In both Italy and Germany black and blue were produced largely by means of woad.

Stringent regulations were enforced in order to secure the permanency of the dyes. Only the most expensive dyes were allowed to be

[9] Thorndike, *Science and thought in the fifteenth century,* chap. xiii, pp. 252–53.
[10] Staley, *Guilds of Florence,* p. 124.

used on the finest cloth. To this day in such Florentine fabrics as have been preserved, the colors are as brilliant as they were in the fifteenth century. The ingredients for the various dyes and mordants were imported from every quarter of the then known globe, and formed some of the principal items of Florentine trade with the East.

Alum was so necessary to the dyeing industry, and its economic importance therefore so great, that a brief discourse on the history of this mineral deposit is necessary. Until the fifteenth century, when alum was first discovered in Europe, the Italian wool manufacturers were absolutely dependent upon importation of alum from other lands, and all these were in Mohammedan possession. In 1255 Rubruck, the Franciscan friar whom St. Louis sent to visit the Mongol khan, found in Iconium on his return trip two merchants—a Genoese named Nicholas de Santo Siro, a native of Acre, and a Venetian named Boniface de Molendino—who had a monopoly of the alum trade there in Asia Minor. Alum which usually cost fifteen bezants was sold by them for fifty. The product was marketed by Greek and Armenian merchants, who, as middlemen, probably made as heavy a profit as the producers. One can get some idea, accordingly, of the price of alum in Italy. Another alum deposit in Asia Minor was at Koutaieh, capital of the principality of Kermian. Aleppo in the hinterland of Syria was another place whence alum was exported to the West. The alum trade out of Egypt was jealously guarded by the Venetians. In fact it was one of the bitterest grounds of feud between Venice and Genoa, and until the Genoese were victoriously excluded from Alexandria by Venice during the Crusades, alum was an important article of Genoese trade. Genoa's revenge came in 1261 when she overthrew the Venetian rule on the Bosphorus and succeeded to Venice's commerce in the Black Sea and Asia Minor. Then the Zaccaria brothers, the same who made a fortune in sugar, made a colossal fortune in the alum of Phocea.

The advance of the Turks in Asia Minor in the fourteenth century was watched with some gratification by Venice, who hoped to see her hated rival Genoa lose the commercial domination which she enjoyed owing to the favorable policy of the Paleologi emperors towards the Ligurian republic. In 1368 a Venetian embassy was sent to the sultan Murad in hope that Venice might acquire license to purchase alum under favorable terms. But Genoa managed to retain the good graces of the Turks and in 1415 we find a Genoese named Giovanni Adorno enjoying the concession to work the alum beds of Phocea. In 1437 the sultan Murad II granted to a company composed exclusively of Genoese the monopoly of all the alum deposits in Asia Minor, except those at Lesbos and Phocea where the Venetians had obtained a concession. But catastrophe overcame the company in 1455 when, after the capture of Constantinople, the Turks, who had so far tolerated the Genoese in the Levant and spared the Genoese island of Chios, changed their tactics and attempted to seize the rich island. The Turks failed to capture Chios, which was not lost until 1566, but both Genoa and Venice were deprived of the alum concessions which they had had. The result was a "Black Friday" in Venice and Genoa. In Venice two merchants of alum failed for 150,000 ducats. It was the failure of the supply of this all-important commodity which was in a large measure responsible for the ultimate decay of the Florentine cloth industry.

Men and women in these textile industries worked together, especially since the looms of Italy were such that they required two people to operate them; hence it was only natural that man and wife, mother and daughter should work together. But as the business grew it became necessary for the women to devote more and more time to the preparation of meals for the workers, and they were crowded out from the industry itself. Into this loophole German workmen stepped and took the place of women at the loom, especially when the Black Plague of 1349 had swept away a great portion of the working population.

When these bankers first went into the cloth business the woolen industry was one of strictly home manufacture. But as the business grew it was seen that the loss of time and disorganization of the work was so great that it would be impossible to compete with better organized countries, and the result was that they worked out an improved factory system. A great part of the work was still done in the home; a regular messenger service was worked out by means of which goods were delivered into the hands of the workers and also called for by messengers when the work was done. In connection with some of the stores there were built up regular central workshops in which the lowest class of workmen were employed under foremen with regulations very similar to the factory rules of the present-day shops. Here part of the rough work such as combing and dyeing was done. The cloth was then sent out from these factories to the homes of the workmen, back again for another process, and then out again, until it was ready to be sold. In the homes it was possible for men who owned their looms to install extra looms, hire men to work them for day wages, and thus set up in business for themselves and become masters.

The statutes of the *Calimala* give us much interesting information upon the mechanism of the Florentine corporation. Every six months the heads of the warehouses and the stores met together to elect their councils. Every warehouse had two votes, every store one; those elected had to serve. The four councils chose one of their number as prior. They were assisted by a general council and a special council. The consuls looked after the interests of the gild and supervised the members of the corporation. Once a month the general assembly of the consuls of all the arts was held. In order to enter the *Calimala* one had to have plied one's trade for a year, but in time eligibility became hereditary. It was forbidden to sell cloths except those imported from beyond the Alps. Gambling was forbidden in the shops. The apprentices had to sleep on the premises and could not go out at night. The life of the apprentices was carefully regulated. This strict discipline gave the arts an excellent organization. Foreign cloths were examined by experts upon their arrival and were then distributed to the various gilds, trimmers, dyers, fullers, carders, *etc.* The dimensions, the luster, the fineness of the cloth when completed was specified. Special officers appointed by the gild fixed the prices, and every bolt of cloth had to bear a tag with the prices fixed, the name of the house, and even of the workman who had handled it.

While engaged in his researches upon the history of the Florentine woolen trade, professor Alfred Doren [11] was struck with the constant recurrence of the names of German workmen in the records of the Florentine cloth workers. That led to the discovery that thousands of German artisans in the fourteenth and fifteenth centuries wended their way to Italy in order to learn better or newer industrial technique. A reviewer, in commenting upon this book, observed:

> It is an interesting matter for speculation and inquiry to what extent medieval Italy was indebted to these foreigñers from the north of the Alps for her remarkable industrial and artistic development. . . . From the second half of the fourteenth century Germans were to be found all over Italy plying almost every conceivable trade and craft. At an early date they seem to have practically monopolized the inn-keeping industry. They found occupation also as weavers, dyers, tailors, furriers, shoemakers, bakers, millers, grocers, soapmakers, provision merchants, butchers rarely, barbers, apothecaries, smiths, turners, carpenters, coopers, potters, curriers, saddlers, stone masons, wood carvers, glass painters, goldsmiths, silversmiths, scribes, illuminators, booksellers, notaries, musicians, physicians, and there is one instance of a German schoolmaster. As cooks they are frequently met with, especially in monasteries.[12]

This great migration of German workmen into Italy seems to have begun about 1370, and was contingent upon two important circumstances. German manufacturing seems to have reached a peak at this time, so much so that the markets were glutted with goods; and secondly, progressive German workmen were eager to learn the superior technique of Italy in many trades. Wherever these immigrants were settled in numbers they formed local brotherhoods, not unlike many

---

[11] *Deutsche Handwerker und Handwerkerbrüderschaften im mittelalterlichen Italien* (Berlin: Prager, 1903).
[12] *English Historical Review*, XIX, p. 153 (a review of the above).

modern "lodges." They were partly social clubs and partly insurance associations to provide care in event of illness, protection in event of trouble, and decent burial to each member. These societies are not to be confused with the industrial gilds, of which the incomers shortly became members. Some of these German workmen brought their families with them, or sent for them after becoming established. But the most were unmarried journeymen who soon married women of Italy, so that within two generations this immigrant class was Italianized. It would be interesting, if it were possible, to ascertain the particular parts of Germany whence these immigrants came. But the records afford no certain evidence on this point. They are all invariably denominated Tedeschi—Germans. It is natural to infer, however, and there is some reason to believe, that most of them came from the cities of South Germany like Nuremberg, Augsburg, Ulm. But there was apparently a plentiful sprinkling of North Germans, too, from Frankfort, Cologne, Hamburg, Bremen. Some Flemish and Dutch workmen must also be included in this category.

CHAPTER XI

THE FISCAL AND ECONOMIC POLICY OF THE PAPACY IN THE FOURTEENTH AND FIFTEENTH CENTURIES

WE have seen in the preceding chapters how from the thirteenth century forward the volume and variety of commerce, trade and industry in every European country increased; how the surplus profits arising from this activity were invested in new methods of economic promotion; how the practice of international loans increased; how every important mercantile point blossomed into a fiscal and banking center.

The Church and the papacy could not escape being influenced by these changes and reflecting these conditions. For although primarily a spiritual institution, the Church was an international state formed of an international society, whose chief executive was a prince as well as a priest. Bishops and abbots were also political rulers, enjoying rights of sovereignty like those exercised by lay princes. Moreover, the Church, too, possessed enormous wealth in the form of landed endowments, market privileges, coinage rights, episcopal and monastic shops whose employés were servile dependents. The volume of manorial, feudal and ecclesiastical revenues imposed by the Church made it the greatest and richest tax collector, the greatest fiscal agency, the richest banker, in Europe.

In this capacity the removal of the papacy from Rome to Avignon in 1309 was of advantage to the popes. Rome was never an important place of commerce in the Middle Ages; it was not situated on any of the high roads of trade, and the States of the Church, when nearly all else of Italy had become a great mart of commerce and hummed with industry, still remained lapt in the old medieval agrarian economy. On the other hand, Avignon was situated upon the Rhône river, from remote times one of the most important commercial arteries of Europe, and the mountain passes connecting North Italy with Provence further contributed to Avignon's commercial prosperity. The Great and Little St. Bernard, the Pass of St. Jean de Maurienne, the Mont Cenis all connected Piedmont with the valley of the Isère, and so with the Rhône. Most important of all these routes was that of Mont Genèvre, the old historic road between Italy and Southern France. To-day it is Route Internationale No. 94, one of the greatest roads of France. The "farm" of these transalpine tolls was one of the sources of papal income in the fourteenth century.

The chief detriment to Avignon's commerce was the swift current of the Rhône, the numerous sandbars, the tolls imposed at Arles and Tarascon, and the heavy pilotage fees exacted by the Arlesians. In order to avoid these difficulties in the fourteenth century the Levantine merchants, notably the Genoese, opened a trade route from Bouc, on one of the arms of the delta, to Avignon, across the Plaine de la Crue. Bouc soon became a port of some consequence for Italian merchants and the Levantine trade. Arles and Tarascon promised to lower their tolls, but no change was made and they were left in the lurch. Still another route from the Riviera to Avignon was that from Nice through Grasse, Draguignan, Aix and Pertuis to the Durance and so to the Rhône at Avignon.

The Venaissin or city and county of Avignon, when the popes came to occupy it, was in a state of dilapidation owing to the ruination resulting from the Albigensian wars. With the papacy came prosperity. As the capital of Christendom, Avignon was thronged with officials—cardinals, chamberlains, chancellery clerks, chaplains, notaries, scriveners, couriers, police, soldiery, to say nothing of visiting bishops and abbots, papal legates returning with their suites to make report, ambassadors, and feudal princes. Nearly three hundred high officials were comprised in the papal entourage, each of whom had his staff of clerks. Moreover, as Avignon was a comfortable place to dwell in, many people from all over Europe settled there as residents. Among these great Roman families like the Colonna and the Orsini were prominent. Naturally French provincials were most numerous. Many of these settled in Avignon to escape the ravages of the English in France. The English were not numerous, but some of the inhabitants of Avignon were immigrants from London, Litchfield and Lincoln. There was a Rue des Allemands, but Germans were not numerous. Italians were almost as numerous as French. Florentine and Lucchese money-changers and bankers were established in the parish of Notre Dame, and there were clusters of Italians from Bergamo, Piacenza, Turin, Genoa, Pisa, Pavia, Bologna, Cesana, Milan, Arezzo, Viterbo, Savona, Rome, Naples, and Sicily. The Jews in Avignon were numerous and better protected than anywhere else in Europe. The popes recognized their remarkable fiscal ability. As the population increased and necessities augmented, Avignon had a remarkable commercial and industrial awakening. There was hardly a trade unrepresented. Petrarch the poet, who was Latin secretary to one of the popes, tells us in one of his letters of the multitude of inn-keepers, spice merchants, fish dealers, furriers, bakers, mercers, soap-makers, leather workers, wool carders, silk weavers, gardeners, and common laborers to be found in Avignon.

The most flourishing business in Avignon was banking, which was almost entirely in the hands of Italians. The great banking firms of

Florence had their representatives there and continued in the four-teenth century as they had been in the thirteenth, to be the chief papal bankers. The papacy suffered seriously when the Bardi and Peruzzi failed in Florence in 1345. As all kinds of merchants frequented Avignon, all sorts of money flowed thither, which it was necessary to convert into papal coin. Over forty money-changers are enumerated in a single papal document of 1327. Foreign merchants from almost every country of Europe had their agents and their warehouses in Avignon. These traders journeyed to the Fairs of Champagne and Beaucaire; they bought dyes, vestments, robes, arms at Montpellier; textiles at Béziers, Albi and Carcassonne; tapestries in Spain; woolen cloth and linens in Flanders; and goods from all the world at Bruges. Along the waterfront of Avignon were piles of timber which had been floated down the Durance and the Isère; tiles, brick. Long strings of mules brought in charcoal from the hills roundabout. All this commer-cial and industrial development was a source of wealth, and Avignon in the fourteenth century boasted of three merchant princes. The book of accounts of one of these has been preserved. We see this prosperity still reflected in the immense and magnificent papal palace in Avignon, the churches, the remains of lesser palaces of cardinals and rich bour-geois of the city, and the stupendous medieval walls which yet sur-round Avignon.

It would be an error, however, to infer that the chief wealth of Avignon was derived from commerce and industry. These were re-sults. The cause of papal prosperity was the money revenue of the popes, which flowed into Avignon like a river of gold from all Latin Christendom. Where there is gold there will merchants be gathered together. Abundance of money not only created a money-lending and banking market at Avignon; it created a market of purchase and sale of all sorts of commodities, especially luxuries.

There were both general and particular reasons for the astonishing development of papal fiscality in the fourteenth century. The capitalis-tic idea and capitalistic practices had been growing apace in Europe ever since the Crusades. The anticapitalistic protests of St. Francis and St. Dominic had gone by the board, although the failure of the almost impossible economic idealism of the former convinced not a few, notably the radical Spiritual Franciscans[1] of the rightness of the teaching. It was unavoidable, indeed inevitable, that the Church and the popes shared in this movement. New taxes to tap the new sources of wealth were a characteristic of the time. All over Europe we find complaint of them—in the France of Philip IV, in the England of Edward I. The French popes, like the kings, under the changed con-

[1] The Fraticelli denied the right of the Church to possess property. John XXII condemned them as heretics.

ditions, were compelled to devise new kinds of taxes in order to provide themselves with revenues; and what is true of the popes is true
of every bishop and abbot. The Church was rich in land, but land
values had diminished under the impact of the great economic revolution which had largely substituted commerce and industry for agriculture as the principal source of wealth. The ancient stream of
manorial revenues of the Church had shrunk to a mere rivulet. In
England and France the kings, in Germany and Italy both princes and
cities, had assumed the right of taxation unto themselves as a political
prerogative. The Church was forced to discover a new sphere of taxation into which the state could not penetrate, and this carried with it
the necessity of inventing new forms of taxation. It was the only way
in which the popes could convert a deficit into a surplus.

The policy of increased papal taxation was not original with the
pontiffs of the fourteenth century. "By the closing years of the twelfth
century the Holy See was finding its old and established revenues
utterly insufficient to meet the cost of rapidly expanding activities.
Fresh sources of supply had to be tapped." [2] The popes before Innocent III had been content with loans or voluntary subsidies contributed by the clergy. Not so Innocent III. During the Crusades new
forms of taxation had been devised to finance those expeditions. Now
that the Crusades were over the papacy had both precedent for the
principle and the machinery for collection in its hands. For nearly a
century the popes had employed all sorts of means to finance the
Crusades. Why not now use the same means to finance the papacy?
"The first expedient was a tax on the incomes of the clergy. Imposed
for the first time in 1199, it was used with increasing frequency
throughout the thirteenth century." [3] A chronological statement will
bring into relief the progress of clerical taxation. There were six several valuations of church property and incomes made in this century:
1216, 1226, 1229, 1256, 1275 and, most famous of all, that of Nicholas
IV in 1291. The growth of the practice not only alarmed temporal
rulers; it gave anxiety to lay lords who were concerned over their
rights of advowson.

The ecclesiastical machinery for the collection of these resources was
perfected by the council of 1274. The dominion of the Latin Church
was divided into revenue districts and collectors assigned to each.
These collectors with the advice of the bishop and two members of
the cathedral chapter appointed in every diocese two deputy collectors.
Payments were to be made in two installments, at St. John's Day
(June 24) and at Christmas. Former valuations were cancelled and
an entirely new valuation made, which marked an increase over the

[2] Lunt, *English Historical Review*, XXX, p. 398.
[3] *Ibid.*

old. There was much protest, much confusion owing to ambiguities in the rules of assessment, and not a little corruption. The moneys collected were stored in sealed bags in cathedrals, monasteries, with the Knights Templar, or sometimes with local Italian bankers to await papal orders. The popes did not always use the money for promoting the Crusades, although that was the avowed purpose of the new assessments. Before 1250 they largely employed the funds to finance their conflict with Frederick II; after that date to support Charles of Anjou's conquest of the kingdom of Naples and Sicily. It was the difficulty of paying for the Sicilian war which led Boniface VIII to divert the proceeds of the tenth imposed in 1300.

All these taxation practices and the machinery necessary to collect the moneys passed over to the French popes at Avignon. One of the early ones, John XXII (1316–34), is justly famous as the wizard of papal finances in the fourteenth century. He understood the world òf his time quite as clearly as the sovereigns, indeed, more clearly.

In the papal court the various separate bureaux which directed the fiscal policy and handled the revenues arising therefrom were together known as the Apostolic Chamber. The two principal officials of this body were the *camerarius,* or chamberlain, and the treasurer. The former was the pope's minister of finance. He was always either an archbishop or a bishop, but could not be a cardinal. Under his authority were not only all the treasury and fiscal officials in Avignon, but also all collectors of the papal revenue throughout Christendom. One of his most important duties was to audit the accounts of these collectors. The treasurer directed the distribution of the papal revenue. Under each of these officials was a host of notaries and clerks.

The papal taxes may be divided into two categories: (1) those paid in directly to the Holy See, (2) those collected in every diocese and remitted to Avignon. In the first category were moneys paid into the Apostolic Chamber by bishops and abbots upon their nomination or confirmation by the pope; chancellery fees paid by every recipient of a papal bull; visitorial payments when coming to the papal court, as every bishop was required to do at certain intervals, and, finally, the fee exacted of every recipient of the archiepiscopal pallium. What this last sum represented may be seen from a few figures. In the fourteenth century the archbishop of Mainz paid 5,000 gold florins, Trèves 7,000, Cologne 10,000. These amounts varied with revaluation of property from time to time. In 1326 Breslau was reduced from 4,000 to 1,785 florins. Martin V, in 1420, raised Mainz and Trèves to the 10,000 florin class. The popes had long exacted a fee for conferring the pallium upon archbishops; fees for the installation of new bishops; the *cens* from monasteries under papal protection; and tithes of episcopal and abbatial revenues, which of course in last analysis were tithes imposed upon all Christians. These were old ecclesiastical taxes. But with the increased wealth of Europe the popes enormously magnified the number and kind of impositions. Many a bishop got into the hands of money-lenders or impoverished his family or mortgaged his house lands in order to pay them.

The second form of papal taxation requires longer description. (1) *Extraordinary Tithes:* These were special assessments and not to be confused with the ordinary tithes. As impositions upon ecclesiastical revenue their origin is to be found in the Crusades. In order to ascertain the approximate value of the wealth of the clergy, the Apostolic Chamber sent inspectors or estimators into every bishopric to make a survey of the resources of every bishop. The tithe was the tenth part, not of the gross but of the net revenue. All clergy except cardinals paid tithe. The crusading orders were exempt. During the reign of Philip VI of France (1328-50) as we have seen, a large portion of the tithe was regularly employed to defray the cost of the war with England, a circumstance which did not enhance the pope's popularity across the Channel. (2) *Annates* were theoretically the whole revenue of a diocese during the first year of a new incumbent, but in practice not more than half as much. John XXII was long given the doubtful credit of having devised this tax. But it is now known that Clement V, the first Avignonese pope, had recourse to it. John XXII made general and systematized a previous practice. (3) *Procurations* were the right of hospitality which the pope might exact when travelling. As the Avignonese popes never travelled they tried with poor success to convert the right into a money payment. It was finally forbidden by the Council of Constance in 1414. (4) *Dona.* These were very various of nature, in theory unsolicited, in practice compulsory requisitions. (5) *Census:* This was of two sorts. The "great census" was collected from lands dependent upon the Holy See; the "small census" was a fee paid by either person or property in return for apostolic protection. Its collection was irregular, and the revenue arising therefrom not large. (6) *Vacancies* were the revenues accruing from ecclesiastical benefices left without an incumbent owing to death or removal of the holder. It was an application to church offices by the popes of the old feudal principle that a suzerain had a right to the revenues of a fief left vacant by the death of a vassal. A not infrequent ecclesiastical abuse of the fourteenth century was that of continuing vacancies.

In addition, the pope sitting *in curia* derived a prodigious revenue from ecclesiastical cases of many sorts, which were appealed to him from episcopal courts. Not all of these would be ecclesiastical cases to-day. But it is to be remembered that in the Middle Ages questions of marriage, separation, inheritance—for wills were not valid unless executed before an ecclesiastical lawyer or notary—were frequently under ecclesiastical jurisdiction. So lucrative was the pope's curial revenue that the Avignonese popes designated a large number of cases as "reserved" cases over which the pope had immediate jurisdiction and which were automatically transferred to Avignon as soon as they arose. This was a practice bitterly condemned by the bishops, who thus were deprived of their fees for sitting on such cases before appealed. The evils of extortion and graft were inseparable from this papal policy.

It must be understood, however, that these papal taxes were solely of an administrative nature and arose quite legitimately in the exercise of ecclesiastical government. One may criticize the management of them as sometimes excessive, or complain of administrative corruption in their enforcement—for which the popes were rarely responsible. But in principle they were legitimate and necessary for the administration and support of the Church.

But when we come to that other group of papal revenues which were derived from the pope's prerogative as spiritual head of the Church the question is not so clear. In the former category we are touching temporal values. In the latter category we are concerned with spiritual values. The greatest of these abuses was the sale of *indulgences*—the practice which probably was most lucrative to the popes. Nothing is here intended in impeachment of the doctrine and principle of indulgence. But abuse of the penitential system and degeneration of granting of indulgences into a business until the spiritual end implied in the grant was eclipsed by the worldly and mercenary nature of the practice seems an almost unavoidable conclusion to one who honestly examines the documentary evidence of the time. It savored too much of using spiritual authority for revenue purposes. This commercialization and fiscal exploitation of "grace" is what so shocked the spiritual sensibilities of the fourteenth century; what reformers inveighed against and heretic groups most condemned.

Another revenue-producing prerogative of the popes was their power of *dispensation*, which was again a function of their spiritual office. In virtue of this prerogative the popes could "dispense" or suspend the canon law, a practice to which they were usually ready to resort if the end justified the means. For example: the canonical prohibitions could be "dispensed" concerning consanguineous marriage, concerning minors holding church benefices, concerning pluralism or the simultaneous possession of many ecclesiastical offices by one man, or concerning the opposite abuse, that of appointing several persons to the same office, only one of whom was the actual incumbent, the rest being merely titulars. Very heavy fees were invariably exacted for such dispensations. The papal revenue arising from appellate cases and dispensations was enormous.

The map of the Church was divided in 1274, as said, into revenue districts known as *collectoria* which rarely conformed to established diocesan or metropolitan lines. But it was not until the fourteenth century that the system acquired form and fixity. The collectors were usually appointed by the *camerarius*, but sometimes by the pope himself. Each collector had a large number of subordinate collectors and was accompanied by a staff of clerks and notaries. Excommunication and interdict were employed on occasion in order to extort taxes.

The transmission of these huge revenues to Avignon was a complex and difficult matter. If the collections had been made in *naturalia*, as they not infrequently were, the products had to be converted into cash on the spot. Accordingly a good collector had to know markets and prices of commodities. When paid in coin the collector had to be on guard lest he receive mutilated or counterfeit money, and in all cases the wide variety of coins which were current required the services of a money-changer to convert the intricate mass of coins into a transmissible sum of money. After the fall of the Templars this was done by Lombard and Florentine bankers, the greatest of which, as we have seen, had their branches abroad. If possible, actual shipment of coin was avoided and bills of exchange used.

Meanwhile how had Rome and the States of the Church fared since the removal of the papacy to Avignon? No more striking contrast is imaginable than that between the luxury prevailing at Avignon and the dire poverty in Rome in the fourteenth century. To all the industrial hum, to all the commercial activity of Italy as a whole in the fourteenth century Rome was a stranger and an anomaly.

There was a want not only of fixed authority, but of those elements of social stability which the other cities of Italy possessed. In the greater republics of Lombardy and Tuscany the bulk of the people were artisans, hard-working orderly people; while above them stood a prosperous middle class engaged mostly in commerce and having in their system of trade gilds an organization both firm and flexible. It was by foreign trade that Genoa, Venice and Pisa became great, as it was the wealth acquired by manufacturing industry that enabled Milan and Florence to overcome and incorporate the territorial aristocracies which surrounded them.[4]

The civil and patrimonial administrative system of the papacy in the States of the Church went to flinders in the anarchy which followed the removal of the pope to Avignon. If things in the States of the Church had followed the course of events elsewhere in Italy, one of the great Roman families like the Colonna or Orsini ought to have arisen, crushed its rivals and established a princedom in Central Italy like that in the Milanais. But the arena was too narrow and the rival

---

[4] Bryce, *Holy Roman Empire*, p. 300, new edition.

families so many that no one of them was able to accomplish this result. Accordingly Rome was torn for decades by the feuds of her unbridled nobility. Their frowning castles not only covered the countryside roundabout, but filled the city of Rome itself. Some of these erections were improvised out of ancient Roman structures. Thus the Frangipani converted the Coliseum into a château. The Septizonium on the Palatine, the Theater of Marcellus, the triumphal arches of Titus, Septimius Severus and Constantine were transformed into bastioned towers. Each family employed hired bravos and mercenaries who, when not warring with other similar bands of ruffians, infested the roads and waylaid pilgrims and travellers, rifled churches and robbed farms of the peasantry. The black anarchy of Rome in the fourteenth century beggars description.[5]

From this pit of despair the republican revolution engineered by Rienzi (1347–53) temporarily and to some degree rescued Rome. But Rienzi cherished too impossible and fantastic ideas to make them effective and in his later years seems to have become mad, unless one believe with some writers that he was a charlatan from the beginning. The partial success of his efforts to introduce law and order into the States of the Church seems, however, to have stirred Clement VI with the hope that something effective might be done to restore the papal domination.

Accordingly in 1353 the pope sent the famous warrior-cardinal Albornoz to Rome for the difficult task. At this time Montefiascone was almost the only place in the States of the Church still recognizing the absentee lordship of the pope. Central Italy was infested with companies of mercenary soldiery. They were highly organized associations of robbers.

The leaders of these *barbuti* (as they were called on account of their helmets), clad in mail from head to foot, were surrounded by a council of four captains for the cavalry and by an equal number for the infantry. Important affairs, moreover, were, according to republican custom, submitted to the parliament of all the corporals. Constables, marshals, corporals formed various grades in this military association, according to the *bandiere* or squadrons into which the company was divided. There were judges and notaries, and treasurers who distributed the booty and salaries and administered the finances. . . . Their motley camp was a market where the spoils of convents and cities were sold by a crowd of merchants, while great Italian banks stood in commercial relations with the captains who deposited their plunder at interest.[6]

Two of these companies were commanded by English soldiers of fortune and were chiefly composed of English troopers out of France.

---

[5] For a remarkable account see the introduction to Bulwer Lytton's *Rienzi*.
[6] Gregorovius, *City of Rome in the Middle Ages*, VI, ii, p. 415.

These captains were Sir John Hawkwood and Hugh Mortimer. The most notorious was Fra Monreale of Albarno, a Provençal and a renegade prior of the Knights of St. John, who came nearer than any other man of the hour to establishing a principality in Rome. In the bank of Perugia he held huge sums which he had extorted from the cities he had blackmailed. Even Florence, Siena, Arezzo and Pisa had purchased immunity from siege and pillage. In 1354 he made 150,000 gold florins by selling the use of his army to Venice against the Visconti under the command of his chief lieutenant, the count of Landau, a German adventurer. When Albornoz sent his envoy asking that he leave the States of the Church in peace the *condottiere* sent back the reply:

My lord, our manner of life in Italy is universally known. To rob, plunder, murder those who resist is our custom. Our revenues depend on mortgages in the provinces which we invade. Those who value their lives buy peace and quiet by heavy tribute. If therefore the Signor Legate wishes to dwell in peace and to secure tranquillity to the cities of His Holiness, then let him do like the rest of the world, that is to say, pay, pay, pay![7]

But Albornoz got his man, not by battle but by a diplomatic ruse and Fra Monreale was sent to the scaffold in 1354. He seized the treasure the knight of St. John had with him and that which he had previously deposited in Rome; it amounted to 100,000 gold florins, 60,000 of which had lately been extorted from Pisa. But the cardinal was not quick enough to get possession of the treasure Fra Monreale had amassed in Perugia, for Florence sequestrated it before the cardinal could reach Siena.

Hope was cherished in some quarters in Italy that the fall of Monreale might be the beginning of the end of the other free companies. As early as 1349 Florence had proposed the formation of a league against them. Albornoz strove for the same object when the emperor Charles IV came to Italy. But the ruffian captains laughed at the emperor's poverty and protests. In 1366 an Italian League composed of Florence, Naples, and Rome seemed on the verge of formation, but Guelf Florence protested against the emperor having any relation with it and the plan dissolved. In spite of this setback, however, the heroic cardinal pursued his course of liberating the States of the Church. It was a shrewd policy of threat and compromise. The first to yield were the Malatesta in Rimini and the March of Ancona. In return for submission to papal authority and for a rent, in 1355, they received the vicariate of Rimini, Fano, Pesaro, and Fosembrone for ten years. The Montefeltri in Urbino and Fermo, and the Manfredi of Faenza yielded soon afterwards under similar conditions. This arrangement

[7] Quoted in Gregorovius, *op. cit.*, VI, ii, p. 416.

palliated their former seizure of papal territory. For in return for conceding title of it to the papacy they received it back as papal rulers (vicars) thereof. Vicars, *i.e.*, local feudal houses, were also installed in the county of Sabina and the mountainous country between Spoleto and Nera. The residue of the papal territory was put under rectors. Associated with them were provincial parliaments in which the churches, monasteries, convents, barons, and towns of the region had representatives. Each rector had his staff of marshal, judges, and tax collectors.

Cardinal Albornoz was as thoroughly imbued with the systematic fiscal ideas current in the fourteenth century as the princes and free cities were. The *Codex Diplomaticus* of the papacy at this time contains a number of interesting documents which cast light on the administration of the papal patrimony. Thus we have a statistical survey made of the March of Ancona in 1356; another of the Romagna and the March made in 1371. The population of the Romagna then numbered 346,444 hearths and its annual revenue was 100,000 florins.

The best evidence for the partial economic recovery of the States of the Church through Albornoz's efforts is found in an event in 1375. The years 1373–75 were years of terrible suffering from crop failures and pestilence in all Southern Europe. Northern Europe seems to have been spared this affliction. Torrential rains alternated with periods of protracted drouth. From Christmas, 1372, until Easter, 1373, no rain at all fell; then it rained almost steadily through April, May and June. At Pisa the price of a measure of wheat rose to four liras in June, 1375; in December it was eight; in February sixteen. The price of wine and olive oil increased in corresponding degree. In Lombardy farming was abandoned and crowds of country folk swarmed into the towns for food. All Italy hungered for bread. Grain was imported by ship-loads from Sardinia and Corsica where the elements had been more propitious. In this singular distress the States of the Church had more wheat than any other part of Italy. Marseilles, Montpellier in France, Genoa, Pisa, Lucca, and Florence petitioned the pope for supplies. Gregory XI replied that he had no more than enough for his own subjects. But Florence loudly protested, and a petty "wheat war" followed in which the papal territory was forcibly despoiled of its grain by the Florentines. The pope was roundly accused of deliberately refusing relief in order to enrich himself by corn speculation, and much of distressed Italy believed the accusation.

Rome lapsed back again into something approaching her former condition of anarchy during the Great Schism (1378–1415). This great cleavage in the history of the Church, although more important ecclesiastically and politically than economically, yet had its economic aspect. Europe was divided between two "obediences," and the revenues and patronage of the Church in each "obedience" exercised not a little influence in protracting the conflict.

If popes and anti-popes had had their way, no Christian man would have been allowed to supply his neighbor with food or fuel; the dead would have remained unburied; war would have been sanctified in its fiercest frenzy, and trade and intercourse between states and cities would have been swept away.[8]

Fortunately, all this acrimony had little effect on the ordinary workaday world. It was said truly that the root of the trouble lay in the fact that neither contestant would part with the revenues, patronage and emoluments of his office. We get a glimpse of the sordid scramble in the time of Alexander V. When he was elected the Spiritual Franciscans went wild with delight, for the new pope was of such humble birth that he knew not who his parents were and hence had no nephews or other relatives to take care of. But his court was soon crowded with office-seekers.

There were one thousand claimants for every vacancy; business was conducted without method; benefices were tossed about; forgeries were abundant; dispensations were allowed for irregular marriages; and everything was soon in complete confusion.[9]

When the Great Schism ended and the papacy returned to Rome, at least two ancient scourges had disappeared. The age of the *condotieri* had passed in Italy by the fifteenth century, and in Rome the old nobility was so broken that never again was it able to raise its head. Unfortunately, however, not even the elements of a middle class existed, as elsewhere in Europe, on which to build a polity. The city of Rome, so far as it was governed at all, was governed by the gilds there. As for the Campagna and the rest of the surrounding territory, it was ruled by petty barons, many of them descended from former vicars and rectors who had localized their power and made it hereditary. Agriculture had almost completely vanished from the Campagna, partly because of the long-continued anarchy, partly because, owing to the profitability of wool-growing, the proprietors deliberately abandoned farming for pasturage. Shepherds from the Alban Hills and the Abruzzi, as in Spain, regularly drove their flocks down from the hills in winter to pasture in the Campagna, and returned with them to the hills again as summer approached. Later popes of the century attempted to remedy this condition. Sixtus IV by law required a third of all lands to be cultivated, reintroduced the constitution of Albornoz,

[8] Wylie, *History of the Reign of Henry IV*, vol. III, p. 4.
[9] Wylie, *op. cit.*, III, p. 391.

reformed the coinage, dredged and leveed the rivers and tried unsuccessfully to drain the pestilent marshes around Foligno and in the
Maritima. He even dreamed of trying to drain the Pontine Marshes.
But the Ager Romanus remained much as it was in the fifteenth century until after the fall of the temporal power of the popes and the
founding of the present monarchy in 1871. When Urban V and Gregory XI visited Rome they returned terrified to Avignon. We have a
remarkable word-picture of the Eternal City about 1400 from the pen
of Adam of Usk, an English bishop who dwelt for some time in Rome
in the pontificates of Boniface IX and Innocent VII. It is a sordid
picture of diminished population, poverty, brigandage, vermin and
wolves. Nocturnal street fights between the wolves and the vagrant
dogs of the city kept him from sleeping, he says. Robbers stripped St.
Peter's of its marble and porphyry. The poverty of the great church
was such that in 1414 only a single lamp could be burned on the day
of the festival of St. Peter and St. Paul. The walls of the Vatican
were so crumbled that wolves invaded the gardens.

Such was the condition of Rome when, in 1420, Martin V entered it
and restored the papacy to its true capital. With the restoration of the
papacy in the fifteenth century Rome entered again not only into
Italian life, but the life of all Europe. The popes became Italian princes
who vied in power and splendor with the Medici and the Visconti;
the papal states became a principality equal to the duchies of Florence
and Milan; Rome increased in population with the concentration of
the administration of the whole Latin Church again in her midst; the
material and moral life which had prevailed at Avignon now prevailed
in Rome, which soon rivalled every other state in Italy for prosperity
and magnificence. The gold of all Central and Western Europe flowed
into the coffers of St. Peter. Abundance of money, crowds of pilgrims
and sight-seers, the coming and going of envoys from every ruler, each
accompanied by a splendid retinue, the number of bishops, abbots and
other ecclesiastics who swarmed to Rome on legitimate business of
the Church or seeking preferments,[10] made business boom. A craze for
house-building and a wave of real estate speculation accompanied this
change. Usurious speculation in wheat was another phenomenon. But
Sixtus IV may be exonerated from the charge of having profited by
such practices, although it must be admitted that graft and abuses

[10] A volume of the greatest historical interest, giving the rules of procedure
in the papal curia, and the actual texts governing the reservation, assumption,
and vacation of benefices, also the procedure in litigation before the papal
courts and the obtainment of dispensations which the pope had reserved, is
Regulae, Ordinationes et Constitutiones Cancelleriae Pauli II (1464–71), printed
at Augsburg in 1476. All these rules are given in full, with the exact amounts
in cash of the fees payable to the papal exchequer. There is a long tariff of
indulgences on folio 139.

on the part of subordinate officials were not unusual. On the whole the permanently resident population of Rome was lightly taxed. The papal incomes were so large that the pope could afford to exempt his own subjects. The French historian, Commines, a shrewd and candid writer, said that the pope's subjects ought to be the happiest on earth since they paid no poll tax and hardly any other kind of tax. This statement must be taken with some qualification, yet it remains true that "hardly anywhere, on an average, was the taxation so low as in the States of the Church." [11] We get a comparative measure of the wealth of the papal state when compared with other Italian principalities in 1464 when a crusade was concerted against the Turks. The pope and Venice were each to contribute 100,000 ducats; Naples, 80,000; Milan, 70,000; Florence, 50,000; Modena, 20,000; Siena, 15,000; Mantua, 10,000; Lucca, 8,000; and Montferrat, 5,000.[12]

The most curious and one of the most lucrative sources of papal wealth in the fifteenth century was the revenue arising from the alum deposits discovered at Tolfa in 1462. In a former chapter we have seen how alum was an indispensable adjunct to the dyeing industry on account of its astringent quality which "set" the colors used. But few alum beds were known in Europe, so that the textile industries of Italy were dependent upon importations at excessively high prices from Asia Minor, principally through Venetian and Genoese merchants. Florence especially suffered from this condition, since it was the greatest textile manufacturing place in Italy. But in 1458 a lucky chance disclosed a small alum deposit at Volterra. Florence promptly declared war on the little town and annexed its territory. The amount thus acquired, however, was insufficient for Florence's needs, and alum was still as high as ever. Then came a new and wonderful find. In 1462 Giovanni da Castro, a Paduan, son of a celebrated jurist, who until 1453 had been manager of a big dye-works in Constantinople, discovered alum at Tolfa in the papal territory. This story is one of the romances of the history of commerce. The facts are related in the Memoirs of Pope Pius II to whom Castro revealed the information. Tramping through the hills Castro found an herb near Cività Vecchia which attracted his attention because he recognized it as one which grew also in the Alum Mountains of Asia Minor. Then he observed in the vicinity a whitish mineral which had a saltish taste. When submitted to fire the substance proved to be alum. Castro hastened to the pope. "Today," he exclaimed, "I bring you victory over the Turk. For annually he receives 300,000 ducats from Christendom for alum. I have found seven hills full of alum, enough to supply

[11] Reumont II, i, p. 279 in Pastor, *History of the Popes,* IV, p. 425 note.
[12] On the Crusade Account Book see Pastor, *History of the Popes,* III, pp. 336–37.

seven-eighths of the world, and plenty of water near at hand. This, and the nearness of the sea for shipping purposes, will make the working of the beds easy. Thus Turkey will be deprived of her profits and new resources for carrying on the holy war against the Turks are furnished." Experiments showed that eighty pounds of the new alum were equal to one hundred pounds of Turkish alum. It was of excellent quality. Within another year there were 8,000 persons employed in the industry. Giovanni da Castro organized a company for exploitation, the shareholders in which were Genoese and Pisans, with whom the pope was a partner. The yearly papal income amounted to 100,000 ducats.

CHAPTER XII

WE must now resume the history of France from 1380. In that year Charles V died. Undoubtedly the economic condition of France had not improved as much in his reign as the political. There was hope that an era of prosperity was about to open. But this hope was soon frustrated. The new king was a boy of eleven years of age. The three brothers of Charles V, the dukes of Anjou, Berry, and Burgundy, and his brother-in-law, the duke of Bourbon, struggled for the power and each one thought only of his own interest. Against these dissipated and incapable nobles the people rebelled on all sides. Paris, which had abdicated its power into the hands of a prince who was a wise and able administrator, would not submit to the exactions of these uncles of the king. Within a short time after his death, the regents of Charles VI, under the influence of popular pressure, were compelled not only to abolish the hearth tax, but also the *gabelle* and the *aides.* The crown with its complicated administration was reduced to the resources of the royal domain. Every new tax was abolished and the lawyers took as texts for their harangues *"Novus rex, nova lex, novum gaudium."* Moreover, the people of the towns were pushed on by the peasantry, who organized jacqueries in the country areas; bloody sedition followed in the towns (1382). Such popular outbreaks were a general phenomenon in Europe at this time. Ghent revolted against the count Louis de Mâle in 1379. In England the peasantry revolted under Wat Tyler in 1381. In Florence there was a popular rising in 1379–82.

In France a long period of agitation began, running roughly from 1380 to 1415. These troubles reacted disastrously upon industry and commerce. During the first part of Charles VI's reign there was no war with England, but it is to be noted that even if there was no general war from 1380 to 1415 there was a partial state of war in a great number of the provinces, occasionally interrupted by truces. The insecurity in Brittany, in Normandy and Poitou was great. The English made unexpected descents on these provinces and pillaged the towns. In 1412 in Lower Normandy, they conceived the barbarous idea of cutting down the apple orchards, which formed one of the chief sources of the wealth of the province.

The French nobility of the epoch of Charles VI displayed a shameless luxury. Never were the entertainments more brilliant than those given at the court at this time; never were the royal entrances into the town of greater splendor. The costumes worn by the nobles were magnificent, and the industry which was fed by this luxury was very prosperous; but the nobles in order to keep it up doubled the taxes on their lands and heavily oppressed the people. Moreover they contracted huge debts which they never paid. The senseless luxury of the time ruined them and the working classes.

The history of industry in the reign of Charles VI consists of the relations of the king with the gilds—relations by turns hostile or friendly. French industry at this time was in a state of complete decay. The workmen had played the principal part in the revolt of 1382. They were the ones who suffered most during the suppression of 1383. They lost their influence in municipal elections and very often their associations were dissolved. Where they survived they were made directly subject to the royal provost. However, little by little the government relaxed its rigor; the gilds in Paris were permitted again, and their confiscated property was restored. They were treated more and more favorably in proportion as the influence of the king's uncles declined, and during the years 1388-90 the gilds recovered their old position. One of them—the Corporation of the Butchers—rose to a position of supreme influence and played a prominent political part in the events which mark the end of the reign of Charles VI.

Before the edict of January, 1383, the butchers had formed various companies scattered in the various seigniories into which the city of Paris was divided. There was first upon the domain of the king the butchers of the Grand Butchery; they dwelt on the right bank of the Seine between the church of St. Jacques de la Boucherie and the river. There were to be found streets with the expressive names of Teurie, Triperie, Tannerie, and the old Place aux Veaux. Then there was the Boucherie Ste. Geneviève, on the hill of that name. At the end of the fourteenth century the members of this corporation, being obliged to kill their animals outside the town, established a slaughter-house at St. Marcel. There were besides special butcheries in the various seigniorial territories, that of the Parvis of Notre Dame on the land of the bishop of Paris, and of St. Germain des Prés on the lands of the abbot of that name.

These butchers enjoyed great privileges and as an organization were very strong. The number of members was limited and membership in the Grande Boucherie succeeded from father to son; the monopoly of butchering in the bourg of St. Germain des Prés was reserved for those who were born in the bourg, or had married a woman there.

The butchering business was a most lucrative one and the leading butchers of Paris were very rich men. Such were Simon Caboche, Thomas Legois, Denis of Chaumont, a skinner, and the heads of the three influential families of the Guerins, the St. Yons and the Deux-Epées, or Two-Swords. Thomas Legois owned a fine house with three gables on the Hill of Ste. Geneviève. William St. Yon, who died in 1380, left a large estate. At his death there was a famous trial before the parlement of Paris, the supreme court of the king, the contest being between his widow and his two sisters. From this process we learn that William St. Yon owned three stalls in the Butchery of St. James, where every week he sold meat worth 200 *livres* (over $920). His profits must have been between $100 and $140 per week. He owned three country houses in addition to his house in town. His silverware was famous, as was his wife's wardrobe. Her jewels were worth over $9000. Besides real and personal property, St. Yon left 300 hides, 800 firkins of tallow, a flock of 800 sheep—for every big butcher was also a stock-raiser with farms in the vicinity of Paris and cattle-pens within the city limits—and a fortune of over $30,000 in hard cash. His widow was accused of having used undue influence with her husband in the making of his will. We do not know how the case came out, but the part of the process which has come down to us throws interesting light on the butchers of medieval Paris.

When a butcher died his son took his place. The twenty-third article of the statutes says that no one can be a butcher of the Grande Boucherie of Paris unless he is a son of a butcher of that Boucherie. If the son was of age he had to give a sumptuous dinner to the other members of the corporation. If the son was a minor his guardian had to pay for two dinners as well as all additional expenses, and give bond that he would do so. At these repasts the provost of Paris, or the king's receiver at the Châtelet were sent presents of wine, cake and game; similar gifts were made to the master and his wife, to the superintendent of the streets of Paris, to the bishop's provost, who administered the bishop's justice, to the cellarer and to the concièrge of the parlement. Other regulations forbade the building of new slaughterhouses, and thus assured a certain monopoly to the corporation.

After the revolt of the Maillotins, however, in virtue of the ordinance of January 27, 1383, the butchers' corporation in spite of its wealth was dissolved, and was not restored until 1388. As it was one of the few corporations having real property, the stalls were confiscated and annexed to the royal domain, and the king pocketed the profits.

The butchers' gild suffered less than many others. But the butchers of Paris never forgave the king. Their day of revenge came years afterwards. Charles VI became a hopeless maniac, and the government was exploited in a most shameful way by the queen, Isabel of Bavaria, and her paramour, Louis, duke of Orléans, who was the king's cousin. But Louis had a bitter rival in the powerful duke of Burgundy.

In 1407 Orléans was assassinated by hired agents of Burgundy. Two factions were formed, one led by Burgundy, the other by the count of Armagnac. The civil war spread from Paris and at last involved most of the provinces of France, too. To complicate the situation Henry V of England revived in France the English wars of the century before.

In 1413, while Henry was besieging Havre at the mouth of the Seine, two years before he won the famous battle of Agincourt over the French, matters came to a climax in Paris. The butchers' gild—partly, one thinks, because of the ancient grudge which it bore towards the crown, and partly because it despaired of any political reform coming from the crown—in 1411 had entered into secret relations with the duke of Burgundy. Although the butchers seem to have taken the initiative, the demand for reform was widespread. The states-general sat from February to May without accomplishing• anything. In this crisis the University of Paris prepared a comprehensive bill of administrative reforms, which the butchers' gild supported with armed forced. Caboche, Legois and St. Yon the Younger, with a large body of partisans, paraded through the city, haranguing the people and condemning the crown and the states-general for their apathy and negligence. On April 28 the crowd assembled before the Bastille, as it was to do again with ominous results in the early days of the French Revolution. They marched to the palace where lived the dauphin who, owing to the madness of Charles VI, was acting-king.

Paris was in a state of turbulence. The butchers were masters of the city. Squads of them patrolled the streets and guarded the bridges and principal buildings. They must have been a formidable sight in their long leather smocks reaching from neck to heel, reeking with the odor of slaying as they caught the chill of the cold spring air, and purple with gouts of blood from the abattoirs. Every man of them carried his long blade, in the use of which he was a master. Seen at a distance their leathern caps might have passed for the steel morion, or iron skull-cap, of real soldiery. Their leather belts were less decorated than those of the knights and gentry, but the effect was just as warlike. No scabbards depended from their belts for the carriage of their swinging steel; they carried their blades in their hands.

On May 26, 1413, the crown accepted the terms of the Grand Ordinance. But unfortunately the butchers' gild, having tasted the sweets of power, was loath to resign its influence. Begun as a justifiable demand for reform, the movement of the Cabochiens became a tyranny. Intense partisans of Burgundy, they opposed every attempt to reconcile the two parties. The mercantile and industrial classes in Paris grew to look upon the butchers' party as a faction of sedition, and rallied to the crown. The Burgundian party began to lose influence, and finally the duke of Burgundy turned traitor and entered into secret negotiations with Henry V of England. This action killed the Cabochiens, for it threw them into alignment with the national foe of France.

Little by little, the crown and the upper classes under the lead of the count of Armagnac gained power, and on September 1, 1413, recovered control of the city and abolished the ordinance. The victorious Armagnacs naturally dealt severely with the Parisian corporations which had backed the duke of Burgundy, who drew his recruits from the lower classes. A new reign of terror followed; long lists of proscription were posted and there were many executions.

On May 13, 1416, the government ordered the destruction of the Grande Boucherie "for the better decoration and embellishment of the streets of Paris, and to remove all infections and corruptions injurious to the public health." The slaughter-houses were removed to more distant parts of the city, and the network of narrow, crooked streets and alleys abolished. Undoubtedly the change was in the interest of the Parisians. The political influence of the butchers' gild was ended. In none of the other famous risings of Paris, neither in the Day of the Barricades, in 1588, nor in the French Revolution, did the butchers play a conspicuous part.

What has been said of industry may be repeated of commerce. At the end of the fourteenth century it seemed as if French commerce was on the verge of a new prosperity. French establishments in Italy were important. The queen of Naples, Jeanne I, by her will transferred her rights in the kingdom of Naples to the second housè of Anjou, to Louis I, and his son, Louis II. The duke of Orléans had married Valentine Visconti, daughter of the duke of Milan, and had received the county of Asti in dowry. Pope Clement VII, the French antipope, dreamed of putting the States of the Church under the suzerainty of France as the "kingdom of Adria." In 1396 French influence was dominant in Genoa, where the marshal Boucicault acquired Savone, Monaco, and the isle of Elba for France, and even tried to seize Pisa and Leghorn. A great future seemed open to French commerce in the Mediterranean. France could dream of rivalling Venice for the domination of the sea. But all these dreams failed. The duke of Anjou was beaten in Lower Italy and could only retain possession of Provence. The duke of Orléans failed in an attempt to wrest the States of the Church from the pope at Rome. In 1400 during the absence of Boucicault a popular rising broke out in Genoa and overthrew French control. In Italy the duke of Orléans was only able to hold on to the county of Asti. From all the attempts of France in Italy, French commerce got nothing. Thus, in spite of appearances, between 1380 and 1415 there was a serious decline of French commerce and industry. From 1415 to 1422, and even down to 1430, when the French victories over the English began, this decay continued.

After 1407, when the duke of Orléans was assassinated, northern France was in a state of civil war. In 1415 the English again invaded the country. Harfleur surrendered to Henry V, and after the battle of Agincourt the whole channel coast fell into English hands, the Castilian merchants at the mouth of the Seine receiving important privileges from England. In 1417 Henry V fell upon Lower Normandy and captured Caen, Bayeux, Argentan, Falaise and, after a long siege, Rouen, which surrendered January 14, 1419. The whole of Normandy was lost to France except Mont St. Michel on the Breton coast, which was never taken by the English. Of all the kingdom of France, Normandy was the richest province; Caen was famed for its cloths and serges; Rouen was the equal of Paris in manufacturing importance, and its cloth trade was very celebrated, while its general commerce extended from Italy to Scandinavia.

The English systematically organized their conquests; those who submitted had nothing to fear, those who refused to recognize English domination were driven out. Many cloth workers were thus compelled to leave Normandy and go into Brittany. Brittany hitherto had produced little cloth except linen, but it soon began to manufacture foreign cloths. This was notably the case at Fougères, where many cloth workers from St. Lo settled and made it an important industrial center.

At the moment when the English completed the conquest of Normandy, the duke of Burgundy was assassinated on the bridge at Montereau, September 10, 1419. This murder broke every connection between the lands of the crown and the provinces of the duke. Henceforth every relation ceased between Flanders and the Ile de France; the valley of the Somme was closed to France. But this was not the worst result of the assassination. Philip the Good threw himself into the arms of England heart and soul.

The treaty of Troyes, May 24, 1420, gave the crown of France to the future son of Henry V, and Catherine of France, daughter of Charles VI. The towns of the Île de France were surrendered to England, and on September 1, Henry V entered Paris. To judge by the reception which the Parisians gave him, one might think that the prosperity of Paris was still great. The bourgeois were clad in rich red, and before the palace a miracle play was performed. But below the surface the state of Paris was miserable. Between 1418 and 1426 the Fair of Lendit was discontinued, and foreign merchants no longer came to France. The Jews, who had been expelled in 1410, migrated to Alsace and other parts of Germany and to Avignon. The Lombards also left and took their banking business to Antwerp, Brussels, and

Geneva. Moreover the English invasion extended. "France" was limited to the southeast and eastern part of the country beyond the Loire, with its capital at Bourges. The only French ports upon the Atlantic were those in Poitou and Aunis—La Rochelle, Niort, St. Jean d'Angely. But these ports rarely saw Portuguese or Castilian vessels. The ships of the Hanseatic League ceased to come there, since the French themselves foolishly stopped their trading because the Hansers also were trading with England. The only ports of profit to France were those on the Mediterranean—Aigues-Mortes, Narbonne, Montpellier. From these sailed the French ships which carried French products to the eastern ports of Egypt and Syria. But even these ports maintained precarious connection with the sea, because of the continual tendency to become silted up. The Fairs of Lyons began to decline, or rather they were transferred to Geneva; those of Montpellier and Beaucaire disappeared. It was the darkest hour of French history, until the coming of Jean Darc and the restoration of government, industry and commercial prosperity under Charles VII and his famed minister, Jaques Coeur.

On August 31, 1422, the hero of Agincourt died at Vincennes, leaving a child of ten months as his heir. This child, the issue of Henry V's marriage with the Princess Catherine of France, succeeded to the English throne as Henry VI. A few weeks later occurred the death of Charles VI, and in accordance with the terms of the treaty of Troyes (1420), the infant Henry VI succeeded to the crown of France.

Upon his deathbed Henry V had designated his brother John, duke of Bedford, as regent of Normandy, and his younger brother Humphrey, duke of Gloucester, regent of England. The council was charged to make no peace with France which would not leave Normandy at least in the possession of Henry VI.

So far as England was concerned, the law gave the dying king no authority thus to dispose of the regency, and the nation refused to be bound strictly by the terms of the will. By an act of Parliament passed in November the duke of Bedford was appointed Protector of the Realm and Defender of the King, Humphrey to act as substitute in his brother's absence. No question seems to have been raised regarding Henry's right to appoint the regent of France and Normandy.

Although a brief episode in medieval history, the history of the regency of John, duke of Bedford, Henry V's brother, in France in the years 1422–35, is of great interest in fifteenth century history. Bedford was committed to a "lost cause" from the beginning. But the history of his endeavor to reconcile France to English domination is the history nevertheless of an honest and noble effort. He is one of the forgotten great men of England.

By character and experience the regent was well fitted for the duties of his position. The third son of Henry IV, he was born in 1389. His first public employment was as constable of England, to which position he was appointed at the age of fourteen. From this time he was constantly engaged in the work of government. In 1404 and 1405 he was in command of troops in active service. In 1408 and 1411 he acted as his father's representative in negotiations with Scotland, and throughout the remainder of the reign he held positions of responsibility in the north of England.

Upon the accession of Henry V, John became his right-hand man. He was lieutenant of the kingdom during Henry V's expedition to France in 1415, and the next summer he himself conducted a naval expedition to the relief of Harfleur, and won a notable victory over the combined fleets of France and Genoa. From July, 1417, to December, 1419, he was again lieutenant of England. During this period occurred the execution of the celebrated Lollard leader, Sir John Oldcastle, at whose trial Bedford presided in person. During the last three years of Henry V's life, Bedford's time was divided between military duty in France and administrative work in England. He took command of the army when Henry V was incapacitated by his last illness, and was with him at his death.

The territory over which Bedford was called to rule embraced Normandy, the district of Calais and Guisnes, Picardy, the Île de France, Chartres, Champagne, and the western portion of Guienne. In addition, the feudal sovereignty of Henry VI was recognized in the extensive territories of the dukes of Brittany and Burgundy and in certain possessions of the duke of Lorraine. The rest of France was in the possession of adherents of *"le roi de Bourges."* In Normandy, Picardy, Champagne and the Île de France, numerous fortresses were held by French lieutenants, and in the midst of the Burgundian possessions, Tournay remained faithful to the French king.

The regent was confronted with two tasks, either of which alone would have taxed his resources to the utmost. He had to complete the military task his brother had begun by establishing the authority of the infant king over the whole of France, and he had to justify the existence of his government by the restoration of order and prosperity in the regions under his control. The story of his military and diplomatic activity is well known. At first he was almost uniformly successful. The outlying Armagnac strongholds in the North were nearly all captured, and by the close of 1424 the dauphin's cause appeared to be hopeless. But the promise of these early years was never fulfilled. Humphrey, duke of Gloucester, was a rash, headstrong, violent man, and his quarrels were of more service to the cause of Charles VII than the sword of his best general. First Gloucester's marriage with

Jacqueline of Holland brought him into violent conflict with the duke of Burgundy, and nearly estranged Bedford's most valuable ally. This affair upset all the regent's plans for the campaign of 1425. Then Gloucester's quarrel with Beaufort necessitated Bedford's presence in England for over a year (1425–27). Chiefly as a result of these distractions, the years following 1424 saw little progress in the conquest. After Bedford returned from England, the remaining French strongholds in Maine were taken and English authority made practically complete north of Orléans.

This was the highwater mark of English authority. In 1429 came the wonderful revival of French national spirit under the leadership of Jean Darc, and in a few months half the English conquests had melted away. The whole Loire basin, Champagne and half the Île de France were lost, and Paris itself was in danger. The campaigns of the next few years strengthened Bedford somewhat, but made no great change in the situation. In 1435 the English cause received its deathblow when Philip of Burgundy made peace with Charles, and just at the moment of the final collapse of his hopes the regent died.

Such in bare outline was the career of John of Lancaster, duke of Bedford. History knows the man chiefly as the executioner of the Maid of Orléans, and as the general who lost to England the fruits of Henry V's victories. But there is another side to Bedford's career which has been neglected—his efforts to effect the political reconstruction of France, and to restore peace, order and economic prosperity. Even in 1358 France had been in no worse condition than in 1422 when Henry V died. Bands of armed ruffians harried the countryside, says the Chronicle of St. Denys: "Treading under foot the fear of God and man they swept over the land with the fury of a tempest; their only thought was of plunder, fire and bloodshed." Some of these bands were well organized like the Free Companies in the previous century. The leader of one of them was no less a person than Enguerran de Monstrelet, the historian, who made a fortune as a freebooter, retired to private life, and took to letters. Another notorious gang was called the "Ecorcheurs," still another the "Flayers." The Journal of a Bourgeois of Paris in the years 1419–49 graphically relates the hardships and sufferings of the time, when wolves even invaded Paris. Thomas Basin, the bishop of Lisieux, relates that

. . . from Chartres on the West to the frontiers of Hainault on the East, and to the North as far as Abbeville, all was a desert. A few patches of cultivated land or vineyard might here and there be seen, but rarely, and never but in the immediate neighborhood of a castle or a walled town. Whenever the laborer ventured out into this enclosure, a watchman took his stand upon the watch-tower that he might blow his horn on the approach of the enemy, never far distant. So familiar had the sound become, so thoroughly was its meaning understood that even the oxen and the sheep hurried homewards when they heard its first warning note.[1]

In spite of the outward tranquillity, the situation confronting Bedford was one of extreme difficulty. His rule was undisguisedly the yoke of a foreigner. So long as Charles VI lived, and the government was carried on in his name, Henry V had been able to put forward a certain claim to the allegiance of patriotic Frenchmen. He had the support of the queen and the duke of Burgundy, and all the weight of royal tradition was in his favor. But when the poor mad king died, the treaty of Troyes had no longer a mask to hide its iniquity. Charles VII was the legitimate and direct heir, and nothing clouded his title to the throne save this treaty, extorted by force from his helpless father. It must have been a most humiliating ordeal for any Frenchman with a spark of national pride in his soul to acknowledge an English duke as regent for an English king. For the present, the bitterness of the Burgundian-Armagnac feud sufficed to stifle the national repugnance to foreign rule, but this was a sandy foundation on which to build a kingdom.

Henry V had organized a systematic government for Normandy after the fall of Rouen in 1419, and had maintained the regular administration at Paris. The estates of Normandy and France were in session during his reign, and the work of the courts appears not to have been seriously interrupted. But outside the cities conditions were only a step removed from anarchy. In the words of Alain Chartier, France was like the sea, *"ou chacun a tant de seigneurie comme il a de force."* The roads were infested with robbers. The chronicles of the period abound with tales of murder, arson, and robbery, while the judicial and administrative records exhibit even more clearly the horror of the times. Henry V executed brigands by hundreds, paying a regular reward for their capture, dead or alive. Receipts for the bounty on outlaws appear in his records side by side and in almost the same terms with records of bounty paid on the scalps of wolves.

Yet all these drastic measures had failed to give relief. Never has a civilized land suffered a more terrible scourge.

Robbery was reduced to a trade; the leader of a band of thieves hired men to serve under him and paid them regular wages. The ecclesiastic abandoned his cowl and his monastery, and bought himself arms and horses with which to follow this new calling.[2]

[1] Stevenson, *Wars of the English in France,* I, introd., p. xl.
[2] Stevenson, *op. cit.,* I, xxxvii. For clergy in arms, see Denifle, *La désolation des monastères pendant la guerre de cent ans,* I, pp. 542 and 554.

Even men of princely blood are named among the captains of the robbers. Common criminals and deserting soldiers made up the worst element of the bands, but their numbers were augmented by starving peasants, artisans out of employment, and ruined gentlemen whom necessity drove to a life of lawlessness.

The only regions which were even comparatively safe were those garrisoned by the soldiery, and there the protectors were scarcely less destructive than were the brigands elsewhere. The duke of Burgundy's troops, even when in friendly territory, had a particularly evil reputation.

The English troops, on account of their better discipline, were less destructive. They were paid with some regularity and were strictly forbidden to pillage the country and levy tribute on the people. When complaints against the soldiery were received, the officers seem to have seriously attempted to render justice. Yet the case of the village of Coulon, pillaged by the English soldiery, and the numerous pardons issued by Bedford to Frenchmen who had slain Englishmen in self-defense, show that it was impossible to restrain the soldiers from acts of violence. Even the captain of a fortress in the English obedience might eke out his income by robbing or ransoming passers-by.

Among the French troops conditions were still worse. The French army was made up of the most heterogeneous elements, Scotch, Italians, Bretons, and Castilians, and was practically without discipline. It was poorly paid, and supported itself by plunder. The soldiery were so dreaded that cities begged to be excused from supporting garrisons for their own defense. Between the robbers properly so called and the "regular" French soldiery there was an intermediate class of guerrillas. In Normandy some of the partisans were well organized, maintained discipline, and kept in touch with Charles VII throughout the period of English domination. Others were distinguished from mere robbers chiefly by their preference for the English as victims. All such partisans the English classed together with common thieves as "brigands," and it is difficult to distinguish the highway robber from the irregular soldier who was really fighting for a principle.

Plainly the regent could hope for little support from that traditional obedience to law and reverence for authority which are the mainstay of every government. Yet had he been strong enough to compel obedience, this very breakdown of law might have worked out to his advantage. Most of the lesser nobility, who personified the old governmental authority in the eyes of the peasantry, were dead or departed, and the ceaseless misery had weakened the Valois dynasty's hold on the affections of the people. Henry V's vigorous, though unsuccessful, efforts to check brigandage and the impartiality of his justice appeared already to have wrought a partial reconciliation. If Bedford could have completed the work of pacification there was hope that self-interest might have outweighed national pride, and the English dynasty in France have secured a more solid basis than the fickle favor of Philip the Good.

There are indications that the English were always more interested in the conquered provinces than in those ceded by the treaty. It has been suggested that this was on account of the ancient connection between Normandy and England, but it seems more likely that Henry V and Bedford foresaw the loss of Paris, but hoped to make the English foothold in Normandy permanent. One of Henry V's last requests was that no peace involving the surrender of Normandy should ever be made. Every effort was made by Bedford to reconcile the occupied territory to English domination. The estates of Normandy were consulted with great frequency; English colonists were settled on the lands of dispossessed Armagnacs; and a new university was founded at Caen. All this labor was of no avail. Though most of the population remained quiet for years, the woods were always full of guerrillas, and in 1434 the peasantry rose in general revolt. They were easily crushed, but the revolt showed clearly the failure of the English plans.

The most urgent task before the regent was the restoration of order. Vigorous measures were undertaken for this purpose. An ordinance was published requiring every person who knew anything of the whereabouts of brigands to report them to the authorities, under pain of fine and imprisonment. Throughout a large portion of Normandy, Bedford stationed companies of fifteen or twenty archers and four or five men-at-arms, who patrolled the roads, furnished guards for merchants, and kept the brigands back in the forests. Bishop Basin says the English used hounds to track down the brigands, and estimates the number put to death in a single year at the impossible figure of 10,000. In 1426 the prévôt of Paris captured two hundred brigands in one expedition. Another expedition in 1431 brought in twenty-nine; another one hundred. Concerning the success of Bedford's efforts Beaurepaire says:

These measures were almost entirely fruitless. The brigands did not cease to spread terror through the plains of Normandy. Many times the estates occupied themselves with this terrible scourge; many times in return for the subsidies granted him, Bedford and his successors renewed the agreement to assure the freedom of the roads and secure to the merchants and cultivators peace and security, but this was a vain promise. Far from diminishing, the evil only increased in proportion as the French took the upper hand, the bonds of discipline relaxed in the English army, and the misery became more profound and general.[3]

[3] Beaurepaire, *Les états de Normandie,* p. 22.

This statement would appear to be overdrawn. It is true that when fortune turned against the English in 1429 and 1430 the regent lost control of the situation, and the last state of France became worse than the first. But during the interval between the battle of Verneuil and the relief of Orléans (1424–29), which is the only period when Bedford really had a chance to do much for the relief of the rural districts, there are distinct indications that conditions were improving. For example, the petition of Jehan de Bonval, a tailor by trade, sets forth that he was driven to brigandage, "seeing that every good and honest person had withdrawn himself from the open country and gone to dwell in a foreign land, and that none knew what to do, where to apply himself, or for whom to labor so as to obtain his livelihood. . . . And because it happened that the said petitioner perceived about four years ago, or thereabouts, that it was possible to work . . . he has devoted himself to his labor and his craft and nothing else." The conclusion seems warranted that while Bedford never succeeded in suppressing the evils and making the country safe, he made an heroic effort and was rewarded by a decided improvement.

The coinage was in a state of intolerable confusion. Charles VII as dauphin had debased the coinage to an enormous extent, and then to correct matters reduced the nominal value of some of his coins to one-fortieth their face. The country was flooded with debased coins of every description and degree of fineness, foreign coins, and counterfeits. Henry V attempted to put out good coins, but withdrew them on the ground that they were being attracted into Armagnac territory.

Pierre Fenin's chronicle gives an interesting account of the economic effects of this fluctuation in the standard of value:

Coins circulated which were worth eighteen *deniers*; but finally they were quoted at two *deniers*, and then it was forbidden to circulate them at all; thus many rich merchants lost heavily. Moreover, the time when money was so debased was very hard on the "signeurs," for their tenants who owed them cash . . . paid a large rent with the proceeds of eight or ten measures (*septiers*) of grain; by which many seigneurs and poor gentlemen received great damage. . . . When coins were restored to their true value, there was much litigation and quarreling concerning sales made in the time of debased money.

Bedford never succeeded in curing this evil. Indeed it is questionable whether it would have been possible for him to do so, even with sufficient resources and adequate knowledge of the laws of finance; for besides the output of innumerable forgers, the country was constantly flooded with base coins issued by Charles VII in close imitation of the coins of Henry VI. The regent issued eighteen ordinances on the subject, fourteen of them in the first year of his incumbency. Concerning the merits of this legislation it is difficult to make any positive statement. In the opinion of M. Huard the English tampered with the coinage, issuing and withdrawing coins to meet the needs of the moment. Stevenson, on the other hand, finds in the legislation of Bedford the "recognition of a policy in advance of his age," and states that he fixed a standard of value proportional to the real value of the bullion. It is certain that a great deal of discontent followed Bedford's changes. Too much weight cannot be attached to this fact, however, for as noted by Fenin, the restoration of base money to its purity caused temporarily no less disturbance and hardship than did its debasement.

England contributed very little toward the expenses of the war. Up to September, 1428, in spite of the enthusiasm created by Bedford's victories, parliament granted the king no regular subsidy, and the clerical grants were very small. For the balance of the period there were direct subsidies estimated to have yielded £25,000 per annum. The average gross revenue of England for the first six years of Henry's reign is estimated at £70,795; for the next twenty-five years at £84,285, certainly not heavy taxation for a nation waging a war of conquest. The maintenance of the garrison at Calais was carried as a part of the domestic expenditure; from 1422 to 1428 it averaged about £16,000 per annum.

Aside from the maintenance of this garrison the English government gave aid chiefly by sending soldiers. The practice seems to have been for the government to advance to commanders of outgoing troops wages for the men for six months. Very little money appears to have been sent from England for the pay of the troops after this six months had expired, and Bedford had to depend on continental resources for the bulk of his funds.

The only available estimates for the whole English territory are a portion of those for the year ending September 30, 1428. The expenditures for that year included 70,000 *livres* for administrative expenses, chiefly connected with the parlement of Paris, and 175,000 *livres* payments to garrisons. The estimate of revenues for the year totals 129,000 *livres*, the most important items being a 25 per cent tax on wine, figured at 100,000 *livres*, and a *gabelle* of 15,000 *livres*.

For Normandy a summarized estimate for 1433–34 shows:

Wine tax and *gabelle*	110,000	livres	tournois
Subsidy and clerical grant	160,000	"	"
Property (fouage) and personal taxes	50,000	"	"
Total	320,000	"	"
Expenses	363,000	"	"
Deficit	43,000	"	"

A considerable amount of information concerning the direct taxes voted by the estates of Normandy is available. In 1421 Henry V was granted a subsidy of 400,000 *livres tournois* from the third estate, with three-tenths from the clergy. In December, 1422, Bedford was still collecting on this grant. He evidently decided that smaller grants would entail less difficulty in collection, as none of his subsidies exceed 200,000 *l. t.* until 1434, when 344,000 *l. t.* was granted. Most of the subsidies range from 60,000 to 150,000 *l. t.*, the larger ones payable in two or three instalments. They were made with sufficient frequency to bring the average up to about 200,000 *l. t.* per annum, besides the clerical grants and certain local subsidies.

The clergy of Normandy granted one-tenth in 1423, 1427, and 1428, and probably oftener. In connection with the last grant the clergy were apparently the victims of some sharp practice. The grant of one-tenth was submitted to the pope for approval before collection, and when the bull of authorization was received, it was found to call for three-tenths; one-tenth for the pope's Bohemian Crusade, and two-tenths for Bedford. This was the occasion of a protest from the chapter of Rouen, but Bedford's extra tenth appears to have been paid.

A preliminary estimate of the finances of Maine for 1433–34 shows receipts from taxes about 56,000 *l. t.* The indirect taxes were very small, the chief revenues being 25,800 *l. t.* from the *taille* and 25,000 *l. t. "receptum de appatismentis."* This item is explained in the estimate as the income from taxes imposed on partisans of the French side who desired to emigrate.

Although a great deal of property was confiscated from the enemy, this does not appear to have resulted in any large income for the treasury, as the property taken was used to reward adherents and give them a solid interest in the permanency of the English rule. In Normandy, at least, it was Bedford's policy to restore confiscated lands to their original owners if possible whenever they chose to make their submission. Some of those whose property was confiscated were men of prominence, such as Jean Jouvenal, Tanneguy du Chatel, and Arthur de Richemont, the duke of Brittany, but many obscure individuals fell under the ban, like the loyalists of the American Revolution, merely for absenting themselves from home.

During the winter of 1428–29 the expenses of the siege of Orléans rose to 40,000 *l. t.* per month. Bedford sacrificed a part of his own fortune and ordered his officers to loan the treasury one-fourth of their wages, the indirect taxes of France and Normandy being pledged for their repayment. Although the home government made heavy payments to finance reinforcing expeditions about this time it appears that the chronic disorder of Bedford's finances became worse and worse after 1430, and that at his death the regent left an accumulation of debts and an empty treasury. The policy of making the conquered country pay most of the expense of conquest, inaugurated by Henry V, negatived Bedford's efforts to reconcile the country to English domination, and was an important factor in the ruin of his plans.

The history of commerce, industry, and agriculture during the regency is little more than the history of the public misery. The constant war, the ravages of brigands and soldiery, the neglect of roads and bridges—everything conspired to destroy economic activity. Unable to till their fields or pasture their cattle in security, many peasants took refuge in the cities and lived on charity, or fled to the woods and lived by plunder. So many striking passages in the chroniclers depict the tribulations of the agricultural population that the modern historian is more apt to overestimate than to minimize the extent of the devastation. The Armagnacs plundered systematically, and the country which formed the scene of active operation suffered terribly from the cruel methods of warfare employed by the English no less than by their enemies. But in the regions which were under English control, the cultivators were protected and agriculture made a considerable recovery. The following passages, which are based on official documents, give a side of the story which we seldom get from the chroniclers:

The English made great efforts to diminish the sufferings of the people and make themselves loved. We have seen that they were readily accepted by the people of Senlis, who with good reasons hated the Armagnacs, for these had lived off the peasantry for twenty years and completely ruined the region. . . . The English, on the contrary, did all they could to cause the war to cease and get the soldiery out of the country.

From 1424 to 1429 the people of the Senlis and Valois region had been able to work in peace toward the recovery of the immense losses they had previously suffered, and in August, 1429, the situation of the country, though far from satisfactory, was already much improved. All was lost when the French came, under the lead of Joan of Arc, to deliver this beautiful country from the English and to ruin it. The Armagnacs had such a reputation for ferocity and were so dreaded that all the peasantry took flight; they cut their grain before it was ripe . . . and took refuge in the fortified towns. . . . The French soldiery conducted themselves in a way to justify the fears of the peasantry.[4]

The cities were protected from the worst effects of the war, but the conditions of life were very hard. Industry had fallen off, prices of food were high, and laborers found none to employ them. The population was greatly reduced. In 1423 the number of good houses standing empty in Paris was estimated at 24,000, besides great numbers which had fallen into ruin or had been converted into stables. The number of empty houses was not due entirely to lack of popu-

[4] Flammermont, *Histoire de Senlis*, pp. 64, 73–74 and 77–78.

lation to occupy them, but in part to peculiarities in the medieval form of real estate tenure. Ownership of city property carried with it fixed monetary obligations, sometimes to several different persons, and with the decline of prosperity the obligations attached to property came to exceed its value. Bedford issued several ordinances attempting to remedy the situation by allowing owners of houses to clear their titles by single payments, but he was only partially successful.

Such commerce as existed consisted chiefly in the transfer of the actual necessities of life from country to city. The devastation of the fields and the insecurity of the highways combined to make the problem of food supply difficult. Bedford was for a time very successful in dealing with this problem. So long as the fortunes of war were in his favor, Paris was fed at lower prices than it had seen for years, and that too, it appears, without frequent recourse to the medieval expedient of a maximum price. From 1421 to 1429 we hear practically nothing of exorbitant prices of food; before and after that period the pages of the Bourgeois de Paris are filled with complaints of the scarcity of bread and the consequent suffering of the poor. Food supplies were brought from Normandy under military escort; in one notable instance in 1431 under the supervision of the regent, at great personal risk to himself.

Within the cities, trade and manufacture experienced a partial revival under Bedford's administration. This is shown by the numerous ordinances for reorganization of gilds and regulation of local trade. Old statutes were confirmed or new ones issued to the woolen workers of Rouen, Beauvais, and Evreux; the silk workers of Paris; the butchers of Evreux, Chartres, and Paris; the barbers of Rouen, the chandlers of Pontoise, the fishermen of Bray-sur-Seine, the hosiers of Bernay, and the surgeons of Paris.

The case of the woolen workers of Beauvais is interesting. Beauvais was famous for woolen goods, but the war had destroyed its prosperity, and many of the skilled workmen had disappeared. Only a part of the drapers had the right to have apprentices, and they abused their privilege by employing apprentices at menial tasks instead of teaching them their trade, and by holding them years beyond their contract. Immigration of new workmen was prohibited by those in control of the gild. The abuse of privilege was so flagrant that the bishop of Beauvais (Pierre Cauchon) prepared an ordinance which abolished the whole mass of existing statutes and opened the city to all workmen of good character who could prove their competence.

In the case of the butchers, political as well as economic considerations were involved. As a result of the "cabochien" affair the ancient rights of the Paris corporation had been abolished by the dauphin in 1416 and the trade placed under the control of the prévôt of Paris.

The old corporation was restored by Henry V, and one of Bedford's first official acts was to confirm its charter, in consideration of the *"bons et aggréables"* services rendered by the butchers to the Anglo-Burgundian cause. Likewise at Chartres the butchers had been punished for partisanship of the duke of Burgundy by letters which opened the trade to any butcher on payment of a small fee. Bedford revoked these letters in 1426 and restored the monopoly.

The statutes of the hosiers of Bernay, confirmed in 1424, may serve as a typical example of the supervision to which industry was subjected. The ordinance contained eleven articles, of which the following is a summary: 1. Hose made of cloth which has not been shrunk and trimmed shall be confiscated. 2. Hose cut and sewed must be well shaped. 3. Hose must be made entirely of one kind of cloth, or at least of one color. 4. No one shall put new cloth and old in the same garment. 5. No one may have an apprentice except a regular hosier who exposes goods for sale at the market every Saturday. 6. No master may have more than one apprentice. Apprentices shall serve three years. 7. The "gardes" shall keep a register of apprentices. 8. No apprentice may change masters. 9. If an apprentice quits the service without permission, *"par jeunesse ou autrement,"* his place shall be held for him one month. 10. Provision is made for examination of apprentices at the end of their service. 11. Workmen moving into the city must pass an examination before being allowed to open places of business.

Some ordinances regulate trade in much greater detail. The statutes of the butchers at Evreux, for example, contained 27 articles, providing for inspection of the markets, and prescribing in detail the precautions necessary to protect the public health. No one except the son or son-in-law of a master butcher could erect a stall without serving a four years' apprenticeship.

When new statutes were issued they appear in every case to have been prepared by the persons interested, and confirmed without change. Most of the ordinances simply confirm old charters, and often it is not clear why the confirmation was necessary. In the case of the chandlers of Pontoise, the old statutes, issued by Charles VI, were lost when the city was captured. Bedford extracted a copy from the archives and reissued them. I find no evidence of any disposition on the part of the English to make innovations in the customary methods of regulating local trade and manufacture.[5] One ordinance affords direct evidence

[5] Except perhaps the case of the horse dealers of Paris. The old ordinance fixed no limit to the number of dealers, in consequence of which the market was thronged with artisans, farmers, laborers, and vagabonds. Numerous persons were cheated, and found that their defrauders could not be identified, or were too poor to make reparation. Bedford reduced the number of dealers to

of the decayed condition of Paris. In 1430 the wine dealers of their own request were reduced in number from sixty to thirty-four, on account of lack of business.

As might be expected, Bedford had little concern with foreign commerce. Excepting licenses granted by the regent in 1433 to export wheat from England to France, on account of the scarcity in the latter kingdom, the only source on this subject is the ordinance of August, 1424, confirming the privileges of the Portuguese merchants trading at Harfleur. Privileges had been granted to Portuguese merchants at this port in 1309, and confirmed with some alterations at various dates in the fourteenth century. The confirmation granted by Bedford added no new features to the previous arrangements. The privileges comprised freedom from port dues and various judicial exemptions, the only feature of special interest being a provision that in the event of hostilities between France and Portugal, the persons and property of the merchants should be inviolable.

Bedford's rank as a statesman cannot fairly be estimated by his actual achievements. He was placed from the beginning in an impossible situation. Into his hands Henry V had committed the task of guarding the English possessions and completing the conquest of France. Until this was accomplished or a permanent peace was reached, his task had to be primarily not civil but military. Far-reaching plans for social and economic reform would have been futile so long as the whole question of the permanency of English domination was hanging in the balance. The most that any ruler could do was to maintain some degree of order, render good justice without disturbing existing institutions, apply provisional remedies to the most glaring evils, and wait for peace to make more thorough reform possible.

Viewed in the light of this situation, the work of the regent entitles him to a position of highest honor. Far more than Henry V he strove to secure for his administration a solid basis in the prosperity of the people. Financial difficulties compelled him to exact oppressive taxes, and military exigencies often checkmated his efforts to restore order, but the work he accomplished shows him to have possessed not only intelligent perception of the needs of the time, but an earnest desire to provide for those needs. The weakness of his government was not in the manner in which he conducted it, but in the lack of moral basis for its existence. Bedford was respected by English and French alike, even his enemies recognizing the incongruity between his personal character and the character of his cause. The treaty of Troyes was a crime, and could not be palliated by conscientiousness in carrying out its provisions. Although repeatedly urged to abandon France and take

twenty-four, and forbade all others to frequent the horse-market. *Ordon.* XIII, p. 41.

the regency in England, Bedford never wavered in what he believed to be his duty. He had pledged himself to Henry V and promised that he would devote his life to the subjugation of France; he had assured the parlement of Paris that he would employ body, soul, and substance for the good of the realm, and he kept both promises. His failure can be charged to no fault of his own.

The desertion of England by the duke of Burgundy in 1435, not the military achievements of Jean Darc, broke the English grip on France. In the next eighteen years the foe was driven out of the country and only Calais remained in their possession. With the political, military and administrative history of the French recovery this chapter need not deal. It may be taken for granted. But it is important to emphasize that no one of these effects would have been accomplished without economic and social integration. In last analysis progress is based upon material welfare. France's restoration was due as much to the rehabilitation of agriculture, commerce, and industry, as to intelligent government and effective military leadership.

In regard to agriculture there is little to say save that the expulsion of the enemy, effective police of town and province, suppression of brigandage, were all that the toiling French peasant required to restore the fields to harvests and the vineyards to vintage. Given peace, agriculture took care of itself.

But in the matter of commerce and industry France, in the reign of Charles VII, experienced an active revival which owed much to the initiative of the crown. The history is found in a series of measures which the crown took for the promotion of commerce and industry. Undoubtedly it is true that Charles VII was primarily interested in the organization of the army, in the restoration of the finances, and in the administration of justice. He put an end to the devastation of the country by the soldiery, by establishing some companies of cavalry in 1445, and in 1448, creating a national infantry in the *francs-archeurs*. He provided the crown with permanent resources by establishing the *taille;* he revised the administration of justice and held officials and magistrates to strict account. But the king was also interested in the revival of commerce and industry. After his great victory over the English, he signed the truce of 1444. This truce was continually extended, and in reality lasted to 1449. Those five years of peace were good years for France. When the war was resumed in 1449 prosperity was not set back. Normandy was reconquered in 1450–51 as well as Guienne, and by 1453 only Calais was left to the English.

With peace, commerce revived. The old fairs were reëstablished. The Foire du Lendit was revived in 1444. Charles VII also attempted to restore the Champagne Fairs. But the commercial life of Champagne had vanished, and Charles VII himself dealt it a mortal blow by protecting the fairs of Lyons. Lyons was admirably situated for commerce. By the valleys of the Rhône and Saône it was in direct relation with the Mediterranean Sea; by the Seine it was easily connected with Paris and Rouen; over the Alps lay Italy. In 1420 when Charles VII was still dauphin he had granted to Lyons two free fairs of six days each, together with all the privileges of the Fairs of Champagne, of Brie, and of Lendit. But everything went to pieces during the war, and in 1444, when commerce was restored, there were three fairs of twenty days each instead of two. It is true that the fairs of Lyons suffered from the competition of those of Geneva, which were then at their height. But Charles VII in 1446 forbade the export of French merchandise to Geneva. At first the prohibition was of little effect, but the king stuck to it. He confirmed the privileges of the fairs of Lyons in 1454, 1457, 1466, and in the reign of Louis XI, Lyons triumphed over Geneva. The number of fairs was increased to four, and at the end of the fifteenth century and during the sixteenth the fairs of Lyons eclipsed all others but Frankfort. Compared with petty local commerce they represented the grand commerce of the kingdom and even international commerce.

Charles VII did not confine himself to restoring the fairs and the markets. He also granted privileges to many individual merchants who frequented them. By letters patent of June 15, 1455, he freed from the tax of twelve pennies per *livre* all merchandise sold in the fairs of Lendit and of St. Laurent in Paris, at the fairs of Champagne and Brie, in that of St. Romain at Rouen, and at the fair of Guibrai near Falaise.

Along with the fairs the king established the old markets. He rebuilt the *halles* of Paris and reinforced the obligation of sale there on certain days. Moreover he took more efficient measures of administration, relieved the merchants of the imposts and the rents which the royal domain collected from the *halles,* and stimulated the circulation of merchandise by making transportation more sure and less costly.

We have already seen how an association of merchants was formed in the fourteenth century along the Loire river. During the Hundred Years' War this association faithfully served the royal cause, for example, furnishing at various times subsidies to the king, who in return favored it. By an edict issued at Suresmes, March 15, 1430, and registered in the parlement of Poitiers on May 11, the king ordered the abolition of "all *péages* levied, imposed, and accrued under whatever color or occasion for the past sixty years under penalty of confiscation of lands and goods." The king was interested in determining what were the old *péages* and what were the new ones. A councillor of the parlement made an investigation which lasted for ten years and at the end of the inquiry the *péages* on the Loire were reduced to

130, as in the fourteenth century. This was still a considerable number, however. The price of salt when transported from Nantes to Orléans was doubled by the cost of freight, or rather the tolls, for the price of transportation was relatively low. Charles VII also caused special commissioners to revise the *péages* on the Garonne, the Lot, and the Tarn rivers. He did the same thing for the rivers of the Île de France and Champagne. He found that on the Seine the price of merchandise was doubled between Paris and Harfleur. The action of the king in making river traffic free put an end to one of the oldest and worst abuses from which French commerce had suffered.

Charles VII also attempted to improve river navigation by encouraging internal improvements upon the affluents of the Seine. The Eure river was made navigable from its confluence with the Seine to within a league of Chartres for boats not carrying more than 25 tonneaux of wine. On the Loire the internal improvements which were superintended by the Association of Merchants of the Loire deepened the bed of the stream and of some of its tributaries, as the Maine, Loir, Sarthe, and Clain. The merchants divided the river into a certain number of sections, over which inspectors were put. These men watched the current, dredged the channel, marked it by stakes, and kept the tow-path in good repair. The association met its expenses by means of a tax imposed on merchandise using the Loire and its branches. Letters patent of Charles VII permitted the levying of these subsidies which came to be called *"droits de boîte"* from the box in which the money was dropped.

The maritime commerce of France, which had declined in the Mediterranean and the Atlantic, was likewise promoted. Charles VII attempted to save the ports of the Mediterranean which had silted up, above all Aigues-Mortes. Regarding this port as the "most beautiful, profitable and safe of Languedoc," in 1445 he imposed a tax of ten per cent upon spices and drugs entering France by any other port than Aigues-Mortes. The result was to give it a monopoly of commerce with the Orient. In 1449 Charles VII set aside the sum of 1,000 *livres* for the improvement of this port, but the money was badly used and the forces of nature were too great to be overcome. The same enlightened policy was followed out at La Rochelle, the best port of France upon the Atlantic until Bordeaux was recovered in 1453. In 1449 he granted La Rochelle the same rights of the eastern trade as Aigues-Mortes. Finally in order to help Narbonne, which still hoped to overcome the capricious doings of the Aude river, he granted the city the *octroi* upon salt and the right to impose a *péage* at the Pont Ferme, for the maintenance of the channel.

In 1437 the English had founded the new town of Granville on a rock almost completely surrounded by water on the coast of Normandy near Mont St. Michel. In 1441 by a daring assault Granville fell into the power of Charles VII, who fortified it. When the truce of Tours was signed in 1444 he sought to ease the condition of the inhabitants there and in March, 1446, declared them free and exempt from all aides and *tailles*. Two annual fairs were established in the town, one on St. Blaise's day in February, and one in September on the Morrow of the Nativity of the Virgin. Moreover, a market was held every week on Saturday. In a short time Granville became one of the most important ports of Normandy.

The trade between Guienne and England dropped to a low point after 1453. Many Gascon merchants, irritated with French commercial persecution and objecting to the aides and the *tailles* they were compelled to pay, removed to England. The Bordelais did not recover its prosperity until the reign of Louis XI.

Charles VII also protected French merchants trading in foreign countries. If they suffered hardship in a foreign country, the government took steps to secure an indemnity. The king especially protected the interest of French commerce in Egypt. He sent some merchants of Montpellier to the Mohammedan chieftains who ruled at Tunis, at Bougia, at Oran, and at Fez. We have few details upon this history, but it seems an exaggeration to argue, as some have, that from 1450 a French company dominated the African coast, where it enjoyed important concessions from the Arabs.

In addition Charles VII gave great attention to the commerce with Italy. As we have already seen, Charles VI had conquered Genoa and the French occupied the city from 1396 to 1409. Charles VII made an attempt to recover the city in 1446 without success. In 1458 the Frejosi, who were French partisans, turned again to France. Jean of Anjou, duke of Lorraine and lieutenant of the king, occupied Genoa and maintained himself there for some time in spite of all the intrigues of Francesco Sforza and the revolt of the Genoese. One of the great maritime republics of Italy was thus in the hands of France, but the occupation was only ephemeral. In 1461 the Genoese again revolted, and then Louis XI renounced his rights over the republic and left the Genoese, as he said, to "the devil, I mean my good friend Francesco Sforza."

Again Charles VII favored commerce in an indirect manner by introducing an honest coinage. During the war everything had been in a state of anarchy. The king himself had speculated upon the variations of the currency. Between 1422 and 1428 there were no less than forty-one changes. Moreover, the feudal mints counterfeited the royal coinage. Foreign coins of every value and every country had been introduced into France and this outside coinage was better than the king's own. At this moment gold and silver were rare, for the old mines of

Europe were exhausted. Moreover, great quantities were buried during the Hundred Years' War and remembrance of the places lost. Again during the luxurious period of the late fourteenth and early fifteenth centuries an enormous amount of gold and silver had been employed in the manufacture of jewelry and plate. As a result there was a monetary crisis in the reign of Charles VII.

Before the war was over the king set himself to remedy this state of affairs. In 1438 a series of ordinances began restoring the coinage, closing all unauthorized mints, and abolishing counterfeit coins. The old money was withdrawn from circulation. Edicts in 1453 and 1456 prohibited the circulation of foreign coin and required that it be taken to the royal mints to be melted. The crown forbade the exportation of the precious metals and continually reaffirmed this prohibition. This is why Charles VII was so pitiless towards Jacques Coeur, why he was opposed to the pope levying the annates in France, and the Pragmatic Sanction was in part a concession to these economic considerations. Thus at the end of the reign of Charles VII the evils of war were repaired. Undoubtedly the population did not reach the density which it had before the conflict, but France showed its capacity to meet and overcome a crisis and to repair its ruins, great as they were.

France, especially southern France, had been a great commercial nation before the disastrous wars with the English, and had even had merchant princes of renown. Such were the Bonis brothers of Montauban, Ponce de Chaparay of Lyons, and Raymond Seraller of Narbonne. But in Jacques Coeur, the great merchant of Bourges in the reign of Charles VII, France not only had its greatest merchant but its greatest minister of commerce and trade before Colbert.

Jacques Coeur belonged to a family of merchants. His father Pierre was a furrier in Bourges and amassed a certain amount of wealth. Jacques Coeur was born in Bourges at the end of the fourteenth century, when the province of Berry was governed by the famous duke John of Berry, an enlightened patron of the arts. Jacques was brought up in his father's shop and had an imperfect education. Thomas Basin says he was almost unlettered, but he adds that he was nimble-witted and had a keen head for business. Jacques Coeur was determined to die rich; he had limitless ambition, and in the realization of this ambition he was without scruple. His business operations were not always honest. A dishonest Maître de Monnaies named Ravaut le Danois, who had been driven out of Normandy by the English and had taken refuge in Bourges, became an early partner of Jacques Coeur in the making of counterfeit money. The government found them out and they were tried and condemned. But in 1429 Charles VII pardoned them and Jacques Coeur had recourse to other means of making a fortune.

He formed an association with the brothers Pierre and Barthelmy Godard to sell furniture, tapestry, and other things to the court, which at this time was very luxurious and extravagant. The king, the queen, and the royal children had each a separate establishment, and each house indulged in prodigal expenditure. The company thus formed dealt in the luxuries of the time. The king's bills were not always paid, but the side profits derived from special privileges were great, and the firm prospered as long as Bourges remained the capital of France, that is to say till 1439.

In 1432 Jacques Coeur went to the East to buy spices, in company with French, Venetian, Genoese, Florentine and Catalan merchants. He sailed on a ship of Narbonne for Alexandria, and counted upon meeting the vessel again at Beirut. But on the return voyage the ship was wrecked on the coast of Corsica; the natives plundered Jacques Coeur of everything, and he returned to France with nothing but courage and ambition left.

Profiting by his old influence he soon obtained an important position at the court and organized a great commercial company, which embraced not only France but the whole known world. He built a fleet of seven merchant ships, of which four were large—the *St. Michel*, the *St. Ouen*, the *St. Jacques*, and the *Madeleine*. These ships plied between East and West, bringing the goods of the Levant—furs and carpets, Arabian perfumes and Chinese porcelain. They also traded in slaves, and transported passengers from port to port along the Mediterranean coast. Through this commerce Jacques Coeur acquired great influence in the East, although he does not himself seem to have gone there after 1432. But he had hundreds of agents there. He made treaties with the Egyptian sultan Abu-Said, and the Knights of St. John in Cyprus, from which he derived great commercial advantage. He secured the favor of Venice by saving the property of some Venetian merchants, which had been confiscated in Egypt. About 1445 his nephew, Jean des Villages, sent to Cairo as Charles VII's ambassador, signed a commercial treaty with the sultan, which guaranteed French merchants protection and liberty of trading in all the Mameluke states. It stipulated for a French consul in Alexandria to judge commercial transactions. Little by little, French vessels began to displace the Venetians and the Genoese. Jacques Coeur also traded with the Turks, who at this time were threatening Constantinople. He obtained an authorization to trade with the infidels from Pope Eugene IV, in spite of the Church's prohibition against the practice, and when in Rome in 1468 secured the renewal of the privilege by Pope Nicholas III. He seems to have driven a thriving trade in the sale of arms to the Turks.

But his commercial operations were not confined to the East. He purchased merchandise throughout all France. He must have been a man of great organizing ability, great initiative, great imagination, and an infinite capacity for detail. In almost every province of France he established a warehouse which centralized the products of the country roundabout. Bourges furnished him cloth and products of the goldsmith's art; Limoges woolen goods; Lyons silks and German importations; at Rouen he had an establishment which connected him with England and Flanders. After the truce of 1444 he put French products on the English market, and it is said that he had a branch establishment at Bruges.

The headquarters of his business was in Montpellier, where he was in close touch with the Orient. In this city he owned a large group of warehouses, with show rooms, spacious cellars, *etc.* He built the Loge des Marchands in the Place au Change, which later became the hôtel de ville of Montpellier. In the last years of his life Jacques Coeur removed his headquarters to Marseilles, where he had an establishment conveniently situated on the harbor. He paid annually 11,000 florins in city taxes, which shows how great his wealth must have been.

In order to direct this immense commerce Jacques Coeur had a staff of at least three hundred persons. There was a factor at the head of each establishment, the most famous of whom was Guillaume de Varge, a native of Bourges, who was attached to the king's silver-plate service (*argenterie*) and superintended the merchandise bought by the court. Later he became comptroller general of the finances in Languedoc. Besides these factors there were the "patrons" of the vessels. The chief of these was Jacques des Villages, who married his master's niece and had a brilliant career. He aided Jean of Calabria in his expedition against Naples, and became grand chamberlain of the duke of Lorraine. Below the patrons was the crowd of employees, such as the purchasing agents in the Levant. This whole staff seems to have been faithful and devoted to Jacques Coeur, who appears to have had a genius for picking men and inspiring them with his own enthusiasm. In order to secure sailors for his ships he often "shanghaied" the wharf-rats and vagabonds along the waterfrint, *coquins, taverniers et autres méchantes gens.*

But Jacques Coeur did not limit himself to commerce. He went into all sorts of speculations. He became a great manufacturer at Montpellier and established dyeing works in which he sought to dye cloths with that brilliant red color so renowned in the Orient. He established a paper factory at Bourges, and paper with his orange trade-mark was widely known. In Florence he established a silk factory, which was superintended by two Florentines, the brothers Bonnatorso, and periodically inspected by two factors, Guillaume de Varge and Pierre Joubert. In central France, at Bourges, Tours, Loches, he collected the king's *gabelle.*

Nor is this all. Three mines of silver, lead and copper were exploited by him in Beaujolais, Lyonnais, and Chessy. Jacques Coeur purchased these mines and paid the king two hundred *livres* per annum in addition to a tenth of the profits. On January 17, 1455, these mines were confiscated by the government, and for a year were worked in the king's name. The producteur-general, Jean Dauvet, on April 19, 1455, drew up a most interesting regulation for the government of these mines.

At the head of the business was a governor and receiver named Pierre Garnier; a comptroller, and a clerk named Nicholas Tharo who was his assistant. The governor superintended the mine-masters and the workmen. He was required to visit the shafts in person, and assure himself that the timber supports were safe. The workmen lived in common; they were given food, drink, and lodgement. The governor was compelled to keep from one to two years' supply of wheat stored up in advance, in order that a sudden rise in the cost of living might not increase the cost of mining. The carpenters, blacksmiths, and metal workers had to be better fed and better lodged than ordinary workmen. The workmen were required to make oath that they would "serve well and loyally . . . and obey the rules." They were under a severe discipline and forbidden to swear in the name of God or the Virgin, forbidden to wear swords or daggers, except a small knife to cut bread and meat, forbidden to injure another, forbidden to fight, or to commit any nuisance in the interior of the mine. Workmen and other employees had to be in bed at a certain hour and be on time at the three meals provided. Article fifty-three provided that no one in the employ of the mine should keep a woman upon the premises. The governor of the mine judged all infractions of the regulations and had the power to fine or imprison. There were police sergeants in each mining community, and appeal could be made from the governor's decision to the bailiff of Mâcon, and the seneschal of Lyons. A complete account of the expenses and receipts of these mines during the year 1455–56, when they were directly exploited by the crown, is preserved. These records contain some very interesting details. It is evident that the miners were well paid, and that their living was comfortable. Their beds were furnished with blankets and pillows, and their food was abundant. But in some other ways the state's exploitation of these mines was unfortunate. The cost of working was too great for profit, and they were farmed out. The crown received a "fermage" and a tenth of the metals produced. In 1457 the mines were restored to Jacques Coeur's children.

Jacques Coeur's wealth was great and his prosperity became a proverb. "Every year he made more than all the other merchants in the kingdom put together," says a contemporary. His wealth has been estimated at a million *écus d'or,* which in intrinsic value in terms of to-day would be more than two million dollars; as to its extrinsic value, that is to say its purchasing power in that time, it is difficult to calculate.

In the days of his prosperity he was famed for the richness of his clothing, which rivalled that of the great nobles; wherever he was he was always served on silver plate. He had houses in most of the important cities of France, as at Lyons, Montpellier, Bourges. In the last city he built that magnificent house which is a marvel of architecture and a national monument. Everywhere the eyes meet with Jacques Coeur's motto, "To the variant heart nothing is impossible." He also owned extensive lands—more than forty seigniories in France, especially in Berry. He pushed his family with him. His brother Nicholas became bishop of Luçon; his eldest son Jean, who took orders, was made archbishop of Bourges in 1446; his second son was a canon of Ste. Chapelle in Bourges; his daughter married the viscount of Bourges; two other sons, Ravout and Geoffrey, continued their father's business. Jacques Coeur was a generous giver. He built the sacristy of the cathedral in Bourges and a chapel for the interment of his family. In Paris he restored the Collège des Bons-Enfants. He lavished presents upon the nobles of the court, and the list of his debtors is a long one. He financed Charles VII's conquest of Normandy from the English in 1449-50. In 1450 he gave the king 60,000 gold pieces for the siege of Cherbourg.

Such a fortune was certain to excite enmity and jealousy. The courtiers complained of his luxury, which they said was an insult to them. The nobles were offended at the haughtiness of this parvenu, and the merchants also were hostile to him. For he created an immense monopoly in France, which ruined a great number of manufacturers and merchants. When he transferred his business headquarters to Marseilles, he incurred the hatred of Montpellier.

Were there political accusations against him? The proof of these is not quite clear. But aside from the jealousy and hatred of him, there were more serious and better-founded accusations. His business methods were far from honest. In the island of Rhodes he made from twenty-five to thirty thousand counterfeit ducats, with which he paid his creditors in Alexandria. In the mint at Montpellier he alloyed the silver ingots. This was the time when the Turks were besieging Constantinople, and he was accused of selling arms to them. When a Christian slave took refuge on one of his ships at Alexandria, in order to please the Egytian sultan he had him sent back.

There were accordingly serious charges against Jacques Coeur. Even the king, who was notorious for selling out his friends, turned against him and brought the most preposterous charge of all, that of poisoning the king's mistress, Agnes Sorel, who, it has been proved, died in childbirth on February 9, 1450, and in her will made Jacques Coeur her executor. On July 30, 1450, he was imprisoned in the château of Taillebourg. In vain he claimed the benefit of the Church's jurisdiction. In vain the archbishop of Tours and the bishop of Poitiers pleaded in his behalf. He was tried before an extraordinary commission. One of them was Antoine de Chabannes, the former commander of the "Ecorcheurs," who was a bitter opponent and a native of Montpellier. The king himself took an active part in the prosecution. From the summer of 1451 to June, 1452, Charles VII was at Lusignan, where Jacques Coeur was in prison. When the process was transferred to Tours, the king was at Plessis-les-Tours. The poisoning accusation fell to the ground, but the other accusations were sustained. On May 29, 1453, the very day that Constantinople was taken by the Turks, the king in council declared Jacques Coeur guilty of the crimes of malversation of the king's revenue, of counterfeiting, of transmitting great quantities of money to the Turks, of taking gold and silver out of the kingdom. Out of regard for his past services and for the sake of the pope, who interceded in his behalf, the death penalty was remitted. But Jacques Coeur was deprived of every office and condemned to plead for mercy with bared head and holding a torch in his hand; he was required to ransom the Christian slave whom he had delivered to Egypt, or another in his place; to restore a hundred thousand gold pieces which he had extorted from the king's subjects; to pay a fine of 300,000 écus; and to remain in prison until full satisfaction had been given. All his property was confiscated and he was condemned to perpetual banishment. The sale of his property took several years, and undoubtedly there were many fictitious condemnations. Antoine de Chabannes, one of the judges, never paid the king for the property which he purchased. Many of the domains were sold at a low price, and the cost of the proceedings almost consumed the price of sale. The merchant vessels belonging to Jacques Coeur, which were not in France, never returned, but put their freight in bond in foreign courts. Nevertheless, some of them were later seized and sold for 9,100 livres to Bernard de Vaulx. One of them, the St. Michel, was later captured by the Turks.

In October, 1454, Jacques Coeur escaped from imprisonment in Poitiers. He was harbored by various convents which he had befriended, and made his way to Beaucaire, where his nephew, Jean des Villages, protected him, and helped him get to Nice whence he sailed for Rome. Pope Nicholas V welcomed him, and his successor, Pope Calixtus III, took advantage of his great talent for organization. He was given command of a fleet prepared against the Turks, and while on this expedition he died at Chios, November 15, 1456.

On his deathbed he recommended his children to the king, but

Charles VII had already in part restored their father's property to them. The king completed the work of restoration and on April 14, 1454, restored Jacques Coeur's house in Bourges and all his property in Berry to his two sons, Ravaut and Geoffrey. Later the crown restored the houses in Lyons and the mines in that region. When Charles VII died, Jacques Coeur's son, the archbishop of Bourges, tried to reopen the process and petitioned the king. The matter came up before parlement, but nothing was ever done. Jacques Coeur had done important work for France, but the history of commerce and industry in the reign of Charles VII is not altogether the history of a single man.

We know much about Charles VII's commercial policy, but little about his industrial policy. However, in the light of certain documents we may assume that industry experienced two opposed and contradictory policies. One tendency pushed towards liberty, the other towards monopoly and regulation.

Let us first study the tendencies towards liberty. As the result of the war workingmen became few and there was a serious stoppage in production. In order to stimulate production the old time restrictions upon the recruiting of workingmen and the liberty of work were abolished. At Rouen in 1407 the provincial estates-general demanded that all foreigners be admitted to every trade, subject simply to surveillance by the guardians of the gild, and in 1408 the king approved this recommendation. In 1416 the bailiff of Chartres, wishing to remedy the depopulation of the city and reduce the cost of food, proclaimed liberty of industry. In 1420 Charles VI permitted night work at Troyes in order to stimulate the leather trade. At Beauvais the cloth manufacture, which had once been so great, had fallen to a very low point. On March 2, 1424, the count-bishop of Beauvais, Pierre Cauchon, in letters patent, opened the city to all foreign merchants. He authorized the manufacture of cheap cloth, distinguished from the better quality by its lighter weight. Charles VII continued this policy.

In these troubled times the working population voluntarily or of necessity abandoned employment, and became less sedentary. Driven out by the English the workmen wandered far in search of employment. Thus at the beginning of the fifteenth century there was a regular exodus of workingmen from the towns of northern France, and these displacements spread the technical arts abroad over France. Local secrets of manufacture thus became open information.

The workmen also left their towns in search of higher wages. When peace came these nomadic habits continued. The working classes were unwilling to establish themselves again in fixed places and it was under Charles VII that journeymen workingmen are first found. Thus the workingmen became detached from his gild and became free. He sometimes ended by settling down in some place far removed from his old home.

This wandering life of the French workingman is interesting. In the eleventh and twelfth centuries there had been some wandering workingmen in France, but they were agricultural laborers who ended by settling down. The English invasions created the nomad artisan. The existence of this class was often very precarious and they were driven to form associations of mutual aid, from which the practice of "compagnonnage" arose. Companionships in general were formed between men of the same trade and were often secret, since they were looked upon with suspicion by the local authorities. Companions of the same trade recognized each other by secret signs and aided one another. A new arrival was found work and aided by money. But the whole question is really very obscure. All sorts of legends have gathered around the practice, and as there are few or no written documents every conclusion is hypothetical. All that we know for certain is that "compagnonnage" dates from the fifteenth century and that it was a result of the nomad life of the workingmen.

Thus the workingmen were no longer attached to the gilds in a strict manner, but escaped and organized themselves. Even in highly industrialized towns the gilds felt the competition of workmen who worked in their own houses or rooms. The gilds made war upon them in the north of France but were unable to suppress these clandestine organizations. However, it is to be remembered in many provinces the gild did not exist, or at least it was an exception. The general rule was free labor. The free trades, of course, did not escape all regulation. But the regulations were imposed by the municipal authorities rather than by the gilds. But if there were liberal measures restraining the power of the gilds for purposes of general interest, there was another current tending towards regulation. In spite of everything the gild system triumphed. When peace was established in 1453 gilds were established in great numbers and the gild system spread all over France. In Poitiers between 1455 and 1497 no less than twelve industrial gilds were founded. At Bourges Charles VII, with the intention of reviving the cloth industry, organized the drapers into gilds. In 1461 the gild system was introduced at Bordeaux and adopted for all the most important trades. The new statutes did not weaken the power of the gilds. On the contrary, the regulations became more strict and more rigorous. The principle of organization and authority triumphed over the principle of freedom of industry. The technique of manufacture was regulated in the minutest fashion, and the gilds sought by every means in their power to secure a monopoly and prevent workmen from becoming masters.

CHAPTER XIII

THE great European states of the Middle Ages were formed by a double process of expansion and consolidation. Even when all cohesion was lost, owing to the supremacy of feudal and particularistic interests over the central authority—as in Germany and Italy, which were reduced to geographical expressions—some reminiscence of their former unity was preserved in tradition and sentiment. But one important state in the later Middle Ages was not so formed. This was the Burgundian state created in the Low Countries by the four dukes of Burgundy: Philip the Bold (1363–1404), John the Fearless (1404–19), Philip the Good (1419–67), and Charles the Bold (1467–77). It was formed neither by expansion nor consolidation, but by agglomeration, like Habsburg Austria in more modern times. Roughly it may be said to have represented on the map of Europe to-day the kingdoms of Belgium and Holland and the French Département du Nord. It was a state of pluralistic origin, uniting territories dependent on Germany like Brabant, Hainaut, Holland, Zeeland, Luxemburg, *etc.*, with regions pertaining to France like Flanders and Artois.

Of a hybrid nature even from this first point of view, the Burgundian state was still more so if we consider the peoples who dwelt in it. It was crossed not only by a political but a linguistic frontier. . . . It united a group of Romanic with a group of Germanic population.[1]

French-speaking Walloons peopled western Flanders, Hainaut, Namur, Artois and southern Brabant; Flemings dwelt in eastern Flanders, northern Brabant and Luxemburg; and Low Dutch in Holland, Zeeland, Gelderland, and Zutphen. It was a "Middle Kingdom" in fact without being so in name, between Germany and France.

Yet in spite of its heterogeneous nature, its dualism, its lack of natural frontiers, the Burgundian state was a genuine political entity and not an amorphous formation. It was the product of a positive historical evolution. The forces which not only neutralized but overcame the natural particularism of this unique state were of an economic nature. In no other region of Western Europe was there denser population, more towns, so congested a commerce and industry. Already as early

[1] Pirenne, "The Burgundian State," *American Historical Review*, XIV, p. 479.

as the twelfth century there were signs of common commercial accord between the towns. The principalities were slower in perfecting economic agreements. It was not local trade that revived commerce; it was the importation of products of distant lands that was decisive. These were such things as wool, tin, copper, salt, and wines. A bourgeoisie developed; class distinctions came into being; violent clashes resulted. Flanders was a region which could not live on its own agricultural products and drew upon the rest of Europe for foodstuffs as well as for wool and metals.

As long as the commerce of the Low Countries was largely an overland commerce anything like common commercial accord was difficult to promote. For while Flanders traded with France and England, Brabant looked towards Aachen and Cologne. What put an end to these opposing tendencies was the development of navigation, both riverain and maritime, which developed Bruges into the most important commercial port in Northern Europe.

Sluys (French Écluse) derived its name from certain sluices or flood-gates constructed in the late thirteenth century at Lammisvliet on the Zwyn, a small village nearly opposite Mude, which was the official seat of the water bailiff (*bailli de l'eau*) of the counts of Flanders. Exactly when these flood-gates were installed is not certain. Sluys is not mentioned in history before 1296, so that it is probable that the sluices were constructed about 1290. What lends probability to this date is a charter of the count of Flanders dated November 23, 1290, constituting Lammisvliet a free town and its inhabitants free burghers having the same laws as Bruges, together with appeal to Bruges as their chief town. But even before these flood-gates were built, as far back as 1270, Hamburger merchants had established a commercial factory at Oostkerke, not far from Damme, on the west bank of the canal which led from the Zwyn to Damme; and Lübeck also had a factory at Houcke, midway between Oostkerke and Mude, on the same bank of the canal. It is evident, therefore, that by the end of the thirteenth century the whole territory around the estuary had become a most important entrepôt, and a place of favorite resort for Flemish, German, French and English merchants.

By the end of the thirteenth century

the coast, where besides Bruges, Antwerp soon formed another outlet on the sea, drew towards it the merchants of the whole country and the whole economic life flowed henceforth in a single stream. . . . The regions of the interior formed henceforth merely the Hinterland of the ports of the Zwyn or the Scheldt. . . . It was a fundamental necessity for all the cities of the region to be able to count on the freedom of the routes leading towards the ports, to see the number of market tolls thereon diminished. . . . After the beginning of the fourteenth century treaties of alliance, of arbitration, of monetary agreement, multiplied between the principalities. Of all these•the most celebrated is that which, in 1339, in the days of James Van Artevelde, established a commercial agreement between Flanders, Brabant, Hainaut, Holland and Zeeland.[2]

The fourteenth century was the period of the great commercial prosperity of Bruges. In the thirteenth century the Hanse of London had been a large purchaser of English fleeces. But in the reign of Edward I the English began to develop a maritime commerce; many vessels were equipped and these ships brought English wool to Bruges. The Flemish merchants, therefore, finding this precious commodity delivered upon the wharves of Damme, gave up London, and the London Hanse disappeared.

The Italian merchants, when they deserted the Champagne Fairs, established direct connection with Bruges, either by the Rhine or preferably by the sea. A regular service was established after 1317 between Venice and Bruges. The Italians carried spices and the products of oriental manufacture. At the same time, the ships of the Hanseatic League brought building timber, wheat, smoked fish, metals, and furs from Germany, Russia, and Sweden. Bruges, situated midway between the Baltic and the Straits of Gibraltar, concentrated the merchandise of the North and South in its port, and became the chief place of exchange in Northern Europe.

It was enormously prosperous. In the canal there were posts indicating the depth of water, and the course of the Zwyn was as well known to sailors as the lagoons of Venice to its gondoliers. Even to this day the high towers of this region are signal posts for vessels. Far out at sea the belfry of Bruges may be descried.

All sorts of languages were spoken in Bruges; all kinds of nationalities paraded there: French, Italians, Castilians, Aragonese, Provençals, English, and especially the Germans. For in 1336 the Hanseatic League established a factory there, and Bruges became a most important base of this powerful maritime league. There was some difficulty in the beginning, and from 1358–1360 the *kontor* was transferred to Dordrecht. But the German Hansa soon returned to Bruges, and stayed there throughout the fourteenth century. The council of Flanders held out important advantages to foreign merchants. They reduced the import tolls, suppressed the right of wreckage, regulated the law of marque, and made wholesale commerce completely free.   This commerce naturally drew men of money to Bruges. The Teutonic Knights had a regular bank there, where they conducted important operations. The papal tithes from all northern Europe were banked at Bruges. There were hundreds of Lombards in the city, and many letters of

[2] Pirenne, *American Historical Review*, XIV, pp. 487–88.

exchange were made payable to Italian bankers there; but there were no Jews in Bruges. They never had any benefits in Flanders.

In the early days Flemish vessels went abroad for wool. In the fourteenth century the ships that sailed up the Zwyn were all foreign. The merchants of Bruges, in a word, were nothing but intermediaries between the merchants of the various nations of Europe. They were the brokers who, in Bruges, played the important social and economic rôle elsewhere played by mere ship-owners. The Brugeois were the great middlemen of Europe.

Outside events also added to this commercial prosperity of Flanders. On December 13, 1355, John III, duke of Brabant, died. The eldest of his daughters was married to Wenzel, duke of Luxemburg and brother of Emperor Charles IV; the two younger were married to the duke of Guelders and Louis, count of Flanders. After two years of war, Wenzel was compelled to yield the seigniory of Malines, to permit the count of Flanders to take the title of Brabant, and to give him Antwerp as a fief. By the annexation of Malines Louis became master of both banks of the river Scheldt, on which Antwerp is situated, and the count of Flanders thought he no longer had to fear Antwerp's rivalry with Bruges.

In spite of internal turbulence arising from the fact that the great Flemish communes were rent by frequent feuds which led them to open hostility with the French king (to whom the oligarchic patriciate jealous of their political and economic mastery appealed for help); in spite of the fact that the needs of the cloth industry necessarily aligned the Flemish towns with England and so drew the country into the vortex of the wars between England and France, Flanders nevertheless soon recovered from the effects of turmoil and invasion. Commerce grew apace in spite of warfare on land and sea, and the cloth industry, which at first had been centered in the great towns like Ghent and Ypres, spread to the surrounding small towns like Cassel, Malines, Commines, *etc.* A peculiar feature of Flemish craftsmanship is that the workmen were paid weekly wages, rather than varying sums for piece work.

This growing economic solidarity was reënforced by the new political authority introduced in 1369. In that year Louis de Mâle, who had no son to succeed him, married his daughter to the French prince, Philip the Bold, duke of Burgundy, a younger brother of Charles V, the French king. But far from being a passive instrument of the French crown the Burgundian dukes labored with every means in their power to detach Flanders from vassalage to the French crown, to expand and consolidate their territories, to build up a powerful and independent state between France and Germany.

It was the misfortune of Flanders at this critical juncture when peace was so necessary to recovery of prosperity and the new ruler required time to set his house in order, that the force of events interfered with both these things. The towns whose liberties the count was determined to restrict were sullen and sore, especially Ghent, whose head was bloody but unbowed after the revolt in 1382. Nearly every town was torn by dissension between the patriciate and the lower classes, while the country areas and small villages hated the great towns. The small towns were not cursed with the narrow regulations which governed gild labor in the large towns, and moreover the country workman was content with lower wages than the town workman. Finally the prospect of new war between France and England loomed large, and Flanders no more now than formerly, could avoid being drawn into it. In fact, Flanders bore the brunt of the brief conflict. The English merchants were expelled from Bruges, and their property confiscated. Calais was in danger, for French forces were at Gravelines and Dunkirk, and a sudden raid upon Calais seemed imminent. The French crown wanted to recover Calais for political and military reasons; Flanders wanted to abolish the English wool staple there since it was a serious injury to her textile industry despite the fact that Flemish influence had always been predominant in Calais, where the weavers still found the raw material so necessary for their looms. Nearly all Flanders lived by draping English wool. The workingmen wanted the "good old times" once more, with "beer and bacon." Among the distressed working classes mutterings were heard, and in the districts of Bourbourg, Bergues, and Cassel the rumor was afloat that they would welcome the English.

In 1383 the English in a cross-channel campaign drove the French out of Gravelines and Dunkirk. Soon the coast from Calais to Blankenberghe was in their hands. Nieuport, Furnes, Bergues, Bourbourg, Poperinghe, Cassel and many other small places surrendered. The loot was enormous. Some of these towns welcomed the English as rulers preferable to the French. A curious backwash of this victorious campaign was that owing to the "hard times" in England, apprentices and servants in London ran away from their masters and hastened across the Channel to better their fortune. Flanders seemed to them an Eldorado of riches. Secret emissaries from Ghent were in the English camp urging immediate English attack on Ypres. Ypres was situated on the main road to Bruges. It was then occupied by a French force. The commercial and ruling class in the city was pro-French, but the artisans were said by the Ghenter agents to be in sympathy with the English, who, it was represented, would restore communal liberties in Flanders. If Ypres were taken, Bruges would fall and the French be driven out.

At this time Ypres was a magnificent place. The great Cloth Hall, finished in 1342, was the most magnificent edifice in the Low Countries.[3] The town was surrounded with beautiful suburbs and was reputed to have 40,000 inhabitants. Ypres prepared to withstand a siege and after two months was still untaken. Fever broke out among the English and there was scarcity of food. Perhaps worst of all was the mob of unarmed English artisans and runaway servants who thronged the English camp, encumbering the English army and aggravating the indiscipline. On August 8, 1383, after a last unsuccessful assault, the English threw up the siege. The French took the offensive and soon the English were reduced again to possession only of Calais.

Peace at least came to a sullen Flanders. But prosperity was yet afar off. The swarm of French-mannered, French-speaking officials in the service of the count-duke nettled the Flemish portion of his subjects, and his magnificence seemed flaunting insolence to an impoverished population. The poverty and exhaustion of the country were the two chief securities of Philip of Burgundy's throne in Flanders.

The first duke of Burgundy was a bold and far-sighted man. The wealth of his new acquisition and the peculiar commercial and industrial interests of his adopted country led to an inevitable deviation of the policy of Burgundy-Flanders from that of France. If politically he was ambitious to make his heterogeneously assorted state independent of France, economically he was ambitious to make Flanders independent by destroying the English wool staple in Calais and compelling English wool to be shipped directly to Flemish ports. To this end, in 1385, he began the construction of formidable fortifications at Sluys, which fronted Sandwich and the entrance to the Thames. Nieuport, Courtrai, and Audenarde completed the quadrilateral of strongholds by means of which the duke hoped to command the Channel and at the same time overawe his turbulent subjects in Ypres and Ghent. In a word, the duke planned to kill two birds with one stone. The English government protested against this fortification of Sluys as vigorously as it protested against the opening of the Scheldt in 1792 and Napoleon's fortification of Antwerp. At the same time the duke put other screws on England in the form of prohibition and embargo. In 1403 a proclamation forbade all commercial intercourse with England. It was hard on his own people, but he hoped thereby to compel the English to transfer the wool staple to Sluys. The English staplers in Calais complained that they were suffering "grievous loss," but the government refused to be moved.

At the height of these strained internal and external relations of Flanders, Philip of Burgundy died (1404) and was succeeded by his son John the Fearless (1404–19). The first act of the new duke was

[3] The destruction of this Cloth Hall in the World War is one of the irreparable losses of civilization.

one of conciliation of his Flemish subjects, even if it was not of any economic relief. Hitherto the seat of government in the Low Countries had been at Bruges, which was a Walloon, not a Flemish town, and, moreover, was notoriously aristocratic in its social attitudes. The language of the court and of the laws had been French. John of Burgundy now fixed his official residence at Audenarde, proclaimed that all communications with his Flemish subjects would be in the Flemish tongue, and finally promised his utmost effort to secure restoration of peace between France and England, with a return of commercial prosperity to Flanders. The first two of these pledges he kept, but the last was incapable of fulfillment even with the best intentions.

It is interesting to observe the growing change in politico-economic ideas in this time. The sober thinking element in the Flemish towns was increasingly coming to the conviction that they had a right to an independent neutrality of trade, in spite of the hostility between France and England. The hardship entailed by the duke's retaliatory policy of prohibition and embargo undoubtedly was a strong influence in developing this new attitude. England, too, was veering around to this state of mind. Pressure was brought to bear on the English council by the Calais merchants, who urged that the staple at Calais was valueless without a truce with Flanders. Even the French government showed symptoms of this new way of thinking, for the principle of a separate treaty between Flanders and England was conceded in 1405. This separate trade treaty or *trêve marchande* as it was called, has been curiously neglected by historians. Yet it is the first document in history which clearly raised the questions of the rights of neutral trade in time of war, and the nature of contraband. The matter of international coöperation for suppression of piracy also entered into the negotiations.

But all good intentions were shortly cancelled by the great feud in Paris between Philip of Burgundy and Louis of Orléans, bitter rivals for control of the government of the mad king Charles VI. This feud culminated in the atrocious murder of Louis by Burgundy's agents in 1407. A protracted civil war ensued between the Burgundian and Armagnac factions, which rent France asunder and provided an opening for Henry V to invade the country. The murder of John the Fearless on the bridge of Montereau in 1419 threw the state of Burgundy-Flanders into military alliance with the English foe.

The political history of Burgundy-Flanders is not germane to this chapter except in so far as some things must be mentioned for sake of clarity. Under Philip the Good the real union of the Low Countries was consummated. He acquired Namur, Brabant, Limburg, Holland, Hainaut, Zeeland, Luxemburg and Antwerp, and really formed and founded the later kingdom of Belgium. He was an uncrowned king as powerful as his royal contemporaries.

His alliance with England enabled him to extend his frontiers and to renew the prosperity of his Flemish towns to such a degree that he died the wealthiest prince in Christendom. Contemporaries estimated his revenue at 900,000 ducats, equal to that of Venice and four times greater than that of Florence. He spent royally upon the splendour of his court the income he derived from the prosperity which was largely due to his statesmanship and enlightened administration.[4]

Philip broke with the English alliance in 1435. He led a joyous and sumptuous life at Bruges, his habitual residence, where he patronized oil-painting, wood-carving, art metal-work, *etc.* Bruges became the art center of all northern Europe. Great painters like Jan Van Eyck, Roger Van der Weyden and Hugo Van der Goes repaid in good measure the princely encouragement they received at the court of Burgundy. The court of Philip became the capital of the chivalry of the fifteenth century, wholly different from the former type. It was a chivalry of parade and tournaments, in the life of which ladies played a very great part. In the Burgundian court etiquette developed those formalities which have survived down to the nineteenth century in the courts of Europe. The regulations of etiquette passed, through the influence of Philip the Good, to the Spanish Court, to the French Court, to the German Court, and to that of Edward VI and Henry VIII of England. To such a degree, indeed, did these rulers impose their wills upon their subjects even in the matter of costume and personal appearance, that when Philip the Good lost his hair, his courtiers were directed to shave their heads.

In Bruges were erected those marvelous structures which to-day delight the tourist: the great belfry tower, the headquarters of the Hanseatic League, the Church of the Holy Sepulchre. The Van Eycks and Memling made the art of Bruges a famous chapter in the history of culture. Some of the most celebrated festivals of the late Middle Ages were celebrated here—in 1430, the marriage of Philip the Good with Isabel of Portugal; in 1468, the marriage of Charles the Bold with Margaret of York. Mediterranean ships sought the harbor of Bruges, bringing Spanish wool, and fruits, oranges, citron, fruit syrup, oriental tapestry; also rare animals which the Portuguese sent from their West African colonies. The marriage of Philip the Good with a Portuguese princess established intimate and active relations between Flanders and Portugal.

How the splendor with which state occasions were celebrated struck a contemporary Englishman is seen from the letter which John Paston the younger wrote to his mother from Bruges after witnessing the week of pageantry and feasting, of dancing and interludes which

[4] Review in *London Times Lit. Sup.,* Sept. 12, 1929, of Otto Cartellieri, "The Court of Burgundy."

marked the occasion of the marriage of Charles the Bold with Margaret of York. "And as for the Duke's Coort, I hert never of non lyek to it, save King Arturys Cort."

But there was another side to this magnificence. The dukes of Burgundy were French in blood, French in mental attitude and "had no traditional sympathy with the memories, no inborn respect for the rights and liberties of any section or class of their subjects."[5] For the movement among the towns—except Bruges—which for more than a century had struggled to establish self-government on popular foundation, they had hatred and fear. Bruges, partly out of tradition, partly out of jealousy of Ghent, was aristocratic and oligarchic and so was inclined to support the political and territorial policy of the duke. But not so the other towns. Neither Philip of Burgundy's effort to arrest the decay of Ypres, nor his Anglo-commercial policy, mollified the towns which resented the strong development of the ducal supremacy. Even Bruges rebelled in 1436, and in 1438 town revolt broke out all over Flanders, only to suffer condign punishment when crushed. Ghent was most stubborn of all. In 1449 when she refused to pay a salt tax to which Bruges and Ypres yielded, four years of conflict ensued which terminated in the ruination of the liberties of the cities throughout Flanders.

The *gabelle* was one of two detested forms of taxation which the dukes introduced from France. The other was the *fouage* or hearth tax, whose incidence we have seen in France in the fourteenth century. This tax was introduced in 1437. Each town and village met the tax collectively by paying so much per hearth and then assessed its inhabitants proportionately. There was some abatement in the case of the very poor. We have the complete data of such assessments for the years 1437, 1464, 1472, 1480, 1486 and 1526. The last three, of course, are post-Burgundian. But taking them all together some luminous conclusions are arrived at. One can follow from decade to decade the progressive decline of Bruges, Ghent, Ypres, Louvain and other towns. By the first quarter of the sixteenth century the population of Ypres, which in the days of its prosperity had been about 100,000, had sunk to 5,000. The Cloth Hall was deserted and grass grew in the streets. Ghent survived as a corn market for the hinterland behind it.

The great commercial and industrial gilds survived these events because they were oligarchic associations of rich bourgeois who had natural affinity with the ducal policy. But commerce and industry had both declined and the gilds held half-empty bags.

Parallel to the industrial decay of Ypres, which is an index of the general decay of the cloth industry in Flanders, is the decay of the

---

[5] *Camb. Modern History*, I, p. 425.

commerce of Bruges. Time was, in the first half of the fourteenth century, when Bruges was the emporium of the north whither came the ships of the Hanseatic League, the galleys of Venice and Genoa, besides sailing craft from the ports of England, France, Portugal, and Spain. Seventeen trading companies had agencies in Bruges. Of 9,300 enumerated burghers over 8,000 were artisans and about 1,000 merchants, which shows that Bruges was also not without importance for its crafts. But the *poorters* or rich merchants dominated everything, although no more than 800 in number. Among these were 243 millionaires, or at least exceedingly rich men. A clique of fifty families ruled the town. The wealthiest of these families were engaged in shipping, merchandising, banking, money-lending, tax-farming, and the purchase of land or rents. The less wealthy were occupied with brewing, the manufacture and sale of cloth, and retailing of foreign imports. Numbered among the excluded artisans must be a crowd of peddlers and hawkers.

It is easy to understand that heavy taxation not only for sustaining the most luxurious court in Europe, but for war, operated disastrously upon Flemish industry and commerce, and that the duke's retaliatory commercial policy towards England fell back on his own head. But the causes of the decline of the commerce and trade of Flanders were deeper than these things. The decline of the Hanseatic League involved Bruges in its own decay. Moreover, under the Lancastrian kings, England ceased more and more to be dependent upon Flanders for weavers and began to fabricate her own cloth, at first with Flemish immigrants who fled across sea from the troubles at home and later with native textile workers. In a word England in the fifteenth century carded, dyed, and wove her own wool. Hence Hanseatic and other merchants long accustomed to resort to Flanders to purchase English cloth, bought it in English ports. Flanders lost her ancient monopoly both as manufacturer and as middleman.

Part of the responsibility for Bruges' decline, however, must be attributed to the narrowness of the oligarchy which governed her business. Bruges clung too tenaciously to old established commercial practices. This oligarchy scrutinized foreign merchants too carefully; it tried to prevent foreign merchants from selling in Bruges goods which had been purchased in the fairs of Antwerp, Berg op-Zoom, or other places of which Bruges was jealous. Most of all the brokerage system, which Bruges introduced, drove trade away. For no commercial transaction effected in Bruges was legal unless made through a local broker who was a burgess of the town. By this tyranny Bruges slowly strangled the goose which laid the golden egg. "The decline of Bruges was due to the development of larger and freer forms of international trade than either Bruges or the Hanse towns were prepared to recognize. A proposal was even entertained in 1477 for erecting a staple that would still further have narrowed the channels of trade; and the formal transfer of the Kontor to Antwerp was delayed half a century after the actual removal of the merchants and the trade by the unwillingness of the League to accept a less privileged position than they had previously enjoyed. In the meantime the Kontor lost its control over the merchants, and many of the more enterprising formed connections with the Rhenish and South German capitalists whose operations dominated the money-market of the sixteenth century. The offer made by the government of Philip II to form an alliance with the Hanse towns against England provided the opportunity for the re-establishment of the control of the Kontor over the German trading community in Antwerp. The inception of this scheme . . . must be connected with the breach between England and the Hanse in 1553–57, and its further development in 1562 with the breach between England and the Netherlands." [6]

Even nature was unkind to Bruges. At the beginning of the fourteenth century the harbor of the Zwyn began to be silted up so that ships had increasing difficulty in reaching the port of Damme. In the winter of 1404–05 all Europe suffered from one of the most terrible and protracted storms on record. The low coast of Flanders was inundated for leagues. The permanent effect of that storm was to open the hitherto shallow estuary of the Scheldt where Antwerp stood and nearly to close the Zwyn. The shoals and islands which had blocked the Scheldt were swept out by the swirling tides, carried up channel and dumped in tremendous masses into the harbors of Sluys, Damme, and other ports. Antwerp then and there became a seaport. Thenceforth shipping swarmed to Antwerp, where a new and more liberal commercial policy was practised, more in harmony with the economic changes. Bruges and Antwerp—these two evoked two different periods and two opposed systems of commerce.

Charles the Bold tried to remedy the evil by opening a second canal, the Zwartegat. He compelled Ghent and Ypres to contribute to the expense though they could ill afford it. But the conditions did not improve. The river got shallower and soon at low tide could be crossed anywhere. Bruges ceased to be a seaport. In 1494 between four and five thousand houses were vacant and fell in ruins.

The banking business hung on longest at Bruges. In the days of the Avignonese popes the tithes of all Northern Europe had been banked there. The Great Schism, when there were first two and then three rival popes, injured this business, for the deposits declined when only one pope banked at Bruges and only part of Europe recognized his

Unwin in *English Hist. Rev.*, XXVII, 814, a review of Rudolf Häpke, *Der deutsche Kaufmann in den Niederlanden*, Leipzig, 1911.

obedience. The real blow to Bruges' banking fell, however, when the popes of the Renaissance withdrew all papal deposits there and deposited them with the Medici bank in Florence and in Rome. Then Bruges became what she has ever since remained, *"Bruges la morte,"* a museum of art treasures and desiccated medieval antiquities.

The striking exception to this almost universal commercial and industrial decline in the Low Countries was Antwerp.

Until 1353 the province of Brabant was an independent principality, for it was not united with Flanders until then. In the swirl of politics, into which almost every principality of the Low Countries was drawn in the fourteenth century, the dukes of Brabant, like other princes, were often compelled to steer between their political obligations and their economic interests. In the early stages of the wars of the English in France the duke of Brabant had adroitly carried water on both shoulders, with the result that his country was spared the internal turmoil and the foreign intervention which vexed Flanders. One reason for this success was the relative economic backwardness of Brabant when compared with Flanders. It was more agrarian than commercial and industrial. But with the increasing importance of commerce and industry Brabant gradually acquired importance, first rivalling and then surpassing Flanders itself in the fifteenth century.

Owing to its position between the two great economic centers in the southern Low Countries, the Meuse and the Scheldt rivers, it was only natural that the duchy of Brabant should, with the great revival of commerce and industry in western Europe, sooner or later become a connecting link between these two important highways. . . . Maestricht, a possession of the dukes since the beginning of the thirteenth century, bore a peculiar relation to the economic development of the duchy. Situated on the left bank of the Meuse where the old Roman road from Boulogne and Rheims passed eastward toward Cologne, it early became important for the transit trade of goods from the Rhinelands and Italy to the towns of Flanders and Brabant.[7]

The weak spot in Brabant was Mechelen (French, Malines), an enclaved fief of the bishop of Liège which had been mortgaged to the count of Hainaut, for acquisition of which the count of 'Flanders and the duke of Brabant were competitors. For in possession of the former it might injure Antwerp by separating its connection with its economic hinterland. This is just what came to pass in 1333 when Count Louis of Flanders bought the mortgage. Twenty years later the counts of Flanders also annexed Brabant and the two states became as one.

With the union of the two provinces, Bruges and Antwerp became natural competitors. The counts of Flanders were desirous of promot-

[7] Lucas, *The Low Countries in the Hundred Years' War*, p. 12.

ing the trade of both towns. But natural advantage and local administrative conditions were both in favor of Antwerp. There gilds were not known; the vexatious restrictions imposed at Bruges upon the conduct of trade were absent. Antwerp offered a fair field and no favor to all merchants. As it owed its primary importance to a fair, so it long remained a sort of great permanent fair in which intercourse was untrammeled by oppressive municipal and gild regulations. Antwerp was soon crowded with mercantile associations and banking houses: the Hanseatic League and the newly founded English company of the Merchant Adventurers were there; the Fuggers and Welsers of Augsburg, the Spinola of Genoa. Finally, after the discovery of America, Antwerp became the greatest commercial city of Europe.

Another rising competitor of Bruges was Amsterdam. In Hanseatic and Flemish shipping records the name of Amsterdam occurs with increasing frequency. Article fifty-four of the Gotland Sea Laws runs: "If a ship loads in Scania or elsewhere, and she is bound for Flanders or another market, and she comes to Amsteldam from stress of weather or from want of necessaries . . ." etc. Evidently the Zuyder Zee was a place of shelter for ships plying between the ports of the Baltic and Flanders, and we know from other sources that by the thirteenth century Amsterdam had become a port of some commercial importance. The construction of the dam on the river Amstel, which made the port, antedated the dam at Sluys by nearly ninety years. For about 1204 Gijsbrecht II, who was the feudal lord of Amstelland, built a castle and a dike at the mouth of the Amstel river, which gave its name to the town. A law of Hamburg, probably of the year 1270, discloses that Hamburger merchants trading with Utrecht, then celebrated for its fine cloths, were accustomed to carry on their trade with Utrecht via the river Vecht, which empties into the Zuyder Zee near Muiden, slightly east of Amsterdam. But this trade was exposed, in winter especially, since sea-going vessels could not ascend the river farther than Marsen, a village on the Vecht, where they were often caught in the ice. The advantage of an open and sheltered harbor like Amsterdam was soon apparent. Moreover, Amsterdam, unlike so many ports, but like Antwerp, was a free port. In 1315 Count Floris of Holland confiscated Amstelland from its lord for treason—real or alleged—and united it with the county of Holland, from which time Amsterdam's greatness may be dated. Amsterdam became a member of the Hanseatic League in 1358 and was the head of a cluster of Hanseatic towns around the Zuyder Zee—Stavoren, Kampen, and Zwolle being the more important—which contributed ships for Lübeck's war with the Danes in 1368.

It would be wrong to infer, though, that Flanders saw her commerce and especially her cloth industry seep away without a struggle. Rural manufacturing of woolens from Spanish wool, free from the narrow protectionism of the towns, supplanted the industry of the great towns. Moreover, Flanders endeavored to compensate for the loss of her woolen trade by promotion of linen manufacturing, especially in the small towns, and by the manufacture of luxurious and costly tapestries. The very word "arras" current in Shakespeare's times for hangings, tells a tale. Arras furnished most of the tapestry for the House of Burgundy. An inventory of 1420 shows that the duke owned four chamber tapestries, fifty-nine hall tapestries and nine tapestries for chapels. The collection was much enlarged by Philip the Good. So valued were these hangings that a "vaulted building of stone" was erected in which they could be stored in safety and protected from fire and dampness. It was after the middle of the century that the decline of Arras became noticeable. There were fifty-nine tapestry workers at Arras between 1462-67, but no new names had been added to the list of master weavers from 1450 to 1467. The remarkable tapestries which decorated the tents of Charles the Bold when the Swiss pillaged his camp after the battles of Granson and Morat were made at Tournai. In Hondschoote a species of cape was manufactured, made of mixed wool and silk, and this trade prospered down to the time of Louis XI. Then the workmen took refuge in the neighboring towns of Lille and especially Amiens. The crowning disaster to the workshops of Arras came in the capture of the town by Louis XI of France in 1477. The taxes and the expulsion of its inhabitants in 1479 "struck a blow at its workshops from which they did not recover." The fall of Arras in 1477 was the end of the first period of the history of European tapestry.

The chief rival of Arras, Brussels, is first mentioned in a purchase of tapestry by the house of Burgundy in 1466. Philip the Good bought a series of six pieces on the "History of Hannibal." "Nevertheless," adds Müntz, "it is certain that from this time the workshops of Brussels rivalled those of Arras, until at length they supplanted them." It has been asserted that there were workshops in Brussels in the fourteenth century, but there is no clear and authentic evidence to support such a statement. However, it is possible that some of the important tapestries in the early collection of the duke of Burgundy were woven in Brabant. Even so, there was no corporation of tapestry weavers as distinguished from the ordinary weavers until the year 1441. On the other hand, though the history is dim, the Brussels tapestries were of sufficient importance to attract the patronage of Philip the Good at a time when he was buying fine hangings from the celebrated Pasquier Grenier of Tournai.

Tournai furnished many fine tapestries during the fifteenth century. One set—the "History of Gideon"—the contract for which was signed by Robert Dary and Jean de l'Ortyle, two master weavers of Tournai, was one of the most highly prized tapestries in the collection of the house of Burgundy. Bruges, Ghent and Antwerp, also, produced a considerable number of hangings in this century. Ghent is said to have had fourteen or fifteen weavers, each employing from ten to twelve workmen. Practically no records remain of the work at Antwerp, but there is evidence that the weavings of Bruges were of great reputation. The impetus to the industry at Bruges came largely through the designs furnished by such painters as the Van Eycks, Roger Van der Weyden, Memling, Thierry, Bouts, and later, Raphael. For from 1420–1500 swarms of tapestry workers who were natives of Arras, Lille, Bruges, Tournai, and Brussels "swooped down on the territory of the marquis of Mantua, the duke of Ferrara, the duke of Urbino, on Venetia, Tuscany, and Umbria." The cause for this general movement lay in the desire to procure the best possible cartoons. Weavers had come to realize that the cartoon was the "most important element in the development of tapestry," and in the design lay the power to determine the success or the failure of the hanging. Italian painters seemed to have had particular fitness for this work, for their paintings showed a balanced grouping, a powerful line, and dramatic feeling. Cartoonists like Cosimo Tura, Mantegna, and Leonardo da Vinci were very popular in Flanders.

There were some efforts to introduce the secrets of the Flemish weavers into England during this century, but undoubtedly the finest tapestries were the products of the Flemish workshops. Many of these Flemish tapestries had come to England as gifts to King Richard II, or to the dukes of Lancaster, of Gloucester, of York, and of Albany. In 1414, Richard, duke of Albany, received from John the Fearless of Burgundy "a chamber of tapestries with figures of fine ladies and little children, sent by the hands of the earl of Bothwell who was at the Burgundian court." Evidently tapestry was of great importance in English life. "It was used for furnishings in everyday life, and for indoor and outdoor decorations on occasions of festivity, pomp and ceremony." The entrance of Elizabeth, queen of Henry VII, into London was a brilliant spectacle, as the old historian describes it: "Al the strets ther, whiche she shulde passe bye wer clenly dressed and beseme with cloth of Tappestrye and Arras, and some streetes as Chepe, hanged with riche clothes of golde and silkes."

The products of the tapestry workshops reveal a variety of themes. In the main the weavers of the thirteenth century had favored religious subjects. But the fourteenth century showed an inclination toward secular themes. Sometimes it was one of romance as the "History of Charlemagne," the "History of Percival of Gaul," or "Theseus and the Golden Eagle." Again it was taken from contemporary life, as "History of Bertrand Duguesclin," or "Battle of Liège," or "Hunting

Scenes." Nature, too, received some attention, especially from the German weavers. In the hanging in the castle of Wartburg the weaver introduced flowers for weapons, and the sward was strewn with flowers among which birds, rabbits and squirrels frolicked. Religious themes were not entirely discarded, however, for among the fashionable subjects were the "Story of Esau and Jacob," "The Life of Jesus Christ," "The Passion," "The Coronation of the Virgin." Also there appeared some allegorical themes as "The Seven Cardinal Sins," and "The Tree of Life."

CHAPTER XIV

SPAIN IN THE FOURTEENTH AND FIFTEENTH CENTURIES

SPAIN is composed of several distinct kingdoms, each of which in earlier times formed a separate and independent realm. Although all except Portugal were ultimately united by marriage, inheritance or conquest, under one crown,[1] the original distinctions, geographical, social and economic, survived, and indeed remained almost unaltered. The cradle of Spain was the principality of the Asturias in the far north of the peninsula. It was—and is yet—largely a mountainous country overspread with thick forests of chestnut and oak, but affording pasturage in the valleys. Hence from time immemorial the Asturias has been a pastoral country. The same is true of Leon, the territory which runs up from the plains of Old Castile into the spurs of the Galician and Asturian Sierras. Here again the rugged slopes, narrow valleys and dreary steppes were fit only for cattle-raising. In both these regions the broken terrain made quantity production of cattle and sheep impracticable. It was quite otherwise with the great central plateau of Old and New Castile, to which one coming from the north descends by one gigantic terrace after another until the great plain of central Spain is reached. The scarcity of rain in central Spain makes all this enormous table-land merely a grazing country, for agriculture never has been a successful occupation. Here was a land of great ranches and rich haciendas spread between walled towns whose sites marked successive stages in the advance of the Christian against the Mohammedan. It was fortunate for Castile that these domains of the great feudal proprietors were scattered over the whole surface of the country, and did not form compact blocks as in France and Germany, for otherwise the royal power would have been too weak to overcome them.

The Cantabrian ports traded with Gascony, Poitou and Normandy in France; with Flanders and England. But this commerce was not large owing to the narrowness and poverty of the coast. It might have been larger if products from interior Spain could have been brought out through the little Biscayan ports. But the mountain ranges cut central Spain off from any but the most difficult access to the northern

---

[1] In the Middle Ages when the word Spain was used, it always signified Castile. Aragon was always thought of as a separate state, and Aragonese were never called Spaniards.

harbors. A tax on sardines and whale oil brought into Cantabrian ports indicates that fishing was the most important industry.

The commerce of Spain did not become of importance until the conquest of Andalusia—Seville in 1248 and Cadiz in 1262—gave the kingdom of Castile outlets on the sea. The ubiquitous Genoese obtained privileges at Seville as early as 1251. Spanish wool and hides were then able to reach the markets of Italy and Flanders. Moreover, Andalusia, unlike central Spain, was a land of fertile soil and delicious climate, so that the olive oil of Seville, the wine of Xerez, the fruits of Malaga became important exports. Castilian agriculture could never more than barely hold its own and was ill-prepared to resist a bad season except in Murcia and Andalusia. The aversion of the Spanish peasant to agriculture became second nature owing to its impracticability. But that impracticability was aggravated by the Mesta or Sheep Owners' Gild, which deliberately discouraged agriculture in the interest of pasturage. The sheep grangers had a habit of burning the trees off to make a young green undergrowth for pasturage. This clash between an agricultural and a pastoral economy is at the root of Castilian economic history. In 1517 the Wool Growers' Gild possessed 2,860,000 migratory sheep. In September the great flocks, rounded up by dogs whose ferocity towards strangers Cervantes has celebrated, were driven from the uplands down into the plains of Estremadura and Andalusia, where the ewes would lamb, and in April were driven north again in search of grass.

The production of wool and other raw materials was the chief undertaking of Spanish industry until the reign of Isabel, when a policy of import duties upon cloth and export duties on wool encouraged native textile manufacture in rivalry with Flemish woollens and Neapolitan, Turkish and Indian silks.[2]

Castilian Spain's industries, aside from those attached to wool, were the building trades, metal-work, tile-making, *etc.* Hence most of the gilds were made up of leather, wool, and metal workers. Excessive regulation of the gilds retarded industry. This evil, unlike gild policy elsewhere in Europe, did not emananate from the jealous and oligarchic spirit of the gilds themselves so much as from the crown. The most skilled workmen of Spain had not been Christians, but Moors and Jews and in skilled industry, as in skilled agriculture, the expulsion of the Jews and the Moors was detrimental. In 1492 "when the united wisdom of Ferdinand and Isabella resolved on the expatriation of the Spanish Moors, they forgot the risk of an exile's vengeance." [3] The

[2] Seaver, *The Great Revolt of Castile*, p. 22.
[3] Lane Poole, *Barbary Corsairs*, p. 7.

Barbary Corsairs of Morocco, the scourge of Mediterranean commerce in the sixteenth century, were the descendants of those exiles.

Society in the kingdoms of Leon and Castile before the great exile in 1492 was divided into four classes: First: clergy, powerful in its political influence, its privileges and its immense wealth. Second: nobility, subdivided into three separate degrees of nobles: (a) magnates or great nobles (*proceres, ricoshombres, optimates*), a military and landed aristocracy which warred against each other and against the crown; (b) hidalgos (*fijosdalgos, infanzones*), neither so rich nor so noble as the former, dependent on the king but exempt from overlordship of the magnates; (c) knights (*caballeros*), a sort of plebeian aristocracy recruited from the urban populace, which originated as town militia and was favored by the crown to make head against the *ricoshombres* and hidalgos. Third: bourgeois of the chartered towns, as everywhere, composed of merchants, artisans, and small free landowners. This class was a social product of the conquest and originally was composed of settlers and colonists introduced into the newly acquired areas and localized in garrison towns to which *fueros* or municipal privileges were granted. Fourth: Jews, Moudejares, and Mozarabs. The Moudejares were Mussulmans who had accepted Christian domination, but preserved their religion and their laws under the conquerors. The Mozarabs were arabized Christians, descended from the early Gothic population which adhered to the Christian religion, but in almost every other aspect had become Mohammedan. All three of these classes were numerous in Castile.

Portugal, the second kingdom in the Spanish peninsula, although a seaboard kingdom, was slow in developing a maritime trade. The earliest evidence of it is an act of 1293 which exempted from taxation ships plying to the ports of Gascony, Poitou, Brittany, Normandy, Flanders, and England. Portuguese merchants were included in the *Charta mercatorum* of Edward I in 1303, and Portugal's commercial relations with England were far closer than with any other country. In 1353 a treaty of commerce and navigation was made between Portugal and England, which in subsequent years was often renewed and cemented by marriage alliances between the reigning houses of the two countries. In 1386 John I, king of Portugal, known as John the Good, married Philippa, a sister of Henry IV of England. English ladies accompanied her and married into Portuguese houses. French was introduced as the court language in Lisbon, as it was at Windsor. The children of this match received alternately Portuguese and English names, which accounts for the appearance of names like Duerte (Edward) and Henry in Portuguese history. Prince Henry the Navigator, the daring Portuguese explorer, was the most distinguished son of this marriage. The chief article of Anglo-Portuguese trade was the wine of Oporto, port wine. Nuts, raisins, various dried fruits, and olive oil were other commodities. The Genoese soon appeared in Portugal, and were followed by the Catalans, Florentines and Venetians. In 1385 the Portuguese established a trading agency at Bruges.

In contrast with Castilian commerce, which was chiefly one of raw products, the commerce of Aragon and Catalonia—for the two were united—was far greater both in volume and variety. Castile was landlocked for centuries. Aragon had had an international and maritime commerce since the period of the Crusades. As the closing years of the reign of King James I approached (died 1276) he could look with pride and satisfaction on the growing cities and busy ports that dotted his lands. The conquest of Majorca had not only extended the Aragonese dominions, but had increased the prestige and influence of the kingdom. Aragonese consuls were stationed in the leading commercial centers of the Mediterranean, and a sturdy merchant marine plied the sea. Although the conqueror had failed to thwart the aggressive advances of the French, he had, in spite of many obstacles and difficulties, maintained the union of Aragon and Catalonia, and left his kingdom firmly established as a Mediterranean commercial and colonial power.

James I of Aragon left the stage set for the second step in the Mediterranean expansion of Aragon. The Sicilian Vespers and the seizure of Sicily occurred in 1282. After much hard fighting the right of a prince of the house of Aragon to sit on the island throne was finally (1302) secured. The importance of this acquisition to Aragonese commerce can hardly be overestimated. Without the naval power afforded by the shipping of Barcelona the great Mediterranean expansion of Aragon would have been an impossibility. What would have been the sequel of the Sicilian Vespers if it had not been for the Catalan fleet? And the possession of Sicily gave Aragon a strategic position in the middle of the Mediterranean.

The history of the commerce of Barcelona in the later Middle Ages is the history of the prosperity, and then the decline, of that commerce. One of the most interesting facts about the reign of James I is that almost every feature of later Barcelonese commercial organization dates from that period. The first law to regulate banking was the decree of 1240, which limited interest to 18 per cent. The Italians, who were expelled from the city in 1265, were the Lombards, Florentines, Sienese, and Lucchesi, whose banking operations in early times were very extensive. In 1268 *all* foreigners were forbidden to do a banking business in Barcelona. The banking history of Barcelona began in James's reign, and, whether or not it was James's intention, the city must have profited a great deal by building up its own banking business, instead of becoming tributary to foreign capital. Another feature of the Barcelonese system which had its beginning in James's reign was the regulation of the brokers or *corredores*. The method adopted of keeping commerce free of fraud was to regulate rigidly the fees to be paid to these men for their services so that they would not, for the sake of a large fee or bribe, take part in a fraudulent deal. The earliest surviving ordinances governing the conduct of the *corredores* date from 1271. There are, however, indications of regulations as early as 1251.

In 1258 the municipal council, acting with the king, put forth the first code of Barcelonese sea law. This ordinance contains twenty-two chapters and touches the most important matters connected with the conduct of shipping, such as the duty of captain, supercargo, pilot, purser, exit from and entrance to ports, landing, loading and unloading, and armament. Again in James's reign we see the first traces of the existence of a mercantile corporation. This body had only four representatives in the city council (of two hundred members). It was, however, to grow. In 1263 James appointed a consul at Alexandria and another at Tunis. These two were the first that went out from Aragon-Catalonia. The consuls were very powerful officials. They were the link which connected the home government with its citizens abroad and to them were delegated most of its powers over them. In 1266 James gave the city council of Barcelona the right annually to elect consuls to govern the shipping proceeding "over sea." This meant giving the city the independent right to regulate its affairs abroad, at least in the Syrian ports and Egypt, the territory then known as "over sea." In 1268 this right was extended to include "Romania" (the Byzantine Empire and its former possessions in Macedonia and Greece), and wherever else Catalan ships might go.

In the meantime, while these innovations were being brought into the Barcelonese commercial organization, the healthy frame of mind in which the city began its commercial career continued. The spirit in which industry was regarded is indicated by the place it held in the city government. Of the two hundred members of the city council which passed the ordinance of 1258 a full majority were representatives of the industrial and trading interests. The make-up of the council shows no trace of a dominant gild merchant. Nevertheless the council fully appreciated the value of commerce. The expansion of industry was rapid as new demands for goods appeared. Barcelona was now a producing center and needed an outlet for her surplus. The production of naval supplies, timber, wrought iron, cordage and rope felt the increase. Hides and wine continued to be important. Manufactures of wool, Catalonia's most substantial and valuable export, flourished especially. The manufacture of finished articles of wood, such as wine casks, grew up. We have hints of the improvement of technique in the other established lines. Industrially Barcelona was ready to face the world. And her goods and commerce soon entered every port. We get some measure of the magnitude of industry in Aragon and Catalonia when it is said that the statutes of the *Gremios y Cofradas de la antigua corona de Aragon* fill the entire fortieth volume of the *Documentos ineditos* of Aragon, and pertain to eighty separate gilds.

But "he who has land has war." Philip IV of France had too many interests elsewhere to go to war with Aragon so he imposed heavy obstacles on Aragonese and Majorcan merchants. James II did not retaliate by going to war. Instead the king and his councillors worked out a reasoned policy by which Aragonese trade could be made independent of France, notably by getting wool from England and Barbary, and by encouraging sheep-raising at home.[4]

Aragon's relations with Genoa were strained. Genoa, which had formerly been the most favored nation in the trade concessions of Sicily, saw the island in the possession of a vigorous and growing rival. The clash was inevitable. Desultory corsairing began almost immediately after Aragon had secured control. When, in 1325, the Aragonese attempted to dispossess the Pisans in Sardinia, a Genoese squadron aided the Pisans in spite of the old enmity between them. For Sardinia, as well as being a stepping-stone between the Aragonese possessions, Majorca and Sicily, in the hands of Aragon would have made a barrier across Genoa's sea front. Two wars were fought (1331–36 and 1351–55), wars which ended in the virtual exhaustion of both parties, but corsairing continued throughout the century.

Aragon had interests further afield than Sicily. From 1326 to 1387 an Aragonese duke held the duchy of Athens. Between 1289–1335 and 1393–1398 Sicily occupied the islands of Gerba and Kerkeni and used them as bases to control eastern Barbary. The action of Aragon often helped make or break an Egyptian sultan. Relations with the Barbary kingdoms were always intimate.

Thus the commerce of Barcelona expanded through the Mediterranean, sure of protection from its enemies and having excellent bases from which to raid enemy commerce. With its safety abroad assured by control of powerful strategic positions the commerce of Barcelona was further encouraged by the wise internal policies of its rulers. It was very much to the advantage of the kings of Aragon to favor commerce and the cities. They needed the military support of the cities, and appreciated the value of a thriving commerce.

In 1283 Peter III abolished all road dues established after 1253. The abolition of the salt *gabelle* the same year proved a great aid to

---

[4] Finke, *Acta Aragonensia*, II, pp. 155–67. Cf. *English Historical Review*, Oct., 1924, p. 600. This long and remarkable document, written in Catalan, fills twelve pages of print.

the fishing industry. In 1295 and 1299 measures were taken which assured the right to export any goods whatsoever to any country except to enemies; but the king reserved the right to hold up exports of grain in times of famine. In 1323 James II freed goods belonging to Barcelonese citizens from all royal or local dues anywhere in the dominions of himself or his successors. In 1343 the privilege of Barcelonese to export silver, coined or in bullion, was established. In 1356 the privilege was given to ship any goods in any ship to any country not an enemy. This liberal commercial policy is in sharp contrast with Castile's mania for regulation.

The merchant gild, which we can distinguish as early as 1258, developed to such an extent that in 1279 it secured the right to elect two of its members as judges to hear marine cases not coming within the scope of ordinary jurisdictions. It was not, however, until 1347 that a consular court was erected in Barcelona. In that year the city council was given the right yearly to elect two consuls of the sea and a judge of appeals, who should have the same jurisdiction as the consular court of Valencia over all maritime cases. In 1354 this jurisdictional competency was made to include "all the seas of the realm." In 1380 Peter IV made the decisions of the court final over all maritime and commercial matters. Appeals from the appellate judge, even to the king himself, were limited to cases of widowhood, wardship, or those involving more than three hundred *libras*.

The benefits derived from this enlightened internal course and vigorous external policy were supplemented by the inherent soundness of Barcelona's system of commercial organization. The merchants' corporation was in 1258 a comparatively uninfluential body. We have seen how it secured the right to a court system for mercantile cases alone. By the fourteenth century it also had considerable power in the city council. Of the (since 1265) one hundred members of that body it elected thirty-two. Entrance to this corporation was comparatively easy. The only qualifications required of a candidate for membership were that he should be actually engaged in the merchant profession, that his blood should be pure in both lines, and that he should have been born in Catalonia. The candidate had to be passed upon favorably by a two-thirds vote of the city council and the corporation.

The efforts to keep Barcelonese commerce free of fraud by securing the integrity of the brokers through whose hands commerce passed still continued. Successive laws were made to limit still further the possibility of a *corregidor* profiting by corrupt practices. He could not, for instance, accept gifts; he could not engage in trade on his own account; he had to levy his charges on both buyer and seller.

Banking developed greatly, and some of the laws made to regulate it were surprisingly modern in principle. In 1290 James II decreed that bankers who could not satisfy their creditors' (depositors') balances should be declared bankrupt and their possessions be sold to meet their indebtedness. Again, by the cortes of Barcelona (1299), bankers were forbidden to keep a double set of books. A banker was to keep his accounts in one book, under oath. In 1301 at the cortes of Lérida bankers were required to give a security of 1,000 silver marks before going into business in Lérida or Barcelona, and 300 marks for the right to do business in other places. The city council also took measures to regulate the banks, such as requiring them to be licensed and to keep certain hours.

The fourteenth century saw the introduction into Catalan banking of the bill of exchange. The form of these bills was very elementary, but they gave the bankers another base for their credit operations besides hard cash. The effect of this innovation was a greater freedom of credit and a consequent falling of the interest rate. James I had made the legal rate 18 per cent; by 1430 it had fallen to 10 per cent. Private banks were a great aid to commerce. But their individual field was too limited to allow them to fill the needs of the credit situation entirely. And so the city council in 1401 founded the famous Taula (*tabula*) or municipal bank. This institution was managed with great success and existed into the nineteenth century.

Manufacturing, especially of wool, Catalonia's staple export, continued to increase. Commerce had a solid base of production. Christians began to enter professions like that of brokerage, which had formerly been despised and left to the Jews. Even the government sent out ships commanded by noblemen to take part in trade.

This prosperity which characterized the commerce of Barcelona in the fourteenth century was the natural result of her intelligent economic and political policy, and was especially noteworthy in the Alexandrian trade. Aragon inherited the old Hohenstaufen policy of friendship with Egypt, and James I preserved amicable relations with the sultans. Peter III continued these relations. Alfonso III (1285–1292) went further still and in 1290 negotiated a defensive and offensive alliance with the sultan, his object being to get help in gold, if not in men, for his struggle against France and the pope. One of the commercial clauses of this treaty provided that the exportation to Egypt of iron, arms, or wood was not to be prohibited. It is doubtful, however, if these negotiations were ratified, as Alfonso very shortly gave up the struggle and agreed to the humiliating terms of the peace of Tarascon. But when James II came to the throne, surrounded by enemies and under the excommunication of the Church, a similar treaty was actually made. Yet again after he had made his peace with the papacy in 1302, he was compelled to promulgate a decree against commerce with the lands of the sultan. But this decree seems to have been for political purposes only, and was not taken seriously. Certainly in 1322 the Irish Franciscan, Simon Simeonis, on his way to the Holy Land found a Catalan *fondaco* in Alexandria. In 1338 another papal prohibition of trade with Egypt was issued, but King Peter was bribed by the sultan not to enforce it. In 1336 Zurita, the great annalist of Aragon, speaks of the volume of the trade with Alexandria. Despatches to the consuls at Alexandria continued to be numerous up to 1381. In 1386 three Barcelonese knights were sent to' Egypt to make a commercial treaty. In spite of the length of the trip (ten or eleven months there and return), the prevalence of piracy, papal bulls, Genoese commercial raiders, Mussulman revolutions, and high tariff rates the trade with Alexandria thrived. The policy of peace and neutrality with all Mussulman princes was perhaps unchristian, but it was very profitable.

In Syria the Catalans had establishments at Beirut and Damascus. The jurisdiction of the Catalan consul in Damascus included Syria and Armenia Minor. Traces of trade with Armenia Minor go back as far as 1293 when James II, in sending an ambassador to the Mongol Khan Geikaton, sent also a letter to the king of Armenia Minor asking for a hall and a quarter for the Catalans and a lowering of duties. This country was under the jurisdiction of the consulate at Famagusta before being put under that of Damascus.

Barcelona had also commercial relations with the islands of the Levant. In 1302 a Cypriote squadron seized a Catalan ship alleged to have been trading between Candia and Egypt. In the next century we find a consul at Candia. Rhodes was at least occasionally visited by Catalan ships; one of the interests here was the transfer of funds between the Spanish estates of the Knights of St. John and their headquarters. But the trade with these islands was slight compared to that which went on with Cyprus, one of the focal points of eastern commerce. When Acre fell in 1291 the western merchants hastened to Famagusta to secure trade concessions or to make sure of those they already possessed. Henry II fixed the tariffs on Catalan merchandise at 2 per cent import or export and 1½ per cent on goods in transit. This act was followed by a rich and continuous commerce until the seizure of Famagusta by the Genoese in 1373.

The promise of an important commerce with Romania may perhaps be inferred from the early date at which Barcelona received the right to have consuls in the Latin Empire. However, we have few facts about this commerce. In 1285 Genoa made financial amends for certain piracies committed by some Genoese on Catalan and Sicilian ships returning from Romania. In 1290 the emperor Andronicus II fixed the duties to be levied on the goods of subjects of the king of Aragon trafficking in his territories at 3 per cent entry and exit. A certain amount of commerce with Constantinople continued after the painful episode of the Catalan Company. This commerce was large enough to make it worth while for the king of Aragon to send a special mission in 1320 to protest against irregularities in the levying of duties, and one of the provisions of the peace treaty between Genoa and Michael Paleologus in 1352 was that Venetian and Catalan commerce should be excluded from the Empire. There was, however, a Catalan consul at least at Pera in 1383. Aside from these data we have no information on Catalan commerce in the Eastern Empire in the fourteenth century. That some adventurous Catalan merchants succeeded in getting into the Black Sea trade was indicated when Tana was sacked by Tamerlane in 1395. It seems impossible, however, because of the jealousy with which Venice and Genoa guarded this trade, that the Catalans' share in it could have been great.

The long career of the Catalan Company, and the fact that from 1326 to 1387 the duchy of Athens was in Catalan hands, might argue that Aragon drew something from Greek commerce. But such was not the case. In the beginning the existence of Catalan rule at Athens was a positive detriment to commerce, and the interests of Barcelona there were never of enough importance to call for a consul. The duchy must, however, have been useful as a naval outpost. Modon in Greece, part of the Venetian spoils in 1204, was an important mercantile center. The good will which existed between Venice and Barcelona (the result of their common enmity towards Genoa) secured for Barcelona a share in this trade, and Modon was a consular town. Thus during the fourteenth century the commerce of Barcelona was well extended in the eastern Mediterranean. Its chief center in the Levant was Alexandria.

The trade of Barcelona in the Italian zone of the Mediterranean made great advances. This was, as might be expected, due to the acquisition of Sicily by the house of Aragon. As a reward for their aid in this venture the Catalans early received trade concessions which assured the prosperity of their Sicilian commerce. In 1285 James I of Sicily gave them the right to have a consul at Palermo. In 1288 Genoese privileges and dues were conceded to the merchants of Barcelona. In 1296 the exportation of grain from Sicily to Barcelona was freed of all dues. Italy drew a great deal of her grain supply from Sicily. This created a coastwise trade which was soon a big item in the Sicilian commerce of the Catalans. In fact, most of the prizes taken by Genoa in her wars with Aragon were grain ships from Sicily or Sardinia. We must not forget, however, that Sicily, especially the port of Messina, was a great market for the exchange of the products of the West against those of the Levant and the Far East. As long as Sicily remained in Aragonese hands the advantages of this trade belonged to Barcelona, much to the dissatisfaction of the Genoese who had formerly enjoyed them. Sicily furnished another market for Catalan wool-stuffs. Her principal exports to Spain were silk and fruits. The Sicilian trade became so important that within fifty years after the establishment of the consulate at Palermo Barcelona had on the island three chief and seventeen subordinate consuls.

One of the effects of the conquest of Sicily was the opening up of the Adriatic to Catalan trade. That meant commerce with Ragusa, Ancona, Manfredonia and Venice. Relations with Venice were always particularly friendly. Trade with the other parts of Italy continued. Commerce with Genoa and Pisa was intermittent in spite of the wars. Trade intercourse between Barcelona, Palermo, and Naples was steady. There were at least two Catalan merchants in the papal states. Florence and Barcelona had especially close trade relations. A commerce with Sardinia and Malta completed the central Mediterranean zone. The food exports of Sardinia—meat, cheese, suet, and grain—were in great demand. The trade with the island was so important that immediately after it came into the possession of Aragon Barcelona established a consul there. Within a short while there were four consuls instead of one. From 1335 to 1511 there were consuls at Malta.

The zone of North African commerce was known of old to the Catalan merchants. We have seen how the policy which James I followed in these regions went beyond making mere commercial treaties and even included military alliances. During the following reigns this policy was continued; in fact, the political relations between the crown of Aragon and the princes of the Magrib became much closer than they had been before. In 1285 a treaty of alliance was made with Tunis; one of its terms was the specific permission of Tunisian warships to refit in Aragonese ports. In 1292, just before the occupation of Sardinia, money was borrowed from the king of Tunis to be used for military expenses. Treaties were made with Bougia in 1309, 1314 and 1323. In 1309 a king of Aragon aided a king of Morocco to recover Ceuta from the Moors of Granada. In 1357 Aragon and Morocco were leagued against Pedro the Cruel. With all this political intimacy between Aragon and Barbary it would have been strange if there had not been also a great deal of trade. The Catalans carried to Barbary cloth, wine, grain, beans, and saffron. They also sold (and even rented) ships to the North Africans. Barbary exported a great variety of articles including oil, wax, sugar, slaves, horses, salt fish, leather, tan-bark, dyeing stuffs, and goods which Berber merchants had imported from farther east. The most important export, however, was coral. In the handling of this commodity the Catalans had a practical monopoly. The trade with Barbary was important, though we must not overvalue it by comparing it to that carried on with the Levant.

As might be expected, the commerce of Aragon with Castile and southern France felt the influence of the expansion of its high sea commerce and itself expanded. In 1282 a consulate was established at Seville. The Catalans took grain and brought back woolstuffs. Consulates were established at Malaga and Almeria in 1327. In southern France we find a consul appointed at Montpellier in 1301, and Catalan commercial interests were large.

The fourteenth century also witnessed a great increase in the Catalan trade beyond the Pillars of Hercules. The most valuable commerce in these regions was with Flanders, where there were Catalan merchants as early as 1267. There is, however, no indication of a permanent trade between Aragon and Flanders earlier than 1300. In 1378–79 in the record of a "capitation tax" levied on the foreign merchants at Bruges we find the following apportionments: Cahorsins 200 *livres,* Florentines 100, Venetians 100, Catalans 100, Milanese 80, Lucchesi 70, and Genoese 50. It will be noted that Castilians are not mentioned in the list. In 1405 the consuls at Bruges, Ypres, and Ghent wrote to the city council of Barcelona complaining about some new trade regulations which the magistracy of Bruges had put in operation and for breaking which thirty-six Catalan merchants had been fined twenty-five *escudos* apiece. In a capitulation of the year 1411 the Venetians at Bruges were assessed a hundred *livres,* the Genoese a hundred, and the Catalans eighty. When, in 1438, Bruges was fined by the duke of Burgundy for rebellion, the foreign merchants helped her pay. Those of Portugal gave 200 *livres,* of Venice 200, of Genoa 150, of Catalonia 100, of Aragon 50.

There were Catalan merchants in England at the beginning of the fourteenth century; a charter of privileges which Edward I granted to foreign traders mentions them. But there are no indications that their trade had any considerable volume. The most frequent mention of England in the commercial annals of the fourteenth century is on the score of her piracies. Without exception every Southern nation having a sea trade with the Low Countries suffered from her attacks. In 1418 Henry V issued letters patent in favor of subjects of the crown of Aragon. We have the instructions sent by the city council of Barcelona to a wool buyer in England in 1441. But these references are not enough to allow us to assign any importance to the trade with England.

In 1418 open war broke out with Genoa. This war was complicated by the entrance of King Alfonso into competition with the Angevin house for the inheritance of Queen Joanna of Naples. At first Alfonso was successful. In 1425 he besieged Genoa. Naples was occupied. Fortune veered, however, and in 1435 the fleet of Aragon was destroyed at Ponza and the king himself taken prisoner. After two years of captivity he was released through the influence of the duke of Milan. Continuing the war he finally (1443) secured peace with undisputed possession of Naples. Aragon was now at the height of her power. Majorca and Roussillon had been reincorporated with the kingdom in 1343, Sicily in 1397. So Don Alfonso's realm included besides his peninsular possessions, Majorca, Roussillon, Sardinia, Sicily, and the kingdom of Naples.

In the south of Italy, as might be expected, the conquests of Alfonso gave a great deal of stimulus to Aragonese commerce. Naples, Gaeta, Ischia, and Otranto were already consular cities. Trade with the ports of the Adriatic, Venice, Ancona, and Ragusa also showed signs of great activity. Ragusa seems to have been especially favored by the Catalan merchants.

Yet no amount of prosperity could counterbalance any substantial injury received by the all-important Egyptian commerce. And there the first half of the fifteenth century was one long record of disaster. This unhappy condition was at the beginning partly the result of the cupidity and fanaticism of certain of the sultans. But the primary cause of the completeness of Barcelona's commercial misfortunes in the eastern Mediterranean was the pernicious activity of Catalan corsairs. Their piracies would have aroused the wrath of an angel, not to mention that of a Mohammedan prince whose income was largely dependent on trade. Hence, except for three short periods, during the whole first half of the fifteenth century the precious markets of Alexandria and Damascus (for Syria was part of the Egyptian realm) were absolutely closed to the Catalans. The Egyptian trade was lost.

This setback was not, however, the only misfortune which occurred to Catalan commerce. The war with Genoa degenerated to chronic piracy. Besides its effects on the morale of Catalan commerce the material losses were heavy. Finally there was the growth of piracy in the Barbary states. This phenomenon was of comparatively late development. Bands of pirates recruited from exiled Spanish Moors, religious fanatics, and the riffraff of the ports infested the African shore and preyed on commerce. By the middle of the fifteenth century they already constituted a real menace.

When Alfonso V died (1458) most of the valuable privileges which he had conceded to the Italians were revoked. Thus another blow was dealt to Catalan commerce. But Alfonso's death brought far worse consequences to his widespread dominions than the loss of Italian trade. If his successor had been of the usual caliber of the kings of Aragon and followed their traditional policy of fostering commerce, the losses of the previous half century of war might have been recouped; the Barbary states might have been forced to abandon piracy; the activity of the Catalan corsairs might have been curbed. In general, the newly acquired territories afforded the means of bringing back a peaceful and orderly condition which would have allowed Aragonese commerce to build up to its former standard of prosperity, to build higher.

This was, however, one of the occasions in history when the personal factor was all-important. Unfortunately John II, Alfonso's brother, to whom he left his possessions in Spain and Sicily and Sardinia, was a despicable character. The Catalans at once rose in revolt, choosing as their leader Don Carlos, the eldest son of Alfonso V. They were so successful that in 1461 an armistice was declared and John consented to an arrangement whereby he recognized all the acts of the Catalans, promised not to set foot in Catalonia again, and nominated Don Carlos to govern the county of Barcelona as his lieutenant. But three months later the young prince died, it was thought, poisoned. Soon there were armies pouring into the kingdom from France and Castile. On June 11, 1462, Catalonia declared itself independent of Aragon. The war continued. The Catalans were, however, unfortunate in their efforts to secure a ruler. Henry of Castile refused their proffered allegiance; Peter the Constable of Portugal died after reigning two and a half years; René of Anjou was a successful leader at first, but later he failed with a consistency which aroused suspicion. Finally in 1472 John wrote a conciliatory letter to the council of Barcelona offering honorable terms; oblivion of the past and confirmation of old laws and privileges. The king was old and blind; the hated Joanna was dead; and Catalonia was very tired of war. And so John's terms were accepted. He reigned until 1479.

This then was the history of Barcelona during the period when peace and order at home and a vigorous foreign policy deliberately encouraging commerce were absolutely essential to her prosperity. Fourteen years of war followed by seven years of John's rule well-nigh finished the Catalan marine. Final and absolute ruin came in the reign of Ferdinand (John's son) and Isabella. The union of Spain did not mean the abolition of intrapeninsular tariff restrictions; each province still regarded the citizens of the other provinces as aliens. Even in Catalonia the towns began an active policy to keep out Barcelonese manufactures and so favor their own products. In 1487 Ferdinand instituted the Inquisition in Catalonia. This was almost the final blow, for it seems that practically the only persons who had been able to keep up any industry or commerce during the period of disaster had been the Jews, or the *"conversos"* of Jewish blood. By the time of the discovery of the Portuguese water route to India the commerce of Barcelona was already a thing of the past.

The transfer of interest to the Atlantic coast practically ruined the Mediterranean trade. Of the fifty-five consulships established during the thirteenth, fourteenth and fifteenth centuries by 1550 only five remained—Marseilles, Messina, Genoa, Palermo, and Naples.

The industrial history of Aragon and Catalonia is less complex than its commercial history. The most important manufacture was woolen goods. In the fifteenth century the Catalans began to imitate foreign cloths, such as *sarga de Irlanda, chamelotes de Reims, de Ostende,* and fabrics of other Flemish cities. In 1522 the list of imitations was even longer, including Italian (Florentine), Flemish and English makes. At this time Catalan cloth was largely used in France, and Lombardy imported Barcelona woolens to the amount of 120,000 Venetian ducats. To protect wool growing, high tariffs were imposed on raw wool, and in 1422 importation of wool was prohibited. The Barcelona cortes, in 1422, decided that no foreign cloth of wool, silk or gold, might enter the country; that no one could use other goods for clothing for himself and family than those made in Catalonia or other provinces of the realm, under penalty.

At a meeting of manufacturers called in that year to devise means of improving their goods, and for the protection of their trade, the cloth manufacturers and dyers drew up ninety-seven articles dealing with the preparation of woolens, the qualities of the different goods, obligations of textile workers, rules for dyeing. Inspectors of the wool gild saw that these regulations were carried out. The dyers of Barcelona became so famous that foreign weaves were sent there to be dyed.

The wool industry was by far the most important trade of Barcelona, but its energetic people and natural resources, especially in minerals, produced other commodities. Among important industries were rope-making, tanning, making of bonnets, armor, cutlery, pottery, glassware, canvas, and cotton goods. The arts of tinners, coppersmiths, steel- and ironworkers were protected from competition, the duty being 50 per cent. This high duty was also in force on imports of leather goods, tanned leather, shoes. Silk, however, was not dutiable. Silk culture was not introduced until the fifteenth century. Yet the Catalans were in constant contact with the Spanish Moors and frequently with the Moors of North Africa. Why did they not learn the art of silk culture earlier?

Another article of export from Barcelona was handworked coral. This coral was brought from the Barbary Coast and other Mediterranean lands. Important exports were salt, which seems to have been shipped abroad in large quantities; bacon, the exportation of which became so great that legislation was passed against it in 1534; saffron, a very important article of export; honey. A cargo of saffron and honey sailing from Barcelona to Alexandria in 1394 was pursued by Genoese pirates. Saffron was also shipped north. There are many indications of its importance. Barcelona's millstones were very famous in the Middle Ages.

There were fulling mills, tanneries, forges, iron works, *etc.*, and artisans of gold and silver work, and pottery. These crafts were mainly exploited by Jews and *Mudéjares*. Other objects were woodenware (including barrels for wine), skins, hides, glassware, ship tackle, rope of hemp and feather grass, salted meats. Paper-making was introduced in the fifteenth century. A ship captured by the Genoese in 1461 had in its cargo 17,000 reeds for writing pens.

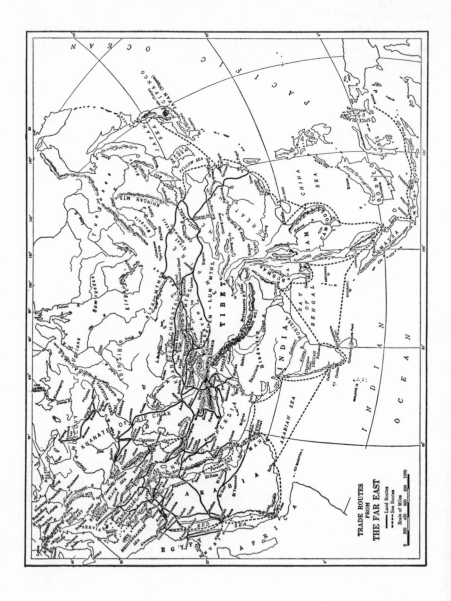

TRADE ROUTES
FROM
THE FAR EAST

——— Land Routes
----- Sea Routes

Scale of Miles

CHAPTER XV

THE BALKAN PENINSULA, GREECE AND THE LEVANT

"THE medieval trade routes between eastern Europe and western and southern Asia fall into two groups: the northern, which passed mainly by land, and the southern, which passed mainly by sea. The former communicated with Central Asia, China, India and Asia Minor; the latter through Syria and Egypt. Each group had branches which entered Asia near Aleppo and diverged in the direction of Tabriz and Baghdad. . . . For most goods the southern routes, especially that by the Red Sea, were cheaper because they ran mostly by sea; but this consideration was less important in the case of the costlier spices, especially as they were liable to suffer damage in the holds of ships."[1]

The northern land routes which served Constantinople were four in number: (1) From Tana at the mouth of the Don and over the head of the Caspian Sea to India or China. (2) From Trebizond to Tabriz and so to the East around the end of the Caspian Sea. (3) From Lajazzo on the Gulf of Alexandretta, via Tabriz, or (4) via Baghdad, to the East, either across Asia or through the Persian Gulf.

Trebizond and Lajazzo were the chief "vestibules to the Mongol lands." Until about 1340, by which time the Mongol Empire had broken up, the conduct of trade between the West and the Far East was regular and not difficult. The Mongols were pagan but tolerant. Even when the western division of the Mongols turned Mohammedan, and the Turks began to expand, intercourse between East and West continued, though not with the same ease as formerly. The Mohammedanized Mongols and Turks were hostile to the presence of Christian merchants among them in the interior, but willing to trade with them in the Black Sea, Aegean and Mediterranean ports. The only country where there was almost complete cessation of commercial relations was Mameluke Egypt. The pope never forgave the Mamelukes for destroying the kingdom of Jerusalem and forbade all commercial intercourse with Egypt. The penalties were excommunication, loss of civil rights, deprivation of inheritance and the right to dispose of property by will. The pope dreamed of creating an international squadron to patrol the Mediterranean and suppress illicit traffic. The fleets of

---

[1] Lybyer, "The Ottoman Turks and the Routes of Trade," *English Historical Review*, XXX, p. 578.

the Hospitallers and the kingdom of Cyprus tried unsuccessfully to carry out this idea. But the trade with Egypt was too lucrative to be stopped. Nicholas IV, Boniface VIII and Benedict XI moderated this embargo and permitted trade with Egypt except in articles which were contraband. Venice, which for centuries had enjoyed almost a monopoly of the trade with Egypt, in 1302 negotiated a new treaty with the sultan. Genoa and Pisa also had consuls in Alexandria which prove the presence of their merchants there. The Christian colony in Alexandria must have been a considerable one, for it is mentioned even in Arabic sources. These prohibitions naturally increased the commerce along the land routes to the profit of Tana, Lajazzo, Trebizond, and ultimately Constantinople, which was the clearing-house of the Levant, upon which all the routes out of the Orient converged.

To gain mastery over this immense Oriental commerce had been the overwhelming motive of Venice in conquering the Byzantine Empire in 1204, as well as the purpose of Genoa in overthrowing Venetian domination on the Golden Horn in 1261.

The Fourth Crusade in 1204 had shattered the Byzantine Empire, but had not wholly destroyed it. While the alien conquerors established themselves at Constantinople, in Greece, and the Archipelago, local dynasties at Trebizond and Nicaea perpetuated the tradition of Byzantine imperialism, and in Epirus a local magnate who dubbed himself "despot" drove the Latins out of Salonika, establishing there another seat of Byzantine imperialism. Although these three states were rivals they had a common enemy in the Latins and each watched the growing weakness of the Latin Empire until the moment should come when it might recover the lost heritage.

When the hour struck in 1261 and the Venetian domination on the Bosphorus was overthrown, it was the Nicene emperor who reunited the Balkan peninsula with Asia Minor to form the restored Byzantine Empire. But the Byzantine Empire never wholly recovered from the blow delivered by the Fourth Crusade. The imperial "restoration" in the person of the Palaeologi emperors was incomplete. The Empire did not recover all its former territorial integrity nor its vanished power. Until its expiration in 1453 it remained a maimed and crippled state. Michael VIII united under his scepter only a fraction of the ancient empire of the Comneni. Thrace was occupied by the Bulgarians and Serbians; the Adriatic coast formed the Despotat of Epirus and was otherwise in dispute between Venice and the kingdom of Sicily; Thessaly was an independent principality. In the Peloponnesus were the duchies of Athens and Achaia under French reigning houses. The great island of Euboea was ruled by princes of Lombard blood. The Archipelago, which collectively formed the duchy of Naxos, was independent. Accordingly the new Byzantine Empire comprehended only the central and eastern portion of the Balkan peninsula, with western Asia Minor, which was reunited to the European part owing to the fact that the revolution of 1261 had proceeded from Nicaea. In a word we distinguish two zones, a Greek zone to the north and east of the Aegean, and a Latin zone to the south and west. Even within this circumscribed sphere the Byzantine Empire's sway was limited. Genoa had exacted in advance enormous commercial privileges in return for having engineered the revolution.

A stroke of the pen transferred from Venice to themselves the monopoly of the Levantine trade. The Ligurian republic, which had taken no part in the labors of the Fourth Crusade, was now granted in return for its pledge to make war against Venice, free trade throughout the Greek Empire and in the Venetian islands of Crete and Negroponte, which the emperor hoped to conquer. The Genoese received permission to found colonies at Anaea, Lesbos and in the rich mastic island of Chios. . . . They obtained the city of Smyrna and were assigned after the conquest of Constantinople the suburb of Galata as their special quarter. Finally, the Black Sea was closed to their enemies. From the treaty of Nymphaion in 1261 dates the growth of Genoa as a Levantine power.[2]

Venice succeeded only in saving the islands of Euboea or Negroponte, and Crete, together with Coron and Modon on the coast of the Peloponnesus[3] from her former dominions. These two great islands were valuable for wheat, oil, wine, wax, honey, raw and worked silk. Coron and Modon were important ports of debarkation of pilgrims going to the Holy Land, and were peopled by a thriving colony of Christian and Jewish tradesmen. Coron was the more important of the two and was famous for its cochineal production.

The enormous hazards and hardships of commerce on land and sea under these divided and complex conditions may be appreciated. A general war in which Venice and Charles of Anjou would be pitted against Genoa and the Byzantine Empire seemed imminent. This was averted by the Sicilian Vespers in 1282, and the paralysis of the Angevin king's power following that event.

In 1294 the long impending war broke out between Venice and Genoa. The latter's fleet assailed Candia in the island of Crete and destroyed a Venetian merchant flotilla in the harbor of Modon. Venice

---

[2] W. Miller, *The Latins in the Levant*, p. 118.
[3] At this time and until much later the Peloponnesus was popularly called the Morea. The term is first found in 1111, and seems originally to have been applied to the coast of Elis whence it was extended to the entire peninsula. The origin of the word Morea is a matter of dispute. See Miller, *op. cit.,* p, 37, note 1.

retaliated by attacking the Genoese colony in Constantinople—the walls of Galata being then unfinished—and ruined the alum works in the island of Phocea belonging to the Zaccaria Brothers of Genoa. Thereupon the emperor sequestrated the goods of Venetian merchants found in the Empire, and the Genoese took a hand with the natives in a general massacre of the Venetians in Constantinople. At last in 1299 Venice and Genoa made peace. But the Byzantine Empire was not a party to it, and Venice continued the war with profit until 1303 when the emperor agreed to pay an indemnity to Venice for the losses she had sustained and to yield four small islands to her. Among the clauses of the treaty was one prohibiting Venetian merchants from trading in the interior of the Empire or dealing in salt and mastic. On these points the emperor was obdurate. But Venice continued to intrigue against the Palaeologi emperors, and for years persisted in cherishing the dream of restoring the Latin Empire again. As late as 1320 she was still plotting to this end.

The commercial rivalry of Venice and Genoa is the key to the history of the Levant in the fourteenth century. Five areas or fields of this rivalry are to be distinguished: The Black Sea territory, the Balkan peninsula, the Aegean islands and the Morea, Syria and the Holy Land, and Egypt. The Turks, Timurlane and the Mamelukes, were important outside factors conditioning this competition—the two former in Asia Minor and the Black Sea area, the latter in Egypt, Palestine and Syria. In Russia the Crim Tartars were an additional factor. The treatment of this intricate history in any other but a topical way would lead to confusion.

We shall begin with the Black Sea region. Here Genoa by the treaty of Nymphaion in 1261 acquired the former Venetian factories on the north coast,[4] of which Tana at the mouth of the Don and Kaffa in the Crimea were the most important. The former was important as the terminus of the trade route out of Central Asia through Astrakhan, and its wares were of an oriental nature. The latter was the locus for traffic in raw stuffs out of Russia like furs, amber, pitch, and hemp, while the Crimea furnished horses and wheat in profusion. To this list slaves and salt fish must be added. But the Crim Tartars and the Mongol Khan of the Golden Horde in the Kipchak both made trouble for Genoa, which was not long in discovering that Venetian intrigue was back of it. In 1343 the Genoese were temporarily driven out of Tana, but returned in 1347. Nevertheless, the Venetians acquired a place of occupation on the opposite bank of the Don, whence they spread to other points, notably Soldaia or Sudak in the Chersonese.

Meanwhile a new diversion in Greece had been created by the in-

---

[4] Thompson, *Economic and Social History of the Middle Ages*, pp. 422-423.

vasion of the Catalan Company in 1302. This notorious army of adventurers and cutthroats ever since 1282 had been engaged in Sicily in thwarting the plans of the Angevin house to recover the island. When that issue was settled in 1302, after twenty years of war, the Catalans found themselves without employment. At this juncture the Asia Minor provinces of the Byzantine Empire for the first time were being pressed by the growing power of the Ottoman Turks and the emperor Andronikos II invited the Catalans to his aid.

In 1306 a Turkish band set foot in Europe for the first time when Roger de Flor, chief of the Catalan Company, recruited them for his own force of freebooters, and instead of aiding the emperor, fell upon Macedonia and Greece. In the latter country the flower of the Frankish chivalry was slaughtered in the battle of Cephisus (1310), from which blow the Latin domination in the Peloponnesus never recovered. The Catalan Grand Company settled in the Morea and founded a state there which endured until the end of the fourteenth century when the Florentine family of the Acciajuoli, who early in the century had got a foothold at Corinth, succeeded to their sway as dukes of Athens.[5] This devastation fell more heavily on Greece than on the Balkan peninsula—on inland more than on seaboard territory—so that in spite of the havoc-wrought, in spite of pirates which infested the Aegean, Venice and Genoa still continued the pursuit of commerce. Galata arose from its ruins. In Constantinople the Venetians now played a secondary rôle to that of Genoa. Genoa also had a quarter in Smyrna after 1346, and possessed the alum territory of Phocea, though both positions were endangered by the Turks.

The progress of the Turks next engages attention. The Turks were an offshoot of the Turcomans who at the beginning of the thirteenth century were dwelling in Khorassan, under their hereditary tribal chieftains, the Ottomans, whence the name Ottoman Turks. At the approach of the Mongols in 1220 they drifted westward, sojourning first in Azerbijan, then in Armenia. From there they invaded the sultanate of Iconium in Asia Minor, which the invasion of the Mongols had disrupted. In the beginning there were not over four hundred Turkish families in all, but as they moved their numbers were increased by the addition of other nomads like themselves. At this time Asia Minor was broken into a swarm of petty principalities. The sultan of Iconium first employed the Turks as mercenaries for the subjugation of his seceded states, but ere long the Turks established their own small principality around Dorylaeum, and began to overrun the Byzantine

---

[5] Athens revived under the Acciajuoli. In a Genoese map of the period the port of the Piraeus, then known as "the port of Athens," is for the first time designated as Porto Leone, so named from the great granite lion now in front of the Arsenal at Venice.

territory in western Asia Minor. The break-up of the Mongol Empire, which was complete by 1340, facilitated the easy expansion of the Turks. But of greater importance is the fact that this disintegration so impaired the through northern route to China that it was nearly abandoned and the roads through Persia became difficult. The result was that the Venetians and Genoese petitioned the pope to moderate his policy towards Egypt and to grant licenses to trade, so that commerce by the southern route improved.

From the middle of the fourteenth century forward, the progress of the Turks was the dominant fact in Levantine history. In 1308 the Turks captured Ephesus. In 1326 Brusa was taken and made their first capital. In 1328 Nicomedia fell. In 1330 Nicea, the ancient city of the council, was captured. About 1330 the sultans created the famous infantry corps known as the Janizaries; it was recruited from captured Christian children educated in Islam and rigorously trained. The discipline and ideals were those of the Templars and Hospitallers in their best days, for like the crusading orders the Janizaries were sworn to celibacy. Dervishes accompanied the battalions and kept their fanatical fires burning. In 1344 Smyrna was taken, but the Genoese were permitted to stay. By this time the Greeks retained nothing in Asia Minor except Scutari and Philadelphia. The small ports of the Black Sea and Propontis were occupied.

Meanwhile, in the southeast angle of Asia Minor the kingdom of Little Armenia, which so far had preserved a precarious independence, was extinguished by the Mamelukes in 1347. This event had no slight influence on Levantine commerce. For with the fall of Acre in 1291 the port of Lajazzo had become one of the principal ports in the East, and its prosperity was increased by the papal ban put upon trading with Egypt. The inhabitants fled to Cyprus. Only two Christian principalities in the Levant survived by the middle of the fourteenth century. These were Rhodes of the Hospitaller Knights and the island kingdom of Cyprus. The former was of slight commercial importance, but Cyprus became the pearl of the East. In Famagusta were the counting-houses and warehouses of every maritime power of the Mediterranean.

As for the Byzantine Empire it seemed to be approaching dissolution in the middle of the fourteenth century.

In Asia Minor Byzantium retained nothing but the suburbs of Scutari, Philadelphia and two towns of Phokaia. Independent emirs ruled the south and centre, the Ottomans the north, whence in seven years they were to cross into Europe, in eight more to transfer their capital to Adrianople. Already the European provinces of Byzantium were cut short by the frontier of the Bulgarian Empire and still more by the rapid advance of Serbia, then the most powerful state in the Balkan peninsula.[6]

[6] W. Miller, "The Genoese in Chios," *English Historical Review*, XXX, p. 419.

As far back as 1329 Stephen Dushan, who boasted that he was "emperor of the Serbs and Greeks," had proposed to partition what was left of the moribund empire between Serbia and Venice. But nothing came of the proposition save a grant to Venice of liberal trading privileges in Serbia. In 1350 the plan would have been futile, for the Turks held the future of the Balkans in their hands.

Yet a curious turn of the tide of events in the Aegean for a short time encouraged Venice and Genoa in the hope that they might secure the reversion of the ruinated Byzantine Empire and checkmate the Turks. The menace of the Turks had become so great in spite of the commercial treaties which each negotiated with them, that for a season Venice and Genoa forgot their differences. Both states saw their concessions and their shipping increasingly jeopardized. This economic self-interest stimulated them to support the crusade which Pope Clement VI was preaching. In 1344 an international fleet was organized composed of four Genoese galleys, six Venetian, four Cypriote, and six of the Knights of Rhodes. The admiral was Martin Zaccaria of Chios, who feared lest he might lose the alum deposits of Phocea to the Turks, and the enormous mastic revenues of Chios for which he had the concession from the emperor. This naval force suddenly appeared in the harbor of Smyrna on October 28, 1344, burned the Turkish shipping there, sacked the port and massacred the inhabitants. Some hardy merchants and bankers set up their business there at once. The counter-assault of the Turks failed, and Smyrna remained in Christian possession under guard of the Hospitallers. Martin Zaccaria soon afterwards was captured by the Turks and put to death.

The news of the Christian recovery of Smyrna was received with enthusiasm in the West and precipitated something like a crusade. The wild rumor was current that the figure of St. John, the patron saint of Smyrna, had appeared at the head of a ghostly legion of 200,000 Christians and slaughtered 1,200,000 infidels. The pope's orders were that the operations of the fleet were to be in the Black Sea for relief of Kaffa, at this time being beset by the Crim Tartars. But the wily Genoese, on the theory that a bird in the hand was worth two in the bush, "diverted" the expedition and instead Chios, which hitherto had pertained to the Byzantine Empire, was seized (1346). Its occupation by Genoa is a curious and interesting story.

The rich products of the island had long been farmed to the great Genoese merchant family, the Zaccaria. It was almost wholly given over to cultivation of mastic, a gum highly prized for its lacquer effect.[7]

---

[7] The company leased to each hamlet a certain area of plantation, and the lessees once a year handed in a certain weight of the precious mastic in proportion to the number of trees. If it were a good year and the yield were greater, they received a fixed price per pound for the excess quantity delivered,

On the mainland opposite to Chios lay Old and New Phocea, or Foglia Vecchia and Foglia Nuova as the Italians denominated them, in which territory were the richest alum deposits in the known world. Promptly some enterprising merchants in Genoa organized a chartered company called the Maona [8] for exploitation of these resources. The shares sold as securities on the bourse in Genoa, but the majority of them were held by the rich Giustiniani family, hence the company was often known as the Giustiniani. In spite of heavy loans at high interest from the Bank of St. George and an annual tribute to the Turks of 14,000 ducats, a dividend of 2,000 ducats was paid on each of the thirteen original shares or preferred stock; while in its best times the small *caratto* or share of common stock, originally worth some thirty Genoese pounds, was quoted at 4,930. One of the resident partners in Chios in 1474 entertained Christopher Columbus, then a simple ship's captain, in his palace there. The maona retained possession of Chios, subject to Turkish tribute, until 1566.

In the meantime—to revert to events in Smyrna—the united fleet of the Christian powers under command of the grand master of the Knights of the Hospital victoriously kept the sea after repulse of the Turkish attempt to recover Smyrna, and in 1347 burned one hundred and fifty Turkish vessels off of the island of Imbros. But the effect of this triumph was largely cancelled by the Mameluke destruction of Lajazzo in the same year.

By this time the Christian forces were exhausted. Their biggest achievement had been the capture of Smyrna, which was not lost to the West until it was sacked by Timurlane in 1403. In 1348 the Hospitallers and the Turks made peace on terms which still allowed Christian merchants to trade in Asia Minor ports, although Pope Clement VI refused to ratify it. In general it may be said that as the Turks annexed Byzantine territory in Asia Minor they took over with the territory the former trade agreements of the Byzantine Empire with Genoa and Venice.

The commercial policy of the Turks . . . was not all one of hostility to trade. They sought, indeed, to exclude foreigners from their internal commerce, as well as from crossing their lands. But such a desire cannot rightly be counted against them. . . . In conquering new regions the Turks regularly renewed the old commercial treaties with foreign powers

but if they failed to deliver the stipulated amount, they had to pay twice that sum. In order to keep up prices in years of over-production, all the mastic over a certain amount was either warehoused or burned. *Op. cit.,* p. 429.

[8] The word is probably a contraction of Madonna, the company being under the protection of Our Lady. The figure of the Virgin stood in the palace of the Giustiniani in Genoa. Other similar companies were the *maona* of Cyprus founded in 1374 and that of Corsica founded in 1378.

and usually observed them faithfully. It is true that with them commerce was secondary and conquest stood first. But they wished to encourage trade for the sake of revenue. They fought with Genoa and Venice, not because these were trading powers, but because they owned lands, cities, and exceptional rights within the area of Turkish political influence. With Florence, Ancona and other commercial cities which had no lands in the Levant and strove for none, relations were uniformly good.[9]

No sooner had peace been made with the Turks than Venice and Genoa again fell into war. Venice was the instigator, for she was frantic with jealousy over Genoa's acquisition of Chios, with which her own Aegean island of Negroponte could not compare in riches.

The emperor Cantacuzene, who chafed under Genoa's arrogant course in Constantinople, joined Venice with hesitation, as did Peter IV of Aragon, whose rule in Sardinia was troubled by revolts instigated by Genoa. In 1352 Pisa came in with her ancient ally. A fierce naval engagement was fought off the port of Pera in which Venice was worsted. In the next year, however, the Genoese were badly defeated off Sardinia. This humiliation in turn was avenged in 1354 by the Genoese admiral Doria, who destroyed a Venetian fleet at Zonchio, the medieval name of Navarino. Finally, in 1355, the duke of Milan succeeded in bringing about an armistice. Later Venice made a secret loan to the emperor, taking the island of Tenedos as security, and in 1375 when payment was defaulted Venice assumed domination of the island, whose value lay not in its commerce but in its location commanding the entrance to the Dardanelles.[10] The last episode of the war between Venice and Genoa was in 1381 when Genoa made a prodigious effort to storm Venice in her island citadel and was routed in the naval battle off Chioggia. The peace of Turin in that year closed the chapter of Genoese-Venetian commercial rivalry. Genoa was well-nigh exhausted by costly war and internicene strife, and in 1396 the French occupied the city.

During the course of these events the Turks were left practically free to conquer the Balkan peninsula without opposition. Wisely refraining from exhausting their resources in besieging Constantinople, the sultans bent all their efforts to the conquest of the Balkan hinterland. In 1365 Adrianople, in the richest plain in the Balkans, was captured, and the Turkish capital was moved thither from Brusa. The Turks had become a European power. In 1387 Thessaly, Boeotia, and Attica were conquered. In 1389 the single battle of Kossovo destroyed Serbia and Bulgaria, and in 1396 the utter defeat of the united armies of France, Germany, and Hungary at Nikopolis established the Turkish

[9] Lybyer, op. cit., p. 582.
[10] For the origin of "Dardanelles" see Revue Historique, CXIX, p. 338.

power in the whole of southeastern Europe. The Turks were in possession of almost all the territory in Europe and Asia Minor which
Byzantium had ruled in its palmiest days. Out of the wreck Genoa
managed to save her commercial privileges at Scutari.

In 1400 Constantinople "seemed to be sinking without possibility of
recovery to its death-gasp." [11] Then suddenly the great Asiatic conqueror, Timurlane, like Ghenghiz Khan, from whom he claimed descent,
loomed out of Asia. Whether a Tartar or a Mongol, it is sufficient to
say that he was kin to the wild and wandering tribes of central and
western Asia. In 1369 he had been the ruler of Samarkand, from which
in ever widening circles he extended his power. Between 1386–93 he
conquered Persia. In 1395 he invaded southern Russia, wrecked Kaffa
and Tana, but had to withdraw because his horses perished.

The limits to the expeditions and conquests of the inhabitants of the
steppes were laid down by the very specialization of their horses, which
made them unable to stand the tropical heat of the plains of Hindustan
or the raw climate and damp moist pastures of the North. This prevented
the penetration of the marauders to the plains of India in the South, while
in the North it saved Muscovy from the hordes of Timurlane, whose horses
succumbed in mass from the wet grass of the forest belt of Russia and
from her damp and foggy nights.[12]

In 1398–99 Timurlane invaded India and took Delhi, whence he returned to the West and fell upon Syria (1400). Christian Europe as
it learned of Timur's conquests was filled with elation, for it saw in
him an ally against the Turks, and curious diplomatic missions were
sent into the East. The papal emissary was John Greenlaw, an English Dominican friar who had carried his life in his hand in the Orient
for years, and who was made archbishop of Soldania or Sultanieh,
the chief city of Azerbijan, near the southwest corner of the Caspian,
on the route to Tabriz, Samarkand, and the East. The city owed its
foundation to the Mongols in 1303 and soon became an important
place of trade. In the summer months an immense fair was held, in
which the products of India and China were displayed. Azerbijan, of
which the seat of government was Tabriz, was governed by Timur's
favorite son Miran, who was openly favorable to Christian merchants
and missionaries, and expressed a willingness to form an alliance with
the English and French sovereigns against the Turks. Even before this
Greenlaw had had an interview with Timur, "thinking it fair to negotiate with one infidel for the ruin of another." Another Western ambassador who came to Samarkand was Ruy Gomez de Clavigo, sent by
Henry III of Castile, whose official account is preserved.

[11] Wylie, op. cit., I, p. 158.
[12] Edinburgh Review, July, 1929.

To the exultation of Christian Europe, the Turkish armies in 1402 were defeated by Timur at Angora, the sultan Bajazet made prisoner and Brusa plundered. But Christian elation was sobered by the sack of Smyrna at the same time. It seemed as if Timur were to supplant the Turks without relief to Byzantium or the West. What saved the Turks was the ambition of Timur to conquer China, although he was now so old that "his eyelids had fallen together." But at Otrar beyond the Syr Daria he fell ill and returned to Samarkand, where he died on February 19, 1405, "leaving behind him ruined cities, wasted countries, mountains of spoil, and pyramids of human skulls."

These embassies which Europe sent to Timur had a double mission —to effect an alliance with Timur against the Turks, and to secure freedom of trade from the ports of Syria and Alexandretta and Lajazzo across Persia to the head of the Persian Gulf and thus to circumvent Egypt. Timur's whirlwind conquests produced a violent change in trade routes in western Asia. His destruction of Tana seriously injured the Black Sea-Far Eastern trade. Nevertheless, Venice doggedly rebuilt Tana in 1410. Similarly his war against Persia disrupted commerce with Syria. He had the definite purpose of making Samarkand the central spot whence radiated caravans for India, China, Persia, Syria, and the West. The vision passed with his death, and the rupture of his empire, with the ensuing anarchy in Persia, nearly ruined the northern routes. Venice and Genoa did not know it, but in the fifteenth century they were fighting for a bag which was getting emptier and emptier.

Timur's empire went to pieces under his sons and grandsons, and the Turks resumed their conquests, while the Christian powers in the Levant wrangled and fought. Cyprus warred with Egypt; on October 7, 1403, a naval engagement off Modon took place between Venetian and Genoese vessels, though the latter now flew the flag of France.

Bajazet's son Mohammed I struggled against his own brothers until his death in 1421. It was Murad II who restored the Turkish power. The years, if not the days, of the Byzantine Empire were numbered. In 1423 the Empire included Constantinople and its suburbs, the peninsula of Mount Athos, Salonika and a few spots in the Peloponnesus. In 1430 Murad II captured Salonika and ominously expelled the Venetian merchants there; the wall across the isthmus of Corinth was forced; Epirus was invaded in 1431 and Janina taken. With it fell the tiny mountain "kingdom" of Albania, which had pertained to the Angevin kings of Naples from 1271 to 1368. After that it was under a dynasty which may have been of Norman descent and preserved its independence until 1431. Venice now trembled for possession of the eastern littoral of the Adriatic. The Turkish conquests were getting close to her.

Even before these dismaying events the Italian cities had been engaged in a mad scramble to safeguard their commercial privileges in the Balkans and the Aegean in anticipation of the collapse of the Byzantine Empire. Soon after the battle of Angora Venice profited by the weakness of the Turks to obtain an advantageous commercial treaty. Pietro Zeno in 1403 negotiated with the Turks in the name of a league formed by the emperor, John Paleologos, Venice, Genoa, and the Knights of Rhodes. The sultan consented to open to ships of the league all the Turkish ports,[13] to restore to Venice the coast opposite Negroponte, to cancel the tributes which Bajazet had imposed on the Genoese in Pera and at Constantinople. Nothing equalled the servility of the Genoese in allowing their colonies in the Aegean to form their own alliances with the Turks. The Genoese communities in Pera and Galata were strongly pro-Turkish.

Venice's policy was somewhat different, because of the territorial power which it still preserved in the Aegean and Peloponnesus. At first allied with the Turks in order to protect her commercial interests, Venice little by little detached herself when those interests were threatened by their progress. In a short time the sultans took the offensive against the Venetians. The Turkish fleet ravaged the Cyclades and Negroponte, and the Turks erected towers on each side of the Dardanelles which thus intercepted all communication with Constantinople and made the Venetian occupation of Tenedos ridiculous. Henceforward the attitude of Venice completely changed. In 1423 Murad II laid siege to Salonika; the inhabitants appealed to the Venetians, who occupied the city, from which the Turks were unable to expel them until 1430.

After that date Venice breathed more freely, for the Turks directed their energies upon the Danubian territories. In 1438 they invaded Transylvania, and besieged Hermannstadt and Belgrade without success. John Hunyadi, voivod of Transylvania and later king of Hungary, was the hope of central Europe. In 1443 the Turks were beaten at Nish and Sofia. These victories gave the Christian forces overconfidence, and the disaster of Nikopolis in 1396 was repeated at Varna in 1444. Europe was exhausted or indifferent to the fate of Constantinople after that. In 1446 the Turks invaded the Morea, burned Corinth and the long Franco-Italian domination in the Peloponnesus was extinguished. In 1448 John Hunyadi made a last supreme effort against the Turks, but a second bloody battle on the field of Kossovo destroyed his army. Five years later, in 1453, Constantinople was taken by the Turks. Within a few years more the Turks completed the subjugation

---

[13] The word used in the treaty was *échelles* which the English corrupted into "scales." The word literally signified the stairs which in every port went down from the quay to the water's edge.

of those islanded territories included within its circle "on the broad line between the limits of the Venetian territory and Trebizond."

After 1453 Venice—Genoa less so—were eager to snatch such fragments of the erstwhile Byzantine Empire as they might, but at the same time trembled lest the Turks seize that which they still possessed in the Levant. They could not help feigning interest in the pope's proposed crusade against the Turks, but at the same time did not want to compromise their trade relations. Hence Venice, while professing interest in the crusade, sent an embassy to Mohammed to get renewal of her old commercial concessions within the fallen empire. Genoa's treasury was empty and she could do nothing. In the readjustment which followed 1453 the political rights of these two cities in the Levant were somewhat curtailed, but their trading privileges were hardly diminished. The commercial policy of the Turks was rather a passive one, and they were more than glad to have others conduct their business for them and thus give them ample opportunity for their warlike occupation. The Venetians continued trading among the Turks. One of the chief articles they handled were slaves, mainly Christians, since they were prohibited by the treaty from dealing in Mohammedan slaves. From time to time the Venetians made some steps towards territorial aggrandizement, which in the long run proved failures. So, for instance, they acquired the island of Cyprus. The sultan, although on good terms with Venice, was by no means loath to make aggressions upon her colonies in the Mediterranean, as well as upon the Genoese colonies. In 1475 Kaffa and Tana on the Black Sea coast were taken by the Turks. But their trade at this time was practically gone.

The Italian princes refused to pay tithes for a new crusade. In vain the pope sent collectors to all the European states. There was general indifference and insignificant results were obtained. In 1462 came news of the fall of Sinope and Trebizond. Soon afterward a powerful Turkish fleet appeared in the Aegean.

The object of this expedition was to put an end to the Genoese rule in Lesbos, to extort a higher tribute from the Maona of Chios and the duke of Naxos, and, if possible, to expel the Knights of St. John from Rhodes and its dependent islands.[14]

Lesbos was taken in 1462. Pius II consecrated the revenues from the newly discovered alum deposits near Cività Vecchia to the crusade. But the whole enterprise fizzled. The Italian cities refused to contribute. While the Turks threatened Ragusa, Venice refused to send transports for the few troops gathered at Ancona. If it had come "an attempt might have been made to secure the Dalmatian coast and Ragusa." [15] Albania was conquered in 1468 after the death of the heroic Skander-

[14] Pastor, op. cit., III, p. 263.
[15] Reumont, op. cit., III, i, p. 151.

beg, who alone had resisted the Turks. In 1479 Venice made her peace with the Turks and devoted her endeavor thenceforth to expanding her power on the mainland of Italy, a policy ultimately ruinous to her. "Venice declined when she ceased to be Levantine and became Italian." [16] In 1480 another attack on Rhodes by the Turks was repulsed, but Otranto was taken, which put the Turks in command of the Adriatic Straits.

From this time the Ottomans left Europe unmolested and turned all their attention to conquest of Persia and Egypt. The former project failed—the history of modern Persia begins with the successful resistance of the first shah, Ismail. The tremendous earthquake which shook Europe and laid much of Constantinople in ruins in 1509 gave a respite to Egypt. In 1516 Selim I conquered Mesopotamia and Syria and finally Egypt in 1517. It was then the turn of Europe again. Belgrade was captured in 1521; Rhodes at last in 1522. In 1528 Hungary was overrun by the Turks and Buda-Pesth captured. But Vienna made a heroic and successful resistance.

Here we may rest the history of the Ottoman Turks. We are well down into modern times. It is of importance, however, before concluding this chapter, to notice the broad effects of the rise of the Ottoman Empire upon the history of commerce. The rise of the Turkish Empire was simultaneous with the great maritime discoveries of the last half of the fifteenth century, and it was long the belief of historians that there was an intimate relation between these two movements; that the Turks intercepted all the great ancient routes of commerce between Europe and the Orient, so that Europe desperately groped for some other way to the East, and finally found it in 1498 when the Portuguese rounded the Cape of Good Hope.

Undeniably this event shifted the route of oriental trade, but there is "little or no connection between the growth of the Turkish power and the causes of the great discoveries. A set of motives quite independent of the rise of the Turks led men like Henry of Portugal and Christopher Columbus to explore the unknown world; and when the new route to India had been established it was found to possess an essential superiority for trade." [17] Even before the Turkish conquest of Egypt, as early as 1502, the Venetians found little spice at Alexandria; in 1504 there was none. The Portuguese had emptied the markets in the East. From that time on an average of twelve ships left Lisbon yearly for India. But the Portuguese were not satisfied with merely buying most of the spices of India, and thus monopolizing the trade; from the year 1507 they blockaded the Red Sea and the Persian Gulf in order not to let any spices pass through along the old routes.

[16] W. Miller, *English Historical Review*, xxxix, p. 136.
[17] Lybyer, *English Historical Review*, XXX, pp. 577–78.

The Venetians might find some spices in Alexandria, but they were very high, while at Lisbon they were comparatively low. Venice knew that she faced ruin, and in vain urged the sultan to build a fleet in the Red Sea and make war upon the Portuguese. She even dreamed of cutting a canal through the isthmus of Suez. Between 1529–32 an Italian traveller named Luigi Roncinotto, when in Egypt, saw thousands of laborers excavating the isthmus. Spain also dallied with the idea of a Suez canal. It was one of the dreams of Cortez, and in 1533 one of his officers, Gaspar de Espinosa, addressed a memoir to Charles V, who ordered a secret survey of the isthmus to be made. Later Philip II appointed a similar commission, which decided that the plan was impracticable. Champlain urged the same design on Henry IV when France and Spain were at war (1588–98). Not the engineering difficulties, but political complications, frustrated this design. For any power having the monopoly of navigation rights through the proposed canal would have had to face a war with the other powers which so immensely profited by the Cape of Good Hope route to the Far East, in which, of course, the Turks would also have been involved.[18]

Genoa's project for restoration of her Levantine commerce was different, but as daring. This was to open trade relations with Muscovy (Russia). In 1520 a Genoese named Paolo Centurione went to Moscow to propose the development of Russo-Indian trade. The projected route was to be up the Indus, over the Hindu Kush, down the Oxus, across the Caspian to Astrakhan, up the Volga and its affluent, the Oka, to Moscow and thence to Riga, where Genoese galleys would meet the products. Apart from the difficulty of this route because of mountains and deserts which would have had to be crossed, a fatal error in the calculation was that the Oxus was thought to flow into the Caspian Sea instead of into the Sea of Aral. But this was not known until 1555, when Jenkinson, the English commercial agent of the Muscovy Company chartered by Philip II and Mary, reached Bokhara from Moscow.[19]

[18] The information in the above paragraphs is derived from a remarkable work by Gustavo Coen, *Le grandi strade del commercio internationale proposte fino dal sec. XVI*. Leghorn, 1888.

[19] It may be of interest to know that Napoleon planned to reach India by this identical route in event of his conquest of Russia in 1812.

CHAPTER XVI

THE BLACK DEATH

WE have reached the brink of modern history. But the student who has read so far must have perceived, partly from allusions in the text, partly from the observation of his own thought, that at least one important event—the Black Death—has not received treatment and that a whole body of social-economic phenomena have been taken for granted rather than explained. These phenomena were so general throughout all Europe that to discuss them at length in chapters which were each devoted to the history of a particular country would have confused the exposition. They were universal conditions, universal factors, which everywhere operated as transforming agencies gradually to change the structure and the content of society. They were simultaneous in their working and cumulative in their effect. Their development and their fusion with the whole civilization of the fourteenth and fifteenth centuries gave the form and the complexion to Europe which it possessed when it emerged into the sixteenth century and the epoch of the Reformation. Hence the succeeding chapters will be devoted to an exposition of these forces or developments, and in the final chapter an effort will be made to make a synthesis, and to combine and appraise the results of all this long and intricate process of transformation.

During the year 1348 and 1349 an infectious disease swept from the East across Europe leaving in its path the heaviest mortality known in history. This disease was called the Black Death because of the purplish-black spots which broke out on the body of the victim. The medical faculty of Paris gives the most concise if not the most logical statement regarding its origin. They said it originated in India.

We have a few exact data which may serve as a possible clue to the source of the disease. In 1333 the country surrounding the Kiang and Hoang Ho rivers in China experienced a parching drouth which devastated the fields and destroyed all vegetable and much animal life. This drying up resulted in a severe famine, which followed very shortly. The following year a heavy rain set in, swelling the rivers and streams until they overflowed in their courses, causing widespread inundations particularly in the vicinity of Canton. In this time of flood and famine it would be only natural that disease in one form or another should break out, and the records show us that in Tche, a Chinese town, a plague developed immediately after the floods, killing five million people, a number almost inconceivable.

From China the disease was carried along the trade routes to the West. There was great freedom of communication between the Far East and Europe at these times because of the enlightened commercial policy of the Mongol Empire that extended from the wall of China to the frontier of Germany. It is possible that the infection might have been carried in bales of silk from the Orient. All of Asia suffered greatly from the plague at this time. Whole villages and towns, even provinces, were entirely depopulated. In some places in India as much as nine-tenths of the population died. The scourge was very heavy in the Mongol Empire also. The disease can be traced westward from China to the Tartars of the Crimea. From the Crimea it was carried by ship to Constantinople and to Genoa. The emperor John Cantacuzene wrote an account of the Black Death in Constantinople. The pestilence spread over Asia Minor, Syria and Egypt.

The disease had reached Sicily and Venice in the latter part of 1347 and the first part of 1348. In Florence it raged from April to September, 1348. All of Italy was afflicted. From Italy the Black Death crossed the Alps and invaded Switzerland, Germany, Poland, and Hungary. In January, 1348, the Black Death was brought by ship to Marseilles. From here it quickly spread northward. The plague reached Avignon in the same month.

In Avignon the contagion was so great that not only by remaining with the sick but even by looking at them people seemed to take it; so much so that many died without any to serve them, and were buried without priests to pray over their graves. A father did not visit his son, nor the son his father. Charity was dead. The mortality was so great that it left hardly a fourth part of the population. Even the doctors did not dare to visit the sick from fear of infection. . . . As for me, to avoid infamy, I did not dare to absent myself, but still I was in continual fear.[1]

The mortality was so great at Avignon that the cemeteries were soon filled and the dead bodies were thrown into the Rhône to prevent putrefaction. The pope opened another cemetery where the bodies were heaped in layers in large trenches. From Gascony the disease crossed the Pyrenees and fell upon Spain. While besieging Gibraltar Alphonso of Castile fell victim to the plague. In France the Black Death reached Paris in October, 1348, and moved on northward through the Low Countries. In August, 1348, the Black Death broke out in Melcombe, England. On January 1, 1349, Edward III wrote to the bishop of Winchester regarding the plague, proroguing the meeting of Parliament to April 27. A later notice was sent on March 16, which declared that

[1] Guy de Chauliac, physician of Clement VI.

because of the ravages of the Black Death the meeting was postponed indefinitely. Soon the number of interments fell behind the ever-increasing death list and the dead were buried in large pits.

The Scots, thinking this an opportune moment to make war on the English when they were stricken with the "Scourge of God," crossed the border, to contract the disease themselves and carry it back to Scotland whence it spread to Ireland. From England the pestilence was carried by ship to Bergen, Norway, in 1349 and thence it spread to Sweden and Denmark, northern Germany and northern Russia, which the Black Death reached again in 1351, thus making a circle through Europe. The plague was also carried by ship from Bergen to Iceland and Greenland.

In Germany and France the medical profession published rules and admonitions to regulate the diet and life of the citizens. An inspection of these rules shows very clearly in how small a degree the nature of the disease was understood; for in the host of regulations which were published regarding the diet and even moral habits of the people, little mention is made of the necessity of cleanliness and hygienic precautions. The doctors prescribed meat "of the proper age" seasoned with pepper, ginger, and cloves. The patient must not sleep in the day time. Light wine, fresh and dried fruits might be used. Cold, moist, watery food was to be avoided. Fat people were advised to sit in the sunshine. "Men must preserve chastity as they value their lives." A physician in Perugia ordered the healthy to wash in vinegar or wine, and to sprinkle the house with vinegar. Camphor was to be smelled often. It was not until the end of the fifteenth century that plague victims were segregated and nurses required to remain away from the healthy for a period of ten days. Huge fires were recommended for the purification of the air. The pope at Avignon is said to have escaped the plague by following this advice and remaining in seclusion.

Sudden and fearful as the infliction of the Great Plague was, it was not without its harbingers. In the first place, for twenty years previously Europe had suffered from periodical famines, most of them more or less local; but that of 1316-17 was general and very severe. It seems necessary to admit that weather conditions in the fourteenth century were unpropitious. The subjoined table will illustrate:

FRANCE		ENGLAND	
1304	Famine		
1305	Famine		
1310	Famine		
1315	Famine	1315-16	Famine, universal. Wheat, 14s, 11d. the quarter in 1315; 16s. in 1316.
1316-17	Long and rigorous winter	1321	Semi-famine. Wheat at 11s.
1325	Drought	1325	Universal drought
1330	Drought. Vines froze		

	FRANCE		ENGLAND
1330–34	Famine	1331	Drought
1334	Famine. Many deaths		
1342	Seine overflowed		
1344	Famine	1344	Drought
1348–49	Black Death	1348	Black Death
1349–51	Famine due to uncultivated fields	1351	Universal famine. **Wheat at** 10s. 2d.
1358–59	Famine	1361–62	Drought
1361–62	Famine and drought		
1363	Hard winter	1369	Famine. Wheat at 11s. 10d.
1371	Famine		
1374	Famine	1374	Drought
1375	Famine	1377	
1390	Famine		Drought

These data in the case of France must be discounted to some degree because of the English ravages in France after 1346. But war would not account for the whole condition, since England reflects similar though not so acute conditions. War has no effect on weather, although weather always powerfully affects war. There was also another forerunner of the Great Plague. This was a plague of rats and mice throughout Europe in the years immediately preceding the Black Death, and the rat has been the symbol of pestilence since remote antiquity. One need go no farther than the Old Testament for evidence of this belief, and the symbolism is attested in ancient art.

The first question which arises for consideration is: What proportion of the population perished? We must certainly be incredulous of the estimates given by contemporary writers who wrote under stress of the terror that stalked in darkness and the pestilence which wasted at noonday. Nothing like one-half, or even one-third, of the population died. It may be doubted whether so much as one-quarter died. The statistical records of the age are so fragmentary, even when they are available at all, that little reliance can be placed upon them. We are compelled to endeavor to ascertain general rather than specific conditions prior to 1349 and after 1349, and then by a process of inverse or backward reasoning, try to come to a comparative determination. We must conclude that the "figures" given of the time are hysterically exaggerated, but at the same time admit that the Black Death caused the heaviest mortality known to history. All particular attempts at calculation must be regarded as mere guess work: as for instance statements that Germany suffered less than other countries; that the mortality was greater in the towns than in the country; that the upper classes and the well-to-do suffered less than the lower classes; that the ascetic life of the clergy protected them from infection more than others.

Let us try to give a general picture of the conditions before inquiring into details. It is easy to see the consequences of the Black Death.

Economic chaos, social unrest, high prices, profiteering, depravation of morals, lack of production, industrial indolence and inefficiency, frenetic gaiety, wild expenditure, luxury, debauchery, social and religious hysteria, greed, avarice, maladministration, decay of manners, followed in the path of the plague. The immediate effect of the Black Death was to lower prices and to glut the market with commodities. The reason is not far to seek. Every civilized society possesses a certain accumulated surplus of goods or produce, enough to last it for some months at least, even if production cease. When the plague had spent its force the surviving population found itself in possession of these accumulated stores, produce, goods, in addition to movable and real property which had once belonged to those who had died.

Men woke up to find themselves rich who had formerly been poor, inasmuch as they were the only surviving heirs. Land, houses, furniture, goods, farm products, cattle, horses, sheep, were without owners. Everything which was movable or which could be driven away on four feet was seized; even landed property was occupied since there was no one to protest, and the very courts of law were stopped. "Then were small prices for everything," records Henry Knighton, the medieval chronicler. "A man could have a horse, which before was worth 40 s. for 6 s. 8 d.; a fat ox for 4 s.; a cow for 12 d.; a heifer for 2 d; a big pig for 5 d; a fat wether for 4 d.; a sheep for 3 d.; a lamb for 2 d.; a stone of wool for 9 d. Sheep and cattle went wandering over fields and through crops, and there was no one to go and drive or gather them." Another writer relates:

In that time there was sold a quarter of wheat for 12 d., a quarter of barley for 9 d., a quarter of beans for 8 d., a quarter of oats for 6 d., a large ox for 40 d., a good horse for six shillings, a good cow for two shillings and even for 18 d. And even at this price buyers were only rarely to be found. And this pestilence lasted for two years and more before England was freed from it. When, by God's mercy, it ceased, there was such a scarcity of labourers that none could be had for agricultural purposes. On account of this scarcity, women, and even small children, were to be seen with the plow and leading the waggons.[2]

The direct result of all this suddenly acquired wealth was a wild orgy of expenditure and debauchery on the part of many. Furs, silks, tapestries, rich furniture, expensive food, jewels, plate, fell within the purchasing power of the poor. Men spent lavishly, luxuriously, insanely. Poor workmen and poorer cotters, living in wretched hovels,

[2] *Eulogium Historiarum* (Rolls Series).

who formerly, like Margery Daw, had slept on straw, now lolled on beds of down and ate from plate that once had decorated the sideboards of nobles. Often, too, they removed from their ancient quarters into vacant houses. The landlord class was hit hard by the plague. "Magnates and lesser lords of the realm who had tenants made abatements of rent in order to keep their tenantry; some half the rent, some more, some less, some for two years, some for three, some for one year, according as they could agree with them."

But this condition of luxury soon passed. Those who survived found themselves personally richer than before; but Europe was immeasurably poorer, for production absolutely ceased for months, even a whole year, and when it was renewed the productive capacity of Europe was found to be much impaired, while the waste had been terrific. When all the accumulated surplus had been consumed or wasted, prices soared and the cost of living, both of commodities and of service, rose enormously. Farm laborers, gild workmen, domestic servants, clerks, even priests, struck for higher wages. "In the following autumn no one could get a reaper for less than 8 d. with his food; a mower for less than 12 d. with his food. Wherefore many crops perished in the fields for want of some one to garner them. But in the pestilence year there was such abundance of all kinds of corn that no one troubled about it. . . . A man could scarcely get a chaplain under ten pounds or ten marks to minister to a church. There was scarcely any one now who was willing to accept a vicarage for twenty pounds." Rents soon went up. Abandoned buildings lapsed into ruin, occupied buildings naturally deteriorated under wear and tear, and the wages of carpenters and other artisans were often so high as to prohibit repairs.

The high prices of staple commodities and the exorbitant demands of the wage-earning class soon reached a pinnacle under the stimulus of profiteering. Accordingly the governments had resort to maximum laws both for commodities and wages. England passed a Statute of Laborers in 1349, France a similar law in 1351.

The social effects of the Black Death were manifold. In the first place, then as now, there was enormous displacement of population. The plague had the effect of an invasion; it either killed or drove out the population. Thousands fled to other places. Infected districts were left deserted. In after-years one finds evidence of this in interesting ways. New place-names, new surnames, even unfamiliar speech in various regions, attest it. One finds evidence of Italian colonies in south German and south French cities; French and Germans in north Italy; Flemings in Normandy; Normans in Picardy, *etc.* Under the stress of fear men were mad to get out of an infected region, and fled, often into another quite as dangerous. We find other evidence of this movement of population in the outcropping of technical industries and crafts, once peculiar to a certain district, in quite another place owing to the flight of workmen from the former to the latter locality.

The texture of society, too, was profoundly modified by the Black Death. In addition to a large class of *nouveaux riches,* the plague opened the door of opportunity to many to get into new lines of employment, or to establish themselves in new kinds of business. Clerks became merchants, former workmen became employers and contractors, farm laborers became gentlemen farmers. The old nobility of Europe, which derived its lineage from the Norman Conquest and the Crusades, largely passed away, leaving their titles and their lands to the kings who gave them out to new favorites, so that a new *noblesse* arose in Europe, a parvenu nobility without the accomplishment, the pride, or the manners of the old *noblesse.* The titles survived, but the blood of the peerage was new, not old; parvenu, not aristocratic. With the passing of the aristocracy passed also the chivalry and courtesy that had distinguished it. The decay of manners in the last half of the fourteenth century is an astonishing fact. The old-fashioned gentility was gone; manners were uncouth, rough, brutal. Familiar speech became rude, lewd, even obscene. Every student of the literature of the fourteenth and fifteenth centuries has observed this. This explains the paradox that books on courtesy were so much in demand in these centuries. The new high society was ignorant of good manners and needed to know. Even fashions reflected the decadent conditions of the age. Refinement and decorum in dress, which marked the distinguished lady and gentleman in the thirteenth century, disappeared. The *nouveaux riches* had a passion for display, for garish colors, for excessive dress, for the wearing of many jewels. Dressmakers and milliners reaped a harvest from this class. The costumes were fabrications to wonder at, but not to admire.

Another characteristic of the late fourteenth century was the protest against political corruption and administrative inefficiency. The cry for reform was widespread and not to be wondered at. The Black Death hit the governments of Europe hard. For two hundred years these governments had been slowly and painfully developing their administrative machinery and training up a skilled class of officials in their employ. Then of a sudden thousands of this technically trained class were cut down, so much so that the governments were crippled beyond what we may imagine; police protection, courts, law-making, the hundred and one everyday activities of an ordered society were arrested. The machinery of the governments nearly stopped. In this emergency two things happened: the offices had to be filled, the government kept running at all cost, so that thousands of ignorant, incompetent, dishonest men were hastily thrust into public offices; moreover, the thousands of vacant offices tempted the job-hunter, the placeman, the professional office-seeker, and this class swarmed into the vacancies with the selfish motive of feathering their own nests and plundering the public. The result was appalling waste, great maladministration, and peculation, with the natural protest of society against these abuses.

The Church was no better off than the governments in this particular. We have already seen that protest arose in Europe in the last half of the fourteenth century against the abuses and corruption in the Church. But the Church is not to be blamed too severely for this condition. It, too, had to keep functioning, and to do so impressed into service all sorts and conditions of men; in the universal terror it could not be overcareful in those whom it selected. And again, church offices were lucrative and influential appointments, and many intruded themselves into church livings for the sake of the material nature of the preferment.

Complaints against political and administrative corruption, the prevalence and increase of crime, lightness of mind, looseness of morals, high prices, profiteering, industrial and farm strikes, extravagance, indolence, or refusal to go to work are common in the fourteenth century. The Black Death wrought a universal upheaval and transformation of society to which nothing else in history is comparable except the influence of the World War.

Even in the field of psychology this analogy holds true. The whole population suffered from "shell shock," from frayed nerves. It is this condition which explains the semi-hysterical state of mind of thousands in Europe, and accounts for their fevered or morbid emotionalism. The old barriers were down, the old inhibitions removed. The superficial yet fevered gaiety, the proneness to debauchery, the wild wave of extravagance, the flamboyant luxury, the gluttony—all these phenomena are readily explicable by the student used to making psychosocial analyses. And as always at such seasons, the phenomena of the Freudian complex are vividly presented. A book could be written solely upon the strange, intense, morbid sex manifestations abroad in Europe in the fourteenth century.

The so-called Flagellant movement was a mixture of religious morbidity and sex stimuli, so widespread in its influence that it reduced thousands to a state of frenzy. Not since the Crusades had Europe witnessed so tremendous a manifestation of mob psychology. In the lapse of all the accustomed inhibitions of church, of state, of society, the thought and conduct of men went off on eccentric tangents. The failure of old authorities gave room for new and self-constituted authorities to establish themselves. Charlatans, mind-readers, sorcerers, witch-doctors, drug-vendors, sprang up like mushrooms, along with perfervid crossroads preachers and soap-box orators each denouncing society and the wrongs around them, and each offering his panacea or remedy. A golden opportunity was afforded to the amateur preacher, the amateur reformer, the pseudo-scientist, the grafter.

The literature of the late Middle Ages is rich in the possession of this kind of psycho-social phenomena, which has not yet been studied. Few even know of it. It may surprise the reader to learn that probably the well-known legend about the Pied Piper of Hamelin is attached to the time of the Black Death. Grotesque and amusing as Browning's famous ballad is, there is yet a tragic pathos underneath the tale, which he failed to divine. Browning, as all his readers, regarded the story as a mere legend. But undeniably there is a basis of real history below the surface. What probably happened at Hamelin was this: the town was infested by rats; the Pied Piper made his appearance (whether a charlatan or a lunatic cannot be said) and offered to charm the rats away. The rats probably stayed, but the Piper's strange costume and stranger power which he claimed to possess, united with the intense, even hysterical emotionalism of the people, worked upon the natural curiosity of children. The sight of such a wondrous spectacle as the Piper in their streets lured them after him and they were scattered, never to return. The poor children were swept away on a wave of crowd psychology, of emotional excitement, to the point of hysteria. Many of them, like those who went on the Children's Crusade, fell into the hands of professional kidnappers and slavers.

In the matter of prices, we may, with a modern scholar,

. . . turn to the general price situation both preceding and following the plague. In considering the fourteenth century it at once becomes evident that prices had been rising generally from 1200, and that they continued so to rise until roughly about 1400, when a period of falling prices set in, lasting approximately until 1475, when they again followed an upward trend. The following table, taken from D'Avenel, *Histoire des prix*, I, p. 27, shows what he believed to be the relative value of money, taking that of 1894 as 1.

1201–1225	4½	
1226–1300	4	Period of rising prices
1301–1350	3½	
1351–1375	3	
1376–1400	4	
1401–1425	4½	Period of falling prices
1426–1450	4½	
1451–1475	6	
1476–1500	5	
1501–1525	4	
1526–1550	3	Period of rising prices
1551–1575	2½	
1576–1600	2½	

Thus while the years of the Black Death are characterized by exceedingly
high prices for foodstuffs, the plague of 1348–51 cannot be said with assurance to have had any permanent effect on the price level itself. In other
words, the devastation so caused seems not to have been of such fundamental importance as to modify the price level of the period. And since
the price level in general is a function of the quantity of money in circulation at any given period, it would be best to ascertain if possible the
condition of the currency during the fourteenth century. Speaking generally, we find that from the ninth to the middle of the twelfth century
the production of silver steadily increased. From 1200 to approximately
1450 the production of silver decreased, apparently because the surface
mines available had been exhausted and because abortive attempts to mine
by hydraulic pressure had flooded many otherwise productive mines. It was
not until the second half of the fifteenth century that silver production
again increased with the discovery of new mines in Sweden, Germany,
Bohemia, and the Tyrol, and subsequently with the importation of precious
metals from America. . . . Such a decrease in the amount of silver in
the coins is in itself an explanation for the rise in prices throughout the
fourteenth century in France, leaving aside any consideration of the effects
of the Black Death itself beyond the spasmodic changes for the actual
years 1348–51. . . . The period 1200–1400 was generally one of rising
prices accompanied by a decrease in the amount of silver produced. . . . It
seems fairly evident that, although the loss of man-power in 1348–51 occasioned a rise in prices, the Black Death did not have a permanent effect
on the price level either in France or in England.[3]

When we pass to an examination of land values we find that there
was no tendency after the Black Death for land values to regain their
former level, as was the case with commodities. Seebohm has said
that English agriculture was permanently impaired. Owing to dearth
of labor and the high wages demanded by those who survived, the landowner had two recourses: either to rent his land in small parcels or
to abandon farming for sheep-raising. This was especially the case in
England, the greatest raw wool producer of the time; but we find the
same thing on a less scale in rural Flanders, in Champagne, in Tuscany, in Lombardy, around Augsburg—indeed wherever sheep pasturage
was close to weaving communities. One other condition promoted this
recourse. Villages and farmsteads went to ruin in the great days of
stress (1348–51) and the cost of reparation was so great afterwards
that owners gave up hope of making repairs. The following table compiled from the assizes preserved in the Tower is quoted from Clutter-
beck's *History of Hertfordshire*. The figures showing the assessed
value per acre were taken at the death of all landowners for purposes
of taxation.

[3] H. R. Bittermann, *Jnl. Polit. Econ.*, XXXVI, pp. 458–59.

	Pence		Pence
1268	9	1348 (Black Death)	
1271	12	1359	9¼
1274	12	1368	10½
1285	6–7½	1381	9¼
1291	9	1417	6
1313	12	1422	4
1330	6–8½	1429	4
1331	8½	1432	6
1336	11½	1446	8
1338	11½		

An analysis of these data, however, will disclose that the Black Death cannot be held to have been solely accountable for the drop in land values in England in the fourteenth century. The recovery to almost normal by 1368 shows this. Evidently some other deranging factor must be taken into account, and this can only have been the rising cost of peasant labor, aggravated by social disorder like the Peasant Revolt in 1381 and the Wars of the Roses in the middle of the fifteenth century. In France the condition was altogether extraordinary between 1346–80 and 1413–53 on account of the ravages of war and of the Free Companies.[4]

The following table has been constructed by Levasseur (*Histoire des classes ouvrières*, I, p. 524, n. 2).

PRICE AND REVENUES OF LAND IN FRANCS PER HECTARE

Periods	Arable Land		Pasture		Vines		Woods	
	Pr.	Rev.	Pr.	Rev.	Pr.	Rev.	Pr.	Rev.
1301–25	222	22 00	......	......	......	......	......	......
1326–50	108	10 80	235	23	463	46	52	5
1351–75	83	8 30	337	33	140	14	84	8
1376–1400	98	9 80	484	48	420	42	53	4
1401–25	89	8 90	136	13	376	37	60	5
1426–50	68	6 80	139	13	218	21	15	1 50
1451–75	48	4 80	218	21	127	12	15	1 50
1476–1500	97	8 10	123	10	228	19	55	4

[4] The effect of the Hundred Years' War as a prime determinant of the economic conditions in France rather than the Black Death is seen most clearly in the fall in the value of land in France during the second quarter of the century. Had the plague been of first importance we should have seen the same phenomenon as in England, a fall in the value of land in the third quarter of the century. But the disturbances of raids, devastation, plundering—all the companions of war—appear to have been of sufficient extent to occasion a definite fall in land values in France. (*Jnl. Pol. Econ.*, XXXVI, p. 477.)

We have considered two important economic phenomena which characterized the years immediately following the Black Death—the price of commodities and the price of land—and have seen that the changes may not be wholly or immediately attributed to the plague. The question of wages and the increasing cost of labor was an important, perhaps the most important, factor. If the evidence of legislation be taken into account this certainly was the case. For the statute books of the fourteenth century in every country of Europe abound with legislation endeavoring to keep wages down and to restrain both peasants and artisans from striking for higher wages. Intimately associated with the effects thereof is the question of commutation of labor services and that of the quickened or retarded emancipation of the villeins. Whether wages were kept down or not, whether emancipation was accelerated by the Black Death or whether that process was independent of it, whether commutation may be ascribed to the influence of the plague or was due to other influences are all moot points among historians. Here, again, one must be cautious of making sweeping statements. On the estates of the bishop of Winchester, at least, the Black Death was not followed by those cataclysmic results rashly attributed to it by early historians. The villeins did not strike nor was there rapid commutation of labor services.[5] All over Europe farm laborers, gild workmen, house servants, even priests struck for more compensation than they had formerly received.

We have evidence of much legislation in restraint of striking laborers and artisans in continental legislation.

In Spain after the pestilence the lords met the need for labor by using slaves, generally Saracens. This amounted to the rejection of the dualistic manorial system and was highly objectionable to the occupying and cultivating classes. In their interest and because they furnished a convenient means of checking the feudal aristocracy, the crown intervened both in Aragon and Castile. On the other hand, the absence of a class of small farmers with capital enough to take over leases, as in England, threw the land made available after the plague into the hands of the townsmen, who worked it by means of servile labor. In these circumstances the government carried through a labor policy, which Kovalevsky believes kept down the normal rise of wages by one, or even two-thirds. Venice alone almost among European states met the consequences of the Black Death by an intelligent economic policy. All the old restrictions were temporarily suspended in favor of a free economic competition. Foreign settlers were attracted by the offer of easy access to the gilds, and indeed to all industrial and commercial rights and even to citizenship. By this means the population of Venice and the Terra Firma was recruited; and in a very few years the conditions prevailing before the pestilence had been restored,

[5] Elizabeth Levett, in Vinogradoff's *Oxford Studies in Social and Legal History*, Vol. V.

and it was possible to return to the old system without any of the social upheavals that afflicted other and less enlightened governments. A somewhat similar policy was pursued at Siena; and at Orvieto, . . . They hit upon a plan for adjusting wages and prices according to a sliding scale.[6]

The two most important statutes of laborers were those of England in 1349 and of France in 1351. Perhaps the fact that England was a pioneer in this form of legislation points to the conclusion that the unrest was greater among the peasantry of the fields than among the workingmen in the towns. It is certainly evidence that England was yet an almost wholly agricultural country. The industrial development of England did not begin until the Lancastrian epoch (1399–1461).

The chronicler Knighton, who has already been quoted, gives a vivid account of this peasant discontent in England:

For the labourers were so lifted up and obstinate that they would not listen to the king's command, but if any one wished to have them he had to give them what they wanted, and either lose his fruit and crops, or satisfy the lofty and covetous wishes of the population . . . and afterwards the king had many labourers arrested and sent them to prison; many withdrew themselves and went into the forests and woods; and those who were taken were heavily fined.

The clamor of the landowners and the turbulence of the peasantry in June, 1349, led to the famous Statute of Laborers, the preamble of which recites that

Whereas a great part of the people, and principally of labourers and servants, is dead of the plague, and that some, seeing the necessity of masters and the scarcity of servants, will not work unless they receive exorbitant wages, and others choosing rather to beg in idleness than to earn their bread by labour . . . we have ordained, by the advice of our prelates and nobles, and other skilled persons, that every able-bodied man and woman of our kingdom, bond or free, under sixty years of age, not living by trading, or having of his or her own wherewithal to live . . . shall, if so required, serve another for the same wages as were the custom in the twentieth year of our reign.

One's sympathy, however, need not go wholly to the working classes. Then, as now, there were two sides to the difficult and complex question of the relation of employer and employed. The trials of the abbess of Shaftesbury, who dared not eject a tenant guilty of flagrant waste lest she lose his labor, make vivid reading in one of the year books. Gild workmen struck not only for higher wages and shorter hours, but

[6] *Political Science Quarterly*, XXVII, p. 323. Cf. Kovalevsky, *Annales internationales d'histoire*, Paris Congress, 1900. 2d sec., pp. 181–212 (Paris, 1902).

even for a less number of days. In Germany the saying went that *"Montag ist Sontag's Bruder*—Monday is Sunday's brother."

The English Statute of Laborers has been so thoroughly studied in comparison with that of France in 1351, and literature pertaining to it is so easily procurable, that it seems justifiable to devote a somewhat extended examination to the French statute, although it applied only to the city and county of Paris and not to the kingdom at large as in England. It is far more searching and complete than the other. How far it was enforced is less clear than in the case of the English law. This may be one of the reasons why even French historians have written little upon it.[7] John the Good's legislation is based in part upon the great ordinance of Philip IV of July 7, 1307. This new ordinance dated January 30, 1351, includes no less than 252 articles in 62 titles.

As the result of the plague working-men's wages and the price of foodstuffs and of manufactured articles rose enormously. John II attempted to regulate wages and prices. He provided what the maximum wages of women employed by the day should be. For domestics employed in households throughout the year, he provided that chamber servants in Paris should receive thirty *sous* annually as the highest price, together with the shoes they had to wear. Nurses were to receive 50 *sous* and no more. Dairy maids were to have 20 *sous* from St. Martin's Day to St. John's Day (November 11 to June 24), and 30 *sous* from St. John's Day to St. Martin's, or 50 *sous* in all. The wages of harvesters and threshers were fixed at the same rate. The best class of farm hands, that is to say, sowers and reapers, could not demand more than 2 *sous*, six pence, by the day.

After having fixed the wages of field hands and domestic servants, the wages of the gilds were fixed. Masons, tilers, slaters, stone-cutters, and carpenters were to be paid 26 pence, and their assistants 16 pence, from St. Martin's Day to Easter; from Easter to St. Martin's, when the days were longer, 32 pence and their assistants 22. All kinds of merchandise were scheduled as to prices, and ordinary objects might not exceed a maximum price. By what principle were these prices fixed? The ordinance expressly says. It was admitted that the day laborer and the artisan were worth more since the plague, but the rise in price of their services must not exceed one-third more. Wages were augmented in the same degree as prices. Thus a maximum price was fixed in the interest of the consumer in order to diminish the general dearness.

But there was another manner of lowering prices: that is, by increasing the number of workmen and abolishing the restrictive regulations

---

[7] Levasseur (*Histoire des classes ouvrières*, I, pp. 501 ff.) seems to have been the first historian to remark its existence. But see *Jnl. Polit. Econ.*, XXXVI, pp. 473–75.

of the gilds, which prevented artisans from increasing in numbers in Paris. Many of the statutes of the arts and trades limited the number of apprentices. This was to reduce the number of competitors in the future, for these apprentices could become future masters. King John, reviving the principles of the ordinance of 1307, decreed in a general fashion that an employer might have as many apprentices as he wanted. All the terms of this article are worthy of remark. The narrow regulations upon the duration of apprenticeship and wages which the apprentice should be paid are abolished. In the case of a special trade, that of the belt-makers and leather curriers, who made belts and soles for shoes, it is provided that "The belt-makers may work at night from All Saints' Day until the middle of March and may have as many apprentices as they wish; these apprentices, at the end of two years may ply their trade and make what they can." Thus we see another narrow rule of the gilds falling to the ground. Night work is specifically authorized, at least in the winter months, and this measure is taken to increase production and to reduce the price of manufactured articles.

But not all the restrictions imposed by the gilds disappeared. Certain old rules still remained. For example, no one could ply two different trades at the same time; merchants could not abuse their artisans or apprentices. A maximum wage of workingmen was fixed, so that no outbidding was possible.

It is to be observed that the ordinance, in the case of certain trades, fixes the number of the masters. This was to give them a monopoly. But observe what these trades are. There are to be thirty wine sellers, who are to sell the wines of the bourgeois at Paris. There are to be sixty wine dealers who are to sell Burgundian wine. There are to be sixty measurers of firewood and no more. But these offices were veritable appointments to which the provost of the merchants appointed, or the royal provost of Paris, or the échevins, and which in consequence were not offices of production. The incumbents thereof were in the public service.

The number of other masters, goldsmiths, drapers, masons was not limited. Every workman who had fulfilled his apprenticeship could establish himself in the city of Paris whether or not his term of apprenticeship had been spent at Paris. He was simply obliged to submit to the general regulations of the corporation and pay an entrance fee.

Thus it is far from true to say that the gilds were destroyed by King John's ordinance. Everything indicates that they continued. At the head of the gilds there remained the *maîtres jurés,* who verified the merchandise put on sale. The *jurés* were chosen by the gildsmen, but they were approved by the provost of the king and took an oath to him. They made reports to the provost concerning violations which they discovered, but the *jurés* themselves were judges of these violations. However, the ultimate judgment was with the provost. In a word, the ordinance of King John tolerated, even respected, the gild system; it merely fixed the price of goods in the interest of the public; it maintained in the gild the principle of the "open door," and abolished certain restrictions.

It has been claimed that the dauphin Charles, developing his father's ordinance, established entire freedom of work, and the letters bearing dates of September, 1358, to the garment-cutters of Paris, at the time he was regent, are cited in proof. The garment-cutters a this time were at outs with the doublet-makers, who had had the monopoly of making doublets and linings. A decision of Charles had recognized this right at one time when doublets were still a new fashion; but now the doublet had become a common garment and the ordinary garment-cutters demanded permission to make them. Charles V appointed the provost of Paris to make an investigation into the question; he decided that the garment-cutters henceforth could also make doublets. Charles did not break the gild by this ordinance, as has been said by some historians; he only permitted both gilds to manufacture such goods after the garment became one of common fashion.

The ordinance of 1351 also contains interesting articles upon purchase and sale in Paris. In order that the maximum prices might not be evaded it was required that sales were to be made in public and by daylight, so that they might be controlled. In consequence, outside merchants could not sell except in the *halles* and markets. Even Parisians who had purchased objects manufactured for sale outside of Paris could not sell them except in the *halles*. The masters of the gilds were to inspect these goods and their authority was backed up by the provost of Paris, the auditor of the Châtelet, the public prosecutor, and the provost of the merchants. The bourgeois of Paris were forbidden to go to outside merchants. The market was not to be opened until after a given signal and only then could transactions begin. The populace of the city had the first right of purchase for their own consumption and then what remained could be sold to others. Hucksters of eggs, butter, and other articles of consumption were not forbidden, but the profit of these peddlers was fixed; they could not make more than two *sous* in twenty *sous*.

The interest which this ordinance presents is great. It is the longest that we have upon the industrial and commercial organizations of the fourteenth century. It goes wonderfully into detail. But it is to be remembered that it was an ordinance rendered under exceptional circumstances, to meet a terrible crisis. It is evident the crown intervened in order to reduce this crisis, but when the crisis was passed the ordinance ceased to be effective, exactly like that of Philip IV in 1307. It was not possible for the crown permanently to fix the price of wages

and manufactured articles. The gilds were unwilling to obey many of
these general articles, for example, that abolishing the limitations upon
apprenticeship. However, one of the intended purposes was achieved
—prices fell. This reduction was less the result of the ordinance than
of external circumstances. The condition of France grew worse—
there followed the rebellion of Paris under Marcel in 1358, the jacquerie, the frightful ravages of the English and the Free Companies
under swashbucklers like Sir Robert Knollys and Armand de Cer-
volles, called the arch-priest. The misery was profound. When the very
necessities of life were wanting, how could luxury survive? Demand
everywhere diminished. The workmen could barely make a living; supply exceeded demand and prices fell so low that in point of fact they
seemed to have been lower than before the Great Plague. There is
evidence of the ineffectiveness in many places of the labor statutes which
limited wages, and of the aggravation of the labor difficulty owing to
imprisonment of sturdy laborers for disobedience of the ordinances.

In the matter of the commutation of old labor rents into money payments and the introduction of farming under lease, the iron logic of
facts cancelled the former contractual relation between lord and villein.
That contract had protected the peasant, by making it impossible for
the lord suddenly to increase the burdens or to alter the form of the
obligation without the will of the tenant already in occupation. But it
did not operate in the opposite direction to protect the lord against exploitation by his villeins in the sudden crisis. Almost everywhere the
peasantry won in this contention between old and new conditions.

The Black Death set the stone rolling in the direction of commutation.
There followed a period of anarchy peculiarly favorable to the assertion
of freedom by the villeins. They deserted their holdings *en masse,* and the
lords, finding the greatest difficulty in keeping up the accustomed services,
consented more and more readily to arrangements on the basis of a money
rent.[8]

But the Black Death did not originate this movement; it merely accelerated a precedent movement. For the gradual economic and social revolution in process in Europe ever since the thirteenth century, to go
no farther back, had already largely substituted the cash nexus for the
old service nexus. There were more free tenant farmers or those owning their own land and less serfs in Europe than is usually supposed.
England was more backward in this slow change than the continent. In
England commutation of labor services did not become general until
the early years of the fifteenth century; and the Church everywhere
lagged behind the laity in yielding to the new condition.

[8] Vinogradoff, *Collected Papers,* I, p. 131.

It would be an error, however, to raise the Black Death to "the dignity of a constant economic force" [9] in and by itself alone. For there were too many other complex phenomena which commingled with it for one to find the Black Death the sole factor or even the supreme factor in the changes of the fourteenth century. There are epochs in history when economic and social forces are so intimately interwoven that the problem created by them eludes solution. The factors are so many and various that they defy social calculus. The historian can only be assured of one thing, namely that no government has ever yet succeeded either in understanding or in mastering organic growth or organic decay. Men die, but the march of time continues. Whether that movement is forward or backward, whether it is "progress" or "decline," who can say? The most that can be said is that it is change.

[9] Vinogradoff, *op. cit.*, p. 136.

CHAPTER XVII

THE GILDS AND THE FORMATION OF THE PATRICIATE IN THE TOWNS. THE PROLETARIAT AND THE CONFLICT OF CLASSES

It is not necessary to repeat here what has been written in the previous volume upon the theories of origin of the medieval gilds.[1]

It being impossible to ascribe the origin of the gilds to any particular seed or root, we may regard the gilds as a spontaneous expression of the medieval tendency towards association, without going further. But whatever the germ—or germs—of the medieval gilds, two facts are clear: that they were coeval with the rise of the bourgeoisie and the formation of the towns, and *when they emerged* they were associations of free merchants or craftsmen organized to protect themselves both against unfree competition and the competition of similar rival groups. Priority in time must be given to the merchant gilds, vague evidences of which we discover in the eleventh century, whereas organizations of free artisans do not appear until late in the twelfth century.

At first all kinds of merchants and all kinds of artisans were associated together. Workers of one trade tended to flock together in one street or one quarter of a town. The occupational names of old streets in every European city is interesting to study. The reasons of such clustering together were, first, convenience of position, and, second, jealousy—the wish to keep an eye on one's fellows and to watch prices. But gradually, yet quite rapidly, a process of differentiation of functions or technique led to the formation of various kinds of gilds until we find highly developed distinctions obtaining. It was kind of work which made the tie that bound them together. Thus in Florence, as we have seen, there were seven major gilds and sixteen minor gilds. The oldest gilds in Germany were those of the fish-dealers of Worms in 1106, and of the shoemakers in Magdeburg in 1128. The first mention in Germany of dealers of cloth in sundry (*kraemer*) or haberdashers, is found at Worms in 1221, and the gild appears at the end of the thirteenth century. At this time we find the apothecaries associated with them. For in the early stages of gild formation, when a group of merchants or artisans was yet not numerous or unimportant, two or more groups would associate together by fusion. In Augsburg we thus find mercers, parchment dealers, spicers, shoemakers, and makers of

[1] Thompson, *Economic and Social History of the Middle Ages*, pp. 788-93.

playing cards combined. In Ulm, which specialized in linen and cotton goods, the cloth dealers (*Gewandschneider*) were the important gild. In Strassburg the chief gild was that of the hatters. In Ulm and Strassburg these two were the richest gilds. The same sort of diversity is found in other towns.[2]

Along with this evolution went also another kindred tendency towards regulation of prices and maintenance of wages to prevent lowering the cost of production, to preserve traditional uniformity and to kill competition.

The end which the gild aimed at was the rule of a proportional equality; hence its minute regulations and exaggerated precautions. The engrossing of raw materials was forbidden. Partnership was looked at askance. The master might engage only a very limited number of men, and follow only a limited number of trades. External as well as internal competition was kept at a distance. Not a foreign workman could be employed when there was scarcity of labor in the commune itself. No articles from without that resembled the home product might be offered for sale. The interests of the purchaser were looked after as well as those of the seller. There were precise instructions regarding the proofs of competence to be furnished by workmen; as far as possible, determination of a price just, and in conformity with the theories of publicists on the legitimacy of all profit. The stability was arranged for as much as it could be, measures being taken to prevent a fall, as well as to check demands for a rise, in their rate.[3]

[2] These merchant and craft gilds must be carefully distinguished from another and more popular form of association. These were the confraternities, which were mutual insurance societies. They multiplied rapidly. The wide prevalence of famine, the Black Death, the intense religious emotionalism abroad account in large measure for their popularity. They were mutual aid societies, insurance companies, burial associations, etc. Sick members received a small stipend per week during illness and a less amount during convalescence. But aid was not given for injuries received in brawls. As an illustration: Two bourgeois of Paris, Raymondin le Monnoyer, an usher of the King's Chamber, and Jacque de Leuge, in July, 1332, founded a confraternity in the Church of St. Paul. Membership was open not merely to workmen but to others. It was sufficient to have decent clothes, to pay five *sous* entrance fee, two pence to the clerk and an assessment of twelve pence. The fee for the annual dinner was three pence. This confraternity provided torches, wax candles, and a pall for funeral purposes. On the Monday following the decease of a member the confraternity paid for the celebration of a requiem mass with a deacon and a sub-deacon. The confraternity assured still other advantages. Its members were under the special protection of the patron saint and celebrated a special mass in his or her honor on the calendar day. This was a grand occasion, for then the chief of the confraternity was inducted into office. At vesper time they sang the Magnificat: *deposuit potentes de sede, etc.,* at which moment the former incumbent quitted office, and when the words of the chant were uttered, *"et exaltavit humiles,"* his successor was installed. This ceremony was called the *"deposuit."* The new president generally gave a present to the society.

[3] E. Nys, *History of Economics,* pp. 103–104 and Vanderkindere, *Le siècle des Artevelde,* p. 106.

It is not necessary, however, to believe that the gilds were all formed after a uniform type, or that gilds were to be found everywhere in the late Middle Ages. Many towns, even of some size, did not have them. There were no gilds in Lyons and Bordeaux until late in the fifteenth century.

As the gilds grew richer and more powerful they became more aristocratic in form and spirit. This cleavage was superinduced by two processes. The rich traders established mercantile and then social connections by marriage with the old landed aristocracy, so that their interests in course of time became identical. Moreover, as workers from manors and farms flocked into the growing towns seeking industrial employment, preferring to be wage earners rather than farm laborers, farm prices declined and many rich traders bought country places outside of town, a practice which further identified them with the landed aristocracy. Interesting studies have been made in the history of certain places, of the fluctuations in the values of land around towns, of the strict control by the town of adjacent agricultural labor, the low wages of the peasantry which operated to keep down the price of labor in the towns, the tendency of small towns and rural villages to welcome incomers and outside trade, as it was the policy of the great towns to exclude them.

Thus a patrician class grew up in the towns. This patriciate cunningly manipulated the regulations of the gilds so as to exclude lower class workmen or traders and assure themselves of monopolistic control of the gild. This was done by recourse to various practices. The entrance fee for membership in the gild was raised to a sum which made it prohibitive for the small man. It was also made more difficult for a workman to become a master by requiring the execution of a *chef d'oeuvre* as a qualification. Professedly this requirement was to preserve quality of work by shutting out all but highly proficient workmen. Actually it was a cartel which barred out all whom the controlling clique wished to exclude. The *chef d'oeuvre* became more and more difficult, so that many artisans were prevented from becoming masters. Then mastership tended to become perpetuated in the same families. The rules were modified in behalf of a master's son, who paid a small fee, much less than that required of an ordinary workman, and who was exempted from the *chef d'oeuvre* if he had had the "right experience." Thus the gilds gradually became a close corporation and mastership an hereditary qualification.

As the gilds multiplied in number and grew richer, more and more they escaped from the control of the governments, whether that government was of royal or of feudal nature. As early as the thirteenth century Bologna passed laws for the punishment of nobles who should offend a gild. This aroused Salimbene's aristocratic spirit to anger, and he declared, "But let the commonality dread lest God's wrath come upon them, for they do against the scriptures (Levit. XIX, 15)." Philip IV was the last king of France who successfully regulated the gilds. They broke the power of the counts of Flanders in the middle of the fourteenth century. The result was that the gilds almost everywhere came to be regulated by the towns. But this condition was a brief one. It was not long before the shoe was on the other foot, and the towns came to be controlled by the gilds. Once in possession of power the first care of the gilds was to establish monopoly of commerce and industry, to limit it to the necessities of the local market, to eliminate competition, either by refusing burgher rights to those who would not conform with such regulations, or by imposing prohibitive tariffs.

Suffrage and eligibility to office was limited to gild members. Municipal legislation was manipulated in the interest of the gilds. Local statute confirmed by law the class regulations governing the *chef d'oeuvre*, fixed wages, the hours of work and the term of apprenticeship. Wages were lowered, and if the wage-earners "struck," outside workers were introduced to keep wages down. The hours of labor were lengthened, not uncommonly from sunrise to sunset in summer. This would make a sixteen-hour day in summer and a long day even in winter. The great bell in the tower of the town hall signalled the opening and closing hour of work. Protracted terms of slackness often intervened. For example, in Flanders and Florence, if the supply of raw wool failed to arrive in season thousands of workmen would be thrown out of employment until the wool arrived.

Abuse of the custom of apprenticeship was a universal grievance. Apprenticeship is defined by Palgrave as "a system by which those intended to follow a particular occupation engage to serve and work under a master for a certain period, and the master engages to teach them during that period the industry or branch of industry in which he is occupied." [4] The original intention of this custom was to provide trained artisans in every craft and at the same time to prevent competition. Accordingly every master had in his service several boys— the number was regulated by gild rules—whom he took into his own home, clothed and fed, and in return trained them up in his own craft. They received no compensation during their period of service. In the beginning the term was two or three years. But the masters lengthened the term of required service of an apprentice to four, five, even seven years with the result that they got skilled employment for almost nothing from experienced apprentices. This evil was further aggravated by the cost imposed to acquire a certificate as a master work-

[4] *Dictionary of Political Economy*, I, p. 45.

man, by the making of a *chef d'oeuvre*. These illustrations make it abundantly evident that the gilds by the fourteenth century had become exploitative monopolistic corporations.

Within the trade everything hangs on the common interests of the masters—the system of apprenticeship, which provided relatively cheap labor; the strict control over the journeymen, prohibiting trade unions or labor on their own account, limiting their wages and their hours and days of work.[5]

All journeymen work was piece-work, and every worker had to produce a set output or be thrown out of a job. A great deal of industry was "cottage" or domestic industry: that is to say the workman worked at home in his own cottage, or in a shop attached to his home. Some industries, however, were such that cottage industry was impracticable. Such was dyeing, for example, which required vats, boilers, presses, *etc.*, and thus more apparatus and more room to work in than an ordinary workman could provide.

As the gilds became more and more narrow and exclusive they made more and more severe regulations. While the gilds aimed to procure as many advantages as possible for themselves, they likewise endeavored to maintain an equality between the masters. No one was permitted to make greater profit than another. The masters of the trade were protected not only against competitors and laborers but against each other, and hence the elaborate provisions against selling on credit, against forestalling and cornering, on the fixing of prices and qualities, on the social functions which fostered their common interests. The gilds guarded lest a master personally enrich himself by too sharp bargaining. Every purchase of materials had to redound to the profit of the entire gild. Commonly the gild purchased in large lots and distributed to the masters. But great as was the influence of these capitalistic gilds, there was one point in which they differed sharply from modern capitalistic concerns—they were purely local in organization. Their monopoly was a city monopoly. A classification of the sources of gild history is needed. Neither the chronology of gild documents, nor the differences between the privileges conferred by the town authorities and the regulations emanating from the gilds themselves have been sufficiently accentuated by historians hitherto. The fact that each town as such had its own special trade policy has not been adequately recognized by economists.

The gilds also tried to maintain the good reputation of a product and decided what conditions governed its fabrication and its sale, determined the length, the breadth of a bolt of cloth, fixed the

[5] *English Historical Review,* XXI, p. 776.

price of each piece, *etc.* In order to maintain the reputation of the gild only duly marked goods were exposed for sale. This is the origin of trade-marks. Shoddy goods and incompetent workmen were not unknown in the Middle Ages. Each craft might manufacture but one kind of article conformed to a certain standard. The master could not adopt new devices or patterns, for the gild rigorously imposed the rules of manufacture. A master could not ply two trades at the same time, and two masters could not combine to increase their profits. Everything was minutely regulated from the raw stuff to the manufactured article, from form and fashion down to price. While perhaps the public was protected by this expert inspection of goods before marketing, on the other hand the requirements of rigid uniformity and suppression of competition checked inventiveness and abridged liberty.

The great gildsmen who controlled the city administration sponsored much wise local legislation.

Civic markets were erected, prices regulated and fixed, and the inspection of wares was also undertaken by the civic authorities. It was necessary for all workers that the food supply should be adequate, and accordingly this was the first care of the administration. They even went farther in most towns and provided municipal mills, bakeries, and slaughterhouses. Nor were the special claims of the industrial workers neglected At a later period we find civic oil mills, fulling mills, grinding mills, saw mills, as well as municipal pressing, dyeing and shearing houses, and frames for cloth dressing. The maintenance of the quality of the raw material formed part of the scheme, and craftsmen were forbidden to take materials or half finished products which had not been stamped by the town authorities, who also sealed the finished article, whether cloth or metal. Their object was to ensure food for all, good raw material for the worker, and protection to the consumer.[6]

But one must not be deceived by appearances. There is no analogy between this policy and modern municipalism. The aim of the latter is philanthropic, or at least hygienic, and looks to the benefit of the poorer classes. The former "was prompted by fear that private enterprise might fail to supply at reasonable cost the necessities of life for the labor which was so essential to capital."

In addition, rich citizens took a pride in promoting local improvements like paving streets, water supply, and sewers, and in erecting magnificent public buildings like hôtels de ville, market houses, and hospitals. In 1338 Florence had thirty hospitals, some of ecclesiastical but more of lay foundation. The *Calimala* alone supported nine hospitals. A light side of gild activity was the social diversions of the gilds. They played a prominent part in public festivities. On June 6,

[6] Rev. of Inama Sternegg, III, pt. 2 in *Economic Journal*, XII, pp. 77–78.

1313, a great celebration was held in Paris when the three sons of Philip IV were knighted; the rhymed chronicle of Geoffrey of Paris has left a description of it. The gilds paraded before the king, each with its special insignia: the leather workers represented characters of the *Roman du Renard;* the weavers depicted scenes from the *Old* and *New Testament*; other gilds depicted Hell, Paradise, *etc.,* on their floats.

The gilds not only took part in all the festivals, but they also played a political part. When the city of Paris, in order to pay the aide of the king, in 1301, imposed upon the inhabitants a *taille* of 100,000 livres, 24 selectmen were chosen from the various gilds—bakers, wine-sellers, corn factors, *etc.,* to control the collection of the tax.

The gild system was spread over all Europe wherever commerce and industry were found in the fourteenth and fifteenth centuries. For, as has been well said: "All highly developed economy is an urban economy. . . . To feudalism belongs the economy of the townless countryside." [7] The gilds in the German towns were no less numerous than those of Italy and Flanders. Little or no difference can be discerned between North and South- Germany. Frankfort had 137, Nuremberg 96, Riga 90, Stralsund 113, Hamburg 114, Lübeck 129. Everywhere where the gild system prevailed, the town governments were controlled by them. The members of the gilds, with their families, formed a local patriciate, a society composed of the upper bourgeoisie, which was rich, politically dominant and socially influential, and intermarried with the local feudal aristocracy to form a single society. The wealthy merchant class became a patriciate, ruling both trade and the local administration.

Between this patriciate and the lower working classes a great gulf was fixed. The "blue nails," as they were called, were economically exploited and socially despised by the patriciate. The arena of class conflict was no longer the country but the town, and the conflict was no longer, as it had been in the feudal age, between baron and peasant, but between the bourgeoisie and the disfranchised commonalty of the towns. It was a conflict between capital and labor as well as a conflict of classes. The feudal age had seen peasant revolts in the country-side. The fourteenth and fifteenth centuries saw riots and rebellions of the lower working classes in the great industrial centers. Against this rich and politically entrenched urban aristocracy the lower classes in the towns, the artisans, craftsmen, and small shopkeepers rebelled, both against the hegemony of the patriciate and against their waste and stealing of the public revenue. The struggle began in the last half of the thirteenth century, endured for over a hundred years, and termi-

[7] Spengler, *Decline of the West,* II, pp. 477, 484.

nated at the end of the fourteenth century with the victory of the patriciate and the gilds.

The delegates of the burgesses of the Prussian towns drew up in 1358 a severe ordinance to terrorize the journeymen who raised a cry about the improvement of their lot, every striker being condemned to have an ear cut off. At Danzig later appeared the coalition of the masters who bound one another to keep their workshops closed for a whole year to suspected workmen. In London in 1387 some journeymen formed themselves into a fraternity, thus declaring themselves in rebellion against the corporations and official gilds. Their example was followed but the bourgeois class lost no time in taking legislative measures in order to silence complaints and demands.[8]

In previous times every peasant revolt had failed; every jacquerie had terminated in bloodshed and suppression. The revolts of the commonalty of the towns, the rebellions of the working classes in the fourteenth century, succeeded no better.

The formation of the group mind among the lower working classes and their rebellion is a striking phenomenon of the fourteenth century. Medieval Europe in the last half of the fourteenth century was stirred almost everywhere by the spread of radical social and political ideas which flared into violent action in Florence between 1379–82, in France at Lyons, Paris, Rouen, and in Cologne and other cities of the Rhine in 1382. These were not risings of country folk, of peasantry, as formerly in the jacquerie and other peasant revolts. Only in England, which was economically and socially more backward than continental countries, did the revolt take the form of a peasant rebellion. They were workmen's riots and the towns were the seat of their manifestations. Crude radical social ideals of a communistic nature not infrequently were commingled with these actions. Many of the popular heresies of the fourteenth century were impregnated with such doctrines, as in the cases of the Flagellants and the Beghards. It was a class war, a war of the poor against the rich, of a crude work-a-day population inflamed with half-baked ideas of liberty and democracy in conflict with a rich bourgeoisie and town patriciate. "Never before the French Revolution," Pirenne has written, "did social hatred revel under more brutal and barbarous forms." Wylie says, "A strange wave of democratic agitation was rolling over Europe bearing crude and violent remedies against tyranny and misrule." Commingled with this agitation were highly emotional manifestations of religious excess like revivalism and the Flagellant outbreak. Heretical movements often were vehicles for expression of economic and social complaint against the wrongs under which the lower European classes labored. This interesting social revolution cannot be circumscribed within nar-

[8] Nys, *op. cit.*, p. 106.

row limits. We find acute manifestations of it in Italy, France, Flanders, Germany. It was a general condition throughout Europe—Worms (1300); Liège (1302); Spires (1304); Ulm (1327); Mainz and Strassburg (1332); Paris (1358); Augsburg (1368); Brunswick (1374); Cologne and Florence (1379); Paris, Rouen, Ghent (1382). It was a widespread movement of a century's duration.

Each and all of these manifestations appeared as simultaneous expressior.s of protest against the abuses for which those who had profited most by the communal revolution were responsible. It was a protest by the underlings, who had contributed to the growth and prosperity of the towns, but who saw the privileges of wealth, ease and comfort, and participation in a government which could secure those privileges, withheld from their grasp. In other words, it was a protest against wealth and power by those who did not have wealth and power but who felt themselves entitled to both; a democratic protest on the part of an economic and social class, which to-day we call the proletariat, against the favored social, economic and political position of another class, which to-day we call the upper middle class. Besides the simultaneity, another fact which strikes one is the universality of this phenomenon. What happened in Florence is exactly what happened in Ghent and Ypres. The same is the case in Germany, in the Hansa towns where the Hanseatic League was the supporter of the local merchant oligarchy. When an uprising took place in Brunswick in 1374 against the ruling council, some of whom were killed and others driven into exile, Brunswick lost its membership in the league and its merchants were excluded from all the markets under the league's control. Mercantile excommunication was a formidable weapon, and the men of Brunswick had to make humble reparation for their democratic aspirations before they could obtain readmission to the confederacy. The movement then was neither sporadic nor aberrant; it was general and was to have been expected. The differences appear only as each uprising is considered in detail. Especially in the matter of taxation the artisan had a grievance. In Flanders the indirect taxes on wine, beer, peat, and grain made up the most considerable part of the town budget, and since these fell most heavily upon the masses, they were looked upon by the people as a method of exploitation by the merchant oligarchy. Some figures for Ghent will make this clear:

1326—Total receipts...	63,000 livres.	Of this 48,000 in "maltôtes"
1333—Total receipts...	65,900 livres.	Of this 54,000 in "maltôtes"
1337—Total receipts...	69,000 livres.	Of this 37,000 in "maltôtes"
1338—Total receipts...	79,000 livres.	Of this 41,000 in "maltôtes"
1339—Total receipts...	139,000 livres.	Of this 38,000 in "maltôtes"
1342—Total receipts...	75,000 livres.	Of this 48,000 in "maltôtes"
1361—Total receipts...	103,000 livres.	Of this 38,000 in "maltôtes"

It must not be inferred that the lower working classes in the medieval towns were like dumb driven cattle. Far from it. The weavers especially were an active and intelligent class of workingmen everywhere in Europe. In France the word *tisserand* was equivalent to radical, and sometimes also meant heretic. The German word *zettel,* meaning the "warp" of a loom, gave birth to the verb *anzetteln,* meaning to contrive or to plot, literally to *warp* or twist a movement. The nature of a weaver's work required intelligence, artistic ability, technical skill, and a power of invention which is not required of the workmen of our machine age. He had some time to think. The environment in his rich and thriving town was not a drab and uninviting one. Whatever taste and feeling for art he had was stimulated by architectural beauty, the popular poetry, and the various festivals which were on every hand.

The close connection of the woollen trade with communistic ideas is a remarkable fact which can be traced through the course of the Middle Ages. . . . Capital was needed to carry it on, and hence the woollen worker became either a sweated workman, receiving the raw material from the dealer and delivering to him the manufactured article, or a cloth producer turned capitalist himself, and employing a large number of journeymen workmen. . . . In every conflict with the then existing municipal and state powers the weavers fought in the front ranks, and they were inclined to welcome any new departure which proclaimed war against the whole reigning order of society.[9]

But weavers made poor soldiers. Aeneas Sylvius in 1451 wrote scornfully of the Taborites in Bohemia:

There are 4000 men in the town capable of bearing arms, but they have become craftsmen, and for the most part gain their living by the weaving of wool, so that they are valueless in war.[10]

The fourteenth century as well as the eighteenth had its philosophies. The literature on which the artisan fed his mind was such as to make him think. As early as the thirteenth century it went as far as to condemn the existing social and political structure as *"contraire à la nature."* This literature was definitely communistic. The *Roman de la Rose* had a conception of kingship which hardly considered the king as reigning by divine right. *Piers Ploughman* and its French counterpart *Le Songe du Vergier* preached the deposition of kings who governed badly. In England were the Lollards, John Ball and Wat the Tyler. In Flanders Van Maerland and the author of the *Spieghel Historical* were outspoken communists of a not very clear-headed type.

[9] Kautsky, *Communism in Central Europe,* p. 54.
[10] *Opera,* p. 662, cited in Kautsky, *Communism in Central Europe,* p. 75.

It is hardly to be supposed that these ideas remained local. Where goods are exchanged so are ideas. There were Gantois in Paris and London. The Fraticelli, the radical mendicants, everywhere took the side of the common people.

They traded on the public discontent. Two and two they tramped the country. . . . Their capacious cowls were stuffed with a little stock of purses, gloves, "*mitaines*," girdles and knives. With these they wheedled their way into the hearts of the women, while in the taverns and places of public resort their music, their physicking both for man and beast, their easy morality and their general good fellowship assured them a ready welcome from the men. They joined in every gossip and mixed in every throng. . . . Thus if they would, they could excite and exasperate the people to the verge of rebellion.[11]

News travelled rapidly in the fourteenth century. The artisan became conscious of his rights as an individual. He became sullen or furious. There was nothing in his ideals to restrain him from using force. Oath-breaking nobles and princes and oath-releasing popes set no example. The bourgeois had shown that rights to which one aspires can be had by force or purchase, and the artisan was not in a position to purchase. He would secure his rights by force of arms, and destroy inequality and privilege.

Florence, as the most industrialized city of Europe, was the most restless and revolutionary. But Paris and Ghent were not far behind it and soon caught up with Florence in political democracy and social radicalism. Throughout this period of discontent when the balance of Europe was unsteady, and urban revolutions were in the air, when workers began talking of natural rights and self-government, the Florentine common laborers were constantly on the verge of revolt. In the first quarter of the fourteenth century we find the working classes in Florence forming trade unions in order to compel concessions from the employers. But the latter, who controlled the government, promptly secured legislation in suppression of such combinations. The richness of the vocabulary used to describe these workmen's associations throws light on how they were regarded by the merchants: *conventicula, lega, dogona, fratellanza, congiura, cospirazione, compagnia, comunella* and *monopolio*. It illustrates also the popularity of the idea of association.[12] This attitude toward association is also exhibited by legislation. In a Florentine statute of 1324 we read: "since frequently under the pretense of lawfulness, violence is practised, every league or society of persons is forbidden if not sanctioned by the public authorities." The

[11] Wylie, *History of the Reign of Henry IV*, I, pp. 272–73.
[12] Rodolico, "The struggle for the right of association in fourteenth century Florence," *History*, VIII, p. 179.

statutes of the *Arte della Lana* (1334) declared that leagues and confederations of workmen were contrary to St. Paul's precepts concerning brotherly love and Christian charity and deplored that too often secret statutes within the gild were made that recognized every one's liberty to work without being subject to the officials and laws of the *Arte*. In 1338 the statutes of the *Lana* prohibited any assembly of workmen even for religious purposes. In 1345 Ciuto Brandini, a woolcarder, with nine others in the employment of the *Lana,* were put to death for attempting to organize the wool carders, wool combers, and other wool laborers into associations. Foreign workingmen were imported as "scab" laborers in order to break the attempts to form unions. The great gilds aimed at expansion of trade, with protective tariffs. The small gilds and the common people detested the wars, which increased taxation and were profitable only to the big manufacturers and the idle rich who lived on their investments instead of by trade.[13]

The bankruptcy of the Bardi and Peruzzi and many other banking houses seriously compromised the upper class, and in 1346 the populace rose against the bourgeoisie, and brought about a democratic revolution, or rather ran amuck. Of the eight priors of the city only two were given to the bourgeoisie; three were allotted to the lower gilds, and three to the common workingmen. This revolution marks the eclipse of the nobles. Many families even changed their names. "See," wrote Villani, the historian, "what becomes of the government of a town when it has artisans, day-laborers and idiots for its lords."

The oligarchic faction rallied and tried to seize the political offices. Then the Black Death befell and for a time everything was paralyzed. Slowly Florence recovered, and resumed its conquering policy towards its neighbors, especially Pisa, which was dealt a heavy blow by the opening of the port of Telamone in 1356. Civil discord soon broke out again. The quarrel of the Ricci and Albizzi families involved the whole city. The Albizzi championed the rich bourgeoisie, the Ricci sustained the cause of the lesser gilds and the masses. With the disappearance of the old noblesse the ancient military aristocracy had passed away and the upper class was undividedly capitalistic.

Things came to a climax in the tumultuous years 1379–82 in the rebellion of the Ciompi,[14] which was at once a democratically engineered political revolution, an economic revolt of the poorer classes against the rich, and a social insurrection of the lower classes against those above them. For three years Florence was in a state of turbulence and civil strife. But by 1382 the great gilds and the *popolani*

---

[13] In Germany this class was called *lediggänger,* or loafers.
[14] The derivation of this word is uncertain. It seems to have been a slang word for wool-carder.

grassi had won out. The rioters included all the lower classes. Macchiavelli estimated that there were 6,000 in one single night's uproar.

The story of the tumult is, briefly, that the mob got control of the city. All business was discontinued, shops were closed, homes fortified and valuables taken to churches and monasteries for safe-keeping. The council became alarmed and considered a redress of grievances. The mob was unruly, went about the city burning and pillaging, broke open prisons and sacked the monastery of Agnoli and the Convent of S. Spirito. Luigi Guicciardini, who had succeeded Salvestro de Medici as *galfonier* of justice, attempted to quiet the people in a speech telling them that their demands had been granted. He seemed to have succeeded and the signory ordered that arms be relinquished, that the shops be opened, and that strangers return to their homes. The mob, still unsatisfied, burned the houses of Guicciardini and others, destroyed the records of the wool trade, and presented further demands. These, too, were granted. The reforms could not go into effect, however, without the consent of the council of the commune, and the law forbade the assembly of two councils on the same day so the meeting had to be deferred. The following day while the council was considering the list of demands the meeting was interrupted, the officers fled for their lives, and the plebs gained control of the palace.

A poor wool-carder, Michele Lando, barefooted and in rags, was at the head of the mob and led them up the steps of the palace. Finding themselves in possession of the palace, they elected Lando *galfonier*. He quieted the mob and introduced reforms, but ruled only a short time, from June 20 to August 31, 1379.

The Ciompi uprising was half strike and half revolution. They demanded the right to form themselves into gilds and to participate in the government. Three new gilds were established: (1) the tailors, shearers, and barbers; (2) wool-combers and dyers; and (3) the Ciompi, which meant all the rest of the lowest class workers. Of the eight priors in the city government, not as before, three were to be chosen from the greater gilds, three from the *arti minori*, and two from the new gilds. Apparently the proletariat and minor gilds had won. But when the revolutionaries' leader, Lando, who was something of a demagogue, resigned, and their leaders began quarrelling among themselves, the vigilance committee, which was controlled by the aristocracy and had dictatorial power, refused to execute the petition of the common class. In the next election the aristocratic party won out, and by 1382 the aristocracy was sure of its power. The luckless leaders of the rebellion were proscribed, notable among whom were Lando and Strozzi. One hundred and sixty-one executions followed. The new gilds were abolished, and by 1393 one may say that the oligarchy was completely in control. Another revolt of the populace under the

Medici in 1397 failed, leaving the magnates definitely entrenched. The aristocracy ruled, but it was always in danger of an uprising under the leadership of some demagogue of these ill-treated common laborers. The way was prepared for the Medici, who were to rise to power through the proletariat's assistance. The Medici capitalized the proletariat's discontent to make themselves princes in all but name. The exhaustion of both factions and the widespread wish for quiet after so much internecine strife paved the way for the mild tyranny of the Medici. Florence preferred peace to liberty.

The rising of the working classes in Paris in 1382 differed from the rebellion of the Ciompi in Florence in that it had a particular rather than a general grievance. But the result was similar. The immediate occasion was resort by the government to the *fouage* and odious sales-taxes again after their abolition in 1380.

Charles V on his deathbed had abolished the *fouage*. On November 14, 1380, the regents were also compelled to abolish the sales-tax upon merchandise in order to abate popular clamor. But the crown could not live without extraordinary taxes, and even if the war against the English were suspended, hostilities yet continued in Brittany. The states-general met at the end of the year 1380 and voted a new *fouage*. The tax was levied, but the amount collected was not sufficient. Then the duke of Anjou reëstablished indirect taxes upon the sale of merchandise and a thirtieth upon salt. These taxes fell heavily upon the lower classes of the towns. The crown had attempted to get the consent of the provost of the merchants and the chief bourgeois and had demanded the consent of the gilds. But they all replied evasively. Accordingly on February 28, 1382, an edict was promulgated and on March 1 the collection of the tax began. That very day Paris revolted. A collector attempted to impose the tax upon an old woman who was selling watercresses in the market; he was set upon and murdered. Other collectors met the same fate. The crowd increased and poured into the Place de Grève, assailed the Hôtel de Ville, and seized twelve thousand leaden mallets which Hugues Aubriot, the provost of the king, had stored there at the time of one of the English raids in France. The furious people committed a thousand excesses. It massacred some Jews and some women; it seized tax lists and account books, jewels, and precious stuffs. The city gates were closed and chains hung across the streets.

The upper class bourgeoisie, who were better minded, attempted to stop these scenes of disorder. Militia of the corps des métiers patrolled the streets with arms under command of their captains of fifty and their captains of twelve and disarmed the *maillotins*. The king, who was at Vincennes, was petitioned to redress these grievances, and promised to return to the "Golden Age of St. Louis," that is to say, to abolish all these new taxes. He also promised amnesty, and the leaders of the movement alone were punished. Order was finally reëstablished after a process of cruel repression. Various persons were beheaded under the pretext that they had been parties or leaders of the movement, and the amnesty of the government was bitterly complained of.

Rouen gave the signal on St. Matthews' Day, February 24, 1382. At the head of the revolt were the coppersmiths and the drapers. The movement spread through the streets of the city. The tocsin was sounded, and the mob pillaged the houses of the leading bourgeois, broached the wine casks, and poured the wine in the streets. Finally the rioters raided the ghetto and plundered the stores of the Jews. This first rising passed, and the more moderate bourgeois entered upon the scene. They forced the chapter of Rouen to renounce an annual rent which was collected from the markets and mills in the city; the abbot of St. Ouen renounced the rights of justice which he exercised in the city. In a great meeting held in the cemetery of St. Ouen the new charter was read and all swore to observe it. The popular anger declined, the rising spent itself and Rouen waited with anxiety to see what the king would do. This rising was called the "Harelle" from an old French word signifying sedition, or trouble.

Peace being restored in Paris, the court went to Normandy to punish Rouen. Before the entry of Charles VI into the city the leaders of the revolt there had been beheaded and their heads set up on the city gates. The great bell in the belfry, which had given the signal for the rising, had been taken down. After Charles VI made his entrance on March 29, 1382, the reprisals continued; there were more executions. The king suppressed the commune of Rouen; the city lost its autonomy and was put under a royal bailiff; this was to remain Rouen's government for centuries. The people were compelled to pay a very heavy fine. The estates of Normandy were forced to lay new taxes upon the sale of merchandise, salt, and drinkables; the commerce and industry of Rouen were well-nigh ruined. The gilds of Rouen had formerly received their statutes from the mayor; the bailiff and viscount ordained these regulations and the gilds lost their independence. Henceforth they were subject to the king, but there was an advantage in the change. The new regulations were less strict and the town favored outside workingmen who wanted to ply their craft.

After Rouen had been punished, the regents sought to humble Paris, but their vengeance could not be applied until after Charles VI's expedition in Flanders, when the king triumphed over the Ghenters in the famous battle of Roosebeke, November 29, 1382. The turbulent Parisians had hoped for a Flemish victory and had corresponded with Ghent. After the victory of Roosebeke they awaited their punishment.

The provost of the merchants, the échevins, and about 500 bourgeois dressed in festal robes, went out to meet the king, when, on January 11, 1383, he prepared to make his entrance into Paris. They wanted to conduct the king into the capital under a magnificent canopy, but the king brutally ordered them to clear the road and to get back to Paris.

Accompanied by twelve thousand men, Charles VI entered Paris as though it had been a conquered city, over the ruins of the dismantled gate of St. Denis. The punishment of Paris then began. All the chains that were hung across the streets were removed and taken to Vincennes; the people were compelled to bring their arms to the Louvre or to the Châtelet; hundreds of arrests were made and the prisons were filled. There were many executions.

On January 20, Charles VI caused a series of new taxes to be cried through the streets—12 pence *per livre* on all merchandise offered for sale; twenty *sous* upon each measure of salt; 12 *sous* on each *queue* of wine sold at retail. These taxes were paid at once and without opposition.

Moreover, the municipal privileges of Paris were abolished. By an ordinance of February 27, 1383, the offices of provost of merchants and of the échevinage were legislated out of existence. The trades, or crafts, which had taken part in the insurrection were all of them smitten. "In our city of Paris henceforth there shall be no *maître des métiers.*" Thus the trades became free in Paris and over these free trades the provost alone had jurisdiction. It was forbidden to form any confraternity, exactly as Philip IV had interdicted them before. Even religious associations were prohibited for fear that they would become centers of plotting. The captains of twelve, the captains of forty, the captains of fifty, formerly employed for the patrol of the city were suppressed; the king henceforth policed Paris.

Terror continued to hang over Paris during all the month of February. Every day three or four persons were executed. Finally on March 1, 1383, a great assembly was held in Paris before the Court of the Palace; one occupant at least for every house in Paris had to be present, which indicates that there must have been many lodging houses in Paris at this time. The chancellor Pierre d'Agemont, in a long harangue, related all the crimes committed by the Parisians since 1380, and then announced a general pardon, from which, however, forty persons were excepted. The others who were accused escaped death by the payment of a very heavy fine which ruined them.

Other towns were also punished by the king because they had followed the example of Paris. Royal commissioners went around making investigation. Laon, Beauvais, and Orléans were heavily fined. Amiens was deprived of its communal government.

There was also a strong movement of agitation in the South. Languedoc protested against the exactions of the duke of Anjou, who was king's lieutenant there. When the duke of Berry was appointed lieutenant in the name of Charles VI there were new troubles at Béziers, Carcassonne, and Nimes. Marauding bands profited by these disorders and haunted the forests. They were recruited from among the unemployed workmen of the faubourgs. In 1383 these marauders were reduced, heavy fines were imposed in the senéchaussées of the South and upon the localities most compromised; these fines were levied as late as 1387. Since the Albigensian crusade Languedoc had not experienced such a régime.

Meantime, violence had broken out in Flanders, especially in Ghent. Flanders had gone through two previous revolutions, one in the time of Philip IV, in which the working classes and the count Louis de Dampierre were united against the bourgeois; the second, between 1339–45, in which, under the leadership of James Van Artevelde, the bourgeois and the workingmen were combined against the count and threw themselves into the arms of Edward III of England. A third revolution, between 1375–85, had to clarify the atmosphere before the dukes of Burgundy were able firmly to establish themselves. In this third revolution the cleavage was between the working classes and the bourgeois or patriciate. It was a democratic rebellion and a social war. The revolt in 1382 was the climax of a series of bitter conflicts between the employers and the proletariat class of daily wage-earners and casual laborers. It was not a war against French domination, although it tended to become so with the Flemish marriage of the French prince, Philip, duke of Burgundy. Nor was it a political struggle. It was a conflict of classes, between the local noblesse, the rich merchant-burghers, and the tax-gatherers on one hand and the lower working classes on the other. Commingled with the latter was a certain proportion of free peasants in West Flanders who feared the tax collector but were not troubled by industrial depression nor worried lest they be thrown out of work or their wages be reduced. Between thousands of artisans and the rich patriciate in many towns, great and small, in Flanders, a political, social, and economic gulf was fixed. The artisans, having no voice in local government, no membership in the gilds which had become enormously rich corporations employing thousands of hands at low wages and for long hours of work, rebelled in 1382. In the first revolution Bruges had first place. In the second and third Ghent was the key to the situation.

Sporadic local uprisings had preceded the great rebellion of 1382, as in 1359 at Ghent and Bruges, in 1366 and 1377 at Ypres. The immediate occasion of the uprising in Flanders was the levy of a special tax upon Ghent by the count to defray the cost of a great tournament to be held on Whitmonday, 1379. Ghent refused to pay it, and the count in anger appealed to Bruges, promising in return for the grant to further Bruges' plan to cut a canal to connect the Lys above Ghent with Bruges and so with the sea. One needs only to examine the map to perceive that this canal, while improving the commerce of Bruges, would have cut off Ghent from much of the produce of Artois and Walloon Flanders which hitherto had found its outlet by the Scheldt. Furthermore, the commercial rivalry between Ghent and Bruges was aggravated by the political antagonism between them. In Ghent the lower classes controlled the town—it was democratic—while Bruges was governed by the local oligarchy of rich bourgeois who controlled the gilds.

Ghent grew furious. The staple of wheat established there was almost certain to be removed to Bruges if the canal were constructed. The bargemen of the lower Lys and the Scheldt were up in arms. Meanwhile the canal was begun by the Brugeois. But after four months of digging a mob of Ghenters attacked the laborers and stopped the construction. This event forced the issue between the count and Ghent, which, once the die was cast, lost no time in organizing rebellion in the whole country. A mob of armed workingmen calling themselves the Whitehoods, under the leadership of one Jahn Yoens, captain of the rivermen, compelled Termonde, Alost, Courtrai, Poperinghe, Ypres and finally even Bruges to join the cause. All urban Flanders was in revolt. In the turmoil a greater man than Yoens arose in the person of Philip Van Artevelde, son of the famous James Van Artevelde. He was well-to-do, living off his rents and the farming of some polders which he owned. He had no economic grievance which impelled him. He may be regarded as a social democrat of that time whose own ideas, more than events, pushed him into the limelight.

It was almost a lost cause when he took hold. For the count, partly by military prowess and partly by adroitly playing the population of the flat countryside against the towns, and the small towns against the larger ones, had gradually acquired an ascendancy. When Philip Van Artevelde took hold of things Ghent stood almost alone in a state of siege threatening reduction by starvation. Active measures to redress the balance of fortune were taken. A body of horsemen, half scouts, half foragers, called *reizers,* was established under a captain named Ackermann, another well-to-do landowner having sympathy with the lower classes like Philip Van Artevelde, and a river fleet organized under a freshwater "admiral" named Koolman, whose particular function was to revictual the half-starved city. Artevelde himself took military command. The count was at Bruges with an army eight times as large as the militia force which Artevelde had. But paucity of numbers was compensated for by effective leadership and desperate courage. A bold attack routed the count; Bruges was captured by the rebels and put to pillage. The tide of events in Flanders was completely turned within a few weeks. For almost all the towns gave in their adhesion to Ghent. Artevelde was declared *Reward* or Guardian of Flanders.

The revolution was an accomplished fact. But the tables were soon turned. The duke of Burgundy, the count's son-in-law, persuaded his nephew Charles VI of France to interfere. Philip Van Artevelde with the precedent of his father's policy before him, appealed to Richard II of England. His commissioners were instructed to ask from Richard, "as lawful king of France," the confirmation of Ghent's liberties and those of other Flemish towns. But no English aid was forthcoming. It may be that the governing class in England had had its fill of social-democratic ideas in the Peasants' Revolt of the previous year. Froissart so says. The French victory at Roosebeke on November 27, 1382, ruined the social-democratic movement in Flanders, although Ghent even after that fought furiously under Franz Ackermann, the sole popular leader left, for Philip Van Artevelde had perished at Roosebeke.

The overthrow of the Ciompi in Florence, the crushing of Paris and Rouen, the day of Roosebeke, were mourned in many shops and factories in Europe. The working classes in the industrial places of Europe had everywhere failed. The bourgeoisie, the capitalists, the employers, the entrepreneur class were in the saddle. Not until the sixteenth century was another such general movement in Europe to occur. Then the Reformation became the vehicle for widespread expression of social discontent.

CHAPTER XVIII

BANKING DURING THE RENAISSANCE

IN the introduction to the present work an attempt was made to show how the origin and genesis of capitalism is to be found as far back as the first century of the Crusades, and in the case of Italy the elements of it may be discerned as early as the eleventh century. It was shown that the fiscal operations of the papacy probably inaugurated the new development; but that the new fiscality of the papal curia would have been impossible without the commercial and industrial awakening of Europe. The papal moneys created the first great available reservoir of resources upon which investment could draw, but the springs and streams contributory to that great pool flowed from the new commerce and industry. Other contributory factors were the conversion of ground-rents, formerly paid in service, into money rents as serfs and villeins became tenant or free farmers, and perhaps even more the unearned increment attached to urban holdings as the towns increased in population and commerce and industry developed within them. Another ancillary factor was increased output of the precious metals, notably in Germany and Bohemia, owing to improved methods of mining.

Commerce—not provincial or national commerce—but international commerce was the foundation of fourteenth and fifteenth century capitalism and the base of the banking operations of the age. Commercial exchanges are a product of a high economic civilization. As a necessary factor for their development commodities must have become *fungibilia* as against *consumptibilia;* that is, they must have been produced with the view of creating commodities of average social or market value, which is only possible with a considerable degree of specialization of labor. This was the case in the mining industries, and also in the manufacture of woolen and linen goods, especially fustians, all of which were highly developed in Germany long before England thought of introducing German miners and fustian weavers with their skill and their methods. Above all other forms of commerce the wool trade and the manufacture of woolen goods were identified with early banking. It was this fact which made Florence the premier banking city of Europe in the thirteenth, fourteenth and fifteenth centuries. The competition of the banking houses there, which were family firms, was the immediate origin of the famous rival parties—the "Blacks" and the "Whites" in Dante's time. And when the Cerchi formed a coalition to combat the monopoly of the three most influential fiscal families of Florence, every other firm ranged itself on one side or the other. The old party names of Guelf and Ghibelline, although they survived, had lost all their ancient significance.[1]

The Lombards had been in the field of the new finance before the Florentines, but the city on the Arno, thanks to its enormous woolen industry, was the first to establish great banking firms, to "develop cosmopolitan trade in goods in combination with cosmopolitan banking practices,"[2] to elevate money-lending from usurious loans to real investment. Florence used her widespread and highly organized business, which covered nearly all Europe, to extend her banking business in conjunction with her commerce. In this development of Florentine banking business, which, at the end of two generations from its beginning around 1250 to the first decade of the fourteenth century, already controlled the credit of all Christian Europe, the *Calimala* and later the *Lana* gild played a rôle hardly less important than that of the Roman Church. The *Lana* first showed the Arno merchants how to win a foremost economic position in England as in the kingdom of Naples. The business of buying raw wool and of manufacturing and selling dressed woolen goods became so lucrative that already in the twelfth century the *Arte di Calimala* included the greatest merchants and had given rise, through its stimulation of commerce, to a number of smaller corporations, including the *Arte del Cambio,* or gild of bankers and money-changers.

The relations between the Florentine banking and Florentine wool trade were interlocking. If the wool trade through its profits assisted the accumulation of capital in sufficient quantities to make it available for money-lending purposes, the interest and gains from the banking operations helped provide the funds which enabled the Arno merchants and industrialists to purchase raw wool and cloth in tremendous quantities, to establish large workshops employing thousands of artisans, and to win for Florence its foremost position in the wool trade.

The wealth of Florence did not give birth to the banking business of the Middle Ages, but it established it. In this field Florence defied all competition. In 1338 there were eighty firms doing a banking and exchange business. The most important were those of the Bardi and Peruzzi. At the end of the fourteenth century the amount of Florentine money in circulation was estimated at two million florins. The Florentines had exchanges everywhere. The Peruzzi alone had sixteen: London, Bruges, Paris, Avignon, Majorca, Pisa, Genoa, Venice,

---

[1] The Guelfs were the "Blacks"; the Ghibellines were the "Whites." See Gino Arias, in *Studi e documenti di storia del diritto.* Florence, 1901.

[2] Davidsohn, *op. cit.,* IV, ii, p. 227.

Famagusta, Cagliari, Naples, Palermo, Clarentza in the Morea, Rhodes, Cyprus, Tunis. Of their agents twenty-seven became priors, seven *gonfaloniers*. The extension of the letter of exchange was the work of Florentine bankers; it increased the security of commerce, and guarded against theft. Loans were readily made by this instrument of credit.

But international banking then, as now, was a speculative, precarious game. Politics as often spelled ruin as profit. Between 1298 and 1326 eighteen banking houses failed—in 1298 the Buonsignori and the Riccardi; in 1302 the Franzesi; in 1303 the Ammanati; in 1305 the Ardinghelli, the Solonanieri, and the Lamberti; in 1307 the Mozzi; in 1309 the Buoncorsi, the Faffi and the Ferrantini; in 1310 the Pulci and the Rimbertini; in 1313 the Sillimani; in 1317 the Macci; in 1318 the Cornacchini; in 1321 the Cerchi Bianchi; in 1326 the Pilastri.

The fall of Boniface VIII, the removal of the papacy to Avignon, the war between Philip IV and Edward I, the French intervention in Flanders, and the misrule of Edward II in England were primary factors in these collapses. In 1311 Edward II expelled the Riccardi and Frescobaldi from England.

In the kingdom of Naples conditions were no more satisfactory for the bankers of Florence. The splendor of the court cost so much that the king was forced to give over more and more political and economic privileges to the bankers, and members of the firms came to occupy important royal offices. At the same time, however, they conducted these offices in such a manner as to alienate the masses of the people and thus sowed the seeds of their own downfall. The beginning of the end is seen in the failure of the house of Scali in 1328. Somewhat later (1341) Florence became involved in a war with Pisa. This city had freed the town of Lucca from Florentine control and the latter wished to bring it back under its domination. Not being strong enough to accomplish the affair alone, Florence sought outside aid. A political crisis ensued which involved an economic one as well, and several of the houses went under. The larger houses survived the crisis, but were badly compromised when the king of Naples repudiated a debt of nearly 200,000 gold florins to the Bardi and Peruzzi. These two houses, however, the greatest in Florence, were able to tide over this adversity owing to their profitable operations in England where they had succeeded the fallen Riccardi and Frescobaldi and for a time caught the tide and rode to fortune.

The Bardi and Peruzzi had first appeared in England in 1290. Between 1290 and 1326 they advanced to the kings sums aggregating at least £72,631, of which only £4,926 was lent before 1311. As time went on the advantages of combination became apparent and they began to act in concert. This custom began about 1337 and was established by 1340. They stood well in the graces of Edward III (1327-77) during the early years of his reign and were accorded many privileges. The laws of the land were relaxed in their favor on several occasions so that they might be safeguarded in the collection of their debts. An example of this took place in 1327 when "the customers of Southampton were ordered to send to the king at once any money in hand of the customs of wool, hides and wool-fells, and of the new custom, and previous assignments notwithstanding, *'except those to the merchants of the Society of the Bardi of Florence.'*" This action of the king was taken in the face of statutes which limited the residence of foreign merchants in the realm and absolutely forbade the assignment of the customs to their credit.

The purposes to which the funds secured from the bankers were assigned were various. In November of 1331 the Bardi agreed to find 1,000 marks a month for the support of the royal household, to cover which they were granted the receipts of certain customs duties at London, Kingston-upon-Hull, Newcastle-upon-Tyne, Hartlepool, and Southampton. Other members of the royal family were supplied by the bankers. The queen, the queen-mother, and the earl of Chester were recipients of advances for which the king acknowledged his indebtedness. The main demands upon the bankers, however, were for carrying on the military operations of the government against France.

By 1336 the Peruzzi had become prominent in affairs, though they seem to have taken little active interest in financing Edward III before this date. They made advances in this year which were guaranteed by the income to be derived from certain parliamentary promises to the king. By the end of the first six months of the year it appears that the king was in their debt to the extent of £32,000. In 1337 their dealings took on added importance due to the increased demand for money growing out of the impending war with France. The only way in which the king could secure an adequate and extended supply of cash was through the manipulation of the wool trade, which was an operation possible only with the consent and coöperation of the Italian merchants who were deeply involved in that branch of business. In March of 1338 the king agreed with the two firms that he would deliver to them all the wool granted to him in England, which they were to sell for his profit.

This situation was the high-water mark of the fortunes of the Italians in England. Even at this time forces were at work in Italy, in France, and in England which conspired together to make their position increasingly untenable. The outbreak of the long war between France and England in 1337 placed the merchants in an embarrassing situation. They could not keep on good terms with both powers. The formal declaration of war saw the arrest of their representatives in

France, a durance from which they escaped only by the payment of huge sums to Philip of Valois. At the same time Edward III began to be more than ever remiss in payment of his debts, of which he insisted on incurring ever more and more. This double trouble was aggravated by the situation in Italy. Financial difficulties were encountered in the city state, and Florentine investments in Naples were endangered. The next development was a war with Pisa, the financing of which put several of the smaller companies out of business (1341), though the more important ones such as the Bardi and Peruzzi managed to keep their heads above water.

It is evident after 1341 that the situation of the Bardi and Peruzzi in England was becoming more precarious in equal ratio to the ever-mounting debts owed them by the king. His wars with Scotland and France not only prevented him from making payment on the debts which he had already contracted, but placed him in the position of requiring more and more funds. To this was added a growing resentment on the part of the rising native merchant class at the favors which the foreigners were receiving from the crown. The actual circumstances are uncertain; there is a possibility that there was a merchant conspiracy in which the king was involved. At any rate the deluge overtook the Italians. They seem to have requested an audit of their accounts at some time between 1343 and 1345. The next development found all their agents in prison, without having any specific charges lodged against them except that they were indebted to the king for large amounts, which, however, Edward acknowledged were much smaller than the sums he owed them. He demanded payment by a fixed date, but later pardoned them. He did not take any measures toward alleviating their distress. It is plainly evident that the imprisonment of the Italians was not based on any misdoings which could not have been condoned, but was rather the result of a wish on the part of the authorities to get rid of a group which had become obnoxious to them.

This episode practically ended the active connection of the two companies with the crown, though they continued to trade in England in a private capacity for some time afterward. Some payments were made both to the Bardi and the Peruzzi after the crash, and they were enabled to make some recompense to the smaller companies which had been involved by their downfall. The Bardi fared less well in this respect than the Peruzzi, as they appear to have received only £150 in return for an acknowledged debt of £50,493 5s. 2½d. In June of 1346 the Peruzzi received £6,375 and in August of 1352 a further payment of £100. The repudiation of the English debt brought matters to a head and it was found necessary to liquidate the assets of the two firms. A panic resulted in Italy as the result of this famous bankruptcy, and a meeting was held at Florence which resulted in an agreement of September 6, 1347, whereby the Bardi paid about 30 per cent on their obligations and the Peruzzi about 20 per cent.

Thus we have seen how four great Italian companies were ruined by their dealings with the kings of England—the Riccardi of Lucca under Edward I, the Frescobaldi of Florence under Edward II, and the Bardi and Peruzzi under Edward III. Figures are available only for the failure of the Bardi and Peruzzi, showing that they advanced to the three Edwards during the years from 1290 to 1345 no less than £433,000. But one must multiply these figures by five in order to appreciate the actual magnitude of the collapse.

The effect of Edward III's repudiation of his Italian debts and the subsequent panic in Europe may be compared with the crash of the Barings in 1892 and our panic of 1893.

The panic in Florence extended far beyond Tuscany. For the ruined firms had branches almost everywhere. Only one banking firm in Florence survived this famous "Black Friday." This was the Medici. For as the transactions of the Bardi and Peruzzi grew in magnitude, partly in order to help them swing the ventures, partly perhaps in order to assure themselves against too great liability, the two major firms had drawn many other banking houses into their English deals. Nearly all of them were involved in the final collapse except the Medici, who at that time were not prominent enough to be considered. The obscurity of the Medici saved them, and upon the ruins of the other Florentine banking firms they rose to riches and to fame. Although the Medici became the princely dynasty of Renaissance Florence, gave two popes to the Holy See and two queens to France, their memory is to-day preserved principally in the three golden balls of the pawnbroker, for six gold balls were the banking and later the heraldic insignia of the Medici house. But the great day of the Medici did not arrive until the removal of the papacy to Rome in 1415.

When the Venetian fleet under command of the doge Domenicho Michael was besieging Tyre during the winter of 1124-25, the supply of money for the fleet was nearly exhausted and the sailors and marines were on the verge of mutiny. In this crisis, with that masterful spirit which so characterized him, Domenicho Michael stamped the seal of Venice upon bits of leather and pledged his word that the senate would redeem every one of these leathern rags—which it did. So far as I know, this is the earliest instance of fiat money in history. The marvel is that the device was not seized upon by Italian princes everywhere to recoup their finances.

Thirty years later (1157) in time of financial stress Venice raised money by a forced loan and established a bank to handle the certificates, which were guaranteed by the state and circulated as bonds.

The original subscribers to the loan were the first stockholders of the bank. What was founded at Venice in the twelfth century was an institution to handle the funded debt of the republic.[3] The state needed money to carry on war and forced loans were made from people who were able to advance the money. Certain revenues of the state, bearing interest, were given to the creditors as security. In the early thirteenth century the names of the creditors and the sums loaned were entered at the Camera degli Impresidi and these credits became negotiable.[4] It was not until 1318 that the term which designates formal banking (*bancherius*) occurs. On September 24 of that year the Venetian senate passed an act recognizing the legality of the receipt of deposits by the *campsores* and making provision for better security for depositors. But this does not signify the establishment of a public bank, but only the existence of an extensive private banking. It was by an act of April 11, 1587, that the so-called Bank of Venice (Banco di Rialto or Banco della Piazza) was established.

In Genoa, as in Venice, the first bank, the Bank of St. George, was established by the creditors of the state. Although not founded until 1407 when the French marshal Boucicault was in occupation, as early as 1371 there is evidence of the circulation of government bonds in Genoa. These *luoghi* increased in the adverse years which followed so that finally Boucicault, in order to stabilize things, consolidated the Genoese debt in this way. The mercantile element was the only stable element amid the party strife. Like the Bank of St. Mark's, the Bank of St. George was not a state bank but a private corporation whose eight directors were elected by the republic's creditors. Its powers were so great that they could not be touched by the government. The Bank of St. George was a state within a state, and far more honestly managed than the government. The magnificent Renaissance palace of the bank still adorns the Piazza Caricamento.

It has been stated by some authors that these first banks were not places of deposit but primarily places of discount for notes. If a merchant owed bills or planned to owe them, as soon as he had purchased stock or raw materials for manufacture, his own notes would not be sufficient to cover them, and his personal note would not pass acceptably. But if he exchanged his personal note for the note of some bank, paying for the transaction through discount, then he could obtain a commercial instrument which would pass from hand to hand. This is an erroneous opinion. There is plenty of early evidence for the double function of banks in the fourteenth century both as places of discount and as places of deposit. Thus Adam of Usk, an English bishop who

---

[3] Molmenti, *History of Venice*, p. 149; Lubbock, *The History of Money*, p. 801.
[4] Pardessus, *Lois Maritimes*, II, Introd., p. cxiii. Levasseur, *Histoire du Commerce de la France*, I, p. 134.

was in Rome about 1400, records in his *Chronicon* that "every man who had wealth kept his money in the merchant's bank ready to further his advancement." [5]

Although Venice funded its public debt and the republic's debentures were marketed through the Bank of St. Mark's, neither that institution nor the Bank of St. George was, strictly speaking, a state bank. Barcelona has the honor of having established the earliest state bank in 1401. This was the Taula di Cambi. The municipal funds deposited therein covered any contingency of loss to private depositaries.

As commerce and industry increased, as the wealth of Europe grew in volume, banks multiplied. In Venice we find private banking houses like the Soranzo, the Priuli, the Pisani, the Lippomani, the Sanudo, the Tiepolo. In Florence every other house was overshadowed by that of the Medici. During the pontificate of Nicholas V it held more than one hundred thousand florins of the wealth of the pope. Giovanni de' Medici left 179,221 gold florins; Cosimo I and Piero each nearly 250,000—and these sums after lavishing enormously upon stately buildings, libraries and works of art. So wide were the transactions of the Medici that they had a branch in Lübeck and another in Milan, which had to be abandoned in 1484 when Lorenzo de' Medici fell into financial and political difficulties. Lorenzo de' Medici shrewdly perceived the importance of low rates of interest in the promotion of business. He rarely charged over 15 per cent and frequently not more than 5 per cent. For this reason Florence was tolerant of the Jews. "A great city like Florence must have Jews," he once said. Owing to the Church's prohibition against exaction of interest—a law which, however, was as much honored in the breach as in the observance— it was convenient for business to have in the community Jews from whom money could be borrowed without compromise, "for when men fail to find money in that manner they are driven to cheating and stealing in order to obtain it," said Lorenzo.

The Medici enjoyed control of two great sources of wealth in the fifteenth century, namely, the power to tax the commercial and industrial wealth of Florence, and as bankers of the popes. The financial affairs of the pope were entrusted to the Roman bank of the Medici; the customs of Rome were farmed out to them and they enjoyed concessions in regard to the papal alum works at Tolfa. In 1472, however, the fiscal relations between the Medici and the popes were abruptly terminated. The breach was due to economic resentment. We have seen in a former chapter that the alum deposits at Tolfa were a lucrative source of the papal revenue and that Florence, having use for large amounts of alum for her dyeing industry, in 1472 made war

[5] *Chronicon*, p. 276.

upon Volterra when a deposit of alum was discovered there, and annexed the territory. Pope Sixtus IV promptly transferred the management of the apostolic exchequer to the bank of the Pazzi family, a business and social rival of the Medici in Florence.

Matters culminated in 1478 in the Pazzi conspiracy, which was an effort on the part of the Pazzi and their partisans, of whom the pope was secretly one, politically and financially to ruin the Medici. The career of Lorenzo de' Medici as a patron of letters and the arts was so great that we are led to think that the "Magnificent" (*Il Magnifico*) must have been a popular ruler. But this is not true. "He cared for no one and tolerated no rival. . . . He interfered in everything, even in the private life of the citizens and in their marriages; nothing could be done without his consent. In the work of casting down the mighty and raising up those of low degree," records Capponi, the Florentine historian, "he refused to act with that consideration which Cosimo had always been careful to observe." The Pazzi, fearing that Lorenzo would plot their ruin, connived against him. Francesco de' Pazzi, the head of the Pazzi bank in Rome, arranged the secret alliance with the pope, who warned them that the business might not be so readily accomplished as they hoped. The papal warning was a prophecy. For the Pazzi conspiracy failed. Lorenzo took terrible reprisal. The gibbet, the rack and the block for twenty-three days in Florence were at their fearful work. The Pazzi family was exterminated, and the wealth of the rival banking house confiscated by Lorenzo the Magnificent. But the Medici never recovered their grip on the papal finances.

The loss of the support of the Medici was embarrassing for the papacy. For the Holy Father by this time, in addition to being an Italian prince with certain sacerdotal authority and functions attached to his office, was also one of the richest princes in Europe, thanks to the thrifty way in which his spiritual prerogatives were capitalized, the sale of ecclesiastical benefices, the imposition of fees, *etc.* In the time of Sixtus IV every pontifical privilege or appointment was purchasable. "Our churches, priests, altars, sacred rites, our prayers, our heaven, our very God are purchasable," exclaimed a scholar of the time. Every office in the papal court had its price, and immense ingenuity was exercised in expanding this market. Sixtus IV bragged that "a pope needs only pen and ink to get what sum he wants." Innocent VIII surpassed his predecessor by establishing a special bank in Rome for the sale of pardons. The papal vice-chancellor when once asked why criminals were permitted to buy pardons instead of being punished, sanctimoniously answered: "God wills not the death of a sinner, but rather *that he should pay* and live."

The wealth of the Roman pontificate in the last half of the fifteenth century was a byword in Europe. Gold flowed into the papal coffers in such volume that there were no taxes in Rome. Much of the revenue derived from the jubilee in 1450 was devoted to the material embellishment of the city. The creation of thirty-nine cardinals by Leo X in 1517 brought him in over 500,000 ducats. When the pope died the Roman bankers had advanced him so much that they were almost ruined. The Bini had loaned him 200,000 ducats; the Gaddi 32,000; the Ricasoli, 10,000; the cardinals Armellini and Santi Quattro 150,000; cardinal Salviati, 80,000.

To the papacy of the high Renaissance, however, we must give the credit of first having established those charitable institutions or "mountains of mercy" known as *monti di pietà*. The earliest of these was founded by Pius II in Orvieto in 1463; that of Perugia was founded by Paul II in the next year. The Franciscans, ever the friends of the poor, were the promoters of these institutions. Sixtus IV opened one in Savona, his native place. In course of time we find others in Assisi, Mantua, Rimini, Ravenna, Pavia, Verona, Alessandria, Ferrara, Parma, Cesena, Montagnana, Chieti, Rieti, Narni, Gubbio, Monfelice, Brescia, Lucca, Aquila, almost always under Franciscan management. "The extraordinary rapid diffusion of these institutions," as Ludwig Pastor has written,[6] "is the best proof that they responded to a real want." But there was none in Florence. It was said that the Jews bribed Lorenzo de' Medici with the sum of 100,000 ducats. The way the Florentine Jews ground the faces of the poor at this time is shown by the fact that according to law they could charge $32\frac{1}{2}$ per cent for loans.

The popes found new bankers to succeed the Medici in the Fuggers of Augsburg. In a previous chapter it has been shown how the cities of southern Germany like Augsburg, Regensburg, Nuremberg, Ulm, waxed fat on commerce and industry in the fourteenth and fifteenth centuries, and had important commercial connections with Italy, Spain, and the Levant. It was natural for the history of the great Italian cities to be repeated in the great German cities. Prosperity created surpluses of money and this money was increased upon itself by loans at interest until in course of time the German cities, too, developed a banking business. Augsburg was easily first. Here, late in the Middle Ages arose those great banking firms of the Fugger, the Welser, the Hochstetter, the Ehinger, and others. Unlike the development in Italy, however, these famous houses owed their resources not to commerce, but to mining.

German mining, particularly silver mining, attained its first great prosperity in the thirteenth century; though important in some places during the fourteenth, that period was on the whole a time of retro-

[6] *History of the Popes*, V, p. 109.

gression. The cause of this failure was that with the rudimentary technique then available only the surface ore was taken, and within two or three generations the mine was exhausted. A second great period, which lasted from 1480–1570, was due to technical improvements. The mechanical inventiveness and technical skill which German mining developed are important points in industrial history. The oldest mines were shallow pits like quarries open to the sky. If the veins radiated out from the mother lode deep trenches called "coffins" were run out from the matrix metal. But such methods availed only for ore lying close to the surface, and shaft-mining became necessary. This "taxed to their utmost the rude machines for drainage then in vogue." If the mine were in the side of a hill and not too deep, a deep trench called a "level" was dug through which the water was run off. Otherwise a windlass was employed, turned either by human power or by horses, bringing up the water in leathern buckets. More effective, but more difficult, was the "adit" (from Latin, *aditus*, approach). This was a drainage tunnel driven through the hillside to the foot of the shaft. "The importance of the adit, not only in a technical sense, but as an incentive to permanent investment of capital in mining, cannot be exaggerated, and its introduction was encouraged by mineral law. But it was too expensive an improvement to be within reach of all, and even when it was employed its usefulness was limited, since when the shaft was driven deeper than the level of free drainage, pumps and windlass had to be employed to bring the water to the adit head." [7] The pump was a series of buckets fastened to an endless chain passing over a notched windlass or over a ratchet wheel. The "rag-and-chain" pump, consisting of an endless chain to which leathern balls were affixed at intervals so that it fitted tightly into a long pipe and was worked by a windlass at the surface, does not appear before 1480. This constantly elevated a column of water up the pipe. In a deep mine a series of such pumps was necessary. If conditions were favorable an overshot water-wheel was substituted for human or horse labor.

The greatest of these mining and banking companies of Germany was that of the Fuggers, who late in the fifteenth century and well down into the sixteenth dominated the money mart of Europe. This celebrated family arose in the middle of the fourteenth century in Augsburg in the person of Johannes Fugger, who was a linen weaver. His son Johannes, who died in 1409, branched out and became a dealer in linen textiles. He was an influential burgher in his native city and when he died left a fortune of 3,000 gold florins. His eldest son Andreas purchased a title of nobility, made a socially advantageous marriage and retired from trade. The business was carried on by his

[7] G. R. Lewis, *The Stanneries*, p. 10.

younger brother, Jakob (died 1460), who made the house of Fugger great. He had seven sons, of whom three—Ulrich, Georg, and Jakob II —enhanced the family fortune both by advantageous marriages and more advantageous loans to the emperor Maximilian I. Jakob Fugger II, who died in 1525, the great-great-grandson of the founder of the house, was probably the most influential financier that ever lived— greater than any Rothschild or Baring or Morgan of more recent times.

In 1494 the Fugger Company was formed. The Fuggers were the financiers of the Habsburgs and rode to fortune. Their loans were repaid by assignment of the silver from the mines of Schwag and Innsbrück at a price which was 25 to 30 per cent below the market value. In return for immediate cash the emperor mortgaged the future revenues of lands, mines and even cities, on which the Fuggers issued instruments of credit which circulated better than coin. The silver, copper, and iron mines of the Habsburg lands in Silesia, Hungary, Carinthia, Tyrol, Bohemia fell wholly into their control. The working of the silver mines in Tyrol began in 1487; copper mining in Hungary was begun in 1497. Soon afterwards the famous gold mine at Reichenstein was acquired. Two other Augsburger firms were at first associated with them, the Welsers and the Hochstetters. The former had begun the working of the mines at Schwag in 1448; at Salzburg, in 1460; in Saxony, in 1471; in 1492, in Bohemia, where the mines had been closed for eighty years because of the Hussite Wars. The Welsers also operated iron forges in Thuringia.

Modern monopolistic practices in business are strikingly illustrated in the operations of these German capitalists. Small mining competitors were bought out by the companies by the payment of the debts of the small operators. In 1498 we find the first attempt to build up a syndicate. The result was a copper combination. At the beginning of the sixteenth century the Fuggers controlled the mines and metal sources of Germany, Austria, Bohemia and Spain—the California, Nevada, Colorado, and Montana of Europe. They owned the quick-silver and silver mines of Almaden and Guadalcaucal in Spain; copper and silver in the Tyrol, and in Hungary. In 1505 they branched out into the East Indian trade. They were the Guggenheims of the age.

Although banking and mining soon absorbed the chief attention of the Fuggers, they still maintained the ancestral weaving and textile business, but added the manufacture of cotton goods to that of woolen and linen cloth, purchasing raw Egyptian cotton in Venice and transporting it to Augsburg for their looms there. In addition they traded in silk, furs, spices, citrus fruits from Spain, arms and ammunition. The emperor Maximilian at first would buy only red cloth from them, but the Fuggers insisted that he must also purchase cloth of other colors to make them fashionable and increase their sales, and the emperor yielded the point. Rare jewels and curiosities sometimes fell into their hands. Thus the Fuggers picked up from the Swiss the girdle taken from the body of Charles the Bold, when he was killed at the battle of Nancy and his camp was plundered by the Swiss soldiery, and sold it to Maximilian.

The Fugger operations in Hungary are the most interesting because there they were not engaged as middlemen but as principals, in partnership with Johann Thurzo, who had got a concession of an old waterlogged copper mine in northwestern Hungary from the crown and the bishop of Fünfkirchen.

We hear of the introduction of capital for the new plant, the operation by which the silver was separated from the copper, and above all of the routes through Pomerania and the Baltic, or through central Germany to the Netherlands, or southwards to Venice. . . . The Venetian trade after a time fell off owing to the jealousy of the Tyrolese government, which wanted an exclusive market, but that with the Netherlands reached enormous proportions. When the Fuggers obtained control of the Swedish copper also, they had practically established a monopoly. . . . The Hanse towns as a rule resented the attempt of the Fuggers to capture the trade of Novgorod and their contribution to the growing prosperity of Antwerp. Yet if Lübeck plundered their ships, Danzig and Hamburg welcomed their caravans of copper. . . . They established an efficient postal service, supplementing or supplanting the official system of Thurn and Taxis, and their early information of important events was of great service to their patrons and doubtless to their own speculations.[8]

It was inevitable that the Fuggers would be drawn to Rome. The breach between the papacy and the Medici was their opportunity. Ulrich and Jakob were certainly in Rome before 1494, but it was in that year that the Roman branch of their banking house was established. Their chief function was to arrange for the remittance of the annates, Peter's pence, tenths, and indulgence revenues, which was done partly in bullion, partly through bills of exchange.

From 1499 the Fuggers are found making advances to the curia on the security of the spiritual revenues which passed through their hands, e.g., they undertook the payment of the sum promised by Alexander VI to Ladislas of Hungary for a crusade in 1501. As usury was forbidden by the Church the question of interest was met by the repayment of an increased sum in the form of capital, the security in this case being the Servitia Communia of Germany, Hungary and Poland. The high rate of interest, the profits of exchange, were not the only advantages reaped by the Fuggers in their new business. From 1503 onwards benefices and prom-

[8] *English Historical Review,* XXVII, pp. 565–66, a review of Max Jansen, *Jakob Fugger der Reiche* (Leipzig, 1910).

ises of benefices were heaped upon the agents and younger members of the house so that their rivals bitterly complained to Maximilian of their simoniacal practices. By the close of Alexander VI's pontificate they were firmly established and were applied to by the camera for loans to meet the expenses of the election of Pius III and Julius II. . . . The functions of the firm were indeed very various. They arranged for the levy and payment of Julius II's Swiss guards, and for the pension granted to men of influence in the country. Their brisk trade in metals made them a natural source of supply for the papal artillery.[9]

The Fuggers played an important part in the inception of the German Reformation. Charles V's inability to execute his schemes in Germany was not a little due to the exhaustion of his credit with the Fuggers, just as the financial difficulties of the papacy led to the widespread sale of indulgences and the scandals which aroused Martin Luther.

As every student of the Lutheran movement is aware, Luther was awakened to protest by the sale of indulgences. Albert of Brandenburg, for the sum of 30,000 ducats borrowed from the Fuggers, had bought from the pope the archiepiscopal pallium of the archbishopric of Mainz. In order to repay the loan in 1517, for a consideration of 10,000 ducats he acquired from the pope the monopoly of the sale of indulgences for certain parts of Germany, among them Saxony and Thuringia. John Tetzel was the dealer in these indulgences and the archbishop's sales agent. He was accompanied on his travels by a representative of the Fuggers, who carried a key to the indulgence box, which was opened in Tetzel's presence and the money turned over to the firm's branch house in Leipzig. Half of the receipts were then paid to the Fugger agent in Rome to be paid into the papal coffers, and the other half retained by the Fuggers as an installment on the archbishop's debt to them. "Of such a nature was the business that started the Reformation." [10]

Having both pope and emperor as their clients in the first quarter of the sixteenth century, the Fuggers sat on top of the world. Already their money had influenced the election of two popes. When Maximilian died in 1519 they were instrumental in securing the election of his grandson Charles V against the competition of Francis I of France. Until the researches of Ehrenberg a mystery had ever been attached to this famous episode. No historian knew how or why the French party was vanquished and vanished from the scene. We now know that the whole affair was a money transaction and that bribery played so huge a part that the electors several times increased their demands.

[9] *English Historical Review*, 1905, p. 88, a review of Aloys Schulte, *Die Fugger in Rom (1494–1523)*. (Leipzig, 1904.)
[10] Ehrenberg, *Zeitalter der Fugger*, I, p. 99.

Charles won through Fugger loans to the extent of 543,000 gold florins. "The formal part of the election, with its display of solemn speeches, was simply a farce intended to delude the people." [11]

The Fugger mining interests in Hungary, the most lucrative investments of this kind which they possessed, were ruined by the Turkish conquest of Hungary in 1526. But the compensation for these losses was found for them by Charles V in Spain, where they almost monopolized the mining industry. In order to reimburse them Charles V leased to the Fuggers the quick-silver mines of Almaden, and the *maestrazgos,* an income the Spanish crown derived from the possessions of the secularized military orders. They even penetrated into the Far East and into America and have a chapter of their own in the history of discovery and Spain's colonial trade in the New World. They helped, with the Welsers, to finance the spice trade in the Moluccas, whose products, for fear of the Portuguese, were not transmitted to Europe by the Cape of Good Hope route but were carried by Spanish galleons to Chile and thence across the isthmus of Panama and so to Seville. In like manner the Welsers received concessions from Charles V for exploitation of reputed gold mines in Venezuela, before Cortez's conquest of Mexico and Pizarro's conquest of Peru regarded as the El Dorado of the New World.

In the meantime, in Europe about the middle of the sixteenth century, in the war of the Reformation and that other war of Charles V with Francis I, the Fugger moneys continued to play an influential rôle. Charles V's victory over Maurice of Saxony and the troops of the Schmalkald League at Mühlberg (1547) was made possible by Fugger gold which enabled him to hire better soldiers than the league had in its service, and in the same way the weight of Fugger gold in the scale discomfited French arms and French diplomacy.

In the middle of the sixteenth century the Fuggers and the Hochstetters formed a Metalgesellschaft or Metal Company which controlled the metal market of Europe. Hundreds of hard-working people, then, as they do now, invested their savings in it and were ruined when the company went bankrupt. "Numbers of farm servants and others," writes Clemens Sender of Augsburg, a contemporary eyewitness of the panic which ensued, "who did not possess over ten florins lent it out to them thinking it would be in safe-keeping, and that they would receive an annual dividend on the investment." The town council of Augsburg had to build a new and larger prison for debtors when the Metalgesellschaft bankruptcy befell.

The total indebtedness of the Spanish Habsburgs alone to the Fuggers in 1563 was 4,445,135 florins. The Spanish venture was the un-

[11] Ehrenberg, *op. cit.,* p. 103.

doing of the Fuggers. In 1562 and again in 1575 Philip II partially repudiated his debts to them, and in 1607 Spain went completely bankrupt. But in addition to the Spanish debts, the Austrian branch of the Habsburgs during the years between 1574 and 1617 had borrowed to the extent of 615,000 florins. In all, the Habsburgs contracted debts which amounted to 8,000,000 florins by the middle of the seventeenth century. Thus what the Fuggers earned during their career over a period of two hundred and fifty years (1409–1650), an amount estimated at five to six million florins in 1550, was lost.

CHAPTER XIX

THE ORIGIN OF MODERN BUSINESS METHODS

THE sources of medieval commercial law are primarily to be found in town charters, private documents, privileges, exemptions, *etc.* All this is another way of saying, as Wilhelm Arnold declared in 1861, "History is the source of law; law is the source of history." [1]

Similar conditions produce similar results and some historians, finding identical provisions in the laws of the ancient Egyptians, Assyrians, and Greeks, have thought to prove the continuity of such institutions. This is labor lost. The law of any ancient people before Rome has only a purely archaeological interest. Between their law and the law of medieval and modern Europe all direct connection is broken. The Middle Ages has the merit of having invented by their own genius the institutions necessary for their own welfare, at least so far as commerce and commercial law are concerned. The fact that the ancient world of Phoenicia and Greece had letters of exchange, banks, consular ports, *etc.*, does not prove their connection with the same institutions in medieval time.

Even in the Middle Ages, so true is it that similar causes produce similar results without its being necessary to establish organic connection, that it seems to have been proved that the peculiar letter of credit developed in Flanders in the thirteenth century, the *lettre de foire,* has no historical connection with the "letter of exchange" which was born in Italy or with the "recognition of debt" of German law. It was an independent evolution and a mixture of the two.

By 1300 the advancement of commerce had reached such dimension in Europe that merchants required clerks who could read and write both Latin and their native tongue. In Flanders an account book was called a "huge." Thus in 1301 Jacques Le Blont of Douai had *"une huge ou il avoit chartes, plusieurs lettres et plusieurs cirographes de dettes con lui devoit en Brabant et ailleurs."* [2] This necessity was one of the reasons for the growing discontent with the schools of the time, which were ecclesiastical. The consequence was that ere long we find progressive cities like Florence and Bruges establishing secular public schools in which the teacher taught the pupils by dictation how to write business letters. The language at first was Latin, but as early as 1204

[1] *Zur Geschichte des Eisentums in den deutschen Städten,* Basel, 1861.
[2] Espinas, *La vie urbaine de Douai au moyen âge,* IV, p. 6.

431

there is an example of the use of the vernacular—the *Distichs of Cato* translated into the vulgar speech. The form of the handwriting was cursive or running Gothic much like modern German schrift.

Modern business methods and practices have their root in the four-teenth and fifteenth centuries, and *not* in the sixteenth, so often set as the fictitious boundary line between medieval and modern history. The sixteenth century developed institutions which were already old; it invented little that was new in business practice.

The history of banking during the fourteenth and fifteenth centuries has been related in the previous chapter. But banking was only one of many instrumentalities of business in the later Middle Ages. It was necessary and inevitable, as the volume and variety of business in-creased in Europe, that new business devices should be invented, or ancient practices, long obsolete, be revived, and new techniques come into vogue in order to facilitate the conduct of trade. The "man in the street" to-day has little or no idea how much he is indebted to the age of the Renaissance for the business methods which he employs. He is as ignorant of the history of early business methods as he is of the history of early banking.

The economic revolution effected in the eleventh and twelfth cen-turies when commerce and industry partly independently, partly stimu-lated by the Crusades, grew enormously in volume, when a money economy gradually began to supplant the older natural economy, re-vived ancient business methods and called new devices into being. In these usages the Italians were the pioneers, since they were preëmi-nently *the* commercial people of the Middle Ages and earliest profited by the Crusades.

In the early history of commerce, trade was merely a matter of exchange of produce. Merchants travelled from place to place with caravans of merchandise which they exchanged for the necessities and luxuries they wished, as well as for other merchandise upon which they would later realize a profit. A certain amount of coin might have been necessary, but there was no general necessity of currency until the time of the Crusades. The first crusaders, having mortgaged or sold their lands, carried their money with them; and so did the early mer-chants. But the risk in so doing was great from loss or robbery by brigands or robber barons. This was less, of course, in the case of crusaders or other nobles who travelled under arms and with a body of retainers, than in the case of merchants. The latter usually travelled in caravans with a squadron of hired guards, or else purchased right of convoy from the lord of the land through whose territories they passed.

The problem of transmitting specie in large quantities was partially solved by the Knights Templar in the twelfth century. With its many fortified commanderies through Europe and the Orient, with its thousands of armed knights, with its own vessels on the sea, the Templar Order in the twelfth century did for Europe what Wells, Fargo and Company did in our own Far West after '49. It carried specie, transmitted money as desired. When Louis VII was in the Orient on the Second Crusade, Suger sent him money by the Templars. In the time of Henry III both the Templars and the Hospitallers were used for the transportation of money between England and Ireland and between England and France. Pope Honorius III used them for the remittance of money to Rome, as did many individuals who were not in official position.

From this practice it was a natural, yet a revolutionary step forward to the substitution of a letter of credit or a bill of exchange for actual cash carried in hand. The appearance of an instrument which could be passed from hand to hand in lieu of wealth marked a revolution in economic affairs. Various forms of documents appear in this century: the bill payable to order, and the promissory note; the ordinary bill drawn in the money of the country where it was payable, and the bill payable in another country at the rate current when due; the bill payable in a place specified, or where cargo was discharged; the bill to mature at date fixed, or the sight draft.[3] The birth of the concept of credit and its conversion to usages of business surely is one of the most important events in European economic history.

There has been much discussion upon the origin of the bill of exchange, and scholars are not agreed. Some claim that it was an Arab practice which was little by little adopted by the Christian world of the west, and in fact the Arab influence was considerable. Many words of commercial language like *traffic, magazine, tariff, douane, fardeau,* are from Arab words. But admitting there is an element of truth in this thesis, the bill of exchange had a multiple origin. There is reason to believe that letters of exchange were framed after the fashion of letters of payment given by kings to their treasurers. In the Anglo-Norman states the king ordered a specified person to pay a certain sum to another specified person in these terms: "Release from our treasury, *etc.—liberate de thesauro nostro,*" etc. These letters were called "liberate letters." When St. Louis went on the Crusade he used the letter patent for his loans. This letter patent was accompanied by a "close letter" addressed to an official of France ordering him to reimburse the bearer for such and such a sum. In other words the document was a letter of payment, or letter of exchange. The money was paid in different currency from the first sum. Some historians have given too much credence to the Florentine historian, Villani, who

[3] Des Marez, *La Lettre de Foire à Ypres au XIIIe Siècle,* p. 31.

attributes the invention of the bill of exchange to the Jews exiled from France by Philip IV, who went to Lombardy and there issued "mandats" or sight drafts in order to recover their property in France. The objection to this theory is that the crown had confiscated the property of the Jews in France, and, further, as the Jews had no status in the law courts, their drafts would not have been honored. Similarly other writers have sought to find the source of the bill of exchange in the practice of the Florentine Guelfs,.who when driven from the city, used this means to recover their property. Hans Prutz, the historian of the Crusades, does not say that the crusaders invented the bill of exchange, yet believes that

. . . it was certainly they who gave to these commercial contrivances, up to that time but little used, a very great practical value, and thereby provided Western Europe, the economic development of which had already been considerable, with a new means of commercial growth.[4]

More specifically still, the honor of devising the bill of exchange has been attributed to the Templars who

. . . seem at an early period to have worked out between their various commanderies a system of money transfers by bills of exchange of which kings, magnates, and also the Italian merchants seem freely to have availed themselves.[5]

The earliest bill of exchange of which we have record—though certainly not the earliest—is one of August 25, 1199, in which King John promises to pay 2,125 marks to some merchants of Piacenza in four installments. This money had been advanced to two bishops at Rome at the command of King Richard.[6] King John seems to have made much use of the letter of credit in his financial dealings. On January 6, 1202, he sent two agents to Rome and gave them a letter addressed "to all merchants" in which he promised to pay all sums advanced to his agents to the amount of five hundred marks "at such time as should be agreed upon, to any person presenting his letter together with the acknowledgment of his agents for the sum received by them."

Another one of the early *"mandats obligatoires"* was found by M. Blancard among the papers of the Manduel family. It is dated February 15, 1220. This documents asserts that *"Bartolomeus Macellarius,*

---

[4] *Economic development of western Europe during the Crusades,* p. 69.

[5] Ferris, "Relations of the Knights Templar to the English Crown," *American Historical Review,* Oct., 1902, p. 12.

[6] Ussher, "Origin of the Bill of Exchange," *Jnl. Polit. Economy,* 1914, p. 569; Macpherson, I, p. 367; Bond, "Extracts from the Liberate Rolls," *Archaeologia,* XXVIII, pp. 216–17.

de Massillia, et Petrus Vitalis, uno consensu et communi voluntate, accepimus mutuo, in urbe Messane, a te Stephano de Mandulio et Guillelmo Benlivenga, MVIC tarenos auri ad pondus Messane. . . ." The debtors promise to pay this sum within a month after the ship on which they are to sail shall have reached Marseilles.[7]

From this time on we have numerous examples of the use of bills of exchange. The form varies slightly, but the main body of the document changes little from one decade to the next. A typical letter of this type is dated Genoa, 1214: *"Ego Symon Rubeus, bancherius, accepi a te, Raimundo de Podiozandino, libras denariorum Janue 34 et denarios 32. Unde promito tibi, vel tuo miso, danti michi hanc cartam, marcos octo boni argenti. . . ."* The place and time of payment is stipulated and the document is witnessed by the usual three persons.

There are some historians, however, who are not willing to concede the honor of having devised the bill of exchange to Italian invention. For a parallel device is found in northern Europe, although not quite so early as 1200, unless it be conceded that the examples which have been preserved are later than types which circulated as early as the twelfth century, but have been lost. These were known as *lettres de foire* or fair-letters, which were promissory notes or drafts drawn by merchants who frequented the Champagne Fairs. The Belgian historian, Des Marez, discovered about eight thousand such documents in the archives of Ypres (which were destroyed during the World War) running from 1249 to 1291. Were there ever earlier ones? In form the document was an indented chirograph, whereof one part was kept by the creditor, while the other remained with the officials of the fair, two of whom had served as witnesses of the bargain. The debtor is mentioned in the third person—*"Sachant tout etc. que N. doit, etc."* He did not seal it, nor did he sign it with his name. The use of these *lettres de foire* made possible a much greater amount of business than had been carried on before, and in turn the importance of the commerce of the fairs stimulated the growth of credit. Instead of being required to pay in actual coin for his purchases a man might go before a magistrate, who was provided for this purpose, and declare himself debtor to another for a specified sum and promise future payment at a given date and place. Some of these letters contained a clause permitting the creditor to transfer his rights to a third person. This may contain the germ of indorsement.

The fairs provided regular places and times for the settlement of such debts, and the transaction was made in a legal way with witnesses and often with a requirement of security to insure the payment. Payment of debts contracted at the Champagne Fairs was widely enforceable. Mas Latrie gives a letter, dated June, 1300, from the guardians of

[7] Fagniez, *Documents*, I, p. 110.

the Champagne Fairs to the king of France demanding that a Venetian who had contracted debts at the Fair of Saint-Jean de Troyes be arrested and that his goods be seized to pay his debts.

The analogy between the Italian bill of exchange and the *lettre de foire* is evident. Are we to see therein two parallel and independent developments? Or was the *lettre de foire* introduced into the Champagne Fairs and Flanders by Italian merchants who resorted to them? There are those who affirm, and those who deny. M. Des Marez believes that the *lettre de foire* was an original credit device which developed independently of Italian influence in the Champagne Fairs and Flanders. "One was a creation of the German mind, the other a product of Latin genius." French business methods and German business methods of the Middle Ages coexisted in Flanders. While at Ypres and Bruges the French system of handwriting and of sealing charters was adopted and remained in vogue down to the very end of the fifteenth century, in Ghent, on the contrary, after 1339 the German system of *Erbbücher*, or registers of accounts, was in vogue. The important thing to observe is that at the beginning of the thirteenth century the principle of credit, *i.e.*, reputation for business probity and solvency, was current in Western Europe, upon which the circulation of letters of credit and bills of exchange was based. In Poggio's *Facetiae* an anecdote is related illustrating this statement:

Messer Piero da Nocera, having to transfer a large sum of ducats at Florence, handed them to the bank of the Medici in Rome and received in exchange a letter of credit, with which he went to Florence. On the journey he began to doubt that he would get his money back. But as soon as he arrived at the bank, everything was duly paid him. So he went to Cosimo and said: "Magna est fides tua." And Cosimo replied: "Messer Piero, trust is the merchant's treasure and the more trust a merchant inspires the richer he is."

In some of these instruments we find the expression, " . . . will pay to you, or to your agent." But our modern practice of allowing the creditor to assign over ownership to a third person, and the third person to a fourth person, and so on, by merely signing the letter of credit, was uncommon. The courts usually insisted that the actual persons contracting the obligations were the only ones that could enforce them. It was necessary that this agency be legally created. Documents creating a legal agent have been found and give an interesting modern touch to the transaction.

Papers have also been found which seem more like transfers of credit than like letters of credit, and which appeared before the beginnings of transference of bank credit. Other documents have the form of drafts. On June 11, 1274 Edward I issued a "Mandate to brother

Warin, treasurer of the New Temple, London, to deliver to Luke de Lukes, king's merchant, 2,000 *l.* out of the money received by him at the mandate of Joseph, prior of the Hospital of St. John of Jerusalem in England, the treasurer, and of Payn de Cadurcis of the tallage assessed upon divers Jews, to take to Paris against the king's arrival there." Pope Alexander IV was mean enough to draw sight drafts on the English bishops from whom he compelled payment under threat of excommunication when he was sustaining Richard of Cornwall in Sicily against Manfred—a policy in which King Henry III abetted him.

We find that at the beginning of the fourteenth century merchants kept account of their commercial operations in books, and that these ledgers were regarded in law as evidence up to a certain sum. We have preserved from this epoch a certain number of these books which have been published and made the object of extended study. It is important to know them.

Among the oldest of these are the ledgers of a Jewish mercantile company with a house at Vesoul and another at Arles. The head of this association was a certain Elias of Vesoul. The operations, of which we have the accounts preserved, run from 1300 to 1310; they extend over all Franche Comté and even beyond the Vosges in the north and into the Saône-et-Loire regions in the south. We find herein written the amount of their loan in Hebrew letters and everything is in order. But in 1310 Philip V expelled the Jews and the edict was applied to Franche Comté. Elias' property was confiscated and given to Queen Jeanne. The account books were taken at the same time, and that is how they were discovered in the archives of the Côte-d'or.

We have the account books of the Bonis Brothers, who were merchants at Montauban in the fifteenth century.[7a] The register, book C, begins in 1339 and runs to 1369. Consequently there were two earlier books, A and B, which have been lost. The Bonis Brothers were great general merchants; they sold the widest variety of products in the Rue de la Faurie—from agricultural products to cloths, spices, shoes, arms, and drugs. They were also dealers in gunpowder, and kept a livery stable; they were undertakers and rented the various objects necessary for funerals. This is not all; they were bankers and loaned money on goods, *i.e.*, they were pawnbrokers, money lenders; they farmed the town taxes and the revenues of the Church. Their book of accounts is accompanied by a book of deposits in which are written the sums entrusted to their bank, and accounts of the estates which they managed. All this accounting is very minutely written out. Every item, whether

[7a] Found in the archives of Tarn et Garonne; published by Edouard Forestie in the *Archives Historiques de la Gascogne* for the years 1890, '93, '94, and separately, 2 volumes.

it was cash or credit, is recorded. This is a document of first importance and a mine of precious information for the history of commerce in the fourteenth century.

The account book of the Boyssel Brothers, merchants at St. Antonin in Rouergue, was discovered by the same scholar. The Boyssel Brothers were wholesale merchants. Another account book is that of Jacques Olivier, a merchant of Béarn. The financial operations indicated in this book run from July, 1391, to July, 1392. Olivier was a manufacturer of cloth. But soon he branched out to the purchase and sale of woolen stuffs and cloths manufactured at Narbonne, and to commercial trading at Alexandria, Beirut, Damascus, and Rhodes. He exported cloth and honey—the celebrated honey of Narbonne—and took spices in return. He had correspondents at Montpellier, Barcelona, and Perpignan; he loaned money, he farmed taxes, he managed estates. He was an important person in his native town.

Two other account books have been found for the former realm of Arles in the fourteenth century. This province, where French was spoken, was intimately connected with France commercially. First there is the day book of Hugo Teralh, who was at the same time a notary and a draper at Forcalquiei. This account book extends from 1330–32. The first column indicates the name of the purchaser, then the amount of the debt, and the character of the merchandise, or indicates the date of the expiration of the debt, whether it be on a saint's day or a fair day, the name of the guarantors when there are any. Often we find the date of delivery and records of account opened or closed. Sometimes instead of these indications, which are in the hands of the merchant himself or his clerk, Hugo Teralh puts a notary's seal upon his register. He was a notary himself, and authenticated the genuineness of his own signature.

In the fourteenth and fifteenth centuries the economic system of the Middle Ages was overthrown. The Church, after its long conflict with the temporal power, proved incapable of governing the world. Human nature refused longer to stand for the general ideas and abstract requirements of the economists; individual energy asserted itself and governments lent their support to commercial practices frowned upon by the Church. Aside from the actual economic changes which took place it is interesting to notice the enormous mass of economic literature which was written at this time. We have treatises on money, on taxation, on the exaction of interest, etc. The most famous economist was Nicholas Oresme, who died in 1382.

Bills of exchange, based on actual transfers of goods, were in general excluded from the category of usury because any discount or interest which might be involved could be considered as payment for work done in transporting money. This brings up one of the most interesting means of evading the canon law—the "wages idea"—by which the taking of a "stipendium" was allowed whenever any labor was involved in the transaction. This led to the business of bill-broking, for it was easy to make a loan upon interest under the form of a bill of exchange.[8]

Even certain forms of papal bulls were negotiable securities. For it was the common practice of the Florentine bankers to buy in the Roman curia the bulls allocating ecclesiastical revenues and to provide for their payment through their business correspondents in the country concerned. This was especially done in England. We learn this interesting information from a very rare pamphlet of thirty-four leaves only, written by one Johannes Consobrinus, a Portuguese who died in 1475. His *Tractatus de justitia commutavia et arte campsoria seu cambiis* was printed in Paris in 1483. It is dedicated to the Venetian patrician Nicolaus Lippomano, "from which you can see what is right and what is wrong in the conduct of trade, in which your city has gained such eminence." The first part of the treatise deals with *"commutationes,"* i.e., exchanges or commercial transactions, and discusses the nature of contracts by which property is transferred from one person or persons to another person or persons; contracts for hire; leases; and the lending of goods or money. In each chapter the author distinguishes between legitimate profit and usury. The second part deals with usury. The fifth chapter of this second part is concerned with the law and ethics of foreign exchange. It is from this that is derived the information that the papal bulls circulated as commercial paper.

A clever device for the evasion of the prohibition of loans at interest was the sale of rent-charges. Many owners of land had tenants who paid a fixed rent which was considered as a right which could be sold. If the landlord were in need of money he would sell his land, including the right to receive the rent, to someone for a certain sum of money. Then the landlord would receive the property back under the condition that in the future he should pay the rent-charge.

Still another form of evasion was the formation of partnerships or companies. A corporation, having no soul, could do many things which fear of the wrath of the Church would prevent an individual from doing. Apart from any consideration of this as a subterfuge to evade the prohibition of usury, the partnership, usually in the form of a *commenda*, had very important results. Business enterprise was given another opportunity for expansion. It brought together men who had money, but little ability or inclination for business affairs. Often it was impossible for a merchant (the *commendator*) to travel with his wares and he did not want to send merely a servant, so he associated with

[8] "The 'false and abominable contract of money,' which 'the more subtly to deceive people, they call exchange,' was attacked by an ordinance of the mayor and aldermen of London in 1364." (Ashley, *Eng. Econ. History,* II, p. 426.)

him someone (the *tractator*) who would conduct the business in return for a certain proportion of the profits. A third means of collecting interest upon a loan without breaking the letter of the law was to give the use of a sum of money without charge until the expiration of a certain time. Then the note was not paid until the money-lender sued for damages for the breaking of the contract.

The amount of business carried on in Europe during the thirteenth, fourteenth, and fifteenth centuries was so great that it outgrew the prohibition on the taking of interest. The loans handled were so large and the business involved was often so complicated that interest at last was openly required without recourse to any of the accepted subterfuges. New ideas of money became general about the fifteenth century. Men began to realize that money had in itself an earning power.

It is necessary to dwell at length on this development of commercial associations. We find them all over Europe by the fifteenth century, especially in the South; they were formed by the great merchants. These merchants trafficked in all sorts of merchandise from cutlery and hardware up to cloths and silk; but they could not sell small articles like knives and scissors except by the gross dozen; spices in bags, cloth stuffs, and silks by the bale, packed just as they came from the country where they were produced.

Strictly speaking these commercial associations may be considered as a form of corporation, to which they have analogous characteristics. Other kinds of associations were formed for business convenience, among which stock companies are to be included. We find various forms of stock company in the Middle Ages. At first the form was very simple. For example, a cattle dealer was loaned money by several men for the purpose of stock-raising; instead of paying in money, both parties divided the profits of the herd. Again, a merchant entrusted some merchandise to a peddler, who betook himself to the fair, or to a sailor who exported the goods. The two associates divided the profits equally. Instead of a pair there might be several persons associated together. Thus capitalistic societies were formed for commercial exploitation. The stock was divided into parts analogous to the practice of to-day and the profits distributed in dividends according to the shares each possessed.

Such societies were formed for the building and equipment of a vessel; they hired a captain who guaranteed them share-profits derived from the sale of merchandise to be transported. But in this case the capitalist alone was responsible. The vessel captain was not liable. However, little by little the principle of limited and distributed responsibility became established. This responsibility, *i.e.*, the certificates of shares in a vessel or trading company, could be sold and passed from hand to hand, and with them passed the benefits and the liabilities. But these principles developed very slowly.

If it be true, as a great German historian of law has written, that "the joint stock company is an institution which throws everything else into the shade, and with whose financial power the world, one might say, can be conquered," [9] then the history of the evolution of partnership is of great importance. As in the case of the origin of the bill of exchange, German and English writers contend that the joint-stock company also was an invention of the Northern peoples of Europe.

W. R. Scott in his three-volume work on *The Joint Stock Companies to 1720* devotes one short introductory paragraph to recognition of the fact that there were organizations of a similar character in existence "in the Italian states" early in the fifteenth century, "if not before that time," and suggests that "when the importance of Italian finance in England at an early period is remembered, allowance must be made for the possibility that, when the time was ripe, the method of constituting a company might have been copied, and that, when an organization of this type was at length founded, it would be, in its main essentials, an importation from abroad and not an indigenous product." He then paradoxically proceeds to endeavor to show in the following fifteen pages that the joint-stock company must have been a native English institution, derived from the *gilda mercatoria*. The author's patriotic zeal has eaten him up. The joint-stock company was an Italian business device, and old long before similar English companies came into existence.

The earliest type of united business enterprise seems to have been the *commenda* or *societas*. At first this was a temporary arrangement for the carrying on of maritime trade, but later came to be adapted to the more permanent uses of internal trade. It may be defined as "a business relationship in which there is an active partner liable without limit, and a capitalist partner whose risk is limited to a fixed sum." [10]

Historically the *commenda* was of Arabic origin. It was existing in the time of Mohammed, and was the form of partnership in vogue among the rich merchants of Mecca. From Arabia the institution spread over the whole Mediterranean world with the conquest of Islam. As later among the western nations, so among the Arabs the *commenda* owed its organization to the endeavor to evade the provisions of Mohammedan law against loans at interest. It was through this type of organization that the work of the Italian financiers was carried on. The Bardi and Peruzzi, who were ruined by the default of Edward III, traded in part only with their own funds; the bulk of their capital was furnished by partners and depositors. This goes far, of course, to

[9] Josef Kohler, *Philosophy of Law*, p. 183.
[10] Palgrave, *Dictionary of Political Economy*, III, p. 67.

explain the widespread disaster which was caused by their downfall. The *commenda* was a very popular form of organization and was tremendously important in the trade of the Middle Ages. It was an all but universal type in the fifteenth century.[11]

A second form of corporate establishment which grew up was that in which the unlimited liability of the partners was recognized. This seems to have found its origin in the family type of mercantile enterprise, in which the term "house" (*casa*) carried its literal meaning. In the original companies only the amount of money which each partner had put up was available to the firm, and the remainder of his goods was under his own control. Likewise the liability of the firm was limited to the common fund to which each member had subscribed. But by a gradual process, which cannot be traced in detail, "the unlimited liability of the partners' separate capital became customary." [12] In course of time the family partnership of unlimited liability was opened up to individuals not united by ties of blood, and this type of organization began in the sixteenth century to rank alongside of the *commenda* form of partnership.

The third type of organization, which developed out of the demands of business and the weaknesses of the other two, was the joint-stock company as we understand it to-day. This type may be described as a company "enjoying corporate rights, and trading with a capital divided into shares—which shares, unlike shares in ordinary partnerships or *commenda* partnerships, were transferable by contract and transmissible on death." [13]

In the history of the origin of European partnership Genoa exercised a predominant influence. Professor Byrne, working in the unpublished records of the Genoese notaries, has written an interesting article on "Commercial contracts in Syria," [14] in which he sets forth the inner workings of the Genoese *societas* and *accomendatio* in the twelfth and early thirteenth centuries. These partnerships were actively contractual in nature, and there is a businesslike atmosphere and broadness of sweep about their transactions that make the English *gilda mercatoria* of the same period, as an evolutionary stage of joint-stock organization, seem petty indeed in comparison.

The general character of the Syrian trade of the twelfth century illustrates the point. It was undertaken only at regular intervals and operated on schedule-time. The long, hazardous, expensive voyages necessitated a protracted stay in Syria, hence a careful preparation of the ship or ships, the assembly of all the merchants engaged in the

[11] Nys, *op. cit.*, p. 285.
[12] Palgrave, *op. cit.*, III, p. 67.
[13] Palgrave, *op. cit.*, III, p. 68.
[14] *Quarterly Jnl. Econ.*, XXXI (1916–17), pp. 128–170.

trade and all the available capital, and in times of war or of particularly active piracy a convoy of the merchant fleet part or all of the way and its being similarly met on the return voyage. Usually the fleet left Genoa in September or October for a Christmas arrival in Syria, perhaps stopping in Sardinia and Sicily, though generally a direct voyage was made. It returned to Genoa in May or June, occasionally stopping at Alexandria, Sicily, or Bougia and Ceuta. The Genoese trade on a large scale in the East began with the formation of the "commune" in 1097, and was probably due chiefly to the activities of the First Crusade. During the next thirteen years, she sent six armed fleets to Syria, varying in size from two to sixty galleys. A few wealthy families at this early date carried on the bulk of the trade.

But a double tendency is notable in the direction of increased volume of trade and an increased number of participants. For instance, for the sailings of the autumn of 1191 thirty-seven contracts representing the dealings of over eighty individuals have been preserved; at the same season of 1203 eighty-one contracts involved about two hundred persons; and in the spring of 1205 one hundred and thirty-two contracts covered the investments of over three hundred investors.[15]

There appear to have been from the middle of the twelfth century two forms of embryonic "companies," the *societas maris* and the *accomendatio*. In the simplest and earliest form the former consisted of two partners: a *socius stans* who furnished two-thirds of the capital of the voyage and remained at home, and the *socius tractans* or *portitor* who supplied the remaining one-third and carried the whole abroad for trading purposes. Byrne denominates the respective partners "investor" and "factor" for convenience. The factor traded, defrayed expenses from the gross proceeds, returned to Genoa, and after disposal there or in the West of the eastern wares secured, shared the net profits half and half with the investor. Each voyage was, prior to 1154, a separate affair.

The next ten years marked the rapid development both in technique and volume of trade. In August, 1158, a *societas* for Syrian trade was formed to last three years, Buronus and de Justa being the contracting principals. A more interesting case was that of Ingo de Volta and Ingo Nocentius. Prior to September, 1156, they formed a *societas* and sent a part of the capital to Syria. In June, 1157, the business was still in operation, the capital having increased from 300 to 810 *livres*. In the autumn, 1160, Nocentius went to Syria under apparently the same *societas* and the capital had further increased to 1,100 *livres*. In opera-

---

[15] Byrne, "Genoese trade with Syria in the twelfth century," *American Historical Review*, XXV, pp. 211–12.

tion for nearly six years, the *societas* was closed on Nocentius' return to Genoa late in 1162. At least two trips had been made, and in the meantime the merchants had been distributing their wares in the West.

From the simple *societas* there developed:

(1) *Societates* of several partners. In case there were two or more *socii stantes* they collectively furnished two-thirds of the capital and at the conclusion of the business received one-half of the net profits to be shared among them. In the late twelfth century there were *societates* with more than one factor.

(2) *Societates* in which the factor might carry goods or money of his own beside his one-third interest in the *societas* proper. Here his additional sum had to share the expenses of the voyage per *lira* invested, but he got all the net profit of his additional sum. The advantage to the *societas* as a whole lay in reducing the expenses for the *socii stantes* interested.

(3) *Societates* in which the investor lent additional sums. In this case the factor received for his trouble one-fourth of the net profits on the additional sum and had his expenses cut as did the investor in the preceding case.

(4) *Societates* in which the factor carried capital for outsiders—*super societatem*—with or without additional capital placed by his original partner or partners or himself. In this case expenses were to be defrayed per *lira* of the total capital and one-fourth of the net profit on the *super societatem* capital was to revert to the *societas*. For all concerned the usual arrangement of equal shares in final settlement applied. This form of partnership became the rule after 1179, and was in reality an *accomendatio*. The *accomendatio* became the more popular form of contractual relation during the last years of the twelfth century for Syrian trade, and its greatest significance lies perhaps in the wholesale extension of participation in foreign trade to men of relatively small means, even the smaller clergy becoming involved. It, too, came to endure for more than one voyage, and marks a very interesting new development in foreign trade—the practice of making consignments in independent vessels by freight to and from Genoa with the factor located in Syria and the investors at Genoa. In case a consignment was not successfully delivered to the consignee, the "sub-factor" of the freighter disposed of the cargo in the usual manner, acting as a factor himself.

Only some new big enterprise was necessary to weld these hustling merchant partnerships into a great organized company. That enterprise came in the fourteenth century and we find ourselves face to face with the *maona*, that of Chios, that of Cyprus, and that of Corsica, flanked at the ends of the century by the full-fledged corporation, the *Casa di S. Giorgio* of the fifteenth.

The earliest instance of the *maona,* that of Ceuta, illustrates well the relation between commerce and politics in Genoa. This *maona* came into existence as a means of saving and enlarging a political holding, valuable because of the expanding commerce of the commune. In 1234, in a time of revolution in Ceuta, the Genoese power there was annihilated by the Saracens. Upon the sultan's refusal to comply with the Genoese demand for compensation, the republic assembled a fleet of a hundred vessels or more and forced an advantageous settlement, the sultan being made to pay a heavy indemnity and all the war costs. All those ship-owners and others who had demands on the sultan, since the Genoese treasury was empty, as usual, were organized into the *maona* of Ceuta. The creditors were registered and might alienate their shares at will. The *dominium utile* of the conquered territory was pledged to the *maona* till the government should discharge its debt to the members. Little is known of this earliest *maona.* We can see more of the inner workings of the system by a brief consideration of the history of its fellow of 1347, the *maona* of Chios.

In 1346 the popular rule in Genoa found itself threatened by an impending invasion of the city at the hands of the Grimaldi, who had been driven from power in Genoa a few years earlier and had established themselves at Monaco. Lacking funds, the Genoese government called upon private citizens to raise a fleet and some forty-four ships were proffered. The masters of twenty-nine of them accepted the terms of the government and sailed under the command of the admiral Simon Vignoso against the invaders. They were, of course, little more than privateers, and their expedition, though having state sanction, was largely a freebooting trip. At the appearance of the fleet the refugees fled once more and thus the expedition was deprived of its *raison d'être* without having satiated its patriotic zeal.

At this point the enterprising Vignoso conceived the brilliant idea that the Near East offered a promising field for Genoese talents. Accordingly he directed the expedition to Negroponte, where he had heard that a combined fleet of Venetian and Rhodian galleys were on the way to take the island of Chios from the Byzantine Empire. This was a double sting to the Genoese, for the island had been lost by Genoa only a few years before, and to see it go to Venice, even for the ostensible purpose of providing a base against the Turks, went sorely against the grain. Vignoso offered to aid the islanders against their approaching enemies on condition that they allow the Genoese flag to be hoisted on the island and permit the landing of a small garrison. The natives refused, and a fight was necessary before the Genoese could land and a three months' siege had to be undertaken before the citadel was reduced. Liberal terms were granted to the people and a governor was appointed to superintend affairs in the name of the Genoese state. To complete the job Old and New Phocea, Samos and Nicaea were annexed.

Thus Genoese supremacy was established in the island. But when the galleys arrived home they found that the exchequer could not repay the sum of 203,000 Genoese pounds which the adventurers had invested. A solution was found in an agreement which provided that for twenty years the government of the island was to be conducted by the company in the name of Genoa. At the end of that time the obligation which the republic had incurred was to be liquidated. In the meantime the collection of the taxes and the monopoly of the mastic (an aromatic gum which was the chief product of the island) were to be in the hands of the twenty-nine associates in the original enterprise, now called the *maona.*[16] Thus a band of freebooters was transformed into a chartered company by having transferred to it virtual sovereignty over a large territory, and being given a respectable source of income through the extensive revenues of that territory. Genoese connection was in theory preserved by the institution of a *podestà* chosen annually by a complicated process. He was to govern in the name of Genoa and try native cases in his court. Financial connection was maintained through two officers known as *massari*, who were to send in annual accounts to the Genoese audit office. The net result of this organization was that, while theoretical sovereignty of the island was in the hands of the home government, the real profits accrued to the chartered company.

The flexibility of the *maona* and the ease with which stock was transferred are illustrated by the turn of events during the eleven years directly following the foundation of the company. The original membership began to tire of their investments. Vignoso died. By 1358 the stock of the concern was concentrated in the possession of eight persons, only one of whom had been a member of the original *maona*. These persons, for the most part absentees living in Genoa, had farmed out the revenue, mainly derived from the mastic, to a second company formed in 1349 and made up of twelve persons. Trouble arose between the two companies, the republic intervened and in 1362 a new agreement was entered into by which the younger company was to control the island for twelve years. The twelve formed themselves into a "house" (*casa*) and, abandoning their family names, called themselves Giustiniani. Attempts were made to regulate the selling of shares in the company. No member could sell his stock to another member, lest the number of stockholders be reduced below twelve. Members were permitted, however, to sell to outsiders of the popular party, with the con-

---

[16] The origin of the term is uncertain. It has been suggested that it is a contraction of "madonna," to whom the trading companies committed themselves for protection. (*English Historical Review*, XXX, p. 421.)

sent of the doge. Each twelfth part was divided into three *karati*,[17] which were subsequently subdivided into eight parts each. The strict provision enjoining the permanency of a twelve-share concern was not lived up to. In 1365 two partners withdrew and returned to Genoa, their shares falling into the hands of one Recanelli, who became the leading spirit of the new company.

In 1373 the new *maona* bought out completely the old organization. By the treaty with the old *maona*, if the government had not redeemed its pledge by 1374, it forfeited its right altogether. To save itself the republic borrowed money from the members of the new *maona*, and became possessed of the territory, leasing the districts again for twenty years to the new *maonesi* who were to deduct from its revenues the amount of the interest and remit the balance, estimated at 2,000 gold ducats to the republic. Seven years' balance was to be paid in advance.

The subsequent history of the new *maona* is somewhat involved. When the time for paying the debt arrived Genoa was in as bad financial condition as at the time it was contracted. The government borrowed from the members of the *maona*, in their private capacity as bankers, sums sufficient to meet the obligation. Thus nominal possession of the island was in the hands of the state, but in order to meet the interest on the new debts the government was compelled to make over the revenues for another twenty year period. Leases were renewed in 1385 which gave the island to the company until 1418, and in 1413 a fresh loan continued the occupation until 1447. Again the company was ceded the island until 1509. In 1513 the republic resolved to pay off the *maonesi* and actually raised the sum required, which, however, the company declined to accept, on the ground that it was at that time, considering the relative money value, not sufficient. The lease was consequently continued and finally in 1528 Chios was leased to the *maona* in perpetuity in consideration of an annual rent of 2,500 ducats. Not only were commercial and administrative affairs in the hands of the *maona;* it administered the foreign policy as well. And this, while it saved the company for a while from the numerous Genose wars, was finally the cause of its fall. Successfully fighting off the Venetians and the Greeks, the *maona* became tributary to the Turks in 1389. The Turkish tribute was not a heavy burden at first, in comparison with the profits, mainly from the alum mines and mastic groves. But it was otherwise by 1566 when the tribute was increased to 14,000 gold ducats and 2,000 ducats' worth of scarlet cloth per year in presents for the Turkish viziers. On default of payment in 1566 the island, already

---

[17] Karato or *caratto* (Arabic qîrât < κεράτιον, a carob-pod): originally a variable unit of weight for gold, silver and pearls. Later it came to mean a share in a partnership or company, usually a twelfth or a twenty-fourth.

disavowed by Genoa, was captured by the Turks. Yet the *maona* even in its later days paid a dividend of 2,000 ducats on each of the thirteen original shares, while "in its best times the small *caratto,* originally worth some thirty Genoese pounds, was quoted at 4,930." [18] The Genoese administration of Chios was an anticipation of the chartered company of the sixteenth century so familiar in the East India Company, the West India Company, and many another similar commercial and colonizing organization.

The essential features of the *maona* of Cyprus were not different. Famagusta was taken over in 1374 and a treaty closed with the king of Cyprus by Peter of Campofregoso "in the name of the commune and of the masters participant in the *maona.*" Besides 90,000 ducats, the expenses of the expedition, the Cyprians were forced to pay the *maona* the tremendous sum of 2,012,400 ducats in twelve yearly installments and to the state 40,000 ducats annually. In the end Cyprus went over altogether to the Genoese under the administration of the *maona,* in 1374 and 1403. In the case of the *maona* of Corsica (1378), that island, already a Genoese possession but ravaged constantly by mountain bandits, was given over to a company of five capitalists headed by Leonello Lomellini with complete administrative authority, even to appointing the governor without ratification by the government at Genoa, although the company recognized the sovereignty of the republic. In 1463 the *compera vecchia di Scio* was created, originally consisting of 415 *luoghi* or shares. In 1498 a new loan of 1,600 *luoghi* was floated paying interest at 4 per cent. It was liquidated in 1513. The same year, however, the paid off shares were reissued and augmented by 460 *luoghi,* a limit being set of 25,000 with 350 of the total to be reserved with the Bank of St. George as a sinking fund. These loan shares, as in the case of the government *compera* previously, became the object of speculation. The system was imitated in Venice where laws against speculation were passed.

Despite the extremely modern management of the *maona* and chartered companies, Sieveking has pointed out that they were not joint-stock companies in the modern sense of the term. The capital of a modern joint-stock company consists of stocks, fixed sums distributed, whereas the *locus* or share of the *maona* was an imaginary unit. The stockholder in a modern company hopes for the highest possible dividend, but the dividend may fluctuate. In Genoa the interest on shares was theoretically fixed; in practice, though, it was not paid regularly nor in full, so that actually the dividend varied, according to the profit of the revenues allotted to the particular shares. This was one cause for the fluctuation of share values.

[18] W. Miller, "The Genoese in Chios" (1346–1566), *English Historical Review,* XXX, p. 418.

Business always hangs together. The prosperity or failure of one form conditions that of other forms. Moreover, there is a natural articulation between business institutions. Superiority in the technique of trade, individual and collective enterprise, the formation of commercial organizations, the establishment of shares in the public debt, double entry bookkeeping, insurance, joint-stock companies—each and all of these institutions are related.

Insurance, which is another cornerstone of modern business, with more colorability than in the case of the bill of exchange and the joint-stock company, is claimed as a German device. Some practice for the insurance of goods was in existence in Bruges in the twelfth and thirteenth centuries, and there is some reason to think that a chartered company was founded in 1310 for the sale of policies of insurance on merchandise against marine or other risks. As with the taking of interest, so insurance encountered opposition from the Church on the ground that it was gambling against God. But there are traces of marine insurance in the *Breve Portus Calleritani* of Pisa in 1318 and in Portugal about 1375. Catalan insurance appears in 1435. A Florentine merchant named Uzzano in 1442 quoted rates of insurance on goods during transit between Pisa and London, and between Milan and Bruges. In the fifteenth century the Genoese merchants at Bruges formed a regular insurance company. In 1456, a certain Marco Gentili, a Genoese, and Charles Lommelino were commanded to pay an insurance indemnity. The Spanish and Florentine merchants also formed companies of insurance. The first English statute of insurance is of 1601 but its language shows that already the practice was old: "Whereas it hathe bene tyme out of mynde an usage amongst merchants both of this realme and of forayne nacions."

History shows that it is beyond the power of a conquering people, who are inferior in culture to the people they have conquered, utterly to destroy their legal and commercial systems. The Roman system of bookkeeping descended to the Church and the barbarian monarchies. The art of bookkeeping has kept pace with the development of commerce. The Romans were familiar with the daybook (*adversaria*), the account book (*tabulae accepti et expensi*), the ledger (*codex*). But the Roman system of keeping accounts disappeared in western Europe apparently in the "iron age" of the seventh century. It was, however, preserved in Constantinople and the Eastern Roman Empire, from which the Arabs borrowed it. When trade began to revive during the Crusades, Italian merchants—Venetians, Genoese, Florentines—reintroduced into the West what had been lost for centuries.

About the year 1000 the use of the abacus or counting-table of the Romans is mentioned, although the figures were Roman and not Arabic numerals. The latter did not become general until the twelfth century, "very possibly transmitted through the operations of trade rather than in academic manuals; but by the end of the century the learned world is divided between the algorists, who upheld the new method of reckoning, and the older abacists, who secured legislation against the use of the new-fangled figures at Florence as late as 1299." [19] In 1202 the oldest known work on bookkeeping, the *Liber abaci*, was published by the Italian mathematician Leonard of Pisa. Part of the city register of Genoa for 1348 shows the current practice. In 1398 an anonymous primer of bookkeeping was widely popular in Italy.

Italian methods of bookkeeping spread to Northern Europe with the expansion of trade. That bookkeeping is Italian in origin the very words employed manifest, as *bank, account, discount, credit, debit, etc.* The first book in English shows this also: James Peele's *Art of Italian Merchant Accounts, or Book-keeping by Double Entry* (London, 1569).

When printing with movable type was discovered arithmetics and manuals of bookkeeping were popular and profitable books to print. The first commercial arithmetic was printed at Treviso in 1478,[20] but that of Pietro Borgo or Borghi, from the Venetian press of Ratoldt in 1484 soon superseded it. No less than sixteen editions were printed between 1484 and 1577. "Although the second commercial arithmetic in point of time, it may properly be called the first one of considerable importance and influence in this field." [21] Pacioli of Venice in 1494 published the first clear exposition of double entry, and he was important enough to have his book on calligraphy illustrated by no less an artist than Leonardo da Vinci. The first printed book which contained an illustration of a banker's office was the *Libro de Mercantie* by Georgio di Lorenzi Chiarini, printed at Florence in 1496. This was the first book to give the customs relating to banking and exchange in use among Florentine merchants in the fifteenth century and is valuable and interesting for showing the practical problems of the period.

The system of book-keeping by double entry which Pacioli described very clearly and accurately, was already in use in northern Italy more than a century and a half before the friar composed his famous treatise.

In the accounts of the Genoese communal stewards for the year 1340 a fully-developed system of double entry is found. The earlier books of the state financial officials of Genoa were burned in a fire which occurred in 1339. There is extant an account-book of the commune for 1278 which has only single entry. Because of the loss of the volumes between 1278 and 1340 it is impossible to determine how early the double-entry system was introduced into the Genoese stewards' accounts.

[19] Haskins, *Renaissance of the Twelfth Century,* p. 312.
[20] David E. Smith, *Isis,* VI, pp. 311–31.
[21] David E. Smith, *op. cit.,* VIII, p. 41.

The original cartulary of 1340 which is now in the Genoese archives, contains 478 pages. The first pages which give the accounts of the stewards, tax-collectors, and notaries are in a poor state of preservation. The accounts of goods purchased for the commune, of various debtors of the city, and of the men-at-arms hired by Genoa are more legible. The Business Historical Society of Harvard University has recently acquired photostats of four of these pages. One contains accounts for goods—pepper, silk, wax, and sugar; another records damages and losses. A third page contains accounts of various debtors, and a fourth lists expenses for soldiers. . . . The entries are in medieval Latin. The debits are on the left half of the page and the credits on the right half. The formula for the debit side is *"debe(n)t nobis pro"* (or *"in"*). For the credit side *"recepimus"* (we have recovered) is used even if there is no previous debit. . . . The diagonal lines canceling the entries indicated that the latter had been transferred to a new ledger or had been balanced out. The entries are crowded together because both debit and credit are on the same page. This differs from the Venetian system as described by Pacioli and as exemplified by carefully and neatly kept Venetian books of the fifteenth and sixteenth centuries. In Venice the debits and credits were entered on different pages facing each other and each entry occupied one or two long lines, instead of being crowded into a narrow space as in the Genoese books.

Venice took the lead in the development of the science of book-keeping and set the style for most of Italy and northern Europe. Indeed book-keeping by double entry was popularly known in the sixteenth century as "book-keeping according to the method of Venice." But the question of the time and place of the origin of double-entry book-keeping in Italy is raised by the fact that the oldest known example of double entry is not Venetian but Genoese—the Genoese stewards' cartulary of 1340, and that the second oldest example is a Florentine ledger of 1390, kept according to the Venetian system, which belonged to the Company of Averardo de' Medici, a money-changer. The question may never be answered because so few early accounts have survived. The oldest Venetian ones date from 1406. Since Venetian and Genoese systems differ somewhat, they may have developed simultaneously and independently. Did the Italians inherit a Roman system or a Byzantine one, or did they really invent book-keeping by double entry? Was double entry first used in official accounts and then adopted for business accounts, or was the reverse the case? At present the evidence is too limited to afford solutions, but further exploration in the Italian archives may result in partial or complete solutions of these and similar interesting problems connected with the early history of modern methods of accountancy.[22]

There was no distinction until very late in the Middle Ages between wholesale and retail trade even in such a city as Nuremberg. The great dealers bought in quantity and sold *en gros* or *en detail* as the chance

[22] Florence Edler, *Bulletin of the Business Historical Society,* Harvard University, Vol. IV, No. 4, June, 1930, pp. 11-12.

to sell came their way. Keutgen's contention that exclusively wholesale merchants existed as early as the fourteenth century is contravened by Below and Uhrliz. When the distinction at last was arrived at, it first appeared among purveyors of foodstuffs. A grosser was a dealer who sold pepper and spices *en gros;* a retail dealer was called a "spicer." It is a pity that the early spelling of the word "grocer" has been lost, for the original form of the word recalls the historical origin of the grocer's business.

As economic condition and necessity gradually organized the private and public business and credit of Europe into something not too remotely resembling the business world of to-day, it is not surprising that we also find something like our stock exchanges. The rise of many of the peasantry, the least speculative of mankind, to the status of bourgeoisie, the growth of industry and commerce, especially of oversea commerce which by nature is more speculative than a land-borne commerce, the growth of a wage-earning class, the replacements of hoards by investment in partnerships and joint-stock companies—all these changes worked together. The first stocks were government bonds; later shares of trading companies were bought and sold. In Venice the names of creditors of the state after 1206 were registered, and the government scrip was negotiable paper capable of being bought and sold and mortgaged or used as security for loans. This practice soon extended to other towns of Italy. Interest on such bonds varied from 3 per cent to 25 per cent, fluctuating according to political conditions. Genoese bonds paid 7 per cent in 1407. The features of negotiability and interest soon created a live speculative market, at least at Florence, and probably in the other cities. In 1345, after the failure of the Bardi and Peruzzi, Florence consolidated its state debt in the form of government bonds to the amount of 570,000 florins bearing 5 per cent interest. Many towns issued bonds hypothecated upon the municipal domains and receipts from *octrois* and *tonlieux*. In 1371 the first stock exchange was founded at Florence. The word "stock" is of English origin. Until as late as 1834 if you lent money to the Bank of England, notched wooden tallies were cut for the amount on the two edges of the stick; the stick was then split into two parts. The bank kept the foil, the lender received the "stock." The two pieces had to fit exactly when payment fell due.[23]

For the inception of international law we must look back to the epoch of the Crusades.

Catalonia first gave birth to a sort of code of maritime law. It was a collection of usages and seafaring customs which, arranged in various chapters, appeared apparently about the middle of the thirteenth cen-

[23] Poole, R. L., *History of the Exchequer*, p. 89.

tury under the title of *Consolato del Mar,* or *The Consulate of the Sea.*
This code seems to have been adopted first by the Venetians in Constantinople in 1255, and was translated into Italian for the purpose.
The Pisans, the Genoese, and other sea-faring people of Europe followed
this example. The Consulate of the Sea became the fundamental law
in all the ports of the Mediterranean. This law, conceived in the midst
of the disorders of a universal piracy, was far from perfection, or the
more liberal disposition of a later age. But at least this code was a law,
and in the articles of private law, offered a guarantee which at this
epoch was a notable benefit to commerce.

Philip IV in various treaties with Aragon, Genoa, and Venice, subjected the letter of marque to certain conditions. It could not be delivered until after several summons addressed to the government interested; the grantee had to give surety that he had complied with all legal
formalities; had to publish a letter throughout all the territory of the
state which had refused him justice in order that every merchant might
be duly informed. He could not exercise it until after a certain period
of delay which permitted the opposite party to secure protection. Merchants going to the fairs could not be troubled for the fault of one of
their compatriots; they were only responsible for their own personal
debts. The letter of marque, moreover, was a warranty. It forbade the
traveller under a false flag from putting himself under the protection
of letters of marque; in case fraud was discovered the vessel and the
cargo were forfeited. The admiralty court in France which appears
under Charles V had cognizance of all affairs, civil and criminal, relating to the sea. A new jurisprudence was formed.

Finally regular treaties of commerce began to be signed at the beginning of the fourteenth century. It is not necessary to see a commercial
treaty in the privileges which Philip IV in January, 1310, granted the
Portuguese merchants established at Harfleur; these were special privileges to attract foreign merchants and the king of Portugal was not
a party. But Charles IV, as we are told by a contemporary, signed
a series of commercial treaties in 1327. On September 8, 1308, a treaty
was made between Haakon, king of Norway and Count Robert of
Flanders. For five years free navigation and commerce were stipulated
between the two peoples. If the king of Norway, or a company, or a
private person had contracted debts of Flemish subjects, their goods
might be sequestrated until the debt was paid. But commerce was to
be continued.

We see, therefore, at the beginning of the fourteenth century the bad
customs of the Middle Ages, which interfered with navigation and deprived maritime trade of all security, were beginning to be abolished.
The European states endeavored to obtain guaranty for their subjects
who sailed in foreign waters or traded abroad.

The medieval consular system was an important factor in the promotion of commerce. It supplied the necessary conditions without which regular trade could hardly have been carried on at all. In a foreign country the medieval merchant had a precarious status. He could not recover his debts; he was liable to be mulcted, not according to the law-merchant which he understood, but by local customs with which he was unfamiliar. This was equally true whether his business took him to another country or only to another city. The Norwich merchant who visited London was as much of a foreigner there as the man from Bruges or Rouen. Thus the consulates became institutions without which trade could not be conducted. In promoting international commerce consular institutions also contributed to the uniformity of laws and customs, and laid the basis for a body of international law later on.

The first period in the history of the consular system has been called the "municipal epoch." Commerce lay outside the tutelage and protection of the state. It had its own consulates based on the system of free association and reciprocity. The sovereign did not appoint the consuls; they were appointed by those whose interests they were to protect.

The extent and importance of Florentine trade may be shown by the number and distribution of her foreign consuls. Between 1423 and 1500 Florentine consuls had been appointed at Alexandria, Naples, Majorca, Constantinople, Cyprus, Black Sea ports, India, Persia, and China. In addition, chancellors, purveyors, interpreters, inspectors, clerks, and soldiers were attached to the service. Each consul was usually assisted by a secretary, who received a salary of four gold florins a month, by two assistants and a native dragoman. The consul was forbidden to carry on trade or to act in any way for another state. His salary was paid by rates levied on merchandise entering and leaving his port. In London, for example, the consul's salary was paid by a tax on bills of exchange and on the value of cargoes bought and sold. Her commerce became so important that in 1421 Florence appointed six maritime consuls for Pisa, over and above the trade consuls already there. In 1426 three of these maritime consuls were moved to Florence. The duties of the three at Pisa were: to watch all commerce, to encourage traders and navigators to use the port, to prevent contraband, to protect Florentine merchandise, to examine bills of lading and ship papers, to inspect crews and supervise wages, to inspect and repair vessels, and to keep an accurate ledger of accounts. The three at Florence had as their duties: to receive and file reports from Pisa, to furnish every sort of shipping information and post it in the loggia of the Mercato Nuovo, to approve the appointment or recall of those named for foreign consulates, to receive complaints and suits on maritime matters and adjudicate thereon, and to make representation to the Council of State in cases requiring official interference.

With the rise of monarchy in the fifteenth century the municipal consul disappeared. He was appointed by the government and represented the sovereign. The appointment of Lorenzo Strozzi, a Florentine, in 1485, to be English consul at Pisa, appears to be the first instance recorded of an official being empowered to undertake this responsibility for Englishmen in the Mediterranean. The English consular system owes its foundation to Richard III.

It was long ago pithily said that "statistics is history standing still; history is statistics in motion." [24] Neither the historian nor the statistician to-day would accept this definition. For the modern historian is not content with describing events; he is as much interested as the economist in discovering conditions. "In the modern sense statistics mean to us a comprehensive inquiry into definite facts capable of expression in numerical terms, within a well-defined geographical area and in a definite period of time." [25] But in a larger, if looser, sense, wherever and whenever the historian finds an orderly arrangement of government or business, he finds evidences of statistics.

The modern statistician, enjoying possession of a plethora of statistical documents poured out to-day by governments, trade organizations, and sociological foundations may deny that any scientific conclusions can be drawn from these early materials. But he would manifest his own ignorance in so doing. Statistics, as a special branch of economic research, may be said to have been founded by Sir William Petty in the seventeenth century, or by Achenwall in the eighteenth, or by Quetelet in the nineteenth, according as one thinks. But statistical documents existed in plenty in the fourteenth and fifteenth centuries, and progressive historians then, as now, perceived their value and made use of them.

The steady growth in variety and mass of documents of a statistical nature, either public or private, from the middle of the twelfth century onward is striking evidence of the increasing wealth of Europe, of the accretion of commerce and industry during the last centuries of the Middle Ages. By 1500 the volume of this material is almost overwhelming to the historian. Yet the losses of such documents indubitably exceed the amount which has been salvaged by the archivist. These documents are unlike the statistical documents of the high feudal age. Then we find registers of fiefs, revindication of fisc, manorial inventories, surveys and extents—in a word, documents reflecting the conditions of an agrarian economy.[26] The statistical documents of the end of the

---

[24] Schlozer in 1804.

[25] R. P. Faulkner, *Penn. Trans. and Reprints*, III, no. 2, introd.

[26] The feudal state of the Middle Ages knew of nothing more than catalogues of seigniorial rights and possessions (*urbaria*); it looked on production as a

Middle Ages, on the contrary, consist of tax lists, princely, ecclesiastical and municipal, tariff or douane lists, registers of navigation kept by various ports for the purpose of levying taxes on shipping, enumerations of population, shipping losses of merchants through wreck and piracy, reclamations and recoveries for damaged goods, merchants' accounts, lists of bank loans, ledger accounts, *etc.* All these kinds of documents are common from 1300.

Rudolph of Habsburg borrowed the idea of registration of fiefs from Frederick II. Charles IV planned a domesday survey of Brandenburg. In 1417 the emperor Sigismund imposed a hearth tax in Austria and Bohemia. In 1418 Albert of Bavaria laid a tax on houses in Groningen and Ommelanden. The revenue of Henry VII of Luxemburg was estimated at 1,900,000 marks; that of his son, Charles IV, after the acquisition of Bohemia, at 3,000,000. The income of Louis IX of France in 1260 has been computed at 3,600,000 *livres*; that of Philip IV at 10,800,000.

The eager interest of governments to acquire statistical information is a characteristic of this age of active commerce and industry. As governments more and more became dependent on resources raised by taxation and on loans borrowed on the security of taxation, statistical knowledge became imperative. In Italy income taxes and proportional taxation based upon such examinations were not a novelty. The new kinds of taxes which were introduced owing to the economic revolution and which so largely substituted a wealth derived from commerce and industry for a wealth formerly derived from land, compelled the governments to make cadastral surveys, inventories, accounts of receipts and expenditures, *etc.* In another place the importance of the *fouage* in France has been noticed; we have seen the care with which Giangaleazzo Visconti kept his ledgers of accounts, applying the method of a banker to the conduct of government; and the valuable amount of statistical matter embodied in the Venetian *Relations*.

Some modern historians who know only the multitude of blue books which every government to-day publishes, are inclined to scoff at the idea that any conception of statistics could have existed so early and to underestimate the value of the documents of this period. While these sources have not the accurate scientific value of modern sources, nevertheless they are not to be despised.

Venice may fairly make good its claim to be the birthplace of statistical science, together, perhaps, with Florence, and followed by the more enlightened despotisms. . . . In the Italian states a clear political conscious-

fixed quantity, which it approximately is, so long as we have to do with landed property only.—Burkhardt, *Renaissance,* p. 69.

ness, the pattern of Mohammedan administration, and the long and active exercise of trade and commerce, combined to produce for the first time a true science of statistics. . . . The writers of the time speak of these things with the greatest freedom. . . . The Italians were, perhaps, the first to reckon, not according to hearths or men able to bear arms, or people able to walk, and so forth, but according to *animae*—souls, and thus to get the most neutral basis for further calculation.[27]

A census of Milan as early as 1288 included house doors, population, men of military age, palaces of nobles, wells, bakeries, wine shops, butchers' shops, fishmongers, the consumption of wheat, dogs, price of salt, wood, hay, and wine; the number of judges, notaries, physicians, school teachers, copying clerks, armorers, smiths, hospitals, monasteries, and other religious corporations, with their endowments.

Northern Europe was slower in awakening to a perception of the value of government statistics. The Hanseatic cities "never got beyond a simple commercial balance sheet. Fleets, armies, political power and influence fall under the debit and credit of a trader's ledger." [28] Even Flanders, although more progressive than any other country in the North, was behind Italy. The Florentine historian Guicchiardini, in the middle of the sixteenth century, expressed astonishment that so little statistical knowledge still was available in the Low Countries.

The great commercial and industrial cities of Italy like Venice, Genoa, and Florence naturally were the places where statistical documents first appeared, and where appreciation of their value was earliest perceived by historians. The historical writers of the epoch of the Italian Renaissance formed their judgments upon observation and experience of men and events. They discuss the merits of different forms of government, the influence of wealth and natural resources, the development of commerce and trade, the nature of taxes, and display a remarkable insight into the nature and value of statistics.

The very first distinguished Florentine historian, Giovanni Villani, shows this renaissance faculty for analyzing the figures of public revenue. It is a just observation of Symonds that "the whole work of Villani remains a monument, unique in medieval literature, of statistical patience and economical sagacity, proving how far in advance of other European nations were the Italians of the period." [29] Thus in 1343 he estimates the receipts of the government at 604,850 gold florins. War devoured the largest portion of this amount. That with Milan cost 600,000 gold florins. He summarizes details as follows:

---

[27] Burckhardt, *op. cit.*, pp. 70–71.
[28] Burckhardt, *op. cit.*, p. 69.
[29] *Age of the Despots*, p. 205.

	Florins
Octroi on comestibles	90,200
Wine taxes	58,300
Salt tax at 40 d. per bushel for citizens and 20 d. for peasants	14,450
Fees for registration of contracts	11,000
Mills	4,250
Taxes on rents	4,250
Slaughterhouses	15,000
Cattle market	2,150
Balconies (shops)	5,550
Drink and fruit shops	450
Passports	3,500
Exemptions from military service	7,000
Licenses to carry arms	1,300
Taxes of citizens of Florence residing in the country roundabout, on rural property, mills, fishing rights, etc	300,000

In another chapter Villani gives figures regarding the cost of administration.

	Florins
Salary of podestà	15,250
Salaries of other offices of government	31,500
Light and heating of palace and the public menagerie	2,400
Police	10,800
Messengers and spies	1,200
Ambassadors	15,000

The statistics of population are no less interesting. After describing the topography of Florence, especially the famous walls, Villani says that there are 25,000 men between 15 and 70 years of age capable of bearing arms, of whom 1,500 are nobles. Not including monks and nuns, the population of Florence is estimated at 90,000 people, plus an average floating population of 1,500. This estimation is based on the amount of bread daily consumed, the figures for which Villani got from the bakeries.[30] Annual births amount to 5,800. Between 8,000 and 10,000 children know how to read; there are six primary schools with an attendance of between 1,000 and 1,200, and four grammar schools with nearly 600 pupils. Florence has 57 parish churches, 5 abbeys, 24 convents, 10 monasteries (the disproportion is interesting), 30 hospitals with over 1,000 beds in them. The wool shops are over 200 in number and annually turn out between 70,000 and 80,000 bolts valued at 1,200,000 florins. More than 30,000 persons are employed in the textile industry. Thirty years before there were as many as 300 shops, but trade has fallen off since then. Again in 1472 we have a most important and complete survey of the commerce and industry of Florence. The income taxes paid by rich Florentines in the years 1427–32 are preserved.[31]

[30] Bk. X, cap. 193.
[31] Ehrenberg, *op. cit.*, I, p. 52 note.

All the great Florentine historians, and there were many, notably Varchi and Guicchiardini, took heavy toll of these statistical documents to be found in the archives. "For the first half of the sixteenth century probably no state in the world possesses a document like the magnificent description of Florence by Varchi." [32] He estimated that Florence had 10,000 *fuochi* or hearths; 50,000 secular population and 20,000 religious. Venice at the same time, according to Giannotti, counted 20,000 hearths. The same historian's comments upon the commercial spirit of Florence and the shop life are penetrating and interesting.

The financial status of the gilds of Florence is recorded in a remarkable document discovered by Davidsohn which shows the assessment on each gild in October, 1321. It is as follows: The woolen gild, 2,000 gold florins; silk gild, 400; physicians and apothecaries, 330; butchers, 325; the *calimala,* or cloth finishers, 320; judges and notaries, 100; bankers, 100; stone and wood dealers, 80; locksmiths and iron-workers, 80; carpenters, 50.

The spirit and extent of Florence's statistical documents during the Renaissance make them the richest of their kind. The lists recur at almost regular intervals of ten years, and are systematically arranged and tabulated. An inventory of 1422 enumerates the seventy-two exchanges which surrounded the Mercato Nuovo; the amount of money in circulation (2,000,000 gold florins); the new industry of gold thread spinning and concludes with an observation on the general prosperity of the republic. From the *Ricordi* of Lorenzo de' Medici estimates of the wealth and business activity of this house between 1434 and 1472 have been worked out.

For richness of statistical information Venetian documents rival, if they do not exceed, those of Florence. The doge Tommaso Mocenigo on his death bed (1423) summarized the economic results of his administration of the Venetian state—four million ducats of previous war loans paid, 6 million surplus. The capital employed in commerce he estimated at ten million ducats per annum. Venice possessed 3,000 small vessels with 17,000 sailors; 300 vessels of medium size with 8,000 sailors; 45 galleys with 11,000 marines. The houses in Venice were valued at ten million ducats and income from rents at 500,000. A thousand Venetians had incomes ranging from 70 to 4,000 ducats. The Zecca's business was over a million ducats a year. The annual commerce of Venice with Florentine amounted to 292,000 ducats.

Marino Sanudo, the greatest Venetian historian, summarizes the statistics of Venice for the year 1423, and gives the income figures for the provinces of Venice on the Italian mainland. The revenue from Padua and its territory amounted to 65,500 ducats, while the cost of administration was not over 14,000. The salt tax brought in 165,000

[32] Burckhardt, *op. cit.*, p. 79.

ducats; the land tax in the dogato (*i.e.,* the immediate territory of Venice) amounted to 25,000, of possessions outside of Italy, 5000. The clergy contributed 22,000, tariffs 16,000, the Jews 11,000. The state lost 6,000 ducats on houses occupied by the very poor.

Corio's *History of Milan* is of a piece with the works of Villani and Varchi for the statistical matter embodied in it. Genoa had no such historians as these, but the mass of Genoese documents of a statistical nature preserved in the archives is enormous. Even for Rome in the depth of the fourteenth century we have the details of a hearth tax (*focaticum*) imposed by Cola di Rienzi, together with his computations of the revenue arising from the salt monopoly in the papal states and the taxes on articles of consumption. For the period when Cardinal Albornoz was rector of the patrimony the remains are fuller. A still more exact document concerning the economic and fiscal condition of the Romagna and the Mark of Ancona was compiled by Cardinal Angelico in 1371. The Romagna in that year numbered 346,444 hearths; its annual revenue amounted to 100,000 gold florins. Schmoller in his epoch-making work,[33] from evidence preserved in the Italian archives has estimated the revenues of the principal states as follows:

Genoa in	1214	600,000 gold florins	
	1293	1,500,000	
	1395	3,000,000	
Pisa in	1293	2,400,000	
Florence in	1340	3,000,000	
	1423	4,000,000	
Pope in	1450	4,000,000	
	1520	4,000,000	
	1590	8,000,000	
Milan in	1423	10,000,000	
	1500	12,000,000 to 15,000,000	
Venice in	1423	11,000,000	
	1500	12,000,000 to 15,000,000	

Even Castilian Spain and England late in the fifteenth century began to keep up with the procession. In 1482, upon command of the catholic sovereigns, Alonso de Quintanilla compiled a census of population of Castile and concluded that there were 1,500,000 *vecinos* or heads of families. As early as 1429 the cortes of Valderrobla ordered a census of Aragon. In 1495 the cortes of Taragona ordered another, which revealed 50,391 *vecinos* as against 42,683 in the previous enumeration. No similar documents exist for other provinces of Spain in the fifteenth century, but by putting together various sources of information of a scattered and fragmentary nature for Granada, Navarre, Alava, and Guipuzcoa, it has been estimated that at the end of the fifteenth cen-

[33] *Grundriss der allgemeinen Volkswirtschaftslehre* (Leipzig, 1901–1904), Vol. I, p. 294.

tury there were 1,800,000 *vecinos* in Spain. If we count five persons per family, the population of the peninsula exclusive of Portugal would then approximate 9,000,000 persons.

In northern Europe our richest statistical information for conditions at the end of the Middle Ages chiefly pertains to the free cities of Germany. German historians have patiently worked out from local records estimates of population, revenues, rates and burdens of taxation for Lübeck, Hamburg, Frankfort, Basel, Dresden, Bern, Mainz, Cologne, Regensburg, Augsburg, Nuremberg, Strassburg, Breslau, Danzig, Rostock, Ulm. From a tax list and census made in Dresden in 1488 the *per capita* wealth has been estimated at 735 marks actual value. The steady increase in the number of free towns in Germany from century to century is in itself an impressive witness to the growth of German commerce and industry. In the year 1000 there were not more than 12 places worthy to be called "towns," though it must be understood that these were not yet free municipalities; in the eleventh century we find 16; in the twelfth century, 28; in the thirteenth century, 119; in the fourteenth century, over 200; in the fifteenth century, nearly 250.[34] London had a population of 46,000 in 1378.[35] On the basis of hearth taxes imposed in these towns interesting estimates of population have been made. Cologne at the end of the fifteenth century was far and away the largest city in Germany, having an estimated population of 52,000. Hegel and Buecher have estimated the population of Nuremberg in 1431 at 22,797, and a later calculation for the year 1499 makes it 20,211; Strassburg, Ulm, and Breslau circa 1475 did not exceed 20,000; Augsburg and Hamburg had not over 18,000; Frankfort not over 14,000; in 1460–61 Lübeck had 20,436; in 1487–88, 22,172; Rostock in 1378 had 10,785; in 1410, 13,935; Danzig in 1416 had 8,549; Dresden in 1489, 4,817; Basel in 1454 had 7,650.[36]

By 1500 it was the business of every ambassador in Europe to acquire all possible information of a financial and other statistical nature pertaining to the country to which he was accredited. The eager interest of governments in acquiring such statistical knowledge is a characteristic phenomenon of the period of discovery and the great international conflict for domination in Italy. Among early Venetian *Relations* are two inventories of the lands and revenues of Charles V giving the imperial income together with that of many nobles.[37] The connection between war and bank-loans was perceived in that day. Geiler von Kaiserberg inveighed against "tainted money" and "shooting fools," or in modern terms, against munition makers and ambitious politicians who battened on war.

[34] Schmoller, *op. cit.,* I, pp. 268–69.
[35] Wylie, *Henry IV,* Vol. III, p. 413 note.
[36] Below, *Vierteljahrschrift,* II (1904), pp. 477 f.
[37] Droysen, *Abhand. d. Sachs. Gesellschaft d. Wiss.,* III (1857).

CHAPTER XX

DURING the latter half of the fifteenth century all the factors and forces which worked to effect the transformation of Europe from medieval to modern were in simultaneous operation, and sometimes were so fused together that it is difficult to distinguish between them. These forces were a blend of conditions, practices, and ideas. This new economic and social condition, this new spirit was general to most of Europe. Everywhere in Europe the development of higher culture is identified with wealth. Where and when the old medieval feudo-ecclesiastical culture is found, there is a backward economic condition and a rigid social structure. The Old Europe is feudal, ecclesiastical, and agricultural. The New, Young Europe is bourgeois, commercial, industrial, and capitalistic. In proportion as capitalism spread over Europe in that proportion Old Europe was transformed and New Europe arose. The Northern Renaissance, whether of Flanders or the rich cities of Germany, was independent of Italy, but it was as intimately identified with commerce and industry, as solidly bourgeois as that of the Italian cities.

In politics a sign of the times is "the new political idea of an undivided state governed by one central and more or less absolute authority, as distinguished from the old feudal kingdom with its loosely knit aggregate of more or less independent fiefs."[1] As feudal history declined, dynastic history rose. This general tendency throughout Europe towards centralized monarchy was most apparent in France, Spain, and England. In these kingdoms it functioned with greatest energy and upon the largest scale. In Italy despotism was more local in its nature, but in spirit it was just as absolute as elsewhere. In Germany it was less general owing to the peculiar nature of German political development. Yet "even Maximilian I could see looming in the distance a dynastically secure universal monarchy of his house."[2] Concentration of political authority and power in the hands of the kings, with territorial consolidation, is everywhere observable. The old feudal provincialism could not hold its own against the new tendency of mon-

---

* For some of the material in this chapter I am indebted to my former student, Dr. Jean Ingram Brookes.

[1] Tilley, *Literature of the French Renaissance*, p. 126.

[2] Spengler, *Decline of the West*, II, p. 382.

archy and nationalism. Except in Germany even the great cities succumbed. In France, after the fall of Charles the Bold, the king had nothing to fear from the great feudal families.

The history of France under Louis XI, Charles VIII, and Louis XII is so typical of the new order of things in Europe in the latter half of the fifteenth century, so pivotal, that it may be treated at some length.

The first concern of the French monarchy was, naturally enough, the securing of its revenue, and the establishment of the arbitrary power of the crown to fix and assess the amount to be collected. Reform as the king might the system of collection on the domain, never again would its contributions be sufficient for even the infrequent times of peace; centralization, militarism, and the state of Europe forced up expenses, and the fiscal policy had to keep pace with the political. Charles VIII in the last months of his reign, making plans to live upon the revenue of the crown lands and duties, and to take from the people annually for the defense of the kingdom not more than 1,200,000 francs, was contemplating an impossible step backward. And though Commines might sententiously remark: "Of all the kings in the world, our sovereign has the least reason to use this expression, 'I have the privilege to raise what money I please upon my subjects,'"[3] by the very simple expedient of not summoning the estates-general the king made the financial power of that body a mere tradition. In preference he negotiated with the provincial estates, which were never able to contradict or to modify the decision of the royal council. The reaction of 1484 saw the reassertion of the money power of the estates-general, but the declaration emanating from Tours was a gesture without real consequences. Such was the extent of the financial power of the national monarchy that it could say, "Thou shalt have no other tax before mine," by forbidding the nobles to levy taxes upon their subjects except by royal consent through letters patent.

There was, then, no one to call a halt on the increasing exactions of the monarchy. Charles VII's total annual revenue had been 1,800,000 *livres*, his *taille* about 1,200,000 *livres*. The statistics for the *taille* from 1462 to 1483 run as follows:

1462	1,200,000 *livres*
1474	2,700,000 *livres*
1481	4,600,000 *livres*
1483	3,900,000 *livres*

The domain brought Louis XI an average of only 100,000 *livres*, as he alienated almost as much of the crown lands as he gained. It is illumi-

[3] Commines, *Mémoires*, I, p. 385.

nating to see how curtly the king writes to the chamber of accounts when it presumes to question his prodigal gifts. The aides and *gabelles*, 655,000 *livres* in 1484, had risen only to 700,000 in 1498—in the face of the growing prosperity of the country, an evidence of much corruption and inefficiency in the collection.

Still the total was not enough, and recourse was had to the old expedients: *décimes*, advances from the bankers, forced loans from the towns. The clergy fared no better than any other part of the nation in the matter of retaining the power of opening its own purse itself: the *décime* was not secured by a demand upon the pope, nor by the consent of the clergy. Amortization taxes and regalian rights over vacant benefices brought in respectable sums. The monarchy naturally, so far as it was possible, resorted preferably to loans from the French towns, loans which were not only exempt from interest charges, but did not have to be repaid at all. The irregularity and the weight of these demands had a highly deleterious effect, not only upon municipal finances, but upon the prosperity of the towns. In 1463 Louis XI secured out of the coffers of the cities the 200,000 *livres* he lacked toward the sum necessary for the redemption of the Somme towns. In 1496 Paris was called on for a contribution of 30,000 crowns. The cities complained to high heaven. But the exactions were not maliciously made; there was a real need of money, and hence the king turned a deaf ear to appeals. It took a catastrophe such as a flood or the plague to make Louis XI reduce his demands, while Charles VIII preferred the comedy of asking for more than was necessary in order to be able generously to reduce the amount.

The most obvious item on the royal budget was the expense of the royal court. Louis XI lived like a bourgeois, but the household expenses swelled from 250,000 *livres* in 1460 to 415,550 in 1481. We find Louis XI grumbling that "workmen arrange things to their own advantage to make the most out of it they can, especially when they have to deal with people who, they think, have a well-lined purse like myself." [4] Charles VIII and Anne wanted to "live like quality," and their expenses went close to the million mark. As it was a recognized policy to bind the nobles to the crown by gifts and pensions, these figured largely in the budget. Charles VIII gave an average of 500,000 *livres* for this purpose annually, so that it is no wonder that Commines said at his death there was "a great mourning for him, for he had been more bountiful to his favorites . . . than any king had ever been before; and indeed he gave them too much." [5]

Foreigners who might be useful or dangerous also had their pensions or their tribute: 16,000 crowns went annually to various English

[4] Letter of January 1, 1479.
[5] Commines, *op. cit.*, II, p. 288.

officials, while 50,000 crowns was the yearly portion of the English king from 1475 to 1483. The Swiss magistrates were insatiable, and Commines calculated that from the battle of Granson to the death of Louis XI, Berne, Lucerne, Freiburg, Zürich and their magistrates had received more than 1,000,000 Rhenish florins. Ordinarily pensions and tributes are monetarily cheaper than war, but Charles VIII's subsidies to foreign powers, in order that he might wage an offensive war of his own choosing, did not have even this justification.

Above all other expenses, however, came the maintenance of the army. The national king was so young in Europe, the national unity so new, that the policies of the government had always to be backed up by the threat of force; the "big stick" had always to be much in evidence. When one adds to this the necessity of showing that right had might behind it, it is clear why the army was a constant preoccupation of Louis XI and Charles VIII. Louis' early measures toward the increase and improvement of the military forces at his disposal were the doubling or tripling of the number of free archers provided by each town, and the organization of a militia in his good city of Paris. Poitiers, which furnished 12 free archers in 1468, sent 23 in 1474; Senlis by 1467 had tripled its quota and provided 18. The king refused firmly to pay anything toward what was considered the intolerable expense of equipping these soldiers. Fagniez has printed the interesting document which provided for the organization of the craftsmen and merchants of Paris in 61 banners, or troops, which were to be always drilled and equipped ready to serve the king. After experience of the ineffectiveness and insubordination of town-bred soldiers, Louis took the fearfully unpopular step of hiring foreign mercenaries, and gave "his kingdom a cruel wound, which will bleed a long time; namely by establishing a terrible band of paid soldiers in imitation of the princes of Italy." [6] The towns found this policy a chastisement of scorpions, for the money drain was much heavier than that in men. In compliance with the reactionary ideas current after the death of Louis, Anne de Beaujeu dismissed the Swiss mercenaries and attempted to organize a local gendarmerie, with little success. An honest effort was made by Charles VIII to maintain discipline so that the term soldier should no longer be synonymous with marauder, but his absence in Italy vitiated all such reforms.

Perhaps the worst of the military abuses arising from the new practices was the billeting of this royal army within or near the towns. The king might send orders for energetic discipline, but so long as the soldiers were not regularly paid, they were bound to take the arrears in one form or another out of the pockets and the peace of the townsmen. There was often an almost complete interruption of commerce

[6] Commines, *op. cit.*, II, p. 43.

when troops were in or near a town, for the merchants would not come in, only to be pillaged. In addition to the billeting, a constant stream of royal commissioners came with requisitions for salt-peter, armor, grain; in Rheims, in 1476, for all the artillery, horses, and carts in the city. The heavy expenses of maintenance of its fortifications was paid by each city, though a royal official might supervise the engineering and secure his share of the graft.

With the expenses of the army grew those of the fleet necessitated by the prevalence of piracy, the desultory conflict with England and Spain, and, finally, the designs on Italy. Louis XI continued the work of Jacques Coeur. Charles VIII went still further, on one occasion calling a master ship-builder from Venice to supervise the construction of three new ships. When in 1491 Charles recruited 500 sailors, the fisc saved itself from any loss by assessing the 200 odd *livres* which was their share of the *taille,* upon the *franches-villes* of that area. For great works, the French fleet was not enough; in 1494 the French used that of Genoa, and Commines reported that the fleet got ready at Genoa cost about 300,000 francs, "which quite exhausted the King's treasury." [7]

The period of Louis XI and Charles VIII was one at best of intermittent war. The results of this situation included more than the pouring out of French resources, and the interruptions to normal economic life caused by the marching and counter-marching of troops the length and breadth of the land. It is to be noticed that war had ceased to be the calling of a class, and become a capitalistic enterprise demanding larger sums of money in a form available more immediately and more conveniently than the national revenue could ever be.[8] Out of this in large measure came the alliance of the national monarchy and the international banker. Wars like those of Louis XI, which added to the unified state such commercially and industrially important provinces as Normandy or the Burgundian lands had some results economically advantageous to the country. Commines says Louis XI's determination to have Normandy was due to the "vast sums of money which are raised in it, for I myself have known it to pay 950,000 francs in one year, and some say more." [9]

Agriculture was the first phase of the economic renaissance to become important, but Louis XI and Charles VIII had little direct influence on its resurrection. Save in the matter of snatching every morsel of property whose holder could not show charters and titles and give them a monetary defense in court, the king showed little positive concern for land. The great energy shown in clearing the *terra*

[7] Commines, *op. cit.,* II, p. 122.
[8] Kaser, *Spätmittelalter,* p. 158.
[9] Commines, *op. cit.,* I, p. 70.

deserta, the breaking up of large fiefs into many holdings, the generalizing of land-holding, the attempt to adjust land revenues to the fluctuations of land values by the introduction of the short-term lease, the sinister prevalence of the *contrat de rente,* these were movements and tendencies with which the monarchy did not concern itself. An entirely futile effort was made to check speculation and corners in grain. Cereal production, particularly wheat, and viticulture grew by leaps and bounds. By 1500 land values had climbed back to their position in 1400, and landed capital was to continue to hold its own in France.

Unlike agriculture, industry felt itself taken in the hollow of the royal hand.

By the close of the fifteenth century a reaction had set in against the freedom of individual activity. Free labor was giving place to regulation by the trade, spontaneous indeed, but encouraged by the crown. Royalty and bourgeoisie combined to crush outside competition with the trades. Commerce underwent a similar reaction. The particularism of the French provinces soon raised a cry for the reimposition of provincial customs and the protection of provincial products. Aliens who had been generously welcomed after the war, are now subjected to harassing disabilities.[10]

The old corporation had been a simple legal association, and the monarchs, with the exception of Philip IV, had either considered the organization of industry not part of public administration, or had been too harassed with other work to attempt interference. Now the impulse toward change came from both sides. The *"métier libre"* was giving way to the *"métier juré"* as the master workmen were bending their efforts to make their group a closed caste and to regulate more minutely the conditions of labor and the quality and quantity of output. Because the lower ranks of the artisan class were very inflammable material, and because the masters controlled town policies by controlling town offices, Louis XI and Charles VIII allied with the masters. The former intervened in many instances to force the free crafts to organize into closed corporations. At Tours, in 1481, he ordered *"que tous les mestriers d'icelle ville . . . fussent jurez."* This system tended to become the common law of industry, extending even to the smaller towns. In this and in his further interference Louis XI was actuated by various motives. It was to the interest of the craft that the number of masters be kept down so that there should be a fair profit for all. The public wanted standard quality and the assurance of a steady supply, to which demand the masters answered that unless free competition were checked they would have to close their shops and leave the town unprovided for. An alliance with the masters not only gave the crown the support of the towns against the seigniors, but out of every rise in

---

[10] *English Historical Review,* XXI, p. 576.

fees and fines sponsored by the former, the royal treasury took a goodly share.

The imperative voice of the royal official was heard on every conceivable point: correcting and approving the statutes and by-laws, settling hours of work and holidays or the use of trade-marks, advising on the processes of manufacture, pronouncing on quality. In Paris Louis XI gave the *garde de la prévôté* police supervision over the gilds. In lesser towns the bailiff or seneschal had the same power. At Lyons the seneschal refused to confirm the statutes presented by the pin-makers and denounced them to the king as contrary to the public welfare. They were not confirmed until the reign of Charles VIII.

In spite of all his wars and counter-wars, Louis XI found time for an enormous legislative activity in regard to the crafts. In the single harried month of June, 1467, the king issued ordinances about shoe-makers, fullers, ball makers, glovers, tailors, doublet-makers. This legislative activity reached its peak in the great ordinance of 1479 regulating the making of woolen cloth all over the kingdom, an ordinance framed after consultation with the cloth-makers of Paris. More and more the system in use in Paris came to be considered the norm, and the government worked to secure a uniformity patterned after the Parisian model.

Louis XI regarded it as axiomatic that a king who made laws and regulations for the gilds should be able to grant dispensations therefrom, in the interest of the king or of the industry. He made favored individuals masters in their craft. At Troyes he authorized the workers in sheep leather to work at night. Louis and Charles being interested in peopling the enlarged town of Orléans, decreed that the workmen in the new faubourgs were free from all gild control—but not from the supervision of royal officials. The newly established silk industry was left a free craft, in the hope of hastening its naturalization.

In the industrial revival so apparent in the period of Louis XI and Charles VIII one may point out as causes not only the growth of corporative organization, the introduction of new industries, the protective measures of the crown, but more than any of these perhaps, the growing demands and expanding markets of late fifteenth century Europe.

The most flourishing of the national industries was the making of woolen cloth, for which Rouen in particular was the greatest center. The prosperity of the cloth towns was so striking as to arouse competition, and Tours, with favors from Louis XI, and Poitiers, to whose cloth gilds Charles VIII in 1488 gave exemption from the duties on wool and dyes, became centers in their turn. Thanks to the effort of the crown, the industrial régime was introduced into Languedoc, so that that province gradually became less tributary to the north and to Italy. In 1477 Louis authorized Nîmes to organize cloth-making; the same favor or command was given to Montpellier in 1476, though there the gild was not successfully organized until 1483. Charles VIII defended this nascent industry against Catalan competition by a prohibitive tariff.

Due to the initiative and perseverance of Louis XI the silk industry was established in France. In December of 1466 the king notified Lyons of the imposition upon that city of the sum of 2,000 *livres tournois* to be used in the establishment of the silk industry in their midst. He expected by this move to enrich the city and to keep money from flowing out of the kingdom, for he estimated that France lost annually to the Italians 400,000 or 500,000 gold crowns by the purchase of silks and cloth of gold. He proclaimed the new industry an honorable craft *"auquel se pourront occuper licitement hommes et femmes de tous estaz, . . . tans gens d'églises, nobles, femmes de religion que autres, qui à present sont oiseux, y auront honneste et prouffitable occupacion."* [11] The following year he imported Genoese, Florentine, and Venetian silk weavers, established them at Lyons, and gave them important privileges. But the Lyonnais considered the whole scheme a rash and expensive innovation, and showed itself both unwilling and incompetent to make a success of the industry, which was therefore moved to Tours within four years after establishment of the craft. There it became firmly rooted, and Charles VIII gave assistance to the making of *"draperie de luxe"* by forbidding the importation of gold or silver cloth, velours, satin, or damask (1485).

The crown exerted itself similarly to encourage the exploitation of the mineral resources of the country. Louis XI's comprehensive ordinance of 1471 created a bureau of mines with the power to grant concessions, and to prospect and exploit mines which the proprietors themselves could not develop. At the same time, he brought in workmen from the Rhine and from Swabia, to whom he gave all the civil rights of citizens and exemptions from taxes and military service. These immunities were renewed by Charles VIII. This hospitality toward foreign skilled labor was a powerful element in the industrial progress of the country. The Italians for ship-building and weaving, the Germans for metal-working and printing, made themselves useful above all others. To the end of the fifteenth century, the mines were worked chiefly by Germans.

The wealthy bourgeois and the nobles developed a passion for *objets d'art* in metal, particularly gold and silver, until, as at Dijon in 1482, the demand and the supply of workers outran the supply of metal. Louis showed his usual calculating prodigality toward other-worldly

[11] *Lettres de Louis XI*, III, pp. 121–122.

powers in his gifts to St. Martin of Tours (1478–1480) : a silver lattice containing 6,776 marks of metal, two gold and silver reliquaries, a statue of the king, kneeling.

France was quick to adopt the new art of printing. From Paris, where it was introduced by a Frenchman and three Germans in 1470, and Lyons where printers from Liège and from Nuremberg established it in 1473, it spread rapidly over the country. Lyons became a book market renowned all over Europe, with more than 160 printers establishing themselves there between 1473 and 1500; and by the end of the reign of Charles VIII, all over the kingdom French printers were supplanting their German rivals.

When the crown turned its attention to commerce the most pressing need was clearly the restoration of the markets and fairs disrupted by the long wars—a consummation devoutly to be wished by king, cities, and nobles alike. Louis founded or reëstablished by royal letter sixty-six fairs, among them the rather sickly growth planted by Charles VII at Lyons. In 1463 Louis wrote to the chamber of accounts that he had granted *"certaines nos lettres patentes . . . aux conseilliers et habitans de notre ville de Lion. . . . Et pour ce que nous avons le fait des dictes foires tres a coeur"* (what a favorite phrase this was with this unsentimental king). The exchequer was to hasten to verify and send on these letters.[12] The making of the grant at that time was connected with Louis' policy toward the fairs at Geneva. The flocking of French merchants, the outpouring of French coin here wrung his mercantilist heart, hence his increase of the number of fairs at Lyons to four, to be held on days coinciding with those of Geneva; his granting of valuable privileges and immunities, and finally the prohibition of any trafficking of French merchants at Geneva. Geneva's frantic protests left him unmoved, though they were useful as a means of blackmailing Lyons into contributions for the king's purposes. The Lyons Fairs suffered an eclipse in 1484 when it was decided that their proximity to the border allowed too much coin to go out of the country, and the fairs were moved to Bourges, then to Troyes, but the privileges of Lyons were restored in 1494. In 1470 the treatment accorded Geneva was repeated in the case of all the great fairs of Flanders, all Normans being forbidden to have any commercial relations with the territory of Charles the Bold, and two free fairs being set up at Caen at a time coinciding with those of Antwerp.

Charters of concession for markets and fairs multiplied under Charles VIII, who granted 125 in the years 1483–90, and 152 between 1490 and 1498. Typical grants of privileges to the fairs included some or all of the following: the right to use foreign money, and to export

[12] *Lettres de Louis XI*, II, p. 109.

precious metals, exemption from the *"droit d'aubain"* and even from the 12 *denier* tax. The creation of free fairs, at which the merchants found not only security and financial exemptions, but in addition the special jurisdiction of judges called *"conservateurs des foires"* enormously stimulated trade and commerce in those areas.

The suppression of the *"droit d'aubain"* in the ports and large cities was widespread, but Louis and Charles went beyond this and multiplied personal exemptions and letters of naturalization to foreign merchants. As Louis XI was never one to let political hostilities interfere unnecessarily with economic processes advantageous to France, he authorized his subjects to maintain commercial relations even with enemy states, and forbade reprisals. In 1470, writing to Troyes, he warned citizens that although the duke of Burgundy had seized the goods of French merchants, Troyes must not interfere with the property of Burgundians, and must restore any goods already seized.

Another stimulus to trade was the dredging of river channels, and the repair of roads and bridges, to which the monarchy contributed. Worse barriers than mud holes and shaky bridges, however, were those of provincial customs duties and an infinite variety of seigniorial tolls, a drain upon the purse and an unsupportable delay to the passage from one point to another. The monarchy was inclined to listen to the clamors of the merchant associations, and the protests of the several estates, for the destruction of provincial duties and of tolls fitted in very well with the unifying, antifeudal purposes of the crown. Yet the work of pushing the customs lines out to the frontier of the country was barely begun in this period, and although Louis XI broke down many of the toll barriers on the Rhône and the Saône, and in 1483 planned for the abolition of all tolls within the kingdom, the repeated legislation of Charles VIII is witness to the fact that the efforts of neither king had been very successful. It was in reality only the long and bitter struggle waged by the. towns and merchant associations which finally eliminated the abuse.

The ordinance of June 19, 1464, establishing postal service in all parts of the kingdom, a thing "which before never had been done," as Commines points out, was, though the service was not yet open to common use, an important step forward. The charge was ten *sous* per horse for four leagues. It is not stated whether or not there was a defioit.

By the last half of the fifteenth century the rulers of the new national states had realized that regulation of the system of international exchange had become a governmental function; and treaties between states began to take the place of the older agreements between cities or hanses. In such treaties the right of commerce, instead of being an arbitrary concession, a toleration of individuals, became the general rule so that any merchant of a friendly power might enter the country, travel about, and set himself up in business.

M. Charles de la Roncière, a French historian, has pictured Louis XI as a confirmed protectionist, whose motto was *"L'industrie, le commerce, le navigage français, aux Français."* [13] Louis XI was one of the earliest mercantilists because of his insistence on the development of national resources to the point of economic independence for France; his demand upon French industry and commerce that they free themselves from, and compete with, the Italian economic world power. But, in Lavisse's phrase, Louis was not a *"protectionist insensé."* Though he wished to make use of all the national resources to enrich his subjects and his treasury and to keep coin from leaving the country, though he protected infant industries, though he evolved a bold scheme for monopolizing the commerce of the Mediterranean, he recognized clearly enough when France needed the coöperation of other nations. His hospitable attitude to foreign merchants, his free trade arrangements with England, his whole series of commercial treaties, are evidence of his determination to free France from the economic isolation to which war and anarchy had reduced her. Charles VIII continued Louis' policy of protection of French industry, but his proclamation in 1484, or rather than of Anne de Beaujeu, of complete liberty of commerce to Frenchman and foreigner alike showed that free trade was winning over protectionism.

Louis XI began his campaign to free France from economic subordination to Italian, particularly Venetian, merchants, by two edicts: that all spices, silks, and other Levantine products must be imported in the "galleys of France" (1464), and that foreigners were forbidden entry to the ports of Languedoc. Four galleys were built, one of which concentrated on the Spanish coast, while the other three, starting from Aigues-Mortes, stopped at Marseilles, Nice, Pisa, Gaeta, Naples, Palermo, Messina, and Rhodes, on the way to Jaffa, Beirut, and Alexandria. Louis XI's attempt to give his protégé, Callioure, the same privileges that Aigues-Mortes enjoyed met with such opposition that the monopoly was restored. But the port was given its death blow when Provence was annexed by the crown. The elimination of foreign traders and foreign shipping was a source of the liveliest discontent on the part of the merchants of Languedoc, who protested that their fairs were ruined and their exports cut in half, and even tried to bribe the king by offering money for the improvement of the harbor of Aigues-Mortes. So obvious was the failure of the plan that Louis XI repealed the ordinance in 1467. But he hoped to strike an even more effective blow at Venice by crippling her ocean commerce: hence French ships

[13] Roncière, in *Rev. des quest. hist.*, LVIII, p. 75.

attacked and plundered the Venetian galleys so often and with such success that the galleys could sail only with an armed guard, and the captains feared an ambush behind every rocky headland. In 1478 Venice secured a peace rather of toleration than of amity. In 1481 king renounced the monopoly of the galleys of France, and tried to more sensible course of urging citizens of every estate to build ships. The year before he had authorized nobles, clerics, and royal officers to go into commerce without losing rank.

Stimulated to new interest in the Levantine trade by the acquisition of Provence, Louis summoned merchant deputies from eleven of the important cities, to meet at Tours in February, 1482. There his representative explained to the assembly the gigantic scheme for a *"Compagnie générale de commerce et de navigation dans la mer du Levant,"* capitalized at 100,000 *livres,* whose merchant ships would secure a complete monopoly of Levantine products and furnish all Western Europe with them. The merchants, who saw the free fairs of Lyons attracting foreigners to the detriment of the maritime towns of the Mediterranean, probably said privately that they wished His Majesty would cease having these hare-brained inspirations in the matter of the Levantine trade; and answered aloud that France was poor, the inland cities could not be interested in the support of such a company, and the better principle, was, after all, complete liberty of commerce. So the great company went no farther.

One other point of interest in Louis' persistent efforts with regard to French trade in the Mediterranean was the sending of an ambassador in 1482 to the "kings" of Tunis and Bona, but no permanent gain resulted.

The whole question of the relation of France to the commerce of the Mediterranean seemed settled when the government of Charles VIII proclaimed liberty of commerce. The only dissenting voice came from Languedoc, fighting a losing battle against the competition of Provence and the shifting of economic equilibrium in the Midi. With the French invasion of Italy, however, the ghost began to walk again.

Relations with Spain, Portugal, England, and the Hanseatic League were the subject of frequent treaties. Early in the reign Majorca and Valencia were opened to the French galleys, and a French consul was sent to Naples. But Louis gradually began to show an aversion to Castilian merchants, whose concentration on articles of luxury took away too much good French money. His attitude led to the closing of Spain to the French. At the same time, however, Portugal was opened; and more cordial commercial relations with Spain were reëstablished after the treaty of Barcelona.

The ports of the west coast were in a bad way since the war, with practically no ships of their own, and the English forbidden entry by

Charles VII. Louis aided La Rochelle by abolishing *"droit de baptisage"* on vessels entering the harbor for the first time, and in 1463 gave all nations the right of entry to Bordeaux, under only the 12 *deniers* duty. Bordeaux later was given a monopoly of export privileges by the decree that all the merchants of the neighboring provinces must ship via Bordeaux all goods for Spain, Portugal, Navarre, Brittany, England, and Flanders.

Louis XI thoroughly approved of the Anglo-French trade, for the English bought the olive oil of the South, wines of Gascony and Champagne, the cloths and haberdashery of the North, but sold in return only less expensive raw materials, such as wool and leather. It became the king's determination to win back the English merchants to France, and even to make the Channel an Anglo-French preserve. When he induced Philip of Burgundy to close the Flemish emporiums to the English, they reluctantly turned to France, but the outbreak of the War of the Public Weal prevented the conclusion of any arrangements. In 1470 he negotiated a truce with Henry VI which provided for absolute free trade between the two countries for six years. In connection with the embassy concluding these arrangements, Louis evolved the novel plan of sending over, under the immunities accorded diplomatic baggage, French products to the value of 25,000 crowns, not to be sold, but merely to be exhibited. The plan was not successful, and Europe was spared this early a development of the "Exposition." Just at that time Edward IV returned and war broke out again, though the commerce of La Rochelle was saved by its being declared a neutral port (1472). In 1475–76 a truce was arranged which provided that only ships belonging to England or to France might trade between the two countries. Charles VIII had more than one reason for desiring the establishment of an entente cordiale with England; and was only too glad to carry through treaties in 1492 and 1497 which did away with all extraordinary charges imposed on the subjects of either king, and established special judges in the ports to handle maritime cases. The governments agreed to take common measures against piracy and to regulate the right of prizes.

Relations with the Flemings were unfriendly throughout most of the reign of Louis XI. Though his prohibition against the fairs in the Low Countries was never completely enforced, Louis denied the petition of the Flemings (1476) for the abolition of the duty of two crowns per cask on wine; and from 1478 to 1483 merchant fleets from the Low Countries were persistently attacked and plundered by the French fleet.

The situation was different with regard to the Hanseatic League. Louis was glad to grant them in successive treaties (1464, 1473, 1483) exemption from all subsidies, aides and *gabelles,* and the payment of the same tariff as that levied on French merchants for the weighing of their merchandise. Hanseatic merchants might acquire any sort of property in France, and dispose of it by will. In case of a war with Germany, they had a year in which to settle up accounts and leave the country. The king assigned them protectors, the admiral, the bailiffs of Rouen, the governor of La Rochelle, and others, who were to handle any cases in which Hanseatic merchants were involved. The French received similar privileges in the Hanseatic cities.

Yet however energetic the treaty-making, its stimulus to commerce was often counterbalanced by the effects of piracy and privateering. Spain and England could always be considered ancient enemies to France, and by the time of the death of Louis XI, the French fleet was pursuing English, Spanish, Portuguese and Italian alike. Not only were diplomatic relations so tense and so shifting that there was always a pretext for a raid on any nearby coast, but the right of reprisal was still recognized on the sea if not on land; and, after all, it was less trouble to subsidize efficient, successful pirate captains to prey only on the shipping of one's friend the enemy, than it was to attempt to capture prominent pirates and dangle them from the yard-arms. The series of treaties negotiated by Charles VIII in 1492–93 were, however, reasonably successful in making the Bay of Biscay and the Channel peaceful and safe for commerce.

Much has been written on the strong connection between Louis XI and the towns of France. On the surface how benevolent the king feels towards his *bonnes villes!* His letters salute them graciously: *"Chiers et bien amez";* how thoughtful he is to thank Lyons for *"le bon recueil que vous avez fait a nostre beau-pere de Savoie, dont nous sommes bien contens de vous."*[14] He pays them the compliment of telling them his troubles: that in spite of an increase in the pension of the duke of Berry, that prince has fled the court; he is quick to warn them that the dukes of Brittany, Berry and Burgundy are using lepers for their emissaries. More than these, he restores privileges, occasionally lowers taxes, proves his confidence in the loyal gildsmen of Paris by organizing them into a militia under a royal officer. Most obvious proof of the trust he feels in the townsmen, and his confidence in their ability, was in 1470, 1479, and 1483, when he called consultative assemblies made up of good business men from the towns.

But beneath the surface there is nothing more kindly than utilitarianism. In his struggle with a feudality determined not to die till sundown, Louis needed the support of the towns; for every aggressive act and the fulfillment of every policy he needed ready money and that could be readily secured only from the town and from the bourgeois

[14] *Lettres de Louis XI,* II, p. 138.

capitalist. Certainly Louis XI laid as firm a hand upon the independence of the towns as he did upon that of any other part of the body politic which might have power to oppose his will. He lent his complete support to the movement which stripped power from the assemblies of citizens to give it to an oligarchical group of the wealthier bourgeois, and in return they took his orders. In elections, justice, and police the king's agent was the power, not even the hidden power. Without any fear of effective contradiction the king could send to Poitiers an order to elect Michau Dauron *"nostre varlet de chambre et receveur en Poitou,"* [15] as mayor, or indicate to Amiens that it would be agreeable to the king to see Jean de Caurroy become mayor.

The agents of the crown began next to turn a righteously honest and efficient eye upon the municipal budgets. Louis XI's officers were present at the submission of accounts, Charles VIII's supervised the assessment of taxes and made inquests into abuses. At the other end, also, the crown controlled municipal finances, for though the central government spent all of its funds on war and *"politique,"* and gave practically no services to the towns, the latter were entirely dependent for the levying of their imposts upon the will of the king. Municipal taxation was based on *octrois* conceded by the crown and determined in kind and amount by the crown. Louis was, however, willing enough to support the contention of the towns that nobles and clergy living within their walls ought to contribute to the expenses of the town, particularly to the maintenance of the fortifications. Ordinarily the king rules that clergy must submit to municipal taxation, that nobles must pay on non-noble holdings within the town or its suburbs, that the ennobled bourgeois—and there were shoals of them—could not claim tax immunity. But the case was very different in regard to members of the bureaucracy or individuals who had been useful to the king. Letters in which he asks Lyons to hold Jean de Garguessalle *"premier escrier de corps et maistre de nostre escuierie,"* and Pierre du Nievre, his father, quit of the aid levied on the city; [16] or asks Troyes to honor the letters of exemption from the *taille* and the duty of watch, and grants a pension to the widow of Antoine Dozenac, are typical examples of very common orders from the king to the towns.

It is difficult to estimate the value of the economic policy of Louis XI and Charles VIII. France in that period, approximately the last forty years of the fifteenth century, had her economic renaissance magnificently furthered, and maddeningly checked by the policies of the crown, so vitally and so commandingly connected had the central government become with the economic life of the country. The polyglot tongue of trade and commerce, the humming of industry sounded

[15] *Ibid.,* II, p. 132.
[16] *Lettres de Louis XI,* III, p. 205.

with a welcome loudness after the stillness of exhaustion caused by a century of war. In M. Imbart de la Tour's apt words: "If Spain *finds* gold, France *creates* it." Cities felt a surge of life, and tore down old town walls to build new streets. The self-made man, with all his pride in achievement, was everywhere apparent. The population increased in town and country. A disconcerting vogue for silks and satins brought out a sumptuary law in 1485 forbidding the wearing of these new costly garments to any who were not of the ancienne noblesse, or chevaliers with an income of 200 *livres*. The cloth-makers of Rouen in 1494 protested that the abandonment of woolen cloth was so great as to cause a crisis in the industry. The standard of living rose for all classes—except the urban proletariat.

These kings were not *"rois des petites gens."* As M. de la Tour points out, in the neatly arranged hierarchy the city masses were always a redoubtable unknown quantity with no stability, no ambitions on which the monarchy could count. They were a menace; they rose often, and with the king's aid were pitilessly suppressed. The aides and *gabelles* of the crown, the *octrois* of the towns, struck the poor with disproportionate force. Low wages with high taxes and high food prices contributed to an alarming increase of pauperism in the towns. Rheims had 2,000 paupers out of a population of 10,000.

One does not need to listen to the jeremiads of the estates-general held at Tours in 1484 to realize that there were other dark spots on the picture. The city budgets showed persistent deficits which were not cured by the thoughtless remedy of mortgaging the municipal incomes; but possibly this condition was as much due to the inability to adjust municipal financial methods to the demands of a new age, as to the heavy exactions made by the crown.

In any case, though the towns might feel they had their grievances, it must be remembered that they were useful to the king and were therefore favored by him. To quote See, *"les grandes cités sont bien moins malheureuses que les bourgs, les bourgs sont moins maltraités que les campagnes."* [17] Political interests might force the king to remit the tax burden of a town, but the fisc must not suffer thereby: the tax was added to those already weighing upon a voiceless countryside. If the situation was bad in those provinces which still had estates to protest in their names, one can imagine how much worse were conditions in the provinces without estates. The country people were brought low by taxes, and crushed to the earth by the man-at-arms.

In the large, then, one has the picture of a France in a period of economic resurrection directed and furthered by the economic actions and policy of the monarchy, but hampered and halted by its political

[17] Henri See, *Louis XI et les villes,* p. 350.

aims and methods. Economic progress was not able to secure the full vitality of a country torn and burdened by the wars which Louis XI could not, and Charles VIII would not, avoid.

Whether that spectacular eruption of the French into Italy in 1494 was a bold move in a bolder scheme of commercial supremacy, or the reckless lust for power of a small mind, has led to wide differences of opinion. It has been argued that France needed to be mistress of one of the great seas [18] that she might oppose to the oceanic commercial monopoly of the Spanish and the Portuguese that of the routes of the Levant, secured by eliminating Italian competition, and that she might free herself from commercial subordination to the Venetians by securing control of the resources of Italy. When every precious-cargoed ship in the Middle Sea should float the royal banner, France would not need to envy the humdrum, work-a-day Spanish and English ships which touched at her western and northern ports. Kaser [19] however, calls the French policy with regard to Italy purely dynastic politics, and the invasion fantastic in goal, barbaric in method, not dictated by any need. Charles VIII was impelled by a blind *"Drang nach Machtvermehrung."* Fueter [20] declares that the prosperous France of the late fifteenth century was defensively, from the economic point of view, invulnerable, and that an imperialistic policy of expansion was a sheer luxury. No other political act of the time, he says, was so dependent upon the free will of the ruling personality instead of upon military or economic necessities, as the French descent upon Italy. The government's decision was due to an error in its judgment of the attainable, and this defect was partially due to the defective organization of the French diplomatic service.

Whether or not Charles VIII inherited the dreams of Louis XI of making the Mediterranean a French lake, the invasion of Italy had economic results. First the consent of, or the neutrality of, the powers had to be bought by the costly concessions of the treaties of Etaples, Barcelona, and Senlis: 745,000 gold crowns to Henry VII, Roussillon and the Cerdagne to Spain without the payment of the mortgage of 300,000 crowns, the yielding of valuable territory to Maximilian. Then, somehow, funds had to be found for the army of 40,100 men, the 100 siege guns, and the fleet of 50 galleys, 24 *gros navires* and 12 galleons. Alienation of crown lands, forced loans from the cities, contributions from Milan, loans from Genoese bankers—the Florentine money market was no longer open since Charles' first overt act had been the spoliation and expulsion of the agents of the bank of the Medici in Lyons—these sources had to be strained to the utmost. For his Italian

---

[18] De la Tour, *Origines de la Reforme*, I, p. 260.
[19] Kaser, *Spät-Mittelalter*, pp. 154, 160.
[20] Fueter, *Gesch. des. Europ. Staatensystems von 1492–1559*, pp. 53, 77.

campaign Charles borrowed 100,000 francs from the Sauli bank in Genoa at 45 per cent interest, and 50,000 ducats from the duke of Milan. The king of France was in such straits that he borrowed the jewels of the duchess of Savoy and the marchioness of Montferrat, to pawn them for 24,000 ducats. Charles was confident that this temporary financial stringency would pass away so soon as the 1,500,000 *livres* of revenue from Naples was in his hands, and even promised to repay from this source the loan gouged out of the unwilling citizens of Troyes. On the other side of the ledger appears the consideration that the intimate contact with commercial and industrial and cultural Italy cannot have failed to force French business technique a step forward, to stimulate French competition with the longer-established Italian industries, to create new wants which Frenchmen would hasten to supply. Charles brought back with him to the castle of Amboise a small army of jewelers, embroiderers, cabinet makers, organ-makers, and very probably other merchants and artisans followed in the wake of the French army. But this year of contact with Italy was more a stimulus and an incentive to activities already in existence than the cause of the creation of new ones; for corporations of painters, wood-carvers, glass-makers, tapestry-makers, French, not foreign, had been multiplying since the days of Charles VII, and the French army found French merchants already well established in Italy.

The protective legislation of Louis XI, united with the jealousy of all Europe against the French on account of their ambitious war of territorial aggrandizement in Italy, resulted in the economic isolation of France. Yet to all outward appearances the new policy paid. The economic prosperity of France in the reign of Louis XII (1498–1515) is indubitable. The glowing picture of the contemporary historian, Claude de Syssel, can be amplified by much other evidence. A modern historian has written of Louis XII's reign:

At no period of her history had France enjoyed such great prosperity. The absence of all civil war for twenty years, the good order maintained by a regular and watchful administration, the security of person and property, the protection afforded to the lowly against the great, to the laborers against the aristocracy and the soldiery, bore marvellous fruit; the population rapidly increased; the cities, straitened in their ramparts, pushed forward their ever-growing suburbs; hamlets and villages arose as if by enchantment in the middle of woods or among once barren wastes. The last trace of the fatal wars which had depopulated France were entirely effaced, and a contemporary writer (Seyssel) states that a third of the kingdom had been brought again under culture in the last thirty years. There was an enormous increase in agricultural produce; the sums paid for farming the taxes were in many places more than two-thirds higher, and the revenues of the royal domain, increasing in the same proportion as those of private individuals, enabled the king to carry on his enterprises without oppressing the nation. Industry and commerce had made similar progress; commercial relations were indefinitely multiplied and merchants made less difficulty of going to Rome or Naples or London than formerly to Lyons or Geneva. The luxury and elegance of the buildings, of furniture and of dress testified to the development of art and the general prosperity.[21]

[21] Henri Martin, *Histoire de France*, VIII, pp. 471–472.

CHAPTER XXI

GERMANY, ITALY AND SPAIN AT THE END OF THE MIDDLE AGES

At the end of the fifteenth century the German people were rich in national possessions, the ground was well cultivated, the wide stretches of forest cleared, and the mines in full working. Of all the countries of Europe Germany had suffered least from the ravages of the Black Death. The German merchant had become the leading commercial person in the west, the Hansa League ruled the northern seas, the south Germans from their factory at Venice distributed eastern spices throughout Europe, German handicraftsmen were celebrated in all lands for their skill and finish, the citizens had their houses filled with costly treasures. Natural economy gave place to money payments as coin, capital and credit became familiar features in business life through the agency of the great German financiers whose customers were the monarchs of Europe.[1]

Commerce made the prosperity of the cities which between the thirteenth and fifteenth centuries are the characteristic economic feature of German life. While the central government was weak, they were strong. The cities had no social homogeneity, the gild wars of the fourteenth century being economic and social as well as political. Nor were they democratic, for wealth made a new aristocracy beneath which was the proletariat, a dangerous element in restless times. The conflict between the cloth-makers and the cloth and wool merchants was really a struggle between labor and capital. In many cities, at the beginning of the sixteenth century, there was a new rising of the proletariat against the council, for the purpose of gaining rights. The cities were strong enough to defy this first manifestation, but a few years later the city proletariat united with the discontented peasants in the Peasants' Revolt (1525).

While the lot of the German burgher class steadily improved in the fourteenth and fifteenth centuries, that of the proletariat and the peasantry grew steadily worse from the thirteenth century forward. The excessive development of local authority, with no check upon it from above, led to intense fiscal exploitation of the peasantry in the form of *zins*, renders, corvées and prestations, a condition which was aggravated by the prevalence of a new kind of petty officials, the ministerials. Thus we observe in Germany in the later Middle Ages a social phenomenon found nowhere else in Europe, at least in the same degree, namely, a widening of the cleavage between the common peasantry and

[1] *Econ. Jnl.*, XII, p. 76.

the burghers, or to put it in other words, a steady elevation of the
burghers and as steady a depression of the peasants. Burghers and
knights between them helped to isolate and make the peasantry more
defenseless than ever. The tillers of the soil, owing to their forced or
inherited political and social inactivity, were caught between the two
vastly more active factors and sadly ground down. Yet of the two, the
burgher class, by its wider interests and its increasing need of performers of manual labor, offered a refuge to the over-oppressed peasant; while the military class, the knights, whose sole fortune consisted
in the peasants settled on their lands, and bound to provide for them,
their household and retainers, in course of time left no scheme untried
for getting all the profit from the transaction which the proprietary
rights of the one party and the dependent and defenseless position of
the other party would present. As the centuries progressed, this peculiar exploitation of labor became aggravated and the harassed and
distracted toiler finally rose in revolt.

The lower aristocracy, the knights, were profoundly influenced by
the political and economic changes of the period, and the shifting of
values from land to commerce. Their estates were subject to division,
their military importance disappeared with the invention of gunpowder.
They lived on their hilltops apart from the city and kept their own
weapons and empty privileges, but poverty and degeneracy lurked
behind their fine exterior.

The result of this class feeling was war between the knights and the
cities. While some of these lower nobles desired their rights only in a
peaceful way, a conspicuous group lived for fighting. There was a great
increase of robbery and private warfare towards the end of the fifteenth
century. These robbers made business in Germany less secure than in
the Low Countries; many of them served without pay, just for the
booty, while their victims, peasants and cities, protested in vain. On
the other hand the knights claimed that the higher nobility were oppressing them, taking away their old rights of hunting and fishing while
still demanding military service.

The condition of the German peasantry is an extremely difficult subject to handle justly, because facts which may be true in one locality
are untrue for another. For instance, the peasant's lot in the Moselle
valley was most gloomy, while those in Swabia had something to lose
and were willing to fight in order to protect their rights. It is impossible to draw general conclusions from local conditions, and equally
impossible to know every local condition. Different writers give widely
varying reports and often neglect to say of what district they are
speaking. Of the rural population in Germany the first class was composed of the few freeholders who had kept their liberty and a little soil.
These proprietary peasants constituted the least numerous body. Of

course the soil belonged almost exclusively to the lords, ecclesiastical and lay; and this was divided into tenures and let out to the second class of peasants, the free tenants, who paid a ground-rent for their holding but were entirely free. In the petty states where there were no land-owning peasants these men ranked after the clergy and nobles. By far the most numerous class, with an infinity of subdivisions, was that of the half-free tenants, who were personally free but bound to the soil. Here the *Hörigen* belong. Lowest in the scale came the serfs, who were under rigorous servitude and subjected to corporal punishment. There were comparatively few in this class, however, except in Pomerania. They could be sold only with the soil. There are instances in the fifteenth century of free tenants being degraded into *Hörigen*, but in general by the end of the century the *Hörigen* of older times had become free tenants, though bound to their holdings by restricted rights of use. And yet as late as 1750, in the bishopric of Hildesheim, out of a total of 8000 peasant farms, some 4500 were cultivated by serfs.

The serfs owed two sorts of duties, a certain proportion of their produce, and a part of their time. To pay the former one-tenth of the grain, of the vegetables, of the cattle went to the lord. In some places the inheritance tax was as high as 30 per cent. The peasant had also to serve with his labor and horses (*Fronpflicht*), his services being claimed in house, kitchen, woods, or vineyard, in hunting, fishing or doing errands generally. Sometimes the service was regulated by custom, sometimes not. It was a burdensome system, especially when unmeasured, for then the peasant was never master of his time; sometimes very severe, the obligations were on the other hand often lightened through personal administration. They are well designated as "chaotic." There is evidence that to meet the increased demands of extravagant living, knights, princes, ecclesiastics attempted to raise the services of their underlings and to make their position more dependent; but probably the real oppression of the peasant dates from the sixteenth century.

At the end of the Middle Ages conditions were such as to give the peasant courage. The increase of population, the enlarged consumption in cities gave him a ready market, which meant the certainty of comfort and the possibility of wealth. Not only all of the country people, but a large proportion of the city dwellers lived from agriculture, consequently large quantities of foodstuffs were raised, and prices were extremely low. In Saxony, about 1500, a pair of shoes cost three *groschen*, a sheep four, and a load of firewood five. Contemporary satirists emphasize the wealth of the peasants, but it must be borne in mind that these writers were not describing their own class. Wimphiling says, "The peasants . . . in many parts of Germany have become through their riches stiff-necked and ease-loving." An Austrian Chronicle of 1478 claims that peasants "wore better garments, drank better wine than their lords." Food was plentiful; a Saxon ordinance of 1482 says that mowers must be content with four dishes at a meal. It was considered necessary to regulate the dress of the common man by sumptuary laws. During the fifteenth century the complaint was made, "No real peasants have been born within thirty years." A satirist deprecates that peasants are addressed as "Gracious Lord." "Why not?" asks the peasant, "I have plenty of money and am dressed like a noble lord." In fact, the peasant of this century, especially in South Germany, was no such poor creature as he became a hundred years later.

The landowners were, from the point of view of the peasants, the most important class. They made it possible for their tenants to earn a livelihood and yet gave ground for the bitterest complaints; for instance, in spite of a bad harvest, hail or storm, the lord must have his dues paid, always in the best quality. The landowners themselves took an active share in commerce and production, but the more active they were, the worse for the peasant, for they became his worst rivals and used their power to drive him from the market. Another grievance was the inclination of the lord to treat the common land as his own and so to narrow the right of the peasant to meadow, wood and water. The gathering of wood was forbidden, the lord's cattle were pastured on the common, and he alone had the privilege of hunting and fishing. His position as judge opened the way to further injustice.

The clergy also demanded heavy tithes of the peasant, the poor vicar must oppress those under him in order to live, and the begging monk relied on the peasant for support. *"Die Kirche kostet dem Bauern viel and leistet ihm wenig."* Perhaps the unhappiness of the peasant was due less to economic need than to lack of freedom; he was powerless against exploitation.

The state, too, in broadening its activities interfered with landowners' rights and encroached on the common land. In Tyrol, in the fifteenth century, woods and brooks were claimed as the possession of the nobility or taken from the community and given to mines or smelters. This state control proved a great thing for the Tyrol, for it saved the forests, but the peasants saw only the loss of their rights. The princes of the same locality also sought control of the waterpower which was necessary for the transport of wood and the smelting of metal. The peasants were forced to give the miners who were newcomers room for their colonies and allow them a share in wood and meadow; but these privileges entailed no obligations and brought about a great contrast between the country people and the miners. The state, in this period, with a greater extent of rights than to-day, was the forerunner of absolutism, but it was not strong enough to protect the peasants from the injustice of landowners. Its zeal for law and justice covered an interest in the fisc, and its demoralized officials merited the aversion of the lower people for all classes above them. Agrarian questions were feebly handled in state legislation, and the peasants are hardly mentioned in the laws of Bavaria (1474, 1501) or of Maximilian (1510, 1518). The only general land ordinance of the Middle Ages, that of Tyrol (1404), was not effective. The state by failing to face the agrarian social problem, increased the class distinctions at the end of the Middle Ages.

As has been shown, the condition of the peasants was perhaps not bad in all places, but it was growing worse through the tendencies of the landowners to increase dues. The direction of the movements in Swabia, Franconia, the Rhine, Tyrol, Steiermark, Upper Austria, was against the infringement on customary usages, statutes, etc. The watchword of the *Vorspiel* as well as of the war of 1525 was, "Away with the new customs, back to the old law!" It is impossible to be sure that the peasants were always right, but when the same demands are made from many districts, the assumption is that they were just. The uprisings before the Reformation were not always of the same sort, but agrarian unrest, a mixing of social and religious elements, many-sided motives, were the characteristics of the trouble of the fifteenth and early sixteenth centuries. The cities had already begun to struggle against the upper classes and proved a power the peasants could not do without. The unrest was caused not by great principles, but by concrete grievances. The peasants had the example of the Hussites and the Swiss, and the struggle for organization came with the recognition of common needs. Success crowned a rising in Salzburg in 1458 against debased coinage, while the Carinthia Bund, ostensibly against the Turks (1478) but also embracing economic and religious demands, brought no improvements. The conditions prevailing on the monastery lands of Kempten were notoriously bad. The villeins were fairly plundered, and free peasants degraded to the position of serfs. The revolt of 1491 was occasioned by an extra tax, and here for the first time the discontented elements of city and country joined, but no improvement resulted, and the same conditions existed until 1525. The signs of a gathering storm increased towards the end of the fifteenth century, the centers seeming to be in the Rhine valley, southwestern Germany and Austria. Sometimes the peasants were dissatisfied because of old dues, sometimes new taxes were the grievance, sometimes it was the loss of the common which pinched. In Austria the country people found allies in the cities and lower clergy, and the path of the discontented was marked by death, murder, robbery, and fire. In his Austrian lands Maximilian attempted to be just in his punishment, and even suggested lightening of burdens. The nobles were of course antagonistic to this course, and in the end the peasants' burdens were heavier than before.

So far the peasants' platform had been conservative, to alleviate local grievances; they had no idea of reforming the world. But fanatics found in disturbed conditions favorable ground for the growth of their wild ideas, and soon there was a widespread demand for the overthrow of all existing institutions. In Bohemia, the scene of Huss's labors, the peasants were worse off than their German brothers. Here the radicals found a willing audience, but after revolting, the peasants' condition was changed only for the worse, while the "Bohemian spirit" was spread into Germany by travelling preachers. The first peasant rising of the fifteenth century, that against the imperial city of Worms, created great excitement.

The Niklaushausen episode is perhaps the most spectacular of the early movements. Hans Böhm was ascetic and fanatic; whether or not he was a deceiver seems open to question. His socialistic preachings, which foretold earthly comfort for all, attracted crowds from the length and breadth of Germany. This important Franconian movement shows as does no other before 1525 emotional excitability, class hatred, and wide-reaching discontent, a combination which meant breakers ahead.

Perhaps examples enough of these risings, which continued steadily, have been cited. The secret organization of the peasants spread over the land. Their banners bore the *"Bundschue"* worn by the country people, which from the time of its appearance near Mühlhausen in 1468 became the emblem of militant discontent. The grievances were more economic than social, more social than religious when looked at in the mass. Such religious complaints as appear are not doctrinal. The peasants were partly on the ground of old rights; they wanted the new taxes removed and longed for the old enjoyment of common woods and pasture, but also there was a Utopian, communistic trend to their demands—they wanted feudalism overthrown and said, *"Die Reichen müssen mit uns teilen."* The laboring classes appeared in these movements as the critics of all above them; they had become self-conscious as a class and realized that what they produced supported the upper classes.

The literature of the period expressed the peasants' complaints against a worldly church, against the feudality, against capital. Peasants and litterateurs with the same ills looked to the same savior, the Kaiser; but in view of the actual conditions, Maximilian's attempts at reform seem singularly ineffective and aloof in their conservatism. Even if he had the will for revolutionary reforms, he had not the necessary power over his independent nobles. Germany was seething with discontent, the people were ripe for union and revolt on the slightest pretext.

This life in Germany in the fifteenth century was complex and many-sided. To reach any comprehensive understanding of conditions it is not sufficient to keep in mind only the grumbling peasants and the city proletariat on the *qui vive* for trouble; one must remember the gay court life of Vienna, the knights who were also highway robbers, the luxurious homes of the burghers. Germany was the land not only of the Fuggers and Welsers, but of Dürer and Melanchthon; the full tide of Renaissance influence in its many phases was flowing north, and Martin Luther was just reaching manhood.

These considerations upon German history may be concluded with some observations upon the "reception" of Roman law in the fifteenth century. For the introduction of Roman law casts an important light upon German commercial conditions. But the nature of the indigenous law which it tended to replace must first be examined. Teutonic law was personal and local in its application. Political decentralization had prevented the formation of a common German law. Towns, cities, districts had their own law, as did the feudality and churchmen. There were no common legal principles. The right of each group of citizens and their own legal ideas is recognized in the variation of law according to social status. For the knights there was the *Lehnrecht,* for the country in general the *Landrecht,* for manors the *Hofrecht,* for cities the *Stadtrecht,* for gilds the *Zünftrecht,* and for peasants the *Bauernrecht.* As a rule these laws were uncodified, and they were so often contradictory that in the beginning of the fifteenth century, at the Council of Basel, unification was proposed by codifying the good laws of all provinces and discarding the bad—a labor of Hercules. By the end of the fifteenth century there was a tendency to make local codes, after the form of the *Sachsenspiegel* and the *Schwabenspiegel.*

In the *Sachsenspiegel,* German law had reached its highest point, and no code was so entirely of the people and free from foreign influence. It was compiled by Eike von Repgow in the thirteenth century, had no precursors, and proved the model for all later forms of German law. Its object was to spread the laws of the free people of Saxony to the exclusion of feudal, seigniorial, or municipal law. Its effect was to arm the northern territories against the inroads of Roman law. During the Interregnum the *Sachsenspiegel,* written originally in Latin, was translated into high German.

Based on Swabian and Bavarian law, the *Schwabenspiegel,* also of the thirteenth century, owed a great debt not only to the *Sachsenspiegel,* but to Roman, canon and imperial law; its object was to spread legal principles beyond mere local communities. The range and thoroughness of these codes may be appreciated by the study of one phase of their legislation. For instance, the *Sachsenspiegel* goes in great detail into the regulations governing mining. In this connection it may be stated that the various and elaborate mine ordinances given in the empire from the thirteenth century on, are of German and not Roman law.

This native law proved inadequate to meet the economic changes involved in the transition Germany underwent in the fourteenth and fifteenth centuries from a natural to a money economy, from agriculture to commerce. The new problems were outside the range of the old agrarian law. The necessary new tool lay ready formed in the Roman law. Of the importance of the introduction of Roman law into Germany there can be no question; its influence extended to economic and political, even to ethical and religious conditions. Feudalism gave way before it. Of complaints against this movement of the upper classes and political authority there are many, but of any general, deep opposition to Roman law, nothing is to be seen. Perhaps the peaceful victory is traceable to the respect in which the laity held scientific learning, and the ecclesiastical superiority of the doctors. The old and general theory is that the introduction of Roman law into Germany worked great hardship for the peasant, by receiving the half-free German to the status of the Roman serf or slave; thus class hostility was developed, and the foundations laid for the Peasants' Revolt. But Fay has shown that this effect on the peasant is only legendary; that the writings of the sixteenth century do not indicate that Roman law in Germany tended to depress the peasants to the status of the Roman slave; that there was no concerted opposition to it; that it was not a cause of the Peasants' Revolt, which may be sufficiently explained on other economic, political and religious grounds. Kaser, the latest to write on the subject, adopts this view, saying, "The reception of Roman law did nothing to make the peasant's condition worse, and does not belong among the causes of the Peasants' Revolt."

From Germany let us pass to Italy. By the end of the fifteenth century Italy manifested clear signs of economic decline, evidences quite independent of adverse events like the French invasion in 1494. Venice had ceased to be Levantine and become Italian, a policy which not only entailed losses in the East, but heavy costs to sustain her extension of power upon the mainland against the dukes of Milan and the popes. Lombardy groaned under the avaricious fiscal exploitation and extravagance of the Visconti, and later the Sforza rulers of the Milanais. Even Florence showed signs of decay. Florence had once enjoyed almost a monopoly of fine cloth weaving, but with improvement of technique in local manufacturing elsewhere, not only in Italy but in Southern Germany, Flanders and the French Midi, that monopoly was broken. Moreover, the spread of a protective policy in Europe, with prohibitive duties in which we are to see the first manifestations of the mercantilist state, operated adversely.

But the Florentines did not stand back and watch apathetically the creeping paralysis of their industry. Like their neighbors they sought a remedy in protection. The export was forbidden of many articles and materials used in the woolen industry, such as wool-pickings and dof-fings, woolen thread, cuttings of woolen cloth, iron-looms, dyes, alum, leaden marks and labels, *etc.*; cloth from Italian cities which discriminated against their merchants was excluded, but this had a detrimental effect, for, being deprived of Florentine cloth, the Italian consumers patronized their home manufacturers and so encouraged their development. With the loss of its foreign markets, the *Calimala* gild sought at least to keep the home market. It attempted to do this through the creation of a monopoly. The first attempt was in 1452 when a certain type of imported yarn was forbidden export. The most drastic measure, however, was the law of August 22, 1458, which the *balia* (city parliament) passed at the insistence of the *Calimala* gild, in return for a payment to the state of 4,000 florins annually. This forbade, with unimportant exceptions, the sale of all foreign cloth in Florence.

Thus we have the logical end of a movement which the wool gild, beginning with the attempt of 1393 to introduce a high protective tariff, initiated in its own interest and protection. Incidentally it also shows the enormous influence of this powerful corporation in being able to have such a drastic law passed. Some authors see in this act of 1458 the death of the *Calimala* gild. If we are to be guided by Doren this is not true. Ever since the beginning of the fifteenth century the affairs of the cloth gild had been on the down-grade. At this time it ceased to import semi-finished foreign cloth and to refine it for resale. Thereafter it concerned itself solely with the wholesale trade in foreign cloth to the North and the Levant, and with every other kind of merchandise that was profitable in the international commerce.[2]

The law of 1458 only completed a process of degeneration and decline that was already near its end. From that time forth the *Calimala* gild pursued purely administrative labors over church buildings and welfare institutions, and in watching over financial affairs. After 1532, when the Republic was abolished, the "grand old gild, after a preponderating position—industrial, commercial, social and political—in the history of Florence for five hundred years and more, drooped slowly but surely; but its death and burial are alike unnoted, and no *Scrivano* has left even one word to tell of its last moments."[3]

The sixteenth century witnessed the complete demise of the wool industry, and with it the wool gild. In the reign of the grand duke Cosimo I, the number of business houses connected with the *Arte della Lana* was reduced to 168; before the end of the century, to 88. As in

[2] Doren, *op. cit.*, p. 422. Davidsohn, *op. cit.*, IV, 2, p. 246.
[3] Staley, *op. cit.*, p. 138.

the case of its ancient rival, the exact date of the suppression of the *Lana* gild is not known, but it probably occurred in the reign of Ferdinand I (1556–64) with the closing of the residence of the consuls and its possession by the canons of Or San Michele.

As for Genoa its state was an appanage of France. Its glory had departed. Yet Italy was still a rich country; indeed its riches were its ruin, for its wealth drew down the invasion of the French in 1494, and later of the Germans and the Spaniards, upon her. The revenue of Naples in 1455 was 310,000 ducats; of Florence, 200,000; of the Papal States, 400,000; of Milan, 500,000; of Venice, 800,000—as much as that of the kings of Spain. In 1492 the revenue of Naples amounted to 600,000 ducats; of Florence, 300,000; of Venice, 1,000,000. But these figures are misleading, for the increased revenue between 1455 and 1494 is not explained by increase of wealth, but by increased pressure of taxation and fiscal exaction. The Italian princes were exhausting their surpluses and drawing upon the capital of their states with ultimately disastrous effect. Rome, unlike the other states, was in the most favorable position, for the popes in ecclesiastical impositions drew upon all Europe and so supplemented the local income from the States of the Church. But the outbreak of the Reformation and the sack of Rome in 1527 brought disaster upon Rome, too, at last.

Spain *found* wealth with the discovery of America—the influence of discovery will be considered later—but it did not produce wealth to any large degree either from agriculture or industry or commerce. Charles I (he was Charles V of the Holy Roman Empire) was a Fleming, not a Spaniard. Betrothed ten times before finally married, he married a princess who brought him no territory. As head of the Habsburg house he had to resist the progress of the Reformation and the advance of the Turks. Spain supplied him with soldiery, but his money came from Flanders. Spain, except the Moorish kingdom, was relatively unproductive, and with the expulsion of the Moors in 1492 the realm lost the most skilled and industrious element of the population.

War in Europe was practically permanent from the death of Louis XII in 1512 to 1559. The policy followed by Charles V, Francis I and Henry VIII was a perfectly simple and material one. Each one was, above all, eager for territory. They had no vision beyond territory, titles and money. They were incapable of foreseeing the broader utility of a conquest. Their policy is that set forth in Macchiavelli's *Prince*, whose models were Caesar Borgia and Ferdinand the Catholic. Wars were made for personal motives. The confusing alliances are without interest. The acts of the sovereigns are without relation to the interest of their states. In fine, the policy of the dynasts was sterile, and ruinous to their subjects. Nevertheless the sovereigns clung to this vicious policy until the wars of religion created new issues. In the policy even of the same government we find internal contradictions and sharp reversals. Thus the Low Countries wanted peace with France, while the Castilian advisers of Charles V clamored for war.

The chief field of action was Germany and Italy. These were the most politically divided countries of Europe. In Italy the great states were Venice, Genoa, Milan, the Papal States, and Naples. There was no noble class to make war, and the country was open to conquest. Naples and Milan excited the cupidity especially of France and Austria. In Germany there was an analogous division. Like Italy, Germany was a geographical expression. The emperor sought to increase his power, but was hampered by the Turks and France. Finally Henry VIII of England revived English claims to the kingdom of France as we see in the campaigns of 1512 and 1520. A long series of wars from 1494 to 1559 replete with dramatic happenings produced no important results. They may be ranged in three grand classes.

Wars for the possession of Naples and Milan. At first France had the advantage, then the Habsburgs. In these wars there was created a new military instrument, the infantry, first employed by the Swiss, armed with pikes. Against them fire-arms had little success. It seemed like a reversion to the ancient tactics of the phalanx. This infantry was imitated in Spain, then in Germany with the *Lanzknechte,* then in France. During these wars Pope Julius II refounded the States of the Church in central Italy.

Francis I was taken prisoner at Pavia in 1515. Rome was sacked in 1527, and a coalition was formed against Charles between the pope and England. An unheard-of event was the alliance of France with the Turks. Twenty years of war followed this coalition, and not until 1559 did France definitely renounce its Italian claims.

The German princes, disquieted by the emperor, leagued with France, and the emperor was forced to renounce every attempt against their independence. In brief, seventy-five years of war had the unique result of transferring the states of Milan and Naples to the house of Austria and consolidating the States of the Church. That was all.

CHAPTER XXII

WE have reached the end of the Middle Ages and are standing on the threshold of modern times. It is a period in which new and great forces are at work which have changed, or are changing, old and fundamental conditions, though powerful and conservative institutions, notably the Church, still cling tenaciously to old ways and practices. Tradition is struggling against innovation. In a word in 1500 Europe is in transition, and that a rapid one. Old things are passing away and all things are becoming new. New earth is under men's feet; new institutions are in vogue around them; they themselves are part of a new society; new ideas are in men's minds. In the sixteenth century, while the political hegemony of Europe was in debate between Spain and France, commercial and industrial leadership passed to Holland and England. The development of the first great international exchanges in Antwerp and Amsterdam, the manner of transacting business at these exchanges, the different forms of credit, the rate of interest, stock-jobbing, the importance of the mining industries, the formation and dissolution of monopolies and trusts, the origin of newspapers (as a sort of commercial stock bulletin), the financial policies of the different countries, the rise of the great fairs at Geneva and Frankfort-on-the-Main, the evolution of national debts—each and all of these are evidences of the changed condition of Europe.

We find these changes registered in various forms. The political change is reflected in the rise of national monarchy and strong monarchical government in western Europe, although not in central Europe or Italy. Important changes are noticeable in the art of war and in military service. The use of infantry has increased and that of cavalry has declined. Army organization no longer is of a feudal nature. The old tie of military service between lord and vassal has been dissolved. Armies are royal and national in spirit and organization. The ancient forty days' service has given way to a system of indentures under which a captain enters into a contract with the king to furnish a certain number of men of his own selection and to keep them provided with arms, horses and food, while the government for its part pays quarterly wages according to an established scale which varies according to the rank and status of each fighting unit. War has become a trade supported by royal taxation and in which immense private capital is invested.[1]

The change is also reflected in the widespread influence of the bourgeoisie. This phenomenon has social and economic implications as well as those of a political nature. The bourgeoisie meant a new class in society; it meant a new economic policy and spirit from that which had obtained in the feudal age. This bourgeoisie is able and willing to expend money for itself and upon itself. Rich merchants build houses which are as palatial as those of the nobles were formerly, like that of Jacques Coeur at Bourges. They have plate upon their tables; they wear furs and silks. There is hardly any sign of general prosperity on which more reliance may be placed than upon a people's willingness to spend money in building. But this new-rich class is indifferent to the erection of churches. They display no zeal for ecclesiastical architecture, as their ancestors had in the thirteenth century. They build for themselves, not for the clergy. They are secular-minded, even anticlerical. Being socially a parvenu class without traditions of higher culture, this bourgeoisie prefers "flamboyant" or "decorative" architecture, a degenerate Gothic.

At the same time this bourgeoisie, which began as a homogeneous social stratum below the clergy and the noblesse, has become laterally cleft. The gild system of production has been supplanted by capitalistic control of commerce and industry, with the result that the vast masses of the working classes everywhere are politically without all but the most meagre rights; socially they are the underdog, and economically they are day-laborers and wage-earners subjected to long hours of work, reduction of wages and unemployment. The lowest edge of this class shades off into a new social element unknown in the Middle Ages. This is the proletariat. The Middle Ages had had its vagabond class, its very poor, its mendicants; but this class was nowhere a densely agglomerated group for the reason that medieval society was a rural, not an urban, society. Now, however, in 1500, with the rise of great cities, the cleavage of the town folk into an upper and a lower stratum, untoward conditions of employment, high prices, we find an urban proletariat almost everywhere. The origin of the proletariat—with the problem of whom the world is still struggling—is to be found in the changed economic conditions of the fourteenth and fifteenth centuries, and is related to the gild system and the growth of capitalism.[2]

Progressive students of society and government during the Renaissance, like Sir Thomas More and the Spaniard Louis Vives, gave

[1] Wylie, *Trans. Royal Hist. Soc.* 3d ser. V, p. 106.
[2] See Ratzinger, *Historische-politische Blaetter für das katholische Deutschland*, XCV (1885); Meyer, *Preuss. Jahrb.* XLVIII (1881); Von Kostanecki, "Arbeit und Armut," *Hist. Ztschft.* CXIII, no. iii (1914).

earnest thought to the problem of the poor. More's ideas were expounded in his *Utopia*. Vives was less idealistic and more practical. In the *De subventione pauperum* he divided the poor into three classes: those in poor-houses and hospitals; the homeless beggar class, and the very poor who yet had some sort of place in which to live. He would have every town make a census of the number of these dependents in each class together with information as to the causes of their distress. He advocated the establishment of central relief organizations under supervision of the local magistrates. Work was to be supplied unto all, and all begging forbidden. The able-bodied poor who knew no craft were to be employed as raw laborers on public works. The undeserving poor were to be put to compulsory hard labor.

Revolutions of an economic nature are less spectacular than political revolutions and far more complex, but it is doubtful whether in the long run they have not been more influential than political revolutions. Commerce was carried on in the fifteenth century less through individual merchants, as formerly, than through great trading corporations like joint-stock companies, the German Hansa, and the Merchant Adventurers out of England, which was a chartered company. These great associations commanded a capital and a political influence which had not existed before. For the European states had awakened to the importance of trade, and strove by means of protective laws and navigation acts to kill competition and promote each its own commerce.

Nevertheless commercial intercourse still labored under some inhibitions which are largely obsolete to-day. Security of life and property, whether on land or water, was much improved, and roads were better. But the wide variety of coin current, especially in Germany and Italy, was both inconvenient and confusing. England was unique in this particular, for there was but one coin of the realm, and—except in Lancaster—only one system of weights and measures (Statute of 1390). Another detriment to commerce was the bewildering maze of different weights and measures in use. The Hanseatic League had never succeeded in establishing a uniform money system or a uniform system of weights and measures. Even Louis XI failed to reform these two evils. Four months before his decease (1483) he summoned a delegation of merchants in order to devise a means of establishing "if it be possible throughout our realm one system of weights and measures and one currency." The king, bare-headed, addressed the assembled company, emphasizing two policies: (1) free internal trade, (2) a uniform system of currency and of weights and measures. But the inertia of long tradition and habit, combined with provincial jealousy was too great to be overcome. Louis XI's design slumbered until 1789.

In the matter of conduct of trade at the end of the Middle Ages the growing number and importance of fairs is to be observed. The fairs grew out of former markets, but they were international in their character. In the high Middle Ages those of Champagne were almost the only fairs of wide influence. But with increase of wealth, better government, territorial consolidation, improved roads, fairs appear in every country of Europe in the fourteenth or fifteenth centuries. The greatest of these was that of Frankfort-on-the-Main, followed by Geneva, Lyons, Antwerp and Frankfort-on-the-Oder. In former times there was a spring fair, an autumn fair, each of several weeks' duration, and sometimes a short midsummer fair. In the fifteenth century the old periodic fair began to be displaced by the year-round commodity market in the greatest centers of trade, where the existence of a credit market facilitated commerce.

In the fifteenth century an agrarian revolution was in progress in Europe, due partly to the production of new forms of wealth derived from commerce and industry, but partly also owing to the disappearance of the communal features of the old manorial economy. There are many evidences of this revolution, not the least important being the land transfers of the period, because they distinguish between pasture, meadow, arable and waste, and give the acreage of each. The alterations in and the relative proportion of the different employments of land are revealed by these sources if they are examined over a considerable series of years. The contrast between fourteenth century transfers and sixteenth century transfers is most marked. In the former the largest number of instances concern the arable land; in the latter meadow, pasture and moorland are objects of conveyance. In other words, the former capacity of these communally enjoyed tracts has disappeared. In the fourteenth century meadow or pasture in severalty was exceptional; by the fifteenth century it was not unusual, even if not yet general Moreover, there is much evidence that merchants were buying up rural property and becoming landowners, either for investment or, in the case of the richest among them, in order to possess country estates and imitate the gentry. Accordingly the tendency was for both the old social and the old economic balance to be upset. An English protest against these tendencies is quaintly worded: "Such was the wisdome and policy of our ancestors to divorce the merchants and handicraftesmen from the husbands (husbandmen) and tythemen, that none of them shold favor of the others gaine; and by this means . . . the country (was) replenished with gentlemen and husbands (husbandmen), which now are inhabited by merchants and men of occupations; soe that noe man is contented with his own estate, which hath brought all things to such extremity as they have bin of many yeares befor."

It is not necessary in these pages to relate the history of discovery and exploration during the fourteenth and fifteenth centuries. The penetration of Asia dates from the missions of those Franciscan friars whom Pope Innocent IV and Louis IX of France sent in the middle of the thirteenth century to the court of the grand Khan in Central Asia. In 1294 Marco Polo returned from seventeen years of residence in China. The *Relations* of Plan Carpini and Rubruck, the two friars, and above all the story of Marco Polo's travels, excited the curiosity and the commercial appetite of Europe. The union of Asia and eastern Europe under the Mongols had facilitated this commerce. But, as has been said, the devastating conquests of Timurlane and the spread of the Ottoman Turks more and more interrupted this traffic, not that the Turks deliberately injured trade, but they had little capacity to promote it.

The crowning event which ruined the old routes to the Orient either across Asia or via the Red Sea or Persian Gulf was the Portuguese discovery of the Cape of Good Hope and Vasco da Gama's voyage to Calicut (India) in 1498. The advantages of the new all-sea route to the Far East, especially cheaper freight rates than those across the whole width of Asia were so great that the discovery changed the front of Europe to the West. Lisbon, Cadiz, Seville, Bordeaux, La Rochelle, St. Malo, Antwerp, Amsterdam, London, Bristol supplanted Venice and Genoa, Constantinople and Alexandria. The trade of the Mediterranean shrank to mere cabotage or coast trade. The Atlantic Ocean and the Indian Ocean were henceforth the broad way to the Far East. The geographical discoveries of the fifteenth century totally altered the commercial situation. It is worth observing that such long voyages would have been impossible without the discovery of the compass, scientific cartography, and a great advance in the art of shipbuilding. Vasco da Gama and Columbus were as much products in their kind of the Renaissance as were Petrarch and Leonardo da Vinci.

Slavery acquired an enormous development during the fourteenth and fifteenth centuries, a fact which is not a comfortable reflection to those who believe in the theory of progress and who think that the period of the Renaissance was so "enlightened." The disruption of the Mongol Empire in 1258, the rise and spread of the Turks, the earth-shaking conquests of Timurlane, pried loose multitudes of people and made them either fugitives or captives. At the same time the Portuguese discoveries along the coast of West Africa brought in many negro slaves. The result was that slavery increased in every Mediterranean country. Circassians, Bulgarians, Serbs, Armenians, Syrians were bought from the Turks and imported by Venetian and Genoese slave dealers. Negroid and negro slaves were sold by Algerian and Moroccan slave dealers to Catalonian and Provençal merchants. The Portuguese brought thousands from Senegambia, the Guinea coast and Nigeria. The word *"moro"* in Italy signified any dark-skinned man; the negro was called *"moro negro."* Was Othello merely a *moro* or was he really an Ethiopian? At the end of the fifteenth century, because of its wealth, Rome was the chief slave mart. Ferdinand the Catholic of Aragon in 1488 sent one hundred Moors as a gift to Pope Innocent VIII, who distributed them among the cardinals and the nobles. The traffic was justified on the ground that most of these captives were Mohammedans or heathens. But it was not true of Armenians, Bulgarians and Serbs. Oriental women were much in demand as household servants, and the fairer among them as mistresses. Some of the licentious nobles in Sicily and Italy had harems of slave women. Rich men prided themselves on having prize wrestlers, jugglers, acrobats, and even jazz orchestras of negro slaves.

A typical manifestation of the late Middle Ages is the large amount of sumptuary legislation. The motive was partly to bridle the excessive and wasteful expenditure of money by the new-rich class upon dress, plate, furniture, jewelry, *etc.* A prevalent notion was the need of maintaining social equilibrium by keeping every man within the bounds of his status and calling. Hence the many artificial codes of dress. It was partly a gesture of austerity of manners and morals in which one discerns the foreshadowing of puritanism. But primarily, perhaps, the motive of these laws was an economic one. Fallacies concerning the nature of wealth have been current in all ages. The economic theory of the fourteenth, fifteenth and sixteenth century—indeed of the seventeenth and eighteenth also—was that the precious metals were actually believed to be wealth itself. The country which sold abroad and gathered gold in return to keep at home grew richer, while a country which exported gold grew poorer. Sumptuary laws were intended to preserve the metal balance in favor of the government. The domestic policy of Elizabethan England, to use Lord Burleigh's words, was "by all pollyces to abridge the use of forrayn commodities as be not necessary for us." It was not until Adam Smith published his *Wealth of Nations* in 1776 that this "mercantilist" theory was shown to be invalid, and it was demonstrated that two countries could each profit by disposing of goods which they possessed in surplus and importing those which they needed. Protection of home industries was another motive of sumptuary legislation. Richer fabrics were usually foreign fabrics.

An interesting social phenomenon of the late Middle Ages is the decline in good manners. The fall of the old feudal aristocracy entailed the eclipse of those old virtues which are the product of long descent and good breeding for many generations. Courtesy, politeness of speech and deportment, gentlemanliness and ladylikeness, declined with the impoverishment and political decay of the "gentle" class. The old noble qualities expressed by the words "honor," "merry," "true," "amorous," "sage," "secret," "large," "prewe," "hardy," "adventurous," "chivalrous," lost their meaning. The virtue in them passed out with the passing of the class which once had cherished them. Each one of these words indicates an aspect of secular grace which vanished. To this very day they are either obsolete or are current in a degraded significance. "Prewe" (*preux*) is not even an archaic word any longer; the conception of "honor" has been greatly changed; the old and the modern meaning of "merry" are very different; "chivalry" is merely a romantic term; and as for "amorous," the present generation could not be trusted with it.

The rise of the burgher class out of a formerly servile peasantry—many of them to high political station and great wealth—brought in a parvenu aristocracy stranger to the traditions of good-breeding which were immemorial among the old aristocracy. Hence courtesy and good manners decayed. Men's conduct became rough, their words and deportment crude and uncouth. But like social climbers in all times the new-rich class aspired to imitate the class which they rivalled or had supplanted. Many an impecunious noble found employment in the household of a rich burgher as a tutor whose duties were less intellectual than moral in their nature. A unique literary phenomenon of the time is the popularity of books on etiquette and courtesy. When printing was invented about 1455 such books were among the best sellers. Examples are Caxton's *Book of Courtesy* in England, *The Book of the Knight of La Tour Landry* in France, and most famous of all Baldasarre Castiglione's *The Perfect Courtier* in Italy. There are many more which might be cited.

Wealth not only makes wealth, but new wealth, combined with the inevitable social changes which result therefrom, also breeds new ideas. The breakdown of medievel ideology gave room for new ideas. The medieval man had been taught to regard the doctrines of the Church as incontestable facts. These doctrines felt as facts colored even the economic life of the age. There is a connection between the ideology of scholasticism and the economic life of the thirteenth century. But the rise of national states, free cities, combined with the decay of scholasticism, created new ideas.

The growing complexity of economic life, even preceding the Reformation, made the maintenance of the old ethical restrictions on economic greed, expounded by St. Thomas Aquinas and recorded in canonical law, increasingly difficult. An ethical social idealism, no matter how valid, which expressed itself specifically in terms gained from the experience of village trade was simply unable to discipline the new international commercialism, with its vast and intricate relationships. Economic life became secularized, therefore, with no law but that of prudential self-interest to guide it, chiefly because Christian idealists were incompetent to fashion new instruments of control when they discovered the old ones impotent.[3]

The rebellion of the business mind of the later Middle Ages against the Church's prohibition of interest is an example. But another idea destined to become of portentous dimension and influence was born in the later Middle Ages. This was anticlericalism.

In a remote sense one may say that the policy of Philip IV and Edward I was anticlerical. But what is here meant by the term "anticlerical" is a growing attitude of mind or public opinion with reference to enormous ecclesiastical wealth, great endowments, profitable economic privileges, and advantageous exemptions which other men were not permitted to enjoy. Increased appropriation of church property for secular uses is one sign of this change. Another, and much more significant sign, is the growth of legislation calculated to reduce or deprive the Church of these material profits. In these days economic and social visionaries endeavor to capture control of governments. In the fifteenth century they tried to capture control of the Church.

Wyclif had long preached that the king not only may, but he must take away its wealth from a delinquent Church that misapplied it, and that any pope or bishop that gainsaid him should be removed as a heretic and disturber of the Church's peace; that the Council should take all land and rent from the dead hand and put it into the hand of the king and the secular arm; that all endowment was a poisoned shackle. . . . Here was a definite scheme to make these waste goods support the Church, the court, the army, and the poor. This plan had really been worked out more than ten years before in a special tract by John Purvey.[4]

Wyclif's followers were not slow to follow up his suggestions.

Many of the knights of Parliament urged that if the king had the wealth that was now wasted by bishops, abbots and priors he could maintain with it 15 earls, 1500 knights, and 6200 squires and have £20,000 a year for his own coffers besides. It was estimated that the disposable funds from the greater monasteries alone would amount to 322,000 marks (£214,666 13 s. 4 d.) per annum. If properly used this money might help every township to maintain its own poor and keep up 100 more almshouses than there were at present, each to be served by two secular priests and endowed with 100 marks per annum, while over and above this amount the smaller religious houses would yield enough to endow 15000 parish priests and clerks, each with the usual stipend of 7 marks a year. These famous figures

[3] *Atlantic Monthly,* review by N. Niebuhr of "Religion and the Rise of Capitalism," by R. H. Tawney. (New York, 1926.)
[4] Wylie, *op. cit.,* III, p. 309.

do not appear on the official roll. The earliest statement of them is given by a biographer of Henry V, who wrote some thirty years later, but the details which he supplies enable us to affirm that the total is only a rough estimate, such as had often to do duty in those days in the absence of exact statistical detail.

In France the Pragmatic Sanction of 1439 by throwing control of church revenues into the hands of the king averted the spread of anti-clericalism there. But in Germany and Italy there are many examples of anti-ecclesiastical legislation. The German cities sought to force ecclesiastical corporations within their jurisdiction to pay something for the protection given them by the city governments. The official record of German imperial cities contain evidence in plenty of attempts to increase municipal revenues by curtailing ecclesiastical exemptions from taxation. The economic background of the Reformation is in these events.

"The motives, both remote and proximate, which led to the Lutheran revolt," it has been truly said,[5] "were largely secular rather than ecclesiastical." The increasing discontent of the people in Germany with the ways and practices of the Church for a full century before the storm broke is perfectly clear. The town of St. Gall in Switzerland in 1529 turned protestant in order to cancel a debt of six thousand florins which it owed to the local monastery. Unfortunately for themselves the clergy failed to read the signs of the times, and bitterly opposed the urban taxes laid upon ecclesiastical property and natural produce or manufactures sold by them. The monasteries within the towns even demanded extension of this immunity to lay brothers, all who dwelt on church property and whose labor was employed by the Church. But the towns insisted on the distinction between property used for strictly ecclesiastical purposes, and income-producing property owned by the clergy. In especial, they were opposed to mortmain, the practice of which was ruinous to the finances of the towns. Feeling often ran high, and more than once monasteries situated within the towns were assailed by mobs. In Augsburg, Ulm, Basel, Freiburg the local governments rigorously insisted on clerical liability to taxation. Basel even required local clergy to perform military service, on the ground that protection was for all and ought to be defrayed by all. This anticlerical sentiment was more pronounced against the monastic clergy than against the secular clergy. In 1493 the great German abbot Trithemius mournfully wrote: "Once princes erected and endowed cloisters. Today they plunder and destroy them." Three years later we find him again deploring that "the days of building cloisters are past. The days of their destruction are nigh." The great disendowment of the English monasteries was

[5] Henry Charles Lea.

not far off. "In this part of the world," wrote Erasmus on September 9, 1517, "I am afraid a great revolution is impending."

The spirit of sixteenth-century business, of which the Calvinist French and Dutch and the English Puritans were the expression, was a by-product of fifteenth-century anticlericalism.

Calvinism took the idea of ascetic conduct out of its monastic environment and placed it in the world. The first and most important principle that followed was that waste of time was a deadly sin. Everyone must work hard in his calling, for hard labour, whether bodily or mental, was the great safeguard against all the sins of uncleanness. But more than that. The elect must take advantage of any opportunity of legitimate profit shown him by God. As Baxter, who is chosen by Weber as a central representative of Protestantism, put it, "if you refuse this and choose a less gainful way, you cross one of the ends of your calling, and you refuse to be God's steward and to accept His gifts and use them for Him when He requireth it." It is easy to see how this attitude would work out in encouraging capitalistic undertakings.[6]

A milder manifestation of anticlericalism is to be found in popular opposition in the towns to the clergy's exclusive control of education. This spirit is manifested as early as the twelfth century. When, in the middle of that century, fire in Ghent destroyed the cathedral school, the burghers profited by the disaster and opened a secular school. But this incensed the local monks of St. Peter's, who hoped that their own school might profit by the destruction of the chapter school and protested to Rome. Alexander III sustained the contention of both groups of clergy against the townsmen. This decree in turn dissatisfied the count of Flanders, and in 1179 he established a secular school, the teacher of which was a notary. In 1195 Ypres founded a municipal school, and by the thirteenth century urban schools were general in Flanders. These were of three classes, primary schools (*scholae parvae*), middle schools (*scholae minores*) and upper schools (*scholae majores*). Renaissance Italy as we have seen was no less progressive.

The purpose of this demand for secular education and secular schools was a utilitarian one. More and more merchants needed to be able to read and write, and required clerks who could do so—not Latin, but the vernacular; not to study theology, but to keep accounts and be able to handle commercial paper. The Renaissance included a utilitarian philosophy of life, a demand for a new policy in education, the wish for industrial and technical training.

A few medieval thinkers of vision had recognized the mastery of a

[6] *London Times Literary Supplem.*, July 10, 1930, Review of "The Protestant Ethic and the Spirit of Capitalism." By Max Weber. Translated by Talcott Parsons.

trade as a genuine part of education. Dunstan (died 988) of England enjoined on every priest the knowledge of some handicraft. Honorius of Autun and Hugo of St. Victor in the twelfth century and Kilwardby, archbishop of Canterbury (1272–79), each drew up a classification of the mechanical arts.

There is no doubt that in the fourteenth and fifteenth centuries technical proficiency had deteriorated from the high place it had possessed in the thirteenth century. The revolution within the gilds by which the masters became capitalist employers and shut out the common workingman was seriously detrimental to intelligent and efficient craftsmanship. For the workman's heart ceased to be in his work. The workingman became a human tool, an industrial drudge, interested in getting as good wages and as short hours as possible, but indifferent to the quality of his work. Skilled artisans and craftsmen became rare except in a few special crafts like that of the armorers. Langland in *Piers Ploughman,* lines 5961–70, voices this complaint. It is a significant fact that the education provided for in the utopian literature which appeared on the threshold of modern times, like More's *Utopia,* included vocational training in the curriculum. Every citizen in Utopia was required not only to have mastered a craft, but also was to understand agriculture.

The conditions which led More to suggest this provision for the industrial education of the masses are revealed clearly in the context. The opening pages of the *Utopia* abound in references to the numerous burdens which oppress the poor—the frequent wars, the idleness and extravagance of the rich, the conversion of corn lands into pasturage and the lack of adequate provision for such a training of the masses as would enable them to secure a livelihood. That interest in the problems arising from these conditions was quite general in More's time is indicated by the fact that the legislation inaugurating the parish apprenticeship system of providing for and training the poor dates from this period.[7]

Rabelais aired his views on education in the *Life of Gargantua,* Chap. xxiv. He would have his pupils taken "to see the drawings of metals or the casting of great ordnance; how the lapidaries did work, as also the goldsmiths and cutters of precious stones," and "to visit the alchymists, money-coiners, upholsterers, weavers, velvet-workers, watchmakers, looking-glass framers, printers, organists and other such kind of artificers." Sir Francis Bacon in the *Novum Organum,* Bk. I, xcviii–cvi, powerfully argued along the same line.

Unfortunately we know all too little of the progress of mechanical invention during the Renaissance. Most familiar engineering devices

[7] Anderson, *School of Society,* XI, p. 371; Cf. Dunlop and Denman, *English Apprenticeship and Child Labor,* p. 248.

used in the Middle Ages had been known to the Romans like the pulley, the screw-jack, the crane. Power was furnished to the last by a treadmill wheel on an axle which was operated either by a group of men or a horse "walking up" and so winding the hoisting rope which ran out over a beam with a pulley at the end, around the axle. By the fifteenth century the crane was in common use in great industrial towns like Bruges, Antwerp and London.[8]

The Romans had known hoisting tackles with three pulleys, two in the upper and one in the lower block; with five pulleys, two in the lower block and three in the upper; and even the "polypaston," or hoisting tackle with many pulleys. These mechanical devices were employed on ships, in mills and in theaters to raise the heavy curtain. The Middle Ages used them similarly. The technical word for crane was "tornamentum." The word "crane" came into parlance from the great town crane of Bruges, the beam of which was decorated with a row of wooden storks (*grue*). Three Cranes Lane in Upper Thames Street, London, derives its name from the cranes once on the waterfront below. In 1438 we find another type of crane in Germany operated by a system of counterweights which were shifted by means of tackle-pulleys.[9]

A medieval architect used a hoisting apparatus called an *avis* or bird to carry up mortar and other material. This is still known in France as a *oiseau*. Woodturning is twice mentioned in Charlemagne's *Capitulare de villis* (§§ 45, 62). St. Gall had a turners' room mentioned in 820. Wire-drawing appeared at Nuremberg in the fifteenth century. Well-boring is mentioned in the town council records of Trier in 1373 and was not unusual in the fifteenth century. A pump made of buckets on an endless chain is pictured in a manuscript of 1438 and the screw-shaft pump was also employed. The ratchet wheel and the sprocket chain wheel, the bevelled gear and the elbow-shaped axle gear were known.[10] The humble wheelbarrow, called a *chiveria*, was common, and it may be a matter of surprise to learn that our common revolving door is as old as the sixth century. In Germany it was called a *"drehthür"* or draw-door.

Textile machines were used in connection with silk-throwing at Lucca as early as 1272. From there their use spread over northern Italy, France, Austria, Switzerland. The water mill first appeared in Italy in the sixth century. The windmill was imported from the Orient during the Crusades. In antiquity and well down through the Middle Ages the sawing of timber was done by hand, the blade hanging from a tripod worked by a man at each end. The Gallic poet Ausonius de-

---

[8] For a picture of that of Bruges see Malcolm Letts, *Bruges*, p. 32.
[9] Feldhaus, F. M. *Die Technik der Vorzeit*, p. 521.
[10] Feldhaus, *op. cit.*, pp. 562, 593.

scribes it in his *Mosella,* verses 361–64. The water-driven saw mill is first mentioned in Germany in 1245. Progressive German cities in the fourteenth and fifteenth centuries established municipal saw mills.[11] Both the over-shot and under-shot wheel were familiar. The revolutionary development of the saw from a hand tool to a mechanical tool took place before the thirteenth century. An illustration from a manuscript of the time is of a machine for sawing planks. The blade is counterbalanced on a lever, the motion of which automatically carries the wood forward to be sawn. This primitive sawmill was evidently meant to be operated by human power, but the application of water-power to similar machines and the use of multiple blades is shown in drawings of the sixteenth century. The paddle wheel boat was invented in the fifteenth century, and several pictures of this invention have come down to us, although the device proved impracticable because the paddles could not be made to revolve fast enough with hand power or the treadmill. The *"bratenwender"* was a mechanical roaster, the spit being turned by a rotary fan in the chimney which revolved under the draught. The screw and the threaded bolt and nut were invented in Germany about 1420.

Among all these impressive economic changes which characterized the history of Europe as it was swinging out of the medieval arc into that of modern times, not the least impressive was the rise in prices and, in general, an increase in the cost of living. This condition was all the more impressive because wages remained stationary. Thus the population was caught between an upper and a nether millstone. Prices had begun to rise as far back as the thirteenth century, but there was some compensation for this in the fact that wages as a whole kept pace with the change in prices until the ravages of the Black Death in the middle of the fourteenth century precipitated a crisis the nature of which has been described in a previous chapter. The aggravation incident to this violent derangement was accentuated by the growing potency of capitalism, whose representatives followed the vicious policy of lowering wages and lengthening hours of labor wherever possible in order to enlarge their profits. The result was the development of a vast amount of economic discontent and social unrest among the working classes, which culminated about 1380 in strikes, riots and even formidable popular uprisings.

A *rapid* rise in prices, however, was checked by two factors. From 1200 to approximately 1450 the production of silver in Europe declined because surface mining had nearly exhausted its possibilities, and the art of shaft-mining had not yet developed to the degree that it could overcome flood conditions in deep mines. Moreover, protracted war, in the East against the Turks, in the West the Hundred Years'

[11] Feldhaus, *op. cit.,* p. 893.

War, so consumed the precious metals that the evils of an inflated currency were not visited upon the people. In France, even after the long conflict with England was over, prices continued slowly to rise and wages to decline. But Louis XI's efficient and sagacious policy gradually wrought stability, and a renewal of prosperity began in the last years of his reign which continued under Charles VIII and through the early years of the reign of Louis XII. Simultaneously throughout Europe there was a slight fall in the price of exchange. Then the upward curve was stopped. The drain of the Italian wars forced a decline again, which of course affected the peninsula also, while as for Germany, the attacks of the Turks upon the flank of Europe (Hungary) acted in like manner.

The burden of taxation imposed by these big campaigns, however, was probably less economically adverse than another development. This was the revolution in German mining methods in the last half of the fifteenth century, by which deep shaft-mining became practicable, with the result that the German, Bohemian and Tyrolean mines under the management of the Fuggers, the Hochstetters and other big mine operators began to pour out upon Europe a volume of the precious metals the like of which Europe had not seen before. The result was inflation and high prices.

These changes (for France) may be indicated in the appended table.[12]

Reigns	Periods	Intrinsic value	Mean intrinsic value per reign	Purchasing power in terms of francs before 1914
Louis XI......	1461–72	6 fr. 097	6 fr. 255	61 fr.
	1473–83	6 fr. 541		
Charles VIII...	1483–86	6 fr. 024		55 fr.
	1487–92	5 fr. 640	5 fr. 651	56 fr.
	1493–95	5 fr. 471		57 fr.
	1496–98	5 fr. 471		
Louis XII.....	1498–1502	5 fr. 471		57 fr.
	1503–07	5 fr. 471		58 fr.
	1508–11	5 fr. 471	5 fr. 433	57 fr.
	1512–15	5 fr. 324		55 fr.

Between 1500 and 1520 one can detect this creeping upward of prices, with which the rise in wages did not keep pace. The increasing cost of foodstuffs and rise of rents without corresponding rise in wages and salaries induced widespread discontent. These culminated in

[12] From Paul Raveau, "La crise des prix au XVIe siècle en Poitou," *Revue Historique*, XLXII, p. 1.

strikes, riots and popular clamor for remedies and relief, which the perplexed governments were unable to accomplish. They were dealing with an invisible enemy. Beneath the regular trades were the casual laborers, who began to constitute a danger. Troops of unemployed and half-employed were hustled from town to town, settling finally in the biggest cities. Vagabondage became a menace to public order. Poor-houses, foundling hospitals, benefit societies and municipal doles only increased the attractiveness of being unemployed, for they confounded those who sought work with those who shunned it. The conditions of labor were permanently out of gear. There is no doubt that after 1500 the standard of living of the masses deteriorated. The trading class was the one which most prospered, as a profiteer class always does in times of economic crisis.

The primary cause of this privation was not the great and protracted wars between Francis I and Charles V, between Valois and Habsburg for ascendancy over Europe, as one might suppose. For heavy as the toll of these conflicts was in the form of burdensome taxation, destruction of capital, interruption of commerce, their effect on the whole was less disastrous than the stupendous inflation due to the flood of silver which began to inundate Europe from the colonies of Spain in America. What the revival of German mining had done on a small scale, the silver from the almost fabulously rich deposits of Potosi and Mexico and the gold of the Inca Empire in Peru did on a scale the like of which the world had never witnessed before, unless when Alexander conquered the East and Rome conquered Greece and Carthage. "Over long periods of time unstable price relationships play a significant rôle in the transformation of institutions and in the realignment of classes. . . . The influx of precious metals into Europe precipitated one of the greatest price revolutions occurring on a specie basis in modern times, if not in all history." [13] In absolute amounts of 16,632,648.20 kilograms of silver and 181,234.95 kilograms of gold were poured upon Europe from the Indies in the sixteenth century—to say nothing of what was smuggled. [14]

The effect of this enormous inflation is discernible in the fearful shrinkage in the purchasing power of the money of the age. In the reign of Francis I (1515–47) the purchasing power of the *livre* shrunk to 47.85 from a previous point of 55 in the reign of his predecessor. Between 1547 and 1559 it fell to 27.50, and between 1559 and 1610 to 12.50. These ratios mean that in terms of the dollar before 1914, the French *livre* shrunk from $12.20 to $2.40 in less than a hundred years. A fortune of 22,000 francs in 1200 was worth 16,000 francs in

---

[13] Hamilton, *Journal of Economic and Business History*, I, p. 1.
[14] See Hamilton, "Imports of American Gold and Silver into Spain," *Quarterly Journal of Economics*, XLIII, p. 436.

1300; 7,500 francs in 1400; 6,500 in 1500. But in the sixteenth century, that is to say in the epoch when Europe was flooded with Spanish-American silver, that fortune of 6,500 francs shrunk to 2,500 francs! And it is to be remembered that what was true of France in this century was true in much the same degree for all Europe.

In Andalusia in 1597 prices were almost five times what they were at the beginning of the century. . . . The trend of French prices during the period . . . seems to be similar. . . . In France during the first quarter of the sixteenth century prices began to rise, reaching their highest point in the last quarter of the century. . . . French prices stopped rising by the end of the sixteenth century, (but) the upward movement in other countries of Northern Europe continued into the seventeenth century.[15]

In England in 1650 when the highest point was reached, prices were 3.31 times as high as in 1451–1500.

We have in these data another reason why the Reformation took on an economic-social aspect and became the vehicle for the expression of widespread discontent. Moreover, it is to be observed that the peak of this distress, which was reached shortly after 1600, coincides with the beginning of the exodus of the working classes from Europe to the colonies in America, where they hoped to find better living conditions, or at least relief from the conditions at home. It is no wonder that the seventeenth century was characterized by emigration of Europe's population to the New World. The settlement of New England, Virginia, indeed all our seaboard states, was more due to the economic distress and social discontent in Europe than to religious persecution.

[15] Hamilton, *Journal of Economic and Business History,* I, pp. 31–32.

BIBLIOGRAPHIES

INTRODUCTION

JAMES WESTFALL THOMPSON, *Economic and Social History of the Middle Ages,* ch. xix; HENRI PIRENNE, "The Stages in the Social History of Capitalism," *American Historical Review,* XIX, 467; P. BOISSONADE, *Life and Work in Medieval Europe* (translation of Eileen Power), bk. ii, pp. 119–278; E. NYS, *Researches in the History of Economics,* chs. vi–ix; W. CUNNINGHAM, *Western Civilization in its Economic Aspects: Medieval and Modern Times,* bk. ii, ch. ii, pp. 70–106; *Growth of English Industry and Commerce* I, sections 95–97; E. EMERTON, *Beginnings of Modern Europe,* preface; R. LODGE, *Close of the Middle Ages,* preface; W. I. BRANDT, "Pierre Dubois, Medieval or Modern?", *American Historical Review,* April, 1930; F. M. POWICKE, "A Medieval Radical," *Manchester University (Owens College) Historical Essays,* pp. 169–192.

CHAPTER I

FRANCE UNDER PHILIP IV (1285–1314) AND THE LAST CAPETIANS

JAMES WESTFALL THOMPSON, *The Middle Ages,* II, ch. xxx; E. LAVISSE, *Histoire de France,* III, ii, livres ii–iii; F FUNCK-BRENTANO, *Les origines de la guerre de cent ans: Phillippe le Bel en Flandre;* J. R. MORETON MACDONALD, *History of France,* I, chs. xi–xii; G. FAGNIEZ, *Documents rélatifs à l'histoire de l'industrie et du commerce,* II, introd. sec. 1; H. C. LEA, *History of the Inquisition,* III, ch. v. (Templars); A. S. TURBERVILLE, *The Templar Order in Europe;* E. J. MARTIN, *The Trial of the Templars;* MANDELL CREIGHTON, *History of the papacy during the period of the Reformation,* I, 27–46; C. W. PREVITÉ-ORTON, "The House of Gaetani," *Edinburgh Review,* October, 1928; F. BAETHGEN, "Zur Geschichte des Hauses Gaetani," *Hist. Ztschft.,* 138 47; ANDRÉ ARTONNE, "Le mouvement de 1314 et les chartes provinciales," *Moyen Age,* IX, 217–57 (a review of Borelli's *Les variations monétaires sous Philippe le Bel);* J. FINOT, *Les rélations commerciales entre la Franca et la Flandre.*

CHAPTER II

THE BACKGROUND OF THE HUNDRED YEARS' WAR

H. S. LUCAS, *The Low Countries and the Hundred Years' War,* chs. i–vii; E. LAVISSE, *Histoire de France,* III, ch. ii, pp. 295–302; SARGEANT, "The wine trade of Gascony," in G. UNWIN, *Finance and Trade under Edward III;* J. G. BLACK, "Edward I and Gascony, *English Hist. Rev.,* XVII, 518; T. F. TOUT, *History of England* (1216–1377) ch. x; W.

Cunningham, "The commercial policy of Edward III," *Trans. Royal Hist. Soc.,* N. S. IV, 197; W. Cunningham, *English Industry and Commerce,* I, sections 98–100; W. Cunningham, *Alien Immigrants in England;* W. J. Ashley, *Early History of English Woollen Industry;* F. R. Barnes, "Taxation of wool," in Unwin, *Finance and Trade under Edward III;* H. Pirenne, *Belgian Democracy,* ch. iv; Whitwell, "The English monasteries and the wool trade," *Vierteljahrschrift f. Sozial und Wirtschaftsgesch.,* II, 1–33 (in English); J. E. T. Rogers, *History of Agriculture and Prices,* I, ch. xxv; T. W. Fulton, *The Sovereignty of the Sea* (cf. *Edinburgh Review,* CCXIV, 357).

CHAPTER III

THE FIRST PERIOD OF THE HUNDRED YEARS' WAR (1337–80)

James Westfall Thompson, *The Middle Ages,* II, ch. xxxi; H. S. Lucas, *The Low Countries and the Hundred Years' War,* ch. viii–xiv; E. Lavisse, *Histoire de France,* IV, i, books i–iii (val. bib.); W. J. Ashley, *James and Philip Van Artevelde;* H. Pirenne, *Belgian Democracy,* chs. v–vi; T. F. Tout, *History of England* (1216–1377), chs. xv–xviii; J. R. Moreton Macdonald, *History of France,* I, chs. xii–xv; J. Mackinnon, *Reign of Edward III;* E. Emerton, *Beginnings of Modern Europe,* ch. vi; G. A. C. Sandeman, *Calais under English Rule;* Hubert Hall, "The English Staple," *Gentleman's Magazine,* vol. cclv, p. 255; A. L. Jenckes, *The Origin, the Organization and the Location of the Staple of England* (Univ. of Penn. dissertation, 1908); Whitwell, "Italian Bankers and the English Crown," *Trans. royal hist. soc.* N. S. vol. xvii, p. 175; W. E. Rhodes, "Italian Bankers in England," *Manchester University (Owens College) Historical Essays;* G. Unwin, *Finance and Trade under Edward III;* H. Belloc, *Paris,* ch. vi; C. H. Pearson, *English history in the fourteenth century; La grande encyclopédie,* art. "Jacquerie"; S. Luce, *La jacquerie;* Hapke, "Die neue Literatur zur Geschichte der Niederlandischen Wollindustrie," *Vierteljahrschrift f. soz. und Wirtschaftsgesch.,* 1912.

CHAPTER IV

TOWN AND TRADE LEAGUES IN GERMANY

On the League of the Rhine see:

F. Menzel, *Geschichte des Rheinischen Städtebundes* (Hanover, 1871); L. Quidde, *Der Schwabische-Rheinische Städtebund im Jahre 1384* (Stuttgart, 1884); Theod. Sommerlad, *Die Rheinzolle im Mittelalter* (Halle, 1895); F. Zurbonsen, "Der Rheinische Landfriedensbund von 1254," *Forschungen zur deutschen Gesch.,* vol. xxiii, p. 289; K. A. Schwab, *Geschichte des grossen Rheinischen Städtebundes,* 2 vols. (Mainz, 1843); A. Busson, *Geschichte des grossen Landfriedensbundes deutscher Städte* (Innsbruck, 1874); J. Weizacker, *Der Rheinische Bund von 1254* (Tübingen, 1879); L. Winterfeldt, "Gottesfrieden und deutsche Stadtverfassung," *Hansische Geschichtsblätter*, vol. xxxii (1897), p. 8; W. BECKER, *Die Initiative bei der Stiftung des Rheinischen Bundes von 1254* (Giessen, 1899).

On the Swabian League see:

WAGNER, *Wittembergische Vierteljahrschrift f. Landesgeschichte*, VI, no. ii (1883); K. KLÜPFEL, Der Schwabische Bund," *Historisches Taschenbuch*, vi folge (Leipzig, 1883); T. LINDNER, "Zur Geschichte des Schwabischen Städtebundes," *Forschungen zur deutschen Gesch.*, vol. XIX, p. 31; W. VISCHER, "Gesch. des Schwabischen Städtebundes," *Ibid.*, II–III; ENGELHARDT, "Histoire du droit fluvial," *Nouvelle revue historique de droit*, 1888, pp. 735–70, and compare an article by Gothein in *Westdeutsche Ztschft.*, XIV, Heft, ch. iii (1895); B. KUSKE, "Die Handelsbeziehungen zwischen Köln und Italien," *Westdeutsche Ztschft.*, vol. xvii (1908).

CHAPTER V

THE HANSEATIC LEAGUE

See valuable bibliographical articles in:

Hansische Geschichtsblätter, LIV, pp. 276–337; *Annales d'histoire économique et sociale*, II, no. viii, October 1930, pp. 494–98; JAMES WESTFALL THOMPSON, *The Middle Ages*, II, ch. xxxii; E. GEE NASH, *The Hanseatic League;* HELMHOLT, *History of the World*, VII, 1–61; DAENELL, "The Policy of the German Hanseatic League respecting the Mercantile Marine," *American Hist. Review*, XV, 47; E. C. SEMPLE, "The Hanse Towns," *Bulletin American Geographical Society*, ch. xxxi, p. 236; R. PAULI, *Pictures of Old England*, ch. vi; D. SCHAEFER, art. "Hansa" in *Handwörterbuch der Staatswissenschaft*, 2d ed., IV, 1117; D. SCHAEFER, *Die Hanse* (1903); J. VON GIERKE, *Die deutsche Hanse;* B. KUSKE, *Quellen zur Gesch. des Kölner Handels und Verkehrs im Mittelalter;* W. STEIN, *Beiträge zur Gesch. der deutschen Hanse bis um die Mitte des 15 Jahrhunderts;* A. KIESSELBACH, *Die wirtschaftlichen Grundlagen der deutschen Hanse und die Handelstellung Hamburgs bis in die 2 Hälfte des 14 Jahrhunderts;* A. HOLM, *Lübeck, die freie und Hansestadt;* F. SCHULZ, *Die Hanse und England von Edward III bis auf Heinrichs VIII Zeit;* F. KEUTGEN, *Die Beziehungen der Hanse zu England im letzten Drittel des 14 Jahrhunderts* (Giessen, 1890); STIEDA, *Hansisch-Venetianische Handelsbeziehungen im 15 Jahrhundert;* J. H. WYLIE, *History of the reign of Henry IV*, I, ch. xl; IV, ch. lxxxviii; K. BAHR, *Handel und Verkehr der deutschen Hanse in Flandern während des 14 Jahrhunderts;* W. BUCK, *Der deutsche Kaufmann in Novgorod* (Berlin, 1891); A. AGATS, *Der hansische Baienhandel;* H. HARTMEYER, *Der Weinhandel im Gebiete der Hanse im Mittelalter;* J. M. LAPPENBERG, *Urkundliche Geschichte des Hansischen Stahlhofes zu London* (Hamburg, 1851); BRINKMANN, "Die älteste Grundbücher von Novgorod," *Vierteljahrschrift f. soz. und wirtsch. Gesch.*, IX (1911), 84; A. BUGGE, "Zur ältester Gesch.

der deutschen Handels-niederlassungen im Ausland und besonders des Kontors zur Bergen in Norwegen," *Vierteljahrschrift f. soz. und wirtsch. Gesch.*, VI (1907) 186; F. VOLLBEHR, "Die Hölländer und die deutsche Hanse," *Pfingsblätter des Hansischen Geschichtsverein*, xxii (1930); C. BRINKMANN, "The Hanseatic League," *Harvard Journal of economic and business history*, II (1930), 590; J. A. WERDENHAGEN, *De rebus publicis Hanseaticis Tractatus, cum Urbium earum Iconismis, Descriptionibus, Tabulis Geographicis et Nauticis* (Frankfurt a.M., 1641). Fol. 6 pts. in I vol. With 191 engraved views of towns, maps and sailing charts of all European coasts with the compass lines and sailing routes marked.

CHAPTER VI

THE TEUTONIC KNIGHTS IN PRUSSIA AND THE BALTIC LANDS

R. LODGE, *Close of the middle ages*, ch. xix; HELMHOLT, *History of the world*, V, 489–97; VI, 285–90; VII, 35–37; H. TUTTLE, *History of Prussia*, I, ch. i; J. H. WYLIE, *History of the reign of Henry IV of England*, IV, ch. lxxxviii; H. G. PLUM, "The Teutonic Order and its Secularization," *University of Iowa historical studies*, 1906; L. VON RANKE, *Weltgeschichte*, VIII, 455–80; WILLY COHN, *Hermann von Salza*; PLEHN, "Zur Geschichte der Agrarverfassung von Ost- und West Preussen," *Forschungen zur Branderburgischen Geschichte*, XVII–XVIII; M. ÖHLER, *Geschichte des deutschen Ritterordens*; A. WERMINGHOFF, *Der deutsche Orden und die Stände in Preussen bis zum 2 Thorner Frieden im Jahre 1466*; W. v. KETRZYNSKI, *Die deutschen Orden und Konrad v. Masovien (1225–1235)*, enlarged German edition (Lemberg, 1904); A. KOCH, *Hermann von Salza, Meister des deutschen Ordens* (1885); K. LOHMEYER, *Geschichte von Ost- und Westpreussen*, vol. I (to 1411), Gotha, 1880, 3rd edition, 1908; A. L. EWALT, *Die Eroberung Preussens durch die Deutschen*, 4 vols., [to 1238], Halle 1872–1886; M. PERLBACH, *Die Statuten des deutschen Ordens*, Halle, 1890; E. LAVISSE, *Revue des deux mondes*, March 15, April 15, May 15, 1879.

For the history of Prussian commerce see:

C. SATTLER, *Handelsrechnungen des deutschen Ordens* (Leipzig, 1887) and his earlier article in *Hansische Geschichtsblätter*, 1877; W. STIEDA, *Schragen der Gilden und Aemter der Stadt Riga bis 1621* (1896); THEODOR HIRSCH, *Handels- und Gewerbsgeschichte Danzigs unter der Herrschaft des deutschen Ordens* (1858).

CHAPTER VII

COMMERCE AND INDUSTRY OF SOUTHERN GERMANY

INAMA STERNEGG, *Deutschewirtschaftsgeschichte*, III, 210–352; SCHULTE, *Geschichte des Mittelalterlieben Handels und Verkehrs zwischen Sud-West Deutschland und Italien*; SIMONSFELD, *Der Fondaco dei Tedeschi in Vene-*

dig, 2 vols. (1887), J. MÜLLER, Augsburger Wärenhandel mit Venedig," *Arch. f. Kulturgeschichte,* I; B. KUSKE, "Die Handelsbeziehungen zwischen Köln und Italien," *Westdeutsche Ztschft.,* XXVII; GEER- ING, *Handel und Industrie der Stadt Basel;* SCHMOLLER, *Die Strassburger Tucher und Weberzunft;* G. VON BELOW, *Grosshändel und Kleinhändel, im deutschen Mittelalter;* H. ECKERT, *Die Krämer in Süddeutschen Städten bis zum Ausgang des Mittelalters;* A. KUNZE, *Die Nordböhmisch-sächs- ische Leinwand und Nürnberger Grosshandel;* G. VON BELOW, "Zur Geschichte der Handelsbeziehungen zwischen Südwestdeutschland und Italien," *Hist. Ztschft.* LIII, (1902); A. SCHULTE, *Geschichte des mittel- alterlichen Handels und Verkehr zwischen Westdeutschland und Italien* (Leipzig, 1900); TH. MAYER, *Der auswärtige Handel des Herzogtums Oesterreich im Mittelalter;* NÜBLING, *Ulms Handel im Mittelalter;* KEUT- GEN, *Grosshändler und Kleinhändler;* FLEGLER, "Die Beziehungen Nürn- bergs zu Venedig," *Anzeiger f. Kunde der deutschen Vorzeit,* 1867, nos. x–xii; G. M. THOMAS, "Beiträge aus dem Ulmer Archiv zur Gesch. des Handelverkehrs zwischen Venedig und der deutschen Nation," *Sitzungsber. der K. Bayer. Akad. d. Wiss.,* 1869; HEYD, *Histoire du commerce du Levant,* vol. ii (use index under place names); HEYD, "Das Haus der deutschen Kaufleuten in Venedig," *Hist. Ztschft.,* XXXII (1874); KRETSCH- MAYER, *Geschichte von Venedig,* 323 f.; 344 f.; 348–74; SIEVEKING, "Der Kaufmann im Mittelalter," *Schmoller's Jahrbuch,* LII (1928), 71; E. BENDER, *Weinhandel und Wirtgewerbe in mittelalterlichen Strassburg;* HÜLLMAN, *Städtewesen im Mittelalter,* 4 vols; H. BRUDER, "Zur Lebens- politik im alten Basel: der Fischandel," *Vierteljahrschrift f. soz. und Wirt- schaftsgesch.,* XI, 157; C. MOLLWO, *Das Handlungsbuch von Hermann und Johann Wittenborg;* SAUR, *Die Wehrverfassung in Schwabischen Städten des Mittelalters;* A. KUNZE, *Die Nordböhmische-Sachsische Lein- wand und der Nürnberger Grosshandel;* A. PÜSCHL, *Das Anwachsen der deutschen Städte;* M. GRUNFELDER, "Die Farberei in Deutschland bis zum Jahre 1300," *Vierteljahrschrift f. soz. und Wirtschaftsgesch.,* XVI, iii; H. V. SAURLAND, "Zu den Mailaender Privilegien für die deutschen Kaufleute," *Quellen und Forschungen aus italienischen Archiven und Bibliotheken herausgegeben vom Königl. Preussischen Historischen Insti- tut in Rom,* V, 269–73; JANSSEN, *History of the German People at the Close of the Middle Ages,* I, 125–30; II, bk. iii, ch. iii; BAX, *German society at the close of the Middle Ages;* MUNRO and SELLERY, *Medieval Civilization,* 358 f.; HEADLAM, *Story of Nuremberg;* W. D. P. BLISS, "Nuremberg, the city of the closed shop," *Outlook,* March 17, 1906; LUISE BARDENHEWER, *Der Safranhandel im Mittelalter,* Bonn diss. 1914.

On Switzerland see:

P. H. SCHEFFEL, *Verkehrsgeschichte der Alpen* (1914); HEKTOR AMMAN, "St. Gallens Wirtschaftstellung im Mittelalter," *Aus sozial- und Wirt- schaftsgeschichte für Georg von Below,* pp. 114–68; P. H. SCHMIDT, *Die Schweiz und die Europäische Handelspolitik* (1914); SIEVEKING, *Jahr- buch f. Schweizergeschichte,* XXXV (1910) on Zürich; FECHT, *Die Ge-*

werbe der Stadt Zürich im Mittelalter; Hauser, *Annales de géographie,* vol. XXV (1916), pp. 413–28; Gilliard, "L'ouverture du St. Gothard," *Annales d'histoire économique et sociale,* April 15, 1929, p. 177 f.; F. Berger, "Die Septimerstrasse," *Jahrbuch f. Schweiz. Gesch.,* vol. xv (1910), pp. 1–180; C. Clare, *The Brenner Pass;* Hoffmann, "The German Alpine Passes in Middle Ages," *Journal polit. economy,* vol. XXXI, pp. 826 f.; J. E. Tyler, *The Alpine Passes;* F. Umlauft, *The Alps, Topography, Geology and History* (1889); Redlow, *Die Brennerpasse im Altertum und Mittelalter;* Oehlmann, *Jahrb. f. Schweiz. Gesch.,* IV (1879); Steinberger, "Die Brennerpasse," *Mitteil. f. oesterr. Gesch.* XXXIII, no. iv (1912); Liebenau, *Archiv. f. Schweiz. Gesch.* XX (1876) (St. Gothard); Heyd, "Die Alpenstrasse der Schweiz," *Ausland,* LV; Arnold Lunn, *Switzerland. Her Topographical, Historical and Literary Landmarks.*

CHAPTER VIII

EASTERN EUROPE

Netta Gheron, *Die Handelsbeziehungen zwischen Leipzig und Ost- und Südost-Europa bis zum Verfall der Wärenmessen;* Jickeli, *Der Handel der Siebenbürger Sächsen bis zur Schlacht bei Mohacs;* Heyd, *Histoire du commerce de Levant,* II (use index); F. Bischoff, "Urkunden zur Gesch. der Armenier in Lemburg," *Archiv. f. oesterr. Gesch.* XXXII, pp. 1–155; Jiricek, *Gesch. der Serben,* vol. I; *Studien z. Kulturgesch. d. 13–14 Jahrh.; Die Handelsstrassen und Bergwerke von Serbien und Bosnien während d. Mittelalters;* Schmidt, *Mittheil. d. Ver. f. Gesch. der Deutschen in Boehmen,* XXIV (1895); Kutrzeba, *Bulletin internat. de l'Académie des sciences de Cracow* (1902); Kaindl, *Geschichte der Deutschen in Karpatenländer;* Th. Mayer, *Der auswärtige Handel des Herzogtums Oesterreich im Mittelalter;* Th. Meyer, *Ztschft. f. Kulturgesch.,* N F II, Heft i (1891); Franz Bastian, "Die Legende vom Donauhandel im Frühmittelalter," *Vierteljahrschrift f. social- und Wirtschaftsgeschichte,* XXII, 289–330; H. Heimpel, "Zur Handelspolitik Kaiser Sigismund," *ibid.,* XXIV, 145–156.

CHAPTER IX

ITALY

There is no general economic and social history of Italy in the later Middle Ages and the subject must be pursued through histories of the various cities. Something, however, may be gleaned from:

J. A. Symonds, *Age of the Despots,* chs. ii–iii; J. Burckhardt, *The Renaissance,* bk. i, ch. vii; P. Villari, *Medieval Italy,* bks. ii–iii; H. B. Cotterill, *Italy from Dante to Tasso;* O. Browning, *Age of the Condottieri;* J. Luchaire, *Les démocraties italiennes* (1920); G. Salvioli, *Storia economica d'Italia nell' alto medievo.*

Special monographs:

Venice

RAWDON BROWN, *Calendar of state papers, Venetian,* vol. I, Introd. lxi f.; cxxxv f.; F. C. HODGSON, *History of Venice in thirteenth and fourteenth centuries;* W. C. HAZLITT, *History of Venetian Republic,* I, 141–87, 362–84; MOLMENTI, *History of Venice,* I, pt. i, chs. vi–vii; C. F. DUNBAR, "Bank of Venice," *Quarterly Journal of Economics,* VI, 308; VII, 210; BURCKHARDT, *The Renaissance,* pp. 62–71; SIMONSFELD, *Die Fondaco dei Tedeschi in Venedig* (1886).

Genoa

J. T. BENT, *Genoa;* W. MILLER, "The Genoese in Chios," *English Hist. Review,* XXX; MANFRONI, "Le relazioni tra Genova, l'impero bizantino e i Turchi," *Atti della Soc. Ligure di St. patria,* XXVIII (1898).

Milan

DOROTHY MUIR, *Milan under the Visconti;* C. M. ADY, *Milan under the Sforza.*

Verona

M. ALLEN, *Verona;* A. WEIL, *History of Verona.*

Pisa

F. C. DIETZ, "Industry of Pisa in fourteenth century," *Quarterly Journal of economics,* xxviii, 360; W. HEYWOOD, *A History of Pisa;* TOMMASINI, *Le colonie pisane d'Africa* (1903).

Siena

F. SCHEVILL, *Siena;* LANGDON DOUGLAS, *History of Siena;* SENIGAGLIA, "Le compagnie bancarie senesi nei secolo XIII e XIV," *Studi Senesi,* XXIV, nos. 3, 4, 5; ROON-BASSERMANN, *Sienische Handelsgesellschaften des 13 Jahrhunderts* (Mannheim, 1912); A. GOTTLOB, "Zur Gesellschaftliste der Buonsignori," *Historisches Jahrbuch,* 1901, p. 722; E. JORDAN, "La faillité des Buonsignori," *Mélanges Paul Fabre,* 432.

Rome

F. GREGOROVIUS, *City of Rome in middle ages,* vols. VI–VIII.

CHAPTER X

THE FLORENTINE WOOLEN INDUSTRY

DOREN, *Studien aus der Florentiner Wirtschaftsgesch.,* (1901); POEHLMANN, *Die Wirtschaftspolitik der Florentiner Renaissance* (1878); DAVIDSOHN, *Geschichte von Florenz,* 4 vols; also his *Forschungen zur Florentinischen Geschichte;* SCAIFE, *Florentine life during the renaissance;* DIXON, "Florentine woollen trade," *Trans. royal hist. society* N. S. XII, pp. 151–79; STALEY, *Guilds of Florence;* PALGRAVE, *Dictionary of political economy,* I, 288 (Ciompi); DAVIDSOHN, "Blüte und Niedergang der Florentiner Tuchindustrie," *Ztschft. f. d. Gesammte Staatswissenschaften,* vol.

LXXXV (1928), pp. 225–56; DOREN, *Deutsche Handwerker und Handwerk-erbrüderschaften im mittelalterlichen Italien* (1903); L. PIGNOTTI, *History of Tuscany*, III, 250 f. (4 vols, 1826, an old but good book); BONOLIS, "Sull' industria della lana in Firenze," *Archivio storico italiano* (1903), p. 379 f. Valuable reviews will be found in *English Historical Review*, XXVI, 371 f.; XXVII, 549 f.; *Moyen Age*, N., S., III, 94 f.; *Vierteljahrschrift f. soz. und Wirtschaftsgeschichte* VII, 183 f.

CHAPTER XI

THE FISCAL AND ECONOMIC POLICY OF THE PAPACY

G. MOLLAT, *Les papes d'Avignon* (with val. bib.); W. E. LUNT, "Financial system of the mediaeval papacy," *Quarterly Journal of economics*, XXIII, 251; G. MOLLAT and C. SAMARAN, *La fiscalité pontificale en France au XIVe siècle* (Paris, 1905); E. HENNIG, *Die päpstlichen Zehnten aus Deutschland im Zeitalter des Avignon-esischen Papsttums und während des grossen Schismas* (Halle, 1909); J. P. KIRSCH, *Die päpstlichen Annaten in Deutschland während des 14 Jahrhunderts*, vol. I (Paderborn, 1903) [part 9 of Quellen und Forschungen Görresgesellschaft]; *Die Einnahmen der apostolischen Kammer unter Johann XXII* [*1316–1334*], edited by E. GÖLLER, 2 vols. (Paderborn, 1910); A. ECKSTEIN, *Zur Finanzlage Felix V und des Basler Konzils* (Berlin, 1912); A. GOTTLOB, *Aus der Camera apostolica des 15 Jahrhunderts* (Innsbruck, 1889); CLEMENS BAUER, "Die Epochen der Papstfinanz," *Hist. Ztschft.* CXXXVIII, pp. 457–503; E. JORDAN, *Le St. Siège et les Banquiers Italiens;* VIARD, "La fiscalité pontificale au XIVe siècle," *Revue des questions historiques*, LXXXI, 566; J. GUIRAUD, *L'état pontificale après le grand schisme* (1895); ANTONELLI, "The papal domination in the patrimony during the Avignonese period," *Archivio della società Rom. di storia patria*, XXXI (1908); W. SOMBART, "Die Campagna im 14 Jahrhundert," *Schmoller's Forschungen* (1888); D. S. MUZZEY, *The Spiritual Franciscans;* MÜNTZ, "L'argent et le luxe à la cour pontificale d'Avignon," *Revue des questions historiques*, LXVI (1899), 5–44; 378–406; E. G. GARDNER, *St. Catherine of Siena;* MARGARET ROBERTS, *St. Catherine of Siena and her times;* N. VALOIS, *Le grand schisme d'Occident*, 4 vols; L. SALEMBIER, *Le grand schisme d'Occident* (bib.); J. H. WYLIE, *Council of Constance;* E. J. KITTS, *In the days of the councils;* G. M. TREVELYAN, *England in the age of Wycliffe;* H. B. WORKMAN, *Dawn of the Reformation;* and his *Age of Hus;* GREGOROVIUS, *City of Rome in the Middle Ages*, vols. VI–VII; PASTOR, *History of the popes*, vols. I–VI; ADOLF GOTTLOB, "Päpstliche Darlehenschulden des 13 Jährhunderts," *Historiches Jahrbuch*, 1899; G. SCHNEIDER, *Die finanzellen Beziehungen der florentinischen Bankiers zur Kirche 1285–1304* (Leipzig, 1899); E. JORDAN, "Le Saint Siège et les banquiers italiens," *III Congrès internat. des Catholiques* (Brussels, 1895), p. 292; G. COLOMBE, *Le palais des papes d' Avignon* (1927); R. BRUN, *Avignon au temps des papes* (Paris), 1928).

CHAPTER XII

SECOND PERIOD OF THE HUNDRED YEARS' WAR (1380–1453)

James Westfall Thompson, *The Middle Ages*, II, ch. xxxi (bib.); Lavisse, *Histoire de France*, IV, i, 267–393 (bib.); IV, ii, 1–320 (bib.); A. Coville, *Les états de Normandie*, 1894; Mirot, "Les émeutes parisiennes de 1380–83," *Mém. de la Soc. de l'histoire de Paris*, XXVIII (1901); Portal, "Les insurrections des Tuchins dans les pays de Languedoc," *Annales du Midi*, IV; Vanderkindere, *Le siècle des Artevelde* (1880); W. J. Ashley, *James and Philip Van Artevelde* (1883); A. M. F. Robinson, *The End of the Middle Ages*; L. Batiffol, *Jean Jouvenel, prévot des marchands* (1360–1431); A. Coville, *Les Cabochiens*; K. H. Vickers, *England in the later Middle Ages*, chs. xix–xxii; J. H. Wylie, *History of the reign of Henry IV*, 4 vols; and Wylie and Waugh, *The Reign of Henry V*; Stevenson, *Wars of the English in France* (3 vols, Rolls series, no. 22), vol. I, introd.; R. A. Newhall, *English Conquest of Normandy*; A. Lang, *Joan of Arc*; F. C. Lowell, *Joan of Arc*; Anatole France, *Jeanne d'Arc*; B. J. H. Rowe, "Discipline in the Norman garrisons under Bedford (1422–35)," *Eng. Hist. Review*, April, 1931, p. 194; E. Cosneau, *Le connétable De Richemont*; E. Costello, *Jacques Coeur and his times*; H. B. Biggar, *Precursors of Jacques Coeur*; Ruth Putnam, *Charles the Bold*, I, chs. i–iv.

CHAPTER XIII

FLANDERS UNDER THE DUKES OF BURGUNDY

Pirenne, "Formation and constitution of the Burgundian state," *American Historical Review*, XIV, 477; Pirenne, *Belgian Democracy*, chs. vii–viii; L. V. D. Owen, *England and Burgundy during the Fifteenth Century*; J. H. Wylie, *History of the reign of Henry IV*, I, chs. xxii, xxviii, xxxiii; II, chs. xli, xlii, xliii; III, chs. lxvi, xc; Ruth Putnam, *Charles the Bold*, 2 vols.; O. Cartellieri, *The Court of the Dukes of Burgundy*; *Cambridge modern history*, I, ch. iii; Häpke, *Brugges Entwicklungsgeschichte zur mittelalterliches Weltmarkt* (1909).

CHAPTER XIV

SPAIN IN THE FOURTEENTH AND FIFTEENTH CENTURIES

R. Altamira, *A history of Spanish Civilization*; Ulick Burke, *History of Spain*, I, 224 f.; C. E. Chapman, *History of Spain*, chs. x–xvii; R. B. Merriman, *Rise of the Spanish Empire*, I, chs. ix and xi; *Cambridge modern history*, I, ch. xi; E. Cheyney, *European background of American history*, 79–113; R. Lodge, *Close of the Middle Ages*, ch. xx; E. Storer, *Pedro the Cruel*; Armitage Smith, *John of Gaunt*; M. A. S. Hume, *Spanish People*, ch. vii; Irene Plunkett, *Isabel of Castile*; Christopher Hare, *A Queen of queens*; Prescott, *Ferdinand and Isabella*;

S. P. Scott, *Moorish Empire*, II, chs. xix–xxii; III, ch. xxvi; H. C. Lea, *History of the Inquisition in Spain;* Sabatini, *Torquemada;* Shillington and Chapman, *Commercial Relations between England and Portugal;* Seaver, *The great revolt of Castile.*

CHAPTER XV

THE BALKAN PENINSULA, GREECE AND THE LEVANT

The Balkan Peninsula and Greece:

W. Heyd, *Histoire du commerce du Levant au moyen-age*, II (1886); F. Schevill, *History of the Balkan Peninsula*, chs. x–xii; W. Miller, *The Latins in the Levant; Essays on the Latin Orient;* G. Finlay, *History of Greece*, IV, chs. v–ix; W. Heyd, *Die italienischen Handels-colonien unter den vier letzten Paläologen* (1341–53) (Stuttgart, n.d.); Ersch and Grüber, *Encyclopädie*, art: "Giustiniani"; C. Diehl, "La colonie venétienne à Constantinople à la fin du XIVe siècle," *Mélanges d'archéologie et d'histoire*, III, 90; H. Monnier, *L'administration des Venétiens dans les îles Ioniennes;* J. Longnon, "Les Français en Grèce au XIIIe siècle," *Revue de l'hist. des colonies françaises*, 1917; Martin, "Les Italiens en Grèce et dans les îles après les croisades," *Revue d'hist. diplomatique*, 1913; M. Silberschmidt, *Das orientalische Problem zur Zeit der Entstehung des türkischen Reiches;* Hirsch, "Die Eröffnung des inneren Asiens für den Europäischen Handelsverkehr," *Hist. Ztschft.*, XLIV, 385; J. B. Bury, "The Lombards and Venetians in Euboea," *Journal Hellenic studies*, vol. VII, p. 352; Vol. VIII, p. 194; vol. IX, p. 91; Tozer, "The Franks in the Peloponnesus," *Ibid.*, IV, 165; W. Miller, "The Serbian Empire in the Middle Ages," *Quarterly Review*, October, 1916.

Turks:

F. Schevill, *History of the Balkan peninsula*, chs. xii–xiii; W. Miller, *The Latins in the Levant*, ch. xiii; H. A. Gibbons, *Foundation of the Ottoman Empire* (1300–1403); E. Pears, *Fall of Constantinople;* and his: *Destruction of the Greek Empire and the story of the capture of Constantinople;* J. B. Bury, "The fall of Constantinople," *Yale Review*, October, 1913; A. H. Lybyer, "The Ottoman Turks and the Routes of Trade," *English Hist. Review*, October, 1915.

Timurlane:

Beazley, *Dawn of modern geography*, III, 333–77; Sir Percy Sykes, *History of Persia*, II, ch. lix; J. H. Wylie, *History of the Reign of Henry IV*, I, ch. lxv, pp. 43–70.

CHAPTER XVI

THE BLACK DEATH

J. W. Thompson, *American Journal of Sociology*, XXVI, 565–72; F. A. Gasquet, *The Great Pestilence;* A. Jessopp, *The Coming of the Friars,* chs. iv–v; J. MACKINNON, *The Reign of Edward III,* ch. xv; J. E. T. ROGERS, *History of Agriculture and Prices,* I, 265–302 and ch. xxviii, and his *Work and Wages,* chs. viii–ix; E. P. CHEYNEY, *Industrial History of England,* pp. 96–134; VINOGRADOFF, *Oxford Studies in Social and Legal History,* V (Levett, The black death); W. J. ASHLEY, *English Economic History,* II, 101 f.; B. H. PUTNAM, *The Enforcement of the Statute of Labourers* (1349–59); H. GRAY, "Commutation of Villeinage in England before the Black Death," *English Hist. Rev.,* October, 1914; M. KOVALEVSKY, *Oekonomische Entwicklung Europas,* vol. V; HELEN ROBBINS [BITTERMANN], *Journal of Polit. Economy,* XXXVI, pp. 458 f.

CHAPTER XVII

THE GILDS AND THE FORMATION OF THE PATRICIATE—THE CONFLICT OF CLASSES

G. UNWIN, *Gilds;* W. MÜLLER, *Zur Frage des Ursprungs der mittelalterliche Zünfte* (1910); KEUTGEN, *Aemter und Zünfte;* S. KRAMER, *English craft gilds and the government;* J. M. LAMBERT, *Two thousand years of gild life* (1891); H. VAN DER LINDEN, *Les gilds marchandes dans le Pays-Bas au moyen age* (1896); K. HEGEL, *Städte und Gilden . . . im Mittelalter* (1891); C. GROSS, *Gild merchant* (1890); R. EBERSTADT, *Ursprung des Zunftwesens und die älteren Handwerkerverbände des Mittelalters* (1900); A. DOREN, *Deutsche Handwerker und Handwerkerbrüderschaften im mittelalterlichen Italien* (Berlin, 1903); *Untersuchungen zur Geschichte der Kaufmannsgilden des Mittelalters; Entwicklung und Organisation der Florentiner Zünfte im 13 und 14 Jahrhundert* (Leipzig, 1897); A. DOREN, *Das Florentiner Zunftwesen* (1908); RÉNARD, *Les corporations à Florence;* W. CUNNINGHAM, "The formation and decay of craft gilds," *Trans. royal historical society,* 1886; J. LUCHAIRE, *Les démocraties italiennes;* N. RODOLICO, "The Struggle for the Right of Association in Fourteenth Century Florence," *History,* VIII; R. H. S. PALGRAVE, *Dictionary of Political Economy,* art. "Ciompi"; G. SCHMOLLER, *Strassburg zur Zeit der Zunftkämpfe* (1875); H. PIRENNE, *Belgian Democracy;* L. MIROT, *Les insurrections urbaines;* A. RÉVILLE, *Les soulèvements des travailleurs d'Angleterre en 1381* (1898); G. ESPINAS, *La vie urbaine de Douai au moyen âge;* K. BÜCHER, *Die Entstehung der Volkswirtschaft* (1893); M. KOVALEVSKY, *Die oekonomische Entwicklung Europas,* Vol. V; BROSCH, *Hist. Ztschft.,* LVI, Heft iii (Ciompi); G. DES MAREZ, "Les luttes sociales en Flandre au moyen âge," *Revue de l'université de Bruxelles,* June and July, 1900; G. SCARAMELLA, "Firenze allo scoppio del tumulto dei Ciompi," *Rivista storica italiana,* 1915, no. 1; SCHMOLLER, in *Sitz. Preuss. Akad. d. Wiss.* (1903), no. 47 (very valuable for class conflict in the cities); LECARPENTIER, "La harelle, révolte rouennais de 1382," *Moyen Age,* 1903, pp. 12 f., 89 f.

CHAPTERS XVIII, XIX

BANKING. ORIGIN OF MODERN BUSINESS METHODS

Rise of capitalism:

W. CUNNINGHAM, *Western civilization*, 182–92; H. PIRENNE, "The Stages in the Social History of Capitalism," *American historical review*, XIX, 467; "Les périodes de l'histoire sociale du capitalisme," *Bull. de l'Acad. roy. de Belgique*, 1914; H. HAUSER, "Les origines du capitalisme moderne en France," *Revue d'économie politique*, 1902; W. SOMBART, *The Quintessence of capitalism;* GEORG VON BELOW, "Die Entstehung des modernen Kapitalismus," *Hist. Ztschft.*, vol. XCI; H. DELBRÜCK, *Preussische Jahrbücher*, vol. XVIII; JAKOB STRIEDER, *Zur Genesis des modernen Kapitalismus; Studien zur Gesch. kapitalischer Organizationsformen;* W. CUNNINGHAM, *The progress of capitalism in England;* R. HÄPKE, "Die Entstehung der grossen bürgerlichen Vermögen im Mittelalter," *Schmoller's Jahrbücher f. Gesetzgebung, Verwaltung und Volkswirtschaft*, vol. XCI; J. A. HOBSON, *Evolution of modern capitalism;* HENRI SEE, *Les origines du capitalisme;* H. SIEVEKING, "Die kapitalistische Entwicklung der italienischen Städte im Mittelalter," *Vierteljahrschrift f. soz und wirt. Gesch.* 1909, pp. 64–93; R. HEYNEN, *Zur Entstehung des Kapitalismus in Venedig;* GRUPP, "Entstehung des Kapitalismus," *Ztschft. f. d. gesammte Staatswissenschaft*, LIII (1897); CARL KOEHNE, "Burgen, Burgmannen und Städte. Ein Beitrag zur Frage der Bedeutung der ländlichen Grundrenten," *Hist. Ztschft.*, CXXXIII, 1.

Rise of banking:

R. H. I. PALGRAVE, *Dictionary of political economy*, art. "Banking"; CONRAD and LEXIS, *Handwörterbuch der Staatswissenschaften*, art. "Bank"; HOOPS, *Real-Lexicon*, art. "Bank"; *Encyclopaedia Britannica*, art. "Banking"; C. F. DUNBAR, "The bank of Venice," *Quarterly jnl. economics*, VI, 308; VII, 310; SCHNEIDER, *Die finanziellen Beziehungen der Florentinischen Bankiers zur Kirche von 1285 bis 1304* (1899); A. SAPORI, *La crisi delle compagnie mercantili dei Bardi e dei Peruzzi* (1926); ARMANDO SAPORI, "I mutui dei mercanti fiorentini del trecento e l'incremento della proprietà fondaria," *Rivista del diritto commerciale e del diritto generale delle obbligazione*, 1928, XXVI, 222–47; A. SAPORI, "L'interesse del denaro a Firenze nel trecento," *Archivio storico italiano*, 1928, X, ch. ii; E. JORDAN, "La faillité des Buonsignori," *Mélanges Paul Fabre*, pp. 416–75; "Le Saint Siège et les banquiers italiens," *Compte rendu du troisième congrès scientifique des catholiques* (Brussels, 1895); ARIAS, *Studi e documenti di storia del diritto* (Florence, 1902); PERUZZI, *Storia dei commercio e dei banchieri di Firenze*, 2 vols. (Florence, 1868); EDWARD BOND, "Extracts from the liberate rolls relative to loans supplied by Italian merchants," *Archaeologia*, XXVIII (1840); W. E. EDWARDS, "The Italian bankers in England and their loans to Edward I and Edward II," *Manchester Univ. Hist. Ser.* No. VI; E. RUSSELL, "The Societies of the Bardi and the Peruzzi and their dealings with Edward III,

327-45," published in G. Unwin, *Finance and trade under Edward III,* ch. xxxii; Emilio Re, "La compagnia dei Ricciardi in Inghilterra e il suo failimento alla fine del secolo XIII," *Archivio della R Società Romana di storia patria,* XXXVII (1914); Luigi Chiapelli, "Una lettera mercantile del 1330 e la crisi del commercio ilaliano nella prima metà del trecento," *Archivio storico italiano,* LXXXII (1924); 7th ser., tome I, 229-56; Melzing, *Das Bankhaus der Medici* (1906); A. Wiszniewski, *Histoire de la Banque de St. George a Paris* (1865); Molard, *Essai sur l'origine de l'organisation de la Banque de St. George à Gênes* (1860).

On the Fuggers:

Ehrenberg, *Das Zeitalter der Fugger* (1898); Max Jansen, *Die Anfänge der Fugger;* Aloys Schulte, *Die Fugger in Rom;* E. Castelot, "La banque des Fugger et les papes de la renaissance," *Journal des économistes,* CXXX (1906), 161 f.

On monti di pietà:

Edwards, *Pawn-broking abroad and at home;* Ashley, *English economic history and theory,* II, 447 f.; Palgrave, *Dictionary of political economy,* article "Mons de Pietà"; Jannet, *Le crédit populaire et les banques en Italie du XVe au XVIIIe siècle,* Paris, 1885; Endemann, in *Hildebrand's Jahrb. f. Nationaloekonomie,* I (1863), 324 f., Wetzer and Welte, *Kirchenlexikon,* VII, 1690 f.; Bruder's *Staatslexikon,* III, 1092 f.; Blaize, *Des monts-de-piété,* Paris, 1856; Pastor, *History of the popes,* V, 108-111.

Insurance:

R. H. I. Palgrave, *Dictionary of political economy,* art. "Insurance"; Schaube, *Ztschft. f. soz. und Wirtschaftsgesch.,* I (1894); Enrico Bensa, *Histoire du contrat d'assurance au moyen âge,* French trans. by Valéry (1896); Jules Lefort, "Les origines de l'assurance," *Revue générale du droit,* 1897; E. Rébouis, *Le credit, le change et l'assurance avant le XVe siècle;* Bonolis, *Archivio storico italiano,* 1898, no. iv; Vance, "Early history of Insurance law," *Essays in Anglo-American Law,* III, 98-108; *Continental Legal History, General Survey,* Part II, secs. 64-65; Part III, sec. 15; *Columbia Law Review,* VIII, 1-17; A. Schaube, "Die Versicherungsgedanke in den Verträgen des Seeverkehrs vor der Versicherungswesens," *Vierteljahrschrift f. Social -und Wirtschaftsgeschichte,* vol. II.

Partnerships and joint stock companies:

R. H. Inglis, *Dictionary of political economy,* s. v.; E. H. Byrne, "Genoese Trade with Syria," *American Historical Review,* XXV, 191; "Commercial Contracts of Genoese Syrian Trade," *Quarterly journal of economics,* XXXI, 128; W. Miller, "The Genoese in Chios," *English historical review,* July, 1915 (on the maona); W. Mitchell, "Early forms of partnership," *Essays in Anglo-American Legal History,* III, 193; S. Williston, "History of the law of business corporations," *Harvard Law Review,* II, 105-24; III, 195; M. Weber, *Zur Gesch. der Handels-*

gesellschaften des Mittelalters; G. Schmoller in *Jahrbuch f. Gesetzgebung,* XVII (1893); J. STRIEDER, *Studien zur Geschichte kapitalistischer Organisationsformen: Monopole, Kartelle und Aktiengesellschaften im Mittelalter und zu Beginn der Neuzeit,* Munich, 1914; ANDRÉ E. SAYOUS, "Les transformations des méthodes commerciales dans l'Italie médievale." *Annales d'Histoire économique et sociale,* I, 166 f.

Bookkeeping, bill of exchange and business methods:

R. H. I. PALGRAVE, *Dictionary of Political Economy,* s. v.; A. P. USHER, "Origin of the Bill of Exchange," *Journal of political economy* (1914); JENKS, "Early History of Negotiable Instruments," *Law quarterly review,* IX, 70; E. NYS, *History of economics,* ch. xii; W. J. ASHLEY, *English economic history,* II, ch. xvi; R. BROWN, *History of accounting and accountants;* ROUSSEL, "Un livre de main au XVIe siècle," *Revue internationale* XIII, 102 f.; 521 f.; 825 f.; LORIA, *Economic synthesis,* 47 f.; DAVID MURRAY, *Chapters in the history of bookkeeping, accountancy and commercial arithmetic;* DAVID E. SMITH, "The First Great Commercial Arithmetic," *Isis,* VIII, 41 f. (1926); SIEVEKING, "Die Handlungsbücher der Medici," *Sitz. d. Akad. d. Wiss., Phil-hist. Kl.,* CLI (1905); SIEVEKING, "Aus venetianischen Handlungsbüchern," *Jahrbuch f. Gesetzgebung, 1901;* EDLER, *Bulletin of the Business Historical Society,* Nov. 1927; HEYKING, *Zur Gesch. der Handelsbilanztheorie.* (cf. *Hist. Ztschft.* N. F. XV (1884).

Commercial law:

For remarkable bibliographical article see *Revue de synthèse historique,* VII, 332 f.; CARTER, "The Early history of the law merchant in England," *Law Quarterly Review,* Vol. LXVII, July, 1901; L. GOLDSCHMIDT, *Handbuch des Handelsrechts* (1891); MOREL, *Les juridictions commerciales au moyen âge* (1897); W. A. LEWIS, *The Romance of the law merchant;* A. FRÉMERY, *Études de droit commercial;* A. DESJARDINS, *Introduction historique à l'étude du droit commercial maritime;* HILDEBRAND, *Recht und Sitte auf den verschiedenen wirtschaftlichen Kulturstoffe* (1896); BONOLIS, *La Giurisdizione della Mercanzia in Firenze nell secolo XIV* (Florence, 1901); LASTIG, *Entwickelungswege und Quellen des Handelsrechts* (1877); VECCHIO and CASANOVA, *Le Rappresaglie nei comuni medievali* (1894).

Trade-marks and patents:

FRANK I. SCHECHTER, *The historical foundations of the law relating to trade marks* (1929); LASTIG, *Markenrecht und Zeichenregister* (1889); BISCARO, *Archivio storico Lombardo,* series iv, no. 34 (1912), (two debates on trade marks); HULME, "Early History of the English patent system," *Law Quarterly Review,* XII, 141–54.

Consular system:

WIRRER, *Ztschft. f. d. gesammte Staatswissenschaft,* vol. L, no. 2 (1894); GLASSON, "Les juges et les consuls des marchands," *Nouvelle revue historique de droit,* 1897; SCHAUBE, "La proxénie au moyen âge,"

Revue de droit internat. et de législation comparée, XXVIII, 527. Consult also various works on international law and encyclopaedias.

Statistics during the fourteenth and fifteenth centuries:

JAKOB BURCKHARDT, *The Renaissance,* pp. 61–87; EMILE GEBHARDT, "Les historiens florentines de la renaissance et les commencements de l'économie politique et sociale," *Séances et travaux de l'Académie des sciences morals et politiques,* CIV (1875), 552 f:; J. A. SYMONDS, *Age of the despots,* 201–05; J. JASTROW, *Die Volkszahl deutscher Städte zu Ende des Mittelalters* (1886); PIRENNE, *Les dénombrements de la population d'Ypres au XVe siècle* (1412–50); STIEDA in *Sitz. Königl. Akad. d. Wiss. zu Berlin* (1902); BELOW in *Vierteljahrschrift f. soz.- und Wirtschaftgesch.,* II, 47 f.; ZOFIA in *Hildebrands Jahrbücher,* LXVI (1896); 489 f.; J. CUVELIER, *Les dénombrements de foyers en Brabant* (1912); INAMA STERNEGG in *Statische Monatschrift,* XII (1886), 387–408; K. ZEUMER, *Die deutschen Städtesteuern, in besondere die städtischen Reichssteuern im 12 und 13 Jahrhundert* (1878); G. SCHONBERG, *Die Finanzverhältnisse der Stadt Basel in 14 und 15 Jahrhundert* (1879); KARL BÜCHER, Der öffentliche Haushalt der Stadt Frankfurt im Mittelalter, *Ztschft. f. d. gesammte Staatswissenschaft* (1896); M. HARTUNG (on finances of Augsburg), *Jahrbuch f. Gesetzgebung* (1895, 1898); PAUL HUBER, "Der Haushalt der Stadt Hildesheim," in Stieda's *Volkswirtschaftliche Abhandlungen* (1901); J. HARTWIG, *Der Lübecker Schoss* (1903); STIEDA (on medieval town finances), *Jahrbuch f. Nationalökonomie* (1899); HEGEL, appendices to volumes of the *Städtechroniken;* CHRISTIAN MEYER, *Stadtrecht von Augsburg* (1872); M. B. MENDL, "Breslau zu Beginn des 15 Jahrhunderts," *Ztschft. f. d. Gesch. Schlesiens* (1929), pp. 154–85 (after a register 1403); G. G. COULTON, *The medieval village,* appendix IX, pp. 440–43.

CHAPTER XX

FRANCE AT THE END OF THE MIDDLE AGES

See bibliography to chapter XII, and LAVISSE, *Histoire de France* IV, pt. ii (with valuable bibliographies); J. S. C. BRIDGES, *History of France from the death of Louis XI,* 3 vols.; IMBART de le Tour, *Les origines de la reforme,* vol. I; *Cambridge modern history,* I, ch. iv, xii.

CHAPTER XXI

GERMANY, ITALY AND SPAIN AT THE END OF THE MIDDLE AGES

See bibliographies to chapters VII, IX and XIV; *Cambridge modern history,* I, chaps. iii, iv, v, vi, vii, viii, ix, x, xi.

CHAPTER XXII

ON THE THRESHOLD OF MODERN TIMES

Cambridge modern history I, chs. i, ii, xv; C. BENOIST, "Les crises de l'histoire moderne," *Séances et travaux de l'Académie des sciences morales et politiques,* vol. 173, p. 191 f.; W. CUNNINGHAM, in *Transactions royal historical society,* ser. III, vol. IV (1910); E. DÉPREZ, "Les grands voyages et les grandes découvertes jusqu' à la fin du XVIIIe siècle," *Bulletin of the international committee of historical studies,* No. ix, June 1930 (Vol. II, part iv), Washington, 1930, p. 555 f.; C. H. HARING, "American gold and silver production in the first half of the sixteenth century," *Quarterly Jnl. Economics* XXIX, 433–79; R. B. MERRIMAN, *Rise of the Spanish Empire* III, 636–37; EARL J. HAMILTON, "Imports of American gold and silver into Spain (1503–1660)," *Quarterly Jnl. Economics* XLIII, 436; EARL J. HAMILTON, "American treasure and Andalusian prices (1503–1660)," *Journal of economic and business history,* I (1929), pp. 1–35; J. BONN, *Spaniens Niedergang während der Preisrevolution des XVI Jahrhunderts,* Stuttgart, Cotta, 1896; CRISTOBAL ESPEJO, "La caristia de la vida en el siglo XVI y medios de abarataria," *Rivista de archivos, bibliotecas y museos,* Madrid, vol. XXIV (1920), XXV (1921); A. E. SAYOUS, Les changes d'Espagne sur l'Amerique au XVIe siècle, *Revue d'économique politique,* 1927; P. RAVEAU, "La crise des prix au XVIe siècle," *Revue Historique* CLXII (1929).

INDEX